The Bill of Rights and American Legal History

A 20-volume
series reproducing over
300 key articles which explore
the 200-year history
of the rights of
American
citizens

EDITED WITH INTRODUCTIONS BY
Paul L. Murphy
University of Minnesota

A Garland Series

Books in the Series

I. The Historic Background of the Bill of Rights

II. Pre-1960 Developments in the Bill of Rights Area
— 2 Volumes —

III. Free Speech
— 4 Volumes —

IV. Free Press
— 3 Volumes —

V. Rights of Assembly, Petition, Arms and Just Compensation

VI. Religious Freedom: Separation and Free Exercise
— 2 Volumes —

VII. The Right to Privacy and the Ninth Amendment
— 2 Volumes —

VIII. Criminal Procedure
— 4 Volumes —

IX. The Bill of Rights and the States

Religious Freedom

Separation and Free Exercise

IN TWO VOLUMES

VOLUME I

EDITED WITH AN INTRODUCTION BY
Paul L. Murphy

GARLAND PUBLISHING, INC.
New York & London
1990

Introduction copyright © 1990 by Paul L. Murphy.
All rights reserved.

The editor and publisher are grateful to the journals and authors cited in the contents for permission to reprint copyright material in this volume. All material is copyright and any further reproduction is prohibited without permission.

Library of Congress Cataloging-in-Publication Data

The Bill of Rights and American legal history /
  edited with introductions by Paul L. Murphy.
  p. cm.
  ISBN 0-8240-5862-3 (v. 6, alk. paper)
  1. Civil rights—United States—History. 2. United States—Constitutional law
  —Amendments—1st–10th—History. I. Murphy, Paul L., 1923–
  Kf47.49.A2B55 1990
  342.73.'085'09—dc20
  [347.3028509]   89-25876

Printed on acid-free, 250-year-life paper.

Manufactured in the United States of America

CONTENTS

VOLUME ONE

Introduction

1. Baker, John W. "Belief and Action: Limitations on the Free Exercise of Religion," in Jaye B. Hensel, ed., *Church, State, and Politics* (Washington, DC: The Roscoe Pound Foundation, 1981), 41–72. 1

2. Cahn, Edmund. "The 'Establishment of Religion' Puzzle," *New York University Law Review* 36 (1961), 1274–1297. 34

3. Choper, Jesse H. "Religion in the Public Schools: A Proposed Constitutional Standard," *Minnesota Law Review* 47 (1963), 329–416. 59

4. Choper, Jesse H. "The Establishment Clause and Aid to Parochial Schools," *California Law Review* 56 (1968), 260–341 148

5. Choper, Jesse H. "The Religion Clauses of the First Amendment: Reconciling the Conflict," *University of Pittsburgh Law Review* 41 (1980), 673–701 231

6. Clark, J. Morris. "Guidelines for the Free Exercise Clause," *Harvard Law Review* 83 (1969), 327–365 261

7. Cord, Robert L. "Church-State Separation: Restoring the 'No Preference' Doctrine of the First Amendment," *Harvard Journal of Law Public Policy* 9 (1986), 129–172 301

8. Corwin, Edward S. "The Supreme Court as National School Board," *Law and Contemporary Problems* 14 (1949), 3–22 345

9. Galanter, Mark. "Religious Freedoms in the United States: A Turning Point?," *Wisconsin Law Review* (1966), 217–296. 365

10. Giannella, Donald A. "Religious Liberty, Nonestablishment, and Doctrinal Development," *Harvard Law Review* 80 (1967), 1381–1431. 445

Volume Two

11. Kauper, Paul G. "The Supreme Court and the Establishment Clause: Back To *Everson?*," *Case Western Reserve Law Review* 25 (1974), 107–129. 1

12. Marcus, Paul. "The Forum of Conscience: Applying Standards Under the Free Exercise Clause," *Duke Law Journal* (1973), 1217–1272. 25

13. McCloskey, Robert G. "Principles, Powers, and Values: The Establishment Clause and the Supreme Court," *Religion and the Public Order* (1964), 3–32. 81

14. Merel, Gail. "The Protection of Individual Choice: A Consistent Understanding of Religion Under the First Amendment," *University of Chicago Law Review* 45 (1978), 805–843. 111

15. Mirsky, Yehudah. "Civil Religion and the Establishment Clause," *Yale Law Journal* 95 (1986), 1237–1257. 151

16. Murray, John Courtney. "Law or Prepossessions," *Law and Contemporary Problems* 14 (1949), 23–43. 173

17. Pfeffer, Leo. "Freedom and/or Separation: The Constitutional Dilemma of the First Amendment," *Minnesota Law Review* 64 (1980), 561–584. 195

18. Riga, Peter J. "Yoder and Free Exercise," *Journal of Law & Education* 6 (1977), 449–472. 219

19. Schwarz, Alan. "No Imposition of Religion: The Establishment Clause Value," *Yale Law Journal* 77 (1968), 692–737. 244

20. Van Alstyne, William. "Trends in the Supreme Court: Mr. Jefferson's Crumbling Wall—A Comment on *Lynch v. Donnelly*," *Duke Law Journal* (1984), 770–787. 290

21. Van Patten, Jonathan K. "In the End is the Beginning: An Inquiry into the Meaning of the Religion Clauses," *St. Louis University Law Journal* 1 (1983), 1–93. 309

22. Waite, Edward F. "The Debt of Constitutional Law to Jehovah's Witnesses," *Minnesota Law Review* 28 (1944), 209–246. 403

INTRODUCTION

The first two rights in the Bill of Rights involve religion. "Congress shall make no law respecting an establishment of religion, or prohibiting the free exercise thereof." This prioritizing reflected the strong feelings of the people in the state ratifying conventions of 1788 and 1789 that the protection of their religious freedom had to be firmly guaranteed. Congress, in ratifying the religion clauses took a longer historical view, feeling the two clauses would serve to avoid the mischief which centuries of experience had demonstrated seemed inevitably to occur when church and state were intertwined. Such a perspective insured the de-politicizing of religion, and thereby defused a potentially explosive situation and, it was hoped, removed religious issues from the ballot box and from politics. It separated government and religion, so that civility could be maintained between believers and unbelievers as well as among the many denominations, sects, and cults that were properly to thrive in this country. In a free government, the security for civil rights must be the same as that for religious rights, James Madison argued. It consists in one case in the multiplicity of interests, and in the other in the multiplicity of sects. Healthy competition in religion and divergent religious approaches was thus endorsed, with a clear understanding that as with other freedoms, governmental hands-off was essential.

Curiously, nineteenth-century America did not see constitutional adjudication on religious issues. The one exception involved Mormon polygamy, which the Supreme Court held, in 1879, was not a constitutionally protected religious practice. Indeed, it was not until the second quarter of the twentieth century that religious issues produced constitutional adjudication.

Religious controversies were primarily local, and religious freedom began to be incorporated against the states in the late 1930s, with a series of cases involving the Jehovah's Witnesses. Their unusual, and to many annoying, proselytizing practices—doorbell ringing, pamphlet peddling, sound trucks, meetings held on public property without permission—were, to the distress of some Americans, generally upheld by the Supreme Court as a permissible form of religious expression. So was the refusal of Jehovah's Witness children to salute the flag in the public schools or be expelled.

But Witness issues, which largely raised free exercise questions, produced mild reaction compared to the separation question. There, starting in 1947, the Supreme Court adopted Jefferson's view of the need to maintain a "wall of separation" between church and state, even though they allowed some preliminary breaches in that wall in condoning busing of parochial school students at public expense, and released time programs in the public schools (as long as the religious instruction they afforded was conducted off of school property). Nationally, as a result, strong sides began to be taken.

By the 1960s, secularists brought to the Supreme Court challenges to the practice of holding religious ceremonies in tax-supported facilities, succeeding not only in having banned the morning prayer in public schools, but subsequently getting bible reading and reciting of the Lord's Prayer removed as violations of the Establishment clause. Such judicial proscription stirred waves of national protest, particularly from conservative religionists, many of whom demanded a constitutional amendment to restore religion to the schools. These advocates were unsuccessful, but the issue did not die. However, it clearly led the Court to draw firmer lines regarding what kind of support for religion the state could legitimately extend. One general distinction was referred to as a "pupil welfare." A state could aid children attending religious schools, as long as that aid went to the child in the form of busing, school lunch programs, police and fire protection for buildings. Other forms of what came to be called "parochial", where money went directly to support the religious programs of the schools, the Court rejected.

The key modern case was *Lemon v. Kurtzman,* in 1971. The case involved state laws in Rhode Island and Pennsylvania which reimbursed non-public schools for salaries, textbooks, and instructional material used in secular courses; and paid teachers of secular subjects in non-public schools a 15 percent salary supplement. The argument was that these would be the same courses students would get in a public school; but clearly they were totally secular courses, so that in no way, it was argued, was this actually subsidizing religion.

The Supreme Court threw out both laws as unconstitutional violations of separation of church and state, but in the process set forth three rules which have been the core of modern religious freedom jurisprudence. They hold that a state statute must have a permissible secular legislative purpose; its principal or primary effect must be one that neither advances nor inhibits religion; and the statute must not foster an excessive governmental entanglement with religion.

Subsequent cases showed the Court interpreting these restrictions relatively rigidly. Posting prominently copies of the Ten Commandments in a public school was impermissible. One enforced minute of silence in which children could pray was also. So were reporting requirements imposed by the state on religious organizations which solicited more than fifty percent of their funds from non-members. The Court had more difficulty when it came to drawing those lines in circumstances involving display of a creche on public property, and attempting to determine when such action constituted endorsement of religion, and when it was simply a reflection of the public celebration of the Christmas holidays in the American historical tradition.

Further variations were revealing. The Court, in 1961, upheld Maryland's "blue laws," contending that they may have been religious initially, but had become secular "to provide a Sunday atmosphere of recreation, cheerfulness, and enjoyment." Tax exemption for church property created only "a minimal and remote involvement between church and state," and had a clear secular purpose, to contribute to the well-being of the community. But the increasingly more conservative Burger, and eventually the Rehnquist, Court moved more to validate indirect support of religion. In a case in 1983, the Court sustained a state law making it possible for taxpayers to deduct tuition, textbooks, transportation, and whatever other expenses were incurred in sending children to public as well as to non-public schools. Rehnquist was convinced this complied with the *Lemon* rule. Four dissenters strongly disagreed. With more conservatives moving into dominance on the Court in the late 1980s, the Rehnquist view seemed destined to prevail.

The free exercise clause raised different questions, but again the trend toward a more conservative Court, oriented more toward non-preferential support of religion generally, affected it. The Warren Court, over some dissent, sustained state laws requiring businesses to be closed on Sunday, even though Jewish petitioners argued that the law was an interference with the free exercise of their religion. But two years later, the Court sustained a claim by a Seventh-Day Adventist woman against a South Carolina law, denying her unemployment compensation because she would not take a job on her sabbath, Saturday.

Showing how ticklish the distinctions sometimes became, the Court also split on two cases involving the Amish. In the *Yoder* case (1972), Chief Justice Burger exempted, partially on religious grounds, Amish children from having to comply with Wisconsin's compulsory school laws after the eighth grade, even though the training they were getting, as arranged by their Amish parents, did not conform to state standards. On the other hand, it sustained a state's claim that an Amish farmer who employed others must pay social security to them, even thought this flew in the face of Amish belief that it was sinful not to provide for their own elderly in the community.

The essays in these volumes probe a range of religious questions from various tangents, and make clear the ongoing, and seemingly, at times, insoluble constitutional problems which the emotional issue of religion continually stirs up.

PAUL L. MURPHY

ADDITIONAL READING

Gerard Bradley, *Church-State Relationships in America* (1987)
Robert Cord, *Separation of Church and State* (1982)
Mark DeW Howe, *The Garden and the Wilderness: Religion and Government in American History* (1965)
Paul Kauper, *Religion and the Constitution* (1964)
John Laubach, *School Prayers: Congress, The Court and the Public* (1969)
Leo Pfeffer, *Church, State, and Freedom* (1967)
Leo Pfeffer, *God, Caesar, and the Constitution* (1975)
Leo Pfeffer, *Religion, State, and the Burger Court* (1984)
Lawrence Rosen, "Continuing the Conversation: Creationism, the Religion Clauses, and the Politics of Culture," *Supreme Court Review* (1988)
Frank Sorauf, *The Wall of Separation* (1976)
Anson Stokes and Leo Pfeffer, *Church and State in the United States* (1965)

BELIEF AND ACTION: LIMITATIONS ON THE FREE EXERCISE OF RELIGION

John W. Baker

Intolerance of differing religious beliefs and practices was an important part of the legacy which the United States received from England.[1] Incipient movements, dating back to the mid-Thirteenth Century,[2] to disestablish an intolerant Roman Catholic Church gained impetus when Henry VIII in 1534 issued the Act of Supremacy.[3] That Act formally severed ties with Rome, and Henry became the supreme head of the Anglican Church—which was as intolerant of divergent views and practices as had been its predecessor.

Henry's ten-year-old son succeeded him as Edward VI, and for the five years he lived as king he reigned under a council of regency whose composition reflected Henry's desire to move the Reformation forward. Mary I, Henry's daughter by Katharine of Aragon, succeeded her brother in 1553, and during her five year reign she and her advisors worked for the restoration of Catholicism in England[4] with such determination that nearly 300 protesting Anglicans were executed. Her title of "Bloody Mary" may have been something of a misnomer, but she did not tolerate religious dissent.[5]

In 1558 Elizabeth I, the Anglican daughter of Henry VIII and Anne Boleyn, assumed the throne. The following year a new Act of Supremacy nullified much of Mary's legislation and revived eight of Henry's reformation statutes.[6] Elizabeth's sex caused Parliament some difficulty in declaring her the Supreme Head of the Church, but the Act did declare her to be "Supreme Governor of this realm...in all spiritual things or causes as temporal...."[7] Although Elizabeth broadened slightly the parameters of acceptable religious expression, the Act of Uniformity of 1559[8] required uniformity in worship and church procedure. Compulsory attendance at and support of the established church remained the law.[9]

The death of Elizabeth in 1603 and the reigns of the first two Stuarts—James I (1603-1625) and Charles I (1625-1649)—did not alter the basic pattern of official religious intolerance. Unofficially the separatists' movement began to grow, and they suffered persecution by the state. Those who wanted to purify the established church and were rejected became the major element and the cohesive force of the revolution led by Oliver Cromwell. The nine year Interregnum under the leadership of Cromwell saw a different set of religious officials but the same basic intolerance of differing religious views and practices.[10]

It was out of this English milieu of religious intolerance that the first permanent English settlement was made at Jamestown in 1607, that the Pilgrims began their settlement in Massachusetts in 1620, and that the major push of North American colonization began. One of the chief motives of those who came to the New World was asserted to be a desire for religious freedom. However, the colonists too often reflected their heritage of religious intolerance, and the desire for religious freedom too often translated into freedom to believe and act in accordance with the religious beliefs and actions of those who established the colony. Roger Williams, an ordained Anglican priest who had become involved in separatist movements, was banished from the Massachusetts theocracy because his religious beliefs differed from those of the separatists who had established that colony.[11]

The colony which Williams then established, Providence Plantations, became a haven for religious freethinkers as well as for those who sought to be free *not* to profess a religious belief and *not* to attend worship services.[12] There were other examples of the recognition of religious liberty in the colonies. Lord Baltimore, a Roman Catholic, permitted a high degree of religious liberty for Christians in his colony of Maryland as did Quaker William Penn in Pennsylvania. However, the free exercise of religion, with all that concept entails, was far from a reality during the American Revolution[13] and under the government which the Articles of Confederation established.

The Articles created a loose confederation of the thirteen states with few actual powers given the national government. The only mention of religion in the document reads:

> The said states hereby severally enter into a firm league of friendship with each other, for their common defence, the security of their Liberties, and their mutual and general welfare, binding themselves to assist each other, against all force offered to, or attacks made upon them, or any of them, on account of religion, sovereignty, trade, or any other pretence whatever.[14]

The degree of religious liberty allowed remained a state matter—determined by the constitution and laws of the individual state.

The most famous of the declarations of rights found in the original states was drafted by George Mason and adopted, with only slight changes and with two entirely new sections, by the Virginia Convention nearly a month before the

Declaration of Independence was signed in Philadelphia. Along with other rights it declares religious liberty for the people:

> That religion, or the duty which we owe to our Creator, and the manner of discharging it, can be directed only by reason and conviction, not by force or violence; and therefore all men are equally entitled to the free exercise of religion, according to the dictates of conscience; and that it is the mutual duty of all to practice Christian forbearance, love, and charity towards each other.[15]

Such a statement on free exercise did not disestablish the Anglican Church in Virginia and did not prevent jailing or otherwise repressing the leaders of minority religions such as Baptists. In 1777 the so-called liberals were able to secure the repeal of state statutes requiring church attendance and universal support of the established church. However, the Anglican Church was not disestablished in Virginia until 1779.

Even this did not satisfy Thomas Jefferson, who prepared a bill for absolute religious freedom and equality. Such an absolute separation of church and state was opposed not only by the Episcopal Church but also by the Presbyterian and some of the other dissenting churches. Jefferson described the struggle for religious freedom as "the severest contest in which I have ever been engaged." It was not until 1786—one year before the Philadelphia Convention—that Jefferson's bill was passed, while he was overseas, by the Virginia Legislature. This broad statute declared in part:

> ...no man shall be compelled to frequent or support any religious worship, place or ministry whatsoever, nor shall be enforced, restrained, molested, or burthened in his body or goods, nor shall otherwise suffer on account of his religious opinions or belief; but that all men shall be free to profess, and by argument to maintain, their opinion in matters of religion, and that the same shall in no wise diminish, enlarge or affect their civil capacities.[16]

Such ideas about the free exercise of religion in Virginia were well ahead of the thinking in the other states but reflected a growing agreement that even though states might maintain an established church they were unable to control the religious activities of a variety of religious organizations.[17]

The Philadelphia Convention in 1787—called because "of the Necessity of revising the Federal Constitution, and adding thereto such further Provisions, as may render the same more adequate to the Exigencies of the Union...."[18]—decided early on to draft a new document and to establish a new type of government. In their discussions religion played only a minor part. According to Madison's notes, religion was mentioned directly only once and that mention occasioned no real debate.

> Mr. Pinkney [sic] moved to add to the art:—"but no religious test shall ever be required as a qualification to any office or public trust under the authority of the U. States." Mr. Sherman thought it unnecessary, the prevailing liberality being a sufficient security agst such tests.[19]

With only minor changes the Pinckney language became a part of the original Constitution.[20]

Debate on a proposal to include a bill of rights in the original document was brief as Madison recorded it. George Mason "wished the plan had been prefaced with a Bill of Rights, & would second a Motion if made for the purpose. It would give great quiet to the people; and with the aid of the State declarations, a bill might be prepared in a few hours."[21] Elbridge Gerry made the motion and Mason seconded it. Roger Sherman alone spoke to the motion.

> Mr. Sherman, was for securing the rights of the people where requisite. The State Declarations of Rights are not repealed by this Constitution; and being in force are sufficient.[22]

There were no state votes in favor of the motion. Massachusetts abstained.

Delaware, Pennsylvania, New Jersey, Georgia, Connecticut, and Maryland ratified the new Constitution in resolutions which approved the document as it was sent to them by the Convention. However, other states, even as they voiced their approval, demanded amendments and changes. Virginia and New York expressed concerns that individual liberties needed to be protected in a bill of rights. The Virginia resolution mentioned religion in much the same words as were found in that state's own Bill of Rights:

> That religion or the duty which we owe to our Creator, and the manner of discharging it can be directed only by reason and conviction, not by force or violence, and therefore all men have an equal, natural and unalienable right to the free exercise of religion according to the dictates of conscience, and that no particular religious sect or society ought to be favored or established by Law in preference to others.[23]

The New York Convention, in approving the new Constitution on July 26, 1788, demanded that rights be protected using similar wording with reference to religion:

> That the People have an equal, natural and unalienable right, freely and peaceably to Exercise their Religion according to the dictates of Conscience, and that no Religious Sect or Society ought to be favoured or established by Law in preference of others.[24]

On June 8, 1789 U.S. Congressman James Madison insisted that the House of Representatives begin consideration of a bill of rights to be added to the new Constitution. The task of getting the new government under way had postponed consideration of amendments until Madison reminded the House that people "...may think we are not sincere in our desire to incorporate such amendments in the constitution as will secure those rights, which they consider as not sufficiently guarded."[25]

Of the nine amendments Madison proposed, the first nonprocedural one stated:

> The civil rights of none shall be abridged on account of religious belief or worship, nor shall any national religion be established, nor shall the full and equal rights of conscience be in any manner, or on any pretext, infringed.[26]

On a motion by Fisher Ames the House wording was, without debate, changed to:

> Congress shall make no law establishing religion, or to prevent the free exercise thereof, or to infringe the rights of conscience.[27]

When the proposed amendment reached the Senate, that body altered the wording to read:

> Congress shall make no law establishing articles of faith or a mode of worship, or prohibiting the free exercise of religion....[28]

A joint conference committee was set up to work out a compromise between the two houses. That committee, chaired by Madison, developed the language which was finally adopted as the religion clauses of the First Amendment: "Congress shall make no law respecting an establishment of religion, or prohibiting the free exercise thereof...."

On September 25, 1789, Congress proposed twelve amendments to the Constitution—without recorded votes—and sent them to the states for their consideration. The ten amendments which we know as the Bill of Rights were ratified by the necessary three-fourths of the states when Virginia voiced its approval on December 15, 1791. Secretary of State Thomas Jefferson authenticated the vote to governors of the states in a circular letter dated March 1, 1792.[29]

The records of the debate are of only marginal help in determining exactly what Congress intended the First Amendment religion clauses to prohibit. The views of Madison and Jefferson, the architects of the Amendment, are clear[30] but those of the other members of Congress and those of the state legislators who approved it are less clear. Thus the courts have had to assume the role of final arbiter in controversies over its meanings.

The dilemma which the Supreme Court has faced in interpreting the religion clauses was detailed by Chief Justice Burger in speaking for the Court in *Walz v. Tax Commission of the City of New York*:

> The Establishment and Free Exercise Clauses of the First Amendment are not the most precisely drawn portions of the Constitution. The sweep of the absolute prohibitions in the Religion Clauses may have been calculated; but the purpose was to state an objective not to write a statute. In attempting to articulate the scope of the two Religion Clauses, the Court's opinions reflect the limitations inherent in formulating general principles on a case-by-case basis. The considerable internal inconsistency in the opinions of the Court derives from what, in retrospect, may have been too sweeping utterances on aspects of these clauses that seemed clear in relation to the particular cases but have limited meaning as general principles.[31]

FREE EXERCISE LIMITATIONS ON GOVERNMENT

Despite the fact that the First Amendment specifically states that "Congress shall make no law..." there were many knowledgeable people who were surprised when the Supreme Court, in *Barron v. Baltimore*,[32] held that the restrictions on government actions found in the Bill of Rights were not applicable to the actions of the several states. While the facts and pleadings in *Barron* dealt only with the constitutional requirement that private property shall not be taken for public use without just compensation,[33] the effect of the decision was to declare that all of the Bill of Rights, including the free exercise of religion clause, protected the people only from the infringements of the national government.[34]

In 1868 the Fourteenth Amendment was added to the Constitution, and in its relevant parts it states:

All persons born or naturalized in the United States, and subject to the jurisdiction thereof, are citizens of the United States and of the State wherein they reside. No State shall make or enforce any law which shall abridge the privileges or immunities of citizens of the United States; nor shall any State deprive any person of life, liberty, or property, without due process of law;....

The Amendment does not make specific reference to religion or to most of the other rights protected by the Bill of Rights. There has been a good deal of disagreement between legal scholars on whether there was any intention that the Fourteenth Amendment be related to the Bill of Rights. There is no question that some of the Amendment's spokesmen saw a relationship. Thaddeus Stevens, who introduced the proposed amendment in the House of Representatives, stated:

> The first section prohibits the States from abridging the privileges and immunities of citizens of the United States, or unlawfully depriving them of life, liberty, or property, or of denying to any person within their jurisdiction the "equal" protection of the laws.
>
> I can hardly believe that any person can be found who will not admit that every one of these provisions is just. They are all asserted, in some form or other, in our Declaration or organic law. But the Constitution limits only the actions of Congress, and is not a limitation on the States. This amendment supplies that defect, and allows Congress to correct the unjust legislation of the States, so far that the law which operates upon one man shall operate *equally* upon all.[35]

A prominent analyst of the Fourteenth Amendment's historical origins declared that one of the major objects the Congress had in submitting the proposed amendment to the states for ratification was the nationalization of the Bill of Rights.[36]

Such conclusions have been strongly challenged by other constitutional scholars who assert that existing evidence does not support the idea that Congress and the states, in adding the Fourteenth Amendment, intended to make the Bill of Rights applicable to the states.[37] Chief Justice Earl Warren suggested that the history of the Fourteenth Amendment is "at best...inconclusive";[38] and Justice Brennan concluded that the "record left by the framers of the Fourteenth Amendment...is...too vague and imprecise," and that the Amendment remains "capable of being interpreted by future generations in accordance with the vision and needs of those generations."[39]

The spirit of Justice Brennan's statement had an earlier expression by the Court in *Cantwell v. Connecticut*,[40] which held that the "liberty" in the Fourteenth Amendment made the religion clauses of the First Amendment applicable to the states. Scholars may argue about the intent of the framers and the ratifying states, but the Court has held that the religion clauses have been nationalized.

FREE EXERCISE OF RELIGION: JUSTIFICATION AND MEANING

Justifications of the Free Exercise Clause: As has been pointed out, one of the motivating drives of those who colonized this nation was an intense desire to protect and practice their own religious beliefs. Such a drive made an indelible mark on the mores of our society. An overwhelming majority of Americans appears to have adopted the ideas of our forebears that a person who is guided by religious beliefs is not a great menace to our society and that he or she should be protected from government infringement of those beliefs and actions.

J. M. Clark has suggested[41] that there are at least three justifications for religious freedom:

1. Religious liberty can be justified because it is inseparable from freedom of speech—a justification for one is a justification for the other. The Court has even considered the two together in several cases.[42] A free society can exist only where there is free speech—and, therefore, where there is religious freedom.

2. Religion represents ideas and idealism which serve as a valuable element in the entire society—even though the society may reject the conclusions of the idealist. For example, many Americans who are not conscientious objectors themselves agree with the idea that a person has the right to choose, for religious reasons, to be a conscientious objector to war.[43] A justification of religious liberty on this basis, however, does not give the courts substantial guidance in deciding religious liberty cases.

3. The most important justification for religious liberty relates to fairness to the individual. As Clark says:

> The violation of a man's religion or conscience often works an exceptional harm to him which, unless justified by the most stringent social needs, constitutes a moral wrong in and of itself.... The moral condemnation implicit in the threat of criminal sanctions is likely to be very painful to one motivated by belief. Furthermore, the cost to a principled individual of failing to do his moral duty is generally severe, in terms of supernatural sanction or the loss of moral self-respect.[44]

These may not be considered as a complete justification of religious liberty to a religious person but they, and particularly the last one, serve as bases for interpretation "by future generations in accordance with the vision and needs of those generations."

"Religion" in the Law: If the free exercise of religion is a "good" worthy of constitutional protection, some brief attempt should be made to define "religion" in terms which aid in discussing the free exercise of that religion.

A leading English legal dictionary does not even attempt to define "religion."[45] *Black's Law Dictionary* defines it as "Man's relation to Divinity, to reverence, worship, obedience, and submission to mandates and precepts of supernatural or superior beings. In its broadest sense includes all forms of belief in the existence of superior beings exercising power over human beings by volition, imposing rules of conduct, with future rewards and punishments." The standard legal definition of the term "religion" is the one given by the Supreme Court: "The term 'religion' has reference to one's views of his relations to his Creator, and to the obligations they impose of reverence for his being and character, and of obedience to his will."[46] However well such a definition may have fitted the concept of religion current in 1890 when it was written, it does not come to grips with the problem of nontheistic religions—a problem which will be discussed below.[47]

Theologian Paul Tillich developed the idea that "religion" should be defined as a person's "ultimate concern."[48] It seems that Judge Augustus N. Hand supported that idea when he said: "Religious belief...is a belief finding expression in a conscience which categorically requires the believer to disregard elementary self-interest and to accept martyrdom in preference to transgressing its tenets."[49]

Such an "ultimate concern" definition is appealing in that it focuses on function rather than content. It does not, thereby, place unnecessary preconceptions on the content of free exercise of religion: "it is adequately limited because it excludes beliefs capable of compromise; and it is consistent with the preferred status given to religious freedom under the First Amendment because of the importance which the law should attach to the ultimate concerns of individuals."[50] There are difficulties from the legal point of view in such a definition. As a definition depending entirely on the psychology of the individual, it becomes entirely too subjective for analysis and puts courts in the difficult position of attempting to determine the sincerity of beliefs. Such a definition also tends to equate the nature of belief with the intensity with which that belief is held and invites inquisitorial methods in direct opposition to constitutional guarantees.[51]

Other scholars have developed different definitions of the term "religion"—all of them with problems of their own. But this is not a theological study. It can rather quickly be concluded that the term "religion" is not subject to a precise, all-inclusive definition. However, there is every indication that the founders *intended* that the word be interpreted broadly by the courts.[52] "The free exercise of religion protected by the First Amendment extends far beyond the freedom of worship; it includes the right to believe, to practice, to preach, and to teach. Moreover, it includes the right of no religion,...[and] it protects disbelief as well."[53]

FREE EXERCISE OF RELIGION: THE SCOPE OF THE PROTECTION

The Supreme Court has stated that the free exercise clause of the First Amendment "embraces two concepts,—freedom to believe and freedom to act. The first is absolute, but, in the nature of things, the second cannot be."[54] It is clear that the problem which confronts a court in hearing a free exercise of religion case is drawing an intelligent and logical distinction between permissible actions based on religious beliefs and impermissible ones.

The Supreme Court has given some guidance. When a court evaluates an assertion that free exercise of religion has been infringed, it will apply the tests developed by the Supreme Court in the establishment cases[55]—i.e., it will look first for a secular primary purpose and effect, and excessive entanglement of government with religion will be considered.[56] If the state's actions pass these tests, the court will apply other tests for determining when state action unconstitutionally burdens, denies, or limits freedom of action based on religious beliefs. These tests were developed over many years[57] and were distilled by the Supreme Court in *Wisconsin v. Yoder*.[58] In *Yoder* can be found a three part test:

(1) The court must determine whether or not a legitimate religious belief is held and whether the activity affected by state action is pervasively religious. (2) The court must inquire as to whether the state action places a burden or inhibition on free exercise rights. (3) Assuming an affirmative response to these two, the court must decide if the burden is justified by a compelling state interest which cannot be served by less restrictive means.

The first of the tests presents some potential problems for a court, but these are largely evidentiary problems. Even though there may be a general uniformity of belief within a sect, a member may hold beliefs which differ from those of his fellows without lessening the validity or viability of those beliefs.[59] Ultimately, the trier of fact must make a judgment on whether a legitimate religious belief is held and whether the activity is pervasively religious. However, "religious beliefs need not be acceptable, logical, consistent, or comprehensible to others in order to merit First Amendment protection."[60]

The second test rests on an objective basis. Does the state action burden or inhibit the free exercise of religion? A *de minimis* burden may be accommodated to the test, but state action which denies "a benefit because of conduct mandated by religious belief, thereby putting substantial pressure on an adherent to modify his behavior and to violate his beliefs," burdens religion. "While the compulsion may be indirect, the infringement upon free exercise is nonetheless substantial."[61]

> The Free Exercise Clause...withdraws from legislative power, state and federal, the exertion of any restraint on the free exercise of religion. Its purpose is to secure religious liberty in the individual by prohibiting any invasions thereof by civil authority. Hence it is necessary in a free exercise case for one to show the coercive effect of the enactment as it operates against him in the practice of his religion.[62]

The third test qualifies somewhat the absolute statement above. Even if there is a burden on religion as a result of state action, the state may justify placing that burden if it can demonstrate a paramount or compelling interest which cannot be served by less restrictive means. Thus, the Court, in its first free exercise case, permitted the government to make illegal the plural marriages sanctioned by the Church of Jesus Christ of Latter-day Saints on the grounds that it had a compelling interest in protecting morals.[63] Similarly, the state interest in protecting the health and safety of its citizens was deemed sufficient to permit the banning of the so-called "snakehandling" cults.[64] The burden of proof of both the compelling state interest and the fact that less restrictive means of serving that interest are not available rests on the state when it infringes on free exercise of religion.

As clear as the free exercise tests may seem, litigation abounds hinging on the question of the legitimate burdens which the state may place on the free exercise of religion. The Supreme Court will hear at least one such case in its next term.[65] The metes and bounds of the protection remain unclear. However, there have been some clear determinations of the scope of the protection in specific cases.

Contributions of the "Mainline" Religious Organizations: For two related principal reasons the so-called "mainline" religious organizations have made very few contributions to the judicial explication of the free exercise clause. In the first place, these organizations have played a major role in determining society's standards. Since they established the norms of religious exercise—the "proper" manner of expressing religious beliefs—they have not felt a need to go to court to protect their free exercise rights. Secondly, until relatively recently the "mainline" religious organizations have been a powerful part of the political establishment. They had large memberships which on some issues could be translated into votes, they had ready access to the media, their membership included prominent financial and political leaders, they had financial resources. Therefore, they simply did not have to cope with government infringement of their free exercise.

When Baptists in Virginia were an unpopular sect—during colonial and early independence times when their leaders were imprisoned for preaching and their churches were harassed—they played a substantial role in laying the groundwork for the proposal and adoption of the religion clauses of the First Amendment. Since that time they have become a part of the religious establishment; and although they have been indirectly involved in litigation under the establishment clause, they have not been involved until very recently in litigation concerning the free exercise clause.[66] The other "establishment" denominations, though not usually subjected to the same kinds of persecution, have also been late in expressing concern over free exercise rights in addition to their concern about establishment rights.[67]

The primary exception to this rule of non-involvement has been in a borderline area of free exercise. The major denominations own—directly or through their member local congregations, depending on their ecclesiology—a substantial amount of real property. This they have sought to protect from schismatics who would leave the denomination and take the local church property with them. Though the litigation has largely involved the question of who owns the property, the churches have emphasized the point that government is forbidden by the free exercise clause from examining or questioning the validity of their beliefs and have insisted that the free exercise clause requires the state to accept their own determination of their polity.[68] They have been essentially successful in this—the Court distinguished hierarchical and connectional churches—until recently, when the Court sanctioned the determination of church property disputes on neutral principles of property law when at all possible.[69]

Contributions of Unpopular Theistic Religious Organizations: The "mainline" denominations have set the standards of "proper" religious belief and action. They have been, as stated above, an important part of the power elite. Religious practices and beliefs which differed from theirs have been suspect, and individuals or organizations which varied from the standards often have become targets for harassment by the state. It is to this group that we are indebted for much of the clarification of the free exercise clause.

Actions based on one of the religious tenets of the Church of Jesus Christ of Latter-day Saints (Mormon) (a persecuted religious group which was forced to flee westward to what is now Utah) were, as mentioned above, at issue in the first free exercise case to reach the Supreme Court. In response to their religious beliefs, the Mormons accepted and practiced polygamy. Bigamy is a felony which is easy to define and identify; and it was a simple matter, in this instance, to distinguish between religious belief and religious action. The Court in *Reynolds v. United States*[70] upheld §5352 of the Revised Statutes which made bigamy punishable by a fine of up to $500 and imprisonment of up to five years. The Court held that religious belief cannot be accepted as a justification of an overt act made criminal by the law of the land.[71] However, because the population in some of the territories was predominately Mormon, it was difficult to impanel a jury which would convict a fellow believer of a bigamy charge. On March 22, 1882 Congress passed an act[72] disfranchising persons living in U.S. territories who were bigamists or polygamists or were cohabiting with more than one woman. Only voters had the right to serve on juries or to vote in territorial elections. The Court sustained the law and held that it was not *ex post facto* even though it was applicable to those persons who entered the territory before March 22, 1882 or who had previously been bigamists or cohabited with more than one person of the opposite sex but were not so cohabiting at the time they attempted to register to vote.[73]

Subsequently, the Court was called on to determine the constitutionality of a conviction under a law passed by the Idaho territorial legislature. At issue was the oath which the law required of all voters. The oath, in relevant part, required a voter to swear:

> ...that I am not a bigamist or polygamist; that I am not a member of any order, organization or association which teaches, advises, counsels or encourages its members, devotees or any other person to commit the crime of bigamy or polygamy, or any other crime defined by law as a duty arising or resulting from membership in such order, organization or association, or which practices bigamy, polygamy or plural or celestial marriages as a doctrinal right of such organization....[74]

The Court stated, "With man's relations to his Maker and the obligations he may think they impose, and the manner in which an expression shall be made by him of his belief on those subjects, no interference can be permitted," and then added the caveat, "However free the exercise of religion may be, it must be subordinate to the criminal laws of the country...."[75] The decision of the District Court of the Territory of Idaho was sustained in an opinion largely devoted to a condemnation of plural marriages: "Bigamy and polygamy are crimes by the laws of all civilized and Christian countries.... To call their advocacy a tenet of religion is to offend the common sense of mankind."[76]

Anti-Mormon/anti-polygamy feelings ran so strong that on February 19, 1887 Congress passed an act which became law without the President's signature.[77] The law provided that the property owned by the Mormon Church which was not actually used for religious worship or burial should escheat to the United States, and that the charter of the Church be revoked.[78] The Court observed that, "The organization of a community for the spread and practice of polygamy is, in a measure, a return to barbarism. It is contrary to the spirit of Christianity and of the civilization which Christianity has produced in the Western World."[79] The Court then sustained a decree of the Supreme Court of the Territory of

Utah that the Corporation of the Church of Jesus Christ of Latter-day Saints be dissolved, that Church property not used for worship or for burials escheat to the United States, and that a receiver be appointed to keep possession of the Church's other real and personal property until a final judicial determination had been made.

The Mormon cases lead to two conclusions: (1) because actions under the free exercise of religion clause are not absolutely protected against state action, the state's criminal laws may be enforced without violating that clause,[80] and (2) the fear which churches have for their freedoms when pitted against an antagonistic government is well founded, unless the state is compelled to demonstrate a paramount, compelling interest in limiting free exercise actions.

The Jehovah's Witnesses, whose ideas and evangelical tactics made them as disturbing to the mainline religions and their society as were the Mormons, have succeeded through recourse to the courts in protecting their own free exercise rights and expanding those of the rest of the religious community. The Jehovah's Witnesses combined free exercise and free speech rights in their demands that they be relatively unfettered in their evangelical outreach.[81] The earliest of their cases raised free exercise issues but were decided strictly on free speech grounds.[82] Though they did not expand free exercise, they gave the Jehovah's Witnesses encouragement in later cases. The leading case, *Cantwell v. Connecticut*,[83] expanded the scope of free exercise in two ways: (1) in it the Court held that the religion clauses of the First Amendment had been made applicable to the states by the Fourteenth Amendment, and (2) the decision limited government restrictions on religious actions.

Cantwell and two other Jehovah's Witnesses were convicted of soliciting funds for religious and charitable purposes under a Connecticut statute which required a permit.[84]

> [T]he Act requires an application to the secretary of the public welfare council of the State; that he is empowered to determine whether the cause is a religious one, and that the issue of a certificate depends upon his affirmative action. If he finds that the cause is not that of religion, to solicit for it becomes a crime. He is not to issue a certificate as a matter of course.[85]

The Court held the solicitation statute invalid in that the official who was responsible for issuing permits had broad discretionary powers to determine what was or was not a religious cause. Because he was given no guidelines, his decision would constitute a censorship of religion and could determine whether or not a particular religious organization survived.

Cantwell alone had been convicted of the common law offense of inciting a breach of the peace. This charge rested on the fact that Cantwell, on a public street in a heavily Roman Catholic section of town, asked two pedestrians separately if he could play a phonograph record for them. Both agreed. The record attacked all organized religions as instruments of Satan and particularly attacked the Roman Catholic Church. The two men were angry and told Cantwell to get out of the area—which he did at once. The Court found "no assault or threatening of bodily harm, no truculent bearing, no intentional discourtesy, no personal abuse." Further, "the petitioner's communication, considered in the light of the constitutional guarantees, raised no...clear and present menace to public peace and order...."[86]

Subsequent decisions of the Court indicated that *Cantwell* did not give carte blanche for all types of evangelical outreach. In its first free exercise case after *Cantwell*, the Court held that a non-discriminatory license fee could be applied to vendors of religious books and pamphlets.[87] Less than one year later the Court vacated its decision and struck down identical fees.[88] The same year the Court invalidated a city ordinance which made it unlawful for a person distributing literature to ring a doorbell or in any way to summon the people in the house to the door to receive that literature even though the literature was leaflets advertising a religious meeting.[89] However, in *Prince v. Massachusetts*[90] a state child labor law was upheld when it had been applied to the guardian of a nine-year-old who was "engaging in the preaching work"—i.e., displaying and attempting to sell copies of "Watchtower" and "Consolation," religious publications of Jehovah's Witnesses. The statute[91] was a general one prohibiting a boy under twelve and a girl under eighteen from participating in any kind of work "in any street or public place." The Court held that the state's interest in child welfare in this case was sufficient to permit it to limit even the religious activities of children.

Further, the Court has been clear that, as long as there is no attempt on the part of government to regulate the content of the religious message being presented and as long as the requirements for licensing and permits are nondiscriminatory, government may regulate "times, places, and manners" of meetings and rallies in public parks and other public places.[92]

The Jehovah's Witnesses also obtained some explication of what the free exercise clause means in reference to exemptions from general government requirements. When the Court was first faced with the question of whether Jehovah's Witnesses' children could be excluded from the Pennsylvania public schools when they refused to participate in the pledge of allegiance to the flag for purely religious reasons, it permitted the exclusion.[93] Only three years later, the Court reversed itself and condemned, on free speech rather than on free exercise grounds, such exclusion of students.[94]

Following the lead of the Jehovah's Witnesses, other religious groups sought judicial protection of their own free exercise exemptions. The Court held that the government could require a person with religious scruples against bearing arms to take an oath that he would do so before he could become a naturalized citizen of the United States.[95] That opinion was overturned fifteen years later when the Court held, in the process of statutory interpretation, that Congress had not intended to bar such conscientious objectors from citizenship.[96] The later decision does not erase the fact that the Court had earlier held that Congress had the power to make a person choose between religious principles and naturalization.

The action in *Braunfeld v. Brown*[97] was based on the contention that the free exercise clause mandated an exemption from Pennsylvania's Sunday closing law[98] for Orthodox Jewish merchants who observed Saturday as the Sabbath.

As a result of their religious beliefs, they were required to close two days out of the week rather than only one. The Court, in its judgment,[99] emphasized that while government action which directly penalizes a religious practice must be subjected to close scrutiny by the judiciary, the requirement of such scrutiny does not make that action unconstitutional per se. The Court pointed out that the law "does not make unlawful any religious practices of appellants; the Sunday law simply regulates a secular activity and, as applied to appellants, operates so as to make the practice of their religious beliefs more expensive."[100] The rule, said the Court, was that "if the State regulates conduct by enacting a general law within its power, the purpose and effect of which is to advance the State's secular goals, the statute is valid despite its indirect burden on religious observance unless the State may accomplish its purpose by means which do not impose such a burden."[101]

By 1963 Justices Frankfurter and Whittaker had been replaced by Justices Goldberg and White. The new Court cast substantial doubt on the continued viability of *Braunfeld* with its decision in *Sherbert v. Verner*[102] and, at the same time, continued the development of a doctrine concerning the relationship between religious exercise and government actions which infringe thereon. Sherbert, a Seventh-day Adventist, was denied unemployment compensation in South Carolina because she refused to work on Saturday, the Sabbath of her faith. The South Carolina Unemployment Compensation Act[103] stated that a claimant must be "able to work, and...available for work" and that a claimant was ineligible for benefits "[i]f...he has failed, without good cause...to accept available suitable work when offered him by the employment office or the employer...." Because Sherbert's religion did not permit her to work on Saturday, she was not able to accept "available suitable work."

The Court stated that if such state action is to withstand a "constitutional challenge, it must be either because her disqualification as a beneficiary represents no infringement by the State of her constitutional rights of free exercise, or because any incidental burden on the free exercise of appellant's religion may be justified by a 'compelling state interest in the regulation of a subject within the State's constitutional power to regulate....' "[104] The Court found the enforcement of the Act in Sherbert's instance imposed a burden on her free exercise of religion and put pressure on her to "choose between following the precepts of her religion and forfeiting benefits, on the one hand, and abandoning one of the precepts of her religion in order to accept work, on the other hand."[105] Also, the State, in the opinion of the Court, did not show a compelling interest. The State's desire to prevent fraudulent claims was not sufficient: "It is basic that no showing merely of a rational relationship to some colorable state interest would suffice; in this highly sensitive constitutional area, '[o]nly the gravest abuses, endangering paramount interests, give occasion for permissible limitation.' "[106] Further, the State did not "demonstrate that no alternative forms of regulation would combat [fraudulent claims] without infringing First Amendment rights."[107]

The Amish, who earlier had quietly allowed their farm horses to be sold to pay taxes to a social security system their religion would not permit them to use, were willing to go to court to protect their rights to refuse, on the basis of religion, to comply with the Wisconsin compulsory school-attendance law which required attendance in a public or private school until age 16.[108] The Amish-run schools went only through the eighth grade; after that the children, then about 14 years of age, were given vocational training suitable for farm life. This practice—as well as their rather simple way of life—was based on their religious belief that they were required to be in the world but not a part of it.[109] Wisconsin stipulated that these beliefs were sincerely held but argued that it had an interest in the education of all children which was sufficiently compelling to justify infringement of the free exercise rights of the Amish.

In deciding *Wisconsin v. Yoder*[110] the Court balanced the rights asserted by the parties in favor of the religious free exercise of the Amish. In so doing, it confirmed its position in *Sherbert* and further limited *Braunfeld*. The Court held that though the state did have a strong interest in compulsory attendance laws,[111] "only those interests of the highest order and those not otherwise served can overbalance legitimate claims to the free exercise of religion."[112] Because the issue was not between education and no education, but rather revolved around two additional years of formal education beyond that provided by the Amish schools, the Court did not believe that the record demonstrated that Wisconsin's interest outweighed the great harm that two years of compulsory attendance in public schools would do to the sincerely held long-term beliefs and practices of the Amish.[113]

Thomas v. Review Board of the Indiana Employment Security Division[114] further strengthened the Court's decisions that unless the state can demonstrate a compelling interest its laws must allow exceptions to persons acting on the basis of religious beliefs. In this case Thomas, a member of Jehovah's Witnesses, had been transferred from the roll foundry of a steel mill to a department which produced turrets for military tanks. Thomas unsuccessfully sought another assignment and then, on the basis of a religious belief against fabricating arms, he quit his job. He applied for unemployment compensation and was denied it because under Indiana law a termination motivated by religion is not for "good cause" objectively related to the work. He then sued to obtain the benefits.[115]

The state argued that there was no tenet of faith of Jehovah's Witnesses against fabricating weapons and that Thomas was expressing a "personal philosophical choice" rather than a religious belief. Further, the state argued that any burden on Thomas' free exercise rights was only indirect and was justified by legitimate state interests.

As noted in a previous section of this paper, the Court held that "the guarantee of free exercise is not limited to beliefs which are shared by all of the members of a religious sect."[116] Although Thomas could not articulate his belief precisely, the Court considered it "religious." The Court rejected the argument of the state that if it paid benefits to Thomas it would be fostering a religious faith[117] and held the state's interest was not sufficiently compelling to justify the burdens placed on the free exercise of religion.

In a sweeping statement the Court declared:

> Where the state conditions receipt of an important benefit upon conduct proscribed by a religious faith, or where it denies such a benefit because of conduct mandated by religious belief, thereby putting substantial pressure on an adherent to modify his behavior and to violate his beliefs, a burden upon religion exists. While the compulsion may be indirect, the infringement upon free exercise is nonetheless substantial.[118]

The solicitation of funds by religious public charities has provided yet another example of court ordered exceptions to general laws. The one case on regulating solicitation of funds by public charities to reach the Supreme Court was not brought by churches—though it directly affected them.[119] Of importance to free exercise concerns was the finding that the claimed substantial governmental interest "in protecting the public from fraud, crime and undue annoyance" is "inadequate and that the ordinance cannot survive scrutiny under the First Amendment."[120] This reasoning is important to religious organizations which, in seeking free exercise exceptions to general laws on solicitation, have had to deal with state interests in protecting against crime, fraud and annoyance.

In seeking to act on these interests to regulate "time, place, and manner," of solicitations, the government has often had confrontations with the International Society for Krishna Consciousness, Inc. (ISKCON). The beliefs of ISKCON require that its members solicit funds directly from individuals and, therefore, ISKCON claims an exception to regulations on "time, place and manner" must be made.

Some forty years ago the Court declared, in a case not involving religious free exercise, that when a government's regulations of actions are not concerned with the content of expression but are only concerned with the circumstances of that expression, the regulations might well pass constitutional muster.[121] But the free exercise clause adds an additional dimension to the regulation of the circumstances of solicitation—content of belief becomes inseparable from the circumstances of time, place, and manner. However, the degree to which the state may validly regulate the circumstances of religious solicitation—if at all—is not clear.

In *Cantwell*[122] solicitation by Jehovah's Witnesses was upheld. However, in 1941, only one year after *Cantwell*, the Court declined to review a circuit court's decision holding that the free exercise of religion may be slightly inconvenienced by requiring a stranger to establish his identity and his authority to represent a public charity before he can solicit funds.[123] However, more recently ISKCON, through a series of lower court cases, has won the points that religious solicitors may not be restricted to booths in airports[124] or to particular sections of a city,[125] and that a state fair cannot restrict religious solicitors to booths on the claim of a compelling interest to prevent frauds.[126] In addition, the government may not require religious solicitors to provide an abundance of information regarding membership, financial affairs, etc.;[127] ordinances which prohibit door-to-door solicitations are invalid when applied to religious groups;[128] and the requirements for obtaining solicitation licenses by religious groups must not intrude on their free exercise of religion.[129]

The lower courts have made it clear that the solicitation of funds for religious purposes is an activity which is protected by the free exercise clause,[130] but the Supreme Court has not yet ruled on the point. Oral arguments were held on April 30, 1981 before the Court[131] on the issue of whether a rule of a state fair which restricts the distribution of literature and the solicitation of funds violates the free exercise clause when applied to the Hare Krishnas. Perhaps clear guidelines will be drawn.

Contributions of Unpopular Nontheistic Religions: The term "nontheistic religions" may seem a contradiction in terms. Therefore, it is necessary to examine further the meaning of "religion." Because religion involves an emotional and personal experience, it is better defined on an individual rather than on a universal basis. Yet there are scholars who attempt universal definitions by examining the elements which make up religion and by viewing those elements from differing perspectives in order to generalize about religion. For example, the positivists, with their disdain for speculation on origins and ultimate causes, conceive of religion as a social phenomenon to be scientifically observed and quantified. The anthropologists look with interest at the social symbols which are a part of religion. Some observers view religion from what is called a "substantive" perspective and others from a "functional" one. While these and other approaches to religion serve specific purposes, they have been of little help to the courts in interpreting the religion clauses of the First Amendment.

Most of the major religious movements in the United States are theistic. That is to say, they recognize the existence of a Supreme Being or God. To some theists God is personal and ever present. Some see God as a remote creator who began the world and its processes—much like the making and winding up of a clock—and then withdrew from the scene. Others see God as a being to be loved, feared, or worshiped—or a combination of these three. All theists agree that a Supreme Being exists and is central to world processes.

Also to be found in the United States are nontheistic philosophical and ethical systems—many having origins in the Orient—which share some moral and ethical concerns with the theistic religions. They do not share with them a belief in a Supreme Being. In spite of this, nontheistic beliefs may be considered as religions both by their adherents and by interpreters of the Constitution.

No case has come before the Supreme Court which has required it to meet head-on the issue of whether nontheistic beliefs constitute a religion within the meaning of the religion clauses of the First Amendment. The Supreme Court has made some statements to the point in cases where this issue was only a collateral one. These statements are *dicta* and not ruling case law. These *dicta*, several strong decisions by lower courts directly on point, Supreme Court decisions on conscientious objection, and substantial scholarly writing support the proposition that the Supreme Court, when it is called on to do so, will hold that nontheistic beliefs constitute religions within First Amendment usage.

There have been three court decisions which give significant insights into the interpretation of the word "religion" as used in the First Amendment: (1) the United States Supreme Court in *Torcaso v. Watkins*,[132] (2) the United States Court of Appeals for the District of Columbia Circuit in *Washington Ethical So-*

ciety v. District of Columbia,[133] and (3) a District Court of Appeals in California in *Fellowship of Humanity v. County of Alameda.*[134]

As was stated *supra*, the courts have tended to equate religion with belief in a Supreme Being.[135] However, the present tendency is to hold that religion does not necessarily posit a belief in a Supreme Being or God.

In *Torcaso*, Torcaso had been denied a commission as a notary public in Maryland because he would not affirm a belief in God as required by Article 37 of the Declaration of Rights of the Constitution of Maryland. Torcaso sued to force the issuance of his commission. The Maryland Circuit Court ruled against Torcaso, and its ruling was sustained by the Maryland Court of Appeals. When the case reached the Supreme Court, it held that Article 37 was an unconstitutional invasion of Torcaso's religious liberty guaranteed by the First Amendment. The Court stated:

> We repeat and again reaffirm that neither a State nor the Federal Government can constitutionally force a person "to profess a belief or disbelief in any religion." Neither can constitutionally pass laws or impose requirements which aid all religions as against non-believers, *and neither can aid those religions based on a belief in the existence of God as against those religions founded on different beliefs.* [footnotes omitted; emphasis added][136]

In a footnote to that statement, the Court indicated in part what it meant by the phrase "...religions founded on different beliefs."

> Among religions in this country which do not teach what would generally be considered a belief in the existence of God are Buddhism, Taoism, Ethical Culture, Secular Humanism and others.[137]

In *Washington Ethical Society*, the Court of Appeals for the District of Columbia Circuit, in a decision written by the present Chief Justice of the Supreme Court, determined that nontheistic beliefs could constitute a religion and that "religious worship" does not require the worship of a deity. Tax exemption on the building in which the Washington Ethical Society conducted services and other related activities had been denied by the Tax Court for the District of Columbia. The Court of Appeals asserted that "The sole issue raised is whether petitioner falls within the definition of a 'church' or a 'religious society' and whether its property is 'regularly used for religious worship.'....."[138] The taxing authority contended that the Society was not a religious society or church because members of the Society did not hold a belief in a Supreme Being and did not use their building for religious worship since "...'religious' and 'worship' require a belief in and teaching of a Supreme Being who controls the universe."[139]

In deciding that the Society was entitled to tax exemption as a church or religious society, the Court of Appeals said:

> Congress in granting tax exemption under this statute, like most of the states, was giving expression to a broad legislative purpose to grant support to elements in the community regarded as good for the community.... To construe exemptions so strictly that unorthodox or minority forms of worship would be denied the exemption benefits granted to those conforming to the majority beliefs might well raise constitutional issues.[140]

Fellowship of Humanity is a lengthy analytical decision which has frequently been cited with approval by other courts. The Fellowship asserted that it was a religion and, as such, should be exempted from certain California taxes. The state denied those exemptions saying, essentially, that because Humanism is nontheistic it cannot be a religion. The Fellowship filed a suit which required the court to determine whether or not Humanism is a religion. The District Court of Appeals in California assumed that "...humanists believe that man contains within himself infinite goodness and controls his own destiny, and that a divine or superhuman being has no place in their beliefs."[141] In arriving at a decision which allowed tax exemption for the Fellowship's buildings, the Court of Appeals said:

> ...there are forms of belief generally and commonly accepted as religions and whose adherents, numbering in the millions, practice what is commonly accepted as religious worship, which do not include or require as essential the belief in a deity. Taoism, classic Buddhism, and Confucianism, are among these religions.[142]

Several cases which have interpreted the statutory phrase "religious training and belief" also support the conclusion that nontheistic beliefs can be classified as religions. Cases arising out of claims of conscientious objection during the Vietnam war required the courts to reach some hard decisions about this phrase. In *United States v. Seeger*[143] the Supreme Court interpreted §6(j) of the Universal Military Training and Service Act as amended. This section of the Code exempts from combat training and service in the armed forces those who are conscientiously opposed to participation in war in any form "by reason of religious training and belief." Such "religious training and belief" includes, according to the Act, "an individual's belief in a relation to a Supreme Being involving duties superior to those arising from any human relation, but does not include essentially political, sociological, or philosophical views or a merely personal moral code."[144]

Seeger, in seeking a conscientious objector classification, did not adopt verbatim the printed Selective Service form. However, he declared that he was conscientiously opposed to participation in war in any form by reason of his religious beliefs. He indicated that he wanted to leave the question of his belief in a Supreme Being open though he did show a "skepticism or disbelief in the existence of God." However, he denied that this skepticism left him with a "lack of faith in anything whatsoever." He cited the writings of Plato, Aristotle, and Spinoza to support his claim to an ethical belief in intellectual and moral integrity "without belief in God, except in the remotest sense."[145] The Court held that this and similar expressions of belief met the test of: "A sincere and meaningful belief which occupies in the life of its possessor a place parallel to that filled by the God of those admittedly qualifying for the exemption...."[146] It also declared that it is the task of the local boards and the courts "...to decide whether the beliefs professed by a registrant are sincerely held and whether they are, in his own scheme of things, religious."[147]

In *Welsh v. United States* the Court further interpreted §6(j) to permit exemption from military service to "...all those whose consciences, spurred by deeply

59

held moral, ethical, or religious beliefs, would give them no rest or peace if they allowed themselves to become a part of an instrument of war."[148] Similarly in *United States v. Sisson*[149] a federal District Court in Massachusetts held that Sisson's refusal to serve in the military on moral but not traditional religious bases was justifiable and quoted with approval Alfred North Whitehead's definition: "...religion is what the individual does with his own solitariness."[150]

The courts, in applying and interpreting §6(j) which permitted exemption from military service based on an individual's "religious training and belief," have equated nontheistic systems of ethical and moral thought with theistic systems of thought and have included both under the rubric of religion. Thus, an assumption that the courts will continue to treat nontheistic systems as religions has a sound basis in precedent.

Additionally, there is considerable authority in modern writings on the subject to warrant the assumption that the courts will incorporate nontheistic beliefs into the definition of "religion" as it is used in the First Amendment:

> A new definition of religion itself is already emerging. Whereas Cicero was satisfied to call it "the pious worship of God," and Menzies only a generation ago won acclaim for terming it "the worship of higher powers from a sense of need," there is a tendency today to question the necessity of including the supernatural in a definition of religion.
>
> * * * *
>
> An inclusive definition, then, must recognize both varieties of religion, theistic and nontheistic.
>
> * * * *
>
> *Religion*: is the endeavor of divided and incomplete human personality to attain unity and completion, usually but not necessarily by seeking the help of an ideally complete divine person or persons.
>
> *Religions* are systems of belief and practice which arise among disciples of some man who has attained a satisfying measure of success in his endeavors to unify and complete his personality.[151]

Professor Donald A. Giannella states:

> Only a particular, fundamental aspect of the realm of the spirit is embodied in the concept of religion. That branch of modern religious thought which is strongly influenced by Paul Tillich's thinking refers to this realm as that area dealing with matters of ultimate concern. In this view religion encompasses those beliefs and world-views which illuminate the "very ground of our being" and which invest life with ultimate meaning and direction.
>
> Although these concepts are very abstract for judges and lawyers, the Supreme Court appears ready to adopt them. In *United States v. Seeger*, the Court admitted that its decision had been influenced by modern theological thought in general and that of Tillich in particular. This development was not too surprising in light of the Court's earlier decision in *Torcaso v. Watkins*, where Mr. Justice Black said that nontheistic religions, such as Buddhism, were included within the protection afforded by the free exercise clause and listed both ethical culture and secular humanism as religions. It is true that the *Seeger* definition is only an interpretation of the term religious belief as used in the Selective Service Act. Nonetheless, it seems

to suggest the Court's ultimate definition of religion for constitutional purposes. [footnotes omitted][152]

A comprehensive note on the problem of governmental definition of religion states, "If the law may not inquire into the content of men's beliefs to determine their verity or reasonableness, it may be inferred that it is improper to use a particular belief, such as a belief in a deity, as a test of religion."[153]

In the process of developing the precedents above, adherents of nontheistic religions have contributed to the evolution of the free exercise clause. By broadening the definition of "religion," nontheists have broadened the scope of free exercise protections. If a philosophical belief plays for an individual the same role which belief in God plays for theists, free exercise rights come into play. The potential for expansion of free exercise rights under such circumstances is theoretically unlimited. The actual contributions of the nontheists will be determined by cases not yet in court.

FREE EXERCISE OF RELIGION: CURRENT PROBLEMS

Despite what seems to be a progressive expansion of the protections of the free exercise clause for both theistic and nontheistic religions, there are many unsettled questions about the degree to which the state can limit, regulate, or control churches[154] and their religious mission. The churches prefer to call any state attempts to so limit, regulate, or control "government intrusion into religion." This is a loaded phrase, but it is indicative of the emotion which the churches bring into existing and potential litigation under the free exercise clause.

At the heart of the church-state conflicts and tensions lies a problem of definition. The state, which must deal with the church in a multitude of ways, would like a clear definition of the word "church." Religious organizations resist having the state make that definition for two basic reasons. First, the Constitution clearly gives to the state only secular powers and specifically denies to it any authority over religious matters. Thus, as they see it, the churches alone have legal competence to define what is church and what is not church. Second, the broad spectrum of ecclesiology, belief, and practice within American religious organizations makes it impossible to arrive at a single definition which will fit all of them. To try to force all of them into a preferred mold would be unconstitutional under the establishment clause alone in addition to inhibiting the free exercise of religion to an unconstitutional degree. Any legislation or administrative regulation which attempts to establish an exclusive definition of "church" will be resisted in the legislatures and in the courts by all segments of organized religion.

Flowing from its determination that the state may not define "church" is the religious community's unshakable belief that the church and only the church must define for itself the nature and content of its religious mission. It is a truism that a definition establishes parameters which are limits. If the state defines the religious mission of a church, it is limiting that mission. Only when the state can demonstrate a compelling interest which cannot be served by less restrictive means may it limit or regulate specific actions which constitute the religious mission of the church, but it cannot under any circumstances develop a definition which sets the metes and bounds of the religious mission of any or all churches.

This problem of definition furnishes a backdrop for an examination of some of the state actions which are in litigation or which will be litigated unless political or administrative remedies become available. The list that follows is not exhaustive but is merely illustrative of the scope of free exercise problems today.

1. *Lobby disclosure and regulation legislation*: Congress has attempted during the last few sessions to reach internal agreement on legislation which would establish a threshold of money and time spent attempting to influence legislation which, when reached, would require a detailed reporting and disclosure of an organization's finances, income sources, and activities. Religious organizations have been included in the proposed bills until the 1981 bill.[155]

Most of the churches consider their efforts to influence the formation of public policy as an integral part of their religious mission and, hence, not subject to governmental control. They do not see a compelling interest in the state's desire to examine their records and books of account.[156] If churches are covered by future lobby disclosure and regulation legislation, most of them will resist and, if the state attempts to enforce the law, they will likely go to the courts for a determination of their rights.

2. *Internal Revenue Service definition of "integrated auxiliaries" of churches*: The Internal Revenue Code provides that §501(c)(3) public charities annually must file extensive informational returns.[157] Mandatorily excluded from filing are "churches, their integrated auxiliaries, conventions and associations of churches."[158] The Internal Revenue Service felt compelled to define the term "integrated auxiliaries"—a new term in the 1969 revision of the Code. In doing so it ran head-on into organized religion's challenge to the legal and philosophical competence of the IRS to define which activities are or are not integral to the religious mission of the church.[159]

After some eighty denominations and religious agencies testified against the proposed regulations containing the definition and no one testified in favor of them, the Service issued final regulations.[160] The churches objected to these as an unconstitutional definition of "church" and "integrated auxiliaries." An agency which one of the mainline denominations considers integral to its religious mission has now been ruled not to be an integrated auxiliary. All administrative remedies have been exhausted, and the General Counsel of the Internal Revenue Service must now determine whether the Service will go to court against a defiant major denomination.

3. *National Labor Relations Board's attempts to exercise jurisdiction over parochial schools*: In 1978 the NLRB insisted on and supervised elections for labor representation for lay teachers in Roman Catholic parochial schools of Chicago. The schools, led by the Bishop of Chicago, refused to recognize or bargain with the union. The NLRB asserted jurisdiction on the grounds that schools were only "religiously associated" and not "completely religious." The Supreme Court held that under the existing statute schools operated by a

church to teach both religious and secular subjects are not within the jurisdiction of the NLRB and that "the Board's exercise of jurisdiction over teachers in church-operated schools would implicate the guarantees of the Religion Clauses."[161] The Court did not reach the point of determining whether such schools *must* be excluded because of the free exercise clause. The Court declined to hear a similar case during the October 1980 term.[162] Churches which operate parochial schools will continue to resist such intrusions.

A recent case gave the Supreme Court an opportunity to decide whether the free exercise clause requires that church schools be exempt from coverage by unemployment compensation laws—and, therefore, indirectly by labor relations law. Petitioners had argued that their school was "church" *per se* and must be exempt on statutory and free exercise grounds. The unanimous Court, in keeping with its rules, relied on statutory interpretation: "Petitioners are eligible for exemption... by virtue of the nature of their relationship to the church bodies that employ them. This makes it unnecessary for us to consider the First Amendment issues raised by petitioners."[163]

4. *State regulation of curriculum content and teacher qualification in church schools*: Though state courts in Ohio, Vermont, and Kentucky have held that the state may not regulate curriculum content in church schools or require that teachers therein hold state teaching certificates,[164] the Supreme Court has not yet seen fit to clarify the issue. The schools' position is that their free exercise of religion rights make it constitutionally beyond the reach of the state to require what, how, and by whom subject matter may be taught in church schools. The state has argued that its concern for the education of its children justifies its actions. State courts have not found this sufficiently compelling to justify regulation of church schools.[165]

5. *Disclosure requirements of federal administrative agencies*: Several federal agencies—the Civil Rights Commission, the Equal Employment Opportunities Commission, the Department of Health and Human Services, and the Department of Education—have attempted to require church-related agencies and institutions, including seminaries, to report their employment and, in the case of schools, admission statistics by race, sex, and religion even though neither the agencies nor the schools received public funds directly. In one case a college with very close denominational ties is appealing a Court of Appeals decision that its free exercise rights permit it to discriminate on religious grounds in hiring and promotion of faculty but that religion may not be used as a pretext for discrimination on other bases.[166] A seminary refused to comply with disclosure requirements and won its free exercise point at the district court level.[167] EEOC's appeal has gone to argument in the 5th Circuit, and a decision should be forthcoming soon. The loser will almost certainly appeal.

6. *State seizure of a church*: The unique assault by the State of California on the Worldwide Church of God is frightening to all religious organizations. California acted under the common law public trust theory which asserts that properties of organizations incorporated as not-for-profit corporations are public trusts—i.e., are held in trust for all the people. Under that theory, if the state has any reason to believe that the trust is not being honored, it can enter,

63

place the corporation in receivership, and seize the property and books of account. Such action was initiated against the Worldwide Church of God and was terminated by a statutory exemption from the theory without a judicial determination.[168] The question of who owns the churches has not been decided, and until it is, religious organizations will not "rest easy."

7. *State authorized "deprogramming"*: A serious threat to the free exercise of religion involves courts granting conservatorship orders giving parents physical custody of their adult children in order that they might be deprogrammed. These conservatorship orders have usually been directed at adherents of unpopular religious movements, but there have been instances in which children have been "deprogrammed" from Roman Catholic and Baptist beliefs. These court-ordered conservatorships and recent legislative attempts to ease the criteria for granting conservatorships over adult children are based on three assumptions: (1) There are 3000 to 5000 "cults" in this country—"evil" religions with which no sane person would get involved. (2) Some people never become old enough to make their own decisions on matters of religion. (3) People who join "cults" have been psychologically kidnapped and forced to join such organizations against their wills.

Despite the admonition that "[i]n the field of beliefs, and particularly religious tenets, it is difficult, if not impossible, to establish a universal truth against which deceit and imposition can be measured,"[169] courts are still granting conservatorships and legislatures are aiding the process. Such an intrusion into an individual's free exercise of religion is of serious concern to the entire spectrum of the religious community.

8. *The Internal Revenue Service's "public policy" criteria for continued tax exemption*: The only statutory qualifications for an organization to be classified as a Tax Code §501(c)(3) organization are that it be a not-for-profit public charity which does not "substantially" attempt to influence legislation and which does not participate in or intervene in any political campaign on behalf of any candidate for public office.[170] The IRS has added a qualification—an organization may not retain tax-exempt status if it goes contrary to what the IRS conceives to be public policy.

For example, the Church of Scientology of California was notified that its §501(c)(3) status was being lifted because several of its leaders had been convicted of felonies—acts which were clearly contrary to public policy.[171]

This public policy approach also has been used in IRS regulations[172] requiring church related schools to demonstrate that they do not discriminate in their enrollment and recruitment practices.[173] Though the regulations have not been adjudicated and are technically still in effect, enforcement has been suspended by amendments to Treasury appropriation acts which direct that none of Treasury's funds be used to enforce the regulations.

The churches assert that if the IRS can determine the composition of the student bodies of institutions integral to their religious missions, it can also determine the standards for membership in the churches themselves and thus the content of their beliefs and ministries.[174] This, they say, threatens their free exercise of religion.

The "public policy" and "integrated auxiliary" confrontations with the IRS have united the broad range of religious organizations. When each of these state actions is adjudicated—which no doubt they will be—religious organizations across the spectrum of beliefs will become directly involved.

9. *Courts' examination of church polity*: The courts have seen fit to redefine ecclesiastical polity so that hierarchical bodies in effect are rendered congregational in polity[175] and dispersed "connectional" churches, such as the United Methodist Church, are deemed to be hierarchical—contrary to their own self-definition.[176] In making that determination, the court laid the basis for its declaration that the entire United Methodist Church could be held liable for the torts of an agency related to a local group of churches.

These actions have been deeply disturbing to organized religion and, because litigation in the major cases was terminated before it reached the Supreme Court,[177] no opportunity for a final determination of the state's power is presently in view.

10. *State regulation of the solicitation of funds*: The law is not clear, as was stated above, on how much the state may limit direct solicitation of funds by religious organizations. Administrative appeals are being pursued on regulations issued by the Federal Aviation Administration limiting solicitation in the airports it operates.[178] The House Committee on Post Office and Civil Service has attempted from time to time to require organizations which solicit through the mails to adopt uniform accounting systems and to make full disclosure of their finances to any potential contributor who asks for the information. Organized religion seems almost anxious to adjudicate the question of the degree to which the free exercise clause allows regulation of solicitation of funds by religious organizations.

This is not an exhaustive list of government intrusions into religion; and none of these developments, taken by itself, is sufficiently alarming to the religious community for it to raise a call to action. There is some consensus that certain restrictions of the free exercise of religion are justified. However, the *pattern* which is formed when all of these intrusions are viewed together is alarming to religious organizations. They feel that they must insure their free exercise rights now lest they be completely eroded in an uncertain future.

CONCLUSIONS

Churches are not above the law, but neither is government above the law. They are both bound by the Constitution and laws "made in pursuance thereof." The churches recognize the difference between religious belief and action on that belief. They would not argue against state control of actions which present a "clear and present danger" to society; but beyond that they insist that the state must clearly demonstrate a compelling interest which cannot be served by less restrictive means before it embarks on efforts to regulate actions based on religious beliefs. The burden of demonstrating that compelling interest lies squarely on the state. The church must not be expected to make the case that the state does not have a compelling interest.

The special status which the First Amendment gives to religion has its disadvantages as well as its advantages. Because an organization is religious, it is forbidden by the establishment clause from receiving public funds. But because an organization is religious, it is protected by the free exercise clause from state demands for reporting or disclosure.

Those organizations or individuals who break the law must expect to pay the penalty set by the law if their offense is not determined to be justified. Religious organizations and their members are no exception. With the exception of claims under the Constitution, they should neither demand nor expect special treatment under the law.

James Madison, the father of the Constitution and of the Bill of Rights, wrote in the famed *Memorial and Remonstrance*: "[I]t is proper to take alarm at the first experiment on our liberties." The churches seem more determined than ever to react strongly to any attempts to unjustifiably limit the free exercise of religion.

FOOTNOTES

[1] W. E. Garrison, *Intolerance* (New York: 1934).

[2] *See* A. L. Smith, *Church and State in the Middle Ages* (Oxford: 1913) and B. D. Hill, *Church and State in the Middle Ages* (New York: 1970).

[3] 26 H.VIII, c. 1, 492.

[4] *See* "First Statute of Repeal," 1 Mary I, c. 2, 202; "Act Reviving the Heresy Laws," 1 and 2 Mary I c. 6, 244; and "Second Statute of Repeal," 1 and 2 Mary I, c. 8, 246.

[5] The 1555 "Act Against Traitorous Words" declared it treason for a subject to pray to God that He "should shorten her days or take her out of the way...or any such like malicious prayer amounting to the same effect...." 1 and 2 Mary I, c. 9, 254.

[6] Elizabeth I was subsequently excommunicated and "deprived of her pretended claim to the aforesaid kingdom and of all lordship, dignity and privilege whatsoever." Bull "Regnans in Excelsis" of Pius V, February 25, 1570, translated and reprinted in S. H. Ehler and J. B. Morrall, *Church and State Through the Centuries* (Westminster, Md.: 1954), 180-183.

[7] 1 Eliz. I, c. 1, 350.

[8] 1 Eliz. I, c. 2, 355.

[9] *See* J. W. Allen, *A History of Political Thought in the Sixteenth Century* (London: 1941).

[10] A. S. P. Woodhouse, *Puritanism and Liberty* (London: 1950).

[11] *See* I. H. Polishook, *Roger Williams, John Cotton and Religious Freedom* (Englewood Cliffs, N. J.: 1967), Part 1, and T. P. Greene, *Roger Williams and the Massachusetts Magistrates* (Boston: 1964).

[12] Williams' *The Bloudy Tenent of Persecution for Cause of Conscience* (London: 1644) speaks strongly of religious liberty and, at 97-116, of the wall of separation which must exist between the garden of the church and the wilderness of the world. The book, published while Williams was in London getting a charter for the colony, was ordered burned at a public ceremony by the English Parliament.

[13] L. J. Moore, Jr., "Religious Liberty: Roger Williams and the Revolutionary Era," XXXIV *Church History* 1, March 1965.

[14] Articles of Confederation, Article III.

[15] Virginia Bill of Rights, sec. 16, June 12, 1776.

[16] Virginia Statute of Religious Liberty, Art. II, January 16, 1786.

[17] *See* S. H. Cobb, *The Rise of Religious Liberty in America* (New York: 1902).

[18] From the Delaware act of February 3, 1787 authorizing and naming "deputies" to the Philadelphia Convention. See *Documents Illustrative of the Formation of the Union of the American States* (Washington: 1927), 66.
[19] *Documents Illustrative*, 647.
[20] U.S. Constitution, Art. VI.
[21] *Documents Illustrative*, 716.
[22] *Id.*
[23] From the Virginia resolution passed on June 27, 1788 printed in *Documents Illustrative*, 1030–1031.
[24] From the New York resolution passed on July 26, 1788 printed in *Documents Illustrative*, 1035.
[25] 1 *Annals of Congress* 444 (June 8, 1789).
[26] *Id.* 451 (June 8, 1789).
[27] *Id.* (August 20, 1789). Irving Brant, Madison's definitive biographer, is certain that this was written by Madison rather than by Ames. See Irving Brant, *James Madison: Father of the Constitution, 1787–1800* (Indianapolis: 1950), 271.
[28] 1 *Journal of the Senate* 77 (September 9, 1789).
[29] The two proposed amendments which were rejected were basically structural and were meant to amplify Art. I, sec. 2, cl. 3 and to add to the provisions of Art. I, sec. 6, cl. 1 the prohibition of varying the pay of members of Congress until a presidential election intervened. They were not rights *per se*.
[30] Jefferson's statement to the Danbury, Connecticut Baptist Association that the First Amendment built "...a wall of separation between Church and State" is found in 8 Works of Jefferson 13 and quoted in *Reynolds v. United States*, 98 U.S. 145, 164 (1878).
[31] 397 U.S. 664, 668 (1970).
[32] U.S. 243 (1833).
[33] U.S. Constitution, Amendment V.
[34] Massachusetts was the last state to give up an established church as a result of an 1833 amendment to its constitution. See J.C. Meyer, *Church and State in Massachusetts* (Cleveland: 1930), 201–220.
[35] Quoted in the appendix to Justice Black's dissent in *Adamson v. California*, 332 U.S. 46, 104 (1947).
[36] H. E. Flack, *The Adoption of the Fourteenth Amendment* (Baltimore: 1908), 94.
[37] C. Fairman, "Does the Fourteenth Amendment Incorporate the Bill of Rights?" II Stan. L. Rev. 5 (1949). See also Graham, "The Antislavery Backgrounds of the Fourteenth Amendment," II Wisc. L. Rev. 610, 659 (1950).
[38] *Brown v. Board of Education*, 347 U.S. 483, 489 (1954).
[39] *Oregon v. Mitchell*, 400 U.S. 112, 278 (1970).
[40] 310 U.S. 296 (1940).
[41] J. M. Clark, "Guidelines for the Free Exercise Clause," 83 Harv. L. Rev. 327, 336, 337 (1969).
[42] See, e.g., *West Virginia Board of Education v. Barnette*, 319 U.S. 624 (1943); *Murdock v. Pennsylvania*, 319 U.S. 105 (1943); *Cantwell*, supra, 310 U.S.
[43] See Mansfield, "Conscientious Objection—the 1964 Term," 3 *Religion and the Public Order* 59 (1965).
[44] Clark, supra, 337.
[45] J. Burke, *Osborn's Concise Law Dictionary*, 6th ed. (London: 1976).
[46] *Davis v. Beason*, 133 U.S. 333, 342 (1890).
[47] For a detailed examination of the problem of definition see S. L. Worthing, "'Religion' and 'Religious Institutions' Under the First Amendment," 7 Pepperdine L. Rev. 313 (1980).
[48] Note, "Toward a Constitutional Definition of Religion," 91 Harv. L. Rev. 1056, 1075 (1978).
[49] *United States v. Kauten*, 133 F.2d 703, 708 (CA 2 1943).

[50] Worthing, supra, 320.
[51] Id. 321.
[52] See "The Meaning of Religion in the First Amendment," *Catholic World*, August 1963. See also XXXII U. Chi. L. Rev. 533 (1965); LVII American Political Science Review 865 (1963).
[53] L. Pfeffer, *Church, State, and Freedom*, rev. ed. (Boston: 1967), 609, 610.
[54] *Cantwell*, supra, 310 U.S., 303, 304.
[55] *Gillette v. United States*, 401 U.S. 437, 462 (1971); *Sherbert v. Verner*, 374 U.S. 398, 408, 409 (1963); *Braunfeld v. Brown*, 366 U.S. 599, 603–608 (1961).
[56] *Lemon v. Kurtzman*, 403 U.S. 602 (1971).
[57] *Sherbert*, supra, 374 U.S., 403; *Surinach v. Pasquera de Busquets*, 604 F.2d 73, 79 (CA 1 1979); *People v. Woody*, 61 Cal.2d 716, 722, 394 P.2d 813, 818, 40 Cal.Rptr. 69, 74 (1977); *NAACP v. Button*, 371 U.S. 415, 438 (1963); *International Society for Krishna Consciousness v. Bowen*, 600 F.2d 667, 670 (CA 7 1979).
[58] 406 U.S. 205 (1972).
[59] *Thomas v. Review Board of the Indiana Employment Security Division*, U.S. (1981), 101 S.Ct. 1425, 1431.
[60] Id. 1430.
[61] Id. 1432.
[62] *Abington v. Schempp*, 374 U.S. 203, 222, 223 (1963).
[63] *Reynolds*, supra, 98 U.S. See also *The Late Corporation of the Church of Jesus Christ of Latter-day Saints v. United States*, 136 U.S. 1 (1890); *Davis*, supra, 133 U.S.
[64] *Pack v. State of Tennessee*, 527 S.W.2d 99, cert. denied, 424 U.S. 954 (1976); *Harden v. State of Tennessee*, 216 S.W.2d 708 (1948).
[65] *Widmar v. Vincent*, S.C. Doc. No. 80-689.
[66] The Baptist Joint Committee on Public Affairs, a confederation of eight Baptist bodies whose mandate involves religious liberty and separation of church and state, has recently filed a brief amicus curiae in *Widmar*, supra, supporting the free exercise rights of college students. In all probability this fall there will be the first *direct* Baptist challenge of government action on free exercise grounds with a major Baptist agency contesting the Internal Revenue Service's regulations defining "integrated auxiliaries" of churches.
[67] In *Pierce v. Society of Sisters*, 268 U.S. 510 (1925), Catholics won the point that parents have the right to send their children to parochial schools. The pleadings in this pre-*Cantwell* case did not stress the religious issue but gave emphasis to property and business rights. Most subsequent parochial school litigation has centered around the establishment clause.
[68] See *Presbyterian Church in the United States v. Mary Elizabeth Blue Hull Memorial Presbyterian Church*, 393 U.S. 440 (1969); *Serbian Eastern Orthodox Diocese v. Milivojevich*, 426 U.S. 696 (1976).
[69] *Jones v. Wolf*, 440 U.S. 903 (1979).
[70] Supra, 98 U.S.
[71] Id. 166, 167.
[72] 22 Stat. 30.
[73] *Murphy v. Ramsey*, 114 U.S. 15 (1884).
[74] *Davis*, supra, 133 U.S., 334.
[75] Id. 342, 343. Quoted with approval but without the caveat in *United States v. Ballard*, 322 U.S. 78, 87 (1944).
[76] *Davis*, supra, 133 U.S., 341. This *dictum* on tenets of faith does not square with the Court's position in *Ballard*, supra, 322 U.S., 87 that if church "doctrines are subject to a trial by a jury charged with finding their truth or falsity, then the same can be done with the religious beliefs of any sect. When the triers of fact undertake that task, they enter a forbidden domain." See also *Founding Church of Scientology of Washington, D.C. v. United States*, 409 F.2d 1146 (CA D.C. 1969), cert. denied, 396 U.S. 963 (1969).
[77] U.S. Constitution, Art. I, Sec. 7.
[78] 24 Stat. 637, 638, 641.

⁷⁹*The Late Corporation, supra*, 136 U.S., 49.

⁸⁰See the line of cases dealing with the use of controlled substances in religious services, e.g., *Randall v. Wyrick*, 441 F. Supp. 312 (DC Mo. 1977); *Lewellyn v. State of Oklahoma*, 592 P.2d 538 (1979).

⁸¹Justice Frankfurter in his opinion concurring with the results in *Niemotko v. State of Maryland*, 340 U.S. 268 (1951), does a thorough job of summarizing, at 276-282, the cases dealing with restrictions on speech in public places.

⁸²*Lovell v. City of Griffin, Georgia*, 303 U.S. 444 (1938); *Schneider v. State of New Jersey*, 308 U.S. 147 (1939).

⁸³*Supra*, 310 U.S.

⁸⁴General Statutes §6294 as amended by §860d of the 1937 supplement.

⁸⁵*Cantwell, supra*, 310 U.S., 305.

⁸⁶*Id.* 311.

⁸⁷*Jones v. Opelika*, 316 U.S. 584 (1942).

⁸⁸*Jones v. Opelika*, 319 U.S. 103 (1943); *Murdock, supra*, 319 U.S.

⁸⁹*Martin v. City of Struthers, Ohio*, 319 U.S. 141 (1943). However, a similar ordinance was sustained when the issue concerned commercial solicitation, *Breard v. City of Alexandria, La.*, 341 U.S. 622 (1951).

⁹⁰321 U.S. 158 (1944).

⁹¹149 Massachusetts General Laws (Ter.Ed.) as amended by Acts and Resolves of 1939, c. 461.

⁹²See, e.g., *Niemotko, supra*, 340 U.S.; *Kunz v. New York*, 340 U.S. 290 (1951); *Henry v. Rock Hill*, 376 U.S. 776 (1964); *Sellers v. Johnson*, 163 F.2d 877 (CA 8 1947), cert. denied, 332 U.S. 851 (1948); *Fowler v. State of Rhode Island*, 345 U.S. 67 (1953); *Poulos v. State of New Hampshire*, 345 U.S. 395 (1953).

⁹³*Minersville School District v. Gobitis*, 310 U.S. 586 (1940).

⁹⁴*Barnette, supra*, 319 U.S. On the same day, June 14, 1943, the Court held that a state may not interfere with distribution by Jehovah's Witnesses of literature aimed at discouraging the flag salute. *Taylor v. State of Mississippi*, 319 U.S. 583 (1943).

⁹⁵*United States v. Macintosh*, 283 U.S. 605 (1931).

⁹⁶*Girouard v. United States*, 328 U.S. 61 (1946).

⁹⁷*Supra*, 366 U.S. The history of Sunday closing laws up until *Braunfeld* is detailed in *McGowan v. Maryland*, 366 U.S. 420, 431-440, 470-551 (1961).

⁹⁸18 Purdon's Pa.Stat.Ann. §4699.10.

⁹⁹Chief Justice Warren was joined by Justices Black, Clark, and Whittaker in the judgment. Justice Frankfurter was joined by Justice Harlan in a concurring opinion. Justice Brennan concurred and dissented. Justices Douglas and Stewart filed separate dissents.

¹⁰⁰*Braunfeld, supra*, 366 U.S., 605.

¹⁰¹*Id.* 607.

¹⁰²*Supra*, 374 U.S. Justice Brennan delivered the opinion. Only Justices Harlan and White dissented.

¹⁰³68 S. C. Code §§68-1 to 68-404.

¹⁰⁴*Sherbert, supra*, 374 U.S., 403. In this statement the Court quotes *NAACP, supra*, 371 U.S.

¹⁰⁵*Sherbert, supra*, 374 U.S., 403, 404.

¹⁰⁶*Id.* 406 quoting from *Thomas v. Collins*, 323 U.S. 516 (1945).

¹⁰⁷*Sherbert, supra*, 374 U.S., 407. At 408 *Braunfeld, supra*, 366 U.S., was distinguished in that the State there had a strong interest "in providing one uniform day of rest for all workers."

¹⁰⁸Wis. Stat. §118.15 (1969).

¹⁰⁹*Yoder, supra*, 406 U.S., 210. See also from the New Testament John 17:14-16.

¹¹⁰*Supra*, 406 U.S.

¹¹¹*Id.* 213, 214.

¹¹²*Id.* 215.

¹¹³*Id.* 221-229.

[114] *Supra*, 101 S.Ct.
[115] The Indiana Court of Appeals, 381 N.E.2d 880 (1980), ordered payment of benefits but that judgment was vacated by the Indiana Supreme Court, 391 N.E.2d 1127 (1980) and *cert.* was granted,　　U.S.　　, 100 S.Ct. 1012 (1980).
[116] *Thomas v. Review Board, supra*, 101 S.Ct., 1431.
[117] *Id.* 1433.
[118] *Id.* 1432.
[119] *Village of Schaumburg v. Citizens for a Better Environment*, 444 U.S. 620 (1980). A substantial number of religious organizations filed *amicus curiae* briefs in this case.
[120] *Id.*, 100 S.Ct., 836.
[121] *Cox v. New Hampshire*, 312 U.S. 569, 576 (1941).
[122] *Supra*, 310 U.S.
[123] *City of Manchester v. Leiby*, 117 F.2d 661 (CA 1 1941), *cert. denied*, 313 U.S. 562 (1941). *See also Sheldon v. Fannin*, 221 F. Supp. 766 (DC Az. 1963) (forbidding prohibition of door-to-door religious solicitation or requiring license).
[124] *ISKCON v. Griffin*, 437 F. Supp. 666 (DC Pa. 1977). *See also Aaron v. Municipal Court of San Jose-Milpitas Judicial District*, 140 Cal. Rptr. 849 (1977). *But see Edwards v. Maryland State Fair*, 476 F. Supp. 153 (DC Md. 1979).
[125] *ISKCON v. City of New Orleans*, 347 F. Supp. 945 (DC La. 1972).
[126] *Bowen, supra*, 600 F.2d (holding the state interest may be served by enforcing state fraud laws). *ISKCON v. Barber*, a case with a similar fact pattern, was argued May 4, 1981 before the Court of Appeals for the Second Circuit (the district court had upheld the New York state fair's limiting of solicitation by the Krishnas due to possibility of fraud).
[127] *ISKCON of Houston v. City of Houston*, 482 F. Supp. 852 (DC Tx. 1979). *See also Westfall v. Board of Commissioners of Clayton County*, 477 F. Supp. 862 (DC Ga. 1979).
[128] *Weissman v. City of Alamogordo*, 472 F. Supp. 425 (DC N.M. 1979).
[129] *Smith v. City of Manchester*, 460 F. Supp. 30 (DC Tn. 1978).
[130] *See ISKCON v. Lentini*, 461 F. Supp. 49 (DC La. 1978); *ISKCON of Berkeley v. Kearnes*, 454 F. Supp. 116 (DC CA. 1978); *ISKCON v. Collins*, 452 F. Supp. 1007 (DC Tx. 1977); *Heritage Village Church and Missionary Fellowship, Inc. v. State of North Carolina*, 263 S.E.2d 726 (1980).
[131] *Heffron v. ISKCON*, S. C. Doc. No. 80-795, 299 N.W.2d 79 (1980), *cert. granted*, U.S.　　, 101 S.Ct. 917 (1981).
[132] 367 U.S. 488 (1961).
[133] 249 F.2d 127 (CA D.C. 1957).
[134] 315 P.2d 394 (1957).
[135] *Davis, supra*, 133 U.S. *See also George v. United States*, 196 F.2d 445 (CA 9 1952). Chief Justice Hughes, in his dissent in *Macintosh, supra*, 283 U.S., 633, 634, stated: "The essence of religion is belief in a relation to God involving duties superior to those arising from any human relation."
[136] *Torcaso, supra*, 367 U.S., 495.
[137] *Id.* 496, n. 11.
[138] *Washington Ethical Society, supra*, 249 F.2d, 127.
[139] *Id.* 128.
[140] *Id.* 129.
[141] *Fellowship of Humanity, supra*, 315 P.2d, 398.
[142] *Id.* 401.
[143] 380 U.S. 163 (1965).
[144] 50 U.S.C. App. §456(j).
[145] *Seeger, supra*, 380 U.S., 166.
[146] *Id.* 176.
[147] *Id.* 185. *See also* Abner Brodie and Harold P. Southerland, "Conscience, the Constitution, and the Supreme Court: The Riddle of *United States v. Seeger*," 1966 Wisc. L. Rev. 306.
[148] 398 U.S. 333, 344 (1970).

[149] 297 F. Supp. 902 (DC Mass. 1969), *appeal denied* for want of jurisdiction, 399 U.S. 267 (1970).

[150] *Id.* 909.

[151] The court in *Fellowship of Humanity, supra,* 315 P.2d, 404, 405, was quoting with approval from Potter, *The Story of Religion* (New York: 1937). The same ideas with essentially the same words are in the more readily available 1958 edition.

[152] D. A. Giannella, "Religious Liberty, Nonestablishment, and Doctrinal Development," 80 Harv. L. Rev. 1381, 1424 (1967).

[153] Note, "Defining Religion: Of God, the Constitution and the D.A.R.," XXXII U. Chi. L. Rev. 533, 545 (1965).

[154] As with the Internal Revenue Code, when the term "church" is used herein it subsumes all types of Christian ecclesiology as well as temples, synagogues, mosques, etc.

[155] H.R. 5 introduced by Rep. Danielson, who is chairman of the Subcommittee on Administrative Law and Governmental Relations of the House Committee on the Judiciary. The 1981 version excluded churches, the 1979 version did not.

[156] Disclosure can have an inhibiting effect on First Amendment rights, *Buckley v. Valeo,* 424 U.S. 1 (1976); it can produce entanglement problems, *Surinach, supra,* 604 F.2d.

[157] §6033 I.R.C. requires a filing of Form 990.

[158] §6033(a)(2)(A)(i). *See also* C. M. Whelan, " 'Church' in the Internal Revenue Code: The Definitional Problem," 45 Fordham L. Rev. 885 (1977).

[159] *See* J. W. Baker, *Government and the Mission of the Churches: The Problem of "Integrated Auxiliaries"* (Washington: 1977) for a detailed account of the struggle and the position which the churches took.

[160] 42 Fed. Reg. 767 (January 4, 1977).

[161] *National Labor Relations Board v. Catholic Bishop of Chicago,* U.S. , 99 S.Ct. 1313, 1322 (1979).

[162] *Lay Faculty Association v. Bishop Ford Central Catholic High School,* 623 F.2d 818 (CA 2 1980), *cert. denied,* U.S. , 101 S,Ct. 1698 (1981).

[163] *St. Martin's Evangelical Lutheran Church v. State of South Dakota,* S. C. Doc. No. 80-120, slip opinion dated May 26, 1981, at 15, 16.

[164] *See State of Ohio v. Whisner,* 351 N.E.2d 750 (1976); *Hinton v. Kentucky State Board of Education,* Civil Action No. 88314, unpublished decision, Franklin Circuit Court.

[165] *But see Faith Baptist Church of Louisville, Nebraska v. Douglas,* S. C. Doc. No. 80-1837, on appeal from the Nebraska Supreme Court, 207 Neb. 802 (1981).

[166] *Mississippi College v. EEOC,* S. C. Doc. No. 80-1703, decision below at 626 F.2d 477 (CA 5 1980).

[167] *EEOC v. Southwestern Baptist Theological Seminary,* F. Supp. (ND Tx. 1980), Civil Action No. CA4-77-141-E, opinion dated January 18, 1980.

[168] *State of California v. Worldwide Church of God.* A California superior court placed the church in receivership, and the church sought relief through the California appellate courts and the Supreme Court. The case ended without published decisions when the Attorney General asked the court to dismiss the case after the legislature passed a law abolishing the public trust theory as it relates to religious organizations. *But see* Scott, *Abridgment of the Law of Trust* (1960) and Bogert, *Law of Trusts* (1973) for a legal argument supporting the Attorney General's theory. For a more detailed examination of the events in the Worldwide Church of God case, *see* S. L. Worthing, "The State Takes Over a Church," 446 *Annals* 136 (1979).

[169] *Katz v. Superior Court,* 73 Cal.App.3d 952, 970, 141 Cal.Rptr. 234, 244 (1977) (voiding superior court conservatorship order on legal rather than constitutional bases).

[170] *See Christian Echoes National Ministry, Inc. v. United States,* 470 F.2d 849 (CA 10 1972), *cert. denied,* 414 U.S. 864 (1973). *See* and compare Treas. Reg. §1.501(c)(3)-1(d)(3); Rev. Rul. 67-71, 1967-1 C.B. 125; Rev. Rul. 75-384, 1975-2 C.B. 204; *Riker v. Commissioner,* 244 F.2d 220 (CA 9 1957).

[171] The Church has challenged this action in a case currently in the Tax Court, *Church*

of Scientology of California v. Commissioner of Internal Revenue, T. C. Doc. No. 3352-78.

[172]44 Fed. Reg. 9451 (February 13, 1979).

[173]This was an outgrowth of court decisions in *Green v. Connally,* 330 F. Supp. 1150 (DC D.C. 1971), *aff'd. mem. sub nom. Coit v. Green,* 404 U.S. 997 (1971) and *Goldsboro Christian Schools, Inc. v. United States,* 436 F. Supp. 1314 (DC N.C. 1977).

[174]'This, they believe, is the main issue in the series of cases involving Bob Jones University and its religiously held beliefs about racial intermingling. *See Bob Jones University v. United States,* F.2d (CA 4 1980), Civil Action Nos. 79-1215, 79-1216, 79-1293, opinion dated December 30, 1980.

[175]In *Worldwide Church of God* the state receiver did not approve of the church's hierarchical polity and declared that he would treat the churches as congregational churches.

[176]*See Barr v. United Methodist Church,* 90 Cal.App. 3d 259, 153 Cal. Rptr. 322 (1979).

[177]The California Attorney General terminated the action in *Worldwide Church of God* and an out-of-court settlement was reached in *Barr.*

[178]The FAA operates Dulles and National airports in Washington, D.C. *See* 45 Fed. Reg. 35314 (May 27, 1980). The Aviation Consumer Action Project has petitioned for reconsideration, 45 Fed. Reg. 59897 (September 11, 1980). That petition is pending.

THE "ESTABLISHMENT OF RELIGION" PUZZLE

EDMOND CAHN

IN PUBLISHING the sixth and final volume[1] of his great life of James Madison, Irving Brant has just completed the most influential American biography of the century. The work has gradually compelled the abler among our judges, lawyers, historians, and political scientists to revise their previous estimates and to appreciate Madison's full eminence of intellect and statesmanship. Chapter by chapter, it has stretched his image from the level of dependable competence to that of authentic greatness. It has proved beyond doubt that the man we used to picture as a mere disciple and lieutenant of Thomas Jefferson was, in fact, an independent, creative, and tough-minded thinker, a forceful personality, and a bold leader at several critical junctures of the nation's destiny.

But this is by no means the whole of Mr. Brant's achievement. The biography has likewise prompted us to confront and reassess Madison's political concepts, to probe again into the fundamental postulates of free government, and to raise in the twentieth century some of the same unsparingly realistic questions that Madison raised in the eighteenth. More and more often, when first principles are at stake, it is Madison whom we find the Justices of the Supreme Court quoting, citing, and contending with. He has become one of the most interesting, most contemporary of our interlocutors. In some respects, his notions are so timely that judges find it hard to keep pace with them.

A Puzzle

There are several instances—one or two, at least, in each of Mr. Brant's volumes—where, with admirable depth of research and brilliance of reasoning, he corrects previous popular misapprehensions, generally-held fallacies, and mistaken historical estimates. Drawing on the wealth of information he provides, I should like to discuss one of the most baffling aspects of recent constitutional doctrine in the Supreme Court. The cases I find so puzzling have arisen under a clause of the Bill of Rights that concerned Madison deeply throughout the busy years of his life, that is, the clause forbidding any law "respecting an establishment of religion." Taking into account the

---

Edmond Cahn is Professor of Law at the New York University School of Law, and author of The Predicament of Democratic Man (1961), The Moral Decision (1955), and The Sense of Injustice (1949).

1. Brant, James Madison, Commander in Chief 1812-1836 (1961) [hereinafter cited as Brant, Madison VI].

whole train of recent "establishment of religion" cases, what one faces is quite a juristic enigma.

In fairness, let me make my own approach plain. It is the same as that of the leading civil liberties organizations who have uniformly advocated a total separation of church and state and have contended that all of the instances of state action which were challenged in recent litigations before the Supreme Court were unconstitutional.[2] The puzzle does not arise merely because the Court has drifted away from a libertarian position; when the Court drifts, one can usually discern a direction. It arises rather because observers see no way to reconcile the voting policy of distinguished Justices in one case with their policy in other cases involving the same clause.

The leading cases on the subject have been *Everson*[3] (permitting state reimbursement of school bus expenses to parents of parochial school pupils), *McCollum*[4] (prohibiting religious instruction on public school premises), *Zorach*[5] (permitting released time for religious instruction elsewhere), and *McGowan*[6] (the 1961 decisions permitting states to enforce general Sunday laws against merchants who were devout observers of a different sabbath day). Where in them is one to seek a consistent pattern of doctrine or analysis? Perhaps, if Justices Jackson and Rutledge had survived to participate in all four decisions, their votes might have provided us with examples of con-

---

2. My reasons are stated in How to Destroy the Churches, Harper's, Nov. 1961, p. 33, adapted from the North Lecture delivered at Franklin and Marshall College on October 26, 1961.
3. Everson v. Board of Educ., 330 U.S. 1 (1947).
4. Illinois ex rel. McCollum v. Board of Educ., 333 U.S. 203 (1948).
5. Zorach v. Clauson, 343 U.S. 306 (1952).
6. McGowan v. Maryland, 366 U.S. 420 (1961), together with Two Guys From Harrison-Allentown v. McGinley, 366 U.S. 582 (1961); Braunfeld v. Brown, 366 U.S. 599 (1961); Gallagher v. Crown Kosher Super Mkt., Inc., 366 U.S. 617 (1961). Separate opinion of Frankfurter, J., at 459; dissenting opinion of Douglas, J., at 561.

I have not listed Doremus v. Board of Educ., 342 U.S. 429 (1952), because in it the majority of the Court, on grounds of mootness and lack of standing to sue, refused to decide the merits (state statute provided for reading five verses of Old Testament at opening of each school day). See Pfeffer, Church, State, and Freedom 169 (1953).

Nor have I included Torcaso v. Watkins, 367 U.S. 488 (1961), where, without a single dissent, the Court struck down a Maryland test-oath requiring "a declaration of belief in the existence of God" in order to qualify for public office (in this instance, the exalted office of notary public). With a friendly pat on McCollum's head, Justice Black, writing for the Court, described the seventeenth and eighteenth century abuses of religious test-oaths and the peculiar odium attached to them by our early settlers. It is an eloquent and moving opinion. Yet the same historical apparatus that embellishes and enriches it likewise operates to narrow the scope of its holding. Following very closely after McGowan, which it cites without reservation, Torcaso indicates no intervening change of attitude. It does reiterate reassuringly the Everson and McCollum statements that government cannot "aid all religions."

tinuity. But this is mere speculation. Moreover, Justice Jackson himself contributed to the general confusion by employing the word "absolute" (usually anathema to him) with approval in his *Everson* dissent,[7] as, for that matter, did Justice Frankfurter (to whom the word is likewise an epithet) in his *McCollum* opinion.[8]

The Sunday law decisions[9] of 1961 provide a typical illustration of the puzzle. Two of the libertarian Justices (Warren and Black) voted to uphold the Sunday laws while the other two (Douglas and Brennan) dissented indignantly. Even between the two libertarian dissenters there was a grave difference. Only Justice Douglas saw the Sunday laws as violating the "establishment of religion" clause as well as the "free exercise" clause.

Three members of the court—Justices Black, Frankfurter, and Douglas—have been on the bench long enough to participate in all of these "establishment" decisions. Seeking to understand their views, one may be tempted to emphasize the opinions handed down in *McCollum* because the outcome was not only correct but also closest of all the decisions to unanimity. Yet even *McCollum* provides no firm footing, for its authority has been compromised, at least in some eyes, by the later decisions in *Zorach* and *McGowan*. If we put *McCollum* aside as a safe and dependable criterion, we are left with the frustrating patterns established in the other cases. Justice Black voted for constitutionality in *Everson*, for unconstitutionality in *Zorach*, and for constitutionality in *McGowan*. Justice Frankfurter voted for unconstitutionality in *Everson* and *Zorach*, only to shift to constitutionality in *McGowan*. Justice Douglas voted for constitutionality in the first two cases and for unconstitutionality in the third.

One might try to dismiss the puzzle by simply insisting that every "establishment" controversy depends on its own facts and circumstances, that judges appraise the diverse facts and circumstances according to their best lights, and that no two types of state legislation touching the subject of religion are quite identical. Did not Justice Black show how close the *Everson* case was by saying that in it the state had approached the very verge of its constitutional power?[10] Did not Justice Jackson, dissenting in the same case, say that his

---

7. He wrote, "This freedom was first in the Bill of Rights because it was first in the forefathers' minds; it was set forth in absolute terms, and its strength is its rigidity." 330 U.S. at 26. This sounds strangely like Justice Black discussing freedom of speech.

8. After referring to "the need for absolute separation," 333 U.S. at 217, he concluded, "We find that the basic Constitutional principle of absolute Separation was violated . . . ." Id. at 231.

9. See note 6 supra.

10. 330 U.S. at 16.

first inclination was to vote for constitutionality and only continued reflection had driven him to the opposite conclusion?[11] Perhaps, in "establishment" contests, the Court has become something like a jury, with a jury's measure of predictability.

I for one find any such exit illusory. While substantial differences of fact might help to account for shifting majorities of the whole Court and shifting votes of a single Justice, they do not adequately explain why Justices like Black and Douglas, whose votes in cases involving freedom of religion, freedom of speech and press, and freedom of association have consistently been on the libertarian side, should fail to provide an intelligible pattern when "establishment of religion" is at issue. Similarly, it is odd that Justice Frankfurter, whose votes in cases falling within the same categories have been rather consistently majoritarian, should oscillate so widely in "establishment" cases. It is not unfair to say that "establishment of religion" is the *only* provision of the First Amendment where the respective working premises of the three Justices seem so volatile.

Background of the "Establishment" Clause

In 1776, while Jefferson was in Philadelphia with the Continental Congress, George Mason headed a committee to frame the Virginia Declaration of Rights and Madison rendered decisive service on the committee. Mason drafted a clause which went no farther than to reflect John Locke's ideal of "toleration" for those who did not belong to the Established Church. Madison succeeded in converting this into a guarantee of freedom of religion, to which "all men are equally entitled . . . according to the dictates of conscience." He also attempted but did not succeed in inserting an explicit condemnation of "peculiar emoluments or privileges" for those who belonged to a particular church.[12]

An unremitting debate ensued between the supporters of establishment, led from time to time by Patrick Henry and Edmund Pendleton, and the disestablishmentarians, led by Mason, Jefferson, and Madison. At almost every session of the Virginia Legislature the former proposed to extend the legal and economic privileges of the church, the latter to remove the remaining vestiges of its special position. In 1779, Jefferson drafted and submitted his celebrated "Bill for Religious Freedom,"[13] which at that time failed even to reach a

---

11. Id. at 18.
12. Brant, Madison I 244-47 (1941); Brant, Madison: On the Separation of Church and State, 8 William & Mary Q. (3d series, No. 1) 3-7 (1951).
13. Reproduced in Appendix A hereof, where the name and text are in conformity with 2 The Papers of Thomas Jefferson 545-47 (Julian P. Boyd ed. 1950) except that

third reading in the Assembly. Jefferson's *Notes On Virginia* (written in 1782 and published in France in 1785) contained a further moving appeal for disestablishment.[14]

In 1784 the sponsors of establishment pressed for enactment of their bill, which would require all persons to pay an annual contribution for the support of the Christian religion or of some Christian church or denomination which the taxpayer might designate. The bill contended, in its preamble, that since organized religion was beneficial to the general welfare, all citizens should be required to participate in supporting it. Thus, the contention which would be put forward in the twentieth century in support of school bus assistance and general Sunday laws (that is, that sectarian education and the sectarian sabbath possessed a strictly secular utility) was advanced, considered, and—as we shall see—rejected in the struggle that led to the First Amendment.

At this stage, George Mason, George Nicholas, and others asked Madison to prepare a statement of the full case for separation of church and state. He produced the epochal "Memorial and Remonstrance Against Religious Assessments" (reproduced in Appendix B

I have divided the preamble into paragraphs and restored roman letters where Dr. Boyd used instructive italics. Thus Appendix A presents the Bill as closely as possible to Jefferson's original version, due allowance being made for the textual uncertainties that Jefferson himself helped to create and that Dr. Boyd recounts for us with characteristic skill. I must emphasize, however, that before the final enactment in 1786 the Bill's preamble suffered certain excisions, which are shown by Dr. Boyd's italics. The uncertainties about the text extend even to the name of the Bill. For sound historical reasons, Justice Black refers to it as Jefferson's Bill for Religious *Liberty*, Everson v. Board of Educ., 330 U.S. 1, 12 (1947), and so does Mr. Brant, Brant, Madison II 354. With profound respect for both of them, I have allowed Dr. Boyd's evidence to convince me that Jefferson (and most of his contemporaries) habitually wrote *Freedom* in referring to the Bill.

By way of comic relief, one of the twentieth century's textual errors caps anything that was perpetrated in the 1780's. The Bill's preamble ends with the following illustrious clause: "errors ceasing to be dangerous when it is permitted freely to contradict them." When the first volume of Claude G. Bowers' biography of Jefferson went through the press, some sleepy or subversive printer's assistant changed the word "contradict" to "circulate"! Bowers, The Young Jefferson, 1743-1789, at 242 (1945).

14. The passage is most conveniently available in The Political Writings of Thomas Jefferson 36-38 (Edward Dumbauld ed. 1955). Among other things, it shows that in 1782 as in 1789 Jefferson consistently advocated a Bill of Rights as a *legal* safeguard, not as a mere basis for appeal to the spirit of the people. Here is his 1782 answer, id. at 38, to what Judge Learned Hand taught on the subject:

[I]s the spirit of the people an infallible, a permanent reliance? Is it government? Is this the kind of protection we receive in return for the rights we give up? Besides, the spirit of the times may alter, will alter. Our rulers will become corrupt, our people careless. A single zealot may commence persecutor, and better men be his victims. It can never be too often repeated that the time for fixing every essential right on a legal basis is while our rulers are honest and ourselves united.

hereof) which was circulated in 1785 and evoked a mighty wave of support for disestablishment. Taking advantage of the tide, Madison called up Jefferson's Bill for Religious Freedom and in 1786 obtained its enactment. Even then, the establishment forces endeavored to enervate the Jefferson bill by changing the word "Lord" in the preamble to "Lord Jesus Christ," only to receive a sharp rebuke from Madison for using such a name as a means of abridging "the natural and equal rights of all men." Jefferson's Bill was adopted without material amendment of its scope. Reporting the struggle and its outcome to Jefferson, who had been serving as American minister to France since 1784, Madison wrote that he flattered himself that the provisions of the Bill "have in this country extinguished forever the ambitious hope of making laws for the human mind."[15] Would that he had been right!

In 1785 Madison showed that he was already committed to total separation of church and state as a *national* principle. A committee of Congress had proposed, in a plan for certain western territories, to set aside one section in each township for support of public schools and one section for religion. When Congress struck out the provision for religion, Madison expressed his amazement that a committee had even proposed a principle "so unjust in itself . . . and smelling so strongly of an antiquated bigotry."[16]

During and after the Philadelphia Convention of 1787, Madison stood against the formulation of a federal bill of rights. One of his chief reasons was the fear that no verbal prohibition of religious establishment could be found quite categorical enough to prevent a narrow interpretation, which in turn would invite further encroachments by aggressive clergymen. Yielding eventually on all other counts, he never felt wholly at ease on this one.[17] Perhaps his misgivings had originated in his 1776 experience with the text of the Virginia Declaration of Rights. At any rate, the debates recorded in the legislative annals of 1789 proved that Madison's semantic anxieties were not imaginary. Various formulations were toyed with to prohibit governmental action in the religious realm, but none seemed entirely free of ambiguity. The experience of the twentieth century has further exposed the semantic complexities of the matter.

---

15. Brant, Madison II 354 (1948). See also references in note 12 supra and Pfeffer, Church, State, and Freedom 97-99 (1953).
16. Brant, Madison II 353 (1948).
17. Of course, the provisions and reservations that eventually became the Ninth and Tenth Amendments were designed to take care of this very difficulty. Yet even as he submitted them to the Congress, Madison again acknowledged his semantic misgivings. 1 Annals of Cong. 456 (1789).

In processing the First Amendment's "establishment" clause, Congress furnished only one completely explicit and illuminating episode. In September of 1789, certain Senators who were supporters of the established churches in New England, backed by Senator Lee of Virginia, who had been a partisan of the 1784 assessment bill, attempted a bold coup. They proposed to begin the First Amendment as follows: "Congress shall make no law establishing articles of faith or a mode of worship or prohibiting the free exercise of religion."[18] This, of course, would have opened the way for government support of churches and church schools. Madison, as chairman of the House conferees, succeeded in defeating the maneuver.

On September 25, 1789, Congress formally submitted the Bill of Rights for ratification. The establishment clause of the First Amendment declared: "Congress shall make no law respecting an establishment of religion." If words can ever confer an absolute tenor on a constitutional prohibition, these were such words.

There is direct proof that when Madison inserted absolute prohibitions in the federal Bill of Rights, he acted with full awareness of what he was doing. On October 17, 1788, only a few months before preparing the document, he had written Jefferson an elaborate statement of his principles and policies.[19] In the final paragraph of his letter, Madison expressed reluctance to frame "*absolute* restrictions in cases that are doubtful, or where emergencies may overrule them." The examples he gave were well chosen, consisting of proposed absolute restrictions against (a) suspension of the writ of habeas corpus, (b) maintenance of a peace-time army, and (c) government grants of monopolies. As his correspondent must agree, none of these ought to be made "absolute." (Madison actually underscored "absolute," as though to wink at the judges and law professors of the twentieth century.) In view of this passage, it is plain that when he drafted and sponsored certain "absolute restrictions" a few months later, he acted advisedly.

How much weight should we attach to Jefferson's and Madison's official behavior when church-and-state issues arose after 1789? This is still a highly debatable question. Obviously, though the subsequent conduct of the two Presidents is pertinent as a kind of practical construction, the people of the United States cannot be said to have adopted it in advance when they ratified the Bill of Rights. Suffice it to say that both men, during their respective administrations, sedulously maintained the libertarian stand for which they had fought

---

18. Brant, Madison III 271 (1950).
19. V The Writings of James Madison 269, 274-75 (Gaillard Hunt ed. 1904).

in the 1780's.[20] Jefferson's felicitous phrase, "a wall of separation between Church and State," uttered during this period,[21] aptly characterizes it. Nevertheless, it seems less controversial for us to concentrate on the two deliberate expositions of their philosophy that were familiar to the congressmen who submitted and the state legislatures who formally ratified the Bill of Rights. These were Jefferson's Bill for Religious Freedom (Appendix A) and Madison's Memorial and Remonstrance (Appendix B).

Explanation Begun: the Biographical Factors

With this outline of the record before us, it may be possible now to explain why the Supreme Court's decisions and the Justices' votes in "establishment of religion" cases seem to lack a consistent pattern. The explanation I am about to offer has nothing to do with reconciling the respective decisions or votes with one another. Believing that by and large they are not really reconcilable, I shall not even make the attempt. My purpose is quite modest; I aim not to dispel but merely to explain the state of confusion.

At the outset, let me say that I do not think the main cause is a conflict of views about the intended meaning of the word "establishment" in the First Amendment. Although once in a while some zealous writer may contend that the First Amendment does not forbid government support of organized religion but only government preference of one religious sect over the others, we may dismiss the argument as summarily as the Supreme Court has.[22] It does not deserve serious consideration if only because in effect it puts forward the same proposal (of non-discriminatory support for all sects) that provoked Madison's Memorial and Remonstrance of 1785.

If not in the meaning of "establishment," where then does the confusion originate? Let me summarize what I believe is the explanation:

The Court and the individual Justices have been working with two different understandings of the scope of "religion" in the "establishment of religion" clause. The narrower understanding may be

---

20. For instances of Madison's acts, see Brant, Madison: On the Separation of Church and State, supra note 12, and references passim in Brant, Madison VI. It is obvious that Madison would have agreed with Judges Dye and Fuld who dissented in Engel v. Vitale, 10 N.Y.2d 174, 176 N.E.2d 579, 218 N.Y.S.2d 659 (1961), petition for cert. filed, 30 U.S.L. Week 3116 (U.S. Oct. 3, 1961) (No. 468) (upholding so-called "non-denominational" prayer in public school classrooms, objecting pupils presumably being excused).
21. The date was January 1, 1802. For the full text in which the phrase occurs, see XVI The Writings of Thomas Jefferson 282 (A. E. Bergh ed. 1907).
22. See, e.g., Everson v. Board of Educ., 330 U.S. 1, 15 (1947).

called the Jeffersonian or Enlightenment view; the broader may be called the Madisonian or Dissenter view. If one adopts the Jeffersonian or Enlightenment view, one treats the "establishment" clause as an adjunct or auxiliary to the clause guaranteeing the "free exercise of religion"; if one adopts the Madisonian or Dissenter view, one treats the "establishment" clause not only as an implement of other guarantees but also as a self-sufficient and independent imperative, meriting the most scrupulous obedience because it safeguards the purity of organized religion itself. Though the difference between the two views is merely one of degree and emphasis, it is quite important enough to determine how a judge will cast his vote in a close case. Consequently, any judge who does not distinguish one view of "religion" from the other is quite likely to oscillate between them in a series of "establishment of religion" litigations.

In offering this explanation, I draw encouragement from Mr. Brant, who likewise seems to sense an underlying difference between the two great Americans in their attitudes toward religion. He says, "In his paramount emphasis upon religious liberty as the core of all freedoms, Madison differed somewhat from Jefferson, whose mind centered on freedom of the press, trial by jury and habeas corpus, and from Mason, who was steeped in generalities about the original principles of government."[23] The data of Madison's biography illustrate this difference rather clearly.

Whereas Jefferson obtained a strictly secular education, Madison spent his formative years at the College of New Jersey (Princeton), an institution that was at least as Presbyterian in general atmosphere as it was liberal and democratic in political influence. His family seems to have been attached to religious interests; a cousin and devoted friend, the Reverend James Madison, became the first Episcopal bishop in Virginia—in 1790, after the church had been disestablished. If during his Princeton stay the young Madison had not developed a vocal disability that permanently limited his oratorical powers, he himself might have followed the then popular vocation of Princeton graduates—the pulpit. (Was the disability merely a psychosomatic proof that he heard the yet-uncertain voice of a different calling? If it was, we can only render thanks that his body knew what his mind was not yet ready to declare.)

At Princeton as at home, establishment appeared not only as an enemy of religious freedom but also as an engine and instrument of

---

23. Brant, Madison: On the Separation of Church and State, supra note 12, at 14. It is not claimed here that Madison was aware of the extent to which he had gone beyond Jefferson's position.

British imperial policy. The established clergy held a vested interest in espousing the cause of the Royalists. No wonder, then, that disestablishment seemed so imperative to the young Madison. In Virginia, he had observed, as Jefferson had, how an established church inevitably violates the freedom of the individual; at Princeton, he could not fail to learn something further, *i.e.*, how it also violates the freedom of other churches and sects.

All this explains the boldness verging on temerity with which Madison, then only 25 years of age,[24] attempted to revise George Mason's article on religious freedom in the Virginia Declaration of Rights of 1776. As we noted, he proposed two drastic changes: (1) the radical advance from Mason's (and Locke's) "toleration" to genuine religious freedom to which "all men are equally entitled," and (2) the abolition of all special privileges enjoyed by the established church, its clergy, or its members. That he succeeded with the first item was, of itself, an historic achievement. As for the second, though rejected at the time, it demonstrated that as early as 1776 Madison was viewing disestablishment not merely as an adjunct to religious freedom but as an independent prerequisite to a free society.

It was three years later that Jefferson introduced his Bill for Religious Freedom as a part or element in an extensive program of statutory reform. The Bill was not enacted until 1786—when Madison, seeing that his own Memorial of 1785 had overwhelmed the supporters of establishment, brought it forward for action. The Bill for Religious Freedom is a noble and beautiful statement, displaying Jefferson's finest gifts of mind and pen.

Yet would it be unfair to suggest that the Bill has occasionally acquired a status that is anachronistic? It is unquestionably more eloquent than Madison's Memorial; moreover, it glows with Jefferson's great charismatic name; of these advantages there can be no doubt. But to regard it as the culminating statement of the disestablishmentarian movement is, I think, anachronistic. Though enacted into law a year after Madison drafted the Memorial, it was actually prepared six years before. The Bill spoke Jefferson's reaction to the scene of 1779. Madison, using much less colorful rhetoric in the Memorial,

---

24. In the splendid summation of Madison's career that concludes the final volume, Mr. Brant comments:

. . . Madison had been inveighing against persecution of Virginia Dissenters at an age when Jefferson's letters were full of belles and dances. The earliest known reference to religious freedom in Jefferson's writings was penned in Philadelphia, two weeks after he read the original draft of that article in the 1776 Virginia Declaration of Rights, which Madison at that time was converting from "toleration of dissent" into a complete guarantee of the rights of conscience.

Brant, Madison VI 526-27 (1961).

absorbed all of Jefferson's arguments and added several important ones of his own. The Memorial is the authentic culminative text not merely because Madison who wrote it also prepared the Bill of Rights; it is definitive because it is both later in date and more comprehensive in scope.

EXPLANATION CONTINUED: THE INTELLECTUAL FACTORS

The intellectual factors are those I had in mind when using "Enlightenment" as a crude label to characterize Jefferson's understanding of religion (reflected in his Bill) and "Dissenter" as an equally crude label to characterize Madison's understanding (reflected in his Memorial). Both understandings have intellectual merit. The two have coincided in application where the free exercise of religion is at issue; their influences have differed only in "establishment" cases. Madison's understanding of religion, being broader in scope than Jefferson's, necessarily leaves less room for state support of church activities.

What were the chief factors that defined religion's scope according to the two views?

A. *The Enlightenment Approach:*

1. *Influence of the Speech-Conduct Dichotomy.*—First among them was the basic Enlightenment theme that political liberty required the drawing of a boundary-line between thought and speech, on one side, where official power ought not to operate, and overt conduct, on the other side, where it ought.

One can rightly say that this was and is the most precious boundary-line that political man ever staked out. Even fearful old Hobbes had recommended making a distinction between thoughts and physical conduct—without indicating to which side he would assign the right of speaking.[25] From Spinoza and Locke to Montesquieu and Voltaire, the whole thrust of Enlightenment doctrine was directed toward the speech-conduct dichotomy. During the seventeenth century, the drive had borrowed a goodly part of religion's zeal, which it never bothered to return. (For example, freedom of speech, which later periods would link automatically with freedom of the press, was historically an offshoot of the demand for free exercise of religion.)[26]

---

25. Hobbes, A Dialogue of the Common Laws, in VI The English Works of Thomas Hobbes 7 (W. Molesworth ed. 1840).

26. Though he baffled Justice Harlan by doing so [see Lathrop v. Donohue, 367 U.S. 820, 852 (1961)], Justice Black was on solid historical ground when, dissenting in International Ass'n of Machinists v. Street, 367 U.S. 740 (1961), he quoted Madison's Memorial and Jefferson's Bill. Id. at 790. To the libertarians of the seventeenth and eighteenth centuries, "establishment" denoted any variety of official compulsion that might violate "the equal rights of conscience."

Accordingly, it would seem quite reasonable to the men of the Enlightenment that the speech-conduct dichotomy might likewise govern when church and state were to be kept apart. Surely, one could not expect the state to respect the immunity of speech unless one conceded it a full right to regulate overt behavior.[27] Thus, if a judge should be presented with a regulation affecting overt behavior only (for example, one of our state Sunday laws), he would feel obliged to inquire merely whether the regulation was reasonable. If it was and if it did not appear to abridge the free exercise of religion, he would be warranted in holding it valid.

2. *Distrust of Corporations.*—The Enlightenment's political program was as individualistic and molecular as its psychology. Associations it viewed with the distrust and hostility that eventually found expression in Revolutionary France's *Loi Le Chapelier* (1791), dissolving all corporate bodies, whether ecclesiastical or secular, as organs of oppression and feudal privilege.[28] Why was disestablishment deemed imperative? Precisely in order to secure religious freedom for the *individual*.

Some of the Enlightenment leaders were atheists, scoffing at religion in all of its forms; some were deists, who by consigning God to an emeritus status had left little room for churches in their scheme of things; some, like Jefferson, were sincerely religious and even more sincerely anti-clerical.[29] None of them was likely to see disestablish-

---

27. The dichotomy was employed explicitly in a leading "free exercise" case: Mr. Jefferson afterwards, in reply to an address to him by a committee of the Danbury Baptist Association (8 id. 113), took occasion to say: "Believing with you that religion is a matter which lies solely between man and his God; that he owes account to none other for his faith or his worship; that the legislative powers of the government reach actions only, and not opinions,—I contemplate with sovereign reverence that act of the whole American people which declared that their legislature should 'make no law respecting an establishment of religion or prohibiting the free exercise thereof,' thus building a wall of separation between church and State. Adhering to this expression of the supreme will of the nation in behalf of the rights of conscience, I shall see with sincere satisfaction the progress of those sentiments which tend to restore man to all his natural rights, convinced he has no natural right in opposition to his social duties." Coming as this does from an acknowledged leader of the advocates of the measure, it may be accepted almost as an authoritative declaration of the scope and effect of the amendment thus secured. Congress was deprived of all legislative power over mere opinion, but was left free to reach actions which were in violation of social duties or subversive of good order.
Reynolds v. United States, 98 U.S. 145, 164 (1878).
It may be significant that when Justice Black quoted Jefferson's "wall of separation" metaphor in Everson, he took it from the Reynolds opinion. 330 U.S. at 16.

28. I dealt with the subject in more detail in The Predicament of Democratic Man 99 (1961).

29. In a wisely equilibrated chapter on the subject, Crane Brinton has perforce to say,
The spirit of the Enlightenment is hostile to organized Christian religion. "In every country and in every age, the priest has been hostile to liberty. He is

ment as a right to which *groups* or sects were entitled. One set of organized superstitions, they would say, or another; it was all the same. On this reasoning, the "establishment of religion" clause would never become a cogent imperative except as an auxiliary to the "free exercise" clause.

3. *Equating the Holy with the True.*—Standing in awe before the grandeur and symmetry of the Newtonian cosmos, many of the atheistic leaders of the Enlightenment evinced a reverence like Plato's for the True. Deistic leaders, on the other hand, would be more likely to equate the Holy with the True, and certain Protestant theologians of the era, who really ought to have known better, seem to have strayed in the same direction.[30] Seen in this shallow fashion, religion could be defined as a specific way of searching for truth. A man's religious "opinions" were comparable to the rest of his opinions; he ought to be free to hold and express them for the same reason that he ought to be free to hold and express aesthetic, scientific, and political views.[31] (Of course, the churches had been inviting some such reductive reaction as this for centuries; they had made it a "religious" proposition that the world was flat, that it stood still, that it was the center of the universe, etc.)

If, then, one assumed that the whole religious enterprise was only a way of searching for truth, one would feel entitled to reduce the role and radius of religion whenever physical science or empirical technique might disclose some new area in which they could do a better job of searching. Ultimately, by applying the formula with consistency, it would be possible to do just what the Senators proposed in vain when the "establishment" clause was being shaped, that is, shrink "religion" to nothing more than "articles of faith or a mode of worship." This accomplished, support for church schools might readily follow.

How remote such a result would be from Jefferson's purpose! Yet, while intending to assert the utmost religious freedom and denounce every conceivable kind of clerical aggression, his Bill for

---

always in alliance with the despot, abetting his abuses in return for protection to his own." Thomas Jefferson is here, of course, using "priest" in a general sense to denote any minister of religion. His statement is by no means extreme, but rather in the center of a spectrum that runs from Voltaire's "Let's eat some Jesuit"—and there are more ferocious extremes than that—to the "natural religion" or deism of professing Catholics like Alexander Pope. The corrosiveness of the Enlightenment is nowhere clearer than in its attacks on Christianity.
Brinton, Ideas and Men 402 (1950).

30. See Pelikan, Fools for Christ 6 (1955).

31. By examining Jefferson's preamble in Appendix A, the reader can see this approach clearly delineated.

Religious Freedom did postulate a dangerously narrow understanding of "religion." Notice, if you please, how often in our times people extract mottoes and apt maxims from its text when the stake they are concerned with is not religion at all but controversial political speech. Eloquent though it is, it offers too meager a criterion of religion for cases under the "establishment" clause.

B. *The Dissenter Approach:*

1. Reliance on Multiplicity.—In order not to exaggerate the difference between the two approaches, we shall begin with the points at which they were closest. Madison matched Jefferson perfectly in a lifelong devotion to the religious freedom of the individual and what he repeatedly called "the rights of conscience." The first five paragraphs of the Memorial offer little more than a vigorous paraphrase of Jefferson's statements in the Bill for Religious Freedom.[32] They leave the purport of the Bill entirely intact. Madison's distinctive achievement consisted in superimposing an *institutional* acceptation of "religion" on Jefferson's monadic acceptation of the term.

For another thing, since like other educated men of the epoch, Madison was conversant with the writings of the *philosophes*, he undoubtedly learned a good deal from them. Madison followed Voltaire[33] in insisting, as he frequently did, that the best possible safeguard of religious freedom was not in legal guarantees but in the sheer multiplicity of religious sects. This conviction Madison retained from early youth to the end of his life; even in old age, he saw fit to regard separation of church and state as a pertinent topic in an essay on the general theme of monopolies![34]

Though he may have come across the reliance on multiplicity of sects in Voltaire[35] or, for that matter, in the manuscript of Jefferson's *Notes On Virginia*,[36] Madison made it wholly his own, fitting it with skill into his pluralistic philosophy of society. He saw that the religious

---

32. But Madison did not adopt the theory of psychological determinism expressed in the opening phrases of Jefferson's Bill (see Appendix A). These phrases were deleted by the Virginia legislature before the Bill was enacted.

33. Brant, Madison: On the Separation of Church and State, supra note 12, at 12.

34. Id. at 21.

35. In 1764, Voltaire (addressing the Christian world tactfully as "Insensés . . . Malheureux . . . . Monstres . . . !") summarized the matter succinctly, "On vous l'a déjà dit, et on n'a autre chose à vous dire: si vous avez deux religions chez vous, elles se couperont la gorge; si vous en avez trente, elles vivront en paix." Voltaire, Dictionnaire Philosophique, verb. Tolérance II, at 269 (J. Benda ed., Paris).

36. The Political Writings of Thomas Jefferson 36-38 (Edward Dumbauld ed. 1955). For understandable reasons, the multiplicity-of-sects analysis was not thought appropriate for mention in either Jefferson's Bill or Madison's Memorial.

sphere had attributes of its own that made it essentially unlike the spheres of economics and of political structure. Granted that in any sphere of human activity the processes of competition, rivalry, and reciprocal checks and balances would serve to restrain monopoly and preserve liberty; nevertheless, when an activity was religious in nature, the government possessed no jurisdiction or warrantable power over it. It had no more right to aid than to hinder the competing sects.

In America, Madison submitted most astutely, the rights of conscience must be kept not only free but *equal* as well. And in view of the endless variations—not only among the numerous sects, but also among the organized activities they pursued and the relative emotional values they attached to their activities—how could any species of government assistance be considered genuinely equal from sect to sect? If, for example, a state should attempt to subsidize all sectarian schools without discrimination, it would necessarily violate the principle of equality because certain sects felt impelled to conduct a large number of such schools, others few, others none. How could the officers of government begin to measure the intangible factors that a true equality of treatment would involve, *i.e.*, the relative intensity of religious attachment to parochial education that the respective groups required of their lay and clerical members? It would be presumptuous even to inquire.[37] Thus, just as in matters of race our belated recognition of intangible factors has finally led us to the maxim "separate therefore unequal," so in matters of religion Madison's immediate recognition of intangible factors led us promptly to the maxim "equal therefore separate." Equality was out of the question without total separation. While, therefore, under Jefferson's individualistic approach it would be extremely difficult to reconcile religious subsidies with the principle of equality, under Madison's institutional approach it would be quite impossible.

2. *The Dissenter Need for Association.*—Of course, when one attaches a Dissenter label to Madison's approach, one does not mean that the Virginia struggle for religious liberty belonged exclusively to the Baptists or any other group. Reading the text of the Memorial, one catches echoes of many noble voices—John Knox and Andrew Melville in Scotland, Peter Wentworth and John Lilburne in England, not to mention the Hebrew prophets who were their common source and inspiration. During the Virginia contest, the Presbyterians of the state were among those who provided significant support for

---

37. In 1790, Madison amended a census bill so as to avoid enumerating clergymen, lest the Government be put in the position of "ascertaining who [are] and who are not ministers of the gospel." Brant, Madison: On the Separation of Church and State, supra note 12, at 17-18.

Madison's efforts. All of these would have rejected a narrow or circumscribed notion of religion's role.

Yet, after we have awarded due credit to the general climate of American thought and Madison's own libertarian genius, there is still much in the particular history of the Baptists that confers depth on the 1785 Memorial and poignancy on the role of religious associations. One understands nothing about so-called "voluntary" associations or their human significance unless one grasps what they mean to the members of a persecuted group. Often, to such a group, church-affiliation is "voluntary" only in the sense that life itself is, or if not life, then the keeping of self-respect. In Revolutionary Virginia, the Baptists were the ones to whom persecution had disclosed not merely the personal but also the corporate value of religion, not merely its individual function as a search but also its group function as a refuge.

The keynote of seventeenth and eighteenth century Baptist experience was sounded at the start. Significantly enough, the first English Baptist Church was organized not by free men in England but by religious exiles in Amsterdam. Their initial confession of faith contained a splendid article on religious liberty and separation of church and state, declaring that "the magistrate is not to meddle with religion, or matters of conscience nor to compel men to this or that form of religion."[38] This, be it noted, as early as the year 1611! The subsequent ordeal of almost unremitting persecution, both in England and in America, only served to reinforce these sound principles and increase the number of adherents.[39] When Madison wrote in his Memorial about the rise of the Christian Church, its independence of government support, and its growth in the face of official persecution, other readers probably recalled the events of the first and second centuries; the Baptists probably recalled those of the seventeenth and eighteenth. Thus the Memorial evoked ideals and loyalties that were not monadic but explicitly social and institutional.

A certain lack of sympathy is to be expected when one tries to convince a very superior mind that the people's understanding of religion does not fully coincide with his. He is likely to dismiss the people's view as merely superstitious. Nevertheless, to the common man and to quite a few uncommon men, religion does possess emotional, ethnic, and cultural aspects—both desirable and undesirable—which cannot be severed from its corporate and communal operations. A

---

38. Encyclopedia Britannica, verb. Baptists, at 87 (1946).

39. In all likelihood, it was the zealous Baptist evangelists, jailed continually for their preachings and preaching continually from their jails, who exemplified the need for an express guarantee of freedom of *speech* in the federal Bill of Rights.

church is far more than a search. Concededly, a temperament like Jefferson's may have needed no fellow-communicants; along with most other intellectuals, he would have approved Alfred North Whitehead's celebrated definition: "Religion is what the individual does with his own solitariness."[40] But this is, at best, a definition suited to the Jeffersons and Whiteheads of the country if there are any, and to others of similar disposition. It is not fit for the remainder of us, or for the judicial enforcement of a clause forbidding "establishment of religion."

3. *Factors of the General Welfare.*—Recognizing organized religion as an ongoing social institution, Madison was much too realistic to overlook the influence it can exert on the general welfare. He proceeded to argue an excellent secular case, proving that here too the establishmentarians were completely mistaken. Religion in a society could indeed serve the general welfare, but government support of religion could serve only the forces of resentment and hatred. Religion could be solidary, but government assistance could be only divisive. These hardheaded considerations, set forth in paragraphs 9 to 15 of the Memorial, have had a massive impact; in fact, they may constitute the main cause why religious liberty has survived in America. Madison warned that anything resembling an establishment would (a) deter persons oppressed in other countries from coming to America,[41] (b) banish some of our citizens from their own land,[42] (c) destroy the harmony we have endeavored to build among highly diverse groups, (d) provoke bitter inter-group hostilities,[43] and (e) weaken the general enforcement of the laws and "slacken the bands of Society."[44]

The argument he concluded with was overwhelming. How could Americans yield on establishment without impairing all the rest of their fundamental rights? Having insisted earlier in the Memorial that even "three pence"[45] for support of an establishment would imperil the people's religious liberty, he now drew the full register of consequences. Since all of our basic rights were held by the self-same constitutional title as freedom of conscience, a compromise on the issue of establishment must jeopardize the entire "basis and foundation of Government."[46]

---

40. Whitehead, Religion in the Making 16 (1926).
41. Memorial (Appendix B) para. 9.
42. Id. para. 10.
43. Id. para. 11, which deserves the most solemn consideration.
44. Id. para. 13.
45. Id. para. 3.
46. Id. para. 15.

RESPECTFULLY SUBMITTED

Only by applying Madison's broader understanding of "religion," which involves full recognition of the term's institutional as well as its individual references, can the Supreme Court realize the just purposes of the "establishment of religion" clause. Acquiescence in a narrower acceptation inevitably works an abridgment of the rights of conscience and a denial of justice. "Justice," wrote Madison, "is the end of government. It is the end of civil society. It ever has been, and ever will be pursued, until it be obtained, or until liberty be lost in the pursuit."[47]

---

47. The Federalist No. 51, at 352 (Cooke ed. 1961). For years, I have restrained my desire to quote this fervent affirmation of Madison's in the 51st Federalist because partisans of Hamilton claimed it for him. Now, however, I feel free to use it. In 1961, the attribution of the 51st Federalist to Madison became not only authoritative but general as well. Brant, Madison VI 428 (1961).

APPENDIX A

Jefferson's Bill for Establishing Religious Freedom

Well aware that the opinions and belief of men depend not on their own will, but follow involuntarily the evidence proposed to their minds;

[T]hat Almighty God hath created the mind free, and manifested his supreme will that free it shall remain by making it altogether insusceptible of restraint;

[T]hat all attempts to influence it by temporal punishments, or burthens, or by civil incapacitations, tend only to beget habits of hypocrisy and meanness, and are a departure from the plan of the holy author of our religion, who being lord both of body and mind, yet chose not to propagate it by coercions on either, as was in his Almighty power to do, but to extend it by its influence on reason alone;

[T]hat the impious presumption of legislators and rulers, civil as well as ecclesiastical, who, being themselves but fallible and uninspired men, have assumed dominion over the faith of others, setting up their own opinions and modes of thinking as the only true and infallible, and as such endeavoring to impose them on others, hath established and maintained false religions over the greatest part of the world and through all time:

That to compel a man to furnish contributions of money for the propagation of opinions which he disbelieves and abhors, is sinful and tyrannical;

[T]hat even the forcing him to support this or that teacher of his own religious persuasion, is depriving him of the comfortable liberty of giving his contributions to the particular pastor whose morals he would make his pattern, and whose powers he feels most persuasive to righteousness; and is withdrawing from the ministry those temporary rewards, which proceeding from an approbation of their personal conduct, are an additional incitement to earnest and unremitting labours for the instruction of mankind;

[T]hat our civil rights have no dependance on our religious opinions, any more than our opinions in physics or geometry; that therefore the proscribing any citizen as unworthy the public confidence by laying upon him an incapacity of being called to offices of trust and emolument, unless he profess or renounce this or that religious opinion, is depriving him injuriously of those privileges and advantages to which, in common with his fellow citizens, he has a natural right;

[T]hat it tends also to corrupt the principles of that very religion it is meant to encourage, by bribing, with a monopoly of worldly honours and emoluments, those who will externally profess and conform to it; that though indeed these are criminal who do not withstand such temptation, yet neither are those innocent who lay the bait in their way;

[T]hat the opinions of men are not the object of civil government, nor under its jurisdiction; that to suffer the civil magistrate to intrude his powers into the field of opinion and to restrain the profession or propagation of principles on supposition of their ill tendency is a dangerous falacy, which at once destroys all religious liberty, because he being of course judge of that tendency will make his opinions the rule of judgment, and approve or condemn the sentiments of others only as they shall square with or differ from his own;

[T]hat it is time enough for the rightful purposes of civil government for its officers to interfere when principles break out into overt acts against peace and good order;

[A]nd finally, that truth is great and will prevail if left to herself; that she is the proper and sufficient antagonist to error, and has nothing to fear from the conflict unless by human interposition disarmed of her natural weapons, free argument and debate; errors ceasing to be dangerous when it is permitted freely to contradict them.

52

We the General Assembly of Virginia do enact that no man shall be compelled to frequent or support any religious worship, place, or ministry whatsoever, nor shall be enforced, restrained, molested, or burthened in his body or goods, nor shall otherwise suffer, on account of his religious opinions or belief; but that all men shall be free to profess, and by argument to maintain, their opinions in matters of religion, and that the same shall in no wise diminish, enlarge, or affect their civil capacities.

And though we well know that this Assembly, elected by the people for the ordinary purposes of legislation only, have no power to restrain the acts of succeeding Assemblies, constituted with powers equal to our own, and that therefore to declare this act irrevocable would be of no effect in law; yet we are free to declare, and do declare, that the rights hereby asserted are of the natural rights of mankind, and that if any act shall be hereafter passed to repeal the present or to narrow its operation, such act will be an infringement of natural right.

APPENDIX B

Madison's Memorial and Remonstrance Against Religious Assessments

To the Honorable the General Assembly
               of
the Commonwealth of Virginia.

A Memorial and Remonstrance.

We, the subscribers, citizens of the said Commonwealth, having taken into serious consideration, a Bill printed by order of the last Session of General Assembly, entitled "A Bill establishing a provision for Teachers of the Christian Religion," and conceiving that the same, if finally armed with the sanctions of a law, will be a dangerous abuse of power, are bound as faithful members of a free State, to remonstrate against it, and to declare the reasons by which we are determined. We remonstrate against the said Bill,

1. Because we hold it for a fundamental and undeniable truth, "that Religion or the duty which we owe to our Creator and the Manner of discharging it, can be directed only by reason and conviction, not by force or violence." The Religion then of every man must be left to the conviction and conscience of every man; and it is the right of every man to exercise it as these may dictate. This right is in its nature an unalienable right. It is unalienable; because the opinions of men, depending only on the evidence contemplated by their own minds, cannot follow the dictates of other men: It is unalienable also; because what is here a right towards men, is a duty towards the Creator. It is the duty of every man to render to the Creator such homage, and such only, as he believes to be acceptable to him. This duty is precedent both in order of time and degree of obligation, to the claims of Civil Society. Before any man can be considered as a member of Civil Society, he must be considered as a subject of the Governor of the Universe: And if a member of Civil Society, who enters into any subordinate Association, must always do it with a reservation of his duty to the general authority; much more must every man who becomes a member of any particular Civil Society, do it with a saving of his allegiance to the Universal Sovereign. We maintain therefore that in matters of Religion, no man's right is abridged by the institution of Civil Society, and that Religion is wholly exempt from its cognizance. True it is, that no other rule exists, by which any question which may divide a Society, can be ultimately determined, but the will of the majority; but it is also true, that the majority may trespass on the rights of the minority.

2. Because if religion be exempt from the authority of the Society at large, still less can it be subject to that of the Legislative Body. The latter are but the creatures and vicegerents of the former. Their jurisdiction is both derivative and limited: it is limited with regard to the co-ordinate departments, more necessarily is it limited with regard to the constituents. The preservation of a free government requires not merely, that the metes and bounds which separate each department of power may be invariably maintained; but more especially, that neither of them be suffered to overleap the great Barrier which defends the rights of the people. The Rulers who are guilty of such an encroachment, exceed the commission from which they derive their authority, and are Tyrants. The People who submit to it are governed by laws made neither by themselves, nor by an authority derived from them, and are slaves.

3. Because, it is proper to take alarm at the first experiment on our liberties. We hold this prudent jealousy to be the first duty of citizens, and one of [the] noblest characteristics of the late Revolution. The freemen of America did not wait till usurped power had strengthened itself by exercise, and entangled the question in precedents. They saw all the consequences in the principle, and they avoided the consequences by denying the principle. We revere this lesson too much, soon to forget it. Who does not see that the same authority which can establish Christianity, in exclusion of all other Religions, may establish with the same ease any particular sect of Christians, in exclusion of all other Sects? That the same authority which can force a citizen to contribute three pence only of his property for the support of any one establishment, may force him to conform to any other establishment in all cases whatsoever?

4. Because, the bill violates that equality which ought to be the basis of every law, and which is more indispensible, in proportion as the validity or expediency of any law is more liable to be impeached. If "all men are by nature equally free and independent," all men are to be considered as entering into Society on equal conditions; as relinquishing no more, and therefore retaining no less, one than another, of their natural rights. Above all are they to be considered as retaining an "*equal* title to the free exercise of Religion according to the dictates of conscience." Whilst we assert for ourselves a freedom to embrace, to profess and to observe the Religion which we believe to be of divine origin, we cannot deny an equal freedom to those whose minds have not yet yielded to the evidence which has convinced us. If this freedom be abused, it is an offence against God, not against man: To God, therefore, not to men, must an account of it be rendered. As the Bill violates equality by subjecting some to peculiar burdens; so it violates the same principle, by granting to others peculiar exemptions. Are the Quakers and Menonists the only sects who think a compulsive support of their religions unnecessary and unwarantable? Can their piety alone be intrusted with the care of public worship? Ought their Religions to be endowed above all others, with extraordinary privileges, by which proselytes may be enticed from all others? We think too favorably of the justice and good sense of these denominations, to believe that they either covet pre-eminencies over their fellow citizens, or that they will be seduced by them, from the common opposition to the measure.

5. Because the bill implies either that the Civil Magistrate is a competent Judge of Religious truth; or that he may employ Religion as an engine of Civil policy. The first is an arrogant pretension falsified by the contradictory opinions of Rulers in all ages, and throughout the world: The second an unhallowed perversion of the means of salvation.

6. Because the establishment proposed by the Bill is not requisite for the support of the Christian Religion. To say that it is, is a contradiction to the Christian Religion itself; for every page of it disavows a dependence on the powers of this world: it is a contradiction to fact; for it is known that this Religion both existed and flourished, not only without the support of human

laws, but in spite of every opposition from them; and not only during the period of miraculous aid, but long after it had been left to its own evidence, and the ordinary care of Providence: Nay, it is a contradiction in terms; for a Religion not invented by human policy, must have pre-existed and been supported, before it was established by human policy. It is moreover to weaken in those who profess this Religion a pious confidence in its innate excellence, and the patronage of its Author; and to foster in those who still reject it, a suspicion that its friends are too conscious of its fallacies, to trust it to its own merits.

7. Because experience witnesseth that ecclesiastical establishments, instead of maintaining the purity and efficacy of Religion, have had a contrary operation. During almost fifteen centuries, has the legal establishment of Christianity been on trial. What have been its fruits? More or less in all places, pride and indolence in the Clergy; ignorance and servility in the laity; in both, superstition, bigotry and persecution. Enquire of the Teachers of Christianity for the ages in which it appeared in its greatest lustre; those of every sect, point to the ages prior to its incorporation with Civil policy. Propose a restoration of this primitive state in which its Teachers depended on the voluntary rewards of their flocks; many of them predict its downfall. On which side ought their testimony to have greatest weight, when for or when against their interest?

8. Because the establishment in question is not necessary for the support of Civil Government. If it be urged as necessary for the support of Civil Government only as it is a means of supporting Religion, and it be not necessary for the latter purpose, it cannot be necessary for the former. If Religion be not within [the] cognizance of Civil Government, how can its legal establishment be said to be necessary to civil Government? What influence in fact have ecclesiastical establishments had on Civil Society? In some instances they have been seen to erect a spiritual tyranny on the ruins of Civil authority; in many instances they have been seen upholding the thrones of political tyranny; in no instance have they been seen the guardians of the liberties of the people. Rulers who wished to subvert the public liberty, may have found an established clergy convenient auxiliaries. A just government, instituted to secure & perpetuate it, needs them not. Such a government will be best supported by protecting every citizen in the enjoyment of his Religion with the same equal hand which protects his person and his property; by neither invading the equal rights of any Sect, nor suffering any Sect to invade those of another.

9. Because the proposed establishment is a departure from that generous policy, which, offering an asylum to the persecuted and oppressed of every Nation and Religion, promised a lustre to our country, and an accession to the number of its citizens. What a melancholy mark is the Bill of sudden degeneracy? Instead of holding forth an asylum to the persecuted, it is itself a signal of persecution. It degrades from the equal rank of Citizens all those whose opinions in Religion do not bend to those of the Legislative authority. Distant as it may be, in its present form, from the Inquisition it differs from it only in degree. The one is the first step, the other the last in the career of intolerance. The magnanimous sufferer under this cruel scourge in foreign Regions, must view the Bill as a Beacon on our Coast, warning him to seek some other haven, where liberty and philanthrophy in their due extent may offer a more certain repose from his troubles.

10. Because, it will have a like tendency to banish our Citizens. The allurements presented by other situations are every day thinning their number. To superadd a fresh motive to emigration, by revoking the liberty which they now enjoy, would be the same species of folly which has dishonoured and depopulated flourishing kingdoms.

11. Because, it will destroy that moderation and harmony which the forbearance of our laws to intermeddle with Religion, has produced amongst its several sects. Torrents of blood have been spilt in the old world, by vain attempts

of the secular arm to extinguish Religious discord, by proscribing all difference in Religious opinions. Time has at length revealed the true remedy. Every relaxation of narrow and rigorous policy, wherever it has been tried, has been found to assuage the disease. The American Theatre has exhibited proofs, that equal and compleat liberty, if it does not wholly eradicate it, sufficiently destroys its malignant influence on the health and prosperity of the State. If with the salutary effects of this system under our own eyes, we begin to contract the bonds of Religious freedom, we know no name that will too severely reproach our folly. At least let warning be taken at the first fruits of the threatened innovation. The very appearance of the Bill has transformed that "Christian forbearance, love and charity," which of late mutually prevailed, into animosities and jealousies, which may not soon be appeased. What mischiefs may not be dreaded should this enemy to the public quiet be armed with the force of a law?

12. Because, the policy of the bill is adverse to the diffusion of the light of Christianity. The first wish of those who enjoy this precious gift, ought to be that it may be imparted to the whole race of mankind. Compare the number of those who have as yet received it with the number still remaining under the dominion of false Religions; and how small is the former! Does the policy of the Bill tend to lessen the disproportion? No; it at once discourages those who are strangers to the light of [revelation] from coming into the Region of it; and countenances, by example the nations who continue in darkness, in shutting out those who might convey it to them. Instead of levelling as far as possible, every obstacle to the victorious progress of truth, the Bill with an ignoble and unchristian timidity would circumscribe it, with a wall of defence, against the encroachments of error.

13. Because attempts to enforce by legal sanctions, acts obnoxious to so great a proportion of Citizens, tend to enervate the laws in general, and to slacken the bands of Society. If it be difficult to execute any law which is not generally deemed necessary or salutary, what must be the case where it is deemed invalid and dangerous? and what may be the effect of so striking an example of impotency in the Government, on its general authority?

14. Because a measure of such singular magnitude and delicacy ought not to be imposed, without the clearest evidence that it is called for by a majority of citizens: and no satisfactory method is yet proposed by which the voice of the majority in this case may be determined, or its influence secured. "The people of the respective counties are indeed requested to signify their opinion respecting the adoption of the Bill to the next Session of Assembly." But the representation must be made equal, before the voice either of the Representatives or of the Counties, will be that of the people. Our hope is that neither of the former will, after due consideration, espouse the dangerous principle of the Bill. Should the event disappoint us, it will still leave us in full confidence, that a fair appeal to the latter will reverse the sentence against our liberties.

15. Because, finally, "the equal right of every citizen to the free exercise of his Religion according to the dictates of conscience" is held by the same tenure with all our other rights. If we recur to its origin, it is equally the gift of nature; if we weigh its importance, it cannot be less dear to us; if we consult the Declaration of those rights which pertain to the good people of Virginia, as the "basis and foundation of Government," it is enumerated with equal solemnity, or rather studied emphasis. Either then, we must say, that the will of the Legislature is the only measure of their authority; and that in the plenitude of this authority, they may sweep away all our fundamental rights; or, that they are bound to leave this particular right untouched and sacred: Either we must say, that they may controul the freedom of the press, may abolish the trial by jury, may swallow up the Executive and Judiciary Powers of the State; nay that they may despoil us of our very right of suffrage, and erect themselves into an independent and hereditary assembly: or we must say, that they have no authority to enact into law the Bill under consideration. We the subscribers say, that the General Assembly of this

Commonwealth have no such authority: And that no effort may be omitted on our part against so dangerous an usurpation, we oppose to it, this remonstrance; earnestly praying, as we are in duty bound, that the Supreme Lawgiver of the Universe, by illuminating those to whom it is addressed, may on the one hand, turn their councils from every act which would affront his holy prerogative, or violate the trust committed to them: and on the other, guide them into every measure which may be worthy of his [blessing, may re]-dound to their own praise, and may establish more firmly the liberties, the prosperity, and the Happiness of the Commonwealth.

Religion in the Public Schools: A Proposed Constitutional Standard

> *The place of religion in the public schools is only one aspect of the problem of Church-State separation, but if the emotional response following last year's United States Supreme Court decision in the Regents' Prayer Case is any indication, it is an important one. In this Article, Professor Choper proposes that, for purposes of testing the constitutional validity of religious activity in the public schools, the first amendment's establishment clause is violated whenever the state engages in "solely religious activity that is likely to result in (1) compromising the student's religious or concientious beliefs or (2) influencing the student's freedom of religious or conscientious choice." After analyzing a number of precedents, Professor Choper applies this standard to various situations that involve religious activity in the public schools; he concludes that the price of abolishing certain religious influences in the schools must be paid to protect religious liberty.*

Jesse H. Choper*

Thirteen years ago, Father John Courtney Murray stated: "No one who knows a bit about the literature on separation of church and state, that for centuries has poured out in all languages, will be inclined to deny that hardly another problem in the religious or political order has received so much misconceived and deformed statement, with the result that the number of bad philosophies in the matter is, like the scriptural number of fools, infinite."[1] Perhaps Father Murray would similarly evaluate the writing that has

---

*Associate Professor, University of Minnesota Law School. The author wishes to express his gratitude to Dean William B. Lockhart and to his colleagues, Professors Yale Kamisar, Robert J. Levy, and Terrance Sandalow, for their valuable suggestions in preparing this Article. He also wishes to thank Stephen I. Dokken, of the second year class, for his helpful research assistance.

1. Murray, *Law or Prepossessions?*, 14 LAW & CONTEMP. PROB. 23 (1949).

appeared since 1949. Whether or not one agrees with his judgment on the merits of the literature, no one would deny that the quantity of discussion is indeed overpowering. With the Supreme Court's recent decision in the *Regents' Prayer Case*,[2] it is inevitable that much more will be forthcoming. This term, the Court has already indicated that it will take a more active role in resolving church-state conflicts.[3] Perhaps the wiser course would be to heed the warning implicit in Father Murray's comment. No doubt, many men of wisdom have declined to express themselves on this issue "so likely to generate heat rather than light."[4] But light, in the form of principled standards to determine the constitutionality, under the first and fourteenth amendments, of the multitude of church-state problems inherent in a democracy such as ours, is sorely needed.

The constitutional standard to be developed in this article is not suggested as a solution for every type of church-state conflict. Rather, it is to be confined to a narrow but exceedingly important segment of the question. The two drives that give rise to the greatest current constitutional controversies regarding the church-state separation commanded by the first amendment, according to Mr. Justice Rutledge,[5] involve the use of the public schools to foster religion and the procurement of public funds to support parochial schools. This article will deal only with the first area.

The proposed constitutional standard is that for problems concerning religious intrusion in the public schools, the establishment clause of the first amendment is violated when the state engages in what may be fairly characterized as *solely religious activity* that is likely to result in (1) *compromising* the student's religious or conscientious beliefs or (2) *influencing* the student's freedom of religious or conscientious choice.[6]

---

2. Engel v. Vitale, 370 U.S. 421 (1962).

3. On October 8, 1962, the Court agreed to hear argument in two cases presenting the issue of the validity of daily Bible reading in the public schools. Schempp v. School Dist., 201 F. Supp. 815 (E.D. Pa.), *prob. juris. noted,* 371 U.S. 807 (1962); Murray v. Curlett, 228 Md. 239, 179 A.2d 698, *cert. granted,* 371 U.S. 809 (1962).

4. Kurland, *Of Church and State and the Supreme Court,* 29 U. CHI. L. REV. 1, 2 (1961).

5. Everson v. Board of Educ., 330 U.S. 1, 63 (1947) (dissenting opinion).

6. Use of the phrase "public schools" is meant to encompass all kindergarten, elementary, and high schools maintained under governmental authority and control. The word "state" is used to designate all that is included

I. DEVELOPMENT OF THE STANDARD

A. SOME SETTLED PROPOSITIONS

Certain preliminary issues must be disposed of at the outset. First, the Supreme Court has decisively settled that the first amendment's mandate that "Congress shall make no law respecting an establishment of religion, or prohibiting the free exercise thereof," has been made wholly applicable to the states by the fourteenth amendment.[7] Although the history, logic, and desirability, of this thesis have been articulately questioned,[8] the Court's consistent position renders further discussion unprofitable. Second, the Court has unequivocally rejected the proposition that the purpose of the

---

within the concept of state action under the fourteenth amendment. See Civil Rights Cases, 109 U.S. 3 (1883). This would cover not only the state legislature and executive, see Virginia v. Rives, 100 U.S. 313 (1879), but also all administrative agencies, Home Tel. & Tel. Co. v. City of Los Angeles, 227 U.S. 278 (1913), political subdivisions, Hague v. CIO, 307 U.S. 496 (1939), and individuals (such as school principals and teachers) acting under color of state authority. See Yick Wo v. Hopkins, 118 U.S. 356 (1886).

7. *E.g.*, Cantwell v. Connecticut, 310 U.S. 296, 303 (1940); Murdock v. Pennsylvania, 319 U.S. 105, 108 (1943); Everson v. Board of Educ., 330 U.S. 1, 5 (1947); Illinois ex rel. McCollum v. Board of Educ., 333 U.S. 203, 210–11 (1948); Zorach v. Clauson, 343 U.S. 306, 309 (1952); Torcaso v. Watkins, 367 U.S. 488, 492 (1961); Engel v. Vitale, 370 U.S. 421, 423, 430 (1962).

The first part of the first amendment will hereinafter be referred to as the "establishment clause"; the second part, as the "free exercise clause."

8. Howe, *The Constitutional Question*, in RELIGION AND THE FREE SOCIETY 49 (1958). The essence of Professor Howe's position is that the language of the fourteenth amendment that "no State shall . . . deprive any person of life, liberty, or property, without due process of law" indicates that its intention was only to bar the states from infringing on those rights that are "implicit in the concept of ordered liberty." Palko v. Connecticut, 302 U.S. 319, 325 (1937). By virtue of the fourteenth amendment, the states not only are forbidden to deny that liberty that is protected by the free exercise clause, but also are powerless to give any aid to religion that would significantly impair the intellectual or spiritual liberties of individuals. The establishment clause, however, may be read to bar many federal aids to religion that do not appreciably affect individual liberties—for example, the granting of tax exemptions to churches and the public schools' permitting the gift of Bibles to willingly receptive pupils. The fourteenth amendment should not be read to prohibit the states from extending these aids to religion.

In answer, it might be suggested that some of the aids to religion that Professor Howe finds to have little impact on the secured rights of individuals—for example, the distribution of Bibles in the public schools—may well have substantial impact. See text accompanying note 509 *infra*. Furthermore, even those aids to religion that have no *immediate* effect on individual liberty—for example, financial assistance to religion in the form of tax exemption or, for that matter, a direct appropriation to a particular church—historically and logically have tended to cause so much strife among religious sects as to ultimately endanger individual liberty. See Everson v. Board of Educ., 330 U.S. 1, 11, 53–54 (1947).

establishment clause is only to forbid governmental preference of one religion over another.[9] Despite heated (and often intemperate) argument to the contrary,[10] the establishment clause bars certain governmental aids to religion even if impartially afforded to all religious sects.[11] Finally, the Court has firmly determined that the ban of the establishment clause extends beyond the setting up of a state church,[12] a proposition with which there has been relatively little disagreement.

B. AIMS OF THE PROPOSED STANDARD

Although it has been suggested that "it is not reason but history that must be consulted"[13] to determine what is right and proper in the field of church-state relations, such a dichotomy neither can nor should be drawn. The precise intentions of the framers of the first amendment are surely of great importance, but scholarly investigation has produced antithetic conclusions.[14] The desirable course is to frame a principle for constitutional adjudication that is not only grounded in the history and language of the first amend-

---

9. Illinois *ex rel.* McCollum v. Board of Educ., 333 U.S. 203, 211 (1948).
10. *E.g.*, O'NEILL, RELIGION AND EDUCATION UNDER THE CONSTITUTION (1949); Corwin, *The Supreme Court as National School Board*, 14 LAW & CONTEMP. PROB. 3, 9–16 (1949); Murray, *supra* note 1, at 23. Disagreement with the Court's interpretation of the establishment clause is not limited to nonjudicial commentators. Recently, the Supreme Court of Florida decided that it was
> not impressed with the language quoted [from four Supreme Court decisions] as being definitive of the "establishment" clause. It goes far beyond the purpose and intent of the authors and beyond any reasonable application to the practical facts of every day life in this country. We feel that the broad language quoted must, in the course of time, be further receded from, if weight is to be accorded the true purpose of the First Amendment.

Chamberlin v. Dade County Bd., 143 So. 2d 21, 24–25 (Fla. Sup. Ct. 1962). See also *id.* at 28; Zorach v. Clauson, 303 N.Y. 161, 179–82, 100 N.E.2d 463, 472–73 (1951) (concurring opinion); 9 U.C.L.A.L. REV. 495, 499 (1962).
11. Everson v. Board of Educ., 330 U.S. 1, 15 (1947); Illinois *ex rel.* McCollum v. Board of Educ., 333 U.S. 203, 210–11 (1948); McGowan v. Maryland, 366 U.S. 420, 443 (1961); Torcaso v. Watkins, 367 U.S. 488, 492–93, 495 (1961).
12. Illinois *ex rel.* McCollum v. Board of Educ., 333 U.S. 203, 213 (1948) (concurring opinion); McGowan v. Maryland, 366 U.S. 420, 442 (1961).
13. Herberg, *Religion, Democracy, and Public Education*, in RELIGION IN AMERICA 118, 142 (Cogley ed. 1958).
14. *Compare* the opinions in Everson v. Board v. Educ., 330 U.S. 1 (1947), *with* the authorities cited in note 10 *supra*. *Compare* Pfeffer, *Church and State: Something Less Than Separation*, 19 U. CHI. L. REV. 1 (1951), *with* PARSONS, THE FIRST FREEDOM (1948). See also Kurland, *The Regents' Prayer Case: "Full of Sound and Fury Signifying . . .,"* 1962 SUPREME COURT REV. 1, 22–25.

ment,[15] but one that is also capable of consistent application to the relevant problems.[16] When applied, the principle should take into account those values now cherished in our society[17] and should not produce decidedly farfetched or unacceptable results.[18] The last criterion is particularly crucial in the emotionally-charged area of religion in the public schools.

The proposed constitutional standard attempts to meet these requirements. If there are any points of general agreement in the field of church-state relationships, they are that probably the paramount purpose for the enactment of the establishment clause was to safeguard freedom of worship and conscience,[19] and that the protection of religious liberty remains our society's major concern in the church-state sphere.[20] By stressing the security of religious and conscientious scruples of public school children, the proposed standard attempts to fulfill both the predominant histori-

---

15. *Cf.* Henkin, *Shelley v. Kraemer: Notes For a Revised Opinion*, 110 U. PA. L. REV. 473 (1962).
16. See LLEWELLYN, THE BRAMBLE BUSH 43–44 (1951). *But see* 51 GEO. L. J. 185 (1962).
17. *Cf.* Wechsler, *Toward Neutral Principles of Constitutional Law*, 73 HARV. L. REV. 1, 31–32 (1959).
18. *Cf.* Henkin, *supra* note 15, at 477.
19. See, *e.g.*, Engel v. Vitale, 370 U.S. 421, 429–30 (1962) (Black, J.); Zorach v. Clauson, 343 U.S. 306, 313–14 (1952) (Douglas, J.); Everson v. Board of Educ., 330 U.S. 1, 8–11 (Black, J.), 53–54 (1947) (Rutledge, J., dissenting); O'NEILL, *op. cit. supra* note 10 at 96; PFEFFER, CHURCH, STATE, AND FREEDOM 122 (1953); Katz, *Freedom of Religion and State Neutrality*, 20 U. CHI. L. REV. 426, 428 (1953); Kurland, *supra* note 4, at 4; Murray, *supra* note 1, at 32; 31 FORDHAM L. REV. 201, 202 (1962).
20. See, *e.g.*, Butts, *The Relation Between Religion and Education*, 33 PROGRESSIVE EDUCATION 140, 141 (1956): "This movement [from the latter part of the 18th century to the early 20th century] toward separation of church and state in education was undertaken in order to preserve freedom for all." Johnson, *Religion and Education*, 33 PROGRESSIVE EDUCATION 143, 145 (1956): "[P]rotection of religious liberty is the beginning and the end of the separation of church and state." Katz, *supra note* 19, at 436, points out that "fear of the Roman Catholic church as a potential threat to religious freedom" probably explains the strict separationist position of those who oppose government aid to religion, such as financial assistance to parochial schools, that seemingly does not result in an impairment of religious liberty. On the other hand, those who attack the strict separationist position on such issues as financial aid to parochial education and public school released time do so on the ground that complete separation violates the religious liberty of those who attend parochial schools or who wish to participate in released time. See, *e.g.*, Bishops of the United States, *The Place of the Private and Church-Related Schools in American Education*, 33 PROGRESSIVE EDUCATION 152 (1956); Hayes, *The Constitutional Permissibility of the Participation of Church-Related Schools in the Administration's Proposed Program of Massive Federal Aid to Education*, 11 DEPAUL L. REV. 161, 162 (1962); Reed, *Church-State and the Zorach Case*, 27 NOTRE DAME LAW. 529, 540 (1952); Slough & McAnany, *Government Aid to Church-Related Schools: An Analysis*, 11 KAN. L. REV. 35, 72 (1962).

cal and contemporary concerns with religious freedom. It prohibits certain governmental action that is likely to result in (1) a student's doing something that is forbidden by his conscientious beliefs, thus *compromising* his scruples or (2) a student's engaging in religious activities that, although not contrary to his religion's beliefs, he would not otherwise undertake, thus *influencing* his freedom of religious participation or choice. The results the proposed standard produces seem to me to be, for the most part, favorable; those that are not are nonetheless acceptable.

C. Delimitation of the Area and Definition of Solely Religious Activity

Many writers have considered the problems of religious infiltration in the public schools and financial aid by government to religious schools to be subject to singular treatment.[21] Some have concluded that the result of both is to "aid" religion, and therefore, both must be measured by the same standard.[22] The contention that both "aid" religion is indisputable, but it cannot follow that "aid to religion" is *the* constitutional determinant.[23] If it were, few governmental activities could withstand constitutional attack.[24]

---

21. *E.g.*, Corwin, *Supra* note 10, at 5; Pfeffer, *Religion, Education and the Constitution*, 8 Law. Guild Rev. 387 (1948); Sullivan, *Religious Education in the Schools*, 14 Law & Contemp. Prob. 92, 109, 111 (1949); Pfeffer, *The New York Regents' Prayer Case (Engel v. Vitale): Its Background, Meaning and Implications*, Committee on Law and Social Action Reports 6 (American Jewish Congress June 26, 1962). For a rather intemperate criticism of the Supreme Court's failure to so treat these questions, see Comment, 9 Ohio St. L.J. 336, 340 (1948).

22. *E.g.*, Boyer, *Religious Education of Public School Pupils in Wisconsin*, 1953 Wis. L. Rev. 181, 240; Note, 1 J. Pub. L. 212, 216 (1952).

23. The source of the confusion is undoubtedly the famous dictum of Mr. Justice Black in Everson v. Board of Educ., 330 U.S. 1, 15 (1947): "Neither [a state nor the federal government] can pass laws which aid one religion, aid all religions, or prefer one religion over another." The dictum was repeated by the Court in Illinois *ex rel.* McCollum v. Board of Educ., 333 U.S. 203, 210 (1948); McGowan v. Maryland, 366 U.S. 420, 443 (1961); and Torcaso v. Watkins, 367 U.S. 488, 492–93 (1961). It has been discussed in virtually all of the church-state literature since *Everson*. Curiously, Mr. Justice Black made no reference to this dictum in Engel v. Vitale.

24. The public fire and police protection afforded parochial schools undeniably "aid" them. The closing of public schools each Saturday and Sunday, which enables Christian and Jewish children to attend their respective churches and synagogues, clearly "aids" attendance at religious services.

The best evidence that the Court never intended the phrase "aid to religion," as commonly understood, to be *the* constitutional determinant, but rather considers "aid" to be a word of art (perhaps poorly chosen), is that in the first two decisions in which the phrase was used, the Court reached opposite conclusions despite the fact that both situations obviously resulted in "aid" to religion. Everson v. Board of Educ., 330 U.S. 1 (1947)

Nor, when more objective standards are available,[25] is it satisfactory merely to say that the question of what kinds of "aid" are constitutional and what kinds are not "is one of degree."[26]

Various forms of public financial assistance to parochial education are permissible under the first amendment because such assistance, despite its resultant aid to religion, has the accomplishment of a nonreligious public purpose[27] as an independent *primary goal,* as distinguished from a dependent *derivative* goal.[28] Thus, the use of tax-raised funds to pay the bus fares of parochial school pupils was upheld by the Supreme Court as "public welfare legislation" protecting "children going to and from church schools from the very real hazards of traffic."[29] Likewise, the argument, whatever its merit, for the constitutional inclusion of religiously affiliated schools in any federal program providing financial assistance for elementary and secondary school buildings and teachers' salaries is that such government support "confers directly and substantially a benefit to citizen education,"[30] and that such an end is within the legitimate scope of federal concern.[31] Although these governmental programs aid religion, *they may not be fairly characterized as solely religious activities.* However, other practices, such as prayer recitation and Bible reading, *must be fairly characterized as solely religious activities having no independent primary nonreligious purpose.* Their exclusive primary goal is to inculcate the students with religious and spiritual ideals or to assist in such inculcation.

(upholding the use of public funds to transport children to parochial schools); Illinois *ex rel.* McCollum v. Board of Educ., 333 U.S. 203 (1948) (invalidating religious instruction during released time in the public schools).

25. *Cf.* Burton v. Wilmington Parking Authority, 365 U.S. 715, 725 (1961), in which the Court treated the problem of what is sufficient state involvement in private action to constitute state action as a question of degree only "because readily applicable formulae may not be fashioned."

26. Zorach v. Clauson, 343 U.S. 306, 314 (1952) (Douglas, J.).

27. See, *e.g.,* 1 BUFFALO L. REV. 198, 200 (1951); 3 RUTGERS L. REV. 115, 119–21 (1949). The aid obtained by religion is often referred to as being merely "incidental."

28. See text accompanying notes 31–37 *infra.*

29. Everson v. Board of Educ., 330 U.S. 1, 16–17 (1947).

30. National Catholic Welfare Conference, *The Constitutionality of the Inclusion of Church-Related Schools in Federal Aid to Education,* 50 GEO. L.J. 397, 422 (1961).

31. For other instances of the use of this position, see Opinion of the Justices, 99 N.H. 519, 113 A.2d 114 (1955); Schade v. Allegheny County Institution Dist., 386 Pa. 507, 126 A.2d 911 (1956); Slough & McAnany, *supra* note 20, at 62–64. See also Cochran v. Louisiana State Bd., 281 U.S. 370 (1930). Evaluation of this thesis is beyond the scope of this article. Since the governmental action with which it deals may not be fairly characterized as "solely religious," it falls outside the constitutional standard proposed herein and is subject to independent consideration.

Contentions proclaiming a public purpose for these solely religious activities are numerous. It has been argued that their intention is to combat juvenile delinquency among American youth;[32] to teach "tolerance, love of fellow men, kindness, responsibility for the welfare of others";[33] to prevent rape and other crimes;[34] and to develop "deep and intelligent convictions" in our children.[35] It has even been suggested that since failure to engage in these practices causes upset and disturbed community reaction, the prevention of such situations is a secular justification for having the religious exercises.[36]

But these arguments ignore the crucial point. The results that follow from the introduction of religion into the public schools are unimportant. What is relevant is the fact that if such effects are produced, they come about only if the primary goal—the implanting of spiritual and religious beliefs—is achieved; the purported seculars ends are derivative from the exclusively religious end.[37]

Perhaps governmental aid to parochial education may be constitutionally justified on the ground that, despite the fact that aid to religion is a necessary effect, an *equally necessary effect* is the promotion of a secular goal. But to uphold the constitutionality of religious incursions into public education on the basis of their alleged secular benefits, despite the fact that they are merely derived from the *sole necessary effect* of advancing religion not only opens "the doctrinal floodgates for infinitely greater aid to religion,"[38] but literally reads the establishment clause out of the first amendment.[39] Such incursions "employ Religion as an engine of Civil policy."[40] If the instilling of moral, ethical, and spiritual values will sustain these solely religious practices,[41] there

---

32. Brief for the Board of Regents of the University of the State of New York as Amicus Curiae, p. 14, Engel v. Vitale, 370 U.S. 421 (1962). See also Gordon v. Board of Educ., 78 Cal. App. 2d 464, 474, 178 P.2d 488, 494 (Ct. App. 1947).
33. Sullivan, *supra* note 21, at 108.
34. W. S. Fleming, quoted in PFEFFER, *op. cit. supra* note 19, at 300–01.
35. Chairman of New York University Department of Religious Education, quoted in Boyer, *supra* note 22, at 232.
36. See Lieberman, *A General Interpretation of Separation of Church and State and Its Implications for Public Education*, 33 PROGRESSIVE EDUCATION 129, 132 (1956).
37. See McGowan v. Maryland, 366 U.S. 420, 466 (1961) (Frankfurter, J., separate opinion); Note, 3 RUTGERS L. REV. 115, 121 (1949).
38. Note, 57 YALE L.J. 1114, 1120 (1948).
39. See generally Pfeffer, *Court, Constitution and Prayer*, 16 RUTGERS L. REV. 735, 746–47 (1962).
40. Madison, *Memorial and Remonstrance Against Religious Assessments*, para. 5, reprinted in Everson v. Board of Educ., 330 U.S. 1, 67 (1947).
41. The argument that this is the saving "public purpose" has been made

would seem to be no reason why a government could not subsidize the church that it feels best inculcates its members with these qualities.[42]

Nor is it a solution to judge these solely religious activities by balancing the public benefit derived against the quantum of aid extended to religion.[43] This test may have some value in the case of governmental action that results directly in both secular and religious benefit, but when the public benefit is derivative—when it is secured only after the religious inculcation is achieved—the secular benefit will always vary directly with the religious benefit, and any balancing is logically impossible.

The reasons calling for separate treatment of the problem of religious activities in the public schools and the problem of financial aid to parochial education are also applicable in severing the former from that presented by other governmental activity that allegedly violates the establishment clause, but has an independent primary nonreligious purpose.[44] Also, since children of elementary and high school age are far less mature and intellectually developed than the public generally,[45] since they are particularly unable to evaluate conflicting religious beliefs objectively,[46] since they are especially susceptible to being influenced in religious choice,[47] and since they are compelled by law to attend the

---

by Creel, *Is It Legal for the Public Schools of Alabama to Provide an Elective Course in Non-Sectarian Bible Instruction*, 10 ALA. LAW. 86, 95 (1949); Harpster, *Religion, Education and the Law*, 36 MARQ. L. REV. 24, 47 (1952); Meiklejohn, *Educational Cooperation Between Church and State*, 14 LAW & CONTEMP. PROB. 61, 67 (1949). See also Hart v. School Dist., 2 Lancaster L. Rev. 346, 352 (Pa. C.P. 1885). The writer in 30 FORDHAM L. REV. 509 (1962), asserts: "It would seem quite arbitrary for the Supreme Court to hold that a general day of rest and relaxation served a public purpose but the acknowledgement of a God by people 'whose institutions presuppose a Supreme Being' was not a public purpose."

42. Professor Kauper suggests this result, although somewhat more cautiously: "Moreover, the notion that government can directly aid religion in order to bolster morale suggests implications of a wider use of public moneys in direct aid of religion." Kauper, *Church, State, and Freedom: A Review*, 52 MICH. L. REV. 829, 837 (1954). See also Pfeiffer v. Board of Educ., 118 Mich. 560, 578, 77 N.W. 250, 257 (1898) (dissenting opinion).

43. See Note, 17 GEO. WASH. L. REV. 516, 529 (1949); 57 YALE L.J. 1114, 1120–21 (1948).

44. *E.g.* Sunday closing laws (see McGowan v. Maryland, 366 U.S. 420 (1961)); appropriations to hospital, maintained under religious auspices, for treating indigent patients (see Bradfield v. Roberts, 175 U.S. 291 (1899)).

45. *Cf.* PFEFFER, *op. cit. supra* note 19, at 423; Cosway & Toepfer, *Religion and the Schools*, 17 U. CINC. L. REV. 117, 137 (1948); Comment, 22 U. CHI. L. REV. 888, 893 (1955). Possible distinctions between elementary school children and high school pupils will be discussed *infra*.

46. *Cf.* 16 GEO. WASH. L. REV. 556, 559 (1948).

47. *Cf.* 25 CAL. OPS. ATT'Y GEN. 324 (1955); Cushman, *The Holy*

site of these religious practices,[48] there is a sound basis for giving distinctive treatment to solely religious practices in the public schools instead of treating them together with similar practices existing in our society generally.[49]

D. THE REGENTS' PRAYER CASE

In 1951, the New York State Board of Regents, the governmental agency that supervises the state's public school system, composed and recommended to all local school boards the following prayer: "Almighty God, we acknowledge our dependence upon Thee, and we beg Thy blessings upon us, our parents, our teachers and our country."[50] In 1958, the New Hyde Park Board of Education instructed all teachers that the prayer be recited aloud by each class at the beginning of every school day. An action in the state courts was instituted by parents of attending students, who were Jewish, Ethical Culturists, Unitarians, or nonbelievers,[51] asserting, *inter alia*, that the practice should cease because it violated the establishment clause.[52] Their claims were rejected at all state levels,[53] although it was made clear that objecting students had the right not to participate.[54] The Supreme Court reversed in *Engel v. Vitale*,[55] holding the practice to be contrary to the establishment clause, a ruling that "aroused more public controversy than any decision since Brown v. Board of Education."[56]

Bible and the Public Schools, 40 CORNELL L.Q. 475, 496 (1955); Kalven, *A Commemorative Case Note*, 27 U. CHI. L. REV. 505, 518 (1960); 74 HARV. L. REV. 611, 614 (1961).

48. *Cf.* Sutherland, *Public Authority and Religious Education: A Brief Survey of Constitutional and Legal Limits*, in THE STUDY OF RELIGION IN THE PUBLIC SCHOOLS: AN APPRAISAL 45 (Brown ed. 1958).

49. Such practices include chaplains in both houses of Congress and in state legislative assemblies and the opening prayer in the United States Supreme Court: "God save the United States and this Honorable Court."

50. Its use was recommended at the commencement of each school day in conjunction with the pledge of allegiance to the flag. Record, p. 28, Engel v. Vitale, 370 U.S. 421 (1962).

51. *Id.* at 12.

52. Other claims presented were that the free exercise clause was violated, that a similar clause of the state constitution, N.Y. CONST. art. I, § 3, was violated, and that the Board of Education had exceeded its statutory power. *Id.* at 16–17.

53. Engel v. Vitale, 18 Misc. 2d 659, 191 N.Y.S.2d 453 (Sup. Ct. 1959), *aff'd*, 11 App. Div. 2d 340, 206 N.Y.S.2d 183 (1960), *aff'd* 10 N.Y.2d 174, 176 N.E.2d 579, 218 N.Y.S.2d 659 (1961) (Dye, J., & Fuld, J. dissenting).

54. 18 Misc. 2d 659, 696, 191 N.Y.S.2d 453, 492–93 (1959).

55. 370 U.S. 421, 424 (1962).

56. 31 U.S.L. WEEK 1038 (1962). The decision was announced on June 25, 1962. Reference to any newspaper or periodical of the time will bear out

At the outset, Mr. Justice Black, writing for the Court,[57] characterized the recitation of the Regents' prayer as "a religious activity."[58] That it was a solely religious activity, having no independent primary nonreligious purpose, is beyond dispute.[59] Examination of the remainder of the opinion, however, leaves somewhat unclear the precise basis and extent of the decision. There is language indicating that the decision holds no more than that the evil in the situation was the fact that a governmental agency had taken it upon itself to *compose* an official prayer for use in the public schools.[60]

---

the Law Week characterization. Many, if not most of the attacks on the case were emotionally oriented and were founded on a basic misunderstanding (unintentional or otherwise) of the decision. Those who found it politically expedient to denounce the "ruling against God" did so, without pausing to learn whether the Court so ruled. Long-time critics of the Court exploited the opportunity to heap further abuse, without regard to the limitations stated in the reasoning and language of the case. For a discussion of this criticism, see Choper, *What Did Court Really Rule on Prayer*, Minneapolis Star, Sept. 15, 1962, p. 6A, col. 5. See generally Kurland, *The Regents' Prayer Case: "Full of Sound and Fury, Signifying . . .,"* in 1962 SUPREME COURT REV. 1; Pfeffer, *supra* note 39.

57. He was joined by Mr. Chief Justice Warren and Justices Clark, Harlan, and Brennan. Mr. Justice Douglas wrote a concurring opinion. Mr. Justice Stewart dissented. For discussion of these last two opinions, see notes 188–89 *infra*. Neither Mr. Justice Frankfurter nor Mr. Justice White participated, the former being ill when the decision was announced and the latter not yet having been appointed when the case was argued.

58. 370 U.S. at 424. The fact that the prayer recitation immediately followed the salute to the flag was not even considered as changing the characterization of the nature of the activity. Record, p. 13, Engel v. Vitale, 370 U.S. at 421. In this connection, see Schempp v. School Dist., 177 F. Supp. 398, 406 (E.D. Pa. 1959). However, the Court's opinion later pointed out that this was an *"unquestioned* religious exercise" (emphasis added) and distinguished this case from "patriotic or ceremonial occasions" such as "singing officially espoused anthems which include the composer's professions of faith in a Supreme Being." 370 U.S. at 435, n.21. Although it appears that this refers only to "The Star-Spangled Banner," the third stanza of which contains references to the Deity, it seems that the Court may be willing to single out those parts of a daily school exercise that are of a religious nature yet unwilling to sever those verses of a song that are solely religious. See text accompanying notes 541–44 *infra*.

59. This was acknowledged in The Regents Statement on Moral and Spiritual Training in the Schools, Record, pp. 28–29, Engel v. Vitale, 370 U.S. 421 (1962).

60.
> The petitioners contend . . . that the . . . prayer must be struck down as a violation of the Establishment Clause because that prayer was composed by government officials as a part of a governmental program to further religious beliefs. . . . We agree with that contention since we think that the [establishment clause] must at least mean that in this country it is no part of the business of government to compose official prayers for any group of the American people to recite as a part of a religious program carried on by government.

370 U.S. at 425.

Even if the Court's holding is this limited, it does not augur well for the closely related public school practices of reading the Bible and reciting other long-established prayers.[61] It can be argued that since the Bible and such prayers as the Lord's Prayer were not *composed* by any governmental agency, they do not fall into the same category as the Regents' prayer,[62] but there seems to be no reason to distinguish between a governmental agency *composing* a religious prayer for use in the schools and that same agency *selecting* a prayer or other religious material composed elsewhere.[63] If anything, the Regents' prayer, which has been described by some as "purely nondenominational,"[64] would be much less objectionable in our religiously pluralistic society than any version of the Bible or the Lord's Prayer, none of which are unobjectionable to all of the major religious faiths.[65] Nor would the circumstances be improved if, instead of the Regents selecting or

---

61. Pfeffer, Committee on Law and Social Action Reports, *supra* note 21, at 5–6, says that it follows from *Engel* that the Lord's Prayer and Bible reading are likewise unconstitutional.

62. See Lewis, *School-Prayer Issue in High Court Again*, N.Y. Times, Oct. 14, 1962, § 4, p. 5, col. 2.

63. It is difficult to believe that the decision in *Engel* would have been different if, instead of the Regents having composed the words of this prayer, they had selected them from a collection of prayers composed by someone else. The opinion laid great emphasis on the bitter controversy in 16th and 17th century England over the governmentally approved Book of Common Prayer. 370 U.S. at 425–27, 429–30. The source of that struggle was the question of what the content of the Book of Common Prayer should be. Surely, it made no difference in that controversy whether the government *composed* prayers that reflected the sentiments of a particular religion or selected prayers already composed of the same kind. See Sutherland, *Establishment According to Engel*, 76 HARV. L. REV. 25, 38 n.36 (1962).

There is language in the opinion to support the conclusion that this distinction should not be drawn.

[O]ne of the greatest dangers to the freedom of the individual to worship in his own way [lies] in the Government's placing its official stamp of approval upon one particular kind of prayer. . . . [N]either the power nor the prestige of the . . . Government [shall] be used to control, support or influence the kinds of prayer the American people can say. . . .

. . . .

[G]overnment . . . is without power to prescribe by law any particular form of prayer which is to be used as an official prayer in carrying on any program of governmentally sponsored religious activity. . . .

. . . .

[E]ach separate government in this county should stay out of the business of writing or sanctioning official prayers. . . .

370 U.S. at 429, 430, 435. See 31 FORDHAM L. REV. 203 n.20 (1962).

64. 9 U.C.L.A.L. REV. 499 (1962). See also Engel v. Vitale, 370 U.S. 421, 430 (1962). *But see* text accompanying notes 66–74 *infra*.

65. See text accompanying notes 258–81, 230–36 *infra*.

composing the prayer, either the teacher or the students made the choice. Indeed, since these people would be much further removed from the pressures of the political process than the Regents, the product of such selection or composition would much more likely be oriented toward the teachings of a particular religious sect.[66]

Certain other observations may be made from an examination of the Court's opinion. The question of whether the prayer was denominationally neutral[67] was sidestepped by the Court.[68] The answer is manifest. Since it involved a supplication to God, it patently favored the theistic religions over those that are nontheistic, such as Ethical Culture (the religion of one of the complaining parents).[69] The conceded "purpose and effect"[70] of this program was "teaching our children . . . that Almighty God is their Creator, and that by Him they have been endowed with their inalienable rights . . . ."[71] Opposition was expressed even among those religions teaching belief in a Supreme Being; some complained that the prayer was ineffectual, while others found it plainly contrary to their religious beliefs.[72] Furthermore, theistic religions differ on the propriety of offering prayers not specifically decreed by the sect and of seeking divine assistance in certain matters.[73]

---

66. *Cf.* Engel v. Vitale, 18 Misc. 2d 659, 699, 191 N.Y.S.2d 453, 495 (1959).

67. Judge Froessel in the New York Court of Appeals found it to be so. Engel v. Vitale, 10 N.Y.2d 174, 183, 176 N.E.2d 579, 583 (1961) (concurring opinion).

68. 370 U.S. at 430.

69. Other nontheistic religions in this country are Buddhism, Taoism, and Secular Humanism. See authorities cited in Torcaso v. Watkins, 367 U.S. 488, 495 n.11 (1961).

70. McGowan v. Maryland, 366 U.S. 420, 443, 445, 449 (1961). See also *id.* at 453.

71. The Regents Statement on Moral and Spiritual Training in the Schools, Record, p. 28, Engel v. Vitale, 370 U.S. 421 (1962).

72. Although the Catholic Church and most Protestant groups warmly endorsed the prayer,
> *The Christian Century* deemed [it] 'likely to deteriorate quickly into an empty formality with little, if any, spiritual significance.' The leaders of the Lutheran Church of Our Redeemer in Peekskill [N.Y.] charged that Christ's name had 'deliberately been omitted to mollify non-Christian elements,' and that the prayer 'therefore is a denial of Christ and His prescription for a proper prayer. As such it is not a prayer but an abomination and a blasphemy.'

PFEFFER, CHURCH, STATE, AND FREEDOM 396 (1953). Opposition was also expressed by the Schenectady (N.Y.) Methodist Church Board, the Liberal Ministers Club (primarily Unitarians and Universalists), and "every important interested Jewish organization in the state." *Ibid.*

73. See the authorities cited in Brief for American Jewish Committee and Anti-Defamation League of B'nai B'rith as Amici Curiae, p. 20 n.6, Engel v. Vitale, 370 U.S. 421 (1962). See also Brief for Synagogue

Thus, the Court could have easily reached its result by use of the generally noncontroversial proposition that the establishment clause forbids governmental preference of some religions over others.[74] However, since the Court had based a decision just one year before on the thesis that a state cannot "constitutionally pass laws or impose requirements which aid all religions as against nonbelievers,"[75] it would be hypercritical to say that, on this ground, the *Engel* holding is too broad.

The holding may be criticized as too broad on another ground, however. A major defense for the constitutionality of the Regents' prayer was the fact that participation in its recitation was wholly voluntary;[76] objecting students were privileged either to remain silent or to be excused from the room.[77] The Court's opinion found "the fact that its observance on the part of the students is voluntary" to be irrelevant.[78] Although recognizing that "when the power, prestige and financial support of government is placed behind a particular religious belief, the indirect coercive pressure upon religious minorities to conform to the prevailing officially approved religion is plain,"[79] Mr. Justice Black stated that "the Establishment Clause, unlike the Free Exercise Clause, does not depend upon any showing of direct governmental compulsion and is violated by the enactment of *laws which establish an official religion* whether those laws operate directly to coerce nonobserving individuals or not."[80] The essence of this position seems to have emanated from the argument by two amici curiae in the case—one finding an establishment clause violation, irrespective of the privilege of nonparticipation, anytime government is engaged in "undertaking or sponsoring religious programs";[81] the other, whenever there is state "participation in religious affairs."[82] This seemingly

---

Council of America and National Community Relations Advisory Council as Amici Curiae, p. 10, Engel v. Vitale, 370 U.S. 421 (1962).
 74. See text accompanying notes 9–11 *supra*.
 75. Torcaso v. Watkins, 367 U.S. 488, 495 (1961). See also authorities cited in note 11 *supra*.
 76. Brief for Respondents, pp. 32–34; Brief for Intervenors-Respondents, pp. 11, 42–43; Brief for The Board of Regents of the University of the State of New York as Amicus Curiae, p. 24, Engel v. Vitale, 370 U.S. 421 (1962).
 77. 370 U.S. at 430.
 78. *Ibid.*
 79. *Id.* at 431.
 80. *Id.* at 430. (Emphasis added.)
 81. Brief for American Jewish Committee and Anti-Defamation League of B'nai B'rith as Amici Curiae, p. 17, Engel v. Vitale, 370 U.S. 421 (1962).
 82. Brief for Synagogue Council of America and National Community Relations Advisory Council as Amici Curiae, p. 15 (Mr. Leo Pfeffer, Attorney), Engel v. Vitale, 370 U.S. 421 (1962).

broad interpretation of the establishment clause was not necessary to the decision in *Engel*.[83] The case could have been more discretely decided specifically on the ground that, regardless of the dissenting student's right of nonparticipation, compulsion did exist;[84] that a showing of actual compulsion was unnecessary because of the "indirect coercive pressure" that this program exerted; that the program would result either in the young children[85] of the minority groups involved taking part in a religious exercise that was contrary to their conscientious beliefs or in their being singled out as "oddballs" by their peers; that this is a cruel choice that no state may constitutionally demand if it engages in a solely religious activity.[86]

II. SUPPORT FOR THE STANDARD

A. INDIRECT COERCION

Although the Supreme Court has never explicitly held that indirect coercive pressure constitutes a violation of the establishment clause,[87] there is a plethora of material to support this rationale.

1. *Existence of Indirect Coercion*

It is universally recognized that such pressures in fact exist. Many writers of widely diverse backgrounds[88] have observed that young people of minority religious groups are extremely sensitive about conspicuously absenting themselves from religious exercises conducted by the majority and that there is a powerful, albeit subtle, pressure to conform. The emotional strain is very frequently so great that it results in unwilling participation in preference to some amount of social ostracism. Student commentators

---

83. See text accompanying notes 189–92 *infra*.
84. *But see* Sutherland, *Establishment According to Engel*, 76 HARV. L. REV. 25, 39 (1962).
85. The parents bringing this suit had a total of ten children attending school. The ages of the children ranged from seven to 15. Record, pp. 11–12, Engel v. Vitale, 370 U.S. 421 (1962).
86. *Cf.* Braunfeld v. Brown, 366 U.S. 599, 616 (1961) (Stewart J., dissenting).
87. This is pointed out in 9 U.C.L.A.L. REV. 500 n.25 (1962).
88. These include Cushman, *The Holy Bible and the Public Schools*, 40 CORNELL L.Q. 475, 495 (1955) (professor of government); Levy, *Views from the Wall – Reflections on Church-State Relationships*, 29 HENNEPIN LAW. 51, 55 (1961) (professor of law); Harpster, *Religion, Education and the Law*, 36 MARQ. L. REV. 24, 42 (1952), and Vishny, *The Constitution and Religion in the Public Schools*, Decalogue J., June-July 1960, pp. 4, 5–6; (practicing attorneys); Lewis, *School-Prayer Issue in High Court Again*, N.Y. Times, Oct. 14, 1962, § E, p. 5, col. 1 (newspaper columnist).

have made the same judgment.[89] A recent opinion by the Attorney General of California stated that "children forced by conscience to leave the room during such exercises would be placed in a position inferior to that of students adhering to the State-endorsed religion."[90]

Social psychologists and sociologists have pointed out that children place great importance on how they are esteemed by their classmates.[91] The urge to conform to their classmates' attitudes is peculiarly strong,[92] and "the fear of being accused by the others of wanting to be 'different' " and the "very strong need to remain a member of one's group"[93] are carried so far as to cause these children to do and say things in accordance with the majority that they are convinced are wrong, even with reference to simple perceptual materials.[94] This is particularly prevalent "where the situation is ambiguous and not very clear-cut."[95] The option either to participate in the majority's religious worship or "to suffer the pain of psychic loneliness"[96] has been recently described by Dr. Robert Bierstedt as forcing these immature students "to choose between equally intolerable alternatives."[97] Even religious educators have warned "that so-called voluntary exemption [from religious observances] does not overcome the compulsion exerted by majority behavior."[98]

The insight is not new. As long ago as 1890, state appellate court judges recognized the fact that a nonparticipant in a reli-

---

89. *E.g.*, 11 AM. U.L. REV. 91 (1962); 28 BROOKLYN L. REV. 146 (1961).
90. 25 CAL. OPS. ATT'Y GEN. 316, 319 (1955).
91. BOSSARD, THE SOCIOLOGY OF CHILD DEVELOPMENT 462 (1948).
92. MURPHY & MURPHY, EXPERIMENTAL SOCIAL PSYCHOLOGY 511–16 (1931). See also Cushman, *The Holy Bible and the Public Schools*, supra note 88, at 495: "A number of psychologists, backed by parents . . . point out the tremendous strength of the pressure to conform."
93. BERENDA, THE INFLUENCE OF THE GROUP ON THE JUDGMENTS OF CHILDREN 30 (1950).
94. *Id.* at 16–33.
95. *Id.* at 32.
96. Address by Professor Robert Bierstedt, *The Use of Public Schools for Religious Purposes*, ACLU Biennial Conference, June 22, 1962, p. 10. Dr. Bierstedt is Chairman of the Department of Sociology and Anthropology at the New York University Graduate School of Arts and Sciences.
97. *Ibid.*
98. Committee on Religion and Public Education of the National Council of the Churches of Christ, *Relation of Religion to Public Education—A Study Document*, INTERNATIONAL J. OF RELIGIOUS EDUCATION, April 1960, pp. 21, 29. See also Murray, *Law or Prepossessions?*, 14 LAW & CONTEMP. PROB. 23, 39 (1949): "Thousand of educators of all religious convictions are increasingly agreed that the atmosphere of public schools is *not* free from pressures."

gious exercise "loses caste with his fellows."[99] Lower federal court judges have also made this observation.[100] Four Justices of the Supreme Court subscribed to this theory when they stated: "That a child is offered an alternative may reduce the constraint; it does not eliminate the operation of influence by the school in matters sacred to conscience and outside the school's domain. The law of imitation operates, and nonconformity is not an outstanding characteristic of children."[101]

The fact that these public school religious practices are inherently compulsive may be empirically demonstrated by examining actual situations in some of the litigated cases. Terry McCollum, whose mother, an ardent atheist, successfully challenged a program of released time religious classes on public school premises in Champaign, Illinois,[102] exercised his right of nonparticipation during the first semester of his fourth grade, but the next semester he did attend religious classes. The following year, he changed schools. In the first semester of his fifth grade, he and only one other pupil declined to attend religious classes; during the second semester, the other boy capitulated.[103] In Terry's school, "children of some thirty-one sects, including Catholic, Jewish, and Protestant, as well as many children without any particular religious preference,"[104] *voluntarily* attended a course teaching the tenets of Protestantism. Donna Schempp's father, a member of the Unitarian faith, challenged Bible reading in the Abington Township, Pennsylvania, public schools as contrary to his family's re-

---

99. State *ex rel.* Weiss v. District Bd., 76 Wis. 177, 200, 44 N.W. 967, 975 (1890). In North v. Board of Trustees, 137 Ill. 296, 304, 27 N.E. 54, 56 (1891), the court observed that it was well-known that public schools conduct religious exercises "and that, with rare exceptions, those attending them yield cheerful obedience thereto, regardless of their personal views on the subject of religion." See also Wilkerson v. City of Rome, 152 Ga. 762, 786, 110 S.E. 895, 906 (1922) (dissenting opinion); People *ex rel.* Ring v. Board of Educ., 245 Ill. 334, 351, 92 N.E. 251, 256 (1910); Knowlton v. Baumhover, 182 Iowa 691, 699–700, 166 N.W. 202, 205 (1918); Herold v. Parish Bd. of School Directors, 136 La. 1034, 1050, 68 So. 116, 121 (1915); Kaplan v. Independent School Dist., 171 Minn. 142, 155–56, 214 N.W. 18, 23 (1927) (dissenting opinion); Engel v. Vitale, 10 N.Y.2d 174, 190, 176 N.E.2d 579, 587 (1961) (dissenting opinion).

100. Schempp v. School Dist., 177 F. Supp. 398, 406 (E.D. Pa. 1959).

101. Opinion of Mr. Justice Frankfurter, in which Justices Jackson, Rutledge, and Burton joined, in Illinois *ex rel.* McCollum v. Board of Educ., 333 U.S. 203, 227 (1948).

102. See Illinois *ex rel.* McCollum v. Board of Educ., 333 U.S. 203 (1948).

103. See People *ex rel.* McCollum v. Board of Educ., 396 Ill. 14, 17, 71 N.E.2d 161, 162 (1947).

104. Record, p. 65, Illinois *ex rel.* McCollum v. Board of Educ., 333 U.S. 203 (1948).

ligious beliefs.[105] Donna had never voiced her objections to school authorities and, on occasion, even volunteered to read the Bible herself.[106] In Southern elementary schools, there are established periods of Christian Bible study; Jewish children have the option of leaving the room, but "some believe that it is better to remain seated than to have forty-three children watch one or two others shuffle out."[107]

2. *The Defenses of Indirect Coercion*

Although there are a few instances of disagreement with the proposition that subtle coercion inheres in these situations,[108] most writers and state judges,[109] unwilling to find a constitutional violation, argue that "these pressures to conform are part of the normal social pattern and part of the price of being a religious nonconformist is the social stigma which all nonconformists have to bear"[110] and that it "is perhaps not a major hardship and is a sacrifice which a minority might well make to a majority."[111] Some argue that "if the State is going to undertake to protect the child at one point, there seems to be no logical reason for its stopping there—it should protect the child from such mental and

---

105. Schempp v. School Dist., 177 F. Supp. 398 (E.D. Pa. 1959).
106. *Id.* at 400. "Indeed the lack of protest may itself attest to the success and the subtlety of the compulsion." *Id.* at 407.
107. Harry L. Golden, quoted in PFEFFER, CHURCH, STATE, AND FREEDOM 304 (1953). "The Christian children wonder why one or two of their number 'do not want to hear about God,' and the Jewish child is also heartsick as well as bewildered." *Ibid.*
108. People *ex rel.* Vollmar v. Stanley, 81 Colo. 276, 293, 255 Pac. 610, 618 (1927): "The shoe is on the other foot. We have known many boys to be ridiculed for complying with religious regulations, but never one for neglecting them or absenting himself from them." For a singularly acrid and sarcastic (although neither very confident nor persuasive) rejection of the fact, see Chamberlin v. Dade County Bd. of Public Instruction, 143 So. 2d 21, 31–33 (Fla. 1962). The suggestion has been made that non-believing children may simply remain silent when religious invocations are being delivered by all of the others and thereby avoid the appearance of "non-conformity." Lewis v. Allen, 5 Misc. 2d 68, 74, 159 N.Y.S.2d 807, 813 (Sup. Ct. 1957). See also 9 U.C.L.A.L. REV. 499–500 (1962). Such advice is extremely naive; remaining silent conspicuously indicates the nonparticipant's status.
109. See Murray v. Curlett, 228 Md. 239, —, 179 A.2d 698, 704 (1962); Engel v. Vitale, 11 App. Div. 2d 340, 349, 206 N.Y.S.2d 183, 191–92 (1960) (separate opinion); Engel v. Vitale, 18 Misc. 2d 659, 695–96, 191 N.Y.S.2d 453, 491–92 (1959).
110. Cushman, *The Holy Bible and the Public Schools*, 40 CORNELL L.Q. 475, 495 (1955).
111. Sutherland, *Public Authority and Religious Education: A Brief Survey of Constitutional and Legal Limits*, in THE STUDY OF RELIGION IN THE PUBLIC SCHOOLS: AN APPRAISAL 33, 51 (Brown ed. 1958). See also Note, 49 COLUM. L. REV. 836, 843–44 (1949).

emotional abuse in all circumstances. But this is totally impossible."[112] The progenitor of this reasoning is the dictum of Mr. Justice Jackson that "it may be doubted whether the Constitution which, of course, protects the right to dissent, can be construed also to protect one from the embarrassment that always attends nonconformity, whether in religion, politics, behavior or dress."[113]

One need not quarrel with the unfortunate truism that it is probably inherent in our society that aberrant religionists and nonbelievers will be subjected to some scorn and derision. Because of this, societal pressures will be brought to bear on religious nonconformists to forsake their beliefs. As long as these societal pressures are initiated by "private action," the Constitution affords no self-executing relief. But when the state or federal government adopts a solely religious program—whose only immediate effect is the promotion of religion and in which benefit to religion is a condition precedent to any possible public benefit—it has approached the brink of its constitutional power. Some would seem to contend that such governmental activity of itself crosses the first amendment's boundary of church-state separation.[114] However, the proposed standard only requires that when this governmental activity unavoidably results in pressures on the immature to abandon their conscientious scruples, or in the influencing of free religious choice, the establishment clause should be deemed violated. It should not be the function of a governmental program to increase "the price of being a religious nonconformist"[115] when

---

112. Harpster, *Religion, Education and the Law*, 36 MARQ. L. REV. 24, 48 (1952).

113. Illinois *ex rel.* McCollum v. Board of Educ., 333 U.S. 203, 233 (1948) (concurring opinion). Mr. Justice Jackson spoke only for himself. It is difficult to reconcile this statement with Justice Jackson's subscription to Mr. Justice Frankfurter's *McCollum* opinion that takes the opposite stand. See text accompanying note 101 *supra*. See also the statement by Mr. Justice Reed that "one can hardly speak of that embarrassment as a prohibition against the free exercise of religion." 333 U.S. at 241. For discussion of the free exercise issue see note 126 *infra*.

It should be made clear that it is not merely "embarrassment" that results in the situations under discussion. To define the problem with that term "tends to assume that a child of tender years has the necessary courage of his convictions—or perhaps more accurately in this situation, the courage of his parents' convictions—to withstand with emotional impunity some very real pressures to conform to group standards and to avoid being marked by his fellows as an 'outsider.' " 11 AM. U.L. REV. 93 (1962).

114. See text accompanying notes 78–82 *supra*.

115. Cushman, *supra* note 110, at 495. *Cf.* Kamisar, *Betts v. Brady Twenty Years Later: The Right to Counsel and Due Process Values*, 61 MICH. L. REV. 219, 246 (1962), who argues that because an indigent crim-

the only immediate results of the program, if any results are forthcoming at all, are aids to religion. Majority will should not be permitted to impose minority sacrifices when that will is expressed through solely religious governmental action in an area afforded specific protection by the first amendment. Neither unorthodox behavior nor dress fits that category; logical distinctions may be drawn. The contrary position amounts to "no less than the surrender of the constitutional protection of the liberty of small minorities to the popular will."[116]

It is not being suggested that, *in vacuo*, the state is obligated to undertake to protect children of religious minorities, or children of the religious majority who have marginal convictions, from the embarrassment and concomitant pressures that nonconformity brings. The Constitution does not demand that the result of every state activity be free from such effects. Solely religious programs should not be confused, as they have been,[117] with those instances in which the state's program has the accomplishment of a secular purpose as its immediate goal.

The *Flag Salute Case*[118] illustrates this distinction. The Supreme Court held that a state could not compel the pledge of allegiance and salute to the flag by public school children who objected because of religious conviction. The result was that objecting children were excused from participation. Since the daily program of saluting the flag continued, there is no doubt that those who conscientiously objected were faced with precisely the same type dilemma as the children whose beliefs precluded participation

---

inal defendant suffers many handicaps that courts are powerless to eliminate is hardly an excuse for enlarging them or perpetuating others.
116. Minersville School Dist. v. Gobitis, 310 U.S. 586, 606 (1940) (Stone, J., dissenting).
117. See Brief for Intervenors-Respondents, pp. 45–47, 51, Engel v. Vitale, 370 U.S. 421 (1962); Corwin, *The Supreme Court as National School Board*, 14 LAW & CONTEMP. PROB. 3, 8 n.25 (1949). *But cf.* Brief for Synagogue Council of America and National Community Relations Advisory Council as Amici Curiae, pp. 16–19, Engel v. Vitale, *supra*.
118. West Virginia State Bd. of Educ. v. Barnette, 319 U.S. 624 (1943). Complainants in the case were Jehovah's Witnesses. Their religious beliefs included a literal version of *Exodus*, 20: 4–5, which says, "Thou shalt not make unto thee any graven image . . .: Thou shalt not bow down thyself to them, nor serve them." They considered the flag as an "image" within this command.
Although the Court stated that the case did not "turn on one's possession of particular religious views or the sincerity with which they are held," 319 U.S. at 634, and found that the state was generally without power to compel *anyone* to salute the flag, *id.* at 642, the case has been often considered, because of its facts, as presenting a free exercise of religion issue. See, *e.g.*, Braunfeld v. Brown, 366 U.S. 599, 603 (1961); Prince v. Massachusetts, 321 U.S. 158, 165 (1944).

in the recitation of the Regents' prayer. School children whose religious scruples forbid them from taking part in military training[119] or from attending classes in physical education,[120] social dancing,[121] or hygiene,[122] suffer similar difficulties. However, since the requirement of pledging allegiance to the flag is imposed to promote patriotism,[123] and since military training and physical education, dancing, and hygiene classes are placed in the public school curriculum to further national and educational goals, these activities of the state must be fairly characterized as secular. In no way do they promote religion, nor do they rely on religious inculcation for their attainment. Such activities, on their face, are unquestionably within the scope of state power. Some children's religious objections to participating in these secular activities may entitle them to be excused on the ground of protecting the free exercise of their religion,[124] but since the state's program is secular, dissenters cannot require the state to abandon it altogether because its continued operation inherently coerces them to join. *This* is the price the deviator must pay. To hold otherwise would indeed be minority oppression of the majority. It is only when the state engages in a solely religious activity that it should bear the full responsibility for the infringements on freedom of religious choice that such a program brings about.[125] It is un-

---

119. *Cf.* Hamilton v. Regents of the Univ. of Cal., 293 U.S. 245 (1934).
120. *Cf.* IOWA CODE § 280.14 (1962).
121. *Cf.* Hardwick v. Board of School Trustees, 54 Cal. App. 696, 205 Pac. 49 (Dist. Ct. App. 1921).
122. *Cf.* ALASKA COMP. LAWS ANN. § 37-7-12 (Supp. 1958); 1 FLA. STAT. § 231.09 (1) (1959); N.Y. EDUC. LAW § 3204 (5); PA. STAT. ANN. tit. 24, § 14–1419 (1962).
123. See 11 AM. U.L. REV. 91, 93 (1962).
124. The question of whether and when the free exercise clause is violated by the compelling of participation in secular activities irrespective of the fact that such participation is forbidden by one's religion is beyond the scope of this article. The issue is one that the Supreme Court appears not yet to have resolved. See Braunfeld v. Brown, 366 U.S. 599, 605 (1961).
125. Professor Kauper rejects this analysis. He agrees that it would be unconstitutional if actual pressure were exerted on any student to take part in the solely religious activity of released time. See text accompanying notes 467–72 *infra*.
But a proper sense of concern for the non-participant does not require rejection of the program on constitutional grounds. A Jehovah's Witness child may not be required to take part in a public school flag salute exercise. He is permitted to abstain. But the public school is not required in deference to his religious convictions to abandon the flag salute exercise even though it carries religious connotations for persons in this category and may, therefore, in this sense be characterized as a religious exercise. Similarly it should be possible to retain a released time program . . . while doing justice to the non-participants.

necessary to determine whether such infringements result in a violation of the free exercise clause.[126] If the activity is both solely religious and inherently compulsive, it should be found to be a violation of the establishment clause.

B. SUPPORT FROM THE SUPREME COURT

1. *The McCollum Case*

As already mentioned, there is no Supreme Court decision that articulates this rationale as its basis. However, examination of the *McCollum* case[127] lends strong support. In that case, the board of education permitted teachers employed by private religious groups to hold weekly religious classes in the public school buildings during regular school hours.[128] The classes were attended by those students whose parents signed cards requesting their permission, and nonparticipants were required to continue their public school studies in other classrooms. The parent of a nonparticipant challenged this program under the establishment clause and was sustained by the Supreme Court.

Some writers have interpreted *McCollum* to stand for the proposition that any use of public property for religious purposes is forbidden.[129] The Court's subsequent decision in the *New York*

Kauper, *Church, State, and Freedom: A Review*, 52 MICH. L. REV. 829, 842 (1954). (Footnotes omitted.)

The difficulty with this approach is the characterization of the flag salute as a "religious exercise," thus putting it in the same category as the Regents' prayer. The two activities are intrinsically different. One furthers religion if it does anything; the other in no way advances any religious cause. To say that any governmental activity that offends some religion is a "religious exercise" would mean that a declaration of war could be so characterized. *Cf.* Hamilton v. Regents of the Univ. of Cal., 293 U.S. 245 (1934).

126. It may well be argued that even though these indirect pressures, which accrue when the privilege of nonparticipation is granted, do not result in a breach of the free exercise clause when the state's activity is secular, free exercise is violated when the state action is solely religious. This would certainly be true if the outcome of free exercise problems "depends upon the balancing of the secular needs of the community against the religious rights of the individual . . . ." Brief for Synagogue Council of America and National Community Relations Advisory Council as Amici Curiae, p. 17, Engel v. Vitale, 370 U.S. 421 (1962).

127. Illinois *ex rel.* McCollum v. Board of Educ., 333 U.S. 203 (1948).

128. Originally, classes had been conducted by Protestant teachers, Catholic priests, and a Jewish rabbi. During the final few years, the Jewish classes had been discontinued. The classes were held for 30 minutes in the lower grades and for 45 minutes in the upper grades. *Id.* at 207–09.

129. *E.g.*, Cosway & Toepfer, *Religion and the Schools*, 17 U. CINC. L. REV. 117, 132–33 (1948); Cushman, *Public Support of Religious Education in American Constitutional Law*, 45 ILL. L. REV. 333, 352 (1950); 25 ALBANY L. REV. 318, 319 (1961).

Released Time Case[130] furnishes credence to this analysis. If this reading is accurate, the Court's decision in *Engel* was predetermined by *McCollum* irrespective of the question of inherent compulsion since the Regents' prayer was concededly a religious exercise being conducted on school property. In fact, the Regents' prayer arguably made greater use of public "property" than the released time program since, in the former case, the teachers conducting the religious exercise were publicly employed.[131] But such a reading of *McCollum* must be rejected. In the *Engel* opinion, *McCollum* was not even cited. Although the Court at several points in its *McCollum* opinion did refer to the fact that tax-supported property was being used for the dissemination of religious doctrines,[132] each time it did so it was careful to couple this fact with a reference to the fact that the public school machinery was being used to foster attendance at religious classes.[133] Furthermore, on several occasions the Court has held that the equal protection clause forbids discriminatory treatment in permitting the use of public parks by religious organizations for religious purposes,[134] thus implying that such use of public property is not constitutionally barred.[135] Indeed, at least one commentator has argued that to deny religious organizations the use of public property while permitting its use by other agencies in the community would itself violate the religion clauses of the first amendment.[136]

Even when religious organizations have made the only nonpublic use of public property (which appears to have been the case in *McCollum*), such use has been sustained by state courts when it did not result in any measurable cost to the taxpayers.[137] In

---

130. Zorach v. Clauson, 343 U.S. 306 (1952).
131. Brief for Petitioner, pp. 24–25, Engel v. Vitale, 370 U.S. 421 (1962); Brief for American Jewish Committee and Anti-Defamation League of B'nai B'rith as Amici Curiae, p. 13, Engel v. Vitale, *supra. But see* note 146 *infra* for evidence of the more extensive use of the public school building in *McCollum*.
132. 333 U.S. at 209, 212.
133. The author of the *McCollum* opinion, Mr. Justice Black, made clear that it was at least *his* intention that the "decision would have been the same if the religious classes had not been held in the school buildings." Zorach v. Clauson, 343 U.S. 306, 316 (1952) (dissenting opinion).
134. Fowler v. Rhode Island, 345 U.S. 67 (1953); Niemotko v. Maryland, 340 U.S. 268 (1951).
135. See Kauper, *Church, State, and Freedom: A Review*, 52 MICH. L. REV. 829, 836 (1954); Sullivan, *Religious Education in the Schools*, 14 LAW & CONTEMP. PROB. 92, 108–09 (1949); Note, 57 YALE L.J. 1114, 1117–18 (1948).
136. Kurland, *Of Church and State and the Supreme Court*, 29 U. CHI. L. REV. 1, 60 (1961).
137. Southside Estates Baptist Church v. Board of Trustees, 115 So. 2d 697 (Fla. 1959) (temporary use of public school buildings by several

his excellent book, Leo Pfeffer contends that the principle of *de minimis non curat lex*[138] has no application when either the establishment clause or the free exercise clause is concerned; "the right sought to be vindicated is a religious right, not an economic one, and it is therefore inappropriate to measure it in economic terms."[139] The Supreme Court, some time ago, indicated its rejection of the *de minimis* maxim in regard to first amendment freedoms.[140] But when governmental activity, even that fairly characterized as "solely religious," does not infringe on religious liberty, either by violating the free exercise clause or by compromising or influencing the freedom of conscientious choice in a manner that arguably does not violate the free exercise clause,[141] the financial expenditure involved must be subject to measurement by the *de minimis* standard. Otherwise, the appearance of "In God We Trust" on our coins would be unconstitutional. Even Pfeffer has found this to be "insignificant almost to the point of being trivial,"[142] thus impliedly invoking the *de minimis* principle. Examination of his analysis reveals that Pfeffer was concerned solely with those religious programs by government that tend to compromise one's religious beliefs. Likewise, the Supreme Court dictum was concerned with the protection of *liberty*. Other recognized authorities have suggested that there must be a place for the *de minimis* doctrine in this area.[143] State courts have specifically accepted its existence,[144] and the *Engel* case need not be read to

---

churches for Sunday religious meetings); Nichols v. School Directors, 93 Ill. 61, 34 Am. Rep. 160 (1879) (occasional use of school houses by different church organizations for religious services); State *ex rel.* Gilbert v. Dilley, 95 Neb. 527, 145 N.W. 999 (1914) (occasional use of school building for Sunday school and religious meetings). *But see* Hysong v. Gallitzin Borough School Dist., 164 Pa. 629, 30 Atl. 482 (1894) (use of public school rooms immediately after regular school hours for Catholic religious instruction to those students of the school who were Catholic by Catholic sisters who were also public school teachers).

It might be suggested that in this final case, unlike the other three, the facts created an atmosphere that resulted in pressures on both Catholic and non-Catholic children to attend the religious classes. See note 461 *infra*.

138. The law does not concern itself with trifles.
139. PFEFFER, CHURCH, STATE, AND FREEDOM 168 (1953).
140. See Thomas v. Collins, 323 U.S. 516, 543 (1945). More recently, the Court appears to have retreated from this position. See, *e.g.*, Barenblatt v. United States, 360 U.S. 109, 134 (1959); Uphaus v. Wyman, 360 U.S. 72, 77–78 (1959).
141. See text accompanying notes 125–26 *supra*.
142. Pfeffer, *Church and State: Something Less Than Separation*, 19 U. CHI. L. REV. 1, 23 (1951).
143. Kauper, *supra* note 135, at 837; Sutherland, *Due Process and Disestablishment*, 62 HARV. L. REV. 1306, 1343 (1949).
144. Southside Estates Baptist Church v. Board of Trustees, 115 So. 2d 697, 699 (Fla. 1959); People *ex rel.* Lewis v. Graves, 219 App. Div.

have rejected it since it may be explained on grounds of inherent compulsion.[145] Therefore, since the operation of the released time program in *McCollum* involved "no direct appropriation of any kind or direct expenditures of money of any kind,"[146] the use of public property there must be considered *de minimis*, and the Supreme Court's decision cannot be explained on the basis of financial aid to religion.[147]

The *McCollum* decision can only be accounted for on the ground that the operation of the released time program—a program having no independent primary secular goal—resulted in compromising the conscientious beliefs of the complainant's child.[148] This inherent effect of released time must have been the "invaluable aid"[149] that the Court found the state was affording "sectarian groups . . . in that it helps to provide pupils for their religious

---

233, 236, 219 N.Y. Supp. 189, 192 (1927); Nichols v. School Directors, 93 Ill. 61, 63, 34 Am. Rep. 160, 162 (1879). In the first case, the court stated that the state constitution would be violated "if the use of the school buildings [for Sunday religious meetings] were permitted for prolonged periods of time, absent evidence of an immediate intention on the part of the Church to construct its own buildings. . . ." 115 So. 2d at 700.

145. But see Pfeffer, *The New York Regents' Prayer Case (Engel v. Vitale): Its Background, Meaning and Implications*, Committee on Law and Social Action Reports 6 (American Jewish Congress, June 26, 1962).

146. People *ex rel.* McCollum v. Board of Educ., 396 Ill. 14, 24, 71 N.E.2d 161, 166 (1947). The court pointed out that

the classes were held in the schoolrooms during the current school period and the rooms were in use during the entire period, and, no doubt, the same cost for lights, heat, janitor service, etc. would exist whether or not the schoolroom was used at the particular time by this particular class. Any additional wear and tear on the floors would seem to be inconsequential. . . . Any additional wear and tear of furniture due to the religious education classes . . . would be negligible.

Ibid. See also Illinois *ex rel.* McCollum v. Board of Educ., 333 U.S. 203, 234 (1948) (Jackson, J., concurring).

147. As this author has suggested elsewhere, the use of the *de minimis* principle in this field may call not only for a measurement of the financial expenditure by government, but also for an examination of the financial benefit to religion. LOCKHART, KAMISAR & CHOPER, SUPPLEMENT TO DODD'S CASES ON CONSTITUTIONAL LAW 358 (1962). Although the former may be negligible, the latter may be quite substantial. See 35 ILL. B.J. 361, 363 (1947). However, this aspect of the problem was not considered at any stage of the *McCollum* litigation. See note 146 *supra*. The Court did find that the released time program afforded unconstitutional aid to religion, but it was not the financial benefit received that turned the decision. See text accompanying notes 148–53 *infra*. *Cf.* Cushman, *supra* note 129, at 352.

148. See Kurland, *The Regents' Prayer Case: "Full of Sound and Fury, Signifying . . .,"* 1962 SUPREME COURT REV. 1, 29–30. For a complete discussion of how and why this is the result of the program's operation, see text accompanying notes 376–87 *infra*.

149. 333 U.S. at 212.

classes through the use of the State's compulsory public school machinery."[150] The Court did state that it was unnecessary to consider the contention that the program "was voluntary in name only because *in fact* subtle pressures were brought to bear on the students to force them to participate in it."[151] This declaration may be explained as a response to appellant's argument that the factual evidence in the case belied the trial court's finding that Terry McCollum's teachers and classmates did nothing to subject him to embarrassment because of his religious opinions.[152] The Court's statement should not be read as rejecting the contention that the released time program was in some way inherently coercive and therefore constitutionally defective. Indeed, other writers have found some form of inherent coercion to be the basis upon which the decision was predicated.[153]

Furthermore, it would seem that the only justification for the Court's finding that appellant had standing to maintain the action was the fact that Terry was subject to certain subtle pressures inherent in the released time program.[154] The existing rule is well settled that a "party who invokes the power [of the federal courts to restrain unconstitutional acts] must be able to show not only that the statute is invalid but that he has sustained or is immediate-

---

150. *Ibid.* Further evidence that the Court relied on the inherent pressures of the activity:
The operation of the State's compulsory education system thus assists and is integrated with the program of religious instruction carried on by separate religious sects. Pupils compelled by law to go to school for secular education are released in part from their legal duty upon the condition that they attend the religious classes.
Id. at 209–10.
151. *Id.* at 207 n.1. (Emphasis added.)
152. The trial court's finding may be found in Record, p. 68, Illinois ex rel. McCollum v. Board of Educ., 333 U.S. 203 (1948). Brief for Appellant, pp. 26–30, advanced the testimony of a number of witnesses that was contrary to this finding and explained how the testimony relied upon by the trial judge was inadequate. Although counsel for appellant interwove this contention with the "inherent compulsion" argument, the Court's statement was addressed only to those of appellant's arguments that took "issue with the facts found by the Illinois courts . . . ." 333 U.S. at 207.
153. *E.g.*, Sutherland, *Public Authority and Religious Education: A Brief Survey of Constitutional and Legal Limits*, in THE STUDY OF RELIGION IN THE PUBLIC SCHOOLS: AN APPRAISAL 49 (Brown ed. 1958); 16 GEO. WASH. L. REV. 556, 558–59 (1948).
154. The Court perfunctorily rejected the contention that appellant had no standing. 333 U.S. at 206. Mr. Justice Black, the author of the Court's opinion, has indicated on other occasions that his standard on the question of standing in the church-state area is considerably more lenient than is the prevailing rule. See McGowan v. Maryland, 366 U.S. 420, 429 n.6 (1961); Two Guys From Harrison-Allentown, Inc. v. McGinley, 366 U.S. 582, 592 n.10 (1961).

ly in danger of sustaining some direct injury as the result of its enforcement, and not merely that he suffers in some indefinite way in common with people generally."[155] The interest of appellant, Terry's mother, was asserted as that of a resident, taxpayer, and parent of a child then enrolled in a public school having a released time program.[156] The record made clear that appellant was an atheist who desired that her child not be indoctrinated with any religious teachings.[157] Although the Court permitted a local taxpayer to challenge local governmental action as being in violation of the establishment clause in *Everson*,[158] that case involved "a measurable appropriation or disbursement of school-district funds."[159] Since the released time program in *McCollum*, like Bible reading in the public schools,[160] did not involve a substantial disbursement, appellant had no standing as a taxpayer. If appellant had sought standing solely on the basis of the fact that she was a parent of an attending child, she would have failed because there could have been absolutely no showing of any direct injury. It could have been accurately said that there was "no assertion that [he] was injured or even offended thereby or that [he] was compelled to accept, approve, or confess agreement with any dogma or creed or even [attend released time religious classes]."[161] Nor, under existing doctrine,[162] could standing have been conferred on appellant on the ground that those who were injured were unable to assert their rights effectively.[163] Appellant satisfied the existing standing prerequisites by alleging the infringement of a constitutionally protected right—the right of her child to be free from certain inherent pressures to participate in a solely religious governmental activity irrespective of any direct coercion. Only by finding the recognition of such a right in *McCollum* may those who questioned appellant's standing be answered[164] and may the decision be satisfactorily explained.[165]

---

155. Massachusetts v. Mellon, 262 U.S. 447, 488 (1923).
156. 333 U.S. at 205.
157. Record, pp. 1–2, Illinois *ex rel.* McCollum v. Board of Educ., 333 U.S. 203 (1948).
158. Everson v. Board of Educ., 330 U.S. 1 (1947). See text accompanying notes 28–29 *supra*.
159. Doremus v. Board of Educ., 342 U.S. 429, 434 (1952).
160. *Cf. id.* at 429.
161. *Id.* at 432 (dictum).
162. See text accompanying notes 219–27 *infra*.
163. *Cf.* NAACP v. Alabama *ex rel.* Patterson, 357 U.S. 449, 459–60 (1958); Barrows v. Jackson, 346 U.S. 249, 257 (1953).
164. Illinois *ex rel.* McCollum v. Board of Educ., 333 U.S. 203, 232–33 (1948) (Jackson, J.); Corwin, *The Supreme Court as National School Board*, 14 LAW & CONTEMP. PROB. 3, 5–9 (1949); Kauper, *supra* note 135, at 834–35.
165. See generally Sutherland, *Establishment According to Engel*,

2. Other Doctrines

There is other support to be found in the decisions of the Supreme Court for the proposed constitutional standard. The Court has unanimously held that, unless justified by some valid overriding interest, a state cannot compel individuals to disclose their membership in an association if such identification, although not directly suppressing the right of free speech protected by the first amendment, nevertheless would have this consequence.[166] It can hardly be said that the state's engaging in a solely religious activity manifests an overriding public interest;[167] in fact, such state activity has been attacked as being in itself invalid.[168] When the state embarks on such a program and then grants the privilege of nonparticipation to conscientious dissenters to avoid problems under the free exercise clause,[169] disclosure of membership in a religious (or nonreligious) group results. Such identification, in turn, tends to compromise religious beliefs[170] that fall within the broad ambit of the first amendment's protection.[171]

This effect is generally unquestioned.[172] The fact that this "re-

---

76 HARV. L. REV. 25, 31–35 (1962). *Cf.* Kurland, *supra* note 148, at 29–30.
166. NAACP v. Alabama *ex rel.* Patterson, 357 U.S. 449 (1958).
167. See text preceding note 114 *supra*.
168. See text accompanying notes 79–82 *supra*.
169. It is undisputed that the free exercise clause, if not also the establishment clause, would be violated if participation in these solely religious activities were governmentally compelled. Engel v. Vitale, 370 U.S. 421, 430–31 (1962); Zorach v. Clauson, 343 U.S. 306, 311–12 (1952); Lewis v. Allen, 5 Misc. 2d 68, 72–73, 159 N.Y.S.2d 807, 811 (Sup. Ct. 1957); Kauper, *Released Time and Religious Liberty: A Further Reply*, 53 MICH. L. REV. 233, 234 (1954); 9 OHIO ST. L.J. 336, 341 (1948).
170. *Cf.* NAACP v. Alabama *ex rel.* Patterson, 357 U.S. 449, 462 (19–58): "Inviolability of privacy in group association may in many circumstances be indispensable to preservation of freedom of association, particularly where a group espouses dissident beliefs."
171. There is persuasive authority for the proposition that it would be unconstitutional for the Government itself to cause a religious nonconformist to be embarrassed, harassed, or humiliated so as to coerce him to compromise his conscientious beliefs. See Bates v. City of Little Rock, 361 U.S. 516, 528 (1960) (concurring opinion); American Communications Ass'n v. Douds, 339 U.S. 382, 402 (1950).
172. See text accompanying notes 87–101 *supra*. *Cf.* NAACP v. Alabama *ex rel.*Patterson, 357 U.S. 449, 462-63 (1958):
> Petitioner has made an uncontroverted showing that on past occasions revelation of the identity of its rank-and-file members has exposed these members to economic reprisal, loss of employment, threat of physical coercion, and other manifestations of public hostility. Under these circumstances, we think it apparent that compelled disclosure of petitioner's Alabama membership is likely to affect adversely the ability of petitioner and its members to pursue their collective effort to foster beliefs which they admittedly have the right to advocate, in that it may

pressive effect . . . follows not from *state* action but from *private* community pressures"[173] is irrelevant;[174] "the crucial factor is the *interplay* of governmental and private action, for it is only after the initial exertion of state power represented by the [introduction of solely religious programs] . . . that private action takes hold."[175]

It is true that all of those Supreme Court decisions in the church-state area that have relied on a compulsion theory to find governmental action to be forbidden by the first amendment have involved instances of compulsion directly imposed by government.[176] However, the Court has shown no inclination to give any weight to differing degrees of governmental compulsion so long as it seems that the state action is likely to compromise conscientious beliefs or influence the freedom of religious choice. Thus, a state requirement that people who wish to become notaries public must declare their belief in God does not as forcefully compel the forsaking or influencing of conscientious beliefs as would be the case if the state prosecuted those who refused to declare their belief;[177] nor does the imposition of a license tax on religious colporteurs compel them as strongly as would a penal provision. But since "the loss of opportunity to obtain private employment . . . may be sufficient to persuade at least some uncommitted persons to adopt a religion,"[178] the Court did not hesitate in *Torcaso v. Watkins*[179] to strike down the required notaries' declaration by a unanimous vote; the license tax was held invalid in *Murdock v. Pennsylvania* because it "tends to suppress" religious practices.[180]

---

induce members to withdraw from the Association and dissuade others from joining it because of fear of exposure of their beliefs shown through their associations and of the consequences of this exposure.
173. *Id.* at 463.
174.
In the domain of these indispensible liberties [under the first amendment], the decisions of this Court recognize that abridgement of such rights, even though unintended, may inevitably follow from varied forms of governmental action. . . . The governmental action challenged may appear to be totally unrelated to protected liberties.
Id. at 461.
175. *Id.* at 463. (Emphasis added.) This same analysis is implicit in the decision holding an ordinance that forbade the distribution of anonymous handbills unconstitutional on the ground that it tended to restrict freedoms protected by the first amendment. Talley v. California, 362 U.S. 60 (1960). See generally Rosenfield, *Separation of Church and State in the Public Schools*, 22 U. PITT. L. REV. 561, 582–84 (1961).
176. See cases cited notes 177–80 *infra*.
177. *Cf.* West Virginia State Bd. of Educ. v. Barnette, 319 U.S. 624 (1943).
178. 74 HARV. L. REV. 611, 614 (1961).
179. 367 U.S. 488 (1961).
180. 319 U.S. 105, 114 (1943).

It would seem to be only a small step to hold, as state courts have done,[181] that when the state engages in a solely religious activity, its action is constitutionally barred if it inherently produces social compulsion to abandon religious convictions.

Before moving on, it should be noted that the constitutional significance of coercion in the area of church-state problems has not escaped attention. Thus, in evaluating several governmental programs that must be fairly characterized as solely religious, Professor Paul Kauper has relied on the absence of any sort of coercion to sustain their constitutionality.[182] On the other hand, he condemns the appropriation of public funds for church buildings or ministers' salaries since "the maintenance of churches is itself not a governmental function and since it coerces the conscience of nonbelieving taxpayers."[183] Professor Robert Levy has concluded that "any program which operates to compel the young and impressionable to orient to religion should be unconstitutional."[184]

3. *Application in Engel v. Vitale*

Thus, the way had been well paved for the Supreme Court specifically to restrict its *Regents' Prayer* decision to the compulsive effect on young children inherent in this solely religious activity by the state. Such a definite limitation would have clearly immuniz-

---

181. *E.g.*, Brown v. Orange County Bd. of Pub. Instruction, 128 So. 2d 181 (Fla. Dist. Ct. App. 1960) (distribution of Gideon Bibles in public schools); Tudor v. Board of Educ., 14 N.J. 31, 100 A.2d 857 (1953) (distribution of Gideon Bibles in public schools).

182. In discussing the chaplains in both houses of Congress, Professor Kauper states that "this is a plain case of spending federal money for religious purposes." Kauper, *supra* note 135, at 837. This seems clearly to indicate that he considers this a solely religious activity. He goes on to state that "it can hardly be considered a substantial use of public funds in aid of religion, and it is not seriously argued that anyone's conscience is coerced by this practice." *Ibid.* The final point is clearly sound although it would not be similarly valid if the chaplains gave daily prayer recitations in the public schools. In raising the question of "substantial use of public funds," Professor Kauper seems to present this as an independent criterion for judging solely religious activities. If it is, as it may well be, one might effectively argue that an annual expenditure of $17,620, see 75 Stat. 320, 324 (1961), is hardly *de minimis*, even when compared to the entire federal budget. See also text accompanying note 147 *supra*.

As to released time programs, Professor Kauper concludes that it has not been demonstrated that they deprive anyone of any liberty. Kauper, *supra* note 135, at 236. An attempted refutation of the conclusion may be found at notes 376–87 *infra*.

183. *Id.* at 846. Here, again, the point made seems to be that this is a solely religious activity.

184. Levy, *Views from the Wall—Reflections on Church-State Separation*, 29 HENNEPIN LAW. 51, 55 (1961). Examination of the context of this statement seems to indicate that Professor Levy was concerned only with those public school "programs" that are solely religious.

ed the Court from the position, taken in the concurring opinion of Mr. Justice Douglas, that government cannot "constitutionally finance a religious exercise . . . whatever form it takes."[185] It would also have effectively distinguished the Regents' prayer situation from most "of the religious traditions of our people, reflected in countless practices of the institutions and officials of our government,"[186] cited by Mr. Justice Stewart in his lone dissent. However, although the language used by the Court appears to be quite comprehensive,[187] it would be rash to conclude that *Engel* passed judgment on (or even hinted at) the long list of governmental activities disapproved by Mr. Justice Douglas[188] or brought forward by Mr. Justice Stewart.[189] The Court's statement that

---

185. Engel v. Vitale, 370 U.S. 421, 437 (1962) (concurring opinion). See note 188 *infra*.
186. Engel v. Vitale, 370 U.S. 421, 446 (1962) (dissenting opinion). See note 189 *infra*.
187. See text accompanying notes 79–80 *supra*.
188. Among the governmental programs and activities that Mr. Justice Douglas would seem to find unconstitutional are congressional and armed service chaplains, use of the Bible for the administration of oaths, "In God We Trust" on coins and currency, and opening prayers in legislative chambers and courts—including the Supreme Court. None of these would seem to produce the inherent pressures that arise from a solely religious activity in the public schools and, thus, are subject to separate consideration. Also included were activities having an independent primary secular goal, such as the availability of funds for parochial schools, G.I. Bill payments to denominational schools, and National School Lunch Act benefits to religious schools. In addition, Mr. Justice Douglas expressed his present disagreement with his vote with the majority in *Everson* (see text accompanying notes 28–29 *supra*), a case raising problems very different from those presented by the Regents' prayer. See text accompanying notes 21–49 *supra*. The evil ingredient that he found to be common to all of these governmental activities was that they "insert a divisive influence into our communities." 370 U.S. at 442, 443. For criticism of this standard, see text accompanying notes 362–65 *infra*.
Mr. Justice Douglas found "no element of compulsion" in the case. 370 U.S. at 438. He stated that there was no more inherent coercion here than there was in the prayers that open sessions of Congress and the Court. *Id.* at 442. This seems to ignore the pertinence of the public school setting and the maturity of the participants. See text accompanying notes 87–107 *supra*.
189. In addition to a number of the matters referred to by Mr. Justice Douglas, Mr. Justice Stewart listed such things as presidential inaugural statements asking the protection and help of God and presidential proclamations of a National Day of Prayer. Neither of these produce effects that are realistically comparable to the social pressures produced in the public school atmosphere. Whether or not constitutional, they must be considered apart from the Regents' prayer.
Mr. Justice Stewart decided that the case was "entirely free of any compulsion . . . including any 'embarrassments and pressures,'" because "the state courts have made clear that those who object to reciting the prayer *must be*" free of these things. 370 U.S. at 445. (Emphasis added.) But no mandate of any court can free this solely religious activity from its concomitant inherent pressures.

"the Establishment Clause . . . does not depend upon any showing of direct governmental compulsion"[190] is entirely consistent with the rationale that the establishment clause is violated by certain laws that produce inherent, albeit *indirect and nongovernmental,* compulsion. So is the Court's pronouncement that the establishment clause "is violated by the enactment of laws which establish an official religion whether those laws operate *directly* to coerce nonobserving individuals or not."[191] Those "laws which establish an official religion" might well be interpreted to mean those laws having no independent primary secular purpose or effect, and the entire pronouncement might not have been intended to deal with those "solely religious laws" that operate *neither directly nor indirectly* to coerce nonobserving persons.[192] In any case, since the governmental program in issue in *Engel* did operate indirectly to compel dissenters, the decision should not, and may not, be read for the proposition that the establishment clause bars all solely religious programs by government.[193]

Close examination of the positions taken by the two amici curiae also indicates that they perhaps meant less than would initially appear. To illustrate the thesis that the establishment clause is violated whenever government undertakes or sponsors a religious program, the argument was made that "the holding of a Mass in a public school during the regular day would violate the Establishment Clause even though all non-Catholic pupils were permitted or required to absent themselves."[194] This would be unconstitutional, but not simply for the reason that the state was "sponsoring [a] religious program"; an establishment clause violation would occur because the minority dissenters would be under the same social pressures from the Catholic majority as the dissenters were in *Engel*.[195] Remove the coercive effect of the public school at-

---

Mr. Justice Stewart chidingly questioned whether "the Court [was] suggesting that the Constitution permits judges and Congressmen and Presidents to join in prayer, but prohibits school children from doing so?" *Id.* at 450 n.9. The answer would seem to be that (1) the case at bar involved only school children and (2) the pressures inherent in the public school setting may constitutionally distinguish it from the other situations mentioned.
190. 370 U.S. at 430.
191. *Ibid.* (Emphasis added.)
192. This conclusion is supported by the opinion's explicit recognition, immediately following its broad statement, that laws that place the "power . . . and prestige of government . . . behind a particular religious belief" plainly result in indirect coercive pressures. 370 U.S. at 431.
193. *But see* Sutherland, *supra* note 165, at 35–36.
194. Brief of American Jewish Committee and Anti-Defamation League of B'nai B'rith as Amici Curiae, p. 17, Engel v. Vitale, 370 U.S. 421 (1962).
195. See 25 CAL. OPS. ATT'Y GEN. 319 (1955). This assumes that a

mosphere and have the Mass held in the public school on Sunday, and a significantly different question is presented.[196] Further, these amici's thesis was documented by citing *McCollum*,[197] as was the proposition advanced by the other amici that the first amendment's ban on establishment would be violated by state "participation in religious affairs."[198] The sound basis for *McCollum*, however, is the presence of inherent compulsion.[199]

C. DISTINGUISHING THE INDISTINGUISHABLE

Acceptance of the proposed constitutional standard not only effectively circumscribes the *Engel* decision, but also provides a ready means for distinguishing between situations heretofore found by some to be indistinguishable. For example, Mr. Justice Jackson,[200] seconded by several commentators,[201] charged that *McCollum's*

---

program of this sort would only be instituted if there were a Catholic majority. *Cf.* Knowlton v. Baumhover, 182 Iowa 691, 695, 166 N.W. 202, 203 (1918); Williams v. Board of Trustees, 172 Ky. 133, 364 Mo. 121, 129–31, 260 S.W.2d 573, 576–78 (1953). If for some reason this were not the case, the result should be the same because of the program's influence on Roman Catholic students who would not attend Mass otherwise, see text accompanying notes 221, 439–53 *infra*, and because of the influence on free religious choice generated by the public school sponsorship of such an activity. See text accompanying notes 244–46 *infra*.

196. See text accompanying notes 129–47 *supra*.
197. Brief of American Jewish Committee and Anti-Defamation League of B'nai B'rith as Amici Curiae, p. 17, Engel v. Vitale, 370 U.S. 421 (1962).
198. Brief of Synagogue Council of America and National Community Relations Advisory Council as Amici Curiae, p. 15, Engel v. Vitale, 370 U.S. 421 (1962).
199. It must be noted, however, that the Pfeffer brief argued that if the state's "conduct is religious, then it is outside the competence or jurisdiction of the State or its instrumentalities, and even if participation were not compulsory, the conduct would be unconstitutional." *Id.* at 17. The scope of this standard is not clear. From the context, it would not seem to apply only to the state's undertaking solely religious activities in the public schools and granting dissenters the right of nonparticipation; it seems to say that all solely religious activities by the state are barred. This is a matter that was clearly not in issue in Engel, and such a thesis is clearly unworkable and unacceptable. See text accompanying notes 140–44 *supra*. Even if this standard is meant to apply only to those governmental activities that require participation (the context of the statement does lend credence to this), query if these can be found to violate the establishment clause if it can be shown that they are neither inherently compulsive (as only mature adults may be involved) nor involve a substantial use of public funds. See note 182 *supra*. It is difficult to differentiate such a case from "In God We Trust" on coins and currency.
200. See Kunz v. New York, 340 U.S. 290, 311 n.10 (1951) (dissenting opinion); Saia v. New York, 334 U.S. 558, 569 (1948) (dissenting opinion).
201. Corwin, *The Supreme Court as National School Board*, 14 LAW & CONTEMP. PROB. 3, 7–8 (1949); Taylor, *Equal Protection of Religion: Today's Public School Problem*, 38 A.B.A.J. 277–78 (1952).

ban from the public schools of the solely religious activity of released time, *a fortiori*, determined the question of whether the state was permitted to bar the solely religious activities of some people in the public streets and parks. The theory was that since *McCollum* forbade the use of tax-supported school property by any and all sects for the propagation of religion, it was patently anomalous for the Court to hold, as it did,[202] that the state was compelled to permit the nondiscriminate use of tax-supported street and park property for that same purpose.[203] It is not difficult to combat this analysis. The effect of the activity in *McCollum* was to coerce those who were either unwilling to participate or uninterested in doing so. This evil—a significant constitutional ingredient—is not present when the public streets or parks are used for religious purposes. No citizen who declines to participate is in any way compelled to do so, and therefore, no person's religious liberty is impaired.

One writer has stated that he is at a loss to determine "why it is constitutional for a public institution to *purchase* a sectarian book [such as the Gideon Bible], but not to enable its pupils to read such books as *gifts* . . . ."[204] The explanation is the same.[205] While no one has ever argued that dissenters are compelled to desert their religious convictions because public school libraries contain sectarian literature, there has been expert testimony that public school sponsorship of the distribution of Bibles creates coercive pressures to do so.[206]

---

202. See cases cited note 200 *supra*.
203. Professor Corwin put it this way:
[T]he discrepancy between the two holdings is apparent. In one [*McCollum*] it is held that a school board may not constitutionally permit religious groups to use on an equal footing any part of a school building for the purpose of religious instruction to *those who wish to receive it*. By the other [*Saia*] the public authorities are under a *constitutional obligation* to turn over public parks for religious propaganda to be hurled at all and sundry whether they wish to receive it or not. The Court seems to cherish a strange tenderness for *outré* religious manifestations which contrasts sharply with its attitude toward organized religion.
Corwin, *supra* note 201, at 8.
204. Lieberman, *A General Interpretation of Separation of Church and State and Its Implications for Public Education*, 33 PROGRESSIVE EDUCATION 129, 131 (1956).
205. Another reason for distinguishing these situations might be that the state has a secular educational aim in placing Bibles in public school libraries—to make this literature available for academic investigation. See text accompanying notes 333-37 *infra*. No such secular purpose is found in sponsoring Bible distribution. The goal of the Gideons International is to "win men and women for the Lord Jesus Christ." Tudor v. Board of Educ., 14 N.J. 31, 33, 100 A.2d 857, 858 (1953).
206. *Id.* at 50, 100 A.2d at 867. See notes 501-09 *infra* and accompanying text.

In upholding the New York released time plan in *Zorach v. Clauson,* the Supreme Court, per Mr. Justice Douglas, implied that such solely religious activity is equivalent to "prayers in our legislative halls; the appeals to the Almighty in the messages of the Chief Executive; [and] the proclamations making Thanksgiving Day a holiday . . . ."[207] Several state courts have sustained public school Bible reading on similar bases.[208] Because of the presence of inherent coercion, it seems that *Zorach* was incorrectly decided[209] and that daily Bible reading in the public schools is also unconstitutional.[210] Whether or not the other activities referred to are constitutionally valid, it is fairly clear that they are not inherently coercive, and therefore, they should not control the disposition of Bible reading and released time.

Relying on the governmental activities referred to by Mr. Justice Douglas, the House Committee on the Judiciary made the same faulty analogy when it stated that the inclusion of the words "under God" in the pledge of allegiance to the flag did not run afoul of the establishment clause.[211] Immature dissenters from the amended flag pledge will surely be subject to the same coercive pressures in the public school as were the children in *Engel.* Because of this, whether the amended pledge to the flag will withstand attack should turn on whether it may be fairly characterized as a solely religious activity.[212]

In a recent comprehensive article dealing with religion in the public schools, one writer has urged that "the Constitution directs the public school to be a completely secular agency" and that it "proscribes the use of public school funds, facilities, personnel, time, sponsorship, auspices, or authority for religious instruction, practice, or ritual, or for any other religious or religiously-oriented purpose, direct or indirect."[213] Under this standard, not only were prayers, Bible reading, and released time found to be unconstitutional, but so also was the objective or academic study of religion.[214] "On the other hand, where information or ideas about religion are intrinsic to the subjects in the school's normal secular

---

207. 343 U.S. 306, 312–13 (1952).
208. *E.g.,* Murray v. Curlett, 228 Md. 239, —, 179 A.2d 698, 702 (1962); Church v. Bullock, 104 Tex. 1, 7, 109 S.W. 115, 118 (1908).
209. See text accompanying notes 397–403 *infra.*
210. See text accompanying notes 61–66 *supra,* 251–94 *infra.*
211. H.R. REP. NO. 1693, 83d Cong., 2d Sess. 3 (1954).
212. For discussion of this question, see text accompanying notes 536–41 *infra.*
213. Rosenfield, *Separation of Church and State in the Public Schools,* 22 U. PITT. L. REV. 561, 570 (1961).
214. *Id.* at 571–78. "Teaching religious doctrine, under any heading, is forbidden." *Id.* at 578.

curriculum, such as history, art, literature, etc., they should be presented factually and objectively."[215] Why a single course in comparative religion makes the school less of a "secular agency" than does the infiltration of religious matter into every other course in the curriculum is unclear. Why the one, and not the other, indirectly instructs in religion is also a mystery. The source of the difficulty seems to be the generality of the standard and the resulting perplexity in its application. Not so, hopefully, with the constitutional standard proposed here.[216]

Finally, it should be noted that use of this suggested standard would even seem to satisfy those, at least for the time being, who contend that since the language of the fourteenth amendment bars only the denial of liberty, "so far as the fourteenth amendment is concerned, states are entirely free to establish religions, provided that they do not deprive anybody of religious liberty."[217]

D. RELIGIOUS PRACTICES CARRIED ON WITHOUT OBJECTION

The seemingly broad standard suggested in *Engel*, as well as the rather sweeping criteria advocated by amici curiae in that case, may be read as stating that any governmental program that is solely religious violates the establishment clause. Under such a reading, there is no question as to the unconstitutionality of such a program, even when no one objects to it. However, since the constitutional principle of the proposed constitutional standard is grounded in the sanctity of the religious and conscientious scruples of public school children, a question does arise as to the extent of its application to a situation in which the public school engages in a solely religious practice and there is no opposition by the attending school children or their parents.

In the two cases in which the Supreme Court has found a practice of this sort to be contrary to the establishment clause, there were conscientious dissenters who instituted the litigation.[218] Thus, if the rationale of these two cases is to be explained on the basis of the proposed constitutional standard, the decisions must be narrowly read to hold no more than that the establishment clause

---

215. *Ibid.*
216. For discussion of the application of the proposed standard to the various religious aspects in the public schools, see text accompanying notes 229–566 *infra.*
217. Corwin, *supra* note 201, at 19. See also note 8 *supra*. It is interesting to theorize whether the establishment of an approved church by a state could be considered an infringement of religious liberty. See text accompanying note 183 *supra*.
218. Engel v. Vitale, 370 U.S. 421 (1962); Illinois *ex rel.* McCollum v. Board of Educ., 333 U.S. 203 (1948).

is violated when a public school engages in a solely religious practice that is objected to by nonconforming students in attendance; if there are no dissenters, the practice may be valid even if, by its nature, it will likely result in compromising of religious beliefs or influencing of the students' freedom of conscientious choice. Furthermore, it may be argued that under prevailing standing requirements, only the parents of a student whose religious beliefs would preclude participation in the school program could be permitted to challenge its constitutionality.[219]

However, the rationale that underlies the proposed constitutional standard calls for rejection of the above conclusions. Despite the fact that the privilege of nonparticipation is extended to religious nonconformists, the societal pressures on children to take part in state-sponsored religious activities often result in their choosing to do so in preference to suffering embarrassment among their peers. This being the fact, if the constitutionality of solely religious activities turns on whether opposition is voiced, these programs most often will be carried on without objection despite the fact that there are nonconformist pupils whose conscientious scruples are being compromised.[220] Even if all the pupils are nominally members of the same religious sect, very likely solely religious programs of that sect conducted in the public schools will result, due to the inherent coercive pressures, in those students with marginal religious convictions being influenced in their freedom of religious choice.[221] Because of these same social pressures, the results of inquiries made by public school officials or parent groups to determine whether all students would be willing to participate in a public school religious activity will probably not reflect the true feelings of those polled.[222] Parents who are

---

219. See text accompanying notes 154–63 *supra.*
220. *Cf.* Kamisar, *The Right to Counsel and the Fourteenth Amendment: A Dialogue on "The Most Pervasive Right" of an Accused,* 30 U. CHI. L. REV. 1, 65–66 (1962), for the view that under the rule of *Betts v. Brady,* 316 U.S. 455 (1942), the uncounselled indigent defendant is caught in a similar vicious circle.
221. Hypothetically, if all of the students of a public school are of the Roman Catholic faith and it is therefore decided to have a daily Mass in the school with attendance being voluntary, the inherent pressures on those non-churchgoing Roman Catholic children to attend this Mass might well be greater than are the pressures on children of minority faiths to take part in majority religious activities.
222. For a decision stating that the unanimous consent of all parents could not save the ceding of public school control to church authorities, see Williams v. Board of Trustees, 173 Ky. 708, 726, 191 S.W. 507, 514 (1917). For a similar case in which the complainant appeared originally to have given his acquiescence, see Knowlton v. Baumhover, 182 Iowa 691, 700, 166 N.W. 202, 205 (1918).

religious dissenters usually refuse to instruct their children to decline to participate because of the fear of their children being subjected to ridicule.[223] Many hesitate to institute litigation because of this and because of "the prospect of disrupted community life, with perhaps devastating consequences to the minority groups themselves, that would result from arbitrary interference with deep-seated community customs."[224] The upshot of all of this would be that those values cherished in our society, which are at the foundation of the standard set forth in this article, would be emasculated by the rule that only those public school religious programs that are in fact objected to by attending students or their parents are unconstitutional. Prophylactic treatment is necessary. The law should be that those solely religious practices in the public schools that are likely to influence free religious choice or to compromise conscientiously held beliefs are per se unconstitutional.

Empirical studies in the church-state field have shown that judicial determinations of unconstitutionality do not substantially deter communities from engaging in patently invalid practices.[225] Thus, the burden of policing falls upon the courts and ultimately upon those willing to risk the time, expense, and hazards, of litigation. If only those parents of attending children who conscientiously oppose public school religious actions were to have standing to attack them, many of these programs would go unchallenged despite the fact that the very values that are afforded the protection of the first amendment are being submerged. The "right" protected in these instances—the "right" to be free from social

---

223.
[T]he children's father testified that after careful consideration he had decided that he should not have [the children] excused from attendance at these morning ceremonies. Among his reasons were the following. He said that he thought his children would be "labelled as 'odd balls' " before their teachers and classmates every school day; that children . . . . were liable "to lump all particular religious difference[s] or religious objections [together] as 'atheism' " and that today the word "atheism" is often connected with "atheistic communism", and has "very bad" connotations, such as "un-American" or "pro-Red", with overtones of possible immorality.
Schempp v. School Dist., 201 F. Supp. 815, 818 (E.D. Pa.), *prob. juris. noted*, 371 U.S. 807 (1962).

224. Johnson, *Summary of Policies and Recommendations of the American Council on Education Committee on Religion and Education*, in THE STUDY OF RELIGION IN THE PUBLIC SCHOOLS: AN APPRAISAL 9 (1958). See also Harry Golden, quoted in PFEFFER, CHURCH, STATE, AND FREEDOM 304 (1953); Sullivan, *Religious Education in the Schools*, 14 LAW & CONTEMP. PROB. 92 (1949). For an extremely forceful documentation of this point, see PFEFFER, *supra* at 402–04.

225. See Sorauf, *Zorach v. Clauson: The Impact of a Supreme Court Decision*, 53 AM. POL. SCI. REV. 777, 784–86 (1959).

pressures to conform to the majority's religious practices that are governmentally sponsored—depends upon anonymity for its effective vindication. To require that it be claimed by those affected themselves would result in substantial nullification of the "right" at the very moment of its assertion.[226] It would therefore be appropriate here for the Court to fashion an exception to the general requirement of standing because of the weighty countervailing policy of adequately securing these "rights."[227]

III. APPLICATION OF THE STANDARD

As has been observed by another proponent of a constitutional standard for church-state controversies, "the genius of ... American constitutional law [is] that its growth and principles are measur-

---

226. *Cf.* NAACP v. Alabama *ex rel.* Patterson, 357 U.S. 449, 459 (1958).
227. See United States v. Raines, 362 U.S. 17, 22 (1960). The precise questions of upon whom standing should be conferred and how this may be accomplished doctrinally is beyond the scope of this article. The Supreme Court has permitted litigants to assert the constitutional rights of others, but none of the decided cases appear to be wholly satisfactory in solving the problem at hand. Professor Kenneth Davis has pointed out that this permission has been, and should be, granted much more liberally once the litigant has properly commenced a proceeding to vindicate his own rights. 3 DAVIS, ADMINISTRATIVE LAW TREATISE § 22.07 (1958). This doctrine is not very helpful here. Other cases may be explained on the basis of the fact that the litigant will suffer direct economic injury as a result of the state enactment. See Pierce v. Society of Sisters, 268 U.S. 510 (1925). These, too, are not very useful.
However, in NAACP v. Alabama *ex rel.* Patterson, 357 U.S. 449 (1958), the Court permitted an association to act as the representative of its members in asserting their rights. Similar to the problem at hand, the rights of the NAACP members would have been nullified if the individuals themselves would have been required to assert them. By analogy, perhaps associations composed of religious dissenters may initiate proceedings. Perhaps it may also be said that such an association "is but the medium through which its individual members seek to make more effective the expression of their own views." 357 U.S. at 459. But *NAACP v. Alabama* also stressed the fact, not likely to be present in the case at hand, that there was "reasonable likelihood that the Association itself through diminished financial support and membership may be adversely affected" by the governmental action. *Id.* at 459–60.
Furthermore, the membership of many associations of minority religious groups is well known. In such instances, an action by the association will redound to the members, thus causing the members to discourage association action for the reasons discussed previously. Granting standing to the parent of any attending child, irrespective of religious conviction, on the ground that to force the parent to assert prejudice will expose the child to opprobrium would also probably be inadequate. Parents would realize that whether or not they were in fact religious dissenters, they would be so publicly regarded. It would seem that full protection can be afforded only by a more relaxed standing criterion. *But see* Sutherland, *Establishment According to Engel*, 76 HARV. L. REV. 25, 42 (1962).

ed in terms of concrete factual situations . . . ."[228] Thus, it would be helpful to examine some of the many actual instances of religious intrusion into the public schools, and to determine their constitutional validity when measured by the proposed constitutional standard.

A. PRAYERS

The prayer at issue in *Engel v. Vitale,* neutral and inoffensive as it was,[229] would fail the proposed constitutional test on several counts. Its purpose and effect was admittedly solely religious. The context in which it was delivered was inherently coercive. Due to its theistic basis, it would likely infringe on the conscientious beliefs of some members of the heterogeneous school population.

However, it need not logically follow that every public school prayer would similarly fail. First, if it were possible to devise a prayer against which no one could raise any conscientious objection, it could not be said that its recitation would result in the compromising or influencing of anyone's religious beliefs or choice. Such a prayer would therefore be free from constitutional attack under the proposed standard. Although projects have been undertaken to attempt to satisfy this requirement,[230] the obstacles appear to be insurmountable. Certainly, the Regents' prayer having been rejected, any prayer that invokes the aid or blessing of the Deity runs afoul of this test. Not only would such a prayer

---

228. Kurland, *Of Church and State and the Supreme Court,* 29 U. CHI. L. REV. 1, 5 (1961).

229. Compare the daily prayer offered by teachers in Hackett v. Brooksville Graded School Dist., 120 Ky. 608, 614–15, 87 S.W. 792, 793 (1905):
> Our Father who art in Heaven, we ask Thy aid in our day's work. Be with us in all we do and say. Give us wisdom and strength and patience to teach these children as they should be taught. May teacher and pupil have mutual love and respect. Watch over these children, both in schoolroom and on the playground. Keep them from being hurt in any way, and at last, when we come to die, may none of our number be missing around Thy Throne. These things we ask for Christ's sake. Amen.

This prayer was found not to be "sectarian," and therefore outside the state constitution's prohibition. Whether or not one agrees with the Kentucky court's definition of "sectarian," there is no question that this prayer is a "religious" exercise under the establishment clause. If recited in the same setting as the Regents' prayer, it would be invalid, under *Engel* or the proposed constitutional standard, even if the reference to Christ were omitted.

230. See Abbott, *A Common Bible Reader For Public Schools,* 56 RELIGIOUS EDUCATION 20 (1961); Note, 22 ALBANY L. REV. 156–57 (1958). Efforts to find a commonly acceptable prayer for American citizens are not confined to our time; Benjamin Franklin was among those who previously made the attempt. See Engel v. Vitale, 18 Misc. 2d 659, 660–62, 191 N.Y.S.2d 453, 459–60 (Sup. Ct. 1959).

cause conscientious objections to be raised by atheists, agnostics,[231] and humanists,[232] but it also appears that at least one of the three chief faiths would have religious objections.[233] It has been shown that when many of the attempts to distill a "common core" or nonsectarian religion are scrutinized, the product "comes to mean the common core of orthodox Protestant belief, and . . . what a substantial majority—not of all, but of the believing—agree upon."[234] Furthermore, theologians[235] and educators[236] have pointed out that aside from the fact that the task is extraordinarily difficult, even if it were possible, the result would probably be the reduction of theology to triviality and the creation of a public school sect that would be objectionable to all religious faiths. Moreover, it is likely that some people would conscientiously resist participation in any public supplication, regardless of its content.

Second, if it were possible to find that the prayer recitation had some independent primary secular purpose, it then could not be characterized as a solely religious activity and would thus avoid this requisite for unconstitutionality. Several endeavors of this nature have already been found wanting.[237] The assertion that the prayer's purpose would be "to prepare the children for their work, to quiet them from the outside,"[238] should probably also

---

231. See Vishny, *The Constitution and Religion in the Public Schools*, Decalogue J., June-July 1960, pp. 4, 6.
232. See Nichols, *Religion and Education in a Free Society*, in RELIGION IN AMERICA 148, 157 (1958).
233.
> Jews believe . . . that when a faith in God is taught, it must be achieved in the context of historical associations accompanied by religious rites and symbols that are related to that particular religious group. . . . We do not appreciate the vague and undefined God to which the "American religion" offers lip service. We do not want our children to think of God only in abstract terms, nor in Christian terms. . . . This is a task, therefore, only for the home, synagogue or church.

Gilbert, *A Catalogue of Church-State Problems*, 56 RELIGIOUS EDUCATION 424, 428 (1961). See also note 73 *supra*.
234. PFEFFER, CHURCH, STATE AND FREEDOM 308 (1953). See also Comm. on Religion and Education, Am. Council on Education, *Religion in Public Education*, 42 RELIGIOUS EDUCATION 129, 161 (1947), which stated that permitting instruction in a common core religion "would be, at best, to assume that the support of an overwhelming majority of the people justified overriding the convictions of a minority."
235. Nichols, *supra* note 232, at 157–58.
236. American Council on Education, quoted in PFEFFER, *op. cit. supra* note 234, at 308–09.
237. See text accompanying notes 32–42 *supra*.
238. Billard v. Board of Educ., 69 Kan. 53, 58, 76 Pac. 422, 423 (1904) (Lord's Prayer and Twenty-Third Psalm). See also Doremus v. Board of Educ., 7 N.J. Super. 442, 454, 71 A.2d 732, 740 (Super. Ct. 1950).

fail, either because of disingenuousness,[239] or because it would seem that if the prayer did produce placidity, it would be due originally to its religious effect.[240]

Third, if the circumstances under which the prayer were to be recited could be so molded as to remove the likelihood that there would be infringement or influencing of any student's religious or conscientious principles, it would be free from challenge despite its solely religious nature. One suggestion toward this end has been that only one student each day be invited to read the prayer while the others simply remain silent.[241] The difficulty with this is that the same social compulsion that operates on students to participate in group recitation would seem to operate here to force a dissenter to take his turn at reading before the class.[242] Even if only the teacher were to recite the prayer, with the students simply listening in silence, the result should probably be the same. It is likely that the conscientious scruples of some students would forbid even this quantum of "participation" in what is clearly a devotional exercise.[243] Therefore, they would be inherently compelled to compromise their scruples. Furthermore, it is most reasonable to believe that the reading of a prayer, each and every day, "buttressed with the authority of the State and, more importantly to children, backed with the authority of their teachers, can hardly do less than inculcate or promote the inculcation of various religious doctrines in childish minds."[244] Educators have

---

239. The proponent of this justification herself conceded that the prayer recitation "was religious to the children that are religious, and to the others it was not." Billard v. Board of Educ., 69 Kan. 53, 58, 76 Pac. 422, 423 (1904). The court, in sustaining the practice did not do so on the ground that the prayer recitation was not a religious activity. Rather, it found that the exercises "were not a form of religious worship or the teaching of sectarian or religious doctrine" as forbidden by the state constitution. *Ibid.*

240. If the mere recitation of *any* reading would accomplish the teacher's goal, then, as indicated in the text, the practice may not be characterized as a solely religious activity and it is not, for that reason, violative of the establishment clause. However, the establishment clause may be violated for another reason. Although the practice would have the immediate secular end of maintaining order, it would also have the immediate effect of promoting religion. Since, by virtue of the above analysis that saves this practice from being a solely religious activity, the secular end *obviously* could be *just as well* attained by means that do not promote religion (*e.g.,* recitation of one of Shakespeare's sonnets), the selection of a reading that furthers religion should be unconstitutional. *Accord,* McGowan v. Maryland, 366 U.S. 420, 466–67 (1961) (Frankfurter, J., separate opinion).

241. See Engel v. Vitale, 11 App. Div. 2d 340, 348–49, 206 N.Y.S.2d 183, 191 (1960) (Beldock, J., separate opinion).

242. This has occurred. See text accompanying note 106 *supra.*

243. See Schempp v. School Dist., 177 F. Supp. 398, 401 (E.D. Pa. 1959).

244. *Id.* at 404. *Cf. The Effects of Segregation and the Consequences of*

expressed the opinion that even a single instance of school approbation of certain religious principles might have this effect.[245] Surely, the daily repetition of devotional exercises will likely result in instilling religious values, thereby affecting the immature students' freedom of conscientious choice.[246] Many students will be influenced to engage more actively in religious endeavors, and the effect of this practice might be to cause pupils of dissenting religious faiths to compromise their scruples.

Several other suggestions merit consideration. One has been "to have each school day commence with a quiet moment that would still the tumult of the playground and start a day of study."[247] Since each student could utilize this moment of silence for any purpose he saw fit, the activity may not be fairly characterized as solely religious, and since no student would really know the subject of his classmates' reflections, no one could in any way be compelled to alter his thoughts. However, the proposal of recitation of the words of a song that invoke or make other hallowed references to the Deity as a replacement for a traditional prayer[248] falls into a different category. Even if the singing of such a song in the public schools were wholly unobjectionable,[249] the recitation of its words as a devotional exercise transforms its entire complexion. This is clearly no more than the designation of an official prayer, irrespective of by whom it is done, and it is invalid for reasons previously mentioned.[250]

Desegregation: A Social Science Statement, 37 MINN. L. REV. 427, 433 (1953):
> The child who, for example, is compelled to attend a segregated school may be able to cope with ordinary expressions of prejudice by regarding the prejudiced person as evil or misguided; but he cannot readily cope with symbols of authority, the full force of the authority of the State—the school or the school board, in this instance—in the same manner.

See also Levy, *Views from the Wall—Reflections on Church-State Relationships*, 29 HENNEPIN LAW. 51, 55 (1961).

245. See Tudor v. Board of Educ., 14 N.J. 31, 51–52, 100 A.2d 857, 868 (1953). *But see* text accompanying notes 524–25 *infra*.

246. *Cf.* Miller v. Cooper, 56 N.M. 355, 244 P.2d 520 (1952), in which the court permitted occasional public school religious activities, but held invalid the continuous availability of religious pamphlets.

247. Editorial, Washington Post, June 28, 1962, § A, p. 22, col. 2. See also N.Y. Times, Aug. 30, 1962, § 1, p. 18, col. 2.

248. See N.Y. Times, July 29, 1962, § 1, p. 36, col. 4; *id.*, Aug. 10, 1962, § 1, p. 21, col. 1; *id.*, Aug. 30, 1962, § 1, p. 18, col. 3.

249. See text accompanying notes 541–44 *infra*.

250. See text accompanying notes 62–66 *supra*.

B. BIBLE READING

Past and present, one of the most prevalent solely religious practices carried on in the public schools has been Bible reading.[251] Its legality and constitutionality have evoked a glut of litigation in the state courts and a surfeit of writing by legal and lay commentators. The Supreme Court has managed to elude the problem in the past,[252] but appears finally to be compelled to adjudicate it on the merits.[253] By any reasonable test, this practice should be unconstitutional.[254]

The prime reason advanced by many state courts for sustaining the practice is that since the Bible is a nonsectarian document, no single religious sect benefits from its use.[255] This factor is crucial under many state constitutional provisions that prohibit "sectarian" teaching in the public schools.[256] However, it is irrelevant as far as the first amendment is concerned since, under the *Everson* dictum, "state action violates the ban . . . if it aids all religions on a nonpreferential basis."[257] Under the proposed constitutional standard, the question of whether the Bible is sectarian is likewise inconsequential. This solely religious practice would be invalid so long as it is likely to cause any student, even if he belongs to no religious sect, to have his conscientious convictions influenced or compromised.[258]

However, it should be made plain that no version of the Bible may be fairly characterized as nonsectarian, even in the sense that none of the *major* religious faiths find it unobjectionable. The earliest challenges to Bible reading in the American public schools were leveled by members of the Roman Catholic faith, who con-

---

251. A recent survey estimates that 42% of American public schools have daily Bible reading. Geographically, the breakdown is: East—68%; South—77%; Midwest—18%; West—11%. Dierenfield, *The Extent of Religious Influence in American Public Schools*, 56 RELIGIOUS EDUCATION 173, 176 (1961).

252. See School Dist. v. Schempp, 364 U.S. 298 (1960); Doremus v. Board of Educ., 342 U.S. 429 (1952).

253. See note 3 *supra*. The Court had little choice but to hear the *Schempp* case since it was appealable as a matter of right under § 1253 of the Judicial Code, and the three-judge court below had found that public school Bible reading was contrary to the establishment clause.

254. See text accompanying notes 60–64 *supra*.

255. See *e.g.*, People *ex rel.* Vollmar v. Stanley, 81 Colo. 276, 255 Pac. 610 (1927); Commonwealth v. Cooke, 7 Am. L. Reg. (o.s.) 417 (Mass. Police Ct. 1859); Doremus v. Board of Educ., 5 N.J. 435, 75 A.2d 880 (1950); State *ex rel.* Weiss v. District Bd., 76 Wis. 177, 44 N.W. 967 (1890).

256. See cases cited in note 255 *supra*; PFEFFER, CHURCH, STATE AND FREEDOM 387 (1953).

257. *Id.* at 391.

258. For examples, see text accompanying notes 105–07 *supra*.

scientiously objected to the use of the King James version.[259] Although there has been some indication that this position is in a state of flux,[260] recent litigation has again been undertaken by Catholic parents.[261] Unitarians,[262] members of the Jewish faith,[263] Buddhists,[264] and atheists[265] have all asserted in the courts that public school Bible reading offends their religious and conscientious beliefs. Universalists and some Lutherans and Baptists also oppose the activity.[266]

A number of state courts, although a minority, have recognized the fact that no version of the Bible is acceptable to everyone.[267] Theologians of all faiths encounter no difficulty in arriving at this conclusion.[268] The Roman Catholic religion finds only the Douay version of the Bible acceptable;[269] despite an assertion to the contrary,[270] "a Catholic child commits a grave sin if he knowingly owns or reads from the Protestant version of the Bible."[271] Very recently, Catholic parents protested a New Jersey community's requirement that their children *listen* to readings from a King James Bible.[272] The Roman Catholic position has

---

259. See *e.g.*, Donahoe v. Richards, 38 Me. 379 (1854); Commonwealth v. Cooke, 7 Am. L. Reg. (o.s.) 417 (Mass. Police Ct. 1859); Nessle v. Hum, 1 Ohio N.P. 140 (C.P. 1894); Hart v. School Dist., 2 Lancaster L. Rev. 346 (Pa. C.P. 1885). See also Boyer, *Religious Education of Public School Pupils in Wisconsin*, 1953 WIS. L. REV. 181.

260. See Reed, *Another Tradition at Stake*, Catholic Action, Feb., 1950, p. 4.

261. *E.g.*, Tudor v. Board of Educ., 14 N.J. 31, 100 A.2d 857 (1953).

262. Schempp v. School Dist., 177 F. Supp. 398 (E.D. Pa. 1959).

263. Herold v. Parish Bd. of School Directors, 136 La. 1034, 68 So. 116 (1915); Church v. Bullock, 100 S.W. 1025 (Tex. Civ. App. 1907).

264. Commonwealth v. Renfrew, 332 Mass. 492, 126 N.E.2d 109 (1955).

265. Murray v. Curlett, 228 Md. 239, 179 A.2d 698 (1962).

266. 2 STOKES, CHURCH AND STATE IN THE UNITED STATES 571 (1950).

267. *E.g.*, Evans v. Selma Union High School Dist., 193 Cal. 54, 222 Pac. 801 (1924); Wilkerson v. City of Rome, 152 Ga. 762, 110 S.E. 895 (1922); People *ex rel.* Ring v. Board of Educ., 245 Ill. 334, 92 N.E. 251 (1910); State *ex rel.* Freeman v. Scheve, 65 Neb. 853, 91 N.W. 846 (1900).

268. See Schempp v. School Dist., 177 F. Supp. 398, 401–02 (E.D. Pa. 1959); Tudor v. Board of Educ., 14 N.J. 31, 46–47, 100 A.2d 857, 865 (1953); Harpster, *Religion, Education and the Law*, 36 MARQ. L. REV. 24, 44 (1952).

269. People *ex rel.* Ring v. Board of Educ., 245 Ill. 334, 343–45, 92 N.E. 251, 254 (1910); State *ex rel.* Dearle v. Frazier, 102 Wash. 369, 383, 173 Pac. 35, 39 (1918).

270. See Herold v. Parish Bd. of School Directors, 136 La. 1034, 1040, 68 So. 116, 118 (1915).

271. PFEFFER, *op. cit. supra* note 256, at 384. See also authorities cited in Rosenfield, *Separation of Church and State in the Public Schools*, 22 U. PITT. L. REV. 561, 571 n.49 (1961).

272. Pfeffer & Baum, Public School Sectarianism and the Jewish Child 31 (American Jewish Congress, May, 1957). Roman Catholics "are forbidden . . . to listen to any version of [the Bible] unauthorized by the

been that the King James version is filled with error and false explanations and is used "as an instrument of proselytism."[273] The Protestant stand regarding the Douay translation of the Bible is similar in many respects to the Roman Catholic feeling about the King James version.[274]

The Jewish faith finds the New Testament, whether it be the Douay or King James version, incompatible with Hebrew teachings.[275] Of course, nonbelievers find the dogmatism of every version of the Bible as an imposition on their conscientious scruples.[276] Nonetheless, the argument has been made that the Old Testament is generally immune from objection.[277] Even discounting those minor religious groups that "in this country . . . are numerically small and, in point of impact upon our national life, negligible,"[278] this argument is far from being accurate. Unitarians have testified that much of the Old Testament's content is contrary to their faith.[279] A Jewish theologian has pointed out that there were specific instances in which the King James Old Testament had been

---

Roman Catholic Church." CATHOLIC ENCYCLOPEDIA 524, cited in Tyree, *Should What Is Rendered To God Be Commanded By Caesar?*, 44 PHI DELTA KAPPAN 74, 76 (1962).

273. Encyclicals of the Popes, quoted in Brief for Plaintiffs, p. 24, Schempp v. School Dist., 177 F. Supp. 398 (E.D. Pa. 1959). See PFEFFER, *op. cit. supra* note 256, at 384:

[T]he translators' dedicatory preface [to the King James version] states that the purpose of the translation was to give 'such a blow unto that Man of Sin (the Pope) as will not be healed [and] to make God's holy truth to be yet more and more known to the people whom they ("Papist persons at home or abroad") desire still to be kept in ignorance.'

274. See People *ex rel.* Ring v. Board of Educ., 245 Ill. 334, 344–45, 92 N.E. 251, 254 (1910); Tudor v. Board of Educ., 14 N.J. 31, 47, 100 A.2d 857, 865 (1953).

275. See Kaplan v. Independent School Dist., 171 Minn. 142, 154–55, 214 N.W. 18, 22–23 (1927) (dissenting opinion); Comment, 43 ILL. L. REV. 374, 382 (1948); 27 TEXAS L. REV. 256, 258 (1948).

276. See Comment, 43 ILL. L. REV. 374, 382 (1948).

277. Doremus v. Board of Educ., 5 N.J. 435, 448, 75 A.2d 880, 886 (1950).

278. *Id.* at 449, 75 A.2d at 887.

279.

In content, the father objected to material in the Old Testament regarding blood sacrifices, uncleanness, and leprosy, together with the whole concept of the Old Testament God which was contrary to the concept of deity which he endeavored to instill in his children. He testified that he did not want his children to acquire an image of Jehovah, the God of vengeance. He pointed out that in the very midst of the Ten Commandments was a verse asserting that God would visit the sins of the father upon the fourth generation . . . and the witness went on to assert that this concept of God was in sharp contrast with the God of his own church . . . .

Brief for Plaintiffs, pp. 5–6, Schempp v. School Dist., 177 F. Supp. 398 (E.D. Pa. 1959).

imbued with a Christological significance.²⁸⁰ Clearly, there is no "English text of the Old Testament accepted fully by the several faiths."²⁸¹

Recognizing this inherent weakness of any complete version of the Bible, it has been suggested that the defect may be remedied by selecting those portions in any version that are in no way religious, but contain only moral principles that are common to *all men*.²⁸² If this could be done, the practice would be valid under the proposed standard. Not only could it not be fairly characterized as solely religious, but no one's conscientious beliefs could possibly be affected. The difficulty is that those who have advocated this course have concluded, somewhat contradictorily, that there is no one competent to select these portions.²⁸³ Even if it be assumed that such Biblical passages may exist, until there is at least a general consensus as to which ones they are, the establishment clause should forbid any individual or group from choosing some and causing them to be read in the public schools. If this were permitted, for reasons previously advanced,²⁸⁴ it is very likely that infractions of religious liberty would occur and go unredressed.

Other attempts have been made to justify the constitutionality of public school Bible reading. They also fail on examination. Several state courts have excused the practice on the ground that dissenters are afforded the right of nonparticipation.²⁸⁵ The inadequacy and fictitiousness of this position have already been belabored.²⁸⁶ Others have attempted to validate the practice because

---

280. Dr. Solomon Grayzel, cited *id.* at p. 10.

281. Committee on Religion and Public Education of the National Council of the Churches of Christ, *Relation of Religion to Public Education —A Study Document,* International J. of Religious Education, Apr. 1960, pp. 21, 28.

282. See People *ex rel.* Vollmar v. Stanley, 81 Colo. 276, 286–93, 255 Pac. 610, 615–17 (1927); Harpster, *supra* note 268, at 45.

283. *Ibid.* See also Comment, 43 ILL. L. REV. 374, 382 (1948): "However carefully selections for reading may be chosen it is inevitable that some students will be forced to listen to portions which they cannot accept."

284. See text accompanying notes 219–24 *supra*.

285. *E.g.*, People *ex rel.* Vollmar v. Stanley, 81 Colo. 276, 293, 255 Pac. 610, 617 (1927); Chamberlin v. Dade County Bd. of Pub. Instruction, 143 So. 2d 21, 31 (Fla. Sup. Ct. 1962); Pfeiffer v. Board of Educ., 118 Mich. 560, 562–63, 77 N.W. 250, 251 (1898); Kaplan v. Independent School Dist., 171 Minn. 142, 151, 214 N.W. 18, 21 (1927).

286. The consistency of holding, on the one hand, that the Bible is nonsectarian and then holding, on the other hand, that it is saved from religious liberty objection because of the right of nonparticipation has long been questioned. See People *ex rel.* Ring v. Board of Educ., 245 Ill. 334, 351, 92 N.E. 251, 256 (1910); Note, 3 RUTGERS L. REV. 115, 125 (1949). This

it does not transform the public school into a "place of worship."[287] While this contention may satisfy some state constitutional prerequisites, it has no bearing vis-a-vis the establishment clause.

A provision that the reading of the Bible be done without comment has often been submitted as a sustaining feature.[288] This argument ignores the fact that to some sects, "the reading in public of any portion of any version of the Scriptures unaccompanied by authoritative comment or explanation, or the reading of it privately by persons not commissioned by the church to do so, is objectionable, and an offense to their religious feelings . . . ."[289] In addition, since other readings in the curriculum are subjected to critical comment and scrutiny, there is reasonable likelihood that the practice of reading the Bible without discerning comment "will tend to the acceptance by those pupils of the statements in the selections as true."[290] Finally, the daily repetition of this activity, in some schools for a substantial segment of time,[291] under the sponsorship of school and teacher will surely have its effect[292] even if done without comment.[293] These points also

---

dilemma would be solved only if Bible reading could be characterized as a secular activity. See text accompanying notes 117–25 *supra*. It is clear that this may not be done.

287. *E.g.*, Moore v. Monroe, 64 Iowa 367, 20 N.W. 475 (1884); Hackett v. Brooksville Graded School Dist., 120 Ky. 608, 87 S.W. 792 (1905).

288. *E.g.*, Carden v. Bland, 199 Tenn. 665, 288 S.W.2d 718 (1956).

289. State *ex rel.* Freeman v. Scheve, 65 Neb. 853, 871, 91 N.W. 846, 847 (1902). For further documentation of this in regard to the Roman Catholic position, see note 272 *supra*; Brief for Plaintiffs, p. 25, Schempp v. School Dist., 177 F. Supp. 398 (E.D. Pa. 1959).

290. Pfeiffer v. Board of Educ., 118 Mich. 560, 578, 77 N.W. 250, 257 (1898) (dissenting opinion). Of interest also is the following statement in State *ex rel.* Weiss v. District Bd., 76 Wis. 177, 194–95, 44 N.W. 967, 973 (1890):

A most forcible demonstration . . . is found in certain reports of the American Bible Society of its work in Catholic countries . . . in which instances are given of the conversion of several persons from 'Romanism' through the reading of the scriptures alone; that is to say, the reading of the Protestant or King James version of the Bible converted Catholics to Protestants without the aid of comment or exposition.

291. In Chamberlin v. Dade County Bd. of Pub. Instruction, 143 So. 2d 21, 31 (Fla. Sup. Ct. 1962), the court noted that Bible reading consumed from three to five minutes each day.

292. Dean Weigle has written that "the message of the Bible is the central thing . . . . The Bible contains the Word of God to man." Quoted in Brief for Plaintiffs, p. 14, Schempp v. School Dist., 177 F. Supp. 398 (E.D. Pa. 1959).

293. Notice again the inconsistency between finding the Bible to be nonsectarian and, at the same time, finding no infringement of religious liberty only because it is read without comment. See note 286 *supra*; Note, 28 GEO. WASH. L. REV. 579, 611 (1960).

overcome the defenses occasionally asserted that the mere reading of the Bible denotes no implication as to the truth or falsity of the subject matter and that merely listening to it compels no student to *believe* in what he has heard.[294]

1. *Teaching of Moral Values*

The argument is frequently made that Bible reading, religious study, and other devotional exercises in the public schools are indispensable to teaching students moral values and qualities, and that this is a vital function of our public schools in teaching good citizenship and in combating "Godless Communism."[295] If this means that the only available method for inculcating students with these values is first to imbue them with religious ideals, then regardless of how important this may be, the establishment clause should forbid the training.[296]

However, the prospects for the public schools' producing good citizens are not quite so bleak. There is ample evidence that religion in general education is unnecessary to produce better child behavior;[297] moral values may be very effectively taught without the aid of religion.[298] "However we [citizens of the American democracy] may disagree on religious creeds, we can agree on moral and spiritual values."[299] Educators and philosophers have shown[300] that such universally accepted values as justice, property rights, respect for law and authority, and brotherhood[301] may be derived from nonreligious sources[302] and may be enforced

---

294. *E.g.*, Donahoe v. Richards, 38 Me. 379, 399 (1854). See also Spiller v. Inhabitants of Woburn, 12 Allen 127 (Mass. 1866).
295. See, *e.g.*, Taylor, *Equal Protection of Religion: Today's Public School Problem*, 38 A.B.A.J. 277, 339 (1952). See also Hart v. School Dist., 2 Lancaster L. Rev. 346, 352 (C.P. 1885).
296. See text accompanying notes 38–42 *supra*.
297. Seminar No. 4, *The Public School and Religious Education*, 49 RELIGIOUS EDUCATION 143, 144–45 (1954).
298. EDUCATIONAL POLICIES COMM'N, NATIONAL EDUCATION ASS'N, MORAL AND SPIRITUAL VALUES IN THE PUBLIC SCHOOLS 17–30 (1951).
299. *Id.* at 33.
300. *Id.* at 37–45.
301. The public school teaches brotherhood as part of the democratic ideal. The churches teach it as a response to God's commandment to love one's neighbor. The secular humanist practices it as an expression of a purely human value. Comm. on Religion and Public Education of the National Council of the Churches of Christ, *Relation of Religion to Public Education—A Study Document*, International J. of Religious Education, Apr. 1960, pp. 21, 25.
302. "After all, if Aristotle, 350 years before the advent of Christianity, could write a rather comprehensive and enduring work on ethics, I do not see why it should be so difficult for modern American secularists of good will to do likewise." Address by F. E. Flynn, Professor of Philosophy, Col-

by nonreligious sanctions.³⁰³ In fact, there is persuasive authority for the view that moral values are better learned through concrete examples during the school day than through lessons that preach them.³⁰⁴

Other generally recognized values, "in the sense that they are common to all segments of our society, irrespective of religious faith or philosophic school,"³⁰⁵ are "responsibility, honesty, temperance, and self-control."³⁰⁶ Thus, while the Illinois legislature demands that "every public school teacher shall teach the pupils honesty, kindness, justice and moral courage for the purpose of lessening crime and raising the standard of good citizenship,"³⁰⁷ it recognizes that this aim may be accomplished on a neutral basis by making clear that the statute "shall not be construed as requiring religious or sectarian teaching."³⁰⁸ Similarly, New York prescribes courses in "partriotism and citizenship," but implies that this goal may be attained by "instruction in the history, meaning, significance and effect of the provisions of the constitution of the United States, [and of the state of New York], the amendments thereto, [and] the declaration of independence."³⁰⁹ Surely it may. While teachers should educate their students about the fact that most of our citizens believe that there are various religious sources and sanctions for our moral values,³¹⁰ they can successfully instill commonly cherished values without engaging in religious indoctrination.

Although one writer, in his intellectual struggle to validate Bible reading, went so far as to concede that the machinations

---

lege of St. Thomas, to the West St. Paul Federation of Teachers, Sept. 20, 1962.

303. "[T]he [ancient] Greeks are an excellent illustration of a people whose principles of conduct were independent of religious sanction . . . . Buddhism is primarily, if not entirely, a system of ethics; one of conduct, without the inducements of rewards and punishments characteristic of Western religions." THAYER, THE ATTACK UPON THE AMERICAN SECULAR SCHOOL 205–06 (1951). See also THAYER, THE CHALLENGE OF THE PRESENT TO PUBLIC EDUCATION 14–16 (1958).

304. See EDUCATIONAL POLICIES COMM'N, *op. cit. supra* note 298, at 60–70; HARTFORD, MORAL VALUES IN PUBLIC EDUCATION *passim* (1958); THAYER, THE ATTACK UPON THE AMERICAN SECULAR SCHOOL 212–18 (1951).

305. *Id.* at 210.
306. *Ibid.*
307. ILL. REV. STAT. ch. 122, § 27–12 (1961).
308. ILL. REV. STAT. ch. 122, § 27–16 (1961).
309. N.Y. EDUC. LAW § 801.
310. See Nichols, *Religion and Education in a Free Society* in RELIGION IN AMERICA 148, 157 (Cogley ed. 1958). *Cf.* Rosenfield, *Separation of Church and State in the Public Schools*, 22 U. PITT. L. REV. 561, 577–78 (1961).

of his proposal were "contrary to reason,"[311] all others seem to have recognized that there are some religious objections to every version of the Bible.[312] When it is read as part of a devotional exercise, the activity must be fairly characterized as solely religious.[313] While teachers no longer beat dissenting students,[314] the fact is that there is an inherent compulsion to participate, and therefore, conscientious scruples are influenced and compromised. The practice should be held to violate the establishment clause.

2. *Academic Study of Religion*

One last area of discussion concerning the place of the Bible in the public schools must be considered. The suggestion has frequently been made that the Bible (and religion generally) is a vital educational tool. If this means "that the highest duty of those who are charged with the responsibility of training the young people . . . in the public schools is in teaching both by precept and example that in the conflicts of life they should not forget God,"[315] then it must be rejected under any reasonable standard. Aside from the fact that this is educationally unacceptable,[316] the Court has made clear that the establishment clause forbids governmental indoctrination of religious beliefs and public school religious instruction.[317] Under the proposed constitutional standard, this effort to inculcate religious beliefs would unquestionably be a solely religious activity likely to influence and compromise the students' freedom of conscientious choice. However, it is totally inaccurate to conclude, as many have done, that this rejection "sanctions [the public schools'] utilization for the purposes of atheists."[318] This would be correct only if the public schools were

---

311. Harpster, *supra* note 268, at 46.
312. *E.g.*, Kauper, *Church, State, and Freedom: A Review*, 52 MICH. L. REV. 829, 842 (1954); Note, 22 ALBANY L. REV. 156, 172 (1958).
313. See Murray v. Curlett, 228 Md. 239, —, 179 A.2d 698, 708 (1962) (dissenting opinion).
314. See Commonwealth v. Cooke, 7 Am. L. Reg. (o.s.) 417 (Mass. Police Ct. 1859).
315. Carden v. Bland, 199 Tenn. 665, 681, 288 S.W.2d 718, 725 (1956). See also Church v. Bullock, 100 S.W. 1025, 1027 (Tex. Civ. App. 1907): "It may be said that said exercises tended to teach that there was an Almighty God; but this cannot be held objectionable . . . ."
316. American public education "disapproves indoctrination with reference to matters of belief." Comm. on Religion and Education, Am. Council on Education, *Religion in Public Education*, 42 RELIGIOUS EDUCATION 129, 161 (1947).
317. Zorach v. Clauson, 343 U.S. 306, 314 (1952).
318. Schmidt, *Religious Liberty and the Supreme Court of the United States*, 17 FORDHAM L. REV. 173, 185 (1948).

either constitutionally permitted or forced to teach that there is *no* God. Obviously, the first amendment forbids this just as much as it forbids exhortations to the contrary. The result, therefore, is one of true neutrality.

It is also error to deduce that this rejection demands "that the child has a 'legal duty' to put all this time in on secular subjects, none on religious subjects";[319] that it results in "the *compulsory exclusion of any religious element* and the consequent promotion and advancement of atheism";[320] that it "surrender[s] these schools to the sectarianism of atheism or irreligion";[321] that it bans all study of God as connected with our principles of government;[322] or that it compels silence about the Bible, religion, and God, thus impressing school children that these matters are insignificant.[323] It can hardly be denied that "we are a religious people whose institutions presuppose a Supreme Being"[324] since it is a matter of "common notoriety"[325] that the great majority of our citizens are religious in the sense that they do believe in God.[326] Although there is some dispute concerning the percentage of our population that is affiliated with organized religious groups,[327] the most recent government survey showed that less than three percent of all persons over the age of 14 reported that they had no religion whatever;[328] almost 95 percent of the population considered themselves to be either Protestant, Roman Catholic, or Jewish.[329] Nor can it be denied that "acknowledgement of a Supreme Being has . . . been a part of our history."[330]

---

319. Murray, *Law or Prepossessions?*, 14 LAW & CONTEMP. PROB. 23, 36 (1949).

320. Engel v. Vitale, 10 N.Y.2d 174, 184, 176 N.E.2d 579, 583 (1961) (Burke, J., concurring opinion).

321. Luther A. Weigle, formerly Dean of Yale Divinity School, quoted in PFEFFER, CHURCH, STATE, AND FREEDOM 291 (1953).

322. Brief for Intervenors-Respondents, pp. 55-56, Engel v. Vitale, 370 U.S. 421 (1962).

323. Schmidt, *supra* note 318, at 187-88. See also PARSONS, WHICH WAY, DEMOCRACY? 11 (1939).

324. Zorach v. Clauson, 343 U.S. 306, 313 (1952).

325. *Cf.* Black, *The Lawfulness of the Segregation Decisions*, 69 YALE L.J. 421, 426 (1960).

326. PFEFFER, *op. cit. supra* note 321, at 289, has acknowledged that "we are a religious people even though our government is secular."

327. Pfeffer contends that the figure is only about 50%. *Id.* at 303. This must be compared with the fact that the various religious bodies claim church membership in 1960 of 64% of the total population. BUREAU OF CENSUS, U.S. DEP'T OF COMMERCE, STATISTICAL ABSTRACT OF THE UNITED STATES 48 (83d ed. 1962).

328. *Id.* at 46.

329. *Ibid.* Query as to how many of these felt "compelled" to make such a disclosure.

330. VIRGINIA COMMISSION ON CONSTITUTIONAL GOVERNMENT, THE NEW YORK PRAYER CASE 4 (1962).

While there is some dispute as to how religious the founding fathers were,[331] the heritage of this country, both in the past and at present, is replete with examples of theistic and religious influences too multitudinous to enumerate fully.[332]

These being the facts, not only would it be virtually impossible, as a practical matter, to obliterate all references to religion from the public schools, but it would be educationally undesirable.[333] But a public school program that seeks to prevent children from growing up as religious illiterates may not be fairly characterized as a solely religious activity. There is a distinct and weighty public purpose in seeing that all school children comprehend the role that religion has played in this country's evolution[334] and that they have some understanding of the nature of the conscientious beliefs possessed by most of our citizens. Under the proposed constitutional standard there would be no constitutional objection[335] to an academic study in comparative religion[336] or to

---

331. See Pfeffer, *Church and State: Something Less Than Separation,* 19 U. CHI. L. REV. 1, 19–20 (1951).

332. A partial list might include the fact that the Declaration of Independence refers to the Deity four times; that the constitutions of 49 states acknowledge the existence of God and many imply that the rights and liberties of the people issue from God and express gratefulness therefore. See Brief for Respondents, pp. 44–54, Engel v. Vitale, 370 U.S. 421 (1962). "In God We Trust" has been impressed on our coins since 1865. In 1956, Congress adopted these words as our national motto. Lincoln's Gettysburg Address referred to God, as did the Mayflower Compact of 1620 and Madison's famous Memorial and Remonstrance Against Religious Assessments. Such national monuments as the Tomb of the Unknown Soldier, the Washington Monument, and the Lincoln and Jefferson Memorials all contain inscriptions mentioning the Deity. The Northwest Ordinance of 1787 stated that religion was necessary to good government. All of our Presidents have asked for the protection or help of God on assuming office. See Engel v. Vitale, 370 U.S. 421, 446–49 (1962) (Stewart, J., dissenting).

333. See the views expressed at a seminar of educators in Seminar No. 4, *The Public School and Religious Education,* 49 RELIGIOUS EDUCATION 143, 144–45 (1954); Cosway & Toepfer, *Religion and the Schools,* 17 U. CINC. L. REV. 117, 142 (1948). "An educated person cannot be religiously illiterate." Comm. on Religion and Education, Am. Council on Education, *supra* note 316, at 160.

334. "A course in the history of California which did not describe the early Catholic missions is unthinkable." 25 CAL. OPS. ATT'Y GEN. 325 (1955). This same report found prayers and Bible reading in the public schools to be contrary to the first amendment.

335. *But see* text acompanying notes 347–48 *infra.*

336. *Accord, e.g.,* PFEFFER, *op. cit. supra* note 321, at 309. Sutherland, *Public Authority and Religious Education,—A Brief Survey of Constitutional and Legal Limits,* 52 RELIGIOUS EDUCATION 256 (1957); Vishny, *The Constitution and Religion in the Public Schools,* 10 Decalogue J. June-July 1960, pp. 4, 6. *But see* Rosenfield, *Separation of Church and State in the Public Schools,* 22 U. PITT. L. REV. 561, 578 (1961).

the study of the Bible as an artistic work.[337] The salient distinction is that this would be teaching objectively *about* religion and the Bible and would not be religious indoctrination.

The academic study of religion may not take the form of teaching "that religion is sacred"[338] nor present religious dogma as factual material.[339] The only purpose for this approach is to inculcate religious beliefs. Nor may daily devotional Bible reading exercises with the privilege of nonparticipation be validated merely by characterizing them as an "elective course in non-sectarian Bible study."[340] The difference between a devotional exercise and an ordinary literature course that examines the Bible, attempting no indoctrination and therefore not exerting pressure on students, is the difference between a solely religious program that is likely to result in the influencing or compromising of students' conscientious scruples and a secular act by government that is within its power.

It is not easy to deny, at least where younger children are concerned, that even an objectively presented academic examination of the Bible, or of religion generally, will result in some indoctrination.[341] But to concede that there is much truth in the contention that "the young mind cannot grasp the nebulous distinction between the Bible as literature and the Bible as sectarian instruction"[342] is not automatically to invalidate a school board's good faith attempt[343] to educate students with "much useful information about the religious faiths, the important part they have played in establishing the moral and spiritual values of American life,

---

337. See Schempp v. School Dist., 177 F. Supp. 398, 404 (E.D. Pa. 1959); 25 CAL. OPS. ATT'Y GEN. 325 (1955).

338. Such was the announced purpose of a program adopted, in the name of academic study of religion, by the Denver school system for "intergroup education." Herberg, *Religion, Democracy, and Public Education,* in RELIGION IN AMERICA 118, 136 (Cogley ed. 1958).

339. See Emerson & Haber, *The Scopes Case in Modern Dress,* 27 U. CHI. L. REV. 522, 523–24 (1960).

340. This was suggested in Creel, *Is It Legal for the Public Schools of Alabama to Provide an Elective Course in Non-Sectarian Bible Instruction?,* 10 ALA. LAW. 86, 94 (1949).

341. PFEFFER, *op. cit. supra* note 321, at 311; Sutherland, *supra* note 336; Vishny, *supra* note 336.

342. Cosway & Toepfer, *supra* note 333, at 137.

343. The problem of dealing with an unconstitutional legislative "motive" of this kind is a vexing one. See Emerson & Haber, *supra* note 339, at 524. However, it is far from insuperable. See, *e.g.,* Gomillion v. Lightfoot, 364 U.S. 339 (1960); Lane v. Wilson, 307 U.S. 268 (1939); Guinn v. United States, 238 U.S. 347 (1915). See generally Israel, *On Charting A Course Through The Mathematical Quagmire: The Future of Baker v. Carr,* 61 MICH. L. REV.107, 140 n.138 (1962).

and their role in the story of mankind."[344] No doubt, indoctrination often results from academic pursuits. Therefore, although the wisdom of reserving this inquiry to the higher grades may be decided by local authorities,[345] it would not seem to be a proper question for the Supreme Court.[346]

However, despite the fact that the activity is secular and thus immunized from the proposed constitutional standard, it may still be in violation of the establishment clause. The thesis suggested is that when a secular activity by government results not only in attainment of a civil objective, but also promotes religion, the establishment clause is violated if the civil goal may be accomplished *just as well* by means that do not promote religion.[347] Thus, it may be argued that the establishment clause demands that the objective study of religion or the Bible be confined to those higher grades where the influencing or compromising of religious beliefs would not occur because the audience is adult enough to distinguish between indoctrination and academic discussion.[348] The contention would be quite convincing if it could be shown that, by so doing, the state's secular objective of making students religiously literate could be just as effectively achieved.

The Roman Catholic church has voiced strong opposition to allowing its children, at any age, to participate in academic courses in religion.[349] It has also been observed that "the objective teaching of religion is likely to be unacceptable to most churches."[350] In the first analysis, this becomes only one factor to be considered in making the legislative choice. If, however, some religious sect demands that its members do not participate in this instruction as a matter of religious dogma, the question becomes

---

344. EDUCATIONAL POLICIES COMM'N, NATIONAL EDUCATIONAL ASS'N, MORAL AND SPIRITUAL VALUES IN THE PUBLIC SCHOOLS 78 (1951).
345.
> The unity of our own country, our understanding of the other nations of the world, and respect for the rich religious traditions of all humanity would be enhanced by instruction about religion in the public schools. Like any other teaching in which deep personal emotions are involved, such instruction should, of course, give due consideration to the varying degrees of maturity of the students.

Id. at 78–79.
346. *Cf.* Braunfeld v. Brown, 366 U.S. 599, 608 (1961). See generally Sutherland, *Public Authority and Religious Education: A Brief Survey of Constitutional and Legal Limits,* in THE STUDY OF RELIGION IN THE PUBLIC SCHOOLS: AN APPRAISAL 67 (Brown ed. 1958).
347. See note 240 *supra.*
348. *Cf.* Kalven, *A Commemorative Case Note, Scopes v. State,* 27 U. CHI. L. REV. 505, 518 (1960). *But cf.* Comment, 32 MARQ. L. REV. 138, 144 (1948).
349. See PFEFFER, *op. cit. supra* note 321, at 310.
350. *Ibid.*

one of whether the free exercise clause is violated by compelling attendance in these courses. Here, as elsewhere,[351] a difficult and delicate free exercise problem is raised when there is a direct conflict between a religious tenet and action compelled by the state—that is, when the state, in pursuit of a secular purpose demands on pain of criminal prosecution that a person compromise his religious scruples.[352] The Supreme Court has not clearly articulated any principle to govern these situations,[353] and the issue is beyond the scope of this article.[354] What should be made plain, however, is that regardless of whether participation in the program may be made mandatory under the free exercise clause, the state is engaging in a secular activity when it introduces the academic study of religion into the public schools. Therefore, with one possible reservation,[355] the establishment clause is not in issue and religious objections to the activity may not result in its abolition.[356]

No doubt there are practical difficulties in administering a program of teaching *about* religion. It may be argued that instructors, who are themselves affiliated with a particular sect, cannot or will not objectively present all points of view;[357] the result, especially

---

351. See text accompanying notes 118–22 *supra*.
352. See Braunfeld v. Brown, 366 U.S. 599, 605 (1961); Prince v. Massachusetts, 321 U.S. 158, 165 (1944).
353. Cases presenting the problem are Prince v. Massachusetts, 321 U.S. 158 (1944); West Virginia State Bd. of Educ. v. Barnette, 319 U.S. 624 (1943); Reynolds v. United States, 98 U.S. 145 (1878).
354. The Court has stated that "legislative power . . . may reach people's actions when they are found to be in violation of important social duties or subversive of good order, even when the actions are demanded by one's religion." Braunfeld v. Brown, 366 U.S. 599, 603–04 (1961) (dictum). If this be the standard, the question of whether the state may demand a religious dissenter to attend classes in the objective study of religion turns on whether the Court feels that any student's failure to attend would be "in violation of important social duties or subversive of good order."
On the other hand, the Court has also noted the importance of whether the religious freedom asserted by the dissenter brings him "into collision with rights asserted by any other individual." West Virginia State Bd. of Educ. v. Barnette, 319 U.S. 624, 630 (1943). It is fairly plain that by absenting themselves from classes engaged in studying about religion, the objectors would not be directly affecting anyone else. Thus, it could be argued that their free exercise claim should be upheld. However, in Reynolds v. United States, 98 U.S. 145 (1878), the Court upheld the conviction of a Mormon polygamist who defended on the ground that the tenets of his church demanded that he practice polygamy. Here it would seem that the defendant's action affected only those persons who volunteered to be affected. For general discussion of this problem, see LOCKHART, KAMISAR & CHOPER, SUPPLEMENT TO DODD'S CASES ON CONSTITUTIONAL LAW 400–01 (1962).
355. See text accompanying notes 347–48 *supra*.
356. See text accompanying notes 117–25 *supra*.
357. See Margolin, Book Review, 72 YALE L.J. 212, 214 (1962).

as far as the younger children are concerned, will be indoctrination at least as powerful as that obtained by a solely religious activity. If the secular purposes of a program of the academic study of religion were inherently subject to abuse, then the only remedy might be to ban the activity.[358] But the alleged defect appears not to be inherent. Educators have stated that "the public school can teach objectively *about* religion without advocating or teaching any religious creed."[359] Theologians "believe that the teachers of the American public school system are, on the whole, qualified to maintain free discussion with genuine respect for religious perspectives."[360] The remedy for teacher abuse is to enjoin it or to get another teacher; it is not to outlaw the program.[361]

Another objection leveled at the academic study of religion in the public schools is that since it is, by its nature, highly controversial, it is likely to engender serious antagonisms among students of the different religious faiths. Instances of this have been recorded.[362] It has been suggested that this matter of "divisiveness" should determine the constitutionality of governmental programs in the religious area.[363] This seems to be neither a desirable nor workable approach to the problem. While this matter is unquestionably relevant to the legislative decision, once a genuinely secular-based program is enacted, it is difficult to see why it should be threatened with preordained abolition under the establishment clause either because some religious group finds it objectionable or because the sensibilities of some students will be offend-

---

358. See Note, 52 COLUM. L. REV. 1033, 1038 (1952); Note, 61 YALE L.J. 412–13 (1952).
359. EDUCATIONAL POLICIES COMM'N, NATIONAL EDUCATIONAL ASS'N, MORAL AND SPIRITUAL VALUES IN THE PUBLIC SCHOOL 77 (1951).
  That religious beliefs are controversial is not an adequate reason for excluding teaching about religion from the public schools. Economic and social questions are taught and studied in the schools on the very sensible theory that students need to know the issues being faced and to get practice in forming sound judgments. Teaching about religion should be approached in the same spirit. General guides on the teaching of all controversial issues may be helpful. If need be, teachers should be provided with special help and information to equip them to teach objectively in this area.
Id. at 78.
360. Nichols, *Religion and Education in a Free Society,* in RELIGION IN AMERICA 148, 159 (Cogley ed. 1958).
361. See Lieberman, *A General Interpretation of Separation of Church and State and Its Implications for Public Education,* 33 PROGRESSIVE EDUCATION 129, 134 (1956); Note, 52 COLUM. L. REV. 1033, 1038 (1952).
362. PFEFFER & BAUM, PUBLIC SCHOOL SECTARIANISM AND THE JEWISH CHILD 34, 37 (1957).
363. See Engel v. Vitale, 370 U.S. 421, 443 (1962) (Douglas, J., concurring opinion). See note 188 *supra.*

ed. If the governmental activity were a solely religious one that would likely result in the influencing or compromising of religious beliefs, the question should be answered differently, as has been maintained throughout this article. But many secular educational programs create dissention and discomfort among students.[364] If the basis of this is due to religious conviction, the free exercise clause may afford individual relief.[365]

Some ardent religionists (and also, undoubtedly some avid non-religionists) have advocated the exclusion of all religious matter from the public school curriculum.[366] This would mean, of course, that the study of European history would ignore the Protestant Reformation and the great religious controversies of the Middle Ages; that American history would be devoid of the struggle for religious freedom in the colonies; that art courses must exclude Da Vinci's "Last Supper" and Michelangelo's "Moses"; and that Beethoven's "Missa Solemnis" and Caruso's rendition of "Adeste Fidelis" could not be played in a music class. This line of reasoning might even prohibit the Bible from the public school library.

Despite the fact that one state court recently could find no difference between studies of this nature and devotional Bible reading,[367] the distinction is quite obvious. The inclusion of that religious material that is an intrinsic part of other disciplines is vitally necessary to a well-rounded education and is, therefore, a secular act.[368] It is thus subject to the same constitutional analysis as the objective study of religion. Unfortunately, from an *educational* standpoint, a recent study of American public education has revealed a "more or less deliberate avoidance of religious subject matter even when it was clearly intrinsic to the discipline concerned."[369] Unfortunately, from a *constitutional* standpoint, the same study "found planned religious activities widely prevalent."[370]

---

364. See note 359 *supra*.
365. See note 354 *supra*.
366. See PFEFFER, *op. cit. supra* note 321, at 287; Johnson, *Religion and Education*, 33 PROGRESSIVE EDUCATION 143, 146 (1956).
367. Chamberlin v. Dade County Bd. of Pub. Instruction, 143 So. 2d 21, 32 (Fla. Sup. Ct. 1962). See also People *ex rel.* Vollmar v. Stanley, 81 Colo. 276, 290, 255 Pac. 610, 616 (1927).
368. See 25 CAL. OPS. ATT'Y GEN. 316, 325 (1955); Johnson, *supra* note 366, at 145.
369. Johnson, *Summary of Policies and Recommendations of the American Council on Education Committee on Religion and Education*, in THE STUDY OF RELIGION IN THE PUBLIC SCHOOLS: AN APPRAISAL 5, 9 (Brown ed. 1958).
370. *Ibid.*

C. Released Time

Prior to the Supreme Court's decision on the Regents' prayer, the Court had decided only two other cases on the merits that concerned the question of religious penetration in the public schools. Both of these cases involved released time programs.[371] Such a program may be defined as "a system of religious education in connection with the public school under which those children desiring to participate in religious instruction are excused from their secular studies for a specified period weekly, while those children not participating in religious instruction remain under the jurisdiction and supervision of the public school for the usual period of secular instruction. No distinction is made in the use of the term between religious instruction classes held within or without the public school building; nor between classes held at the first or last period of the school day and those held sometime between these two periods."[372]

Under the proposed constitutional standard, all released time plans should be held in violation of the establishment clause. The only immediate purposes of such a program are to "encourage religious instruction"[373] and to aid in the religious indoctrination of school children. In upholding the constitutionality of these programs, neither the Supreme Court[374] nor the state appellate courts[375] have denied this fact, nor have the many commentators

---

371. Zorach v. Clauson, 343 U.S. 306 (1952); Illinois *ex rel.* McCollum v. Board of Educ., 333 U.S. 203 (1948).
372. PFEFFER, CHURCH, STATE, AND FREEDOM 315 (1953). For a general history of the program, see *id.* at 313–27. Research has revealed one "first-hour-of-the-day" released time program which was said to be voluntary. Nonetheless, "no pupil . . . has refused or failed to attend such morning services for religious instruction." State *ex rel.* Johnson v. Boyd, 217 Ind. 348, 359–60, 28 N.E.2d 256, 261–62 (1940).
373. Zorach v. Clauson, 343 U.S. 306, 314 (1952).
374. *Ibid.*
375. Gordon v. Board of Educ., 78 Cal. App. 2d 464, 178 P.2d 488 (Ct. App. 1947); People *ex rel.* McCollum v. Board of Educ., 396 Ill. 14, 71 N.E.2d 161 (1947); People *ex rel.* Latimer v. Board of Educ., 394 Ill. 228, 68 N.E.2d 305 (1946); Zorach v. Clauson, 278 App. Div. 573, 102 N.Y.S.2d 27 (1951), *aff'd*, 303 N.Y. 161, 100 N.E.2d 463 (1951); People *ex rel.* Lewis v. Graves, 219 App. Div. 233, 219 N.Y. Supp. 189 (1927), *aff'd*, 245 N.Y. 195, 156 N.E. 663 (1927); Perry v. School Dist. No. 81, 54 Wash. 2d 886, 344 P.2d 1036 (1959). Examination of those reported state trial court opinions that have sustained released time programs also bears out this contention. Zorach v. Clauson, 198 Misc. 631, 99 N.Y.S.2d 339 (Sup. Ct. 1950); Lewis v. Spaulding, 193 Misc. 66, 85 N.Y.S.2d 682 (Sup. Ct. 1948); Lewis v. Graves, 127 Misc. 135, 215 N.Y. Supp. 632 (Sup. Ct. 1926). Research reveals only one reported state case striking down a released time program. The grounds for the decision were that (1) since report cards were printed during school hours upon school presses, the state constitutional provision barring state aid to denomination-

who have defended these decisions. That a system of released time is inherently coercive, thereby compromising the students' freedom of religious choice, has already been mentioned and somewhat demonstrated above.[376] Further evidence of its influencing and compromising nature is not lacking. The existence of compulsion has been found in the fact that religious leaders have so strenuously pressed for the establishment of released time systems.[377] While this is not necessarily valid when measured by the strict rules of logic,[378] it is nonetheless quite persuasive. Religious educators who are proponents of the system have noted that released time programs have a "remarkable evangelistic record,"[379] for in those schools where they operate, a substantial percentage of students attend religious classes who would not otherwise do so.[380] Religious leaders who oppose released time view it as "a means of applying public pressures to non-conformists so as to make them 'give in.' "[381] Schools with released time programs have reported "a considerable percentage of pupils in attendance whose parents do not belong to any church."[382] "They want to go to the church with their schoolmates and ask their parents to sign release cards."[383] Where released time systems have been abandoned, attendance at religious classes has declined.[384] Children of minority religious faiths have been known to enroll in the majority's religious classes because they did "not wish to be marked."[385] The

---

al schools was violated and (2) the program violated the state education law's provision requiring public school attendance during the entire time of the school session. Stein v. Brown, 125 Misc. 692, 211 N.Y. Supp. 822 (Sup. Ct. 1925).

376. See text accompanying notes 102–04, 148 *supra*.

377. See PFEFFER, *op. cit. supra* note 372, at 373; Cushman, *The Holy Bible and the Public Schools*, 40 CORNELL L.Q. 475, 497 (1955).

378. Religious leaders may have any one of a multitude of reasons for seeking the establishment of the released time system, and even if their reason is that they believe the system is compulsive, that does not in fact make it true.

379. Dr. Erwin L. Shaver of the International Council of Religious Education, quoted in PFEFFER, *op. cit. supra* note 372, at 328.

380. *Ibid*. Dr. Shaver points out that before a released time system, half of the school population receives no religious training; when the system is instituted, an average of one-third of this neglected half is reached.

381. Glenn Archer, Executive Director of Protestants and Other Americans United, quoted in PFEFFER, *op. cit. supra* note 372, at 332.

382. JACKSON & MALMBERG, RELIGIOUS EDUCATION AND THE STATE 39 (1928).

383. Sullivan, *Religious Education in the Schools*, 14 LAW & CONTEMP. PROB. 92, 94 (1949).

384. See *id*. at 111.

385. PFEFFER & BAUM, PUBLIC SCHOOL SECTARIANISM AND THE JEWISH CHILD 19 (1957). See Record, p. 135, Illinois *ex rel*. McCollum v.

fact that some may not have done so in no way refutes the existence of the inherent pressure.[386] Those who chose not to enroll, or who were forbidden by their parents from doing so, have told of being "ostracized by the other children in after-school activities."[387]

Examination of the reasoning utilized by those few who defend the constitutionality of released time by denying the presence of coercion is revealing. The Illinois Supreme Court, in *McCollum*, "proved" the nonexistence of any coercion by (1) saying that it was no more present there than it was in a prior, similar case, and (2) referring to some testimony by Terry's mother.[388] The first reason, of course, merely avoids the issue, and aside from the fact that the quoted testimony failed to support the court's contention,[389] there was overwhelming evidence to the contrary.[390] Father Murray has taken the position that no threat to any personal rights was visible in *McCollum*,[391] Terry was not pressured into doing anything he did not want to do.[392] However, he then

---

Board of Educ., 333 U.S. 203 (1948), in which Terry McCollum's teacher testified that she spoke to Terry's mother about "the fact that allowing him to take the religious education course might help him to become a member of the group. He was not accepted as a member of our class. I thought if he did the same things that they were doing that might help."

386. The argument that this disproves the existence of coercion was made by Chief Judge Desmond, concurring in Zorach v. Clauson, 303 N.Y. 161, 176, 100 N.E.2d 463, 470 (1951).

387. Affidavit quoted in PFEFFER, *op. cit. supra* note 372, at 357.

When the released time students departed . . . I felt left behind. The released children made remarks about my being Jewish and I was made very much aware of the fact that I did not participate with them in the released time program. I endured a great deal of anguish as a result of this and decided that I would like to go along with the other children to the church center rather than continue to expose myself to such harassment. I asked my mother for permission to participate in the released time program and to accompany my Catholic classmates to their religious center, but she forbade it.

Id. at 356; *accord, id.* at 356–67. *Contra*, Corcoran, Social Relationships of Elementary School Children and the Released-Time Religious Education Program (unpublished doctorial dissertation in Stanford University Library), abstracted in 56 RELIGIOUS EDUCATION 363–64 (1961), concluding that the "degree of participation in the released-time program was not demonstrably related to the sociometric status of elementary school children."

388. People *ex rel.* McCollum v. Board of Educ., 396 Ill. 14, 23, 71 N.E.2d 161, 165 (1947).

389. Mrs. McCollum had testified that, "I do not know it [released time] would bother him [Terry] one way or the other. I *did* not know it *until in court.*" *Ibid.* (Emphasis added.)

390. See, *e.g.*, notes 103, 385 *supra.*

391. Murray, *Law or Prepossessions?*, 14 LAW & CONTEMP. PROB. 23, 24 n.7 (1949).

392. *Id.* at 39.

recognizes that there was "pressure by the school system in the interest of religious sects,"[393] but justifies its existence by stating that the public schools' "sheer omission of religion from the curriculum is itself a pressure against religion,"[394] and that "the system as such has become a formidable ally of secularism."[395] This position may be refuted simply by denying the premises. As has been pointed out, the establishment clause does not demand that the public schools omit religion from their curriculum, nor does it forbid them from objectively educating children as to the important role religion plays and has played in our civilization and in others. And so long as the establishment clause forbids the indoctrination of pupils with the ideas that there is no God or that, if there is, His influence is unimportant,[396] the public schools may not fairly be said to be allied with secularism.

While the Supreme Court did find the *McCollum* released time system in violation of the establishment clause, it sustained the program at issue in *Zorach v. Clauson*.[397] The only significant difference between the cases, so recognized by the Court majority,[398] was that in *McCollum* the public school classrooms were used for religious instruction, whereas in *Zorach* the religious classes were held away from the public school premises. It has already been shown that these cases cannot be meaningfully distinguished on the basis of the use of public property.[399] It may be true that "if the location of the school building makes the trip to a church long or hazardous because of dangerous street crossings, attendance will be improved by securing permission to teach in the school building."[400] But the fact that the system in *McCollum* may have more effectively promoted religious education does not mean that the *Zorach* plan did not promote it at all. It could be argued that the holding of the religious sessions in the same classrooms in which the ordinary daily school activities took place suggested that the religious instruction was an integral part of the public school program and, therefore, created a greater compulsive pressure on dissenters. This may make the result in *McCollum* more understandable, but it does not erase the "ineradicable built-in pressure to 'sign-up' for religious instruction"[401]

---

393. *Ibid.*
394. *Ibid.*
395. *Ibid.*
396. See text accompanying note 318 *supra*.
397. 343 U.S. 306 (1952).
398. *Id.* at 315.
399. See text accompanying notes 129–47 *supra*.
400. Sullivan, *supra* note 383, at 94.
401. Rosenfield, *Separation of Church and State in the Public Schools*, 22 U. PITT. L. REV. 561, 574 (1961).

in *Zorach*. Even those who favor the result in *Zorach*[402] agree with those who do not[403] that the decisions are irreconcilable on the matter of inherent coercion.

Probably the most frequently voiced argument in support of the constitutionality of released time is that its validity is dictated by the Supreme Court's landmark decision in *Pierce v. Society of Sisters*.[404] That case held an Oregon statute requiring public school attendance for children of certain ages unconstitutional on the ground that the fourteenth amendment gives parents the right to direct the education of their children and, therefore, the right to send their children to private or parochial schools that meet state qualifications. One aspect of the argument is that the right recognized in *Pierce* was a right guaranteed by the free exercise clause of the first amendment; to deny the availability of religious instruction in the public schools to those parents who, for financial or other reasons, send their children there, is to confine this right "to parents who can afford to send their children to parochial or other private schools . . . ."[405] The contention that rights protected by the free exercise clause would be suppressed by forbidding released time and other religious programs in the public schools has also been made by a number of others without the aid of the *Pierce* case.[406]

Apart from the question of whether *Pierce* really upheld a free exercise claim,[407] the argument must fail. The shortest answer is that released time programs violate the establishment clause and that ends the matter. Although this point seemingly begs the question, it is strengthened by the fact that the two most articulate proponents of the free exercise argument recognize that the validity of their argument turns on whether the continued operation of re-

---

402. *E.g.*, Kauper, *Church, State, and Freedom: A Review*, 52 MICH. L. REV. 829, 839 (1954).
403. *E.g.*, Zorach v. Clauson, 303 N.Y. 161, 187–88, 100 N.E.2d 463, 477 (1951) (Fuld, J., dissenting); Kurland, *Of Church and State and the Supreme Court*, 29 U. CHI. L. REV. 1, 77 (1961); Comment, 7 ALA. L. REV. 99, 107 (1954); Note, 52 COLUM. L. REV. 1033, 1038–39 (1952); Note, 61 YALE L.J. 405, 413–16 (1952); 74 HARV. L. REV. 611, 614 (1961); 31 TEXAS L. REV. 327, 329–30 (1953).
404. 268 U.S. 510 (1925).
405. Corwin, *The Supreme Court As National School Board*, 14 LAW & CONTEMP. PROB. 3, 20 (1949).
406. *E.g.*, Zorach v. Clauson, 303 N.Y. 161, 178, 100 N.E.2d 463, 471(1951) (Desmond, J., concurring); Zorach v. Clauson, 198 Misc. 631, 636–37, 99 N.Y.S.2d 339, 344 (Sup. Ct. 1950); Harpster, *Religion, Education and the Law*, 36 MARQ. L. REV. 24, 53 (1952); Murray, *supra* note 391, at 33; Reed, *Church-State and the Zorach Case*, 27 NOTRE DAME LAW. 529, 540 (1952).
407. See Kurland, *supra* note 403, at 13–14; Pfeffer, *Released Time and Religious Liberty: A Reply*, 53 MICH. L. REV. 91, 93–94 (1954).

leased time programs infringes on the rights of anyone else.[408] While it has not been contended that the program's imposition on nonconformists violates their rights specifically guaranteed by the free exercise clause,[409] it has been amply shown that the system of released time does infringe on their conscientious scruples.

The more authoritative answer to the argument based on *Pierce* is that the Court has specifically rejected a similar free exercise contention. If the free exercise clause is not violated by a law that "simply regulates a secular activity and, as applied to appellants, operates so as to make the practice of their religious beliefs more expensive,"[410] a decision by the Court to uphold the establishment clause surely must not fail because it has this effect.[411] It may be true that the rights guaranteed by *Pierce* would forbid a state from so regulating its public school system "as to make religious education or exercise impracticable or to limit such education or exercise to Saturday or Sunday"[412] and would preclude a state from "the pre-empting of the whole of the child's time so as to leave no adequate part for religion."[413] Such regulation would effectively bar action "demanded by one's religion."[414] But, since no religion demands that its children be excused early from school to attend religious classes, the abolition of released time "does not make unlawful any religious practices . . . ."[415] At most, the denial of a released time program may be said to impose "only an indirect burden on the exercise of religion . . . ."[416] Clearly, neither the purpose nor the effect of the denial of a released time program "is to impede the observance of

---

408. Zorach v. Clauson, 303 N.Y. 161, 178, 100 N.E.2d 463, 471 (1951) (Desmond, J., concurring); Corwin, note 405 *supra*. See also Johnson, *Summary of Policies and Recommendations of the American Council on Education Committee on Religion and Education*, in THE STUDY OF RELIGION IN THE PUBLIC SCHOOLS: AN APPRAISAL 5, 16–17 (Brown ed. 1958).

409. *But see* Pfeffer, *supra* note 407, at 96–97. See also 1 BAYLOR L. REV. 79, 81 (1948).

410. Braunfeld v. Brown, 366 U.S. 599, 605 (1961).

411. To adopt this free exercise rationale, see text accompanying note 405 *supra*, would be tantamount to saying that the free exercise rights of indigent Roman Catholics would be denied by the state's failure to provide free parochial schools.

412. Fahy, *Religion, Education, and the Supreme Court*, 14 LAW & CONTEMP. PROB. 73, 84–85 (1949).

413. PFEFFER, *op. cit. supra* note 372, at 289.

414. Braunfeld v. Brown, 366 U.S. 599, 604 (1961). Even here, the Court has stated that this is not an absolute test for determining free exercise clause violations. 366 U.S. at 605. See text accompanying notes 351–52 *supra*.

415. 366 U.S. at 605. See also Pfeffer, *supra* note 407, at 96.

416. 366 U.S. at 606. See also Note, 61 YALE L.J. 410–11 (1952).

one or all religions or is to discriminate invidiously between religions . . . ." If it were, the free exercise clause might be violated.[417] Rather, the purpose and effect is to prevent a violation of the establishment clause.[418] Since this "nonreligious" purpose would plainly be thwarted by any program of released time, under the standards set forth by the Supreme Court,[419] there is no credence to the contention that any person's free exercise rights are denied by the exclusion of released time programs.[420]

Another aspect of the argument based on *Pierce* deals with the matter of compulsion. The rationale articulated by the Court in striking down the program in *McCollum* was that "the operation of the State's compulsory education system . . . assists and is integrated with the program of religious instruction carried on by separate religious sects. Pupils compelled by law to go to school for secular education are released in part from their legal duty upon the condition that they attend the religious classes. This is beyond all question a utilization of the tax-established and tax-supported public school system to aid religious groups to spread their faith."[421] The Court concluded that, by the system, "the State . . . affords sectarian groups an invaluable aid in that it helps to provide pupils for their religious classes through use of the State's compulsory public school machinery. This is not separation of Church and State."[422] The argument advanced is that if the *McCollum* plan was defective because it conditioned absence from the public school upon attendance at religious classes, then, *a fortiori*, the parochial school attendance upheld in *Pierce* is also constitutionally defective for precisely the same reason, for it permits children to satisfy the compulsory school attendance law by attending religious classes.[423] Both arrangements produce attend-

---

417. See 366 U.S. at 607.
418. *Cf.* 366 U.S. at 609.
419. If the nonreligious purpose (preventing an establishment clause violation) could be accomplished by means that do not impose an indirect burden on religious observance (exclusion of released time programs may be said to impose such a burden, see text accompanying note 416 *supra*), the Court has indicated that failure to employ the alternative means would violate the free exercise clause. Braunfeld v. Brown, 366 U.S. 599, 607 (1961).
420. *Accord,* Kauper, *supra* note 402, at 848.
421. Illinois *ex rel.* McCollum v. Board of Educ., 333 U.S. 203, 209–10 (1948).
422. 333 U.S. at 212.
423. See Zorach v. Clauson, 303 N.Y. 161, 173–74, 100 N.E.2d 463, 468–69 (1951); Corwin, *supra* note 405, at 20; Meiklejohn, *Educational Cooperation Between Church and State,* 14 LAW & CONTEMP. PROB. 61, 67–68 (1949); Sullivan, *supra* note 383, at 109; 22 So. CAL. L. REV. 423, 440 (1949).

ance at religious classes by discharging parents from their obligation under the compulsory school provisions. "It is not merely fanciful or frivolous to suggest that [*Pierce*] . . . represents one hundred percent released time."[424]

This line of argument is not wholly unpersuasive. If *McCollum* were based on nothing more than the compulsory education law, it would seem to jeopardize *Pierce*. Or if the main thrust of *McCollum* were that truancy regulations were enforced by reports of attendance at religious classes being made to the public school[425] and that "knowledge that an official record is kept of his attendance necessarily places pressure on the child—accustomed as he is to the discipline of school—to attend these religious classes,"[426] then again the system upheld in *Pierce* might seem to be faulty.

But, even accepting the validity of these bases, the situations are distinguishable. Under the system of released time, the only alternative to remaining in the public school is to attend religious classes. This is not the case in the *Pierce* context. There, children who were excused from public school attendance had a broader range of alternatives; they could attend any accredited private school as well as parochial school.[427] A true analogy between released time and the situation in *Pierce* would exist only if religious classes were but one of several desirable choices available to students.[428] A school board program that would permit students to be released for a certain period of time each week on condition that they attend one of a group of extra-curricular education classes—for example, classes in music, art, religion, drama[429]— might well be valid under the establishment clause.[430] Indeed, the reasoning of one noted commentator suggests that the exclu-

---

424. Kauper, *supra* note 402, at 841.
425. See Illinois *ex rel.* McCollum v. Board of Educ., 333 U.S. 203, 209 n.5 (1948).
426. Zorach v. Clauson, 303 N.Y. 161, 188, 100 N.E.2d 463, 477 (1951) (dissenting opinion).
427. The case itself was prosecuted by both a parochial school and a military training school.
428. Here, again, the question of legislative motive becomes relevant. See note 343 *supra*.
429. "Released time as now practiced had its origin in Gary, Indiana, in 1913 when the Superintendent of Schools directed the dismissal of children an hour earlier one day of each week to enable them to pursue their individual interests such as religion, music or art." Pfeffer, *Religion, Education and the Constitution*, 8 LAW. GUILD REV. 387, 396–97 (1948).
430. The New York courts have upheld released time programs on this basis. People *ex rel.* Lewis v. Graves, 219 App. Div. 233, 239, 219 N.Y. Supp. 189, 195–96, *aff'd*, 245 N.Y. 195, 198, 156 N.E. 663, 664 (1927). See also Cushman, *The Holy Bible and the Public Schools*, 40 CORNELL L.Q. 475, 494 (1955).

sion of religious education as one of the alternatives would violate constitutionally protected religious freedom.[431] Most importantly in regard to the proposed constitutional standard, the difference that might make this program valid is that the provision of attractive alternatives to religious education would remove the inherently coercive element in released time. Students who were religious nonconformists and students with marginal beliefs would not be faced with the choice of either receiving religious instruction, which would compromise or influence their conscientious scruples, or being regarded as "oddballs."[432] They could join with those of their friends of the religious majority who preferred to study art, music, or drama rather than religion.[433] It may be that by instituting such a program, more children would attend religious classes than would be the case otherwise. This is undoubtedly the result of the decision in *Pierce*.[434] But, despite the fact that this represents aid to religion, the absence of coercion calls for a favorable constitutional judgment under the proposed constitutional standard. State action of this nature may be fairly characterized as merely an "accommodation."[435]

However, there is a more compelling distinction between the *Pierce* situation and released time, again based on compulsion. Regardless of the presence of alternative choices, no child of a minority religious faith (or of no faith at all) feels *compelled* to attend a parochial school simply because, under the *Pierce* case, the government must permit him to do so. But, in the released time situation, nonconforming pupils do feel compelled to accept religious instruction, thus compromising their conscientious beliefs.[436] This last argument has been rejected on the ground that

431. Kurland, *supra* note 403, at 5.
432. Those children of minority religious faiths who choose to go home to receive religious instruction from their parents, a plan suggested by the counsel for the school board in *Zorach*, would be just as "oddballish" as those who were forced to remain in school because their parents had no religion to impart to them. See PFEFFER, *op. cit. supra* note 372, at 355.
433. In light of the fact that only about half of the public school population would accept religious education without a program of released time, see note 380 *supra*, if attractive alternatives to religious education were available to released students, it is most likely that many religious conformists would accompany the dissenters to the nonreligious classes.
434. It is obvious that if the Court had upheld the statute in *Pierce*, parochial school attendance would be diminished.
435. See text accompanying notes 463–72 *infra*.
436. It might be argued that by the Supreme Court's action in *Pierce*, removing any legal impediment to full time parochial education, the clergy was left free to exert strenuous pressures on their parishioners to send their children to parochial schools and that, in this way, governmental action resulted in private pressures being brought to bear on those

it "is based on the premise that the public school represents a kind of involuntary imprisonment, release from which may be effected by attending religious education classes,"[437] and that it may not "be accepted as an unquestioned proposition of fact that religious instruction is so attractive and public school education so repressive that parents and children will invariably respond by choosing to escape the public school classroom."[438] This is not the premise advanced here. The inherent compulsion does not necessarily arise from the unattractiveness of the public school, but from the urge of the nonconforming students, who would otherwise be left behind, to join the group. Thus, released time is a solely religious activity that is likely to result in compromising and influencing religious beliefs.

Of course, if it could be shown that in those schools that have adopted released time[439] there is majority nonparticipation, it would be difficult to maintain that those students who remain behind will be considered "oddballs" by their colleagues. As a practical matter, it would seem that unless a large proportion of the school were "willing" to participate, the program would be discontinued.[440] For the most part, the available statistics bear out the assumption that most children attend.[441] Those involved in the program have stated that "the enrollment of 90 to 99 percent of the public school constituency in the weekday church school is quite common. To reach less than 80 percent is the excep-

---

members of the faith with marginal convictions, thus influencing the freedom of religious participation; this then would be no different than that aspect of released time. This argument may be rebutted by pointing out that the *Pierce* decision was dictated by a serious free exercise claim: since the Roman Catholic religion demands that its children attend parochial schools, the Oregon statute was in direct conflict with the religious practice. See text accompanying notes 479–81 *infra*. It has already been pointed out that denial of released time presents no comparable free exercise claim. See generally text accompanying notes 410–20 *supra*. Thus, although released time must be characterized as a solely religious activity, the purpose of the decision in *Pierce* may be fairly characterized as "nonreligious."

437. Kauper, *supra* note 402, at 839.
438. *Ibid.*
439. A recent survey indicates that about 30% of American public schools have released time programs. Dierenfield, *The Extent of Religious Influence in American Public Schools*, 56 RELIGIOUS EDUCATION 173, 177 (1961).
440. In fact, this often happens. See PFEFFER, *op. cit. supra* note 372, at 336–37.
441. There appear to be no published national statistics on the percentage of participation in those schools that do have released time programs. See generally *id.* at 317–21.

tion."[442] Reports from such cities as Spokane, Washington,[443] Champaign, Illinois,[444] Salina, Kansas,[445] and Van Wert, Ohio,[446] confirm this. On the other hand, some schools in Berkeley, California,[447] Mount Vernon, New York,[448] Minneapolis,[449] and Chicago[450] report minority participation. Released time should nonetheless be invalid in most of those schools with minority participation because of the consequences of the unpleasant atmosphere that exists for those pupils, many of them members of the religious majorities, who remain. Educators have complained that one of the major problems involved in the administration of released time programs is what to do with the nonparticipants.[451] The dilemma facing them is that if special programs or normal educational activities are conducted, this in effect penalizes those who attend religious classes; on the other hand, it is unfair to the nonparticipants "to keep them occupied solely with 'busy' work."[452] If the latter course is taken, an unattractive environment is produced for those left behind, thereby influencing attendance at religious classes. Furthermore, if regular school courses are continued, although the religious school may be intrinsically no more attractive than the public school, it is likely that the mere opportunity to change environment and "escape from the classroom and school routine"[453] will act as an incentive to students to go elsewhere. These being the less attractive alternatives available in the public schools, the solely religious program of released time will likely influence the student with marginal re-

---

442. Dr. W. Dyer Blair, Director of the Department of Weekday Religious Education of the International Council of Religious Education, in 1940, quoted in *id.* at 335.
443. "In most instances . . . there are but few children remaining." Perry v. School Dist. No. 81, 54 Wash. 2d 886, 889, 344 P.2d 1036, 1038 (1959).
444. See text accompanying note 103 *supra*.
445. 95%. JACKSON & MALMBERG, *op. cit. supra* note 382, at 50.
446. 81–96%. *Ibid.*
447. Just over 25%. See Nelson, *The Fourth "R" —Religion—In Education*, 51 RELIGIOUS EDUCATION 40, 41 (1956).
448. Over 25%. See Larson, *A Superintendent Looks at the Week-day School of Religion*, 51 RELIGIOUS EDUCATION 43 (1956).
449. Overall, about 50%. But individual schools vary from 12 to 94%. A majority of them are above 50%. Greater Minneapolis Council of Churches, Comparison of Weekday Church School Enrollment with Public School Enrollment, Nov. 13–17, 1961.
450. Less than 10%. See PFEFFER, CHURCH, STATE, AND FREEDOM 348 (1953).
451. See Nelson, *supra* note 447, at 41.
452. PFEFFER, *op. cit. supra* note 450, at 325.
453. Note, 52 COLUM. L. REV. 1033, 1038 (1952). See also Cushman, *supra* note 430, at 496.

ligious beliefs to attend religious classes—something he would not otherwise do.

The same cannot be said for a program of dismissed time, "the system under which, on one or more days, the public school is closed earlier [or opened later][454] than usual, and all children are dismissed, with the expectation—but not the requirement —that some will use the dismissed period for participation in religious instruction."[455] It is no surprise, therefore, that there is general agreement, even among those who find released time unconstitutional, that dismissed time is valid.[456] True, such a program will probably result in greater attendance at religious classes than would otherwise occur.[457] Moreover, it might be demonstrated that the school board's purpose in early closing was solely religious.[458] Nevertheless, the element of state-caused compulsion is absent. Students are not faced with the publicly imposed choice of either going to religious school or remaining behind in an unenticing setting. If they choose to attend religious classes, they will do so in preference to other equally alluring, and, in many cases, more than equally alluring, alternatives.[459] Perhaps dissenters will nonetheless be subject to pressures from their conforming colleagues who choose to attend religious classes,[460] but this would exist even if the schools closed at the regular hour. Unlike the case of released time, the coercion may not be attributed to governmental action.[461] The argument has been made that a

---

454. See City of New Haven v. Town of Torrington, 132 Conn. 194, 197, 43 A.2d 455, 457 (1945).
455. PFEFFER, op. cit. supra note 450, at 315.
456. Zorach v. Clauson, 303 N.Y. 161, 190, 100 N.E.2d 463, 478 (1951) (Fuld, J., dissenting); Cushman, *Public Support of Religious Education in American Constitutional Law*, 45 ILL. L. REV. 333, 354, 356 (1950); Sullivan, *Religious Education in the Schools*, 14 LAW & CONTEMP. PROB. 92, 93 (1949); Note, 52 COLUM. L. REV. 1033, 1039 (1952); Comment, 43 ILL. L. REV. 374, 386 (1948); 46 MICH. L. REV. 828, 829-30 (1948); 27 TEXAS L. REV. 256, 259 (1948); Note, 57 YALE L.J. 1114, 1119 (1948).
457. See Katz, *Freedom of Religion and State Neutrality*, 20 U. CHI. L. REV. 426, 439 (1953).
458. A decision to hold the school picnic on Sunday *afternoon*, so as to enable those students who wish to go to church to do so, seems to have a solely religious purpose. But since this action does not inherently compel church attendance, it could not be said to violate the establishment clause under the proposed standard.
459. "[R]eligion can compete more successfully with arithmetic than with recreation." Note, 57 YALE L.J. 1114, 1119 (1948).
460. See generally 31 TEXAS L. REV. 329 (1953).
461. Query if the same could be said if the public school rented its premises for religious classes to commence immediately following the end of the public school day. Would not the coercive pressures here be attributable to the school board's action? See note 137 *supra*.

dismissed time plan "could not be used *if* the effect of the dismissal were to make the total time in school less than that required as compulsory attendance."[462] This would be irrelevant under the proposed consitutional standard because it has no bearing on the matter of compulsion. In any case, it is difficult to determine what merit the argument has since the required time for school attendance could easily be reduced.

There has been much discussion, particularly with reference to released time and other religious infiltration in the public schools, about the state's assuming a role of "neutrality" in this conflict and about the state's making an "accommodation" between the competing interests.[463] While this may have an abstract appeal, it does not adequately substitute for analysis under a principled standard.[464] The New York courts have upheld the constitutionality of the Regents' prayer[465] and released time[466] on this basis. Professor Kauper, a most articulate advocate for the constitutional validity of released time, agrees that it aids religion, but justifies it as a "reasonable accommodation."[467] It is true that "in matters of public education due respect for the democratic process should

---

462. Cosway & Toepfer, *Religion and the Schools*, 17 U. CINC. L. REV. 117, 141 (1948).
463. See, *e.g.*, 9 U.C.L.A.L. REV. 495, 501 & n.30 (1962) and authorities cited therein.
464. Professor Robert F. Cushman calls for "a doctrine of state neutrality." Cushman, *supra* note 430, at 490. He argues that "if all social groups, without regard to purpose, were allowed to come into the schools and conduct meetings which the students could attend, religious groups, since they are social groups, would be included." Perhaps so. But under this same principle, it would be valid for the Community Sandlot Baseball League, the Model Railroad Club (two of Cushman's examples, *id.* at 491), and the Roman Catholic Church (my example) to come into the public schools to prosyletize for members. Professor Philip Kurland's "neutral principle of equality" would appear to call for the same result. Kurland, *Of Church and State and the Supreme Court*, 29 U. CHI. L. REV. 1, 4–5 (1961). Under the principle proposed in this article, the establishment clause would forbid the inclusion of the Church. There is nothing in the Constitution prohibiting the use of the public schools for Little League proselyting; the first amendment stands in the way of any religion doing the same thing. Nor would the prohibition violate the free exercise clause under any Supreme Court interpretation of it. At most, this would be "only an indirect burden on the exercise of religion." Braunfeld v. Brown, 366 U.S. 599, 606 (1961). See generally text accompanying notes 415–20 *supra*.
465. Engel v. Vitale, 18 Misc. 2d 659, 694, 191 N.Y.S.2d 453, 491 (Sup. Ct. 1959).
466. Lewis v. Spaulding, 193 Misc. 66, 73, 85 N.Y.S.2d 682, 690 (Sup. Ct. 1948).
467. Kauper, *Church, State, and Freedom: A Review*, 52 MICH. L. REV. 829, 841 (1954). See also Kauper, *Released Time and Religious Liberty: A Further Reply*, 53 MICH. L. REV. 233, 236 (1954).

permit some discretion to the community in shaping its educational policies,"[468] and that "the interest of parents in the religious education of their children is a legitimate legislative concern."[469] Dismissed time satisfies these appeals. Professor Kauper agrees that "no actual pressure [should be] placed on any student to attend classes in religious education."[470] But he states that "a proper sense of concern for the non-participant does not require rejection of the [released time] program on constitutional grounds,"[471] since "it remains to be demonstrated that the optional released time privilege deprives anyone of [religious liberty]."[472] Hopefully, it has been demonstrated here.

1. *Excusing Children for Religious Holidays*

The argument has often been advanced[473] that excusing children from the public schools for observance of their particular religious holidays is merely an "instance of released time but on a smaller scale,"[474] and, therefore, this practice stands or falls with released time. But there are many distinguishing features. Released time is inherently coercive because it operates to single out the nonconformists *against their will* and compels them to attend religious classes *against their will*. When children are excused from classes on religious holidays, they *ask* to be singled out because they *wish* to attend religious services. Assuming that the public school act of excusing them has a solely religious purpose, the act is requested by the religious nonconformists themselves.

In the case of released time, majority participation works to coerce minority attendance. Minority participation usually results in the practice of excusing children for religious holidays since the public schools ordinarily close on the majority's religious holidays.[475] However, for the same reasons that operated in the re-

---

468. Kauper, *Church, State, and Freedom: A Review, supra* note 467, at 839.
469. Kauper, *Released Time and Religious Liberty: A Further Reply, supra* note 467, at 236.
470. Kauper, *Church, State, and Freedom: A Review, supra* note 467, at 842.
471. *Ibid.*
472. Kauper, *Released Time and Religious Liberty: A Further Reply, supra* note 467, at 236. See also Katz, *supra* note 457, at 439.
473. Zorach v. Clauson, 343 U.S. 306, 313 (1952); Zorach v. Clauson, 303 N.Y. 161, 173, 100 N.E.2d 463, 468 (1951); 20 FORDHAM L. REV. 328, 331 (1951); Brief for Intervenors-Respondents, p. 43, Engel v. Vitale, 370 U.S. 421 (1962).
474. Kauper, *Church, State, and Freedom: A Review, supra* note 467, at 840.
475. Professor Kurland would probably also distinguish these situations, but on other grounds. Since released time makes only religious education

leased time context, it may be that permitting children of religious minorities to be excused from the public school to attend religious services will likely influence students of these religious minorities with marginal beliefs to attend the church or synagogue of their faith.[476] Nonetheless, the situations are distinguishable because, while it has been shown that there is no colorable claim that denial of released time infringes on rights under the free exercise clause,[477] denying children of minority religious faiths their wish to attend holiday religious services does raise a serious free exercise question.[478] Even those who have argued that the two situations are otherwise similar recognize this difference.[479] Attendance at religious services is often an act demanded by one's religion. By the public schools' refusal to permit such attendance, the student faces the choice of either violating his religious principles or receiving whatever penalties the school chooses to impose. The Supreme Court has not held that, in a situation of this nature, the free exercise claim must prevail, but it has recognized that "in such cases, to make accommodation between the religious action and an exercise of state authority is a particularly delicate task."[480] The free exercise claim here does appear to be quite substantial and persuasive because it can hardly be said that a student's action in absenting himself from school for one day is "in violation of important social duties or subversive of good order."[481] For

---

available, he would likely find it invalid because "it is . . . forbidden the state to confer favors [only] upon religious activity." Kurland, *Of Church and State and the Supreme Court*, 29 U. CHI. L. REV. 1, 5 (1961). Since pupils may be excused from the public schools for many reasons (*e.g.*, funerals, dental appointments), he would likely say that the first amendment *demands* that they also be excused for religious holidays because "inhibitions [may] not be placed by the state on [only] religious activity." *Ibid.* However, it would seem that if the public school forbade absence for *all* extracurricular activities, Professor Kurland's thesis not only would permit the schools to deny excusing children for religious observances, but would actually forbid the schools from granting it. Since there is a substantial and persuasive, albeit not conclusive, free exercise argument for granting children absence from the public schools to observe their religious holidays, see text accompanying notes 478–81 *infra,* one might well disagree with this last point. See LOCKHART, KAMISAR & CHOPER, SUPPLEMENT TO DODD'S CASES ON CONSTITUTIONAL LAW 399 (1962).

476. Of course, if there is majority participation, inherent coercion will exist.

477. See text accompanying notes 414–20 *supra*.

478. See Zorach v. Clauson, 303 N.Y. 161, 191–92, 100 N.E.2d 463, 479 (1951) (Fuld, J., dissenting); Cosway & Toepfer, *Religion and the Schools*, 17 U. CINC. L. REV. 117, 141 (1948).

479. Zorach v. Clauson, 303 N.Y. 161, 173, 100 N.E.2d 463, 468 (1951); Kauper, *Church, State, and Freedom: A Review, supra* note 467, at 840, 848.

480. Braunfeld v. Brown, 366 U.S. 599, 605 (1961).

481. 366 U.S. at 603.

these reasons, the establishment clause may well permit a state to excuse children from school for religious observances despite the influence it may have on them and other pupils. No comparable "nonreligious" justification exists for released time.[482]

2. *Shared Time*

The newly adopted program of "shared time,"[483] under which parochial school students come to the public schools each day to take certain secular classes, merits brief consideration. As presently constituted, the plan involves a relatively small number of Catholic students[484] joining their public school associates for a few hours each day. There would seem to be no constitutional objection under the proposed constitutional standard in these circumstances, since the activity may not be characterized as being solely religious and it is unlikely that public school students will feel compelled to join their Catholic colleagues when the latter return to the parochial school.[485]

One might suggest that, since the experience over the years with released time has revealed teachers' persistent application of direct pressures on pupils to attend religious classes, despite the fact that teachers have been specifically prohibited from so doing,[486] the program is inherently subject to abuse and, therefore, unconstitutional.[487] However, we need not go this far. Despite the warning that "the critical constitutional issues with respect to released time cannot be solved by any play of language in using the word 'compulsion,'"[488] it is submitted that this solely religious activity should fail, principally for that reason.

D. TEACHERS WEARING RELIGIOUS GARB

Next to Bible reading, the issue involving religious infusion in the public schools probably most often brought before the state courts is whether the schools may employ teachers who wear religious garb.[489] The reason commonly given for the invalidity of

---

482. *Cf.* note 436 *supra*.
483. Philadelphia Inquirer, Sept. 5, 1962, p. 25, col. 1.
484. About 10% of those in attendance in the public school. *Ibid.*
485. The question of whether this program constitutes unconstitutional financial aid to parochial schools is beyond the scope of this article.
486. For extensive documentation, see PFEFFER, CHURCH, STATE, AND FREEDOM 356–67 (1953); Note, 61 YALE L.J. 405, 412–13 (1952).
487. See Note, 52 COLUM. L. REV. 1033, 1038 (1952).
488. Kauper, *Released Time and Religious Liberty: A Further Reply*, 53 MICH. L. REV. 233, 236 (1954).
489. "A recent survey showed that members of religious orders in

this practice is that "the distinctive garbs, so exclusively peculiar to the Roman Catholic Church, create a religious atmosphere in the schoolroom. They have a subtle influence upon the tender minds being taught and trained by the nuns. In and of themselves they proclaim the Catholic Church and the representative character of the teachers in the schoolroom. They silently promulgate sectarianism."[490]

There is by no means the same general consensus on this point, however, as there is about those practices previously discussed. The pressures on the religiously nonconforming child that are created by his failure to join his colleagues in a particular activity are absent here. Nor can it be said here, as it was in connection with Bible reading, that by engaging teachers who wear religious garb, the state influences the student's freedom of conscientious choice by placing its "stamp of approval" on the Roman Catholic faith. It should be clear to students in the upper grades that when public school teachers are employed, the state approves only of their intellectual qualifications; the state does not endorse their sex, political beliefs, or religious affiliations any more than it sanctions the clothes that they wear or the street on which they live. As to those students in the lower grades, it would seem that any influence of the religious garb would not differ substantially from that produced by the pupils' knowledge of their teacher's religious devotion acquired elsewhere—from statements the teacher has made, from religious insignia the teacher wears, or from general community information.[491] The evidence that this practice is likely to compromise religious beliefs or influence conscientious choice is not very strong.

Even if the evidence were more convincing, the practice of permitting teachers to wear religious garb in the schools would not violate the establishment clause under the proposed constitutional standard unless it could be fairly characterized as solely religious. The practice has been defended on the ground "that to prohibit

---

religious garb were employed as teachers to some extent in the public schools of sixteen states and territories." Fahy, *Religion, Education, and the Supreme Court*, 14 LAW & CONTEMP. PROB. 73, 89 (1949).

490. Rawlings v. Butler, 290 S.W.2d 801, 809 (Ky. 1956) (dissenting opinion). See also Zellers v. Huff, 55 N.M. 501, 523–25, 236 P.2d 947, 963–65 (1951); O'Connor v. Hendrick, 184 N.Y. 421, 428, 77 N.E. 612, 614 (1906); O'Connor v. Hendrick, 109 App. Div. 361, 371–72, 96 N.Y. Supp. 161, 169 (1905); Cosway & Toepfer, *Religion and the Schools*, 17 U. CINC. L. REV. 117, 138 (1948); Comment, 22 U. CHI. L. REV. 888, 893–94 (1955).

491. See Hysong v. Gallitzin Borough School Dist., 164 Pa. 629, 657, 30 Atl. 482, 484 (1894); Harpster, *Religion, Education and the Law*, 36 MARQ. L. REV. 24, 54–55 (1952).

a teaching Sister from wearing the garb would infringe the free exercise of religion."[492] If this premise is valid, it would seem to be a "nonreligious" justification for the practice. However, while it is quite clear that the Constitution prohibits state discrimination against its employees on the basis of religion,[493] it is not clear that the free exercise clause requires the state to permit its teachers to do anything that their religion demands.[494] Aside from the fact that barring teachers who wear religious garb from the public schools would constitute only a rather minor disability,[495] there is some indication that Catholic Sisters may receive dispensation to wear lay clothing while teaching in the public schools.[496] These being the facts, if further research revealed that the wearing of religious garb was likely to act as a compromising or influencing factor, it seems doubtful that the free exercise clause could be read to prohibit a state from barring religious garb from the public schools.[497] If this be true, the wearing of the garb in the schools might fairly be characterized as a solely religious practice.

In any case, if it is found that the practice is influential or coercive, it may be that the establishment clause is violated despite the activity's arguably secular foundation. The secular objective (qualified teachers) may be attained just as well by employing those who do not wear religious garb and, by so doing, the objectionable effects would be eliminated.[498] As of now, the factual premises remain unproven.

The fact that Roman Catholic Sisters contribute their net income from public school teaching to the church should have no bearing whatever on the constitutional validity of the practice.[499] Persons should be able to spend their income for any legal purpose. In fact, the argument may well be made that "to deny the right to make such contribution would in itself constitute a denial of that right of religious liberty which the Constitution guarantees."[500]

---

492. Fahy, *supra* note 489, at 90. *But see* Commonwealth v. Herr, 229 Pa. 132, 78 Atl. 68 (1910); Comment, 22 U. CHI. L. REV. 888, 894 (1955).
493. See Wieman v. Updegraff, 344 U.S. 183, 191–92 (1952); United Pub. Workers v. Mitchell, 330 U.S. 75, 100 (1947).
494. Query if the state could not bar a teacher whose religious faith required that she proselyte while teaching. See Harfst v. Hoegen, 349 Mo. 808, 816, 163 S.W.2d 609, 614 (1942).
495. See text accompanying note 410 *supra*.
496. It has been granted in New York and North Dakota. AMERICAN CIVIL LIBERTIES UNION, 41ST ANNUAL REPORT 28–29 (1961).
497. See generally Braunfeld v. Brown, 366 U.S. 599, 603–07 (1961).
498. See text following note 346 *supra*.
499. Rawlings v. Butler, 290 S.W.2d 801, 806 (Ky. 1956); Zellers v. Huff, 55 N.M. 501, 522, 236 P.2d 949, 961–62 (1951); Hysong v. Gallitzen Borough School Dist., 164 Pa. 629, 656–57, 30 Atl. 482, 483–84 (1894).
500. Gerhardt v. Heid, 66 N.D. 444, 460, 267 N.W. 127, 135 (1936).

The whole discussion of this subject has dealt only with the single practice of teachers wearing religious garb. The result suggested here may be different if the totality of the circumstances in the public school environment, of which the teacher's attire is merely one element, is likely to compromise or influence the conscientious convictions of the students.[501]

E. DISTRIBUTION OF BIBLES

In a recent survey of over 2,000 public school superintendents throughout the country, over 40 percent admitted that the distribution of Gideon Bibles to students was permitted through their schools.[502] This practice is unquestionably solely religious,[503] and the only two cases considering the problem that have reached the appellate level have found it to be in violation of the establishment clause.[504]

There should be no dispute that the King James version of the Bible, which is the version distributed by the Gideons, is objectionable to a large number of religious faiths, and that the scruples of Roman Catholic children will be compromised by receipt of a copy.[505] However, one might agree that this activity is, at best, mildly compulsive on the objectors as compared with some of those programs previously discussed.[506] Consider the situation in *Engel*; it would seem much less likely that a child, during the prayer recitation, would leave the room to stand outside with nothing to do,[507] than that he would decline acceptance of a Bible. This would seem particularly true when the procedures for acquisition of the Bible were carefully drafted so as to avoid the singling

---

501. See Note, 22 U. CHI. L. REV. 888, 890 (1955); text accompanying notes 560–63 *infra*.
502. Dierenfield, *The Extent of Religious Influence in American Public Schools*, 56 RELIGIOUS EDUCATION 173, 175 (1961).
503.
  The Gideons International is a nonprofit corporation . . . whose object is "to win men and women for the Lord Jesus Christ, through . . . (c) placing the Bible—God's Holy Words—or portions thereof in hotels, hospitals, schools, institutions, and also through the distribution of same for personal use."
Tudor v. Board of Educ., 14 N.J. 31, 33, 100 A.2d 857, 858 (1953).
504. Brown v. Orange County Bd. of Pub. Instruction, 128 So. 2d 181 (Fla. Dist. Ct. App. 1960); Tudor v. Board of Educ., 14 N.J. 31, 100 A.2d 857 (1953).
505. See text accompanying note 271 *supra*.
506. See Levy, *Views From the Wall—Reflections on Church-State Relationships*, 29 HENNEPIN LAW. 51, 55–56 (1961).
507. In fact, no child requested such permission although it had been provided for. Brief for Petitioners, p. 31, Engel v. Vitale, 370 U.S. 421 (1962).

out of nonconformists.[508] Nonetheless, there has been expert testimony that the program, as administered, generated pressures to conform.[509] If this factual premise remains unshaken, under the proposed constitutional standard the practice must cease.

F. SCHOOL CREDIT FOR OUTSIDE RELIGIOUS INSTRUCTION

It has been reported that "in a number of communities the public school—generally at the high school level—will give credit toward graduation for religious instruction obtained after public school hours or during week ends under the auspices of the child's church."[510] The purpose and effect of this program—sectarian indoctrination—is solely religious. If those students who do not participate will have to spend extra time in the public school acquiring these credits while the participants are dismissed, this program is no different from released time. Nonparticipants will be conspicuous and, if in the religious minorities, will be subject to pressures to compromise their beliefs. If there is only minority participation, the opportunity to avoid public school routine will likely influence free religious choice. But despite the unquestioned aid that religion would receive, these results would not follow if the public school arranged its schedule so that all students, regardless of whether they participated in outside religious classes, remained in school during the entire school day. Furthermore, if the school were to give credit for a number of extra-curricular educational courses that were of generally equal attractiveness, all pressures and incentives would seem to be removed, and the program should pass the proposed constitutional standard.

The fact that some time of public school administrators and teachers may be taken in insuring that the instruction is being taken by the students and being given by qualified personnel must be excused as *de minimis*.[511] However, if the public schools insist on examining and grading the students on the basis of what they have learned,[512] the program should probably be invalid. In such cases, pupils whose religious beliefs differ from those of the public school teacher will very likely be tempted to learn what they

---

508. In *Tudor*, parents simply had to sign a permission slip. Children whose parents had signed reported to a room "at the close of the session." No other students were present. No reason was to be stated when the announcement calling the students was made. 14 N.J. at 34–35, 100 A.2d at 858–59.
509. 14 N.J. at 50–52, 100 A.2d at 867–68.
510. PFEFFER, CHURCH, STATE, AND FREEDOM 305 (1953).
511. See text accompanying notes 141–47 *supra*.
512. *Cf.* State *ex rel.* Dearle v. Frazier, 102 Wash. 369, 173 Pac. 35 (1918).

believe will be generally acceptable or at least to assert this for examination purposes. Such a compromising element should be barred.

G. BACCALAUREATE AND GRADUATION

Baccalaureate exercises, under public school auspices, are widespread[513] and have divided communities "with bitter conflict and tension."[514] Many of these programs are "occasions to impart spiritual truths"[515] and ordinarily include all the elements of a Protestant church service—processional hymn, invocation prayer, choral hymns, Bible reading, address by a clergyman, benediction prayer, and recessional hymn.[516] These must be fairly characterized as solely religious activities whether the service is held on public school or church property. Certain faiths, particularly the Roman Catholic, forbid participation in exercises of this kind.[517] Although nonparticipation is often permitted,[518] it would likely be ineffective as far as inherent compulsion is concerned for reasons previously discussed.[519] Thus, since participation would directly compromise some students' religious scruples, the establishment clause would be violated under the proposed constitutional standard.[520] Of course, this would neither bar the individual churches from conducting baccalaureate services for members of their own faith nor prevent the public schools from having a nonreligious assembly program that is called a baccalaureate.

---

513. Almost 87% of school superintendents polled stated that the activity was engaged in in their school systems. Dierenfield, *The Extent of Religious Influence in American Public Schools*, 56 RELIGIOUS EDUCATION 173, 175 (1961).
514. Boyer, *Religious Education of Public School Pupils in Wisconsin*, 1953 WIS. L. REV. 181, 196.
515. Sample comment by public school supervisor, quoted in Dierenfield, *supra* note 513, at 179.
516. See PFEFFER, CHURCH, STATE, AND FREEDOM 418 (1953). See also Rosenfield, *Separation of Church and State in the Public Schools*, 22 U. PITT. L. REV. 561, 573 (1961).
517. Boyer, *supra* note 514 at 196, 205.
518. See Chamberlin v. Dade County School Bd., 17 Fla. Supp. 183, 197 (Cir. Ct. 1961). However, in West Virginia and Pennsylvania, recent instances are reported in which nonparticipating Catholic students were denied public awarding of their diplomas. See AMERICAN CIVIL LIBERTIES UNION, 37TH ANNUAL REPORT 64 (1957); PFEFFER, *op. cit. supra* note 516, at 420.
519. However, it may be argued that the pressures on a nonconforming student to attend a single program are virtually nonexistent, especially when compared to the pressures generated to participate in an activity that occurs every day or once each week.
520. An opinion of the Attorney General of the state of Washington, April 20, 1962, agrees. See Jurisdictional Statement, p. 18, Chamberlin v. Dade County Bd. of Pub. Instruction, *appeal docketed*, 31 U.S.L. WEEK 3139 (U.S. Oct. 15, 1962)(No. 520).

There have been several reports of public schools conducting their graduation exercises in church buildings.[521] It this were the only available site for the occasion,[522] it would be difficult to argue that this is a solely religious practice. Moreover, if this be the fact, the alternative argument for establishment clause violation is likewise inadmissible;[523] despite any religious objections to the practice, the secular objective of having a suitable building may not be attained by alternative means.

Graduation invocations delivered by clergymen present a somewhat different problem. This part of the graduation program must be considered as solely religious despite efforts to make it nonsectarian. But there are several reasons why this program may be defended under the proposed constitutional standard. Research has not revealed that listening to the invocation is contrary to anyone's religious or conscientious beliefs. If this is true, the practice could not possibly result in compromising any student's conscientious scruples. And even if there were some objection, the atmosphere is not conducive to inherent compulsion to attend the invocation. The dissenting pupil need not absent himself from the entire program, and he will likely have the comfort of his parents' and relatives' presence and will be in the midst of many people outside his peer group.[524] Finally, the fact that this is but a small segment of a program that a student attends but once makes fairly unpersuasive the "stamp of approval" argument for influencing religious beliefs advanced in connection with daily religious exercises in public school classes.[525]

H. RELIGIOUS INSIGNIA

A North Dakota staute requires "a placard containing the ten commandments of the Christian religion to be displayed in a conspicuous place in every schoolroom, classroom, or other place where classes convene for instruction."[526] Not long ago, a New York school board passed a resolution that a neutral version of the Ten

---

521. See State *ex rel.* Conway v. District Bd., 162 Wis. 482, 156 N.W. 477 (1916); AMERICAN CIVIL LIBERTIES UNION, 34TH ANNUAL REPORT 51 (1954).
522. See Miller v. Cooper, 56 N.M. 355, 244 P.2d 520 (1952).
523. See text following note 346 *supra.*
524. The situation has been accurately compared to an opening of Congress or a presidential inauguration. Committee on Religion and Public Education of the National Council of the Churches of Christ, *Relation of Religion to Public Education—A Study Document,* International J. of Religious Education, Apr. 1960, pp. 21, 29.
525. See State *ex rel.* Conway v. District Bd., 162 Wis. 482, 495, 156 N.W. 477, 481 (1916).
526. N.D. CENT. CODE § 15–47–10 (1960).

Commandments, amalgamating and modifying the Jewish, Catholic, and Protestant versions, be placed in each classroom.[527] There has been a proposal in Massachusetts to place the words "In God We Trust" in every public schoolroom.[528] All of these practices must be fairly characterized as solely religious,[529] and all of these mottoes undoubtedly would be found violative of someone's conscientious scruples.[530] Aside from the fact that they arguably violate the establishment clause because they involve a measurable and perhaps substantial expenditure of public funds solely in aid of religion,[531] it would seem that they would also fail under the standard proposed herein.

The identification of the public schools with these religiously oriented mottoes,[532] constantly in view of immature students with malleable minds and highest regard for the public school institution, is likely to result in influencing or compromising their religious beliefs.[533] This should be contrasted with the placing of a Christmas creche on the public school lawn that "was not erected or displayed while school was in session"[534] and where "no public funds were expended, nor was the time of any public employee involved in its erection or display."[535] The compromising or influencing potential here seems minimal indeed, as it probably also would if the creche were displayed within the school for a few days while classes were in session.[536]

---

527. See Note, 22 ALBANY L. REV. 156 (1958).
528. See AMERICAN CIVIL LIBERTIES UNION, 37TH ANNUAL REPORT 64 (1957).
529. The announced purpose of the New York program "was to strengthen the moral and spiritual values of the students in the school district." See Note, 22 ALBANY L. REV. 156 (1958).
530. See *ibid*. Note that those theses that propose "neutrality" as the constitutional determinant would seem to permit all of these since there is no constitutional bar to other symbols such as the American or state flag or the sign of the Red Cross or Heart Fund. Indeed, this analysis might well permit the permanent erection of a Crucifix or Star of David or of any extremely sectarian motto. See note 464 *supra*.
531. See note 182 *supra;* 3 N.D. CENT. CODE § 15–47–10 (1960): "The superintendent of public instruction may cause such placards to be printed and may charge an amount therefor that will cover the cost of printing and distribution."
532. *Cf.* Note, 49 COLUM. L. REV. 836, 840 (1949).
533. See text accompanying notes 243–46, 291–94 *supra*.
534. Baer v. Kolmorgen, 14 Misc. 2d 1015, 1019, 181 N.Y.S.2d 230, 236 (Sup. Ct. 1958).
535. *Ibid*.
536. See AMERICAN CIVIL LIBERTIES UNION, 39TH ANNUAL REPORT 39 (1959).

I. FLAG PLEDGE AND PATRIOTIC SONGS

In 1954, Congress amended the pledge of allegiance to the flag to include the words "under God." Whether as a general matter this is unconstitutional is not the question to be considered here. Rather, the issue is whether a school board's requirement that the pledge be stated each day in the public schools violates the establishment clause. This is a difficult question when measured by the proposed constitutional standard. If the only purpose and effect of the inclusion of these words is to have the student recognize the existence of God and to inculcate religious beliefs, then the words should be stricken for reasons previously examined. However, it could be argued that this activity is not solely religious; that, unlike the Regents' prayer that required an invocation of the Deity and a supplication to God,[537] the flag pledge merely requires the recitation of an historical fact—that this nation was believed to have been founded "under God" and that most of our people currently believe this still to be the case. The recitation of the flag pledge would then be no different from the recitation of Lincoln's Gettysburg Address which, while involving the mention of God, does not demand that the student swear allegiance to Him but merely requires the student to learn American history. On this characterization, the activity is secular, and, under the proposed standard, the establishment clause would not demand its exclusion. If some student's conscientious beliefs forbid participation,[538] the free exercise clause demands that he be excused.[539] The fact that he may be inherently compelled to participate is unfortunate but irrelevant.[540]

Even accepting this line of argument, the issue may not be fully resolved. The distinction presented is exceedingly subtle, very likely too fine to be perceived by even an above-average student. There is little doubt that the inclusion of the words "under God" in a daily school exercise will result in compromising of some students' conscientious scruples. Therefore, the argument that the establishment clause is violated because the state may accomplish its secular purpose—teaching students that the founding fathers and

---

537. "The 'Regents prayer' is an acknowledgement of our dependence upon Almighty God and a petition for the bestowal of His blessings." Engel v. Vitale, 10 N.Y.2d 174, 180, 176 N.E.2d 579, 581 (1961).

538. Objections have been raised. See Lewis v. Allen, 5 Misc. 2d 68, 159 N.Y.S.2d 807 (Sup. Ct. 1957), aff'd, 11 App. Div. 2d 447, 207 N.Y.S. 2d 862 (1960).

539. West Virginia State Bd. of Educ. v. Barnette, 319 U.S. 624 (1943).

540. See text accompanying notes 118–26 supra.

most citizens believe that this nation exists under God—just as effectively by less obtrusive means is quite forceful.[541]

An even closer question is presented by the public school activity of singing certain songs as part of the daily opening exercises. Some very popular patriotic compositions, such as "God Bless America" and the final stanza of "America,"[542] undeniably involve supplications to the Deity. This is probably true also of any number of songs. Nevertheless, it seems fair to contend that neither the purpose nor the effect of these is solely religious; the thrust of these songs is to instill love of country and not love of God. This argument becomes even more persuasive when the entire content and spirit of the remaining parts of the opening exercises is nonreligious. Perhaps this argument stretches the principle a bit. But even ardent separationists agree that this activity is secular.[543] Therefore, while the free exercise clause may demand the right of nonparticipation for students whose scruples forbid them from taking part, under the proposed standard, the establishment clause does not forbid the practice. The alternative position for establishment clause violation may also be satisfied by the contention that, since these songs have become something of an American tradition, it is doubtful that the state's secular purpose may be achieved *just as effectively* with their elimination. As to the third stanza of "The Star-Spangled Banner,"[544] the analysis above is even more forceful, especially since the words do not involve an invocation to God but are more like the recitation of historical facts.

J. HOLIDAY OBSERVANCE

The commemoration of certain religious holidays is a very com-

---

541. See text following note 346 *supra*.
542.
Our fathers' God! to Thee
Author of Liberty,
To Thee we sing;
Long may our land be bright
With freedom's holy light;
Protect us by Thy might,
Great God, our King!
543. See Pfeffer, *Court, Constitution and Prayer*, 16 RUTGERS L. REV. 735, 750 (1962); *cf.* McCluskey, quoted in THE STUDY OF RELIGION IN THE PUBLIC SCHOOLS: AN APPRAISAL 25 (Brown ed. 1958). See also Sutherland, *Establishment According to Engel*, 76 HARV. L. REV. 25, 38 (1962).
544.
Blest with victory and peace, may the heav'n rescued land
Praise the Power that hath made and preserved us a nation!
Then conquer we must, when our cause it is just,
And this be our motto—"In God is our Trust."

mon public school practice.[545] Many of the forms that this takes may not be fairly characterized as solely religious. Nor do many of these practices lend themselves to student participation. The presence of these two factors would clearly preclude an establishment clause violation under the proposed principle. Thus, the placing of a Christmas tree or an Easter bunny in the public school has virtually no religious significance and, even if it did, its short lived presence, combined with its scant religious import, would seem to have minimal effect.

The singing of religious songs and the staging of religious pageants are entirely another matter. While the tenor of some holiday songs (for example, "White Christmas" and "Jingle Bells") and of some plays (for example, Dickens' "Christmas Carol") is quite clearly associated with our people's culture rather than with their religious beliefs,[546] this cannot fairly be said of those whose language and purport is Christological, devotional, or otherwise religious. The evidence of the inherent compulsion on members of religious minorities to participate in these songs and pageants is substantial. At a school *in which Jewish children were in the majority,* a sixth grade pupil asked to be excused from the singing of Christmas hymns;[547] after class, she "was belabored by her classmates with such epithets as 'Christ-killer who refuses to sing hymns to Jesus Christ.' "[548] In reaction to or in anticipation of such occurrences, "many Jewish children, with the blend of ingenuousness and ingenuity natural to their age, . . . often engage in one or another subterfuge to produce the appearance of cooperation in the school celebration without at the same time genuinely participating in violation of their religious convictions."[549] The emotional ambivalence

---

545. A recent study showed that Christmas was celebrated in 88% of the public schools polled; Easter, 58%; Hanukkah, 5%; Passover, 2%. Dierenfield, *The Extent of Religious Influence in American Public Schools,* 56 RELIGIOUS EDUCATION 173, 176–77 (1961).

546. THE AMERICAN COLLEGE DICTIONARY 214 (Barnhart ed. 1959) gives, as a definition of Christmas: "Dec. 25 (Christmas Day), now generally observed as an occasion for gifts, greetings, etc." See also PFEFFER, CHURCH, STATE, AND FREEDOM 407 (1953); Rosenfield, *Separation of Church and State in the Public Schools,* 22 U. PITT. L. REV. 561, 573 (1961).

547. *Cf.* PFEFFER, *op. cit. supra* note 546, at 406:
Nor can any non-Jew rightfully assert that such singing ["Come, let us adore Him, Christ the Lord," or "Born is the King of Israel"] will not violate the Jewish child's religious conscience, any more than the school principals in the 19th century could rightfully assert that the Catholic child's religious conscience would not be violated by reading from the King James Bible.

548. *Id.* at 407.

549. PFEFFER & BAUM, PUBLIC SCHOOL SECTARIANISM AND THE JEWISH CHILD 6 (1957). See examples cited *id.* at 7–9; Franck, quoted in

that this produces is quite obvious. No doubt, many less determined children fully sacrifice their religious scruples by joining their colleagues. These solely religious activities that require student participation, whether it be the singing of hymns or the acting in plays, are likely to result in compromising conscientious convictions.[550] Nor is the practice validated under the establishment clause by celebrating the holidays of a greater number of religious faiths. Since religious leaders of all faiths have objected to this,[551] it would only seem to compound the difficulty.

Nothing that has been said would deter examination, in the public school curriculum, of certain aspects of religious holidays as an academic matter. Thus, the singing and learning of religious hymns in a music class, as part of the study of different types of musical compositions, must be fairly characterized as secular activity.[552] Likewise, the occasional showing of motion pictures that depict various religious happenings may be of considerable educational value,[553] and, even if not, the quantum of participation required would be so slight that it is unlikely that the compromising or influencing of conscientious scruples would occur. This last instance is to be contrasted with a public school group activity of making religious cut-outs to be pasted on the schoolroom windows and walls.[554] Here, the element of inherent compulsion seems quite powerful, and under the proposed constitutional standard, *if the children were required to make only religiously significant pictures,* and this practice were contrary to their religious beliefs, the establishment clause would be violated.

K. PUBLIC SCHOOLS IN PAROCHIAL BUILDINGS

In a small percentage of school districts throughout the country, public school classes are held in church owned buildings.[555]

THE STUDY OF RELIGION IN THE PUBLIC SCHOOLS: AN APPRAISAL 60 (Brown ed. 1958); Gilbert, *A Catalogue of Church-State Problems,* 56 RELIGIOUS EDUCATION 424, 429 (1961).

550. *But see* Levy, *Views From the Wall—Reflections on Church-State Relationships,* 29 HENNEPIN LAW. 51, 56 (1961).

551. See PFEFFER, *op. cit. supra* note 546, at 410–12; AMERICAN CIVIL LIBERTIES UNION, 41ST ANNUAL REPORT 27–28 (1961).

552. See Pfeffer, *Court, Constitution and Prayer,* 16 RUTGERS L. REV. 735, 750 (1962).

553. *But see* Chamberlin v. Dade County School Bd., 17 Fla. Supp. 183, 196 (Cir. Ct. 1961).

554. *Cf.* Sutherland, *Due Process and Disestablishment,* 62 HARV. L. REV. 1306, 1344 (1949).

555. Dierenfield, *The Extent of Religious Influence in American Public Schools,* 56 RELIGIOUS EDUCATION 173, 177 (1961), reports almost 8%.

This practice has spawned a good deal of litigation in the state courts. If the practice involves no more than the school board's renting the only available property,[556] it may hardly be fairly characterized as solely religious. Thus, there would be no violation of the establishment clause, either under the proposed constitutional standard or under the alternative test previously discussed.[557] The fact that the school rooms have religious pictures and decorations[558] would possibly not alter these conclusions, despite the fact that their placement in an ordinary public school would be objectionable; if, irrespective of the religious decor, the church building is still found to be the best available space, the issue is entirely different.[559] It may be reasonably argued that no matter how great the amount of religious infusion in the environment due to quasi-control by the church, the school board's practice of using parochial buildings cannot be said to be solely religious, either in purpose or in effect; in each instance, it is the considered judgment of the public school board that, on balance, these are the best available facilities for public education. Perhaps this would immunize the practice under the proposed standard.

This may not be the case in regard to the alternative criterion for establishment clause violation. It is ultimately the function of the Court to determine whether "on balance, these are the best available facilities" and whether the secular end may not be attained by less objectionable means. It has been suggested that the solution here is: "that which is legally tolerable ends where the religious infusion becomes unreasonably great."[560] But certain guidelines may be established. Public officials should not be permitted to abdicate their responsibility of selecting teachers and textbooks to clerical authorities.[561] The potentiality for unchecked religious indoctrination of public school students in these cir-

---

556. See Rawlings v. Butler, 290 S.W.2d 801, 806–07 (Ky. 1956).
557. See text accompanying note 523 *supra*.
558. See State *ex rel*. Johnson v. Boyd, 217 Ind. 348, 359, 28 N.E.2d 256, 261 (1940).
559. This line of argument assumes, of course, that the pictures and decorations are there without the consent of the public school officials. If they had control over these matters, then the retention of these decorations could be accurately described as a solely religious activity.
560. Sutherland, *Public Authority and Religious Education: A Brief Survey of Constitutional and Legal Limits*, in THE STUDY OF RELIGION IN THE PUBLIC SCHOOLS: AN APPRAISAL 33, 43 (Brown ed. 1958).
561. See Millard v. Board of Educ., 121 Ill. 297, 301, 10 N.E. 669, 671 (1887); State *ex rel*. Johnson v. Boyd, 217 Ind. 348, 358, 28 N.E.2d 256, 261 (1940); Berghorn v. Reorganized School Dist., 364 Mo. 121, 130, 260 S.W.2d 573, 576 (1953). Compare Crain v. Walker, 222 Ky. 828, 839, 2 S.W.2d 654, 659 (1928).

cumstances would seem so great[562] that no justification for it should be held acceptable, perhaps even if the result is tantamount to the temporary suspension of the so-called "public" education. The same, of course, must be said if the result of the use of the parochial buildings is compulsory religious teaching.[563] In such cases, the Court should find that alternative means (for example, construction of an independent public school building or arranging for public education in another school district) must be used to accomplish the secular end of providing a public education. Even if the Constitution permits the use of public funds to aid parochial education, this is no authority for the proposition that the state may demand that children of all faiths who wish a "public education" attend a publicly supported institution that is essentially no different from a parochial school.

On the other hand, if the unalterable consequences of using church property for public education are that the schools, granting the right of nonparticipation, engage in certain solely religious practices such as prayers and worship in daily chapel exercises[564] or programs of religious instruction akin to released time,[565] the Court should place a heavy burden on the state to demonstrate that less objectionable means do not exist. Otherwise, all the protections afforded religious liberty in the public schools that have been discussed may be easily circumvented by turning over some of the control of public education to the clergy of a particular religious faith.[566]

---

562. See, *e.g.*, Knowlton v. Baumhover, 182 Iowa 691, 703, 166 N.W. 202, 206 (1918); Harfst v. Hoegen, 349 Mo. 808, 811, 163 S.W.2d 609, 610 (1942); Zellers v. Huff, 55 N.M. 501, 506, 236 P.2d 949, 952 (1951); Boyer, *Religious Education of Public School Pupils in Wisconsin*, 1953 WIS. L. REV. 181, 217–225.
563. See cases cited note 562 *supra*.
564. See Williams v. Board of Trustees, 172 Ky. 133, 134, 188 S.W. 1058 (1916); Berghorn v. Reorganized School Dist., 364 Mo. 121, 131–32, 260 S.W.2d 573, 577–78 (1953).
565. See Millard v. Board of Educ., 121 Ill. 297, 302, 10 N.E. 669, 671 (1887); State *ex rel.* Johnson v. Boyd, 217 Ind. 348, 359, 28 N.E.2d 256, 261–62 (1940); Zellers v. Huff, 55 N.M. 501, 507–08, 236 P.2d 949, 953 (1951); Boyer, *supra* note 562.
566. *Cf.* Knowlton v. Baumhover, 182 Iowa 691, 725–26, 166 N.W. 202, 213 (1918):

> [W]henever the adherents of any particular creed can command a majority of any school board, it may abandon the schoolhouse provided for the common and equal use of all the people, move the school into some church or some parochial or private building established for sectarian use, put in charge of it trained ecclesiastics bound by solemn vows to devote their lives, their services, and all their God-given powers to the advancement of the interest of their church, fill the school with distinctive emblems of their faith, and by a multitude

CONCLUSION

The purpose of this article has not been to reconcile the myriad of state court decisions involving the problems of religion and the public schools. There has been no attempt to demonstrate the existence of an internal consistency even within the very few cases decided by the Supreme Court. Nor has the endeavor been to predict the outcome of future litigation. While the recent decision in *Engel v. Vitale* has been examined, it has not been suggested that the case permits of only one interpretation. Rather, the purpose here has been to submit a rational and desirable standard for constitutional adjudication in this area, and to demonstrate its application in some specific situations. In many of these instances, "nice" distinctions have been drawn. But a "boundary line is none the worse for being narrow."[567] It should be made clear that "the principle offered is meant to provide a starting point for solutions to problems brought before the Court, not a mechanical answer to them."[568] If some of the underlying factual premises advanced here are shown to be incorrect, the results suggested must be changed. But the principle should be adhered to.

Central to the theme of this article has been the fact that it is vital to the preservation of religious liberty to recognize that although "you send your child to the schoolmaster . . . 'tis the schoolboys who educate him."[569] Voluntariness is a concept, not merely a word. "Compulsion which comes from circumstances can be as real as compulsion which comes from a command."[570] If the price for the protection of religious liberty in the public schools is the abolition of certain religious influences,[571] that price must be paid. Although this conclusion may be said to manifest no more than "the traditional American weakness of identifying our own preferences and predilections with the Constitution,"[572] the effort has been made to submerge these preferences and predilections in favor of historical and contemporary national goals.

---

of influences, silent as well as expressed, shape the plastic minds and characters of the young children committed to their care in accordance with their own religious views, and saddle the expense of this sectarian education upon the taxpayers.

567. McLeod v. J. E. Dilworth Co., 322 U.S. 327, 329 (1944).
568. Kurland, *Of Church and State and the Supreme Court*, 29 U. CHI. L. REV. 1, 6 (1961).
569. EMERSON, THE CONDUCT OF LIFE 123 (1860).
570. Public Util. Comm'n v. Pollak, 343 U.S. 451, 468 (1962) (Douglas, J., dissenting).
571. See Kirven, *Freedom of Religion or Freedom from Religion?*, 48 A.B.A.J. 816, 819 (1962).
572. Kauper, *Church, State, and Freedom: A Review*, 52 MICH. L. REV. 829, 848 (1954).

The Establishment Clause and Aid to Parochial Schools

Jesse H. Choper*

I

INTRODUCTION

IN 1947, MR. JUSTICE RUTLEDGE found "[t]wo great drives . . . constantly in motion to abridge . . . the complete division of religion and civil authority which our forefathers made. One is to introduce religious education and observances into the public schools. The other, to obtain public funds for the aid and support of various private religious schools."[1] *Everson v. Board of Education*, the occasion for his observation, was the first significant decision of the Supreme Court in current history interpreting the establishment clause of the first amendment. Involving bussing of children to parochial schools, it concerned the second of the Justice's "two great drives."

Since 1947, the Court has addressed itself extensively to the first of the two issues in controversy—the influence of religion in the public schools.[2] Although litigation on that question continues to arise,[3] the Court's pronouncements, despite some criticism,[4] seem largely to have resolved the

---

* B.S., 1957, Wilkes College; LL.B., 1960, University of Pennsylvania; D.Hu.Litt., 1967, Wilkes College; Professor of Law, University of California, Berkeley. The author wishes to express his gratitude to his colleague, Frank I. Goodman, for his very helpful comments and to Alan S. Koenig, of the third year class, for his excellent and exceptionally thorough research assistance.

[1] Everson v. Board of Educ., 330 U.S. 1, 63 (1947) (dissenting opinion). *See also id.* at 14.

[2] *See* McCollum v. Board of Educ., 333 U.S. 203 (1948) (on-premises released time); Zorach v. Clauson, 343 U.S. 306 (1952) (off-premises released time); Engel v. Vitale, 370 U.S. 421 (1962) (Regents' prayer); School Dist. v. Schempp, 374 U.S. 203 (1963) (Bible reading and Lord's Prayer).

[3] *See* Chamberlin v. Dade County Bd. of Pub. Instruction, 377 U.S. 402 (1964) (baccalaureate services); DeSpain v. DeKalb, 384 F.2d 837 (7th Cir. 1967) (compulsory recitation of thankful-type verse); Stein v. Oshinsky, 348 F.2d 999 (2d Cir.), *cert. denied*, 382 U.S. 957 (1965); Reed v. Van Hoven, 237 F. Supp. 48 (W.D. Mich. 1965) (prayers before school begins); Lewis v. Allen, 14 N.Y.2d 867, 200 N.E.2d 767, *cert. denied*, 379 U.S. 923 (1964) ("under God" in pledge of allegiance). *See generally* Ladd, *Public Education and Religion*, 13 J. Pub. L. 310 (1964); Note, 20 VAND. L. REV. 1078 (1967).

[4] For various views, see Brown, *Quis Custodiet Ipsos Custodes?—The School Prayer Case*, 1963 SUP. CT. REV. 1; Choper, *Religion in the Public Schools: A Proposed Constitutional Standard*, 47 MINN. L. REV. 329 (1963); Fordham, *The Implications of the Supreme Court Decisions Dealing with Religious Practices in the Public Schools*, 6 J. CHURCH & ST. 44 (1964); Griswold, *Absolute is in the Dark—A Discussion of the Approach of the Supreme Court to Constitutional Questions*, 8 UTAH L. REV. 167 (1963); Kauper, *Prayer, Public Schools and the Supreme Court*, 61 MICH. L. REV. 1031 (1963); Kurland, *The Regents'*

260

matter. Therefore, it is evident that the most sensitive issue involving religion and government today is, as in *Everson*, that of public aid to parochial schools.[5] Intense interest in the constitutional aspect of the topic is reflected in a recent pamphlet reporting that as of December 1, 1967, at least a score of cases involving the establishment clause question were pending in state and lower federal courts.[6] And, on January 15, 1968, the Supreme Court, for the first time in over twenty years, agreed to hear argument on the subject.[7]

A. The Concept of Aid

Forcefully emphasized and oft-repeated language in Supreme Court opinions, beginning with *Everson*, appears to permit little room for debate about aid to religion:

> The "establishment of religion" clause of the First Amendment means at least this: Neither a state nor the Federal Government .... can pass laws which aid one religion, aid all religions, or prefer one religion over another .... No tax in any amount, large or small, can be levied to support any religious activities or institutions, whatever they may be called, or whatever form they may adopt to teach or practice religion.[8]

On this basis, President John F. Kennedy declared in 1961 that a "clear prohibition of the Constitution"[9] forbade the allocation of federal funds for parochial schools.

What constitutes aid or support, however, is "obviously a sophisticated and not a simple literal concept."[10] In the *Everson* decision itself, for

---

Prayer Case: "Full of Sound and Fury, Signifying . . . ," 1962 SUP. CT. REV. 1; Pollak, *Foreword: Public Prayers in Public Schools*, 77 HARV. L. REV. 62 (1963); Sutherland, *Establishment According to Engel*, 76 HARV. L. REV. 25 (1962).

There has been virtually no disagreement with the Court's firm determination that the ban of the establishment clause extends beyond the setting up of a state church. *See* McGowan v. Maryland, 366 U.S. 420, 442 (1961).

[5] *See* P. KAUPER, RELIGION AND THE CONSTITUTION 109 (1964); Oaks, *Introduction* to THE WALL BETWEEN CHURCH AND STATE 1, 5 (D. Oaks ed. 1963).

[6] American Jewish Congress Commission on Law and Social Action, Litigation Docket of Pending Cases Affecting Freedom of Religion and Separation of Church and State, Dec. 1, 1967, at i-ii.

[7] Board of Educ. v. Allen, 20 N.Y.2d 109, 228 N.E.2d 791, 281 N.Y.S.2d 799 (1967), *prob. juris. noted*, 36 U.S.L.W. 3278 (U.S. Jan. 15, 1968).

[8] Everson v. Board of Educ., 330 U.S. 1, 15-16 (1947); *accord*, Torcaso v. Watkins, 367 U.S. 488, 492-93 (1961); McGowan v. Maryland, 366 U.S. 420, 443 (1961); McCollum v. Board of Educ., 333 U.S. 203, 210 (1948). *See also* School Dist. v. Schempp, 374 U.S. 203, 216 (1963).

[9] 107 CONG. REC. 2430 (1961).

[10] Hayes, *The Constitutional Permissibility of the Participation of Church-Related Schools in the Administration's Proposed Program of Massive Federal Aid to Education*, 11 DE PAUL L. REV. 161, 168 (1962).

example, the Court upheld public reimbursement to parents for the expense of bussing their children both to public schools and to Catholic parochial schools; yet the Court acknowledged the "possibility that some of the children might not be sent to the church schools if the parents were compelled to pay their children's bus fares out of their own pockets when transportation to a public school would have been paid for by the State."[11] Even the *Everson* dissenters seemed to agree that the furnishing of police and fire protection and of water and sewage services to churches and church schools conformed with the establishment clause.[12] Yet it may plausibly be said that all of these "in fact give aid and encouragement to religious instruction."[13] Neither the fact of a "continuing and increasing demand for the state to assume" their cost,[14] nor the fact that their provision by state funds affords the church "greater strength in our society than it would have by relying on its members alone"[15] demonstrates their unconstitutionality. Some additional ingredient—some brighter line of demarcation—is necessary for invalidation of the expenditure of tax funds.[16]

Thus, despite the Court's rather insistent declarations, "[p]redictability is still elusive."[17] It is not clear that "a non-preferential expenditure of public moneys to religious institutions in furtherance of purposes in which government and the churches have concurrent interests may . . . so deeply involve government in religious matters as to violate what the Court conceives to be the basic values served by the First Amendment."[18] In sum, it does not appear that the Court has firmly foreclosed the issue of the constitutionality of aid to parochial education.[19]

B. *The Relevance of "History" and "Experience"*

Despite the fact that the Court has not absolutely precluded inquiry into the constitutionality of aid to parochial schools, it could be argued

---

[11] 330 U.S. at 17.
[12] *See id.* at 60-61 (dissenting opinion of Rutledge, J.).
[13] *Id.* at 45.
[14] *Id.* at 46.
[15] School Dist. v. Schempp, 374 U.S. 203, 229 (1963) (concurring opinion of Douglas, J.).
[16] *See* Lardner, *How Far Does the Constitution Separate Church and State?*, 45 Am. Pol. Sci. Rev. 110, 129 (1951).
[17] Kempner, *The Supreme Court and the Establishment and Free Exercise of Religion*, in Religion and the Free Society, July 1958, at 65, 91 (pamphlet issued by The Fund for the Republic, New York, N.Y.).
[18] Kauper, *Schempp and Sherbert: Studies in Neutrality and Accommodation*, in 1963 Religion & Pub. Order 3, 28-29 (D. Giannella ed.).
[19] For further discussion, see text accompanying notes 285-318 *infra*. Professor Kurland has observed that "[a]nyone suggesting that the answer [to whether government may contribute financially to parochial education, directly or indirectly], as a matter of constitutional law, is clear one way or the other is either deluding or deluded." Kurland, *Of Church and State and the Supreme Court*, 29 U. Chi. L. Rev. 1, 96 (1961).

that the history of the religion clauses of the first amendment has already determined the outcome. It has been contended that "history and experience may be sounder guides to locating Jefferson's 'wall of separation between church and state' than abstract logic."[20] But reliance on history alone is futile. Perhaps it is true that "[n]o provision of the Constitution is more closely tied to or given content by its generating history than the religious clause of the First Amendment. It is at once the refined product and the terse summation of that history."[21] But a recent, detailed inquiry into the practices, preferences, fears, and experiences of the entire generation that promulgated the religion clauses catalogues a wide assortment of possible explanations for their phraseology and concludes that "it is impossible to give a dogmatic interpretation of the First Amendment, and to state with any accuracy the intention of the men who framed it . . . ."[22]

The historical facts are that free public education was virtually nonexistent during the early years of independence,[23] and where it did occur it had a distinctly religious orientation.[24] The relevance of the latter fact for the meaning of the establishment clause, however, is unconvincing in light of the further fact that established religions and churches flourished in the colonies,[25] persisting at times into the nineteenth century.[26] And, if experience is to be our guide, it is perplexing to find that, despite provisions in almost all state constitutions which arguably, and often explicitly, prohibit public aid to sectarian schools,[27] it was calculated twenty years

[20] U.S. Dep't of Health, Education & Welfare, *Memorandum on the Impact of the First Amendment to the Constitution upon Federal Aid to Education,* 50 GEO. L.J. 349, 357 (1961). *See also* Herberg, *Religion, Democracy, and Public Education,* in RELIGION IN AMERICA 118, 142 (J. Cogley ed. 1958).

[21] Everson v. Board of Educ., 330 U.S. 1, 33 (1947) (dissenting opinion of Rutledge, J.).

[22] C. ANTIEAU, A. DOWNEY & E. ROBERTS, FREEDOM FROM FEDERAL ESTABLISHMENT 142 (1964). *See generally id.* at 123-42. Also, *compare* C. MOEHLMAN, THE WALL OF SEPARATION BETWEEN CHURCH AND STATE (1951), *and* Pfeffer, *Church and State: Something Less than Separation,* 19 U. CHI. L. REV. 1 (1951), *with* J. O'NEILL, RELIGION AND EDUCATION UNDER THE CONSTITUTION (1949), *and* W. PARSONS, THE FIRST FREEDOM (1948).

[23] *See* School Dist. v. Schempp, 374 U.S. 203, 238 & n.7 (1963) (concurring opinion of Brennan, J.). *See also* Brown v. Board of Educ., 347 U.S. 483, 489-90 (1954).

[24] C. ANTIEAU, A. DOWNEY & E. ROBERTS, *supra* note 22, at 71.

[25] *See* Engel v. Vitale, 370 U.S. 421, 428 & n.10 (1962).

[26] L. PFEFFER, CHURCH, STATE AND FREEDOM 141 (rev. ed. 1967).

[27] A. STOKES & L. PFEFFER, CHURCH AND STATE IN THE UNITED STATES 423-24 (rev. ed. 1964); F. BEACH & R. WILL, THE STATE AND NONPUBLIC SCHOOLS 15-19 (HEW, Office of Education Misc. No. 28, 1958). *See also* Note, *Catholic Schools and Public Money,* 50 YALE L.J. 917 (1941).

It may be urged that the existence of explicit constitutional prohibitions against aid to parochial schools in over 80% of the states, *see* A. STOKES & L. PFEFFER, *supra,* presents compelling evidence as to the construction, in view of widespread tradition, that should be given to the establishment clause in respect to this issue. But there are several reasons why the point is not persuasive. First, the language of the establishment clause is far from being as specifically opposed to such aid as are many of the state mandates. *See, e.g.,* MINN. CONST. art. 8,

ago that both federal and state funds "are actually being allocated, in no less than 350 instances, to American parochial schools today."[28] And it is reasonable to assume that increased public concern with education has caused that number to grow significantly.

Most assuredly, however, history occupies a prominent role in the formulation of establishment clause principles. It has been properly utilized by the Court, not to discover the precise intention of the framers as to the controversial religious questions of today,[29] but rather to "divulge a broad philosophy of church-state relations."[30] History should furnish the informed perspective needed to fashion a rational constitutional standard that serves several purposes, including cognizance of the evil consequences feared by the framers,[31] appreciation of values presently cherished, and capability of consistent application to the relevant problems.[32] Too strong a reliance on history and experience, given their detailed inconsistencies which cannot be rationalized on principled grounds, will result only in ad hoc, unreasoned rulings. Such rulings conceal value judgments that, although inevitable in constitutional decisionmaking, should be laid bare by the articulation of general principles.

C. *The Purpose of the Article*

It has been seen, at the threshold, that both Supreme Court rulings and first amendment history leave open the constitutional question of aid

§ 2: "But in no case shall . . . any public moneys or property, be appropriated or used for the support of schools wherein the distinctive doctrines, creeds or tenets of any particular Christian or other religious sect are promulgated or taught." This is evidenced by the fact that despite the Court's interpretation of the establishment clause in 1947 in Everson v. Board of Educ., 330 U.S. 1, permitting public payment of bus transportation of children to parochial schools, a number of state courts have subsequently held the practice invalid under their state constitutions. *See, e.g.,* Matthews v. Quinton, 362 P.2d 932 (Alas. 1961), *appeal dismissed and cert. denied,* 368 U.S. 517 (1962); State *ex rel.* Reynolds v. Nusbaum, 17 Wis. 2d 148, 115 N.W.2d 761 (1962). Further, whereas the historical background of the establishment clause is virtually devoid of problems of education, see text at notes 23-24 *supra,* many of the state constitutional limitations were a direct response to Catholic efforts to obtain public funds for parochial education. Note, *Catholic Schools and Public Money,* 50 YALE L.J. 917, 919-20 (1941). Thus, both the wording and setting of many of the state prohibitions, in contrast to the first amendment, clearly preclude any argument that certain aid to parochial schools is valid because it is nonreligious and serves a public purpose. Reed, *The "Permeation" Issue in Federal Aid to Education,* 8 CATHOLIC LAW. 197, 203-04 (1962). *See also* note 33 *infra.*

[28] A. JOHNSON & F. YOST, SEPARATION OF CHURCH AND STATE IN THE UNITED STATES 112 (1948).

[29] *See* School Dist. v. Schempp, 374 U.S. 203, 241 (1963) (concurring opinion of Brennan, J.).

[30] C. ANTIEAU, A. DOWNEY & E. ROBERTS, *supra* note 22, at xi; *see, e.g.,* Engel v. Vitale, 370 U.S. 421 (1962); McGowan v. Maryland, 366 U.S. 420 (1961); Everson v. Board of Educ., 330 U.S. 1 (1947).

[31] School Dist. v. Schempp, 374 U.S. 203, 236 (1963) (concurring opinion of Brennan, J.).

[32] The specific role which each of these sometimes conflicting elements should play in constitutional adjudication is indeed a topic of substantial independent inquiry.

to parochial schools. This article will propose a rule under the establishment clause[33] for testing the constitutionality of aid to those parochial schools that provide at least some secular education. It is particularly appropriate, in dealing with this topic of aid to parochial schools, to recall Mr. Justice Frankfurter's warning that "preoccupation by our people with the constitutionality, instead of with the wisdom, of legislation or executive action is preoccupation with a false value."[34] But it is constitutionality alone that must concern us here, irrespective of any preference as to the desirability of assisting nonpublic schools.[35] Perhaps in resolving this issue "the members of the Court must have recourse to their own convictions about the place of religion in education and public life,"[36] but surely not to the exclusion of other, more consequential determinants.

In brief, my proposal is that governmental financial aid may be extended directly or indirectly to support parochial schools without violation

---

[33] As has already been observed, see note 27 *supra*, the question under the various state constitutions may be wholly different. Because of the specificity of many of them, decisions thereunder may require a drawing of lines that will not withstand the test of being capable of "consistent application," see text accompanying note 32 *supra*, to a broad range of rationally similar problems. *See* the comment of Professor Jaffe in Dorsen, *The Arthur Garfield Hays Civil Liberties Conference: Public Aid to Parochial Schools and Standing to Bring Suit*, 12 BUFFALO L. REV. 35, 41 (1962).

The question under the establishment clause arises when a state aid program survives the state constitutional test, *see, e.g.*, Board of Educ. v. Allen, 20 N.Y.2d 109, 228 N.E.2d 791, 281 N.Y.S.2d 799 (1967), *prob. juris. noted*, 36 U.S.L.W. 3278 (U.S. Jan. 15, 1968), or in connection with the myriad of federal programs under which institutions with religious affiliation receive federal funds through grants or loans. For a fairly complete listing of such programs, see *Hearings Before the Ad Hoc Subcomm. on Study of Shared-Time Education of the House Comm. on Education and Labor*, 88th Cong., 2d Sess. 32-48 (1964). *See also* text accompanying notes 559-69 *infra*. Especially important in this latter group is the Elementary and Secondary Education Act of 1965, 20 U.S.C. §§ 236-44, 331-32b, 821-27, 841-48, 861-70, 881-85 (Supp. I, 1965), under challenge in six cases pending at the end of 1967. *See* American Jewish Congress, *supra* note 6.

[34] *Quoted in* THE SUPREME COURT ON CHURCH AND STATE vii (J. Tussman ed. 1962).

[35] *See* Kauper, *Church and State: Cooperative Separatism*, 60 MICH. L. REV. 1, 39-40 (1961). A mass of literature and debate exists on the question of wisdom and legislative policy. An excellent brief summary may be found in L. PFEFFER, CHURCH, STATE, AND FREEDOM 521-29 (rev. ed. 1967). *See generally*, FEDERAL AID AND CATHOLIC SCHOOLS (D. Callahan ed. 1964). Personally, I have no firm nor even well-informed judgment on the matter, although, as a believer in the virtues of a strong public educational system, I am troubled by the argument that the distribution of tax funds to private and parochial schools would result in their proliferation to the detriment of the public schools. *See, e.g., Hearings on H.R. 2361 and H.R. 2362 Before the General Subcomm. on Education of the House Comm. on Education and Labor*, 89th Cong., 1st Sess. 1533 (1965) (Statement on Behalf of the American Jewish Congress).

[36] Drinan, *State and Federal Aid to Parochial Schools*, 7 J. CHURCH & ST. 67, 71 (1965). *Cf.* Jones, *The Constitutional Status of Public Funds for Church-Related Schools*, 6 J. CHURCH & ST. 61, 70 (1964): "In the interpretation of the 'no establishment' clause, as in the interpretation of any other provision of the Constitution, it is impossible to achieve a surgically pure separation of 'law' from 'policy.'"

of the establishment clause so long as such aid does not exceed the value of the secular educational service rendered by the school.

The general theorem is not advanced as being wholly novel. It has been suggested by other commentators[37] and implicitly relied upon by state courts facing the question under state constitutions.[38] But a thorough examination of its implications in light of history, precedent, principle, and intricacies in application is called for.[39] No attempt will be made here to predict the Court's future course of action. Rather, the proposed rule seeks to take account of "past event and initial purpose"[40] and, in this light, to elaborate, as dispassionately as possible, a constitutional rationale "suitable for the government of the future."[41]

Part II of the article explores a general rationale for the broad scope of the establishment clause, with particular emphasis on its historical and contemporary goals, and with incidental reference to the fourteenth amendment and to doctrines of standing. Part III describes the functioning of this establishment clause rationale. Part IV discusses the specific

---

[37] The clearest statements appear in Blum, *Our Federal Constitution and Equal Justice in Education*, in EDUCATIONAL FREEDOM AND THE CASE FOR GOVERNMENT AID TO STUDENTS IN INDEPENDENT SCHOOLS 138-43 (D. McGarry & L. Ward eds. 1966); National Catholic Welfare Conference, *The Constitutionality of the Inclusion of Church-Related Schools in Federal Aid to Education*, 50 GEO. L.J. 397, 411, 434-35 (1961); Note, 36 GEO. L.J. 631, 645-46 (1948). See also Johnson, *A Problem of Culture*, in Religion and the Schools, April 1959, at 64, 70 (pamphlet issued by The Fund for the Republic, New York, N.Y.); Blum, *Bus Rides for All Children*, SCHOOL ACTIVITIES, Apr. 1967, at 6; Costanzo, *Wholesome Neutrality: Law and Education*, 43 N.D.L. REV. 605, 620 (1967); Rafalko, *The Federal Aid to Private Schools Controversy: A Look*, 3 DUQUESNE L. REV. 211, 222 (1965); Slough & McAnany, *Government Aid to Church-Related Schools: An Analysis*, 11 KAN. L. REV. 35, 69 (1962); NEW REPUBLIC, Mar. 2, 1963, at 4-5.

[38] *See* St. Hedwig's Indus. School v. Cook County, 289 Ill. 432, 124 N.E. 629 (1919); Trost v. Ketteler Manual Training School, 282 Ill. 504, 118 N.E. 743 (1918); Dunn v. Addison Manual Training School, 281 Ill. 352, 117 N.E. 993 (1917); Dunn v. Chicago Indus. School, 280 Ill. 613, 117 N.E. 735 (1917); Murrow Indian Orphans Home v. Childers, 197 Okla. 249, 171 P.2d 600 (1946). *See also* Community Council v. Jordan, 432 P.2d 460 (Ariz. 1967). In several of these cases, the facts indicated that not only was public aid given to the religiously affiliated "schools" involved, but children of all religious faiths were committed to them by the juvenile court. Thus, although the matter was not raised, first amendment issues —free exercise and establishment—were there present that do not exist in the "ordinary" aid to parochial school case. See text at note 551 *infra*.

For state cases refusing to accept the proposed rationale, see Bennett v. City of La Grange, 153 Ga. 428, 112 S.E. 482 (1922); Synod v. State, 2 S.D. 366, 50 N.W. 632 (1891).

[39] Without such an inquiry, one might agree with Mr. Justice Holmes that "no general proposition is worth a damn." 2 HOLMES-POLLOCK LETTERS 59 (M. Howe 1st ed. 1961).

[40] M. HOWE, THE GARDEN AND THE WILDERNESS 3 (1965).

[41] *Id*. I do not believe that the discussion that follows derives in any significant part from my "own prepossessions about the wisdom of encouraging the maintenance of private schools with public funds." Drinan, *supra* note 36, at 71. Nor do I believe that "the underlying [constitutional] issue of the struggle is brutally simple: are parochial schools to be encouraged or not?" Note, *Public Funds for Sectarian Schools*, 60 HARV. L. REV. 793, 800 (1947). *See also* note 35 *supra*.

operation of the proposed rule for parochial schools. Part V places the rule for aid to parochial schools in juxtaposition to competing theories, examining the efficacy of these other approaches and more fully illustrating the workings of the thesis advocated. Finally, Part VI briefly summarizes existing federal programs in aid of parochial education, measuring them against the rule proposed herein.

II

AN ESTABLISHMENT CLAUSE RATIONALE

A proposal permitting governmental financial assistance to parochial schools not exceeding the value of secular services they render comports with a general rationale for the establishment clause that reflects both contemporary and historical aims.

A. Historical Support

Although the indistinctness of the precise historical designs of the establishment clause has already been noted, several aims emerge quite lucidly. Its paramount purpose then, like its major concern today, was to safeguard freedom of worship and conscience—in a word, to protect religious liberty.[42] And it is equally clear that this purpose comprehended the intention that "the conscience of individuals should not be coerced by forcing them to pay taxes in support of a religious establishment or religious activities."[43] In other words, as part of the general attempt to safeguard religious belief, the establishment clause sought to protect taxpayers from being forced by the federal government to support religion. This is cogently confirmed by Thomas Jefferson's "Virginia Bill for Religious Liberty" which proclaimed "that to compel a man to furnish contributions of money for the propagation of opinions which he disbelieves, is sinful and tyrannical";[44] by James Madison's "Memorial and Remonstrance Against Religious Assessments" (whose title is itself revealing) which condemned even forcing "a citizen to contribute three pence only of his property" to support any religious establishment;[45] by Thomas Cooley's *Constitutional*

---

[42] *See* P. KAUPER, *supra* note 5, at 77; RELIGION AND AMERICAN SOCIETY 41 (Center for the Study of Democratic Institutions 1961); Dunsford, *The Establishment Syndrome and Religious Liberty*, 2 DUQUESNE L. REV. 139, 203-12 (1964); Sky, *The Establishment Clause, The Congress and the Schools: An Historical Perspective*, 52 VA. L. REV. 1395, 1426-27 (1966). For further discussion and citation of authority, *see* Choper, *supra* note 4, at 333 nn.19-20.

[43] Kauper, *supra* note 35, at 9. *See also id.* at 5-6. "The most serious infringement upon religious liberty before our Bill of Rights was adopted was the use of tax-raised funds for religious purposes." Pfeffer, *Some Current Issues in Church and State*, 13 W. RES. L. REV. 9, 18 (1961).

[44] 12 HENING, STATUTES OF VIRGINIA 84 (1823). *But cf.* M. HOWE, *supra* note 40, at 26.

[45] ¶ 3, set forth in Everson v. Board of Educ., 330 U.S. 1, 65-66 (1947) (app.). *See also*

Limitations which found clearly unlawful "under any of the American constitutions . . . [c]ompulsory support, by taxation or otherwise, of religious instruction";[46] and by many important Supreme Court opinions in the church-state field—majority, concurring, and dissenting.[47] Whatever other historical bases for the establishment ban,[48] it is beyond reasonable dispute that it purported to secure religious liberty, in particular by prohibiting taxation for religious purposes.[49] That historical intent conforms with the contemporary American view that "it is a violation of religious liberty to compel people to pay taxes to support religious activties or institutions."[50]

B. *The Scope of the Establishment Clause*

Given this background, the broad philosophy of church-state relations reflected in the nonestablishment precept becomes manifest: Governmental action for *religious* purposes is highly suspect;[51] it is constitutionally objectionable when it impinges on religious liberty either, as I have

---

Pfeffer, *Federal Funds for Parochial Schools? No*, 37 NOTRE DAME LAW. 309, 310-11 (1962); Flast v. Gardner, 271 F. Supp. 1, 6-7 (S.D.N.Y. 1967) (dissenting opinion of Frankel, J.): "It is now familiar to all who have touched this subject that a central concern—perhaps the most central concern—of the Establishment Clause is to ban utterly the use of public moneys to support any religion or all religions. . . .

. . . .

. . . .

" 'Support' by use of taxpayers' money lay at the heart of Jefferson's and Madison's concern."

[46] T. COOLEY, A TREATISE ON THE CONSTITUTIONAL LIMITATIONS 663-64 (7th ed. 1903).

[47] *See, e.g.*, Engel v. Vitale, 370 U.S. 421, 442 n.7 (1962) (concurring opinion of Douglas, J.); McGowan v. Maryland, 366 U.S. 420, 453 (1961) (opinion of the Court by Warren, C. J.); McCollum v. Board of Educ., 333 U.S. 203, 248, 249 (1948) (dissenting opinion of Reed, J.); Everson v. Board of Educ., 330 U.S. 1, 8, 10-12 (1947) (opinion of the Court by Black, J.); *id.* at 33, 41, 44, 52, 53 (dissenting opinion of Rutledge, J.).

[48] The contention has been advanced that the clause's purpose was to prevent Congress from interfering with the then existing state establishments. *See, e.g.*, W. KATZ, RELIGION AND AMERICAN CONSTITUTIONS 8-10 (1964); Snee, *Religious Disestablishment and the Fourteenth Amendment*, 1954 WASH. U.L.Q. 371; Note, 61 NW. U.L. REV. 760, 769-70 (1966). The late Professor Howe found this argument "[g]rammatically persuasive . . . [but] historically unconvincing," and suggested that the language drafted supported "a related, but less radical, interpretation of the prevailing policy" concerning the power of federal courts "to respect state law when it happened to sustain a religious enterprise." M. HOWE, *supra* note 40, at 23.

[49] *See generally*, C. ANTIEAU, A. DOWNEY & E. ROBERTS, *supra* note 22, at 1-29.

[50] P. KAUPER, *supra* note 5, at 14. *See also*, R. DRINAN, RELIGION, THE COURTS, AND PUBLIC POLICY 231 (1963).

[51] The contention is not made that every governmental action that may be fairly characterized as being exclusively for religious ends violates the establishment clause. If neither of the additional elements discussed in text accompanying notes 52-53 *infra* is present, it may persuasively be argued that, even though the governmental purpose is religious, it does not threaten the evils at which the establishment clause (or the free exercise clause) was directed, at least not in any meaningful sense. *See also* notes 53, 55 *infra;* Mansfield, Book Review, 52 CALIF. L. REV. 212, 219 (1964).

argued elsewhere,[52] by compromising the individual's religious beliefs, or, as outlined above, by directly coercing the individual to support religion by allocating tax funds for sectarian use.[53] On the other hand, governmental action for *secular* purposes does not fall within the core of the establishment clause's concern[54]—the "nonestablishment guarantee is directed at public aid to the *religious* activities of religious groups."[55]

1. Conflicting Approaches

(a) *Absolutism.*—This circumscription of the establishment clause has not met with universal approval. Some would have the clause invalidate

---

[52] Choper, *supra* note 4.

[53] This should be subject to a de minimis test. *See id.*, at 351-53.

[54] If compliance with such governmental action involves compromise of religious or conscientious beliefs, a free exercise violation may result. *See, e.g.,* Sherbert v. Verner, 374 U.S. 398 (1963); *In re* Jenison, 265 Minn. 96, 120 N.W.2d 515, *vacated and remanded,* 375 U.S. 14, *rev'd,* 267 Minn. 136, 125 N.W.2d 588 (1963).

Whether such governmental action may still violate the establishment clause because alternative means to obtain its secular end are available that less directly affect religion is discussed in text accompanying notes 325-345 *infra*.

[55] P. FREUND, RELIGION AND THE PUBLIC SCHOOLS 11 (1965) (emphasis added). *See also* Sky, *supra* note 42, at 1433: "[T]here is double historical support for the proposition that a law providing tax funds to religious organizations for the specific purpose of supporting *religious* functions is a 'law respecting an establishment of religion.'" (Emphasis added.)

The basic establishment clause rationale just outlined is meant generally to deal with problems traditionally considered as arising under the nonestablishment ban—matters such as direct or indirect public financial assistance to religious groups or institutions, religious activities sponsored by government, religious pronouncements by public officials, coercive state action coinciding with religious precepts—rather than with issues of alleged infringement of individual religious liberty, conventionally adjudicated under the free exercise clause. No comprehensive or final articulation of the establishment clause's every application is intended. That task may not be undertaken without thorough consideration of the fundamental question of the interrelationship between the establishment and free exercise clauses and the seeming "dilemmas" not infrequently posed thereby. *See generally* W. LOCKHART, Y. KAMISAR & J. CHOPER, CONSTITUTIONAL LAW 1183-85 (2d ed. 1967).

In resolving a conflict between practices demanded by one's religion and civil regulation, the Court has acknowledged that "to make accommodation between the religious action and an exercise of state authority is a particularly delicate task." Braunfeld v. Brown, 366 U.S. 599, 605 (1961). Decision in favor of the former requires the state to serve the religious interest of the individual. Such state action to prevent a free exercise clause violation may be "defined" as being for a "nonreligious" purpose. *See* Choper, *supra* note 4, at 393, 402. *See also* Moore, *The Supreme Court and the Relationship Between the "Establishment" and "Free Exercise" Clauses,* 42 TEXAS L. REV. 142, 196-97 (1963). In other instances, a state may be permitted, although not required, to facilitate personal liberty by relieving a serious burden placed on religious exercise by government action. *See* Mansfield, *Conscientious Objection—1964 Term,* 1965 RELIGION & PUB. ORDER 3, 70-71 (D. Giannella ed.). *See generally* Katz, *Freedom of Religion and State Neutrality,* 20 U. CHI. L. REV. 426 (1953). Such a course may be characterized as being for a "restorative or equalizing" purpose. *See* Galanter, *Religious Freedoms in the United States: A Turning Point?* 1966 WIS. L. REV. 217, 290-91. These matters may well call for some qualification of the literal reach of the establishment clause rationale set forth above. *But cf.* note 199 *infra* (last three paragraphs).

any governmental support to certain institutions controlled by a church or religious organization "[e]ven if a completely secular part of [the institution's services] could be isolated."[56] This seemingly "absolutist" theory will be discussed below.[57]

(b) Neutralism.—Another highly respectable thesis falls on the opposite side of the spectrum. Under the doctrine developed by Professor Kurland, which states simply "that government cannot utilize religion as a standard for action or inaction,"[58] it would seem that government could constitutionally finance the entire operational costs of all state-accredited educational institutions, including those controlled by a religious organization, because the classification—state-accredited educational institutions—which includes most ordinary parochial schools, is not in the religious terms which his doctrine forbids.[59]

---

[56] G. LaNoue, Public Funds for Parochial Schools? 32 (1963).

[57] See text accompanying notes 346-353 *infra*.

[58] Kurland, *supra* note 19, at 6. See also Hutchins, *The Future of the Wall*, in The Wall between Church and State 17, 22 (D. Oaks ed. 1963).

[59] Professor Kurland's doctrine also addresses itself to a proper construction of the free exercise clause, urging that it be considered abridged by a government "classification in terms of religion . . . to impose a burden." Kurland, *supra* note 19, at 6. Under this test, he would find a free exercise violation if government extended financial support to all state-accredited schools except those that are church-related. *Id.* at 15 n.57, 70. *See also* Kauper, *Separation of Church and State—A Constitutional View*, 9 Catholic Law. 32, 42 (1963). But he would find no violation if the government classification were "in terms of public and non-public schools." Kurland, *supra* note 19, at 15 n.57.

A discussion of the implications of the free exercise clause on the aid to parochial school question is generally beyond the scope of this article. It has been stated that the free exercise rights of parents wishing to have their children educated in parochial schools are infringed if aid equivalent to that given to public schools is not also extended to parochial schools. However, it has been vociferously maintained that the suggestion is "wholly unjustified," Letter from Professor Howe to Senator Wayne Morse, in S. Doc. No. 29, 87th Cong., 1st Sess., at 50 (1961), and that the free exercise contention "elevate[s]" an argument based on concepts of equity to the dignity of a contention grounded in the Constitution." *Id. See also* U.S. Dep't of Health, Education & Welfare, *supra* note 20, at 374-75; Pfeffer, *supra* note 43, at 14-18. But the contention is by no means "clearly without foundation," W. Katz, *supra* note 48, at 75.

Although the argument has been extant for some time, *see* V. Blum, Freedom of Choice in Education 38-61, 106-32 (1958); W. Parsons, The First Freedom 122 (1948); Henle, *American Principles and Religious Schools*, 3 St. Louis U.L.J. 237 (1955); Weclew, *Church and State: How Much Separation?*, 10 De Paul L. Rev. 1, 19 (1960); 1 Bill of Rights Rev. 309 (1941), it has gained significant force from the Supreme Court's decision in Sherbert v. Verner, 374 U.S. 398 (1963). *Sherbert* involved a state's denial of unemployment compensation benefits to a Seventh Day Adventist who would not work on Saturday, the Sabbath Day of her faith; the state commissioner thus found that she had failed "without good cause, to accept 'suitable work' . . . ." *Id.* at 401. The Court, in holding that her rights under the free exercise clause were violated, made several salient points relevant to the aid to parochial schools issue: First, it pointed out that Mrs. Sherbert's "ineligibility for benefits derives solely from the practice of her religion." *Id.* at 404. Similarly, a Catholic child attending a parochial school is ineligible for the financial benefits granted other state-accredited schools (*i.e.*, public schools) solely because of the dictates of his religion; that

A shortcoming of this approach is that it permits the employment of tax-raised funds for strictly religious purposes. Seemingly, this doctrine would allow the use of public money for the construction of churches and synagogues if the legislative classification were broad enough—say, a statute allocating funds for new structures to house all voluntary associations, enacted on the ground that members lacked requisite resources for

---

Catholic parents have "the duty of entrusting their children to Catholic schools wherever and whenever it is possible," Pope Paul VI, Decree on Christian Education (1965), *reprinted in* 1 T. EMERSON, D. HABER, & N. DORSEN, POLITICAL AND CIVIL RIGHTS IN THE UNITED STATES 1079, 1081 (3d ed. 1967), hardly requires citation. See also the Canon Laws of the Roman Catholic Church, reproduced in Everson v. Board of Educ., 330 U.S. 1, 22-23 (1947) (dissenting opinion of Jackson, J.). *But cf.* R. DRINAN, *supra* note 50, at 190-92. Second, the Court noted that "the pressure upon [Mrs. Sherbert] to forego [her religious] practice is unmistakable," 374 U.S. at 404. Given the well-publicized financial predicament of parochial schools and the importance of effective education to children, a similar pressure exists to attend a better financed public school. Third, as in *Sherbert*, denying financial aid to parochial schools "forces [the Catholic child] to choose between following the precepts of [his] religion and forfeiting benefits, on the one hand, and abandoning one of the precepts of [his] religion . . . on the other hand." *Id.* Finally, the *Sherbert* Court concludes that "to condition the availability of benefits upon this appellant's willingness to violate a cardinal principle of her religious faith effectively penalizes the free exercise of her constitutional liberties." *Id.* at 406. It is not difficult to reach a similar conclusion in respect to denying public aid to Catholic parochial schools. *See generally* School Dist. v. Schempp, 374 U.S. 203, 312-13 (1963) (dissenting opinion of Stewart, J.); Blum, *Our Federal Constitution and Equal Justice in Education,* in EDUCATIONAL FREEDOM AND THE CASE FOR GOVERNMENT AID TO STUDENTS IN INDEPENDENT SCHOOLS 154-57 (D. McGarry & L. Ward eds. 1966) [hereinafter cited as EDUCATIONAL FREEDOM]; Blum, *Freedom and Equality,* in FEDERAL AID AND CATHOLIC SCHOOLS 43, 51-54 (D. Callahan ed. 1964); Drinan, *Does State Aid to Church-Related Colleges Constitute an Establishment of Religion?—Reflections on the Maryland College Cases,* 1967 UTAH L. REV. 491, 511-15; Farhat, *The Michigan School Bus Law,* MICH. STATE B.J., Apr. 1964, at 28, 31; Regan, *Religious Neutrality,* 110 AMERICA 74 (1964); Rice, *The New York State Constitution and Aid to Church-Related Schools,* 12 CATHOLIC LAW. 272, 321 (1966); 19 S.C.L. REV. 242 (1967).

It may even be argued that the free exercise claim for aid to parochial schools is yet more compelling than Mrs. Sherbert's successful claim. When the state sends Mrs. Sherbert her unemployment compensation check, as the Court ordered that it do, thus excusing her from taking "suitable work" because of her conscientious scruples, the state's action is taken solely to facilitate religious exercise—the state's purpose may be said to be *religious.* See note 55 *supra.* In the view of some analysts, such action raises serious establishment clause problems. *See* Kurland, *supra* note 19, at 94; *cf.* Sherbert v. Verner, *supra,* at 415 (concurring opinion of Stewart, J.). But when the state finances the nonreligious aspects of education in parochial schools, its purpose, as will be demonstrated *infra,* see text at notes 145-149, is *secular,* thus removing this possible objection. *See* W. LOCKHART, Y. KAMISAR & J. CHOPER, CONSTITUTIONAL LAW 1185-86 (2d ed. 1967).

It is not meant by this brief discursiveness to speculate as to the Court's resolution of the free exercise claim if it were advanced. In fact, the Court's denial of certiorari in Swart v. South Burlington Town School Dist., 122 Vt. 177, 167 A.2d 514, *cert. denied,* 366 U.S. 925 (1961), in which the state court rejected the contention, does not bode well for its ultimate success. *See also* Dickman v. School Dist., 223 Ore. 347, 366 P.2d 533 (1961), *cert. denied,* 371 U.S. 823 (1962). Nor is it meant to suggest that the persuasiveness of the free exercise argument follows conclusively from *Sherbert.* Perhaps a "compelling state interest," 374 U.S. at 406, found necessary but wanting in *Sherbert,* to justify the "sub-

such undertaking.[60] Although such a statute may not be said to give intentional and purposeful support to religion,[61] in the sense that it "singles out a religion, or religions generally, for direct financial assistance,"[62] this particular statute's clear effect contradicts a vital value underlying the establishment clause.[63] The breadth of the classification—using tax funds to support buildings for the Rotary, Odd Fellows, and Chamber of Commerce, in addition to recognized (and nonconformist) religions—would seem to many people only to add pocketbook insult to constitutional injury.[64] Even the most avid proponents of aid to parochial schools would seem to agree that such subsidies of religion are not permissible.[65] Whether consciously or not, the "official support of the State or Federal Govern-

---

stantial infringement," *id.*, of the free exercise right will be shown in the aid to parochial schools context—perhaps the essentiality of conserving the public fisc, perhaps the notion (with which I disagree) that to grant the aid would itself violate the letter or spirit of the establishment clause. The point is that the free exercise allegation is surely not "sheer sophistry," 78 CHRISTIAN CENTURY 508 (1961) (editorial).

Father Drinan has made the following contention for the constitutional compulsion of aid to parochial schools: because "of clear Supreme Court rulings precluding sectarian teaching and religious practices in public schools it can be persuasively argued that the granting of funds only to the public school is a violation of the establishment clause because such a policy endorses and prefers one educational and philosophical orthodoxy [a "religion . . . of secularism," R. DRINAN, *supra* note 50, at 193] over all others." Drinan, *The Constitutionality of Public Aid to Parochial Schools*, in THE WALL BETWEEN CHURCH AND STATE 55, 72 (D. Oaks ed. 1963). Even if the "religion of secularism" assumption were to be valid, *but see* note 224 *infra*, the contention as a plea for financial aid must fail. It ignores the Court's unequivocal pronouncement that the establishment clause forbids governmental support of all religions, not merely preference of one religion over another. School Dist. v. Schempp, 374 U.S. 203, 216 (1963). *See also* S. HOOK, RELIGION IN A FREE SOCIETY 16 (1967).

[60] *See* LaNoue, *The Child Benefit Theory Revisited: Textbooks, Transportation and Medical Care*, 13 J. PUB. L. 76, 89 (1964).

With respect to the free exercise clause, the Kurland thesis has been recently rejected by the Court in Sherbert v. Verner, 374 U.S. 398 (1963). With respect to the establishment clause, the Court, consistent with the Kurland thesis, has to date invalidated only governmental action strictly directed to religious ends. McCollum v. Board of Educ., 333 U.S. 203 (1948); Torcaso v. Watkins, 367 U.S. 488 (1961); Engel v. Vitale, 370 U.S. 421 (1962); School Dist. v. Schempp, 374 U.S. 203 (1963). But it is fair to note that the thesis has never really been put to the test in the establishment cases, as in a situation just hypothesized in the text.

[61] *Cf.* McCollum v. Board of Educ., 333 U.S. 203, 248 (1948) (dissenting opinion of Reed, J.).

[62] Dunsford, *supra* note 42, at 205.

[63] See text accompanying notes 43-50 *supra*. *See also* U.S. Dep't of Health, Education & Welfare, *supra* note 20, at 373.

[64] *But cf.* 77 HARV. L. REV. 1353, 1357-58 (1964).

[65] *See Hearings on H.R. 2361, supra* note 35, at 821 (Statement of Msgr. McManus). *See also* R. DRINAN, *supra* note 50, at 231; statement of Msgr. Gallagher, quoted in *id.* at 29. The fact that a public subsidy of religion may attract more people to it, thus resulting in a net increase in the operating costs of the church, *see* Matthews v. Quinton, 362 P.2d 932, 953 (Alas. 1961) (dissenting opinion), is, of course, irrelevant to the analysis.

ment would be placed behind the tenets of one or of all orthodoxies. This the Establishment Clause prohibits."[66]

(c) *Divisiveness*.—It has frequently been declared that the function of the establishment clause is "above all, to keep bitter religious controversy out of public life by denying to every denomination any advantage from getting control of public policy or the public purse."[67] The conflict among religions brought about by a struggle for public funds is surely unfortunate and undesirable.[68] And upholding the constitutionality of some amounts of aid to parochial schools or to the children that attend them might well push in this direction.[69] One might agree that "if government interferes in matters spiritual, it will be a divisive force,"[70] thus making such action constitutionally suspect. But to make "divisiveness" determinative of constitutionality, despite the secular nature of the governmental program in controversy, is neither a desirable nor a workable approach to the problem.[71]

Whether rightly or wrongly, the various churches and religious groups have exerted powerful political influence in national and state legislative halls[72]—frequently in disagreement with one another—concerning such causes as Sunday closing,[73] gambling, prohibition, abolition, integration, overpopulation, birth control, sterilization, marriage, and divorce. Surely such legislation is not therefore invalid. Nor would a denial of aid to parochial schools largely diminish the extent of religious political activity. In fact, it "might lead to greater political ruptures caused by the alienation of segments of the religious community."[74] Those who send their children to parochial schools might intensify opposition to increased governmental aid to public education on the ground that it raises their taxes without direct personal benefit, decreases their financial ability to support the parochial schools, and augments the operational costs of parochial schools seeking to maintain qualitative parity with the improved public schools.[75]

---

[66] School Dist. v. Schempp, 374 U.S. 203, 222 (1963).

[67] Everson v. Board of Educ., 330 U.S. 1, 27 (1947) (dissenting opinion of Jackson, J.). *See also* McCollum v. Board of Educ., 333 U.S. 203, 228 (1948) (concurring opinion of Frankfurter, J.).

[68] *See* Van Alstyne, *Constitutional Separation of Church and State: The Quest for a Coherent Position*, 57 AM. POL. SCI. REV. 865, 868 (1963).

[69] *See* Everson v. Board of Educ., 330 U.S. 1, 53-55 (1947) (dissenting opinion of Rutledge, J.); A. JOHNSON & F. YOST, *supra* note 28, at 113.

[70] Engel v. Vitale, 370 U.S. 421, 443 (1962) (concurring opinion of Douglas, J.).

[71] *See* Choper, *supra* note 4, at 385-86.

[72] *See* M. HOWE, *supra* note 40, at 62; P. KAUPER, *supra* note 5, at 83-85; RELIGION AND AMERICAN SOCIETY, *supra* note 42, at 71; see text accompanying notes 100-01 *infra*.

[73] *See* McGowan v. Maryland, 366 U.S. 420, 435 (1961).

[74] 77 HARV. L. REV. 1357 (1964).

[75] *Cf.* Mitchell, *Religion and Federal Aid to Education*, 14 LAW & CONTEMP. PROB. 113, 122-27 (1949); Whelan, *School Question: Stage Two*, 105 AMERICA 17 (1961).

2. Application to the States

Before proceeding further, certain other peripheral matters may be treated. The discussion to this point has assumed that the first amendment's mandate, that "Congress shall make no law respecting an establishment of religion," is equally applicable, through the fourteenth amendment, to action by the states. This has been the Court's consistent position and, in view of this, the Court has recently noted that contrary arguments "seem entirely untenable and of value only as academic exercises."[76]

Examination of the dispute, however, may help to clarify the scope of the establishment clause. The relevant fourteenth amendment language is that "no State shall . . . deprive any person of life, liberty, or property, without due process of law. . . ." It is therefore asserted that the fourteenth amendment should forbid only those violations of the first amendment's establishment clause that "significantly affect the secured liberties of individuals"[77] so as to deprive them of such liberty without due process of law—the implication being that some establishment clause infractions do not significantly impair fourteenth amendment liberties.[78] It is this suggestion that may be challenged.

The suggestion assumes that while the fourteenth amendment prevents infringements of liberty which "significantly affect" the individual, the first amendment forbids abridgements which do not do so. It bears repeating, however, that a central design of the establishment clause was that it act "as a co-guarantor, with the Free Exercise Clause, of religious liberty,"[79] by preventing the government generally from coercing religious belief and specifically from compulsorily taxing individuals for strictly religious purposes.[80] If nonsecular federal action involves either of these consequences, I would suggest that it has "significantly" affected indi-

---

[76] School Dist. v. Schempp, 374 U.S. 203, 217 (1963). *See generally id.* at 215-16.

[77] Howe, *The Constitutional Question,* in Religion and the Free Society, *supra* note 17, at 49, 61. *See also* P. KAUPER, *supra* note 5, at 56.

[78] *See* M. HOWE, *supra* note 40, at 138.

[79] School Dist. v. Schempp, 374 U.S. 203, 256 (1963) (concurring opinion of Brennan, J.). *See also id.* at 227 (concurring opinion of Douglas, J.); *id.* at 312 (dissenting opinion of Stewart, J.); Lardner, *How Far Does the Constitution Separate Church and State?,* 45 AM. POL. SCI. REV. 110, 128 (1951); note 42 *supra.*

Whatever the historical foundation for the notion that the clause was intended to bar Congress from disestablishing the state establishments, see note 48 *supra,* it is of little pragmatic relevance today because of the nonexistence, and patent invalidity under the fourteenth amendment, of any formal state establishment. Of course, as a matter of logic, this purported goal of the establishment clause could not be made applicable to the states through the fourteenth amendment. *See* W. KATZ, *supra* note 48, at 11.

[80] See text accompanying notes 43-50 *supra.*

vidual freedom.[81] Thus, if such state action involves either,[82] it has seemingly violated the fourteenth amendment by "significantly" affecting personal liberty.[83] However, if federal action involves neither consequence, then I would suggest that the establishment clause itself—as a matter of constitutional construction—has probably not been breached. The establishment clause, in sum, may well ban no activity that should not also be held to violate the fourteenth amendment, consistent literally with the latter's relevant language.[84]

3. Standing of Federal Taxpayers

The question of a federal taxpayer's standing to challenge federal aid to parochial schools—or, for that matter, aid for church construction itself—is generally beyond the scope of the discussion.[85] But again, brief inquiry may be enlightening in examining the reach of the establishment bar.

Frothingham v. Mellon[86] holds that a taxpayer's interest in federal appropriations is too minute, remote, uncertain, and indeterminable to support a suit challenging federal spending. Whether the decision rests on a finding that the matter therefore does not meet the "case or controversy" requirement of article III of the Constitution, or whether it is

---

[81] See note 51 *supra*. *See* School Dist. v. Schempp, 374 U.S. 203, 295 (1963) (concurring opinion of Brennan, J.); *id.* at 308 (concurring opinion of Goldberg, J.). *See also* Choper, *supra* note 4, at 331 n.8. *Cf.* text accompanying note 333 *infra*.

[82] See text accompanying notes 51-53 *supra*.

[83] Such use of tax funds might also be characterized as a deprivation of property without due process of law.

[84] For an interesting and novel analysis that would make the religion clauses of the first amendment applicable to the states via the equal protection clause of the fourteenth amendment, see Kauper, *The Constitutionality of Tax Exemptions for Religious Activities*, in THE WALL BETWEEN CHURCH AND STATE 95, 101-02 (D. Oaks ed. 1963).

[85] The issue of whether the rule of Frothingham v. Mellon, 262 U.S. 447 (1923), bars a suit by a federal taxpayer challenging aid to parochial schools is specifically presented in a case now pending before the Supreme Court. Flast v. Gardner, 271 F. Supp. 1 (S.D.N.Y.), *prob. juris. noted*, 389 U.S. 895 (1967). *See also* Elliott v. White, 23 F.2d 997 (D.C. Cir. 1928) (no standing); Protestants and Other Americans United v. O'Brien, 272 F. Supp. 712 (D.D.C. 1967) (no standing); Protestants and Other Americans United v. United States, 266 F. Supp. 473 (S.D. Ohio 1967) (no standing).

That local and state taxpayers have standing in the Supreme Court, if granted standing in the state court, to challenge local and state expenditures seems clear from the decided cases, Everson v. Board of Educ., 330 U.S. 1 (1947); Cochran v. Louisiana State Bd. of Educ., 281 U.S. 370 (1930), although the issue has rarely been discussed by the Court. *See* Doremus v. Board of Educ., 342 U.S. 429 (1952). The possibility that a taxpayer's suit to enjoin state expenditures allegedly in violation of the establishment clause might lie in the federal district courts despite the state's refusal to recognize such an action is discussed in Sutherland, *Due Process and Disestablishment*, 62 HARV. L. REV. 1306, 1330-35 (1949).

[86] 262 U.S. 447 (1923).

based only on a judicial rule of self-limitation, is unclear.[87] But even if it is the former, a taxpayer's suit based on an alleged establishment clause violation is arguably distinguishable from *Frothingham*.

The ordinary federal taxpayer's suit urges simply that the congressional appropriation is ultra vires—beyond the national power and thus "reserved to the States" by the tenth amendment. The gravamen of the claim is that there has been a violation of states' rights (although the allegation is frequently added that this results in a deprivation to the individual of property without due process of law[88]). In such circumstances, the Court has good reason to decline jurisdiction[89]—to find "essentially a matter of public and not of individual concern";[90] to require the taxpayer "to show . . . that he has sustained or is immediately in danger of sustaining some direct injury . . . and not merely that he suffers in some indefinite way in common with people generally."[91]

When the federal taxpayer's suit urges that the congressional appropriation violates the establishment clause, however, his claim is not merely one of ultra vires. The expenditure of compulsorily raised tax funds for religious purposes, both historically and contemporarily, may well be characterized as an abridgment of individual religious liberty.[92] The issue is not only one of states' rights; it may be one of alleged governmental infringement of individual rights protected by the Constitution.[93] "Direct injury" has allegedly been "suffered"—and not "in some indefinite way."[94] Mr. Justice Jackson recognized that "[o]ne of our basic

---

[87] This issue would be crucial were Congress to enact a statute authorizing taxpayers to attack federal expenditures on establishment grounds. Such legislation has, at different times, passed the House, H.R. 4643, 81st Cong., 1st Sess. § 5 (1949), and the Senate, S. 2097, 89th Cong., 2d Sess. (1966), but never both houses together. If *Frothingham* were based on article III, such legislation would be unconstitutional. *Compare* Manning, *Aid to Education—Federal Fashion*, 29 FORDHAM L. REV. 495, 506 (1961); U.S. Dep't of Health, Education & Welfare, *supra* note 20, at 381; Comment, 8 VILL. L. REV. 224, 230-31 (1962-63), *with* Professor Jaffe's view in Dorsen, *supra* note 33, at 51. On this possibility, a number of legislative devices, other than a taxpayer's suit, have been developed as conceivable avenues for testing federal expenditures under the establishment clause. *See* Jaffe, *supra*, at 64-65; U.S. Dep't of Health, Education, & Welfare, *supra* note 20, at 382; 77 HARV. L. REV. 1357, 1360 (1964). *See also* TIME, Nov. 25, 1966, at 55-56. The Elementary and Secondary Education Act of 1965, 20 U.S.C. §§ 241k, 827, 869 (Supp. I, 1965), presents this potential. *See* Drinan, *Standing to Sue in Establishment Cases*, 1965 RELIGION & PUB. ORDER 161, 165 (D. Giannella ed.).

[88] *E.g.*, Frothingham v. Mellon, 262 U.S. 447, 482, 486 (1923). *See generally* Lewis, *Constitutional Rights and the Misuse of "Standing*," 14 STAN. L. REV. 433 (1962).

[89] *See* Choper, *On the Warren Court and Judicial Review*, 17 CATHOLIC U.L. REV. 20, 39-40 (1967).

[90] Frothingham v. Mellon, 262 U.S. 447, 487 (1923).

[91] *Id.* at 488.

[92] See text accompanying notes 43-50, 79-80 *supra*.

[93] *See* Choper, *supra* note 89, at 39-41.

[94] Frothingham v. Mellon, 262 U.S. 477, 488 (1923).

rights is to be free of taxation to support a transgression"⁹⁵ of the establishment clause; that the Court "had jurisdiction" "[w]here a complainant is deprived of property by being taxed . . . to support a religious establishment."⁹⁶ Thus, *Frothingham* may be inapplicable to a suit based not on the tenth amendment, but rather on the establishment clause.⁹⁷

The establishment clause rationale described herein concludes that the clause generally forbids nonsecular governmental action which infringes religious beliefs and specifically bars coercive taxation for strictly religious purposes. Under this rationale, governmental spending for secular purposes is permissible. This rationale is not only consistent with contemporary and historical values underlying the establishment clause, but also affords an evaluative perspective for the problems of the role of the fourteenth amendment and the question of standing to sue.

III

DEFINITION OF SECULAR PURPOSE

The broad establishment clause rationale described above would generally forbid government expenditures for strictly religious purposes and would bar governmental action for these purposes if infringements of religious liberty followed. On the other hand, it would generally permit the state to act for secular purposes. Thus, it is analytically critical to decide what constitutes a secular purpose and how it should be determined. This is frequently a perplexing inquiry because a law may be enacted for a multiplicity of purposes and may produce a multiplicity of effects.⁹⁸ A Sunday closing law, for example, may have the secular purpose of promoting the general welfare by creating a day of respite or the religious purpose of forbidding work to enhance church attendance.⁹⁹

Certain aspects of the problem are quite clear. The fact that religious groups sponsored a law—or even were its sole sponsors—does not make its purpose nonsecular;¹⁰⁰ the Civil Rights Act of 1964 might not have passed without the support of churchmen.¹⁰¹ Nor, with the rare and

---

⁹⁵ Everson v. Board of Educ., 330 U.S. 1, 22 (1947) (dissenting opinion).
⁹⁶ McCollum v. Board of Educ., 333 U.S. 203, 233-34 (1948) (concurring opinion).
⁹⁷ An allegation that federal funds are being expended for religious purposes, sufficient to support standing, should not, of course, be misidentified with the question of whether the money is in fact being so used—which goes to the merits of the case. *But see* Drinan, *supra* note 87, at 172.
⁹⁸ *See* Van Alstyne, *supra* note 68, at 875.
⁹⁹ *See* McGowan v. Maryland, 366 U.S. 420 (1961).
¹⁰⁰ See text following note 72 *supra*.
¹⁰¹ *See* Carroll, *The Constitution, The Supreme Court, and Religion*, 61 AM. POL. SCI. REV. 657, 662 (1967).

limited qualification to be noted below,[102] should existence of a secular purpose turn on judicial examination of legislative motives[103]—a long, forbidden psychoanalytic attempt to find the *"real* reason," articulated or unspoken, for passing a law.[104] Rather, whether government action is secular or religious should generally be determined by the nature of its *independent* or *primary* effect (a term to be illustrated below, and not to be confused with "principle" or "paramount" effect). If the primary effect is to accomplish a nonreligious public purpose, the action should generally be held immune from establishment clause attack.[105] But if the primary effect is to serve a religious end, the action's purpose should not be characterized as secular even though an *ultimate* or *derivative* public benefit may be produced.[106]

A. *Illustrations*

Specific instances are necessary to illustrate the point. It has been maintained that public school prayer recitation and Bible reading serve the secular purpose of producing profound convictions in children, thus making them better citizens.[107] But if such are the effects, they come about only if the primary goal of these practices—the implanting of spiritual and religious beliefs—is achieved; the purported secular ends are derivative from the primary religious effect. Thus, under the analysis suggested above, the purpose of the governmental action is religious.

Sunday closing laws also serve an undeniably religious end by encouraging church attendance in removing the obstacle of having to report for work. But they also produce an independent secular effect—"a Sunday atmosphere of recreation, cheerfulness, repose and enjoyment."[108] And this secular effect is in no way dependent on or derived from the religious impact of the statute.

Governmental actions whose secular benefits flow from the achievement of a primary religious effect must be suspect under the establishment clause.[109] Such actions "employ Religion as an engine of Civil

---

[102] See text accompanying note 114-24 *infra.*

[103] Van Alstyne, *supra* note 68, at 876.

[104] *See* McGowan v. Maryland, 366 U.S. 420, 466, 469 (1961) (concurring opinion of Frankfurter, J.); A. BICKEL, THE LEAST DANGEROUS BRANCH 208-21 (1962).

[105] See text accompanying notes 325-45 *infra.*

[106] *See* Choper, *supra* note 4, at 334-38. *See also* Hammett, *The Homogenized Wall,* 53 A.B.A.J. 929, 933 (1967).

[107] *See* discussion in Choper, *supra* note 4, at 336.

[108] McGowan v. Maryland, 366 U.S. 420, 448 (1961).

[109] I have argued that such actions should be invalid if either of two additional factors are present. See text accompanying notes 51-53 *supra*. This distinction should satisfy the objection of Lardner, *supra* note 79, at 132, that "the public welfare argument amounts to the automatic validity of all legislation" because "[a]ll legislation in a democracy arises

policy."[110] Allowing such actions would literally read the clause out of the first amendment; it would justify government subsidization of that church that the government found best inculcates its members with the deep convictions that make for better citizenship.[111] But governmental action that produces independent secular efforts should generally be unassailable even if an equally necessary or inevitable effect is the benefitting of religion. If not, the fire department could not protect burning churches.

B. *Judicial Determinations*

This is not to say that the task of distinguishing primary religious and secular effects is always free of difficulty. But usually it is. Thus, in *Torcaso v. Watkins*, the Court observed that there could be "no dispute about the [religious] purpose or effect"[112] of a requirement that public officeholders declare a belief in God. And in *Engle v. Vitale*, the Court had "no doubt that . . . daily classroom invocation of . . . the Regents' prayer is a religious activity."[113]

On occasion, governmental action with a primary religious effect may be wrapped "in the verbal cellophane"[114] of a secular purpose. Thus, in the *Bible Reading Cases* the state argued secular purpose—"the promotion of moral values, the contradiction to the materialistic trends of our times, the perpetuation of our institutions and the teaching of literature."[115] The Court easily rejected the assertion, agreeing instead with the trial court's finding that the exercises had a religious character.[116]

In such instances, the Court is not—nor should it be—making the

---

from the belief that it promotes the public welfare," and that of Carroll, *supra* note 101, at 662-63.

[110] J. MADISON, MEMORIAL AND REMONSTRANCE AGAINST RELIGIOUS ASSESSMENTS, ¶ 5, set forth in Everson v. Board of Educ., 330 U.S. 1, 67 (1947) (app.).

[111] See text at note 107 *supra*. See also McCloskey, *Principles, Powers, and Values: The Establishment Clause and the Supreme Court*, 1964 RELIGION & PUB. ORDER 3, 26 (D Giannella ed.): "[A] religious law for a religious end . . . . offends one religious conscience in the name of another, and unless we reject the sovereignty of religious belief, we must find this blameworthy. Nor is such a law vindicated by the contention that it employs religious means to a secular end, *i.e.*, the development of a moral citizenry which will in turn produce a just and happy society. For whatever tendency the means have to accomplish that end may be canceled by their simultaneous tendency to generate the bitterness that makes such a society difficult." *See also* School Dist. v. Schempp, 374 U.S. 203, 278-81 (1963) (concurring opinion of Brennan, J.).

[112] 367 U.S. 488, 489 (1961).

[113] 370 U.S. 421, 424 (1962).

[114] United States v. Kahriger, 345 U.S. 22, 38 (1953) (dissenting opinion of Frankfurter, J.).

[115] School Dist. v. Schempp, 374 U.S. 203, 223 (1963).

[116] *Id.* Similarly, I suggest that the Court would reject the contention that requiring the memorization of the Catechism in public schools serves the secular purpose of teaching the technique of memory. *But cf.* Paul v. Dade County, 202 So. 2d 833 (Fla. Dist. Ct. App. 1967).

judgment that any secular purpose of the law fails to be paramount over whatever religious end the church obtains by the regulated conduct.[117] For the Court to engage in such an ad hoc balancing process[118]—relying only on the Justices' subjective notions of paramountcy—to treat the problem as "one of degree,"[119] is not satisfactory when more objective standards are available.[120] Even where a religious purpose exists, the state's secular purpose need not be dominant or paramount;[121] the existence of a "legitimate" independent primary secular purpose should be sufficient. The determination of "legitimacy" by the Court undeniably involves the making of a not wholly objective judgment. But, unlike the "dominancy-paramountcy" inquiry, it is a judgment of a quite limited nature, mainly disposed of by common sense and observation of the obvious effects of the enactment.[122] Although the inquiry is necessitated by a recognition that a disingenuous legislature can easily find secular purposes to cover any religious interest it wishes to further,[123] such a cover is almost always revealed as cellophane.[124]

A few additional illustrations may be helpful. In 1921, the California legislature appropriated 10,000 dollars for the restoration of the San Diego Mission,[125] resulting in an unquestionable financial benefit of a strictly religious nature to the Roman Catholic Church, which owned and controlled the mission for the use of its parishioners. There was also an independent primary secular effect, however, in no way derived from the religious impact of the action, which could not be fairly characterized as a mere "cover." As the court noted, the missions have significant architectural, historical, and educational value, and the aid therefore served a secular esthetic purpose. Under the proposed analysis, this should generally be adequate to establish constitutional validity.[126] It might be added, as a persuasive rather than a constitutional argument,[127] that it is reasonable to believe that reconditioning the mission would pay financial dividends to the state treasury, by increased tourism, in excess of its cost. The mission case thus involved no possible infringement

---

[117] *But see* Hammett, *supra* note 106, at 932. *See also* Note, *The Elementary and Secondary Education Act of 1965 and the First Amendment*, 41 IND. L.J. 302, 324 (1966).
[118] See text accompanying note 447 *infra*.
[119] Zorach v. Clauson, 343 U.S. 306, 314 (1952) (Douglas, J.).
[120] *See* Choper, *supra* note 4, at 335.
[121] *But see* Hammett, *supra* note 106, at 932.
[122] *See, e.g.*, School Dist. v. Schempp, 374 U.S. 203, 223-25 (1963). See text following note 231 *infra*.
[123] LaNoue, *supra* note 60, at 77-78.
[124] *See generally* Van Alstyne, *supra* note 68, at 876-77.
[125] Frohligher v. Richardson, 63 Cal. App. 209, 218 P. 497 (1923).
[126] The California court, however, found the action violative of the state constitution.
[127] See text following note 158 *infra*.

of religious or conscientious scruples, either directly or through diversion of tax funds to religious purposes.[128]

A municipality should not, however, be permitted to allocate public funds to build houses of worship for the purpose of encouraging church-going people to live in the community. In contrast to the mission restoration example discussed above, which attracted people by appealing to their esthetic and educational interests, this plan would publicly finance the religious needs of individuals in order ultimately to derive a secular goal. Even though the plan might increase the general tax base in the community,[129] thus compensating the public for its religious expenditure, its primary effect—from which the secular end would be derived—would be religious.[130]

Finally, it has been suggested that, as part of a state's mental health budget, funds might be granted to the Roman Catholic Church and the Protestant Episcopal Church to subsidize confession costs because of their therapeutic value.[131] But it would seem here that the purported therapeutic benefit—which we may concede is secular—would come about only as a result of the confessor's having obtained spiritual satisfaction. The exclusive primary effect is religious.[132]

C. *Supreme Court Rationale*

The rather specific rationale of several decisions of the Supreme Court is consistent with this "secular purpose" approach. In the *School Bus Case*,[133] the Court acknowledged that the governmental program substantially benefitted religion in the "possibility that some of the children might not be sent to the church schools if the parents were com-

---

[128] Similarly, an expenditure by the Utah legislature to construct a building for the preservation and display of relics, highly important to the Mormon religion but also of great historical significance in the state's development, serves an independent primary secular goal. *See* Thomas v. Daughters of Utah Pioneers, 114 Utah 108, 197 P.2d 477 (1948). So, too, would an appropriation by the Los Angeles County Board of Supervisors to a religious association for the purpose of preparing a motion picture film of the latter's annual sectarian-oriented Christmas parade, if the film were to be distributed throughout the country "to exploit and make known the resources of the County and thereby increase its trade and commerce." County of Los Angeles v. Hollinger, 221 Cal. App. 2d 154, 156, 34 Cal. Rptr. 387, 389 (1963) (invalid under state constitution). *See also* 37 Op. Cal. Att'y Gen. 105 (1965).

[129] Murray v. Comptroller of the Treasury, 241 Md. 383, 402-04, 216 A.2d 897, 908-09, *cert. denied*, 385 U.S. 816 (1966).

[130] See text following note 158 *infra*.

[131] Davidow, *Governmental Aid to Church-Affiliated Colleges: An Analysis of a Possible Answer to the Constitutional Question*, 43 N.D.L. Rev. 659, 679 (1967).

[132] This should be contrasted with public aid to divinity schools to train students to recognize mental illness. *See* U.S. Dep't of Health, Education & Welfare, *supra* note 20, at 375-76 n.18.

[133] Everson v. Board of Educ., 330 U.S. 1 (1947).

pelled to pay their children's bus fares out of their own pockets when transportation to a public school would have been paid for by the State."[134] Yet, the Court upheld public payment of the bus fares of parochial school pupils as "public welfare legislation" protecting "children going to and from church schools from the very real hazards of traffic."[135] There was a legitimate independent primary secular purpose and effect.[136] The Court utilized the same analysis in the *Sunday Closing Law Case*,[137] recognizing that the establishment clause "does not ban federal or state regulation of conduct whose reason or effect merely happens to coincide or harmonize with the tenets of some or all religions."[138]

In the *Bible Reading Case*,[139] the Court was most explicit. It laid down a "test" as follows: "what are the purpose and primary effect of the enactment? If either is the advancement or inhibition of religion then the enactment exceeds the scope of legislative power as circumscribed by the Constitution. That is to say that to withstand the strictures of the Establishment Clause there must be a secular legislative purpose and a primary effect that neither advances nor inhibits religion."[140]

If the Court meant that there is an establishment clause violation if *the* purpose and primary effect is religious but that there is no such violation if *a* secular legislative purpose and primary effect exists, and if the Court used the word "primary" as I have used it in the discussion above—that is, as distinguished from "ultimate" or "derivative"[141]—then the Court's test essentially states the reasoning that I have employed.[142]

In fairness, this places undue weight on tiny words which usually denote no such significance. The Court may perhaps have drafted the test not for the specific situation in *Schempp*, but for the question of aid

---

[134] *Id.* at 17.
[135] *Id.* at 16-17.
[136] *See* note 510 *infra*; Comment, 45 MICH. L. REV. 1001, 1021 n.89 (1947).
[137] McGowan v. Maryland, 366 U.S. 420 (1961).
[138] *Id.* at 442. Neither, it would seem, should the clause ban "federal or state [financial aid] whose reason or effect merely happens to coincide or harmonize with" the aims of some or all religions, if a primary effect of such aid is for "the general welfare of society," *Id.*
[139] School Dist. v. Schempp, 374 U.S. 203 (1963).
[140] *Id.* at 222.
[141] Mr. Hammett argues, *supra* note 106, at 933, that the Court's intention on this point was to assure that the enactment does not enhance the financial strength of the church to a greater extent than it augments the influence of or benefit to the state. How the Court is to measure these relative increases in power is not clear. He may mean, as I have suggested, that there must be an independent secular benefit commensurate with the state aid. But if he means that the members of the Court must individually weigh these church and state factors in each case, then serious objection may be raised. See text accompanying notes 117-20 *supra*.
[142] For support of this view, see Kauper, *supra* note 18, at 12-13. *See also* Kauper, *Religion, Higher Education and the Constitution*, 19 ALA. L. REV. 275, 288 (1967).

to parochial schools.[143] Even so, because of differing inferences that may be drawn, it provides no ready answer. Perhaps, on the other hand, the Court was concerned only with the problem before it.[144] In any case, my only contention is that the *Schempp* "test" is not inconsonant with the "secular purpose" approach proposed herein.

IV

AID TO PAROCHIAL SCHOOLS

A. Secular Purpose

At least some governmental aid to support parochial education serves a primary or independent secular purpose. No one can deny the state's legitimate interest in improving the educational quality of all schools,[145] or the benefits to society in general from education,[146] or even the national defense interest in an enlightened citizenry.[147] The fact is that "parochial elementary and secondary schools educate one out of every eight future citizens of this country, and that the teacher and classroom needs of parochial school systems are possibly even more serious than are those of the public school systems."[148]

Even Mr. Justice Rutledge, in his vigorous dissent in *Everson*, admitted that "it is much too late to urge that legislation designed to facilitate the opportunities of children to secure a secular education serves no public purpose."[149] His position was that the establishment clause

---

[143] Sky, *supra* note 42, at 1441.
[144] *See* Horace Mann League v. Board of Pub. Works, 242 Md. 645, 220 A.2d 51, 64, *cert. denied*, 385 U.S. 97 (1966); LaNoue, *supra* note 60, at 78-79.
[145] Board of Educ. v. Allen, 20 N.Y.2d 109, 116, 228 N.E.2d 791, 794, 281 N.Y.S.2d 799, 804 (1967), *prob. juris. noted*, 36 U.S.L.W. 3278 (U.S. Jan. 15, 1968). *See also* Amdursky, *The First Amendment and Federal Aid to Church-Related Schools*, 17 SYRACUSE L. REV. 609, 624 (1966).
[146] Malloy, *How to Talk About Federal Aid*, 105 AMERICA 421, 422 (1962).
[147] Sky, *supra* note 42, at 1448.
[148] Actions of the General Assembly of the United Presbyterian Church in the U.S.A. Supporting Federal Aid to Public Primary and Secondary Education, in 5 *Hearings on S. 370 Before the Subcomm. on Education of the Senate Comm. on Labor and Public Welfare*, 89th Cong., 1st Sess., at 2890 (1965). It is not the purpose here to document the alleged need of parochial schools for financial assistance. But several interesting facts might be mentioned: (a) The U.S. Commissioner of Education recently observed that "[a]t all levels of education, effective teaching has become increasingly contingent on well-stocked libraries. . . ." 2 *id.* at 848. His statistics revealed that 29.6% of public school pupils and 37.2% of nonpublic school pupils attended schools that had no libraries. *Id.* at 849. (b) Children from "deprived neighborhoods" attending both public and parochial schools "are losing points on their IQ, particularly between the third and sixth grades, and by the time they get to the eighth grade, they are apt to be 2 or 3 or 4 or 5 years behind." 5 *id.* at 2540 (question by Senator Robert F. Kennedy).
[149] 330 U.S. at 50.

forbids state support for "religious training, teaching or observance."[150] I agree. But, "[i]f the fact alone be determinative that religious schools are engaged in education," he could "see no possible basis, except one of dubious legislative policy, for the state's refusal to make full appropriation for support of private, religious schools, just as is done for public instruction."[151] I disagree.

Parochial schools perform a dual function, providing some religious education and some secular education. Government may finance the latter,[152] but the establishment clause forbids it to finance the former. That government money may be used for partial support of church schools does not mean that "it can also be used for the support of our churches, and that we are moving toward a union of church and state in America."[153] Conceding Mr. Justice Jackson's premise that "Catholic education is the rock on which the whole structure rests,"[154] his conclusion does not follow that rendering "tax aid to its Church school is indistinguishable . . . from rendering the same aid to the Church itself."

It must be perceived that by using tax funds to support the secular aspects of parochial education, the state expends no more than would be required either to support parochial school pupils if they attended existing public schools, or to establish additional public schools at various sites for all pupils presently attending parochial schools,[155] neither of which alternatives raises colorable constitutional objection. This point is not made to prove that either the free exercise clause or political fairness demands government aid for parochial schools. Rather, it demonstrates that, where the state affords public money to finance the secular aspects of education in church-related schools, it imposes a tax burden essentially identical with that which it could constitutionally impose for separate secular facilities. To do so in no way violates the historical and contemporary policy underlying the establishment clause against infringing religious liberty through taxation for religious purposes.[156]

---

[150] *Id.* at 52.

[151] *Id.* at 49-50. Justice O'Connell makes a similar contention in Dickman v. School Dist., 232 Ore. 238, 255-56, 366 P.2d 533, 542 (1961), *cert. denied*, 371 U.S. 823 (1962).

[152] This is considered in detail in text accompanying notes 200-80 *infra*.

[153] A. JOHNSON & F. YOST, *supra* note 28, at 151.

[154] Everson v. Board of Educ., 330 U.S. 1, 24 (1947) (dissenting opinion of Jackson, J.).

[155] *See* Snapper, *Contributions of Independent Education*, in EDUCATIONAL FREEDOM 103, 104-05 (D. McGarry & L. Ward eds. 1966); *cf.* Freeman, *Tax Credits and the School Aid Deadlock*, 194 CATHOLIC WORLD 201, 203 (1962).

[156] Thus, Professor Sutherland could write of a proposal granting limited aid to parochial education that it "would not impair any person's free exercise of religion, it would have to be judged as a question of 'ultra vires.'" Letter to Senator Morse, in S. Doc. No. 29, 87th Cong., 1st Sess. 52, 61 (1961). *See also* Corley, *Objection to Aid Answered*, in EDU-

In addition, it is possible that, by affording some state aid to nonpublic schools (but substantially less than the per capita public school cost),[157] a net decrease in the tax burden would result; a number of nonpublic pupils who are now shifting to public schools for economic reasons might cease doing so and, as is frequently predicted, many public school children might transfer to parochial or private schools.[158] Of course, this latter argument is not of constitutional scope, because a net increase in tax burden should be equally constitutional if the public aid were limited to the secular aspects of education in parochial schools. Nor could government finance religion in the hope, or even with the assurance, that it would in some way produce a smaller overall tax burden. Economically, the argument is appealing. Constitutionally, however, I know of no dissent from the proposition that it would be a patent use of religion as an engine of civil policy in violation of the establishment clause.

B. Discrimination Among Recipient Schools

The proposal contained in this article assumes that any governmental aid will be extended to parochial schools on a constitutionally nondiscriminatory basis. For the legislature to single out, say, Lutheran parochial schools or their students for aid, while refusing to afford equal privilege to other similarly situated church-related or private schools, would be a patent violation of the establishment clause, as would giving aid only to church-related schools while denying it to others similarly situated. The former action would "prefer one religion over another."[159] The latter would "aid all religions as against non-believers."[160]

This is not to say that if aid is to be extended beyond the realm of public schools it must be afforded nondiscriminatorily to all nonpublic schools. The statute in the *Everson* case itself distinguished between nonpublic schools "operated for profit in whole or in part"[161] and those that were not, as does Title III of the Elementary and Secondary Education Act of 1965.[162] Such a classification, not based on religion, should not

---

CATIONAL FREEDOM 184, 186 (D. McGarry & L. Ward eds. 1966). *But see* Editorial, . . . *And in Maryland,* Washington Post, Oct. 11, 1967, at A 16, col. 1.

[157] Calculation and allocation of costs in parochial schools that may be publicly financed is discussed in text accompanying notes 200-84 *infra*.

[158] *See* McDonough, *Economy of Government Aid to Independent Education: A Taxpayers' Savings Plan,* in EDUCATIONAL FREEDOM 122 (D. McGarry & L. Ward eds. 1966).

[159] Everson v. Board of Educ., 330 U.S. 1, 15 (1947).

[160] Torcaso v. Watkins, 367 U.S. 488, 495 (1961). *See also* Tarshis v. New York, 24 App. Div. 2d 644, 262 N.Y.S.2d 538 (1965). *But cf.* Packer Collegiate Institute v. University of State of N.Y., 273 App. Div. 203, 208-09, 76 N.Y.S.2d 499, 505 (1948).

[161] 330 U.S. 1, 3 n.1 (1947).

[162] 20 U.S.C. §§ 841, 843(b)(5) (Supp. I, 1965).

violate the establishment clause.¹⁶³ Nor, despite suggestions to the contrary,¹⁶⁴ should such an economic differentiation be held to contravene the equal protection clause of the fourteenth amendment.¹⁶⁵ Perhaps wealth is "a capricious or irrelevant factor" to measure a voter's qualifications¹⁶⁶ or to determine certain rights of those accused of crime.¹⁶⁷ But surely it is not such a factor for the purpose of distribution of public largesse. It has been suggested that equal protection forbids discrimination both for and against Negroes,¹⁶⁸ but never seriously that it makes poverty an equally neutral factor.¹⁶⁹

It is true that this profit-nonprofit classification turns on the character of the school, which is the immediate recipient of the aid, rather than on the particular needs of each child in attendance, and that some needy students will be enrolled in schools operated for profit while some affluent children will be registered in nonprofit institutions.¹⁷⁰ Although a more perfect system might look to the individual child rather than base its judgment on the assumption that nonprofit schools educate more needy children,¹⁷¹ this would be much more difficult to administer.¹⁷² In the context of an essentially economic classification,¹⁷³ equal protection "is offended only if the classification rests on grounds wholly irrelevant to the achievement of the State's objective."¹⁷⁴ "It is by . . . practical con-

---

¹⁶³ *See* Kurland, *supra* note 19, at 70. *Contra*, Stout, *The Establishment of Religion Under the Constitution*, 37 KY. L.J. 220, 231-32 (1949). However, if the amount of aid given to a parochial school within this classification exceeds the value of the secular educational service it renders, the establishment clause would be violated under the terms of the proposal advanced in this article.

¹⁶⁴ *See* Comment, *The School-Bus Law: Transportation of Parochial and Private School Pupils in Pennsylvania*, 27 U. PITT. L. REV. 71, 79 (1965). The statute in *Everson* was not attacked on this ground, but the Court indicated that such a challenge might not be wholly frivolous, 330 U.S. at 4 n.4, 4-5; *see* Comment, *Constitutional Law—Establishment of Religion, Due Process, and Equal Protection—Public Aid to Parochial Schools*, 45 MICH. L. REV. 1001, 1014 (1947).

¹⁶⁵ Or, in the case of a federal statute, the due process clause of the fifth amendment. *See* Bolling v. Sharpe, 347 U.S. 497 (1954).

¹⁶⁶ Harper v. Virginia Bd. of Elections, 383 U.S. 663, 668 (1966).

¹⁶⁷ *See* Douglas v. California, 372 U.S. 353 (1963); Griffin v. Illinois, 351 U.S. 12 (1956).

¹⁶⁸ *See* Kaplan, *Segregation Litigation and the Schools—Part II: The General Northern Problem*, 58 NW. U.L. REV. 157 (1963).

¹⁶⁹ *But cf.* Edwards v. California, 314 U.S. 160, 184-85 (1941) (concurring opinion of Jackson, J.).

¹⁷⁰ *See* Everson v. Board of Educ., 330 U.S. 1, 20-21 (1947) (dissenting opinion of Jackson, J.); *id.* at 62 n.58 (dissenting opinion of Rutledge, J.); Allen & Marshall, *"Child Benefit" Has Lost Its Glitter*, 44 PHI DELTA KAPPAN 77, 78 (1962).

¹⁷¹ *See* 5 *Hearings on S. 370*, *supra* note 148, at 2895 (Statement of Lawrence Speiser, Director, ACLU).

¹⁷² *See* T. POWELL, THE SCHOOL BUS LAW 75 (1960).

¹⁷³ *But cf.* Horowitz, *Unseparate but Unequal—The Emerging Fourteenth Amendment Issue in Public School Education*, 13 U.C.L.A.L. REV. 1147 (1966).

¹⁷⁴ McGowan v. Maryland, 366 U.S. 420, 425 (1961).

siderations based on experience rather than by theoretical inconsistencies that the question of equal protection is to be answered."[175]

Statutes constitutionally neutral on their face, however, may be invalid in effect.[176] Under a proper statutory definition, for example, the only "nonprofit" school in town may be a parochial school. Absent a judicial finding that the legitimate statutory definition merely camouflaged an illegitimate preference of religion violating the establishment clause,[177] the statute should not be held invalid. A public appropriation for a primary secular purpose should not be void merely because, under an appropriate neutral standard, a religiously controlled institution happens to be the only recipient.[178]

A more difficult issue, but one apparently of no great consequence, arises where an aid statute by its terms names the parochial schools of one church only, or names only parochial schools, and it is unknown from the statute or its available legislative history whether other similarly situated schools exist.[179] The Court could: (a) strike down the statute, thus forcing the legislature to redraft properly if it can;[180] (b) strike down the statute, unless it were shown that there were no others similarly situated;[181] (c) uphold the statute, unless it were shown that there were others similarly situated.[182]

C. *The Compensable Amount*

The constitutional principle proposed herein speaks of the secular educational services rendered by the church-affiliated school. Assuming that these services may be isolated,[183] little difficulty arises where their cost is the same to the parochial school as to the public school system. Because government may properly finance the secular education of all

---

[175] Railway Express Agency v. New York, 336 U.S. 106, 110 (1949). *See* Rhoades v. School Dist., 424 Pa. 202, 225, 226 A.2d 53, 66, *appeal dismissed per curiam*, 389 U.S. 11 (1967).

[176] *See* Lane v. Wilson, 307 U.S. 268 (1939).

[177] Herein, the question of "motive." See text at notes 114-24 *supra*; W. LOCKHART, Y. KAMISAR & J. CHOPER, CONSTITUTIONAL LAW 1209 (2d ed. 1967). For an example, see State *ex rel.* Reynolds v. Nusbaum, 17 Wis. 2d 148, 158, 115 N.W.2d 761, 766 (1962).

[178] *See* Kintzele v. City of St. Louis, 347 S.W.2d 695 (Mo. 1961) (redevelopment authority gave benefit to university, within relevant geographic area, which happened to be religiously affiliated). *See also* 79 CHRISTIAN CENTURY 1057 (1962) (editorial); 78 *id.* at 1135 (1961) (editorial).

[179] This was in fact the situation in *Everson*. The township resolution authorized reimbursement only for parents of public and Catholic schools pupils. 330 U.S. at 4 n.2.

[180] *See id.* at 21 (dissenting opinion of Jackson, J.); *cf.* McLeod v. J.E. Dilworth Co., 322 U.S. 327 (1944).

[181] Everson v. Board of Educ., 330 U.S. 1, 62-63 n.61 (1947) (dissenting opinion of Rutledge, J.).

[182] This is the action the *Everson* Court took. *Id.* at 4 n.2.

[183] For discussion of this issue, see text accompanying notes 200-284 *infra*.

children, whatever their religious faith, payment to a parochial school under these circumstances of the same amount that such education costs in the public schools should be immune from establishment clause protest: No tax funds are being expended for strictly religious purposes; no more tax funds are being used than would be if the pupils were in public schools;[184] the church obtains no financial benefit except compensation for the cost of secular services rendered.[185] A fortiori, there is no difficulty if the cost of providing this service in the parochial school is less than it is in the public school system, as is not unlikely, and government pays the parochial school only this lesser amount.

But suppose that the cost of providing secular educational services in the parochial school is less than is the cost in the public school system and government pays the parochial school the latter amount.[186] Although here also no more tax funds are being expended than would be if the pupils were in public schools, the church obtains a net financial benefit. Nevertheless, this should not violate the establishment clause. Literally thousands of church-related agencies offer secular services that are funded—or purchased, if you will—by government.[187] If any organization—profit or nonprofit, religious or nonsectarian—provides a secular service to government at the "going rate," and is able to profit thereby because of low labor costs, efficiency, or any other reason, the Constitution should not be held to prohibit it.[188] In fact, for government to refuse

---

[184] *Cf.* Cook County v. Chicago Indus. School for Girls, 125 Ill. 540, 569-71, 18 N.E. 183, 196-97 (1888).

[185] *See* Schade v. Allegheny County Institution Dist., 386 Pa. 507, 512, 126 A.2d 911, 914 (1956); Cushman, *Public Support of Religious Education in American Constitutional Law*, 45 ILL. L. REV. 333, 336 (1950). It may not be denied that the public financing may permit the church now to use funds formerly spent for secular educational purposes for strictly religious purposes. This "freed funds" issue, whose effect is irrelevant to the rationale proposed herein and is produced by every concededly valid direct or indirect public aid to religiously-affiliated institutions, is further considered at text accompanying notes 407-15 *infra*. Neither may it be denied that, as a result of this governmental action, the church will be significantly aided in a nonfinancial way, for gaining attendants at parochial schools "is a powerful instrumentality in the successful prosecution of the work of [many churches]." Bennett v. City of La Grange, 153 Ga. 428, 437, 112 S.E. 482, 486-87 (1922). But, since the government's action has a primary secular effect, the equally present benefit to religion should not invalidate it. See text following note 111 *supra*.

[186] *Cf.* 2 U.S.C. § 88a(c) (1964), providing that congressional pages may "attend a private or parochial school of their own choice" and that "such . . . school shall be reimbursed" by Congress "in the same amount as would be paid if the page or pages were attending a public school."

[187] *See* R. DRINAN, *supra* note 50, at 27. *See also* Hammett, *supra* note 106, at 936.

[188] Thus, a religiously-affiliated institution may be the successful bidder in a redevelopment project, satisfying a valid public purpose, and this should not violate the establishment clause because the institution thereby acquired valuable property at a lower price than it would have had to pay by negotiation with the private owners, who got full value for the property from the public redevelopment authority. *See* Ellis v. City of Grand Rapids, 257

to deal on equal terms with an organization providing public services because that organization is religiously-affiliated might even be seen as a violation of the free exercise clause.

It must be recalled that government assistance to religion which neither infringes religious liberty nor expends tax funds for strictly religious purposes should not be considered violative of the establishment bar.[189] Thus, in the context of the immediate discussion, it is the "cost" to the public and not the "aid" to religion that is determinative.[190] As long as the government receives in full the secular services purchased, the relative cost or profit to religion of supplying those services should have no relevance to the establishment clause. Its prohibition should be satisfied by a showing that the government is getting the secular services it paid for. Consequently, where something costs the government little or nothing, it should make no difference what secular services it receives. For example, the government may allow religious organizations temporarily to use vacant public buildings for strictly religious purposes. Such occasional use of public buildings may substantially "aid" religious groups, and it may save them significant rental fees. But, if the use is not "regular and extended in duration,"[191] the "cost" to the public is nil or de minimis,[192] and there should be no establishment breach.[193] It may be argued that, even though the use of the building cost the state nothing, it could charge these religious organizations measurable rental fees. But the establishment clause should not require that government profit at religion's expense. It should merely forbid public expenditures for strictly religious purposes.

Therefore, if the government lends money at a rate of interest equal to or above the government borrowing rate but below the commercial

---

F. Supp. 564, 569-70 (W.D. Mich. 1966); 64th St. Residences, Inc. v. City of New York, 4 N.Y.2d 268, 150 N.E.2d 396, 174 N.Y.S.2d 1 (1958). *See also* Adams v. County Comm'rs, 180 Md. 550, 26 A.2d 377, 380 (1942).

[189] See text accompanying notes 43-50, 79-80 *supra*.

[190] *But cf.* McVey v. Hawkins, 364 Mo. 44, 54, 258 S.W.2d 927, 932-33 (1953).

[191] L. PFEFFER, *supra* note 26, at 207.

[192] *See* note 53 *supra*. *But cf.* Engel v. Vitale, 370 U.S. 421, 441 (1962) (concurring opinion of Douglas, J.).

[193] *See* Southside Estates Baptist Church v. Board of Trustees, 115 So. 2d 697 (Fla. 1959); Nichols v. School Directors, 93 Ill. 61, 34 Am. Rep. 160 (1879); State *ex rel.* Gilbert v. Dilley, 95 Neb. 527, 145 N.W. 999 (1914); People *ex rel.* Lewis v. Graves, 219 App. Div. 233, 236, 219 N.Y.S. 189, 192 (1927).

Similarly, if public funds were used to construct a research laboratory on the campus of a church-affiliated university, and the building were used for this purpose to the extent contemplated and demanded by the research project, the full secular purpose that the state bargained for will have been achieved. This being so, even a regular use of these facilities (say, on evenings or weekends) by the school for religious purposes should be valid. *But see* Kratz, *Research and Service Programs and Public Funds in the Church-Related School*, 7 J. CHURCH & ST. 207, 211-12 (1965).

rate, it may so lend to sectarian groups, *even though they use the money for strictly religious purposes*. The church benefits, but at no cost to the state. This should not be confused with government loans for *secular* purposes.[194] Since, as to these, grants would be unobjectionable, loans at any rate are obviously valid.[195] It follows that a state may buy textbooks—even religious ones—at quantity prices and sell them to parochial schools at the discounted price.

Finally, suppose that the cost of providing secular educational services in the parochial school exceeds the cost in the public school system[196] and government pays the parochial school the former amount. Although the church here does not obtain funds that may be used for strictly religious purposes, more tax funds are being expended than would be if the children were in public schools. There should, nonetheless, be no violation of the establishment clause.[197] So long as the state expenditure is in fact for a primary secular goal,[198] no tax funds are being used for strictly religious purposes.[199]

---

[194] *See* Hayes, *supra* note 10, at 174. *See also* provisions of the Housing Act of 1950, 64 Stat. 77, 12 U.S.C. § 1749 (1964); the National Defense Education Act of 1958, 20 U.S.C. §§ 421-29 (1964).

[195] The National Defense Education Act of 1958, 20 U.S.C. § 445(b)(3) (1964) sets the interest rate for loans to nonprofit private schools at one fourth of 1% above the average government borrowing rate.

[196] This might result because the marginal additional cost of adding even all the parochial students to the public schools could well be less than the cost of duplicative facilities in the parochial school. Or the per capita cost of transportation for parochial school students might be higher. *See Hearings on H.R. 13160 and H.R. 13161 Before the General Subcomm. on Education of the House Comm. on Education and Labor*, 89th Cong., 2d Sess., at 56 (1966).

[197] *Contra, 5 Hearings on S. 370, supra* note 148, at 2896 (statement of Lawrence Speiser, Director, ACLU).

[198] In fact, an additional secular purpose might be advanced in that, even though there may be duplicative facilities, there is an educational advantage in smaller classes and diversified and experimental techniques and programs—although the diversified style may not be such as to produce religious rather than secular education, see text accompanying notes 200-80 *infra—see* Snapper, *supra* note 155, at 106-07.

[199] See text accompanying note 155 *supra*.

The entire discussion assumes that the total funds provided by all levels of government—federal, state, and local—including the value of tax exemptions (and such benefits as preferential mailing rates, see Weclew, *Church and State: How Much Separation?*, 10 DE PAUL L. REV. 1, 23-24 (1960)) given parochial school property and activity, will not exceed the cost of the secular educational services rendered by the church-affiliated school. The general topic of tax exemptions for church property and religious activities is beyond the scope of this discussion. But brief reference to certain aspects of the problem may be helpful.

There appears to be no analytically meaningful way to distinguish a tax exemption from a direct subsidy. Exemptions afford financial benefits and increase the tax burden of others. Murray v. Comptroller of Treasury, 241 Md. 399, 216 A.2d 897, 906, *cert. denied*, 385 U.S. 816 (1966). *But see* Snyder v. Town of Newtown, 147 Conn. 397, 161 A.2d 770, 781 (1960) (dissenting opinion) (1960), *appeal dismissed*, 365 U.S. 299 (1961); *cf.* Everson v. Board of Educ., 330 U.S. 1, 61 n.57 (1947) (dissenting opinion of Rutledge, J.). Unlike the sporadic

D. The Permeation Issue

1. The Facts

Probably the most complex matter concerning public financial assistance to parochial education is the permeation (or integration) issue. It is frequently contended that "official Catholic doctrine refuses to recognize any distinction between secular and religious teaching."[200] Pope

---

church use of public buildings, see text accompanying notes 189-93 *supra*, tax exemption thus clearly results in out-of-pocket cost to taxpayers. It may be true that by tax exemption "the state merely refrains from diverting to its own uses income independently generated by the churches through voluntary contributions." Giannella, *Religious Liberty, Nonestablishment and Doctrinal Development—Part II. The Nonestablishment Principle*, 81 HARV. L. REV. 513, 553 (1968). But, by augmenting the assessment on others, tax exemption effectively "forcibly diverts the income of both believers and nonbelievers to churches." *Id.* Thus, in reference to governmental financial assistance to parochial education, tax exemptions must be computed with other funds provided. *But cf.* Lundberg v. County of Alameda, 46 Cal. 2d 644, 298 P.2d 1, *appeal dismissed sub nom.* Heisy v. County of Alameda, 352 U.S. 921 (1956).

It has been said that, "No entirely satisfactory rationale for tax exemption has ever been stated in any American judicial decision," R. DRINAN, *supra* note 50, at 9, and its constitutionality has been seriously questioned. Korbel, *Do the Federal Income Tax Laws Involve an "Establishment of Religion"?*, 53 A.B.A.J. 1018 (1967). *But see* General Finance Corp. v. Archetto, 93 R.I. 392, 176 A.2d 73 (1961), *appeal dismissed*, 369 U.S. 423 (1962). There is some indication that, at least in some forms, the Court considers it required by the free exercise clause. *See* Follett v. McCormick, 321 U.S. 573 (1944); Murdock v. Pennsylvania, 319 U.S. 105 (1943). When afforded to church or synagogue buildings themselves, perhaps it is justified as "compensation" for the public welfare (purely secular) services performed by these religious organizations. *See* Murray v. Comptroller of Treasury, 241 Md. 383, 401-02, 216 A.2d 897, 907-08, *cert. denied*, 385 U.S. 816 (1966); Kauper, *supra* note 84, at 97, 108, 112-13. For an excellent general discussion, *see* Kauper, *supra* note 84; *see also* Note, 61 Nw. U.L. REV. 777, 787-93 (1966).

Professor Van Alstyne has introduced an extremely provocative and penetrating consideration, which logically goes not only to justification of "tax accommodations [for religion] which currently exist in many state and federal laws," Van Alstyne, *supra* note 68, at 882, but is relevant also to the entire question of expenditure of public funds in aid of religion. He observes that "as more of the economy and environment is occupied by the increasing public, governmental sector of our society, the net effect of the shift is to confine religion to the ever shrinking domain of the relatively diminishing private sector," and that "to the extent that the tax revenues thus collected may not be spent by government to support religious enterprises, but must be used exclusively for secular purposes, the net effect, arguably, is to reduce the relative supply of funds available to religion." *Id.* at 881.

Professor Giannella amplifies this point in advancing, as central to his thesis, that "the no-aid aspects of the separation principle should be relaxed in direct proportion to the extent of governmental regulation." Giannella, *supra* at 522. *See generally id.* at 522-26, 537-55.

The rationale is indeed an intriguing one and unquestionably merits further exploration. But, like others, "Once loosed, the idea ... is not easily cabined." Cox, *Foreword: Constitutional Adjudication and the Promotion of Human Rights*, 80 HARV. L. REV. 91 (1966). Apart from judicial limitations that are essentially intuitive and involve "large and imponderable factors," Giannella, *supra* at 527, it would suggest that government literally may finance many strictly sectarian efforts of organized religion. It is seemingly a thesis demanding extensive, if not total, reevaluation of the broadly conceived establishment clause goals in light of changed and changing circumstances.

[200] Konvitz, *Separation of Church and State: The First Freedom*, 14 LAW & CONTEMP.

Pius XI and Pope Leo XIII are quoted as ordering "that every . . . subject taught, be permeated with Christian piety,"[201] as are Catholic educators, theologians and philosophers.[202] A Lutheran school manual demands "that all areas of the curriculum reflect an adequate philosophy of Christian education."[203] Seventh Day Adventists declare their "endeavor to permeate all branches of learning with a spiritual outlook."[204] After all, it is asked, "if religion is taught only one or two hours a day in church schools, what is the point of maintaining the separate parochial school system?"[205]

But there is less than universal agreement as to the facts. Others familiar with Catholic—and Jewish[206]—parochial school education explain that the pupil there "learns essentially the same arithmetic, spelling, English, history, civics, foreign languages, geography, and science" as is taught in the public schools, but in addition learns religion "and the religious dimensions of secular knowledge."[207] In the Lutheran school sys-

---

PROB. 44, 58 (1949). *See also* Konvitz, *Whittling Away Religious Freedom*, COMMENTARY, June 1946, at 4, 6-7.

[201] Konvitz, *Separation of Church and State: The First Freedom*, 14 LAW & CONTEMP. PROB. 44, 58 (1949). *See also* Drinan, *Should the State Aid Private Schools?*, 37 CONN. B.J. 361, 366 (1963); Hayes, *Law and the Parochial School: A Formulation of Conflicting Positions*, 3 CATHOLIC LAW. 99, 100 (1957); Slough & McAnany, *supra* note 37, at 61-62.

[202] *See* A. STOKES & L. PFEFFER, *supra* note 27, at 444; Pfeffer, *Religion, Education and the Constitution*, 8 LAW. GUILD REV. 387, 396 (1948); *Hearings on H.R. 6074 Before the Ad Hoc Subcomm. on Study of Shared-Time Education of the House Comm. on Education and Labor*, 88th Cong., 2d Sess., at 55 (1964).

[203] Quoted in G. LANOUE, *supra* note 56, at 31.

[204] *Id.*

[205] *Id. See also* Gordis, *Education for a Nation of Nations*, in Religion and the Schools, *supra* note 37, at 5, 23.

[206] *See* paper by Dr. Nichols, *summarized in* Religion and Freedom 22 (Report by D. McDonald on a Seminar sponsored by the Fund for the Republic, New York, N.Y., May 5-9, 1958); Gilbert, *Symposium: Shared Time*, 57 RELIGIOUS EDUC. 14, 15 (1962). *But see* Brickman, *id.* at 20, 21, who says that some Jewish parochial school leaders would object to their students taking courses in literature, science, and social studies outside of the Hebrew day school because they "should not be exposed in secular courses to any heterodox or heretical ideas or doctrines."

[207] National Catholic Welfare Conference, *supra* note 37, at 408. *See also* McCluskey, *A Changing Pattern*, in FEDERAL AID AND CATHOLIC SCHOOLS 31, 39-40 (D. Callahan ed. 1964); Copass, *Church Schools Have No Claim on Public Funds*, NATION'S SCHOOLS, Aug. 1945, at 29; Coughlan, *Religion and the Schools*, LIFE, June 16, 1961, at 110, 122; D'Amour, *Tempest in a Textbook*, 107 AMERICA 443 (1962); Hayes, *supra* note 10, at 176; Kauper, *supra* note 35, at 36; Williams, *Should the Federal Government Aid Parochial Schools*, 111 FORUM 100 (1949). The following statement illustrates the point well: "The Christian teacher of the law, therefore, should know the positive legal fact, but he must also have some concern for the law as an expression of justice. The Christian biologist must know the facts of evolution, but he must also be aware of theological discussion of human creation. The Christian physicist must know his nuclear science, but he must be aware that its applications have had a social and ultimately moral impact on the whole world." Fidelian, *Christian Schools, Secular Subjects*, 81 COMMONWEAL 566, 568 (1965).

tem, it is said that "the main features of the public school curriculum are reproduced."[208] In response to a study showing that many "secular course" textbooks used in parochial schools are permeated with religious symbols, concepts, and doctrines,[209] it has been said that the examples "were highly arbitrary and not representative," and that "Catholic educators . . . as a whole, do not favor textbooks in which dabs of spurious religion serve only to distort the essential subject matter. . . ."[210]

Further evidence that secular subjects in parochial schools need be little different than their counterpart public school offerings is found in the fact that, as part of shared time programs, many parochial school students actually take such courses as mathematics, physics, science, foreign languages, music, industrial arts, home economics, and physical education in the public school itself.[211] Catholic educators have observed that "basic instruction" in such courses as literature and history could well be undertaken in shared time programs in the public schools "with the church adding the distinctive note which it can bear to the revelation

---

A teacher's manual for a mathematics text prepared for use in Catholic schools begins by pointing out that "the authors . . . have recognized that first and foremost, an arithmetic program for Catholic schools must be mathematically sound. Over and above this, they have recognized that . . . these situations present opportunities for the exercise of Christian virtues." LaNoue, *Religious Schools and "Secular" Subjects*, 32 HARV. EDUC. REV. 255, 274 (1962).

[208] A. STOKES & L. PFEFFER, *supra* note 27, at 419. Lutheran teachers are instructed to "'constantly search for materials that can be correlated with basic texts,'" LaNoue, *supra* note 207, at 281, thus implying that religious values are added to basic secular instruction.

[209] See discussion accompanying note 207 *supra* and notes 252-278 *infra*.

[210] Ball, *Federal Aid—1964*, 61 NAT'L CATHOLIC EDUC. ASS'N BULL. 228, 229 (1964). See also Gallagher, *Observations Arising from the Horace Mann Case*, 63 NAT'L CATHOLIC EDUC. ASS'N BULL. 232, 236 (1966): "A flat judgment concerning the morality or sinfulness of a particular practice simply has no place in the history classroom or the science laboratory." Downey, *Suppose Parochial Schools Receive Federal Aid . . .* , CATHOLIC SCHOOL J., March 1967, at 44, takes the position that parochial schools, "in developing explanations of the life of Christ . . . [should not] step over into anti-Semitism," nor should they in treating "doctrinal differences among Christians, [step] into attack upon the sincerity of Protestants as persons." *Id.* at 50. Further, he points out that the "pursuit of secular learning should be considered hallowed in itself both because of its origin in the Divine Intellect and because it is imparted in a setting sponsored by the teaching Church. Well-meaning attempts at introducing additional devotion and piety into geography, arithmetic, etc." are unnecessary, *id.* at 51. For a similar attitude of Christian Reformed parochial school education, see LaNoue, *supra* note 207, at 284.

The recent testimony of supervising administrators of the Catholic school systems in Chicago and Pittsburgh was that a large percentage of the textbooks used in their elementary and secondary schools was also widely used in the public schools. 2 *Hearings on H.R. 2361*, *supra* note 35, at 809, 810.

[211] *Hearings on H.R. 6074*, *supra* note 202, at 55, 263. In a recent Chicago shared time plan, all courses except English, social studies, music and art were taken in the public school. *See* Morton v. Board of Educ., 69 Ill. App. 2d 38, 216 N.E.2d 305 (1966).

of God in these areas" in the parochial school.[212] Thus, it is concluded, the reason for maintaining a separate parochial school system is not for the purpose of teaching a wholly different curriculum. Rather, it is to add "the most important of the four R's,"[213] the feeling being that children attending public schools that taught only secular subjects five days a week would consider religious training unimportant, and that this impression could not be overcome by a few after school hours or Sunday school.[214]

Several facts emerge clearly from the foregoing discussion. First, "permeation" is a word of varied and imprecise meaning. Father Drinan can state as "the undeniable fact that secular instruction in a Catholic school is 'permeated' by a Catholic atmosphere and Catholic attitudes,"[215] yet urge that "permeation should avoid every suggestion of quasi-coercion or 'indoctrination.'"[216] Second, the secular courses taught in parochial schools rarely, if ever, mirror exactly the courses taught in the public schools. Third, although "no scientific study has ever been done on the extent of the permeation of sectarian teaching in the instruction in secular subjects in Catholic schools,"[217] it is likely that some secular subject courses in some parochial schools are so "permeated" that they are in reality courses of sectarian indoctrination,[218] despite the regulatory power

---

[212] Smith, *Symposium, supra* note 206, at 10, 11. *See also* Geoghegan, *id.* at 24, 25.

[213] 2 *Hearings on S. 181 and S. 717 Before the Senate Comm. on Education and Labor*, 79th Cong., 1st Sess., at 651 (1945) (testimony of Edward S. Heffron, Executive Secretary, National Council of Catholic Men).

[214] *See* Mitchell, *Religion and Federal Aid to Education*, 14 LAW & CONTEMP. PROB. 113, 132-33 (1949).

[215] R. DRINAN, *supra* note 50, at 229.

[216] Drinan, *The Challenge to Catholic Educators in the Maryland College Case*, NAT'L CATHOLIC EDUC. ASS'N BULL., May 1967, at 3, 7. The following interesting definition of the term's objectives reveals its latent ambiguity: "We want religion to permeate the curriculum of our schools, so that our children may have the opportunity to learn how to construct for themselves a world view that is rationally theistic, in contrast to the shattering dichotomy between religion and science, between ethics and business or politics, between the supernatural and the natural, that characterizes the world view of so large a part of society today." Hanlon, *Federal Aid?*, 110 AMERICA 418 (1964). That the federal government does not regard "permeated" parochial education as intrinsically a religious activity is evidenced by the fact that tuition contributions to its support are not deductible for income tax purposes as religious contributions. *See* G. LANOUE, *supra* note 56, at 43.

[217] Drinan, *The Constitutionality of Public Aid to Parochial Schools*, in THE WALL BETWEEN CHURCH AND STATE 55, 64 (D. Oaks ed. 1963).

[218] An article by Sister Carolyn, *Lay Teachers Have a Spiritual Role*, CATHOLIC SCHOOL J., Jan. 1963, at 43, 44, urges that secular course instructors "so teach that the Christian principles become guiding principles. . . . Convinced that Christian principles must be the motivation for acts, you teach differently from a textbook teacher. Your teaching is structured upon principles, the truths of a Christian life. By a gradual buildup of understandings which shape into a generalization, you lead the child to discover truth rather than impose or patch on him a fact of information. . . . All of our units of study are directed to form a person who thinks, judges, and acts like Christ."

of the state—whether exercised or not;[219] that some courses are completely, bona fide secular;[220] that some courses fall between these extremes. Fourth, the problem of the parochial school secular courses being turned into nothing more than religious instruction is not inherent; no religion demands it, nor constitutionally could a religion demand it if contrary to reasonable state requirements.[221]

2. Extent of Permissible Aid

Under the rationale proposed in this article, public financial assistance to parochial education may not exceed the value of the secular educational service rendered. One relatively effortless way of avoiding the whole problem of permeation in this connection is simply to ignore it by taking the position that "the secular character of secular subjects is not changed by a moral or religious permeation"; "that it is impossible to study and interpret man and his activities apart from his moral and religious values"; and that "the National Merit Scholarship competition . . . is clear evidence that students who attend church-related schools receive a secular education as good as that received by students in our public schools."[222] On this reasoning, there would be no prohibition to financing accredited parochial schools on a lump-sum parity with public schools without further investigation.[223]

---

[219] See A. STOKES & L. PFEFFER, supra note 27, at 413 But see Hayes, supra note 10, at 175 n.33; Kenealy, Equal Justice Under Law—Aid to Education, 11 LOYOLA L. REV. 183, 198 (1962-63). For discussion of the exercise of state regulatory power over nonpublic schools, see text accompanying notes 472-89 infra.

[220] An article by Sister Alice, Modern Art in the Religious Class, CATHOLIC SCHOOL J., Jan. 1963, at 46, 48, recommends that "regardless of our feelings toward modern art, we will not impose our likes, dislikes, and prejudices upon our students." An article by Sister Paulinus, Bacteriology in the High School, id. at 49, gives a fully objective account of the technical problems of studying the subject. For similarly written instructional essays by Catholic educators, quite divorced from religious influences, see O'Neill, The Homeroom in the Guidance Program, id. at 60; Sister Ruth, Budding Poets, id. at 67; Phillips, Written Recitation in Teaching Science, id. at 68; Sister Christina Marie, Geometric Forms Taught in First Grade, id., Feb. 1963, at 46; Sister Marion Beiter, Teacher Training for Secondary Mathematics, id. at 50; Sister Marie Joseph, How We Teach Russian, id. at 51; Sister M. Martin, Freshmen Really Read, id. at 54.

[221] See discussion in text accompanying notes 477-89 infra. See also Drinan, Does State Aid to Church-Related Colleges Constitute an Establishment of Religion?—Reflections on the Maryland College Cases, 1967 UTAH L. REV. 491, 494, 505; Manning, Aid to Education—Federal Fashion, 29 FORDHAM L. REV. 495, 523-24 (1961).

[222] Blum, supra note 37, at 153. See also id. at 140; 2 Hearings, on H.R. 2361, supra note 35, at 819-20 (testimony of Msgr. Frederick G. Hochwalt).

[223] Until recently, there has been no comprehensive published study comparing the academic and other achievements of parochial school students to those of public school students. See Jencks, Catholics and Our Schools, NEW REPUBLIC, Mar. 19, 1962, at 21, 22. Such a major sociological study, comparing Catholic school Catholics and public school Catholics, entitled THE EDUCATION OF CATHOLIC AMERICANS, by Andrew M. Greeley, a

But this may be too simple. Competitive examinations and sociological studies are not so exact as to determine conclusively that the educational services rendered in parochial schools are as complete and effective and have the same impact from a nonreligious perspective on the overall development of the student as does public school education. Viewed from the basis of per-hour input, it is reasonable to assume that this is not the case, given the parochial school time spent on religious instruction. And it is clear that the state may not subsidize religious instruction or indoctrination, no matter where undertaken.

The establishment clause prohibition against using tax funds for strictly religious purposes appears to require a more careful scrutiny to

---

Catholic priest, and Peter H. Rossi, a Protestant, was published in 1966 under the auspices of the National Opinion Research Center.

The monograph lends support to the contention just discussed in text accompanying note 222 *supra*. Among the controlled findings were that Catholic school Catholics increased their social class margin over other Catholics, *id.* at 57; that those who went to Catholic primary schools were more likely to graduate from high school than other Catholics and were just about as likely to do so as public school Protestants, *id.* at 49-50; that those who went to Catholic high schools were more likely to go to college than Catholics and almost all classes of Protestants who went to public high schools, *id.* at 50; that Catholic school Catholics scored significantly higher on a brief general knowledge test than did public school Catholics, *id.* at 120; that Catholic school Catholics ranked measurably higher on an occupational-prestige index than did public school Catholics, *id.* at 140. The authors conclude that "there is no evidence that Catholic education interferes with occupational or educational achievement." *Id.* at 146. Relevant thereto is the judgment of Catholic high school Catholics indicating that their schools are no more "repressive" or "authoritarian" than other schools. "There are no significant differences in the proportions saying they are free to disagree in class, that all students are treated equally, or that they are free to talk to the teacher if they think they have been treated unfairly. Indeed, in two of the three instances, the slight associations that do exist suggest that Catholic schools may be somewhat *more* liberal in these matters." *Id.* at 193.

The survey also revealed interesting results as to attitudes. It found no evidence that Catholic school Catholics were less tolerant of members of other groups, *id.* at 122; were less likely to defend civil liberties, were more given to extremist religious attitudes or to distrusting world and worldly effort, or were more rigid in their child-rearing practices, *id.* at 125; that, while Catholic school Catholics do interact less with other Americans while in school, this does not continue in later life, *id.* at 121. Other studies have shown that differences between Catholic and non-Catholic schooling, in respect to such matters as participation in the community, values concerning occupational achievement, or the political goals of American society, are nonexistent. *See* J. FICHTER, PAROCHIAL SCHOOLS: A SOCIOLOGICAL STUDY 116 (1958); Rossi & Rossi, *Some Effects of Parochial School Education in America*, 90 DAEDALUS 300 (1961); Rossi & Rossi, *Background and Consequences of Parochial School Education*, 27 HARV. EDUC. REV. 195 (1957). *See also* A. GREELEY & P. ROSSI, THE EDUCATION OF CATHOLIC AMERICANS 8-9 (1966).

Finally, it must be observed that the Catholic school education did produce religious consequences. Catholic school Catholics were more likely to engage in sacramental activity, *id.* at 56-57, 71, were more "loyal" to the ecclesiastical system, *id.* at 60, were better informed on the "fine points" of religious knowledge, *id.* at 61, and were more orthodox in their moral beliefs, *id.* at 63. *See also* Kelley, *Protestants and Parochial Schools*, in FEDERAL AID AND CATHOLIC SCHOOLS 71, 77 (D. Callahan ed. 1964).

assure that only the secular aspects of parochial school education will be publicly financed.[224] But to admit "an admixture of religious with secular teaching"[225] is the beginning, not the end, of the inquiry. To concede that "commingling the religious with the secular teaching does not divest the whole [course or activity] of its religious permeation and emphasis,"[226] is not to conclude that no part of the course or activity may be aided with public money.

A secular subject parochial school course or activity may concurrently serve independent, dual purposes—that is, full secular value may be obtained for the time and resources expended, and religious interests may also be served. If such is the case, the entire course or activity serves a primary secular purpose—and may therefore be fully financed—the aid to religion notwithstanding.[227] On the other hand, a secular subject parochial school course or activity may partially serve both religious and secular ends. Here, an allocation must be made; only the secular product may be publicly financed.[228] Of course, if a "secular subject" parochial school course or activity is in reality religious instruction, it cannot be publicly funded at all; and if it is exclusively secular in purpose, it may be totally funded.

(a) *The Relevance of "Atmosphere."*—Before applying this approach, certain other matters should be considered. That the general atmosphere of parochial schools—as created by religious symbols, teachers in religious attire, and compulsory religious exercises and courses—is oriented toward religious goals[229] should not affect the constitutional judgment

---

[224] It is not an adequate response to say that, since classroom religious neutrality is impossible in interpreting any subject matter, a secularist religion is being taught in the public schools; therefore, the fact that a religious orientation is given a parochial school subject should not disqualify it from full public support. See Blum, *Freedom and Equality,* in FEDERAL AID AND CATHOLIC SCHOOLS 43, 45-47 (D. Callahan ed. 1964); *cf.* note 59 *supra* (last paragraph). Perhaps public schools should avoid any indoctrination in ultimate values, *see* Kauper, *supra* note 18, at 23; but if a public school teacher illustrates points by calling on universally accepted moral values, derived from classically neutral nonreligious sources, this is not religious indoctrination in the accepted sense. See Choper, *supra* note 4, at 377-79. That a publicly accepted and espoused behavioral standard is adopted by a religious group (say, the Secular Humanists) as its own moral or ideological tenet, does not make it a "religious" tenet for all purposes. *Cf.* McGowan v. Maryland, 366 U.S. 420, 442, 445 (1961); School Dist. v. Schempp, 374 U.S. 203, 225 (1963). *See generally* Giannella, *supra* note 199, at 562-63; Note, 61 Nw. U.L. REV. 705 (1966). *See also* note 59 *supra* (last paragraph).

[225] Everson v. Board of Educ., 330 U.S. 1, 47 (1947) (dissenting opinion of Rutledge, J.).

[226] *Id.*

[227] See discussion at notes 105, 108, 111, 125-28, 133-38 *supra*. "The real issue is whether the philosophy of education professed in any way diminishes the content and methodology of the secular subjects taught at these church-connected institutions." Costanzo, *supra* note 37, at 649. *See also id.* at 635. *But see* Note, 62 Nw. U.L. REV. 253, 262 (1967).

[228] *See* Note, 22 LA. L. REV. 266, 269 (1961).

[229] *See* G. LANOUE, *supra* note 56, at 32; Gordon, *The Unconstitutionality of Public Aid*

as to whether the particular course or activity may be publicly funded. The clearly sectarian purpose of these accouterments produces no infringement of religious liberty, since students attend the parochial schools of their own volition.[230] And since public funds are not used to subsidize these items, but only for the proven secular aspects of the educational experience, no expenditure of tax money for religious purposes results.

(b) *Judicial Definition of "Religion."*—Under the analysis proposed herein, the question whether a particular course or activity serves a primary secular purpose, a primary religious purpose, or mixed purposes must ultimately be for the Court. It "must be ready to define religion, religious teaching and religious commitment."[231] But this would not be a novel exercise for the judiciary.

As has already been noted,[232] the Court has on a number of occasions labeled particular governmental activity religious or secular. In the *Sunday Closing Law Cases*, the Court expressed its willingness and obligation to engage in "close scrutiny"[233] to determine if an action's purpose and "its operative effect"[234] were religious. So, too, should the Court examine challenged parochial school courses and activities when necessary.[235]

In the *Regents' Prayer Case*, which is closely analogous to the question in issue, the Court passed judgment on such public school activities as recitation of the Declaration of Independence (or the Gettysburg Address) and the singing of the Star Spangled Banner—all of which are somewhat religiously "permeated"—and concluded that these exercises were "patriotic or ceremonial" rather than "religious."[236] In the *Bible Reading Cases*, the Court ruled that study of the Bible and religion "as

to Parochial Schools, in THE WALL BETWEEN CHURCH AND STATE 73, 90 (D. Oaks ed. 1963); Slough & McAnany, *supra* note 37, at 61-62.

[230] *See also* discussion in text accompanying note 551 *infra*.

[231] Kauper, *supra* note 142, at 294.

[232] See discussion in text accompanying notes 112-16 *supra*.

[233] McGowan v. Maryland, 366 U.S. 420, 449 (1961).

[234] *Id.* at 453. *See also* Two Guys from Harrison-Allentown, Inc. v. McGinley, 366 U.S. 582, 592 (1961); Gallagher v. Crown Kosher Market, 366 U.S. 617, 630 (1961). "After all, the labels a State places on its laws [or a parochial school places on its courses and activities] are not binding on us when we are confronted with a constitutional decision. We reach our own conclusion as to the character, effect, and practical operation of the regulation [course, activity] in determining its constitutionality." 366 U.S. at 573 (dissenting opinion of Douglas, J.).

[235] *Cf., e.g.*, Sherbert v. Verner, 374 U.S. 398, 399 n.1 (1961) (practice was found to be a "basic tenet" of religious creed); Murdock v. Pennsylvania, 319 U.S. 105, 108 (1943) (practice was found to be an "age-old form of missionary evangelism").

[236] Engel v. Vitale, 370 U.S. 421, 435 n.21 (1962). Mr. Justice Douglas found the words "under God" in the pledge of allegiance to have a religious purpose. *Id.* at 440 n.4 (concurring opinion); *cf.* Mr. Justice Brennan's discussion in School Dist. v. Schempp, 374 U.S. 203, 304 (1963) (concurring opinion).

part of a secular program of education"[237] was proper, thus addressing itself to the very matter under discussion here.

It has been argued that it is extremely difficult to distinguish religious from secular textbooks;[238] that "the task of separating the secular from the religious in education is one of magnitude, intricacy and delicacy."[239] But just as the Court, if called upon to do so, must determine whether a public school textbook is religiously indoctrinatory,[240] or whether a public school history course is really religious instruction, it should make the same constitutional judgment in respect to parochial school affairs.[241] When a public school action is found religious the remedy is to enjoin; when a parochial school practice is held religious, to forbid its public subsidization.

The general undesirability of requiring the Court to define what is religious and what is not need not be disputed. But, although the Court "can and must avoid passing on the truth of particular religious beliefs,"[242] it cannot escape the former task. "This necessity arises out of the constitutional language itself, which sets down religion as a subject for special treatment."[243] A judicial definition must be fashioned under the "absolutist" theory,[244] which bars all aid to "religion." It must be determined under Professor Kurland's thesis,[245] which forbids classifications in terms of "religion."[246] And it must be faced under the rationale proposed herein.[247]

---

[237] School Dist. v. Schempp, 374 U.S. 203, 225 (1963). *See also* the lengthy discussion by Mr. Justice Brennan, *id.* at 266-78 (concurring opinion).

[238] Board of Educ. v. Allen, 20 N.Y.2d 109, 122, 228 N.E.2d 791, 798, 281 N.Y.S.2d 799, 809 (1967) (dissenting opinion), *prob. juris. noted*, 36 U.S.L.W. 3278 (U.S. Jan. 15, 1968). *See also* U.S. Dep't of Health, Education & Welfare, *supra* note 20, at 358: "[I]t is readily apparent that what one person would classify as simply secular knowledge another would regard as religious instruction." *But see* Kenealy, *supra* note 219, at 204.

[239] McCollum v. Board of Educ., 333 U.S. 203, 237 (1948) (concurring opinion of Jackson, J.).

[240] It has been asserted that, "Many of the public school textbooks present Protestantism in a more favorable light than Catholicism and Christianity more favorably than Judaism . . . . There are definite sectarian tendencies in the textbooks." Corley, *Objections to Aid Answered*, in EDUCATIONAL FREEDOM 184, 192-93 (D. McGarry & L. Ward eds. 1966) (emphasis omitted). *See also* Pflug, *Religion in Missouri Textbooks*, 36 PHI DELTA KAPPAN 258 (1955).

[241] The Court has said of its religious "neutrality" rule that its application "requires interpretation of a delicate sort," School Dist. v. Schempp, 374 U.S. 203, 226 (1963).

[242] Mansfield, Book Review, 52 CALIF. L. REV. 212, 216 (1964), *referring to* United States v. Ballard, 322 U.S. 78 (1944).

[243] Mansfield, *supra* note 242, at 216.

[244] See text accompanying notes 346-53 *infra*.

[245] See text accompanying note 58 *supra*.

[246] *See generally* Mansfield, *supra* note 242, at 215-16.

[247] It would undoubtedly ease judicial administration if parochial school students took all secular courses in public schools as part of a shared time program and then returned to

As has been the case concerning the Court's handling of the issue of religious exercises and activities in public schools, most decisions under the proposed rationale for adjudicating these problems in parochial schools will not be difficult. The Court, guided by common sense and the obvious effects of the activity,[248] rather than by its own "prepossessions,"[249] may set the standard in a few cases. If abuses occur, they may be checked by federal or state aid administrators,[250] reviewed by state and lower federal courts, with ultimate review always available in the Supreme Court.[251]

Pragmatically, the issue should rarely arise, at least in the foreseeable future, for it is highly unlikely, as a matter of political reality, that the total amount of governmental assistance to parochial education will even approach the conceded value of the secular educational services it renders.

(c) *Illustrations.*—Keeping this last point in mind, some specific illustrations of problems that could arise under the proposed rationale may be helpful. The second grade arithmetic text assigned in a Catholic parochial school may use sectarian characters, illustrations or examples, phrasing arithmetic problems in terms of rosary beads instead of apples,[252] and using pictures of parochial schools instead of public schools. Or, if the text is "clean," the teacher may use these illustrations. Trumpet instruction may involve an unusual amount of religiously-oriented music, and French language instruction may include a high concentration of religiously-significant words or reading.[253]

---

the parochial school for the requisite "permeation" and other religious instruction. *See* G. LaNoue, *supra* note 56, at 44. But, when essentially the same secular public school course may be offered in the parochial school, there is little justification for elevating a rule of administrative convenience into a constitutional mandate. And see text following note 251 *infra.*

[248] See text accompanying note 122 *supra.*

[249] McCollum v. Board of Educ., 333 U.S. 203, 238 (1948) (concurring opinion of Jackson, J.).

[250] Mr. LaNoue suggests that a major flaw in granting aid to parochial schools would be that "an authority would have to be set up to supervise local curricula, to censor textbooks for religious material and to investigate infractions and abuses with public money." LaNoue, *supra* note 207, at 291. In respect to the rationale proposed herein, this is an overstatement. Perhaps such a public agency should be set up, irrespective of public financing, as it already is for public schools, to assure that parochial schools offer a sound educational program. See text accompanying notes 472-75 *infra.* If public aid is given, however, the only necessary desideratum (although not, of course, constitutionally required) is to constitute an official to check abuses.

[251] *See* McCollum v. Board of Educ., 333 U.S. 203, 238 (1948) (dissenting opinion of Reed, J.).

[252] *See* 107 America 1201 (1962). *See also* J. Fichter, *supra* note 223, at 86; LaNoue, *supra* note 207, at 272-73, 275.

[253] *See* LaNoue, *supra* note 207, at 276. *See also* McGowan v. Maryland, 366 U.S. 420, 445 (1961) (statutes use religiously oriented terms).

Considerations of religious liberty, not present in voluntarily-attended parochial schools, might prevent all or some of this in public schools.²⁵⁴ But in the examples above, full secular value seems to have been obtained for the time and resources expended, despite the fact that religious interests may also have been served.²⁵⁵

(1) Burden of Justification.—Some educators might urge that the above uses of sectarian material did not afford the parochial pupils a secular educational experience completely analogous to that offered in the public schools. If such a case is made, the state or federal financing agency and the recipient parochial school should have the burden of justifying allocation of the full cost of the course to the secular side of the ledger. Although legislative and executive action ordinarily carries a much stronger presumption of constitutionality,²⁵⁶ the Court has forcefully held that this is not the case when the precious personal freedoms of speech, press, and religion are at stake.²⁵⁷

It may seem to some that individual liberty is only indirectly affected when governmental grants to religious bodies are challenged under the establishment clause,²⁵⁸ thus vindicating use of the usual presumption of constitutionality or something close to it. But the prohibition against the use of compulsorily raised tax funds for strictly religious purposes, central to the concept of nonestablishment as an important guarantor of religious liberty, suggests that here, too, the regular presumption should be modified.²⁵⁹ Thus, after an opponent of aid initially demonstrates that a parochial school course or activity is in whole or part primarily religious, in the sense used in this article, the obligation of rebuttal should rest with those defending aid. In cases of uncertainty, the issue should be resolved against the public funding.²⁶⁰

---

²⁵⁴ *Cf.* Dickman v. School Dist., 232 Ore. 238, 243, 366 P.2d 533, 536 (1961), *cert. denied*, 371 U.S. 823 (1962).

²⁵⁵ *But see* S. Hook, *supra* note 59, at 111. The constitutional effect would seem to be little different than if a parochial school mathematics, music, or language teacher is trained at public expense, *see* 20 U.S.C. § 425(b)(3) (1964); *id.* § 1111 (Supp. I, 1965), and then uses the techniques discussed in teaching his parochial school class.

²⁵⁶ Metropolitan Cas. Ins. Co. v. Brownell, 294 U.S. 580, 584 (1935), and cases there cited.

²⁵⁷ Cases cited by Justice Frankfurter in his concurring opinion in Kovacs v. Cooper, 336 U.S. 77, 90-96 (1949).

²⁵⁸ *See* Comment, 13 U.C.L.A.L. Rev. 1100, 1113-14 (1966).

²⁵⁹ *See* Comment, 21 S. Cal. L. Rev. 61, 67 (1947); *cf.* Sullivan, *Religious Education in the Schools*, 14 Law & Contemp. Prob. 92, 107 (1949). *But see* Reed, *The "Permeation" Issue in Federal Aid to Education*, 8 Catholic Law. 197, 201 (1962).

²⁶⁰ *But cf.* Mitchell v. Consolidated School Dist., 17 Wash. 2d 61, 75, 78, 80, 135 P.2d 79, 85, 86, 87 (1943) (dissenting opinions); State *ex rel.* Reynolds v. Nusbaum, 17 Wis. 2d 148, 171-72, 11 N.W.2d 761, 773 (1962) (dissenting opinion).

(2) *Examples.*—In a parochial school biology text or course, after a full explanation of the theory of evolution, the church's perspective on the matter may also be fully articulated.[261] Or, in the civics course, the concept of racial equal protection may be amplified by presenting both the relevant secular and theological values. Since there would seem to be no constitutional objection to such an objective presentation in the public schools,[262] there should likewise be none here, despite the concurrent religious educational value, and despite the fact that these matters may never be mentioned in the average public school class.[263] They still have significant secular educational value.[264] Even a parochial school course in "religion" itself may so qualify if properly handled.[265]

There is a very fine line, however, between objective presentation and subtle commitment,[266] and this truth is not confined to parochial schools. Some texts used in public schools[267]—and, undoubtedly, some teachers—unintentionally emphasize Humanistic or antireligious values.[268] Undoubtedly, the opposite is also true. Such emphasis will vary from public school to public school, dependent in part on the cultural, religious and racial composition of the students and teachers.[269] To the extent that this is constitutionally permissible, effectively unavoidable, or de minimis in the public schools, it should be similarly unobjectionable in the parochial schools for the purpose of public funding—subject always to the burden of justification discussed above.[270]

---

[261] *See* LaNoue, *supra* note 207, at 465.

[262] *Cf.* McCollum v. Board of Educ., 333 U.S. 203, 235-36 (1948) (concurring opinion of Jackson, J.).

[263] Smith, *Catholic Science Textbooks?*, 110 AMERICA 78 (1964), suggests that some public school textbooks in the natural sciences (that are also used in some parochial schools) fail to mention any relevant religious views. *See also* the view of Mr. Justice Brennan that "to what extent, and at what points in the curriculum, religious materials should be cited are matters which the courts ought to entrust very largely to the experienced officials who superintend our Nation's public schools." School Dist. v. Schempp, 374 U.S. 203, 300 (1963) (concurring opinion).

[264] *See* Reed, *supra* note 259, at 197. Even if virtually every parochial school course contains an objective presentation of the religious viewpoint, *see* LaNoue, *supra* note 207, at 290, it might well pass muster so long as it is not done to the detriment of a reasonably well rounded secular education. Separate courses on "the lives of the Saints," *see* CATHOLIC SCHOOL J., Feb. 1963, at 24 (advertisement), or "the evils of Communism," see *id.*, Jan. 1963, at 22 (advertisement), would present this problem. The defense burden of justification is here relevant. See discussion in text accompanying notes 256-60 *supra*.

[265] *See* McQuilken, *Religious Instruction*, 86 COMMONWEAL 48 (1967).

[266] "It is too much to expect that mortals will teach subjects about which their contemporaries have passionate controversies with the detachment they may summon to teaching about remote subjects . . . ." McCollum v. Board of Educ., 333 U.S. 203, 236 (1948) (concurring opinion of Jackson, J.).

[267] These are sometimes also used in parochial schools. Smith, *supra* note 263.

[268] *Id.*

[269] *See* McCollum v. Board of Educ., 333 U.S. 203, 237 (1948) (concurring opinion of Jackson, J.).

[270] See discussion in text accompanying notes 256-60 *supra*.

A parochial school history course or text may teach that all major events are related to or produced by one of the basic truths of the religion,[271] or may emphasize the contribution of one religion over all others.[272] Parochial school texts in English composition may "stress Catholic religious words and teachings,"[273] or a current events class may use a weekly magazine whose articles are "Catholic-oriented."[274] An advanced biology text or course may omit all references to birth control, sterilization, and euthanasia,[275] or specifically reject most parts of evolutionary theory and shift scientific concepts so that they appear to be based on religious tenets.[276] A parochial school geography text may describe only Catholic families in various cultures,[277] or the teacher may ask the students to map all Catholic churches in the state of Nebraska.[278]

Clearly, some[279] or all of these parochial school activities, as well as some referred to earlier,[280] cannot be fully supported with public funds. Either the quantity of religious perspective has deprived the course of full secular educational value, or the quality of sectarian permeation has so slanted the material as to have partially undermined or even fully destroyed its secular content. The very description of these courses and texts appears to state a sufficient case to shift the burden of justifying any quantum of secular value to those defending governmental support.

E. Allocation

It must be reemphasized that, as a realistic matter, problems of the nature just discussed will arise rarely,[281] as will problems of allocating cost between religious and secular parts of "mixed" parochial school activity. As with the issue of permeation, the burden of justifying both the propriety of the allocation and the method used should be on the government or recipient defendant once the assailant has made the requisite initial demonstration.

Several problems of allocation that have disturbed courts may serve as brief illustrations. The cost of bus transportation to parochial schools, for example, cannot be allocated in "proportional shares as between the

---

[271] See Albert, *Teaching History in the Elementary School*, 51 CATHOLIC SCHOOL J. 10 (1951).
[272] See A. STOKES & L. PFEFFER, *supra* note 27, at 411.
[273] See CATHOLIC SCHOOL J., Jan. 1963, at 86 (advertisement).
[274] See *id.* at 88.
[275] See LaNoue, *supra* note 207, at 265.
[276] See *id.* at 284.
[277] See *id.* at 271.
[278] Sister Julian, *Does Johnny Like Geography?*, CATHOLIC SCHOOL J., Jan. 1963, at 66.
[279] The most obviously suspect are those discussed in text accompanying notes 271, 272, 274, 276, and 277 *supra*.
[280] See text accompanying notes 207, 218 *supra*.
[281] See text following note 251 *supra*. But see G. LaNoue, *supra* note 56, at 32.

secular and religious instruction."[282] The reason is that, as will be amply shown,[283] the activity fully serves an independent secular purpose. Thus, its value, if provided by the parochial school while public school children are bussed at public expense, may be completely listed in the secular services column. No allocation is necessary.

Suppose that public funds are used to construct a building for educational research on the campus of a church-affiliated college, title being vested in the school.[284] If the building is always used for this purpose as contemplated, no allocation problem arises. But suppose, after three years, the building is to be converted into a chapel and utilized exclusively for religious purposes. If in the building's three years as a research center, the total governmental contribution to the college, including the full amount of the grant for the building, did not exceed the value of the secular educational service rendered by the college, the matter is closed. The fact that the building will now be used for religious purposes is irrelevant. The taxpayers have gotten at least full secular value for their contribution. But, if in those three years the total governmental contribution, including the grant, exceeded the value of the college's secular educational services, the building may not be used for religious purposes until the college reimburses the government for the excess amount or some other proper arrangement is made. The science of accounting, with judicial review when appropriate, is neither above nor below the needed task.

F. Relevant Supreme Court Decisions

Reference has previously been made to passing remarks by some observers suggesting that existing Supreme Court opinions have already resolved the problem of aid in parochial schools.[285] It is *Everson v. Board of Education*[286] that is most frequently cited for this proposition—by advocates on both sides of the issue. The brief of the National Catholic Welfare Conference reasons: "The underlying principle of the case is plain: government aid may be rendered to a citizen in furtherance of his obtaining education in a church-related school."[287] It points out that the majority opinion's stringent interpretation of the establishment clause,[288] although more than a mere dictum, "must be read in the light of the

---

[282] Everson v. Board of Educ., 330 U.S. 1, 46 (1947) (dissenting opinion of Rutledge, J.).

[283] See note 510 *infra*.

[284] Horace Mann League v. Board of Pub. Works, 242 Md. 645, 683, 220 A.2d 51, 72, *cert. denied*, 385 U.S. 97 (1966).

[285] See text accompanying notes 9, 143 *supra*.

[286] 330 U.S. 1 (1947).

[287] National Catholic Welfare Conference, *supra* note 37, at 417.

[288] The language is set forth in text accompanying note 8 *supra*.

actual result of the case .... [which is that] secular education in church-related schools ... is supportable by government,"[289] and in light of the opinion's edict that the state "cannot exclude ... [persons], *because of their faith, or lack of it,* from receiving the benefits of public welfare legislation";[290] that there was "careful avoidance by the majority of any rule which would preclude aid [for] ... secular subject training."[291] Finally, it reads the Court's language barring any tax support for "any religious activities or institutions, whatever they may be called, or whatever form they may adopt to teach or practice religion,"[292] as only excluding "aid in support of (a) the teaching or practicing of religion ... ; (b) religious institutions *as* religious institutions."[293]

The argument is incisive and not unpersuasive. But it is by no means conclusive. An argument at least as convincing can be made the other way: The whole tone of the majority opinion[294] strongly implied that bus transportation marked the outermost limit of permissible governmental aid. The Court suggested that the plan at bar went to the "verge"[295] of the state's constitutional power. The Court said, albeit in dictum, that the establishment clause forbade a state to "contribute tax-raised funds to the support of an institution which teaches the tenets and faith of any church";[296] that the line to be drawn is "between tax legislation which provides funds for the welfare of the general public and that which is designed to support institutions which teach religion."[297] The latter point seems directly to contradict the "religious institutions *as* religious institutions"[298] conclusion. In the bussing situation presented

---

[289] National Catholic Welfare Conference, *supra* note 37, at 418. Mr. Pfeffer concedes that the result leads logically to that conclusion. L. PFEFFER, *supra* note 26, at 568.

[290] 330 U.S. at 16.

[291] National Catholic Welfare Conference, *supra* note 37, at 420.

[292] See note 8 *supra* and accompanying text.

[293] National Catholic Welfare Conference, *supra* note 37, at 420-21. *See also* Costanzo, *supra* note 37, at 620-26; Drinan, *The Constitutionality of Public Aid to Parochial Schools,* in THE WALL BETWEEN CHURCH AND STATE 55, 66 (D. Oaks ed. 1963). *Contra,* AMERICAN JEWISH CONGRESS, SCHOOLS, SUBSIDIES AND SEPARATION 3 (1965); 5 *Hearings on S. 370, supra* note 148, at 2750 (Statement of Dr. C. Stanley Lowell, Associate Director, Protestants and Other Americans United for Separation of Church and State). *See also* W. KATZ, *supra* note 48, at 70-71: "This sentence [in *Everson*] is certainly not free from ambiguity. The question is whether the thrust is against *support of religious teaching* or, more broadly, against any *support of institutions* which give such teaching. The latter interpretation is perhaps more easily justified as a matter of grammar." *See also* R. DRINAN, *supra* note 50, at 131-33; Davidow, *supra* note 131, at 678.

[294] *See* Jones, *Church-State Relations: Our Constitutional Heritage,* in RELIGION AND CONTEMPORARY SOCIETY 156, 194 (H. Stahmer ed. 1963); Gordon, *supra* note 229, at 85; Pfeffer, in Dorsen, *supra* note 33, at 38-39.

[295] 330 U.S. at 16.

[296] *Id.*

[297] *See id.* at 14.

[298] See text accompanying note 293 *supra.*

by *Everson* the Court stressed that the state "contributes no money to the schools,"[299] and that the services provided were "indisputably marked off from the religious function"[300] of parochial schools.

In respect to the proposal advanced in this article for aid to parochial schools, the best that can be said of the *Everson* opinion [301] is that all discussion by the majority beyond that vital to the result of the case itself was dictum and that discussion in subsequent Supreme Court opinions[302] lends some credence to the proposal urged herein.

Advocates on both sides of the issue also rely on *Bradfield v. Roberts*,[303] which held that federal appropriations for ward construction and care of indigent patients to a hospital in the District of Columbia operated by the Roman Catholic Church did not violate the establishment clause. The National Catholic Welfare Conference contends that the Court recognized that "the church exercises great and perhaps controlling influence over the management of the hospital."[304] Thus, it concludes that the Court "did not rule that a direct appropriation to a sectarian institution would be unconstitutional."[305] The Conference asserts therefore that *Bradfield* and *Everson* are *"clear precedent for aid."*[306]

The language relied on in *Bradfield*, however, may represent not the Court's conclusion, but its statement of the complainant's allegation. For the Court carefully explained that the hospital, incorporated by act of Congress, was simply "a secular corporation being managed by people who hold to the doctrines of the Roman Catholic Church, but who nevertheless are managing the corporation according to the law under which it exists";[307] and that its "property and its business are to be managed in its own way, subject to no visitation, supervision or control by any ecclesiastical authority whatever, but only to that of the Government which created it."[308] This surely may not be said of parochial schools. But neither may it be said, as opponents of aid allege, that "[i]mplicit in this decision is the holding that the Constitution would be violated by a

---

[299] 330 U.S. at 18. *See also* Opinion of the Justices, 233 A.2d 832, 835-36 (N.H. 1967).

[300] 330 U.S. at 18. For specific reliance on this point, *see* Rhoades v. School Dist., 424 Pa. 202, 233, 226 A.2d 53, 70 (concurring opinion of Roberts, J.), *appeal dismissed*, 389 U.S. 11 (1967).

[301] That one member of the five man majority has recently indicated a change of view, *see* Engel v. Vitale, 370 U.S. 421, 443 (1962) (concurring opinion of Douglas, J.), is of little relevance since only he and Mr. Justice Black presently remain on the Court.

[302] See text accompanying notes 137-42 *supra*.

[303] 175 U.S. 291 (1899).

[304] *Id.* at 298.

[305] National Catholic Welfare Conference, *supra* note 37, at 416.

[306] *Id.* at 422.

[307] 175 U.S. at 298-99.

[308] *Id.* at 299.

grant of Federal money . . . to an institution controlled by a sectarian organization"[309] or "subject to ecclesiastical authority."[310]

A more reasonable conclusion is that *Bradfield* leaves open the aid to parochial schools question.[311]

A number of writers consider Supreme Court decisions involving religion in the public schools as bearing directly on the question of aid to parochial schools. It is true that *McCollum v. Board of Education*—in which the Court invalidated "on-premises" released time—does refer disapprovingly to "the use of tax-supported property for religious instruction."[312] But the entire opinion makes clear that it was an additional factor, the "utilization of the tax-established and tax-supported *public school system* to aid religious groups to spread their faith,"[313] that was conclusive.[314]

Zorach v. Clauson—in which the Court refused to invalidate the New York "off-premises" released time plan—does contain the dictum that "[g]overnment may not finance religious groups . . . ."[315] But it is inaccurate to contend that the *Zorach* Court distinguished *McCollum* on the ground that "public . . . funds were not used in New York."[316] Rather, the Court stressed that in *McCollum* "the force of the public school was used to promote [religious] instruction,"[317] whereas the Court found this not to be so in New York.[318]

Under the rationale proposed in this article the cases dealing with religion in the public schools are clearly distinct from the question of

---

[309] L. Pfeffer, *supra* note 26, at 534.

[310] G. LaNoue, *supra* note 56, at 16.

[311] The case of Quick Bear v. Leupp, 210 U.S. 50 (1908), is also advanced to support the position that aid to parochial schools violates the establishment clause. The case held that the federal government could disburse treaty funds, held in trust for Indians and legally belonging to them, to church-affiliated schools designated by the Indians to pay tuition costs. The opinion provides no support for the assertion by Mr. Justice Rutledge, in Everson v. Board of Educ., 330 U.S. at 43 n.35, that "it was stated also that such a use of public [rather than tribal] moneys would violate . . . the First Amendment," nor does careful reading of the Court's language relied on by Mr. Pfeffer, *supra* note 26, at 535.

[312] 333 U.S. 203, 209 (1948).

[313] *Id.* at 210 (emphasis added).

[314] *See also id.* at 209-10, 212. The author of the *McCollum* opinion thought that he had made "categorically clear [that] the *McCollum* decision would have been the same if the religious classes had not been held in the school buildings." Zorach v. Clauson, 343 U.S. 306, 316 (1952) (dissenting opinion of Black, J.).

[315] 343 U.S. 306, 314 (1952). Two authors cite this statement as indicative of the Court's attitude with regard to the invalidity of aid to parochial schools. G. LaNoue, *supra* note 56, at 23; L. Pfeffer, *supra* note 26, at 535.

[316] G. LaNoue, *supra* note 56, at 23; *see* L. Pfeffer, *supra* note 26, at 535.

[317] 343 U.S. at 315.

[318] This "deeper difference" has recently been emphasized by Mr. Justice Brennan, concurring in School Dist. v. Schempp, 374 U.S. 203, 262 (1963). *See also id.* at 223 (opinion of the Court by Clark, J.).

aid to parochial schools.[319] That the former involve governmental programs lacking independent primary secular purpose has been documented elsewhere.[320] That at least certain amounts of governmental financial aid for parochial education serves a primary secular purpose has been documented above.[321] Moreover, religion in the public schools involves infringements of religious liberty by compromising students' conscientious beliefs.[322] Although aid to parochial schools involves the expenditure of public money, it has been noted above[323] that use of tax funds for secular purposes does not violate the constitutionally protected right of conscience.[324]

G. *The Doctrine of Alternative Means*

Several members of the Court have employed an "alternative means" rationale in establishment clause cases.[325] Mr. Justice Frankfurter has theorized that "[i]f a statute furthers both secular and religious ends by means unnecessary to the effectuation of the secular ends alone . . . the statute cannot stand."[326] Mr. Justice Brennan has opined that "[t]he Constitution enjoins those involvements of religious with secular institutions which . . . use essentially religious means to serve governmental ends where secular means would suffice."[327]

Using this doctrine, opponents of aid for parochial schools have urged its unconstitutionality. They reason that the state's secular goal of maintaining and improving the quality of education for all students may be

---

[319] Thus, the fact that the Court has invalidated public school prayer and Bible reading, Engel v. Vitale, 370 U.S. 421 (1962); School Dist. v. Schempp, 374 U.S. 203 (1963), does not render it "most unconvincing to argue that the Court will turn around and permit the government to subsidize" parochial schools. G. LaNoue, *supra* note 56, at 23.

[320] Choper, *supra* note 4, at 335, 368-77, 387-400.

[321] See text accompanying notes 145-49, 200-80 *supra*. For this distinction see Korbel, *supra* note 199, at 1021; Sky, *supra* note 42, at 1465.

[322] For a fuller discussion of this problem, see Choper, *supra* note 4, at 368-77, 387-400.

[323] See text accompanying notes 155-56 *supra*.

[324] This reconciles the difficulty of some who find the expenditure of any public funds in aid of parochial education a much wider breach of the "wall of separation" than the on-premises released time condemned in *McCollum* or the distribution of Bibles invalidated in Tudor v. Board of Educ., 14 N.J. 31, 100 A.2d 857 (1953), *cert. denied*, 348 U.S. 816 (1954). *See* G. Spicer, The Supreme Court and Fundamental Freedoms 82 (1959); Bryson, *Mending the Breach*, 65 Christian Century 649, 650 (1948). *See also* Choper, *supra* note 4, at 361-62.

Since public schools are available to all and are wholly financed by public funds, granting some public aid to parochial schools will not produce "pressures to conform—*i.e.*, to affiliate with some groups which are aided." Davidow, *supra* note 131, at 687. See also text accompanying notes 375-77 *infra*.

[325] *See generally* Wormuth & Mirkin, *The Doctrine of the Reasonable Alternative*, 9 Utah L. Rev. 254 (1964).

[326] McGowan v. Maryland, 366 U.S. 420, 466-67 (1961) (concurring opinion).

[327] School Dist. v. Schempp, 374 U.S. 203, 231 (1963) (concurring opinion).

achieved without extending governmental financial assistance to parochial schools—that is, without the use of what they characterize as essentially religious means. They recognize that the state is constitutionally forbidden to require all students to attend public schools.[328] But they conclude that the state need only channel aid to the public schools, thus improving their quality, and concomitantly raise the standards of accreditation for private and parochial schools to a similar level.[329]

There are several points to be made in response. First, a majority of the Court has never employed the "alternative means" rationale in an establishment clause case.[330] Second, a close reading of Mr. Justice Frankfurter's reasoning indicates that he was only suggesting the doctrine's use when a statute's *primary effect* was religious and the purported secular end was *derivative*,[331] as I have used these terms herein. Third, in respect to government programs that directly serve independent secular ends, Mr. Justice Brennan stresses utilization of the doctrine when the program jeopardizes "the religious liberties of any members of the community."[332]

If a statute's primary purpose is religious, and it presents no real danger to individual religious and conscientious beliefs, perhaps it should be invalid if nonreligious alternative means are available.[333] And, if a

---

[328] Pierce v. Society of Sisters, 268 U.S. 510 (1925); *cf.* Truitt v. Board of Public Works, 243 Md. 375, 410, 221 A.2d 370, 391 (1966). *But cf.* U.S. Dep't of Health, Education & Welfare, *supra* note 20, at 379.

[329] *See* L. Pfeffer, *supra* note 26, at 569.

[330] *See* McGowan v. Maryland, 366 U.S. 420, 450 (1961) in which the Court replied to the argument that it should be used, "However relevant this argument may be, we believe that the factual basis on which it rests is not supportable." *Cf.* School Dist. v. Schempp, 374 U.S. 203, 224 (1963). Professor Van Alstyne has pointed out that "application of the 'alternative means' idea might well have produced a different result in the *Everson* case, itself," *supra* note 68, at 879.

[331] His principal illustration concerned the use of a religion as an engine of civil policy: "A State may not endow a church although that church might inculcate in its parishioners moral concepts deemed to make them better citizens, because the very *raison d'être* of a church, as opposed to any other school of civilly serviceable morals, is the predication of religious doctrine." 366 U.S. at 467. Further, he acknowledged that "the State may guard its people's safety by extending fire and police protection to the churches," *id.* In this instance, where there was an independent primary secular purpose—guarding safety—and an equally necessary and inevitable aid to religion, the Justice would not require the use of an alternative means—demanding that churches obtain private police and fire protection. Finally, he concludes his discussion of "alternative means" with the statement that the "'establishment' contention can prevail only if the absence of any substantial legislative purpose other than a religious one is made to appear." *Id.* at 468. Thus, he would find that if there is a legitimate, independent primary secular purpose, the statute is immune from establishment attack despite the existence of alternative means.

[332] 374 U.S. at 281. He also applies his rationale to action whose primary effect is religious, that is, action that uses religion as an engine of civil policy—and which endangers religious liberty. See his discussion of Torcaso v. Watkins, 367 U.S. 488 (1961), in this context, 374 U.S. at 265.

[333] *But see* note 51 *supra;* text following note 83 *supra*.

statute's primary purpose is secular, and it presents threats to religious freedom, a persuasive argument may be made that the alternative means doctrine should be employed.[334] But if a statute's primary purpose is religious, and it is likely to result in compromising the individual's religious or conscientious beliefs, as I have argued here[335] and elsewhere,[336] it should violate the establishment clause even in the absence of an alternative means. And, finally, if a statute's primary purpose is secular, and it does not impinge on rights of conscience, I would suggest that the alternative means doctrine should not apply even though the statute inevitably affords some aid to religion. Such a statute presents none of the evils at the core of the establishment ban, and to subject all such legislation to judicial review, for a search for alternative means that afford no aid whatever to religion, would bring innumerable measures before the Court and unnecessarily involve it in an essentially legislative task.[337] Governmental aid to support the secular aspects of parochial education falls into this final category.

Even if the alternative means rationale were applicable to this final category, it is not clear that aid to parochial schools would be invalid. Mr. Justice Brennan apparently did not exclude this final category discussed above from the doctrine's coverage,[338] but he did state that the means used would be invalid only if the secular objectives of the state could be *"effectively* achieved in modern society"[339] by the alternative nonreligious means. So, too, Mr. Justice Frankfurter would have applied his thesis only "where the same secular ends could *equally* be attained by means which do not have consequences for promotion of religion."[340] Similarly, commentators speak in terms of *"practical* alternatives less likely to offend the first amendment," and achievement of the public purpose "by nonsectarian methods without unreasonably increasing costs or administrative burdens."[341]

A forceful argument may be made that it would be highly ineffective

---

[334] *See* Choper, *supra* note 4, at 370 n.240, 383; Moore, *The Supreme Court and the Relationship Between the "Establishment" and "Free Exercise" Clauses*, 42 TEXAS L. REV. 142, 188 (1963).

[335] See text accompanying note 53 *supra*.

[336] Choper, *supra* note 4, at 332-34, 348-50.

[337] *Cf.* Southern Pac. Co. v. Arizona, 325 U.S. 761, 794 (1945) (dissenting opinion of Black, J.). For example, challenge to the constitutionality of fire protection for church buildings could be made on this basis, see note 331 *supra*.

[338] He treated the establishment clause objection to Sunday closing laws which conceded "secular purpose"—and did not comprehend a violation of religious liberty claim (which was made by Sabbatarians under the free exercise clause, *see* Braunfeld v. Brown, 366 U.S. 599 (1961))—as being subject to the "alternatives" rationale. 374 U.S. at 265.

[339] 374 U.S. at 265 (emphasis added). *See also id.* at 281.

[340] 366 U.S. at 467 (emphasis added).

[341] Comment, 13 U.C.L.A.L. REV. 1100, 1109 (1966) (emphasis added). *See also* Truitt v. Board of Pub. Works, 243 Md. 375, 221 A.2d 370 (1966).

and impractical to aid only public schools and simultaneously raise the accreditation standards for all others.[342] Apart from the limits that the free exercise clause might place on the state's ability so to regulate parochial schools,[343] such action could well result in a large influx of private and parochial school students to the public schools. Tax funds would have to be used for construction of expanded public school facilities, and an inefficient and uneconomic waste of existing parochial school facilities would result.[344] "Such pragmatic considerations would be irrelevant if the command of the Constitution were clear . . . [but] the lack of an effective alternative should be highly relevant when a plausible constitutional defense can be made . . . ."[345]

To summarize briefly, the establishment clause should be held to prohibit nonsecular government action that infringes religious belief, and to forbid taxing for strictly religious purposes. Therefore, as applied to questions of parochial school aid, the establishment clause should not be held to prevent government from subsidizing these schools to the extent that they provide secular services. As long as the government gets its money's worth of things secular, it should make no difference that the supplying institution is somehow religious in nature. The establishment clause, rather than asking whether religious institutions inevitably benefit thereby, should instead ask whether the government is receiving the full value of secular services purchased. The question, consequently, is not *whether* to aid parochial schools which supply secular services, but rather *how much* aid to extend. In resolving that inquiry, the courts must first characterize an educational service or activity as generally religious or secular. If secular, the government may subsidize it at full value; if religious, those defending the aid should carry the burden of showing that the activity contains specific secular aspects entitled to aid. In conclusion, however, it must be remembered as a political reality that the necessity for such allocation will generally remain academic as long as parochial schools continue to provide considerably more in secular services than they receive in aid.

V

OTHER THEORIES

Earlier discussion has traced the operation of a proposed rule for testing the constitutionality under the establishment clause of aid to

---

[342] On the question of whether the state may obtain its educational objectives by merely aiding public schools and doing nothing in respect to parochial schools, *compare* Van Alstyne, *supra* note 68, at 878, *with* Kauper, *Religion, Higher Education and the Constitution*, 19 ALA. L. REV. 275, 288 (1967).
[343] See discussion at notes 479-89 *infra*. *See also* Sky, *supra* note 42, at 1448-49.
[344] Note, 41 N.Y.U.L. REV. 983, 987 (1966).
[345] 77 HARV. L. REV. 1353, 1358 (1964).

parochial schools. Reference will now be made to other theories involving aid to parochial schools and the establishment clause, with particular examination of their own internal consistency and viability and with the intention of further illuminating certain aspects of the constitutional proposals made in this article.

A. Absolutism

The so-called "absolutist" theory, mentioned earlier,[346] would prohibit all aid which benefits religious institutions either directly or indirectly,[347] sustaining "appropriations only when it can be found that in fact they do not aid, promote, encourage or sustain religious teaching or observances, be the amount large or small."[348] This view "assumes both that state and religion coexist in mutually exclusive and self-contained spheres and that each sphere can be sharply defined."[349] It would seemingly invalidate use of public library books for reading assigned by a parochial school teacher,[350] the stationing of policemen near parochial schools, fire protection and other municipal services for parochial schools,[351] and the laying of sidewalks at public expense in front of parochial schools. All these publicly funded activities may fairly be said directly or indirectly to benefit parochial schools and aid, promote and encourage the religious teaching that takes place therein.[352] It may accurately be concluded that the absolutist theory is "of such far-reaching consequence, and in conflict with so many practices, that it is neither administratively, politically, nor ethically [nor constitutionally] tenable."[353]

---

[346] See text accompanying note 57 *supra*.

[347] *See* Greenawalt, in Dorsen, *supra* note 33, at 44.

[348] Everson v. Board of Educ., 330 U.S. 1, 53 (1947) (dissenting opinion of Rutledge, J.).

[349] 77 HARV. L. REV. 1353, 1357 (1964).

[350] *Cf.* Linde, *Constitutional Rights in the Public Sector: Justice Douglas on Liberty in the Welfare State*, 40 WASH. L. REV. 10, 28 n.239 (1965).

[351] It does not do to distinguish these as "matters of common right, part of the general need for safety. Certainly the fire department must not stand idly by while the church burns." Everson v. Board of Educ., 330 U.S. 1, 60-61 (1947) (dissenting opinion of Rutledge, J.). Secular education is as much a matter of common right, part of the general need for an intelligent citizenry. Certainly the state must not stand idly by while children are inadequately educated.

Nor does it do to say that "education which includes religious training and teaching" has been made a matter "of private right and function" by the free exercise clause, *see* Pierce v. Society of Sisters, 268 U.S. 510 (1925), and that the use of public funds to defray its cost, therefore, cannot be said to be "for a public purpose." Everson v. Board of Educ., 330 U.S. 1, 51 (1947) (dissenting opinion of Rutledge, J.). Eating fish on Friday may also have been a matter of private right protected by the free exercise clause. But government distribution for health purposes (a primary secular purpose) would not have been barred by the establishment clause.

[352] *See* National Catholic Welfare Conference, *supra* note 37, at 455; Comment, *A Constitutional Analysis of the Wisconsin Bus Law*, 1962 WIS. L. REV. 500, 516.

[353] LaNoue, *supra* note 60, at 79.

B. Child Benefit v. Aid to School Itself

The so-called "child-benefit theory"[354] also fails in its purpose of both presenting a viable constitutional test and confining the amount of permissible public aid for parochial education. This approach takes several forms. Principally, the theory distinguishes between valid public assistance to aid the child and invalid public assistance to aid the parochial school itself. Under it, "lunches, textbooks, bus transportation, and health services" are "clearly constitutional";[355] appropriations for "language instruction and laboratory facilities"[356] are uncertain; grants "for building, maintenance and teachers' salaries are foreclosed."[357]

Although this theory may be characterized as "a workable compromise interpretation of the First Amendment,"[358] it places form over substance. The hard fact is that aid for any secular educational purpose, from transportation and textbooks to construction of a science laboratory and payment of a Spanish teacher's salary, helps the child to take his proper place in society.[359] "There is no logical stopping point."[360] The "child benefit theory" thus has no reasoned limits and misses "the real issue, which is the nature of the benefit and its relationship to the 'Establishment Clause.' "[361] a subject already discussed at length herein.

The implicit rationale of the majority in the *Everson* decision suffers the same defect. It upheld public payment of bus transportation on the ground that the children were merely "receiving the benefits of public welfare legislation,"[362] yet suggested, in strongest dictum,[363] that this was as far as the establishment clause would extend. But it must be granted that state subsidization of all secular education similarly affords

---

[354] For judicial development of the theory, *see* Cushman, *supra* note 185, at 337-39. For description of the congressional attempt to fashion the Elementary and Secondary Education Act of 1965 to fit the theory, see Kelley & LaNoue, *The Church-State Settlement in the Federal Aid to Education Act*, 1965 RELIGION & PUB. ORDER 110 (D. Giannella ed.) ; Taylor, *Federal Aid for Children and Teachers in All Schools*, 12 CATHOLIC LAW. 193, 195 (1966).

[355] Jones, *The Constitutional Status of Public Funds for Church-Related Schools*, 6 J. CHURCH & ST. 61, 72 (1964).

[356] *Id.*

[357] Jones, *supra* note 294, at 196.

[358] *Id. See also* Giannella, *supra* note 199, at 572-81.

[359] *See, e.g.,* Note, 12 Mo. L. REV. 465, 468 (1947); Comment, 6 U. DET. L.J. 174, 176 (1943).

[360] Everson v. Board of Educ., 133 N.J.L. 350, 359, 44 A.2d 333, 339 (1945) (dissenting opinion). *See also* 35 CONN. B.J. 119, 125 (1961); 1 BILL OF RIGHTS REV. 307, 309 (1941).

[361] Note, 41 IND. L.J. 302, 309 (1966).

[362] 330 U.S. at 16.

[363] See text accompanying notes 294-300 *supra.*

children the benefits of public welfare legislation.[364] The establishment clause should forbid no aid in that category.[365]

The *Everson* majority seemingly also sought to draw a line by emphasizing that in the case at bar "the State contributes no money to the schools."[366] On the basis of this reasoning, it has been concluded that "direct grants to sectarian schools are prohibited,"[367] and that "grants for assistance in the construction of general school facilities and for increasing teachers' salaries, to be administered by governmental agencies and made available directly to sectarian schools, are the clear case of what is proscribed by the Constitution."[368]

Closely akin to the "child benefit theory,"[369] this rationale also places form over substance. The constitutional result turns on the payee of money or recipient of property, whatever the primary effect of the government action or whoever the true ultimate beneficiary.[370] It would invalidate a consignment of microscopes to a parochial school or a grant of funds to construct a science laboratory regardless of the clear secular purpose. "Similarly, if the only reasonable or practicable means of providing fire and police protection were to give a religious school public funds and have it perform this function itself,"[371] such granting of funds would also be unconstitutional. Surely, it should make no constitutional difference if arithmetic textbooks are given to the parochial school rather than to the pupil or a public library from which he may withdraw them.[372]

It is argued by some that if direct grants to parochial schools do not violate the establishment ban, then nothing does except discrimination among religions,[373] thus challenging the Supreme Court's unequivocal position that governmental support of all religions is forbidden.[374] Not true. Under the rationale I propose, governmental aid may not exceed the value of the secular services even where given to every religion.

It is contended that providing school bussing or laboratory equip-

---

[364] *See, e.g.,* P. KAUPER, FRONTIERS OF CONSTITUTIONAL LIBERTY 136 (1956); Boyer, *Public Transportation of Parochial School Pupils,* 1952 WIS. L. REV. 64, 85; Comment, 21 S. CAL. L. REV. 61, 75 (1947); Note, 60 HARV. L. REV. 793, 800 (1947); 3 INTRA. L. REV. 147, 153 (1948).

[365] *See* Katz, *Freedom of Religion and State Neutrality,* 20 U. CHI. L. REV. 426, 440 (1953).

[366] 330 U.S. at 18. See text accompanying notes 296-99 *supra.*

[367] U.S. Dep't of Health, Education & Welfare, *supra* note 20, at 361.

[368] *Id.* at 373. *Cf.* P. KAUPER, *supra* note 5, at 106-07.

[369] *See* Cushman, *supra* note 185, at 347.

[370] *See* Everson v. Board of Educ., 330 U.S. 1, 55-56 n.50 (1947) (dissenting opinion of Rutledge, J.).

[371] Comment, 11 ST. LOUIS U.L.J. 464, 471 (1967).

[372] *Cf.* Sky, *supra* note 42, at 1457-58. See text accompanying notes 530-33 *infra.*

[373] U.S. Dep't of Health, Education & Welfare, *supra* note 20, at 373-74.

[374] See note 59 *supra* (last paragraph).

ment to a parochial school should be invalid because this makes "access to this public welfare benefit . . . dependent on conditions set by a religious group. These conditions will generally involve conformity to a religious creed or practice as the price for admission to the school and its publicly donated equipment."[375] It may be true that "placing citizens in the position of having to accept church authority in order to obtain necessary public welfare benefits . . . constitutes an establishment of religion."[376] But it is not true that providing parochial schools with secular educational services has this effect. Under the rationale I propose, parochial schools would get no greater benefits than are already accorded public schools. Thus, access to the benefits is in no way dependent on the acceptance of church authority.[377]

Perhaps the greatest weakness in the "child benefit theory" and the "no money to the parochial school" rationale[378] is that they permit public funds to be used for strictly religious purposes, beyond use for secular purposes, in contravention of a basic thrust of the establishment clause. Proponents of the "aid the child" approach advocate direct state subsidies to parents who may then choose any school for their children's education,[379] subject to the state's right of accreditation.[380] "Thus the schools would in no way be subsidized with public funds; only parents and their children would be subsidized."[381]

No one denies that these subsidies would ultimately reach the parochial school's treasury; such a result would probably be a specific condition of the awards.[382] After all, that is their precise purpose. Thus, if

---

[375] LaNoue, *supra* note 60, at 91.

[376] *Id.* at 91-92. The free exercise claim is even more apparent.

[377] Other considerations are present if the church-related school is in fact the only realistically available school. See text accompanying notes 436-39 *infra*.

[378] As is true of other approaches to be discussed, both the "child benefit" and "no money to parochial school" rationales fail to fulfill their purported aims because of the freed funds factor, which produces precisely the effects they seek to avoid. See text accompanying notes 407-15 *infra*.

[379] V. BLUM, FREEDOM OF CHOICE IN EDUCATION 29-30 (1958). *See also* Hayes, *supra* note 201, at 111; Note, 29 FORDHAM L. REV. 578, 580 (1961).

[380] The subsidy may take several analytically indistinguishable forms: (a) Direct appropriation. (b) Tax Credit. For discussion, *see* V. BLUM, *supra* note 379, at 19-22 *passim*. *See also* Freeman, *Tax Credits and the School-Aid Deadlock*, 194 CATHOLIC WORLD 201, 207 (1962), for the view that a tax credit is "free from constitutional challenge . . . because it funnels out no public money and avoids contact between government and the private school." (c) Tax deduction.

[381] V. BLUM, *supra* note 379, at 30.

[382] *See* Brown, *State Constitutions and Religion in Education*, in EDUCATIONAL FREEDOM 163, 183 (D. McGarry & L. Ward eds. 1966). "Since tuition charges are flexible and in Roman Catholic schools are often far below operating costs, the charges could readily be adjusted upward to take advantage of the parents' subsidies." Nelson, *Proposal on the School-Aid Impasse*, 78 CHRISTIAN CENTURY 448, 449 (1961). *See also* Almond v. Day, 197

the public subsidy exceeds the value of the secular educational service rendered, tax funds are being utilized for strictly religious purposes.[383] The parent subsidy theory fails to recognize this difficulty. Tax funds could be used for religion even if the amount given is only "equal to the sum expended on every child who attends the free schools,"[384] because there is no guarantee that the parochial school offers the same quantum of secular education as the public schools, nor that the lesser quantum offered costs the parochial school as much as the sum made available to it.[385] The strictly religious use of tax monies could result even if the amount given is only "*part* of a tuition which is itself considerably less than the cost of education at the school attended,"[386] because even this smaller governmental subsidy might exceed the cost or value of the secular educational service rendered.[387]

A "subsidy-to-the-parent-for-school-tuition" plan is not analogous to a government old age assistance program.[388] In the latter instance the subsidized citizen may spend the money in any way he wishes, save it, or give it away. Government does not condition its grant, as it does the parent subsidy scheme, on the recipient's channeling the funds to a specific, limited class of ultimate beneficiaries, which class includes church-affiliated institutions.

That a person receiving old age assistance donates a portion to his church presents no colorable establishment clause issue. It is analytically

---

Va. 419, 426, 89 S.E.2d 851, 856-57 (1955); Lowell & Southgate, *POAU Position on Church-State Relations*, 5 J. CHURCH & ST. 41, 51 (1963); Note, 36 FORDHAM L. REV. 129, 131 (1967); Note, 42 VA. L. REV. 437, 438-39 (1956).

[383] This may explain the result in Swart v. South Burlington Town School Dist., 122 Vt. 177, 167 A.2d 514, *cert. denied*, 366 U.S. 925 (1961), which invalidated a tuition plan. The Vermont statute authorized payment of full tuition "but not in excess of $325.00 unless authorized by a vote of the town school district," 122 Vt. at 179, 167 A.2d at 515. The amounts appropriated to Roman Catholic high schools may have covered both secular and religious educational costs, although the opinion gives no indication. It has been argued that "without doubt the real reason for the decision lay in the fact that tuition payments, which were made directly to the schools, were not in some manner apportioned to support of the nonreligious instruction given." Slough & McAnany, *supra* note 37, at 69. *See also* Alciatore, *Federal Aid to Church-Related Schools and the Constitution*, 65 CATHOLIC EDUC. REV. 383, 393 (1967); National Catholic Welfare Conference, *supra* note 37, at 420 n.54. The court's opinion affords scanty support for this view.

[384] R. DRINAN, *supra* note 50, at 196.
[385] See discussion accompanying notes 183-199 *supra*.
[386] V. BLUM, *supra* note 379, at 28.
[387] It has been argued that a tax deduction, see note 380 *supra*, "would not corrupt the Constitution any more than the tax deduction now allowed those who make charitable donations to churches." THE REPORTER, Mar. 30, 1961, at 12. Perhaps the latter deduction survives attack on the ground that the benefit to the ultimate beneficiary religious groups does not exceed the value of the secular services they render. The topic, although obviously pertinent, is generally beyond the scope of the discussion.
[388] *Contra*, V. BLUM, *supra* note 379, at 32-34.

identical to a public employee's donating a portion of his compensation to his church.[389] There is not the slightest government compulsion to ultilize tax funds for religious purposes. But a government condition that a tuition subsidy be transferred to some school of the parent's choice (including a parochial school) is analytically identical to a state payment to any voluntary association that a recipient joins (including his church or synagogue). Government has thereby restricted full freedom of choice as to how tax funds will be spent. It has singled out religion, albeit as part of a somewhat larger category, for government financial aid. If the ultimate religiously-affiliated beneficiary does not render secular services in return, tax raised funds will be used for strictly religious purposes. As has already been observed,[390] this result is contrary to the underlying purposes of the establishment clause.

For these reasons, under the theory advanced in this article, certain provisions of the old "G. I. Bill of Rights"[391] seem to violate the establishment clause.[392] Under that bill, as reportedly administered, the government paid tuition directly to the veteran's school, even if it was a theological seminary.[393] This was not a case in which "GI's are paid a certain amount which they can use in any way they want . . . [as] compensation for their serving in the armed forces."[394] That would be like old age assistance. The G. I. Bill, however, was a case of "conditioned" benefits, within a fairly limited category, as described above.[395]

The funneling of tax money to theological seminaries appears to serve a strictly religious purpose.[396] That this is "education they would

---

[389] *Cf.* Rawlings v. Butler, 290 S.W.2d 801, 806 (Ky. 1956); Zellers v. Huff, 55 N.M. 501, 522, 236 P.2d 949, 961-62 (1951); Hysong v. Gallitzen Borough School Dist., 164 Pa. 629, 656-57, 30 A. 482, 483-84 (1894).

[390] See text accompanying note 60-66 *supra.*

[391] Serviceman's Readjustment Act of 1944, 58 Stat. 287.

[392] *See* Sullivan, *Religious Education in the Schools,* 14 LAW & CONTEMP. PROB. 92, 109-10 (1949). *But see* Blum, *Academic Freedom and Tax Support for Independent Education,* 40 PHI DELTA KAPPAN, 349, 353 (1959).

[393] Secretary of Health, Education & Welfare, Federal Programs Under Which Institutions With Religious Affiliation Receive Federal Funds Through Grants or Loans, March 28, 1961 (memorandum), in S. Doc. No. 29, 87th Cong., 1st Sess. 37, 44 (1961). Blum, *supra* note 392, at 352, reports that "approximately 36,000 veterans used federal money to pay for training as Protestant ministers. . . ."

[394] Comment of Mr. Pfeffer, in Religion and Freedom, *supra* note 206, at 13.

[395] It is of interest to note that the Higher Education Act of 1963, 20 U.S.C. § 751(a)(2) (1964), bars funds for use in divinity schools. *See also* PA. CONST. art. III, § 18.

[396] For the suggestion that there might be some exception due to an exercise of the war power, *see* Note, 8 LA. L. REV. 141 n.20 (1947); *cf.* Bowker v. Baker, 73 Cal. App. 2d 653, 655, 167 P.2d 256, 257 (1946). *But cf.* Ex parte Milligan, 71 U.S. (4 Wall.) 2 (1866). Perhaps all or some of the tuition might be justified on the ground that clergymen perform a number of primary secular services. *See also* note 132 *supra.*

have undertaken had they not been taken in the Army"[397] is irrelevant. On this theory, the government could make contributions to any voluntary association to which the veteran had belonged because he would have done so had he been at home. Moreover, excluding theological seminaries from the Bill would not appear to have been a denial of free exercise for religion does not demand attendance there.[398] Further, every veteran, whatever his religion, could have his tuition paid for secular education at any accredited institution, including those that are church-related.[399]

C. "Earmarking"

1. Restricted Grants

Another effort to draw a line regarding the constitutionality of aid to parochial education may be described as the "restricted purpose" or "earmarking" theory. Its thrust is that, where the public funds awarded to church-affiliated schools—or to students attending them—are designated for specific secular purposes, the nonestablishment precept is satisfied because such grants, unlike more general grants, would not finance religious functions.[400] Thus, allocation of public funds for improving secular educational methods, construction of dormitories, acquisition of science, mathematics and foreign language equipment,[401] textbooks also used in public schools,[402] and scientific and medical research[403] are valid.[404] On the other hand, governmental appropriations "with no restrictions and no direction as to the purposes for which the money can be spent would be unconstitutional."[405]

The majority opinion in *Everson* lends some support to this "restricted purpose" theory. It spoke of bus transportation, ordinary police and fire protection, connections for sewage disposal, and public highways

---

[397] 2 *Hearings on H.R. 2361, supra* note 35, at 1614.

[398] *Cf.* note 59 *supra*. *See also* note 55 *supra*.

[399] *See* State *ex rel.* Atwood v. Johnson, 170 Wis. 251, 176 N.W. 224 (1920).

[400] 52 Ia. L. Rev. 571, 574 (1966). *Cf.* Kauper, *Separation of Church and State—A Constitutional View*, 9 Catholic Law. 32, 42 (1963).

[401] *See* U.S. Dep't of Health, Education & Welfare, *supra* note 20, at 375-76.

[402] *See id.* at 368; Borden v. Louisiana State Bd. of Educ., 168 La. 1005, 123 So. 655, 661 (1929).

[403] *See* Lowell & Southgate, *supra* note 382, at 52-55.

[404] Some would distinguish among these items. Thus, of those items mentioned in the text, Protestants and Other Americans United (POAU), see *id.*, would seem to approve only of research grants. But since all serve strictly primary secular purposes, they appear analytically indistinguishable. In fact, it has been pointed out that research grants afford the recipient institution significant additional assistance in attracting strong faculty, "enriching the educational program, developing better facilities, drawing higher quality students, and diversifying sources of income." Kratz, *supra* note 193, at 210.

[405] *S. Hearings on S. 370, supra* note 148, at 2524 (Statement of Senator Morse).

and sidewalks as "general government services . . . separate and . . . indisputably marked off from the religious function."[406]

2. Freeing of Funds

The "restricted purpose" or "earmarking" rationale, however, is not a viable constitutional test. Although use of the public funds may be strictly limited to the ends designated, their allocation releases additional church funds for strictly religious purposes[407]—be it for religious proselytizing, the purchase of religious insignia, or any of a countless number of other purely religious ends. Because of this "freed funds" effect—hardly a matter that may be deemed "immaterial"[408] by the advocates of this rationale—the theory effectively fails to fulfill its own purposes and places form over substance.

To avoid this consequence, it has been argued that a grant may be "earmarked for a specific purpose which would not otherwise be undertaken by the recipient . . . ."[409] But this is an inquiry more easily stated than demonstrated. For example, that the cost of textbooks or transportation had formerly been borne by the parents,[410] does not mean that their provision now by the state will not provide additional funds to the religious institution.[411] The latter could now easily and justifiably increase its tuition charge, thus providing it with funds available for strictly religious use.[412]

Even if the property or service which the government finances had not previously been part of the parochial school's—or parents'—activities, it cannot be said with any confidence that funds are not freed. It

---

[406] 330 U.S. at 17-18. Since these serve strictly secular purposes, it is difficult to distinguish them, on this "earmarking" analysis, from other such services. *But see* text accompanying note 443 *infra.*

[407] *See* Letter from Professor Sutherland to Senator Morse, in S. Doc. No. 29, 87th Cong., 1st Sess. 60 (1961); 79 CHRISTIAN CENTURY 617 (1962) (editorial); 77 HARV. L. REV. 1353, 1354 (1964); 59 MICH. L. REV. 1254, 1255 (1961).

[408] Opinion of the Justices, 99 N.H. 519, 522, 113 A.2d 114, 116 (1955).

[409] U.S. Dep't of Health, Education & Welfare, *supra* note 20, at 370. *See also* Moore, *supra* note 334, at 161. The Elementary and Secondary Education Act of 1965 attempts to meet this qualification. It forbids grants for instructional materials if institutional funds would ordinarily have been used for like materials, 20 U.S.C. § 823(a)(5) (Supp. I, 1965), and for specialized educational services if normally provided by the nonpublic school, 45 C.F.R. § 116.19(d) (1967).

[410] In respect to textbooks, see Board of Educ. v. Allen, 27 App. Div. 2d 69, 72, 276 N.Y.S.2d 234, 238 (1966). Regarding transportation, *compare* Comment, *Hospital Aid and the Establishment Clause: Conflict or Accomodation,* 13 U.C.L.A.L. REV. 1100, 1107 (1966), *with* L. PFEFFER, *supra* note 26, at 178; State *ex rel.* Reynolds v. Nusbaum, 17 Wis. 2d 148, 152, 115 N.W.2d 761, 763 (1962).

[411] *But see* Cochran v. Board of Educ., 281 U.S. 370, 375 (1930); LaNoue, *supra* note 60, at 80; 36 KY. L.J. 228, 330-31 (1948).

[412] See note 382 *supra.*

would be extremely difficult to prove that the parochial school, or the parent, would not have itself undertaken the matter in the near future[413] —the question not infrequently turning on the subjective thoughts of the school's administrators or all parents, or on the credibility of their testimony in respect thereto. In addition, a court may "be compelled to examine the financial structure of the school, its previous success or failure in fund-raising campaigns, and the proposed allocation of its resources."[414] This approach might produce an undesirable situation whereby the parochial school administrators or the parents would defer providing a particular service because to provide it now would make a subsequent government subsidy unconstitutional. Finally, it would be virtually impossible to prove that the parochial school would never have itself undertaken the project—be it special remedial reading, field trips, special tutoring, or even a "head-start" program.[415] It is more natural to assume that any service provided by public schools is also within the reasonable contemplation of parochial schools.

"Earmarking" is of no consequence under the rationale proposed in this article. Nor is the freeing of funds which is an effect of even police and fire protection.[416] Rather, the crucial inquiry is whether the total government assistance exceeds the value of the secular educational service rendered. The state funds may be paid to the parent or directly to the school so long as they serve a primary or independent secular purpose, as defined herein.

Even if the parochial school endorsed the government's bank draft directly to a seller of religious books or insignia, it should be of no constitutional significance;[417] this is logically no different than the school's endorsing the draft to a seller of dictionaries or bus transportation, and then drawing a check on funds in its own account—which it would otherwise have used for the dictionaries or bus transportation—to pay for the religious books or insignia. Even if the state, at the parochial school's request, were itself to supply religious tracts to the school[418]— unlikely as this may be—there should be no issue if the total public appropriation to the school were not greater than the value of the secular services rendered; this is analytically the same as the state supplying dictionaries to the parochial school and the school then buying the reli-

---

[413] See Note, *The Elementary and Secondary Education Act of 1965 and the First Amendment*, 41 IND. L.J. 302, 314-315 (1966); Comment, *supra* note 410, at 1107.
[414] 41 N.Y.U.L. REV. 983, 986 (1966).
[415] See CATHOLIC SCHOOL J., June 1965, at 13-15.
[416] See note 185 *supra*.
[417] *Cf.* State *ex rel.* Nevada Orphan Asylum v. Hallock, 16 Nev. 373, 387-88 (1882).
[418] *But see* Board of Educ. v. Allen, 20 N.Y.2d 109, 121, 228 N.E.2d 791, 797, 281 N.Y.S.2d 799, 808 (1967) (dissenting opinion).

gious tracts with the funds freed. Of course, the state should not be able to condition its grant on use for religious purposes. In that case, although the parochial school might use the funds thus freed for secular purposes, the grant would not assure this result. Only a religious end would be guaranteed, and by conscious government dictate. This the establishment clause forbids without further inquiry or computations.[419]

D. Child Benefit "Revisited"

Having considered the "child benefit" and "earmarking" theories, what may be termed the "LaNoue-child benefit revisited" theory merits some attention. Mr. LaNoue submits three criteria as the bases for a constitutional formulation respecting aid to parochial schools:[420] First, if the aid goes directly to the parent or child, no religious institution should acquire new property through the state action. (The shortcomings of this criterion have already been fully explored.[421]) Second, all control over administration and spending of the public funds should remain with the state—for example, the state should select any textbooks provided.[422] (But, whoever the selecting agency, establishment clause values are preserved if the book is to be used for a primary secular purpose.[423]) Third, no religious use should be made of what the state provides. (This ignores the freed funds effect.[424])

E. Aid to Hospitals Distinguished

Government grants and loans for hospital construction, to institutions including those that are church-affiliated,[425] generally conceded to present no establishment clause problems,[426] are analogous to public financing of the secular aspects of parochial education.[427] Just as the state may

---

[419] *Cf.* text following note 158.
[420] LaNoue, *supra* note 60, at 90-91.
[421] See discussion in text accompanying notes 354-390 *supra*.
[422] *Cf.* Chance v. Mississippi State Textbook Rating & Purchasing Bd., 190 Miss. 453, 462, 200 So. 706, 708 (1941); Board of Educ. v. Allen, 20 N.Y.2d 109, 116, 228 N.E.2d 791, 794, 281 N.Y.S.2d 799, 804 (1967); W. VA. CODE ANN. § 1782(2) (1961).
[423] For elaboration, see discussion accompanying notes 200-80 *supra*. See also text accompanying notes 464-65, 520-33 *infra*.
[424] See text accompanying notes 407-15 *supra*.
[425] The Hospital Survey and Construction Act, 42 U.S.C. § 291 (1964), better known as the Hill-Burton Act, authorizes grants and loans for up to two-thirds of the cost of construction of general hospitals and other medical facilities.
[426] See text accompanying notes 303-11 *supra*.
[427] In Quick Bear v. Leupp, 210 U.S. 50, 74 (1908), the Solicitor General argued, "A school, like a hospital, is neither an establishment of religion nor a religious establishment, although along with secular education there might be, as there commonly is, instruction in morality and religion, just as in a hospital there would be religious ministrations." While there may be differences in degree beyond those he indicated, they should not be consequential for establishment clause purposes. See discussion at notes 428-39 *infra*.

"care for the destitute ill,"[428] so, too, may it provide for the educational advancement of its citizenry. To paraphrase Mr. Pfeffer, "As long as the sum paid to the denominational [school for the cost of its nonreligious education] does not exceed the amount the state would be required to expend to [provide this education in public schools], the [parochial school] is not really receiving government aid."[429]

The cases have been distinguished by some, principally on the grounds that admission to religiously-affiliated hospitals is on a nonsectarian basis and that the hospitals make no attempt to promote religious dogmas.[430] Apart from the facts that at least Catholic parochial schools are not restricted to members of that faith,[431] and that sectarian hospitals not infrequently have religious insignia in the rooms,[432] have religiously significant requirements for doctors who may enter,[433] and follow medical codes differing from that of the American Medical Association,[434] there is a more constitutionally relevant response. When government funds are being expended only for primary secular purposes—either ministering to the sick or serving the secular educational needs of the young—the religious affiliation of the recipient institutions or those in attendance should be inconsequential—as should be the fact that "parochial schools are created specifically for religious as well as secular purposes."[435]

Religious restrictions on admission to an institution supported by public funds or such an institution's general religious tone should be similarly irrelevant constitutionally so long as the benefits provided may conveniently be obtained elsewhere.[436] On the other hand, if "the gov-

---

[428] L. PFEFFER, *supra* note 26, at 201.
[429] *Id.*
[430] *Id.* See also Lien v. City of Ketchikan, 383 P.2d 721 (Alas. 1963); Kentucky Bldg. Comm'n v. Effron, 310 Ky. 355, 358, 220 S.W.2d 836, 838 (1949); Truitt v. Board of Pub. Works, 243 Md. 375, 404, 221 A.2d 370, 387-88 (1966); 62 Nw. U.L. REV. 256 (1967); Comment, *supra* note 410, at 1116.
[431] For statistics, *see* 5 *Hearings on S. 370, supra* note 148, at 2547.
[432] L. PFEFFER, *supra* note 26, at 201-02.
[433] *Id.* at 202.
[434] Lowell & Southgate, *supra* note 382, at 54.
[435] Note, *The Elementary and Secondary Education Act of 1965 and the First Amendment*, 41 IND. L.J. 302, 321 (1966).
[436] See text accompanying notes 375-77 *infra*. But see Giannella, *supra* note 199, at 528, 554, 589. Likewise, the fact that denominational social welfare units "believe that all children of their faith should be cared for by agencies representing the same faith," R. WERNER, PUBLIC FINANCING OF VOLUNTARY AGENCY FOSTER CARE 141-42 (1961), should not disqualify them for public financial assistance.

The decision in Simkins v. Moses H. Cone Memorial Hospital, 323 F.2d 959 (4th Cir. 1963), *cert. denied*, 376 U.S. 938 (1964)—holding that "private" hospitals receiving Hill-Burton Act funds and participating in a federal-state program for satisfying community hospital needs were sufficiently involved with "state action" to be subject to the fifth and fourteenth amendments' prohibitions against racial discrimination—is sometimes cited for the proposition that religious institutions receiving governmental aid may similarly be charged

ernment has chosen to aid a religious institution to save the expense of building new public facilities"[437] or has "granted a government financed monopoly over certain services in a particular geographical area,"[438] the result may be different. Under these circumstances, an otherwise private institution is performing what has traditionally been, or what has effectively become, a "public function." Therefore, there is a forceful argument that it should be subject to the "state action" restrictions of the Constitution[439]—that either governmental assistance must be terminated or the institution must be bound by the constitutional obligations of the state.

F. Balancing

Probably the most forthright school of thought that wishes to have the Constitution permit some public financial assistance to parochial

---

with the obligations of the state. Thus, it is argued that publicly assisted church-related schools and hospitals may constitutionally be barred from giving any religious preference in the choice of admittees, administrators and staff, from conducting religious observances, and even from placing religious symbols in rooms. Comment, *Public Control of Private Sectarian Institutions Receiving Public Funds*, 63 MICH. L. REV. 142 (1964). *See also* P. KAUPER, *supra* note 5, at 116-18; Kelley, *Protestants and Parochial Schools*, 79 Commonweal 520 (1964).

But the *Simkins* case is distinguishable on several grounds. First, the court noted that it did not merely rely on the fact that the recipient hospitals were publicly financed. It stressed that the hospitals operated "as integral parts of comprehensive joint or intermeshing state and federal plans or programs designed to effect a proper allocation of available medical and hospital resources for the best possible promotion and maintenance of public health." 323 F.2d at 967. Thus, the court was impressed with the argument that these private hospitals were performing a "State function," *id.* at 968, that is, that they served in fact as substitute facilities for those the state would have otherwise provided and that the state selected them to be put to this use. See text at notes 437-39 *infra. See also* Lewis, *The Meaning of State Action*, 60 COLUM. L. REV. 1083, 1104 n.77 (1960). This "state function" notion is not to be confused with the fact that these hospitals (like nonpublic schools or other private hospitals) were simply rendering public services that other existing state institutions also happen to provide. *But see* Comment, *supra*, at 146-47.

Further, even if the fact that the hospitals were publicly financed is considered to be the crucial ingredient, there is a vital distinction between "state action" of this kind involving racial discrimination and "state action" of this kind involving religious preferences and observances. A publicly supported "private" institution's claim of right to racial discrimination is weak at best. But a publicly supported church-affiliated school's contention that religious preference for students and faculty is necessary or desirable for execution of its purposes raises a substantial claim under the free exercise clause. Similar and even stronger claims may be made for religious observances and insignia. *See generally* Henkin, *Shelley v. Kraemer: Notes for a Revised Opinion*, 110 U. PA. L. REV. 473 (1963); Horowitz, *Fourteenth Amendment Aspects of Racial Discrimination in "Private" Housing*, 52 CALIF. L. REV. 1 (1964); Van Alstyne & Karst, *State Action*, 14 STAN. L. REV. 3 (1961).

[437] LaNoue, *supra* note 60, at 92 n.75.
[438] *Id.*
[439] *See* Evans v. Newton, 382 U.S. 296 (1966); Public Utilities Comm'n v. Pollak, 343 U.S. 451 (1952); note 436 *supra*. The "public function" issue is generally beyond the scope of the discussion. For further consideration, see W. LOCKHART, Y. KAMISAR & J. CHOPER, CONSTITUTIONAL LAW 1235, 1290, 1293, 1322-25 (2d ed. 1967).

education but forbid public subsidization of all the secular aspects is
that which contends that "today . . . most of the distinctions of the law
are distinctions of degree."[440] The view is that the Court must decide
"when a little becomes too much,"[441] and must engage in "the process of
balancing the many competing considerations and ultimately weighing
them on policy considerations."[442] The *Everson* majority's clear implication that bus transportation lay at the brink of unconstitutionality[443]
may be relied on for substantiation.[444]

This test is sometimes phrased in terms of a "direct-indirect"[445] or
"active-passive" standard.[446] But, in essence, the approach requires the
Court to juggle a nearly infinite number of diverse factors—for example,
whether the state's purpose is religious or secular, the importance in terms
of priorities of the public purpose, the relative probability of its accomplishment, the type and quantum of benefit given to religion, whether
funds will be freed, the relative strength of sectarian influences operative
within a particular recipient institution, the relationship of the benefit to
the religious aspects of the institution aided, the extent to which the state
selects the institutions to be aided. These, in turn, must be measured by
the implications of the free exercise clause as tempered by the force of
the establishment clause, considered in light of the existence and
adequacy of alternative means, and perhaps bolstered by a presumption
of unconstitutionality (or maybe constitutionality).[447]

The defect of this approach is by now apparent. If "the method of
weighing constitutional objectives in order to choose among them affords
no guidance for further action, except on what Holmes called a 'pots and
pans' basis,"[448] then subjective assessment of the multitudinous elements
at issue here is presumptively inappropriate for an independent judiciary
as we know it. Only in limited and compelling circumstances is such a
process even justifiable, much less desirable.[449] The advocates of this
approach themselves acknowledge that, as applied to aid to parochial

---

[440] Panhandle Oil Co. v. Knox, 277 U.S. 218, 223 (1918) (dissenting opinion of Holmes, J.).

[441] Sutherland, *supra* note 85, at 1310.

[442] Note, 52 CORNELL L.Q. 814, 826 (1967). *See also* Moore, *supra* note 334, at 192-93.

[443] See discussion at note 295 *supra*.

[444] *See* U.S. Dep't of Health, Education & Welfare, *supra* note 20, at 368-69. *See also* Horace Mann League v. Board of Pub. Works, 242 Md. 645, 671, 220 A.2d 51, 65, *cert. denied*, 385 U.S. 97 (1966).

[445] *See* Hayes, *supra* note 201, at 108.

[446] *See* Note, 8 LA. L. REV. 136, 140 (1947).

[447] *See generally* U.S. Dep't of Health, Education & Welfare, *supra* note 20, at 365-73; Comment, *supra* note 410, at 1109-14. *See also* Note, 52 CORNELL L.Q. 814, 826 (1967); Note, 8 LA. L. REV. 136, 140 (1947).

[448] Kurland, *supra* note 19, at 96.

[449] See text accompanying notes 32, 117-20, 337 *supra*.

schools, "it is futile to hazard a prediction of the outcome"[450] and that the consolation to "[t]hose who see no distinction between transportation and any other form of assistance whatsoever [is that they] should keep in mind that, apparently, the Court [in *Everson*] did."[451]

G. *Horace Mann*

The recent, celebrated *Horace Mann* decision in Maryland,[452] invalidating under the establishment clause the allocation of state funds to three of four church-related colleges for construction of science and classroom buildings, a dining hall, and a dormitory, employed a somewhat more limited but analytically similar balancing approach. The state court, interpreting the relevant Supreme Court opinions as barring any direct grants to "sectarian" institutions,[453] utilized a six-criteria formula to determine whether each recipient college met this test.[454] The court itself recognized the inappropriateness of this constitutional approach—"to decide each case upon the totality of its attendant circumstances."[455] It admitted that application of its test was "a rather elusive matter, being somewhat ephemeral in nature."[456]

The more basic defect in the *Horace Mann* decision was that, for establishment clause purposes,[457] it ignored the fact that, no matter how "sectarian" the recipient college, the state expenditures seemingly served a primary secular purpose;[458] undoubtedly, the colleges found to be "sectarian" receive many indirect public benefits that "aid" them as significantly as the funds in issue.[459] Thus, to bar all direct governmental

---

[450] Moore, *supra* note 334, at 193.
[451] U.S. Dep't of Health, Education & Welfare, *supra* note 20, at 369.
[452] Horace Mann League v. Board of Pub. Works, 242 Md. 645, 220 A.2d 51, *cert. denied*, 385 U.S. 97 (1966).
[453] 242 Md. at 654-72, 220 A.2d at 55-66.
[454] The court examined in detail (a) the college's stated purposes, (b) the college personnel, (c) the college's relationships with religious organizations and groups, (d) the place of religion in the college's program, (e) the product of the college program vis-à-vis accreditation and character of activities of alumni, (f) the work and image of the college in the community. *Id.* at 672, 220 A.2d at 65-66. For a more direct, less complicated approach, under a state constitutional provision, see Collins v. Kephart, 271 Pa. 428, 117 A. 440 (1921).
[455] 242 Md. at 678, 220 A.2d at 69.
[456] *Id.*
[457] The court, in rejecting attacks under the Maryland constitution, held that the expenditures were "for public purposes." 242 Md. at 685, 220 A.2d at 73.
[458] *See* Drinan, *The Challenge to Catholic Education in the Maryland College Case*, NAT'L CATHOLIC EDUC. ASS'N. BULL., May 1967, at 3, 5.
[459] For example, various forms of student scholarships and assistance. *See* note 382 *supra;* Brown, *supra* note 382, at 182-83; Blum, *supra* note 37, at 147-48; 3 *Hearings on S. 600 Before the Subcomm. on Educ. of the Senate Comm. on Labor and Public Welfare*, 89th Cong., 1st Sess., at 1226 (1965) (Statement of Lawrence Speiser, Director, Washington ACLU).

grants to church-affiliated educational institutions simply because they engage in certain practices that foster religion, while acknowledging that "not every activity of a religious group is necessarily a religious activity,"[460] not only jeopardizes a host of existing state and federal programs,[461] but places form over substance and is constitutionally unsatisfactory.

H. *Manipulation*

1. *Lending Textbooks*

The test for determining whether governmental assistance to religion breaches that neutrality demanded by the first amendment, it has recently been argued, should be whether "the aid could be manipulated by church or state to dominate the other."[462] The aid involved, for example, in the *Allen* case now pending before the Supreme Court[463]—lending secular textbooks to parochial school students—is found to violate that standard on several counts.

First, "since textbooks are used in the classrooms as an integral feature of the educational process, there is no certainty that they would not be manipulated for religious instruction in parochial schools."[464] True. But even assuming that similar manipulation could not occur with respect to state-provided school lunches (by prayers in connection therewith, for example), or state-financed school medical examinations (by their illustrative use in classroom theological discussions), or state-laid sidewalks providing access to the denominational school, the point is not well taken. Even public aid that is itself immune from sectarian manipulation frees church funds either for uses subject to manipulation, or for strictly religious uses. This being so, the attempted limitation only formalistically accomplishes the end sought. The sole criterion should be whether the total public support exceeds the value of the secular service rendered. If allegedly secular activities are so manipulated as to be no longer fairly characterized as nonreligious, they may not be included in valuing the secular service provided.[465]

Second, it is contended that lending textbooks "will create and foster a pressure to dominate the choosing of books that shall be used in the public schools (so that they may also be used in parochial schools)."[466]

---

[460] 3 *Hearings on S. 600, supra* note 459, at 1223 (Statement of Lawrence Speiser, Director, Washington ACLU).

[461] *See* Davidow, *supra* note 131, at 668-69.

[462] Note, 36 GEO. WASH. L. REV. 246, 250 (1967).

[463] Board of Educ. v. Allen, 20 N.Y.2d 109, 228 N.E.2d 791, 281 N.Y.S.2d 799 (1967), *prob. juris. noted*, 36 U.S.L.W. 3278 (U.S. Jan. 15, 1968).

[464] Note, 36 GEO. WASH. L. REV. 246, 249 (1967).

[465] See text accompanying notes 200-80 *supra*.

[466] Note, 36 GEO. WASH. L. REV. 246, 250 (1967), quoting from the dissenting opinion

That may be true. But if such pressures occur and are unconstitutional,[467] they should be dealt with specifically rather than by striking an entire program. And, however irresistible such pressures would be, they seemingly exist even in the absence of the program because approximately half of Catholic children presently attend public schools.[468]

2. Control Follows Aid

Finally, it is urged that if "parochial schools become dependent on state financing of books for children, manipulative conditions could attach which would compel sectarian schools to restrict religious instruction or which could ultimately result in dissolution of a separate parochial system altogether."[469] This "control follows aid" assertion, frequently heard[470] and already referred to,[471] deserves further consideration.

It was said ten years ago that "examination of the state constitutional and statutory provisions reveals little public control of private schools and teachers."[472] An authoritative and comprehensive federal study reported at that time that in only five states do departments of education "have explicit statutory responsibilities for the certification of teachers of nonpublic schools,"[473] and indicated that curriculum regulation was indeed minimal.[474] And there is little reason to believe that much significant change has taken place since then.[475]

It is argued that increased state financial assistance to parochial schools will bring additional state supervision because it is "discrimi-

---

in Board of Educ. v. Allen, 20 N.Y.2d 109, 123, 228 N.E.2d 791, 798, 281 N.Y.S.2d 799, 810 (1967) *prob. juris. noted*, 36 U.S.L.W. 3278 (U.S. Jan. 15, 1968).

[467] *See also* discussion in text accompanying notes 67-74 *supra*.

[468] L. PFEFFER, *supra* note 26, at 510.

[469] Note, 36 GEO. WASH. L. REV. 246, 249-50 (1967).

[470] *See, e.g.*, Everson v. Board of Educ., 330 U.S. 1, 27 (1947) (dissenting opinion of Jackson, J.); Gurney v. Ferguson, 190 Okla. 254, 256, 122 P.2d 1002, 1005 (1941); Davidow, *supra* note 131, at 683.

[471] See note 436 *supra*.

[472] Kohlbrenner, *Some Practical Aspects of the Public Character of Private Education*, 86 SCHOOL & SOC'Y 348, 351 (1958). In 1956, the National Education Association concluded that state supervision of nonpublic schools was "conspicuous by its absence rather than by its presence." *State and Sectarian Education*, 34 N.E.A. RESEARCH BULL. 210 (1956).

[473] F. BEACH & R. WILL, *supra* note 27, at 26.

[474] *Id.* at 25.

[475] A 1964 study of state curriculum requirements for nonpublic schools showed that 41 states provided for some regulation. But the instructional areas covered included only the following: common branches of education (31 states), U.S. Constitution (27), English language (26), American history (16), state constitution (16), other national documents (15), state and national civics (15), safety education (10), moral education (6), state history (6), other areas of special state interest (6), physical education (4). Stolee, *Nonpublic Schools: What Must They Teach?*, 92 SCHOOL & SOC'Y 274, 275 (1964), *reprinted in* 1 *Hearings on S. 370*, *supra* note 148, at 469. Further, in 15 of these 41 states, there was no enforcement whatever of the regulations. *Id.* at 470.

natory . . . to allow public funds to be spent by private schools without public control and yet insist on such public control for public schools."[476] Perhaps this will be true as a realistic political matter. However, government may believe controls are unnecessary or undesirable, and aid conditioned on controls thought unsatisfactory by the recipient may be refused. More importantly, as a constitutional matter, the state's power to regulate nonpublic schools is wholly independent of any allocation of public funds.[477] This is confirmed in practice by requirements already noted[478] and by a number of others.[479] On the other hand, public aid or not, the Constitution forbids unreasonable restriction of religious instruction or dissolution of the parochial school system.

The landmark decision of *Pierce v. Society of Sisters*[480] is relevant on both counts. Invalidating a state requirement of compulsory public school education, the case held that due process of law forbids unreasonable state interference with parents' liberty to direct their children's education. The parental right being grounded in the Constitution, state authority to curtail it would not appear to be augmented by the grant of governmental funds.[481] But *Pierce* also recognized state authority "reasonably to regulate all schools, to inspect, supervise and examine them, their teachers and pupils; to require . . . that certain studies plainly essential to good citizenship must be taught, and that nothing be taught which is manifestly inimical to the public welfare."[482]

Those whose conscientious scruples constitutionally entitle them to attend a church-related school plainly have no absolute right under the free exercise clause to maintain those schools free of state regulation,[483] whatever the amount of public financial support given them. Although the state may have no right "to standardize its children by forcing them to accept instruction from public teachers only,"[484] to attain important

---

[476] Bemis, *What is Discrimination?*, 42 PHI DELTA KAPPAN 329 (1961).
[477] *See* Brickman, *Public Aid to Religious Schools*, 55 RELIGIOUS EDUC. 279, 287 (1960). *See also* Whelan, *Textbooks and the Constitution*, 107 AMERICA 399, 401 (1962).
[478] See note 475 *supra*.
[479] *See, e.g.*, 20 ME. REV. STAT. ANN. § 1281 (1965) (commissioner shall establish requirements for accreditation including quality of instruction, school facilities and curriculum content); MICH. COMP. LAWS ANN. §§ 340.732(a), 388.551 (1967) (courses of study shall be comparable to and of same standard as in public schools); NEV. REV. STAT. § 394.130 (1963) (same instruction as is required in public schools, *but no right to share in public school funds*); N.Y. EDUC. LAW § 3204 (McKinney 1953), *as amended*, (McKinney Supp. 1967) (course of study for first eight years must include twelve designated subjects); N.C. GEN. STAT. § 115-255 (1966) (*religious instruction should not be interfered with* but minimum standards for courses of study must be met).
[480] 268 U.S. 510 (1925).
[481] See note 490 *infra*.
[482] 268 U.S. at 534.
[483] *But see* A. JOHNSON & F. YOST, *supra* note 28, at 139.
[484] Pierce v. Society of Sisters, 268 U.S. 510, 535 (1925).

societal goals it clearly may regulate action demanded by religion or conscience.[485] This is especially true where the interests of children are concerned.[486] Although the free exercise and due process clauses may assure private or sectarian schools the liberty "to inculcate whatever values they wish,"[487] those clauses do not hamper the state's power reasonably[488] to promote children's welfare through basic secular education.[489] Thus, the "control follows aid" argument, as least as to its constitutional relevance, loses its force.[490]

I. Accreditation

By virtue of *Pierce v. Society of Sisters*,[491] states must make it possible for parochial schools to gain accreditation. It is therefore contended that "public money . . . cannot logically be withheld from the private school if it is publicly accredited as an institution where children may fulfill their legal duty to attend school."[492] This reasoning, acclaimed as the

---

[485] Braunfeld v. Brown, 366 U.S. 599, 603-04 (1961); Cantwell v. Connecticut, 310 U.S. 296, 303-04 (1940).

[486] Prince v. Massachusetts, 321 U.S. 158, 168 (1944).

[487] School Dist. v. Schempp, 374 U.S. 203, 242 (1963) (concurring opinion of Brennan, J.).

[488] In making the "accommodation between the religious action and an exercise of state authority [which] is a particularly delicate task," Braunfeld v. Brown, 366 U.S. 599, 605 (1961), the state's interest in demanding that certain courses be taught would seem more substantial than its concern in forbidding inquiry into some field of knowledge. *See* Meyer v. Nebraska, 262 U.S. 390, 392 (1923) (argument for plaintiff in error). State control "need not be so restrictive that the independent school is precluded from having ample flexibility in determining how these common learnings will be taught, what additional subjects will be offered, what personal values will be imbued, and what experiments will be conducted." Fountain, *A Plea for Public Support of Pluralism in America*, 44 Phi Delta Kappan 415, 418 (1963). *See* Farrington v. Tokushige, 273 U.S. 284, 298 (1927). Nor should the state's requirements be so onerous as to preempt time for religious instruction. *See* Choper, *supra* note 4, at 392-93.

[489] *See* State v. Garber, 197 Kan. 567, 419 P.2d 896 (1966), *cert. denied*, 389 U.S. 51 (1967), and cases there cited, 197 Kan. at 574-75, 419 P.2d at 902. *See also* 5 *Hearings on S. 370*, *supra* note 148, at 2073 n.21 (Statement of Edgar Fuller).

[490] It has been contended that public financial assistance to parochial schools with resultant controls would be contrary to the prohibition in Everson v. Board of Educ., 330 U.S. at 16, of government participation "in the affairs of any religious organizations or groups and *vice versa*." Lowell & Southgate, *supra* note 382, at 50. But the *Everson* opinion itself recognized that parochial schools must meet "the secular educational requirements which the state has power to impose." 330 U.S. at 18. With or without financial assistance, this is not the government participation in religious affairs obviously referred to by the Court, its exact language notwithstanding. Further, if the state enters into a contract with a religious organization (here, for secular education), the state may enforce reasonable terms. Just as surely, the state may not "condition the availability of benefits upon . . . [the recipient's] willingness to violate a cardinal principle of . . . religious faith." Sherbert v. Verner, 374 U.S. 398, 406 (1963).

[491] 268 U.S. 510 (1925).

[492] Drinan, *The Constitutionality of Public Aid to Parochial Schools*, in The Wall Between Church and State 55, 60 (D. Oaks ed. 1963).

"strongest argument to sustain . . . general aid to parochial schools,"[493] may be misleading.

The fact of accreditation should not be determinative. Under the establishment clause analysis proposed herein, a state could constitutionally "accredit" a parochial school course in religious instruction for the purpose of satisfying the minimum number of units required for graduation under state law. Since the purpose and effect of such a course could be religious—sectarian indoctrination—accreditation by the state would serve a primary religious end. But it would neither compromise anyone's religious scruples nor involve the use of compulsorily raised tax funds.[494] However, for the state to support such an accredited course with public funds would have the latter effect and, therefore, should be held to violate the bar against establishment of religion. Similarly, accreditation of a parochial school should not necessarily permit its being financed with public money on a par with schools that are not church-affiliated. The establishment clause should bar any grant of public funds exceeding the value of the secular services rendered.

J. The Public Welfare-Educational Process Distinction

Many opponents of public aid to parochial education, conceding the validity of certain " 'health' measures"[495] like free medical and dental services and free hot lunches for children in parochial schools, would draw the line there. Aid beyond this—in the form of school bus transportation, textbooks, or science equipment—is aid "to the educational process itself"[496] and falls within the constitutional ban. Medical care and hot lunches are "true welfare benefits," it is contended, needed by a child "whether he goes to a public school, to a parochial school, or to no school at all."[497] But school transportation and textbooks "are essential aids to the function of education as such . . . [and] cannot constitutionally be provided where the education is religious, since the function [aided] thus becomes religious education."[498]

---

[493] Kurland, *Politics and the Constitution: Federal Aid to Parochial Schools*, 1 LAND & WATER L. REV. 475, 491 (1966).

[494] See text accompanying notes 51-53 *supra*; Choper, *supra* note 4, at 406-07.

[495] Archer, *Protestants Reply: The Bishops Demand Subsidy*, U.S. NEWS & WORLD REPORT, Dec. 2, 1955, at 104, 105.

[496] Statement of Mr. Greenawalt, in Dorsen, *supra* note 33, at 44. *See also* Tockman, *The Constitutionality of Furnishing Publicly Financed Transportation to Private and Parochial School Students in Missouri*, 1963 WASH. U.L.Q. 455, 491-92, 505; 33 CORNELL L.Q. 128 (1947); Comment, *A Constitutional Analysis of the Wisconsin School Bus Law*, 1962 WIS. L. REV. 500, 516.

[497] L. PFEFFER, *supra* note 26, at 570.

[498] Rosenfield, *Separation of Church and State in the Public Schools*, 22 U. PITT. L. REV. 561, 580 (1961). This "which function is aided" theory seems first to have been developed at length by Cushman, *supra* note 185, at 348-49.

This rationale may be challenged on a number of grounds. First, it is inconsistent with a conclusion drawn by its own advocates. The public welfare-education distinction would invalidate all school medical, nurse and dental care and milk and hot lunch programs for parochial school students. Although such services may be needed by every child, these state and federal programs do not "go to pupils as minor citizens . . . [but rather] to them as school-children."[499] They are not provided to the unfortunately substantial number of school-age children not enrolled in any school,[500] nor to children absent from school, nor to any children on those days when schools are closed.[501] Similarly, this thesis would disqualify parochial school students from the benefit of such municipal services as school area traffic control devices[502]—including stationing traffic officers on school corners[503]—home instruction for those temporarily unable to attend school, the public library school bookmobile, school driver training,[504] reduced rates by a publicly owned system for pupils traveling to school or school activities,[505] and publicly sponsored educational television programs for classroom use.[506]

Conceding that "transportation, where it is needed, is as essential to education as any other element,"[507] this is equally true of medical care and hot lunches. Hot lunches in particular, we know today, are no less important for many children than, as Mr. Justice Rutledge said of transportation, "the very teaching in the classroom or payment of the teacher's sustenance. Many types of equipment, now considered essential, better could be done without."[508] Any distinction between them does not hold.[509]

But the more basic objection to distinguishing between medical care and school lunches, on the one hand, and bus transportation, science

---

[499] Williams, *Church-State Separation and Religion in the Schools of Our Democracy*, 51 RELIGIOUS EDUC. 369, 373 (1956), who states the converse as being the fact.

[500] In 1949, the National Education Association pointed out that there were then 4 million such children. 66 CHRISTIAN CENTURY 166 (1949) (editorial).

[501] For illustrative description, see T. POWELL, THE SCHOOL BUS LAW 69-74 (1960).

[502] *See* Rhoades v. School Dist., 424 Pa. 202, 211, 226 A.2d 53, 59, *cert. denied*, 389 U.S. 11 (1967).

[503] *See* 25 NOTRE DAME LAW. 367-68 (1950); 11 U. PITT. L. REV. 321 (1950).

[504] *See* R. DRINAN, *supra* note 50, at 138.

[505] *See id.* at 139.

[506] *See* 5 *Hearings on S. 370, supra* note 148, at 2538.

[507] Everson v. Board of Educ., 330 U.S. 1, 47 (1947) (dissenting opinion of Rutledge, J.). Its cost has been estimated at "10 to 15 per cent of total school costs." *Christian and Public Schools: Some Specific Problems*, 40 PHI DELTA KAPPAN 302, 303 (1959).

[508] Everson v. Board of Educ., 330 U.S. 1, 48 (1947) (dissenting opinion).

[509] *See* Johnson, *Religion and Public Education*, BULL. OF NAT'L ASS'N OF SECONDARY SCHOOL PRINCIPALS, April 1947, at 95, 97, suggesting that a lunch program should be viewed as direct aid to the school because "without it they would be forced by the competition of public schools to provide lunches at their own expense." *See also* Blum, *Religious Liberty and Bus Transportation*, 30 NOTRE DAME LAW. 384, 420 (1955).

equipment, and the like, on the other, is that all of these items fulfill independent primary secular purposes.[510] Even if they are all classified as essential to the educational function,[511] none has the primary effect of aiding religious education in violation of the establishment clause.[512] A child needs secular education "whether he goes to a public school, to a parochial school, or to no school at all"; secular education is a "true welfare benefit."[513]

The *Everson* dissenters found the bussing plan the same as furnishing "free carriage to those who attend a Church,"[514] or paying "the cost of transportation to Sunday school, to weekday special classes at the church or parish house, or to the meetings of various young people's religious societies."[515] State action of these sorts would obviously violate the

---

[510] The *Everson* dissenters complained that the reimbursement of parents for bus transportation costs was in no way related to "the child's safety or expedition in transit," 330 U.S. at 20 (Jackson, J.), because riding on public busses was "subject to all the hazards and delays of the highway and the streets." 330 U.S. at 60 (Rutledge, J.). But the New Jersey plan assured that children would ride busses to school whereas without compensation they might walk, drive their own cars, or be transported by busy parents or friends. Surely, the state could find that public busses provided for greater safety than the first two, and it was reasonable to believe that it might be more secure than the last. That the parochial school or the religious education therein was also benefited should be of no constitutional consequence. See Nichols v. Henry, 301 Ky. 434, 443, 191 S.W.2d 930, 934-35 (1946).

Even if the motivating consideration or main effect was not protecting children from traffic hazards but rather relieving the hardship of distance, see Board of Educ. v. Wheat, 174 Md. 314, 326, 199 A. 628, 634 (1938) (dissenting opinion); L. PFEFFER, *supra* note 26, at 567, the primary purpose is no less secular. Perhaps "a child going to visit a neighbor or to a motion picture theatre is just as much subject to the hazards of the road as a child going to school," L. PFEFFER, *supra* note 26, at 566. See also Pfeffer, *supra* note 202, at 395-96. *But see* LaNoue, *supra* note 60, at 89. However, the fact that the state chooses only to safeguard the child going to school does not contradict its secular purpose. "The legislature may do what it can to accomplish what is deemed necessary for the public welfare, and stop short of those cases where the detriment to a few, not afforded state aid, is considered less important than the expense or inconvenience to the state which might result if the rule laid down were mathematically exact." Matthews v. Quinton, 362 P.2d 932, 957 (Alas. 1961) (dissenting opinion), *cert. denied*, 368 U.S. 517 (1962). See discussion in text accompanying notes 170-75 *supra*. Thus, the state may provide bus transportation for all school children, all poor school children, all school children who attend nonprofit schools (see discussion in text accompanying notes 170-75 *supra*. *But see* Rhoades v. School Dist., 424 Pa. 202, 250, 226 A.2d 53, 85 (dissenting opinion), *cert. denied*, 389 U.S. 11 (1967)), or all nonpublic school children who live on existing public school bus routes. *But see* Matthews v. Quinton, 362 P.2d 932, 940 (Alas. 1961), *cert. denied*, 368 U.S. 517 (1962). Public undertaking of any of these programs, like public funding of all secular educational costs, serves a primary nonreligious purpose.

[511] *See* Sherrard v. Jefferson County Bd. of Educ., 294 Ky. 469, 478, 171 S.W.2d 963, 967 (1943); Gurney v. Ferguson, 190 Okla. 254, 255, 122 P.2d 1002, 1004 (1942).

[512] See discussion in text accompanying note 498 *supra*.

[513] L. PFEFFER, *supra* note 497.

[514] 330 U.S. at 24 (Jackson, J.). *See also* Powell, *Public Rides to Private Schools*, 17 HARV. EDUC. REV. 73, 82 (1947).

[515] 330 U.S. at 47 (Rutledge, J.).

establishment clause. Although a secular purpose would be served (convenience of citizens, protection against traffic hazards), it would be accomplished by unconstitutionally singling out one religion or all religions for preferential advantage.[516]

Aid to all schools, or all school children, or all school children in nonprofit schools does not so discriminate. Such aid is as constitutionally nonpreferential as providing free carriage to all citizens or subsidizing all public transportation costs. Because these general programs have a primary secular purpose, they should not violate the establishment bar when the transportation happens to be used to get to church, to religious meetings, or to parochial schools. The programs are logically the same as all other municipal services afforded all property without classification reflecting its religious ownership.[517]

It appears both logically and pragmatically ironical to contend[518] that bus transportation for school children alone violates the establishment clause but that bus transportation for everybody, including school children, does not. The latter not only provides the same benefit to religious education as the former, but, unlike the former, it also subsidizes trips to Sunday school and church services.[519] These apparent inconsistencies disappear under a rationale that looks to whether the government service provided—transportation and textbooks, for example—serves a primary secular purpose.

K. The "Who Controls" Test

Whether "it is the church (or church institution) or the state that performs or controls the performance of the services paid for by the state" has been submitted as the "ultimate test,"[520] under the establishment clause, for permitting public financial assistance to parochial education. Its basis is that "[i]t is reasonable to assume that services performed or controlled by a religious institution could and would be used to further the religious objectives of that institution, whereas services performed or controlled by a public body would be secular in purpose and form."[521] This thesis would permit "the transportation of school children

---

[516] See text accompanying notes 159-60 *supra*.
[517] State *ex rel.* Reynolds v. Nusbaum, 17 Wis. 2d 148, 157, 115 N.W.2d 761, 766 (1962). To say that, for religious property or activities, the establishment clause "forbids support, not protection from interference or destruction," Everson v. Board of Educ., 330 U.S. 1, 61 n.56 (1947) (dissenting opinion of Rutledge, J.), is effectively to urge an untenable distinction between sidewalks and fire protection.
[518] See discussion in text accompanying notes 495-98 *supra*.
[519] *See* LaNoue, *supra* note 60, at 89.
[520] Gordon, *supra* note 229, at 92.
[521] *Id.*

by a *public* bus,"[522] despite the fact that this would be "ultimately beneficial to parochial school students and incidentally or indirectly of aid to the church institutions they attend."[523] But it would forbid the supplying of textbooks because "the use of texts in an educational context which is privately, rather than publicly, managed and administered directly serves a religious educational purpose."[524]

1. General Criticism

The principal difficulty with this proposal is in its basic assumption. It is possible that a parochial school will so structure its services as to further, exclusively or partially, its religious objectives. If so, as was discussed earlier,[525] such services cannot be supported by government to a greater extent than the value of the secular ends served. Further, it is clear beyond doubt that public schools may also so structure some of their services.[526] If so, the courts must intervene when called upon. And it is also manifest that services controlled by a religious institution frequently do in fact further society's nonreligious objectives.[527] If not, public financial support could not even be given to a religiously-affiliated hospital, a result apparently required by this thesis.

Transportation of parochial school children in a bus leased by the school would probably be described, under this approach, as a service "controlled" by the religious institution and thus the rental fee could not be paid by government.[528] But bus transportation would nonetheless have a secular purpose. Even religious instruction given during the bus ride would not affect the primary secular purpose of safety and convenience. And if the government closed its fire department and instead paid any

---

[522] *Id.*
[523] *Id.*
[524] *Id.* at 93.
[525] See text accompanying notes 200-80 *supra.*
[526] *See, e.g.,* cases cited note 2 *supra.*
[527] The fact that a parochial school, in contrast to a public school, may have controlled admission policies and religious exercises and instruction to further its religious objectives, *see* G. LaNoue, *supra* note 56, at 29-30, should not affect the result. See discussion in text accompanying notes 375-77, 436-39 *supra.* To say that a school may not serve a public purpose or function because of these factors, *see* G. LaNoue, *supra* note 56 at 34-35, is a misleading use of the word "public." Government is not restricted to supporting only activities that are "open to the *public.*" It may finance action for a secular or public purpose even though undertaken by an institution not subject to public management or to the constitutional responsibilities of the state itself. *See* note 436 *supra;* Herberg, in Religion and Freedom 18 (D. McDonald ed. 1958). May a person, wholly supported by public welfare be forbidden to discriminate racially in the purchase of necessary food and services?
[528] Query, under this approach, if a publicly financed program of hot lunches, taken in the parochial school building, is a service controlled by church or state, especially if a school-directed blessing precedes and concludes it.

private fire protection agency selected by the parochial school, the establishment clause should not invalidate this action.[529]

The "who controls" approach has also been applied to library books. Mr. LaNoue argues that a constitutional distinction should be drawn between housing books in a parochial school library on " 'indefinite' or 'permanent' loan"[530] and having books "housed in public buildings" being "removed . . . only for the period necessary for reasonable educational use . . . for a textbook one semester or one year."[531] But the purpose of either alternative is plainly secular; the "control" exerted over the books by the parochial school seems essentially the same;[532] the public cost of each program appears identical, as does the benefit to the child and his school. This should not be the stuff of which constitutional distinctions are made.

He asserts that "since the books will not be centrally catalogued, students and teachers from other schools will be unable to borrow the public materials."[533] True. But so long as the primary purpose is secular and parochial schools are not given preference over other schools similarly situated, the fact should be of no constitutional significance.

2. Shared Time

Proponents of the "who controls" rationale would permit public financing of shared time or dual enrollment programs[534] in which parochial school pupils take part of their course work in the public schools.[535] Yet, not only would they bar use of these funds to pay for secular services of parochial schools, they would also invoke the establishment clause to

---

[529] *But see* Gordon, *supra* note 229, at 92.

[530] LaNoue, *The Title II Trap*, 47 PHI DELTA KAPPAN 558, 561 (1966).

[531] *Id.* at 562. Mr. Pfeffer would distinguish constitutionally between public library books lent to parochial pupils for up to two weeks and those lent for six months. The latter is "in effect taking that book out of the public domain and putting it into private domain." 2 *Hearings on H.R. 2361, supra* note 35, at 1631. But, contrary to his analogy, if adequate books are provided for all to borrow on a six month basis, this is not the same as a religious group appropriating a public park for six months. See also text accompanying note 532 *infra*, and following note 533 *infra*.

[532] Mr. Pfeffer would find a constitutional difference between public library loans to parochial school students of books, records and magnetic tapes, on the one hand, and equipment for playing the records and tapes, on the other. 2 *Hearings on H.R. 2361, supra* note 35, at 1619. This surely is irrelevant in terms of "who controls." It would seem, under that theory, that libraries would be barred from any loans to parochial school students for school use.

[533] LaNoue, *supra* note 530.

[534] *See* G. LaNoue, *supra* note 56, at 43-44; L. Pfeffer, *supra* note 26, at 578-79. *See also* Note, 65 MICH. L. REV. 1224, 1231 (1967). *But see* American Civil Liberties Union, Position on Shared Time, Apr. 4, 1965.

[535] For discussion of rulings under state constitutions, *see* Katz, *Note on the Constitutionality of Shared Time*, 1964 RELIGION & PUB. ORDER 85, 89-94 (D. Giannella ed.).

forbid public school instructors teaching courses in the parochial schools themselves.[536] Therefore, the very same public school teacher who taught, say, a section of a course in home economics or geography to a class including parochial school students, as part of a shared time program in the public school, could not teach the same course at the parochial school at what might very well be the same total public expense. Nor would it appear that a publicly hired speech therapy[537] or driver training[538] teacher could instruct parochial pupils at the church-affiliated school.[539] Of course, these results would not obtain under the establishment clause approach suggested in this article.[540]

(a) Parochial School Representation.—The fact that a parochial school representative may participate with public school officials in the planning and administration of shared time programs[541] has been condemned under the establishment clause.[542] But this is not the type of religious participation in the affairs of government[543] that must be thwarted. If the participant seeks to inject religion into the shared time curriculum, he may not do so. But if his participation is addressed to secular educa-

---

[536] 2 *Hearings on H.R. 2361, supra* note 35, at 1618 (testimony of Leo Pfeffer).

[537] *See* Special Dist. v. Wheeler, 408 S.W.2d 60 (Mo. 1966). Under the Elementary and Secondary Education Act of 1965, public school personnel are providing remedial instruction in mathematics and reading on parochial school premises. The question is raised in Polier v. Board of Educ., a pending case described in American Jewish Congress, *supra* note 6, at 4. The National Defense Education Act of 1958 finances state plans for academic testing of nonpublic school students. 20 U.S.C. §§ 483(a)(1), 484(b) (1965). Apparently this could be done by public personnel in parochial schools. *See generally*, 1 *Hearings on S. 370, supra* note 148, at 471-72.

[538] *But see* 2 *Hearings on H.R. 2361, supra* note 35, at 815.

[539] Query as to extension of home teaching services to physically handicapped children who will return to parochial schools. *See* Scales v. Board of Educ., 41 Misc. 2d 391, 245 N.Y.S.2d 449 (Sup. Ct. 1963).

[540] Professor Kurland suggests that shared time programs "have no rationale except benefit for church schools," (*supra* note 493, at 494. *See also* Burton, *Public Funds for Public Schools Only*, 78 CHRISTIAN CENTURY 415, 417 (1961)) and therefore violate the first amendment. But, while seemingly judging legislative "motive," see text accompanying notes 103-04 *supra*, this disregards the clear effect of these programs which seek broader distribution of public funds to the goal of an improved secular education for all. If only parochial school students could participate, the issue would be different. See text at notes 159-60 *supra*. The dual enrollment provision in Title I of the Elementary and Secondary Education Act of 1965 requires participation "of educationally deprived children . . . who are enrolled in *private* elementary and secondary schools" 20 U.S.C. § 241e(a)(2) (Supp. I, 1965) (emphasis added).

[541] *See* Elementary and Secondary Education Act of 1965, 20 U.S.C. § 844(a) (Supp. I, 1965).

[542] 1 *Hearings on H.R. 13160 and H.R. 13161 Before the General Subcomm. on Education of the House Comm. on Education and Labor*, 89th Cong., 2d Sess., at 340 (1966); 2 *Hearings, on H.R. 2361, supra* note 35, at 1610-11; Note, *supra* note 435, at 316.

[543] See note 490 *supra*.

tional concerns, no establishment issue should arise. Surely, a meeting of government officials and community leaders to discuss publicly funded programs for riot prevention may constitutionally include church representatives, who may suggest a secular role that their institutions might play.

(b) Preference to Catholicism.—Especially in respect to shared time,[544] it has been alleged that public financial aid to parochial schools is in fact preferential aid to Roman Catholicism because that religion is the principal one engaged in the field of education[545] whereas other denominations emphasize different endeavors.[546] But numerous civil regulations for secular purposes affect the interests of different religious groups disproportionately—obvious examples being laws requiring Sunday closing, enforcing monogamy, and prohibiting usury.[547] So long as the state's purpose and primary effect is nonreligious, the establishment ban should be held satisfied.

L. *Higher Education Distinguished*

It is frequently asserted that aid to church-related colleges and universities is constitutionally distinguishable from aid to elementary and secondary parochial schools.[548] The principal reason advanced is that college attendance is voluntary,[549] whereas public support of parochial schools is support of coerced religious instruction.[550] There is little doubt that, if children are assigned by public authority—that is, coerced—to attend what is in effect a parochial school, their first amendment rights of religious liberty have been breached, whatever their religious faith. Public support of the school under those circumstances merely compounds the evil.[551] But, in the usual case, government compulsory education laws coerce no child to attend a parochial school, and public aid to both public and parochial schools "would not make attendance at either

---

[544] *See* Archer, *The Truth about Shared Time,* EDUC. DIG., Nov. 1966, at 10, 12.

[545] A recent estimate placed 5½ to 6 million children in Catholic schools; 310,000 in Protestant schools (mostly Lutheran, also Seventh Day Adventist, Reformed Church and Mennonite); 50,000 in Jewish day schools. L. PFEFFER, *supra* note 26, at 509-10.

[546] Kelley, *supra* note 223, at 78.

[547] *See* McGowan v. Maryland, 366 U.S. 420, 462 (1961) (concurring opinion of Frankfurter, J.).

[548] *See generally* Giannella, *supra* note 199, at 581-90.

[549] *See* U.S. Dep't of Health, Education & Welfare, *supra* note 20, at 377-78; National Catholic Welfare Conference, *supra* note 37, at 450.

[550] The argument is articulated by P. KAUPER, *supra* note 5, at 115.

[551] Such was the case in Millard v. Board of Educ., 121 Ill. 297, 10 N.E. 669 (1887); Knowlton v. Baumhover, 182 Ia. 691, 166 N.W. 202 (1918); Harfst v. Hoegen, 349 Mo. 808, 163 S.W.2d 609 (1942); State *ex rel.* Pub. School Dist. v. Taylor, 122 Neb. 454, 240 N.W. 573 (1932); *cf.* Berghorn v. Reorganized School Dist., 364 Mo. 121, 260 S.W.2d 573 (1953); Moore v. Board of Educ., 4 Ohio Misc. 257, 212 N.E.2d 833 (1965).

type of institution any more or less compulsory."[552] For both higher and lower levels of education, a public purpose is achieved if the amount of governmental financial assistance does not exceed the value of the secular educational service rendered.[553]

The further argument is made that, since a much higher percentage of students is enrolled in private colleges than in private elementary and secondary schools, the national interest in affording the former financial assistance is much stronger.[554] But, again, a secular purpose would be served in both instances.[555] Finally, there are two responses to the argument that "church colleges are not in the business of religious indoctrination, unlike church grammar and high schools."[556] First, it may be contradicted by the facts: "[I]n many church-related colleges, religion is just as central a part of the educational program and objectives as it is in parochial schools."[557] Second, as has already been shown, the "permeation" issue should not act as a complete bar to aid.[558]

VI

EXISTING FEDERAL PROGRAMS

It has recently been calculated that at present there are more than one hundred federal programs allocating property or funds worth billions of dollars to religiously-affiliated institutions, the Department of Health, Education, and Welfare alone aiding close to two thousand church-connected educational agencies.[559] Those programs involving the transfer of commodities or equipment for the achievement of specific secular goals, clearly fall within the class of permissibility under the establishment

---

[552] S. Doc. No. 29, 87th Cong., 1st Sess. 69 (1961) (Senator Keating).

[553] *See* State *ex rel.* Johnson v. Boyd, 217 Ind. 348, 28 N.E.2d 256 (1940). *Cf.* Wright v. School Dist., 151 Kan. 485, 99 P.2d 737 (1940), where it is obvious that the public aid exceeded the secular value.

[554] U.S. Dep't of Health, Education & Welfare, *supra* note 20, at 379.

[555] Former Senator Keating has pointed out that "it is about as unrealistic to plan a comprehensive aid-to-education bill at the elementary school level which isolates" the "more than 5 million children" attending sectarian schools "as it would be to plan an aid to higher education which ignored . . . students attending sectarian colleges." S. Doc. No. 29, *supra* note 552, at 69. Professor Kauper has noted that the "enrollment" argument "will be weakened as time goes on, since more and more public institutions will have to assume the lion's share of meeting increased demands for college education." P. KAUPER, *supra* note 5, at 115.

[556] Note, 61 Nw. U.L. REV. 777, 787 (1967). *See also* U.S. Dep't of Health, Education & Welfare, *supra* note 20, at 380.

[557] Kauper, *supra* note 35, at 37.

[558] The distinction between colleges on the one hand and grammar and high schools on the other may be relevant under state constitutional provisions. *See In re* Opinion of the Justices, 214 Mass. 599, 601, 102 N.E. 464, 465 (1913).

[559] *See* Ervin, *Mrs. Frothingham and Federal Aid to Church Schools*, 43 N.D.L. REV. 691, 692-93 (1967).

clause approach proposed herein, as do others affording direct grants for research of a designated nonreligious nature[560] and for training personnel for these purposes.[561] Taxpayers' dollars are plainly not being used for religious purposes. Nor are they so being utilized when public funds are appropriated for the construction or purchase of facilities or property that will be employed for strictly secular purposes[562] or for the establishment of special programs for the achievement of public ends.[563]

Somewhat more suspect, at least in principle, are those plans that grant money to church-affiliated educational institutions for part-time employment assistance to students.[564] It is possible under such programs that public funds will be employed for strictly religious purposes—for example, to pay a student assistant in a religious indoctrination course. But the statutory scheme may protect against this,[565] and even if it does not, it is highly unlikely, given present realities and those of the foreseeable future in respect to the quantum of public financial assistance, that any establishment clause issue would arise under the proposed rationale.[566]

A substantial number of current federal programs pay tuition grants to deserving students.[567] The possible dangers inherent in this form of government monetary assistance have already been discussed.[568] But,

---

[560] See, e.g., 16 U.S.C. §§ 581, 581a (1964) (agriculture and forestry); 42 U.S.C. §§ 1891-93 (1964) (science and national defense); 42 U.S.C. §§ 702(b), 712(b), 726, 729a (1964) (child and maternal welfare); 42 U.S.C. § 241 (1964) (health); 42 U.S.C. § 1310 (1964) (public welfare and social security); 42 U.S.C. § 1857 (1964) (air pollution); 20 U.S.C. §§ 331-32 (1964) (education); 42 U.S.C. § 712 (1964) (crippled children); 42 U.S.C. §§ 2542-44 (1964) (juvenile delinquency); 20 U.S.C. 512 (1964) (foreign languages); 20 U.S.C. § 542 (1964) (communications media for educational services); 20 U.S.C. § 35c(c) (1964) (vocational education); 29 U.S.C. § 34 (1964) (rehabilitative medicine); 42 U.S.C. § 2473(b)(5) (1964) (aeronautics and space).

[561] See, e.g., 10 U.S.C. § 4382 (1964) (ROTC); 42 U.S.C. §§ 2801-07 (1964) (teachers of illiterates); 42 U.S.C. § 242(d) (1964) (nurses); 42 U.S.C. §§ 282-83 (1964) (cancer control); 20 U.S.C. §§ 1031-34 (1964) (library science); 20 U.S.C. § 611 (teachers of physically handicapped).

[562] See, e.g., 42 U.S.C. §§ 292-93 (1964) (medical training); 20 U.S.C. §§ 701-33 (Supp. I, 1965) (construction of higher education facilities).

[563] See, e.g., 42 U.S.C. § 2000b (1964) (racial desegregation in education).

[564] See, e.g., Economic Opportunity Act of 1964, 42 U.S.C. §§ 2751-56 (1964) (work-study).

[565] 42 U.S.C. § 2754(a) (1964) provides "that no such work shall involve the construction, operation, or maintenance of so much of any facility used or to be used for sectarian instruction or as a place for religious worship."

[566] See text following note 251 supra.

[567] See, e.g., 20 U.S.C. §§ 1061-69 (Supp. I, 1965) (needy students in higher education); 20 U.S.C. § 511(b) (1964) (modern foreign languages); 20 U.S.C. § 464 (1964) (national defense). See also the "Delaney proposal," H.R. 9803, 87th Cong. 2d Sess. (1962) ($20 annually for each elementary and secondary school child); the "Church proposal," H.R. 4978 & H.R. 340, 87th Cong., 1st Sess. (1961) (tax benefits for parents of all students).

[568] See discussion in text accompanying notes 379-87 supra.

again, as a practical matter, there should be no real nonestablishment problems.[569] In conclusion, whatever the eventual judicial decision concerning the constitutionality of parochial school aid, the federal legislature has long given implicit recognition to its administrative viability, in respect to the rule proposed herein.

CONCLUSION

This article has attempted to serve several purposes. One has been to explore the broad scope of the first amendment's mandate that "Congress shall make no law respecting an establishment of religion," from both a traditional and normative perspective, accounting for both historical and contemporary goals. As a rationale for the constitutional adjudication of issues arising under the establishment clause, it suggests that a distinction be drawn between state action for religious and secular purposes and that the first amendment was designed to safeguard personal religious liberty by preventing the government from coercing religious belief and from taxing for religious purposes. The recommended approach is advanced, however, only as a point of departure. It does not mechanically produce answers, nor is it intended to articulate a "completely coherent system applicable across the board."[570] Further, it demands a delicate judicial judgment in close cases, although it would seem that the really difficult applications are more frequently created by imaginative hypotheticals than by the authentic dynamics of government action.

The article's second major purpose has been to propose a constitutional rule for the thorny political issue of governmental financial assistance to parochial education. Specifically, the rule advises that governmental aid to parochial schools is constitutional to the extent that it does not exceed the value of their secular services. Whatever the incidental benefits to religious institutions, the establishment clause should be satisfied by ensuring that government receive secular returns from those institutions commensurate with its financial expenditure.

It is easier to describe briefly what tasks have deliberately been omitted. No reconciliation of the pertinent state, federal, or Supreme Court decisions has been attempted. No prediction as to the outcome of

---

[569] More substantial issues have been presented by the Ordinances for the Northwest and Southwest territories which set aside land grants for the support of religious education and by 18th and 19th century congressional support of religious education of Indians by Christian missionaries. *See* Costanzo, *Federal Aid to Education and Religious Liberty*, 36 U. DET. L.J. 1, 34 (1958). *See also* 16 U.S.C. § 479 (1964), authorizing a group of persons residing in the vicinity of national forests to use forest land for the erection of a church. The primary effect of these programs would appear to be the employment of tax funds for religious purposes.

[570] Deutsch, *Neutrality, Legitimacy, and the Supreme Court: Some Intersections Between Law and Political Science*, 20 STAN. L. REV. 169, 190 (1968).

Supreme Court decisions in relevant present and future litigation has been advanced. I have not endeavored to make a carefully balanced appraisal, on the basis of my own likes or dislikes or those of others, of what is a desirable, feasible or politic legislative course.[571]

If the constitutional rationale advocated will sustain enactments thought unwise by some, they must be reminded that it does not command results thought abhorrent by others. For the Court to decide that some parochial school aid may be constitutional does not preclude the legislature from finding that it is unwise or improper. The realm of what is sound and just in this highly complex and emotionally charged area should remain open for informed debate and expedient resolution so long as the basic underlying freedom guarded by the establishment clause is preserved.

---

[571] *See* Oaks, *supra* note 5, at 8.

ARTICLE

THE RELIGION CLAUSES OF THE FIRST AMENDMENT: RECONCILING THE CONFLICT*†

*Jesse H. Choper***

The Religion Clauses of the first amendment, having been held fully applicable to the states[1] as well as to the national government, forbid government from enacting laws "respecting an establishment of religion, or prohibiting the free exercise thereof."[2] In this paper, I wish to confront the ineluctable tension that exists between the two provisions—a conflict that the Court has conceded in observing that the Religion Clauses "are cast in absolute terms, and either . . . , if expanded to a logical extreme, would tend to clash with the other."[3]

I.

In the main, the Court has tended to view the Religion Clauses as embodying two independent mandates. Consequently, it has developed separate tests for determining whether government action violates either provision. As for the Establishment Clause, the three-prong test that has evolved is that, in order to pass constitutional muster, government action (1) must have a secular, rather than a religious, purpose, (2) may not have the principal or primary effect of advancing or inhibiting religion, and (3) may not involve "excessive entanglement" between government and

---

* This paper, slightly modified, was delivered as the Louis H. Caplan Lecture, at the University of Pittsburgh School of Law, April 10, 1980.
† Copyright 1980 by University of Pittsburgh. All rights reserved.
** Professor of Law, University of California, Berkeley; B.S. 1957, Wilkes College; LL.B. 1960, University of Pennsylvania; D.Hu.Litt. 1967, Wilkes College. I wish to thank Judith Z. Gold of the class of 1980 for her exceptionally able and extremely valuable assistance in the preparation of this paper. I have greatly benefitted from many discussions with my colleague, Michael E. Smith, on the subject. My thanks also to John E. Coons, Paul J. Mishkin and Stephen D. Sugarman for their very helpful criticism of an earlier draft.
 1. *See generally* School Dist. of Abington Twp. v. Schempp, 374 U.S. 203, 215-17 (1963).
 2. U.S. CONST. amend. I.
 3. *See* Walz v. Tax Comm'n, 397 U.S. 664, 668-69 (1970).

religion.[4]

As for the Free Exercise Clause, the Court has made clear that if the purpose of a law "is to impede the observance of one or all religions or is to discriminate invidiously between religions, that law is constitutionally invalid."[5] It is equally plain that a law that attempts to regulate religious *beliefs* is unqualifiedly forbidden.[6] Very few laws, however, single out religion for adverse treatment,[7] deliberately prejudice persons because of their particular religious scruples, or penalize religious *beliefs*.[8] Rather, most issues under the Free Exercise Clause arise when a general government regulation, undertaken for genuinely secular purposes, either penalizes (or otherwise burdens) *conduct* that is dictated by some religious belief or specifically requires (or otherwise encourages) *conduct* that is forbidden by some religious belief. The Court has recognized that while "[the freedom to believe] is absolute . . . , in the nature of things, the . . . [freedom to act] cannot be."[9] In this context, the Court has employed "a balancing process"[10] and ruled that if a government regulation of general applicability burdens the exercise of religion then, in the absence of a state interest "of the highest order,"[11] government must accommodate the religious interest by granting it an exemption from the general rule.

Thus, the seemingly irreconcilable conflict: on the one hand the Court has said that the Establishment Clause forbids government action whose purpose is to aid religion, but on the other hand the Court has held that the Free Exercise Clause may require government action to accommodate religion. Unfortunately, the Court's separate tests for the Religion Clauses have provided virtually no guidance for determining when an accommodation for religion, seemingly required under the Free Exercise Clause, constitutes impermissible aid to religion under the Establishment Clause.[12] Nor has the Court adequately explained why aid to religion, seemingly violative of the Establishment Clause, is not actually re-

---

4. *See, e.g.,* Lemon v. Kurtzman, 403 U.S. 602, 612-13 (1971).
5. Braunfeld v. Brown, 366 U.S. 599, 607 (1961).
6. Cantwell v. Connecticut, 310 U.S. 296, 303 (1940).
7. *But see* McDaniel v. Paty, 435 U.S. 618 (1978).
8. *But see* West Virginia State Bd. of Educ. v. Barnette, 319 U.S. 624 (1943).
9. Cantwell v. Connecticut, 310 U.S. 296, 303-04 (1940).
10. Wisconsin v. Yoder, 406 U.S. 205, 214 (1972).
11. *Id.* at 215.
12. *See, e.g.,* Wisconsin v. Yoder, 406 U.S. 205 (1972); Sherbert v. Verner, 374 U.S. 398 (1963).

quired by the Free Exercise Clause.[13]

II.

Nearly twenty years ago, I proposed an interpretation of the Establishment Clause for testing the validity of religious practices in the public schools.[14] The interpretation was that such activities should be held unconstitutional if (1) they were *solely religious,* that is, if their "primary" purpose was religious even if "derivative" secular benefits might flow from their promotion of religion,[15] *and* if (2) they were likely to *compromise* or *influence* students' religious beliefs. Under this test, students' religious beliefs are "compromised" if they do something that is forbidden by their religion; their religious beliefs are "influenced" if they engage in religious activities that, although not contrary to their religion, they would not otherwise undertake.

Several years later, I proposed a rule for testing the validity of government financial aid to religious institutions, particularly parochial schools.[16] It reasoned that government expenditures for "solely religious" purposes—as ordinarily evidenced by their "primary" effect even if "derivative" public goals were advanced[17]—result in *coercing* taxpayers to support religion and thereby infringe religious liberty. My approach concluded that government assistance to parochial schools should not be held violative of the Establishment Clause so long as it did not exceed the value of the secular educational services provided by the schools because, in such case, the primary purpose and effect was nonreligious.

Taken together, both proposals encompass a single principle: *the Establishment Clause should forbid only government action whose purpose is solely religious and that is likely to impair religious freedom by coercing, compromising, or influencing religious beliefs.* My main goal in this paper is to suggest why I believe this principle should also be used to resolve the conflict between the Establishment and Free Exercise Clauses.

---

13. *See, e.g.,* Lemon v. Kurtzman, 403 U.S. 602 (1971); School Dist. of Abington Twp. v. Schempp, 374 U.S. 203 (1963); McCollum v. Board of Educ., 333 U.S. 203 (1948).
14. Choper, *Religion in the Public Schools: A Proposed Constitutional Standard,* 47 MINN. L. REV. 329 (1963).
15. *Id.* at 334-38.
16. Choper, *The Establishment Clause and Aid to Parochial Schools,* 56 CALIF. L. REV. 260 (1968).
17. *Id.* at 277-78.

III.

It is both appropriate and useful to begin all constitutional interpretation by consulting the historical intent of the Framers. Indeed, perhaps "[n]o provision of the Constitution is more closely tied to or given content by its generating history than the religious clause of the First Amendment."[18] But, as is so often true, "[a] too literal quest for the advice of the Founding Fathers [may be] futile and misdirected,"[19] because there is no clear record as to the Framers' intent, and such history as there is reflects several varying purposes.[20]

For example, a number of states had established churches until long after the Revolution.[21] There is some evidence that an original purpose of the Establishment Clause was to immunize these state-sponsored churches from the authority of the newly ordained national government.[22] After application of the Establishment Clause to the states through the fourteenth amendment,[23] the fulfillment of this original purpose becomes painfully complicated. Thus, dogmatic insistence on implementing the Framers' precise intent, if such is discernible, might jeopardize values that we now perceive as unconditionally protected by the Establishment Clause. Perhaps because our nation has become far more religiously heterogeneous, "practices which may have been objectionable to no one in the time of Jefferson and Madison may today be highly offensive to . . . the deeply devout and the nonbelievers alike."[24]

Moreover, even if the Framers' intent were unanimous, unambiguous, and totally in accord with contemporary values, it could provide no ready answers for the resolution of many of today's church-state problems. For example, since public education was virtually nonexistent until long after the Revolution,[25] the Framers could have no specific position on the subject of religious activities in the public schools—one of the most frequently litigated and

---

18. Everson v. Board of Educ., 330 U.S. 1, 33 (1947) (Rutledge, J., dissenting).
19. School Dist. of Abington Twp. v. Schempp, 374 U.S. 203, 237 (1963) (Brennan, J., concurring).
20. *See* L. TRIBE, AMERICAN CONSTITUTIONAL LAW § 14-3 (1978).
21. L. PFEFFER, CHURCH, STATE, AND FREEDOM 141 (rev. ed. 1967).
22. *Compare* W. KATZ, RELIGION AND AMERICAN CONSTITUTIONS 8-10 (1964) *with* M. HOWE, THE GARDEN AND THE WILDERNESS 23 (1965).
23. *See* Everson v. Board of Educ., 330 U.S. 1 (1947).
24. School Dist. of Abington Twp. v. Schempp, 374 U.S. 203, 241 (1963) (Brennan, J., concurring).
25. *See id.* at 238 & n.7.

emotionally charged modern Establishment Clause questions. Nor did the Framers foresee the development of such social and regulatory programs as unemployment insurance,[26] antidiscrimination laws,[27] or the National Labor Relations Act,[28] all of which have generated thorny church-state issues.

Nonetheless, history does "divulge a broad philosophy of church-state relations."[29] One tenet that emerges most clearly is that a central purpose of the Establishment Clause (as well as of the Free Exercise Clause) was to protect religious liberty—to prohibit the coercion of religious practice or conscience,[30] a goal that remains paramount today.[31] "Cruel persecutions," observed the Court in its first major Establishment Clause decision, "were the inevitable result of government-established religions."[32] As Justice Brennan concluded in his influential examination of the Religion Clauses, "[the Establishment and Free Exercise Clauses], although distinct in their objectives and their applicability, emerged together from a common panorama of history. The inclusion of both restraints . . . shows unmistakably that the Framers of the First Amendment were not content to rest the protection of religious liberty exclusively upon either clause."[33]

The practice perceived by the Framers as perhaps the most serious infringement of religious liberty sought to be corrected by the Establishment Clause was forcing the people to support religion by the use of compulsory taxes for purely sectarian purposes.[34] Thus, Madison abhorred obliging "a citizen to contribute three pence only of his property"[35] for nonsecular ends; Jefferson

---

26. *See* Sherbert v. Verner, 374 U.S. 398 (1963).
27. *See* Trans-World Airlines, Inc. v. Hardison, 432 U.S. 63 (1977).
28. *See* NLRB v. Catholic Bishop of Chicago, 440 U.S. 490 (1979).
29. C. ANTIEAU, A. DOWNEY, & E. ROBERTS, FREEDOM FROM FEDERAL ESTABLISHMENT at xi (1964).
30. *See* Engel v. Vitale, 370 U.S. 421, 429-30 (1962); Zorach v. Clauson, 343 U.S. 306, 313-14 (1952); Everson v. Board of Educ., 330 U.S. 1, 8-11 (1947); *Id.* at 53-54 (Rutledge, J., dissenting); L. PFEFFER, CHURCH, STATE, AND FREEDOM 122 (1953); Dunsford, *The Establishment Syndrome and Religious Liberty*, 2 DUQ. L. REV. 139, 203-12 (1964); Katz, *Freedom of Religion and State Neutrality*, 20 U. CHI. L. REV. 426, 428 (1953).
31. *See* Choper, *supra* note 14, at 333-34 & n.20.
32. Everson v. Board of Educ., 330 U.S. 1, 12 (1947).
33. School Dist. of Abington Twp. v. Schempp, 374 U.S. 203, 232 (1963) (Brennan, J., concurring).
34. *See* Kauper, *Church and State: Cooperative Separatism*, 60 MICH. L. REV. 1, 5-6, 9 (1961); Pfeffer, *Some Current Issues in Church and State*, 13 W. RES. L. REV. 9, 18 (1961).
35. Everson v. Board of Educ., 330 U.S. 1, 65-66 app. (1947) (Rutledge, J., dissenting)

insisted that "to compel a man to furnish contributions of money for the propagation of opinions which he disbelieves, is sinful and tyrannical;"[36] and the Court has repeatedly expressed this basic ideal by confirming that the Establishment Clause means at least that "[n]o tax in any amount, large or small, can be levied to support any religious activities or institutions, whatever they may be called, or whatever form they may adopt to teach or practice religion."[37] While public subsidy of religion may not directly influence people's beliefs or practices, it plainly coerces taxpayers either to contribute indirectly to their own religions or, worse, to support sectarian doctrines and causes that are antithetical to their own convictions. As a matter of both historical design and present constitutional policy, the Establishment Clause forbids so basic an infringement of religious liberty.

IV.

My proposals—based on the principle that the Establishment Clause should forbid government action whose purpose is religious and that is likely to impair religious freedom—sought to fulfill the central aim of the Religion Clauses: protection of religious liberty. Before exploring how this principle may help resolve the tension between the Establishment and Free Exercise Clauses, I should like briefly to compare my proposals to the paths the Court has taken in the past two decades.

With respect to religious practices in the public schools, most of the results reached by the Court—invalidating "on-premises" released time, and prayer and Bible reading programs[38]—have been in accord with my approach; but the Court's rationale, at least read literally, has been somewhat at variance with it. My proposed standard would forbid public school practices only when sectarian purpose is coupled with an infringement of religious liberty—*i.e.*, when it is shown that religiously motivated programs such as released time, Bible reading, and prayer will likely compromise or influence religious beliefs. Under the Court's articulated

---

(Memorial and Remonstrance Against Religious Assessments ¶ 3).

36. *An Act for Establishing Religious Freedom*, 12 W. HENING, STATUTES AT LARGE, LAWS OF VIRGINIA 84, 85 (Richmond 1823).

37. Everson v. Board of Educ., 330 U.S. 1, 16 (1947).

38. McCollum v. Board of Educ., 333 U.S. 203 (1948) (released time); Engel v. Vitale, 370 U.S. 421 (1962) (prayer); School Dist. of Abington Twp. v. Schempp, 374 U.S. 203 (1963) (Bible reading).

test, however, religious purpose alone condemns the programs.[39] I have already indicated how this position raises severe problems in reconciling the tension between the Establishment and Free Exercise Clauses, and I shall expand on this shortly. At this point, however, it is enough to observe that although the Court has *stated* in its major opinions in this area that coercion of religious belief—which is central under my proposal—is unnecessary for an Establishment Clause violation,[40] it has often carefully catalogued the coercive elements of the programs that it has held invalid.[41] Indeed, in *Zorach v. Clauson*,[42] in which the Court upheld an "off-premises" released time program, the Court effectively conceded that the program's purpose was religious,[43] but emphasized, wrongly in my view,[44] that it involved no "coercion to get public school students into religious classrooms."[45] Thus, on closer examination, I find substantial consonance between the Court's approach and my own.

With respect to aid to parochial schools, however, I must take considerably less comfort both from what the Court has said and also from what it has done. Under my proposal, since spending public funds for religious purposes is, as has been discussed,[46] a form of religious coercion, the Establishment Clause would forbid government aid to church-related schools if the money were used for sectarian ends. A state appropriation that would be used in this way would be government action for religious purposes with the consequent threat to religious freedom. If it could be shown, however, that the state receives full secular value for its money, then its expenditure would be for a nonreligious purpose and there would be no danger to religious liberty—and thus there would be no violation of the Establishment Clause. Under my proposal, all of the many aid programs to elementary and secondary parochial schools that the Court has invalidated since 1971[47] would have

---

39. School Dist. of Abington Twp. v. Schempp, 374 U.S. 203, 222 (1963). *See also* text accompanying note 4 *supra*.
40. School Dist. of Abington Twp. v. Schempp, 374 U.S. 203, 221-23 (1963); Engel v. Vitale, 370 U.S. 421, 430-31 (1962).
41. Engel v. Vitale, 370 U.S. 421, 430-31 (1962).
42. 343 U.S. 306 (1952).
43. *Id.* at 314.
44. *See* Choper, *supra* note 14, at 387-90.
45. 343 U.S. at 311.
46. *See* notes 34-37 and accompanying text *supra*.
47. For a summary of these decisions, *see* W. LOCKHART, Y. KAMISAR & J. CHOPER, CONSTITUTIONAL LAW: CASES-COMMENTS-QUESTIONS 1191-1210 (5th ed. 1980).

probably survived constitutional challenge.

How has the Court's approach differed from mine? In every case in which it has disapproved of aid to parochial schools, it has found that the first prong of its test—that the program have a secular purpose—has been met. In some of the cases, however, the Court has condemned the programs because they failed the second prong of its test; *i.e.,* the Court has found that the aid plans might have the primary effect of advancing religion (an effect which, if not prevented by the state, would also produce invalidity under my standard). But, as we shall see, it has been the third prong of the Court's Establishment Clause test—"excessive entanglement" between government and religion—that has effectively posed the greatest obstacle for aid to parochial schools. Since this factor plays no proscriptive role under my proposal, it accounts for the fundamental difference between the Court's approach and mine.

The Court has observed that the major beneficiaries of aid to nonpublic elementary and secondary schools are those operated by the Roman Catholic Church and has found that Catholic schools are "permeated" with religion. The Court has therefore reasoned that in order to insure that government aid does not advance the inculcation of religious doctrine (and thus run afoul of the second prong of its test), the state would have to engage in comprehensive surveillance of the recipient schools. This would foster an impermissible degree of administrative entanglement between church and state (thus failing the third prong of the Court's test). As a consequence, a state that wishes to aid parochial schools is faced with an insoluble dilemma. Since church-related elementary and secondary schools are presumably "permeated" with religion, the Court often requires that even the most neutral forms of aid[48] be continually monitored so as to ensure that they will not be used for religious purposes; but such monitoring engenders "excessive entanglement" and thus renders the program invalid.

V.

Without cataloguing the school aid cases in detail, I think it is fair to say that application of the Court's three-prong test has generated ad hoc judgments which are incapable of being reconciled on any principled basis. For example, a provision for therapeutic and diagnostic health services to parochial school pupils by public em-

---

48. *See, e.g.,* Meek v. Pittenger, 421 U.S. 349 (1975) (maps, tape recorders).

ployees is invalid if provided *in* the parochial school,[49] but not if offered at a neutral site, even if in a mobile unit adjacent to the parochial school.[50] Reimbursement to parochial schools for the expense of administering teacher-prepared tests required by state law is invalid,[51] but the state may reimburse parochial schools for the expense of administering state-prepared tests.[52] The state may lend school textbooks to parochial school pupils because, the Court has explained, the books can be checked in advance for religious content and are "self-policing";[53] but the state may not lend other seemingly self-policing instructional items such as tape recorders and maps.[54] The state may pay the cost of bus transportation to parochial schools,[55] which the Court has ruled are "permeated" with religion; but the state is forbidden to pay for field trip transportation visits "to governmental, industrial, cultural, and scientific centers designed to enrich the secular studies of students."[56] I hope that these illustrations are sufficiently striking to demonstrate the unpredictability of the Court's approach. Indeed, in an unusually candid recent dictum, the Court forthrightly conceded that its approach in this area "sacrifices clarity and predictability for flexibility"[57]—a euphemism, I suggest, for expressly admitting the absence of any principled rationale for its product.

VI.

The conceptual chaos forged by the Court's test—effectively attributable to its "entanglement" prong—is not, however, its chief shortcoming. A more fundamental objection is that avoidance of administrative entanglement between government and religion neither should, nor can, represent a value to be judicially secured by the Establishment Clause.

Administrative entanglement between government and religion has sometimes been seen as threatening the values underlying the constitutional separation of church and state because of the fear that religious institutions will capture their public regulators

---

49. *Id.*
50. Wolman v. Walter, 433 U.S. 229 (1977).
51. Levitt v. Committee for Pub. Educ., 413 U.S. 472 (1973).
52. Committee for Pub. Educ. v. Regan, 444 U.S. 646 (1980).
53. Board of Educ. v. Allen, 392 U.S. 236 (1968).
54. *See* note 48 *supra.*
55. Everson v. Board of Educ., 330 U.S. 1 (1947).
56. Wolman v. Walter, 433 U.S. 229, 252 (1977).
57. Committee for Pub. Educ. v. Regan, 444 U.S. 646, 662 (1980).

by taking advantage of the widely noted tendency of administrators to develop a mutuality of interest with those they are supposed to regulate.[58] This concern, however, is unfounded, both doctrinally and empirically. First, it has long been held that the Constitution permits the state to regulate church-related institutions even if it provides them no financial assistance whatever.[59] Second, parochial school curricula, for example, have long been regulated,[60] without any significant evidence of the church capturing the state.[61] Thus, while the values underlying the Establishment Clause should forbid the state from abdicating to the church by permitting public funds to be used for religious purposes, they should not prevent meaningful government regulation of church-related institutions.

Another evil, it is often argued, arising from entanglement is that administrative regulation impairs the free exercise of religion.[62] Here, again, there is no real evidence that the regulation of religious bodies which has taken place—albeit in the absence of substantial amounts of aid[63]—has produced this result. If it did, it would be unconstitutional whether or not the regulation were tied to aid. Although, "as a political matter, aid may prompt constitutional regulation theretofore absent, . . . [t]his consideration is relevant to the question of whether a religious institution should apply for aid; it is not relevant to whether the aid may constitutionally be granted."[64]

Another form of administrative entanglement occurs when the state seeks to distinguish religion from nonreligion in order to grant a religious exemption from burdensome civil regulations. Although government scrutiny of religious beliefs and practices may

---

58. J. NOWAK, R. ROTUNDA, & J. YOUNG, CONSTITUTIONAL LAW 865 & n.5 (1978), and authorities there cited.

59. Pierce v. Society of Sisters, 268 U.S. 510, 534 (1925).

60. A 1964 study of state curriculum requirements for non-public schools showed that 41 states provided for some regulation. See Stolec, *Non-Public Schools: What Must They Teach?* 92 SCHOOL & SOC'Y 274, 275 (1964).

61. It may be argued that when regulation is coupled with aid, the religious institution has a greater incentive to attempt a "capture." But when compliance with regulation not accompanied by aid is costly, the incentive is substantially the same.

62. See Everson v. Board of Educ., 330 U.S. 1, 53 (1947) (Rutledge, J., dissenting); *Id.* at 26-27 (Jackson, J., dissenting); Kurland, *Of Church and State and the Supreme Court,* 29 U. CHI. L. REV. 1, 4 (1961).

63. See note 61 *supra.*

64. Schwartz, *No Imposition of Religion: The Establishment Clause Value,* 77 YALE L.J. 692, 710 (1968).

be a sensitive and unwelcome task, its "necessity arises out of the constitutional language itself, which sets down religion as a subject for special treatment."⁶⁵ Here, again, the Court has never doubted that government may become entangled with religion in this way.⁶⁶

In sum, scrupulous avoidance of all administrative "entanglement" between church and state might well require abandonment of virtually all regulation of religious activities, even for such desirable purposes as ensuring minimum educational standards for all school children. Even avoidance of only "substantial" entanglement would probably prevent government from characterizing certain beliefs as religious in order to exempt them from onerous and unnecessary secular rules. This would result either in confining such exemptions to members of long-established churches whose religiosity was universally conceded, or, indeed, in eliminating Free Exercise Clause exemptions altogether. I believe that avoidance of church-state entanglement, at the expense of forsaking legitimate secular pursuits or the more general value of preserving religious liberty, is mandated neither by the Establishment Clause nor good sense.

VII.

The "entanglement" prong of the Court's Establishment Clause test also contains a somewhat separate element, which may be labeled "political divisiveness," under which government action may be held invalid if it promotes political fragmentation along religious lines.⁶⁷ It is somewhat unclear whether the Court is using this "political divisiveness" as an independent test of constitutionality, a "warning signal"⁶⁸ calling for stricter application of other tests, or only to reinforce its conclusions. I believe, however, that, like its companion element of administrative entanglement, avoidance of political strife along religious lines neither should, nor can, represent a value to be judicially secured by the Establishment Clause. Indeed, if government were to actually ban religious conflict in the legislative process, this would raise serious questions under those provisions of the first amendment that guarantee

---

65. Mansfield, Book Review, 52 CALIF. L. REV. 212, 216 (1964).
66. *See* Wisconsin v. Yoder, 406 U.S. 205, 240 (1972) (White, J., concurring).
67. *See* Lemon v. Kurtzman, 403 U.S. 602, 622-23 (1971). *See also, e.g.*, Meek v. Pittenger, 421 U.S. 349, 365 n.15, 372 (1975); Committee for Pub. Educ. v. Nyquist, 413 U.S. 756, 795-97 (1973).
68. Lemon v. Kurtzman, 403 U.S. 602, 625 (1971).

political, as well as religious, liberty.

Practical considerations, however, more than doctrinal ones, demonstrate the futility of making "political divisiveness" a constitutional determinant under the Establishment Clause. Surely, legislation is not invalid simply because a religious organization supported or opposed it. Conflict among sectarian groups—whether it arises on the issue of how public funds should be expended or on the question of whether to grant a religious exemption from laws of general application—may well be unfortunate. But such discord is neither meaningfully different nor more dangerous than the disagreements among religious groups that are inevitably generated when government pursues many concededly secular ends. Religious groups have differed concerning a wide variety of political issues—including Sunday closing, gambling, pornography, drug control, gun control, the draft, prohibition, abolition of slavery, racial integration, prostitution, overpopulation, sterilization, abortion, birth control, marriage, divorce, the Equal Rights Amendment, and capital punishment, to name but a few. Undoubtedly, organized churches and other religious groups have markedly influenced the resolution of some of these issues.[69] The participation of such groups in the legislative process may well be relevant in determining whether a law should be subject to scrutiny under the Establishment Clause because it promotes a religious purpose.[70] But if a law serves genuinely secular purposes—or impairs no one's religious liberty by coercing, compromising or influencing religious beliefs—there is no persuasive reason to hold it unconstitutional simply because its proponents and opponents were divided along religious lines.

Furthermore, even if government could or should eliminate political fragmentation along religious lines, the Establishment Clause would be a most ineffective tool for the task. For example, forbidding laws granting aid to parochial schools does not effect a truce, but only moves the battleground. There is every reason to believe that the failure to assist church-related schools antagonizes many citizens who feel that their taxes are being used to subsidize

---

69. *See* CENTER FOR THE STUDY OF DEMOCRATIC INSTITUTIONS, RELIGION AND AMERICAN SOCIETY 71 (1961); M. HOWE, THE GARDEN AND THE WILDERNESS 62 (1965); P. KAUPER, RELIGION AND THE CONSTITUTION 83-85 (1962).

70. *See* Village of Arlington Heights v. Metropolitan Hous. Dev. Corp., 429 U.S. 252 (1977).

an alien dogma of secularism.[71] Since funding only public schools places parents whose children attend parochial schools at a competitive disadvantage, they will tend to oppose legislation benefitting public schools.[72]

Similarly, Christian groups may lobby for a Sunday closing law, believing that their religious obligation to abstain from work on Sundays places them at a disadvantage in the marketplace. Moreover, it is in their interest, and in the interest of nonreligious people, vigorously to oppose an exemption from the law for Sabbatarians, who might gain a competitive advantage from being open on Sundays. But if the exemption is denied, Sabbatarians will just as vigorously oppose enactment of the Sunday closing law.

In sum, religious antagonism in the political arena, though perhaps regrettable, is a fact of life in our pluralistic governmental system which cannot be effectively suppressed through the Establishment Clause.

VIII.

To turn now to my principal subject, while it has been the "entanglement" prong of the Court's Establishment Clause test that has plagued the Court's efforts on the question of aid to parochial schools, it is the "secular purpose" prong that is most troublesome in respect to reconciling the seeming antipathy between the Establishment and Free Exercise Clauses. Because this part of the Court's test flatly prohibits any government action that has a religious purpose, it would make virtually *all* accommodations for religion unconstitutional. Since, as we shall see,[73] the primary goal of nearly all accommodations for religion is to avoid burdening religious activity, it is plain that their purpose is to assist religion. Thus, taken literally, the "secular purpose" requirement of the Court's Establishment Clause test would, for example, forbid the exemption of conscientious objectors from military service[74] and Amish school children from compulsory education laws.[75] As we have seen,[76] the Court's interpretation of the Free Exercise Clause

---

71. Schwartz, *supra* note 64, at 700-01.
72. *See* Choper, *supra* note 16, at 260, 273-74; *see also* J. NOWAK, R. ROTUNDA & J. YOUNG, *supra* note 58, at 867-68.
73. *See* text accompanying notes 115-17 *infra*.
74. *But see* Selective Service Draft Law Cases, 245 U.S. 366, 389-90 (1918), and discussion at notes 111-26 *infra*.
75. *But see* Wisconsin v. Yoder, 406 U.S. 205 (1972), and discussion at note 110 *infra*.
76. *See* text accompanying notes 9-11 *supra*. *But see* Anderson v. General Dynamics,

243

rejects these implications of its Establishment Clause test. Indeed, the Court has not only mandated religious exemptions under the Free Exercise Clause but has also strongly indicated its approval of a number of government accommodations for religion that were not constitutionally required.[77]

The Court's apparent inconsistency may be rationalized by concluding that its Establishment Clause principles simply give way in the face of a serious (or even arguably substantial) Free Exercise Clause claim.[78] Indeed, this approach may be endorsed as wisely fulfilling the historic and contemporary aims of both clauses to further religious liberty. But while I do not believe that the Establishment Clause should be read to bar all exemptions for religion, I am also unwilling to totally ignore the Establishment Clause simply because government's purpose is to accommodate religion. Precisely because the Establishment Clause is designed to protect religious liberty, I believe that it should not be automatically read as subordinate to the Free Exercise Clause, but rather as limiting the extent to which government may act in behalf of religion.

My discussion will focus on the Establishment Clause. It makes no attempt to determine, once it is found that a religious accommodation is *permissible* under the Establishment Clause, when such accommodation may be *required* under the Free Exercise Clause. Rather, it concerns the Free Exercise Clause only by confining its scope.

IX.

My proposal, once again, is that the Establishment Clause should forbid government action that is undertaken for a religious purpose *and* that is likely to result in coercing, compromising, or influencing religious beliefs. Thus, I disagree with the Court's articulated view that religious purpose alone renders government action invalid. Rather, it is only when religious purpose is coupled with threatened impairment of religious freedom that government action should be held to violate the Establishment Clause.

I wish to make clear that my position is not grounded in the

---

489 F. Supp. 782 (S.D. Cal. 1980).

77. *See, e.g.*, Gillette v. United States, 401 U.S. 437, 461 n.23 (1971) (draft exemption); Arlans Dep't Store, Inc. v. Kentucky, 371 U.S. 218 (1962) (dismissing for want of a substantial federal question an appeal testing the constitutionality of a Sabbatarian exemption from a Sunday closing law); Zorach v. Clauson, 343 U.S. 306 (1952) (released time program).

78. *See* L. TRIBE, AMERICAN CONSTITUTIONAL LAW § 14-4, at 822-23 (1978).

idea that government promotion of religion serves secular ends by producing public benefits. If legislation designed to assist religion jeopardizes religious freedom, no public benefit should save it. Conversely, if state satisfaction of the religious needs of either the majority or a minority does not jeopardize any Establishment Clause values that have been identified, it should be held constitutionally permissible regardless of whether it serves some independent secular goal. Thus, the key to an Establishment Clause violation should be whether the government action endangers religious freedom.

To illustrate my view—and specifically to contrast it with prevailing judicial doctrine—I believe that *Epperson v. Arkansas*[79] was wrongly decided. In *Epperson*, the Court held that Arkansas' "anti-evolution" statute, which made it unlawful to teach the theory of Charles Darwin in the public schools, violated the Religion Clauses. The Court rested its conclusion on the ground that it was "clear that fundamentalist sectarian conviction was and is the law's reason for existence."[80] I would not dispute the Court's finding that the statute had a solely religious purpose even if it could be shown that it produced derivative secular benefits such as the promotion of classroom harmony.[81] But to rely on the nonestablishment precept to invalidate a religiously motivated law that creates none of the dangers the Establishment Clause was designed to prevent represents, in my view, an "untutored devotion to the concept of neutrality"[82] between church and state. Conceding that the law in *Epperson* "aided" fundamentalist religions, there was no evidence that religious beliefs were either coerced, compromised or influenced. That is, it was not shown, nor do I believe that it could be persuasively argued, that the anti-evolution law either (1) induced children of fundamentalist religions to accept the biblical theory of creation, or (2) conditioned other children for conversion to fundamentalism. In contrast to other situations to be discussed below,[83] those whose religious interests were not advanced by the law appeared to suffer no *religious* harm. Therefore, while the accommodation for religion in *Epperson* may not have been constitu-

---

79. 393 U.S. 97 (1968).
80. *Id.* at 107-08.
81. *See* text following note 14 *supra*.
82. School Dist. of Abington Twp. v. Schempp, 374 U.S. 203, 306 (1963) (Goldberg, J., concurring).
83. *See* text following note 101 *infra*.

tionally required by the Free Exercise Clause,[84] the law should have survived the Establishment Clause challenge. Even though it satisfied a private religious need, it did not, given the above factual premises, threaten religious liberty.

X.

Although the Court has seldom explored the tension between the Religion Clauses, the problem has by no means gone unnoticed. It should be helpful in defining the contours of my proposal to contrast it with some of the major scholarly attempts to reconcile the conflict.

Nearly twenty years ago, an influential article by Philip Kurland urged that the Religion Clauses be read together to state a single principle of neutrality, mandating that "government cannot utilize religion as a standard for action or inaction because these clauses prohibit classification in terms of religion either to confer a benefit or to impose a burden."[85] Although there is much to be said for this rule of "religion-blindness," it has, in my view, two serious shortcomings. In requiring government impartiality respecting religion, the rule produces results hostile to religion without serving nonestablishment values and permits forms of aid that subvert historical and contemporary aims of the Establishment Clause.

The neutrality principle produces hostility to religion by flatly prohibiting all solely religious exemptions from general regulations no matter how greatly they burden religious exercise and no matter how insubstantial the competing state interest may be. In advancing the admirable goals of government neutrality and impartiality, it downgrades the positive value that both Religion Clauses assign to religious liberty.

Consider a simple illustration: Suppose that a school regulation requires pupils to wear shorts during gym class for the aesthetic effect of uniform dress and that one child requests an exemption because her religious scruples forbid her to bare her legs.[86] The "religion-blindness" rule would allow a broadly worded exemption for "all children whose modesty makes the wearing of shorts uncomfortable" or for "all children whose parents request exemption." Either of these would protect the religious objector,

---

84. See note 77 and accompanying text supra.
85. Kurland, supra note 58, at 6.
86. See Mitchell v. McCall, 273 Ala. 604, 143 So. 2d 629 (1962).

but so many other children might also take advantage of the exemption that the regulation's aesthetic goal would be destroyed. Even if the school believed that it could exempt children who objected on religious grounds and still achieve its overall aesthetic purpose, such an exemption would constitute an impermissible classification under the neutrality principle. Thus, the school board would seemingly be faced with the choice of either protecting the religious child by abandoning its concededly valid purpose, or compromising the religious child's beliefs even though denying the exemption is unnecessary to serve its purpose. The "religion-blindness" rule would appear to demand these equally unsatisfying alternatives even though granting a religious exemption would neither coerce, compromise, nor influence the religious beliefs of any school children. I doubt that it could plausibly be argued that children would change their religions in order to obtain an exemption, or that the beliefs of those granted the religious exemption would thereby be intensified. Therefore, a religious exemption—admittedly undertaken for nonsecular purposes—would in no way impair religious freedom. Pursuant to my proposal, it would be permitted by the Establishment Clause.

Paradoxically, the neutrality principle not only requires hostility to religion at odds with the values of the Free Exercise Clause, but also permits aid to religion in conflict with values of the Establishment Clause. It would apparently allow the use of tax funds for the purely religious functions of church organizations, so long as the legislative classification is broad enough. For example, suppose the state allocated public funds to all private associations for the purpose of distributing replicas of their insignia to their members. The Rotary Club, the League of Women Voters, and religious groups would all be beneficiaries. Under the "religion-blindness" rule, denial of funds to religious groups would constitute an impermissible religious classification, yet including such groups would designate tax funds to be used to purchase crosses and Stars of David. If our economy were to reach such a stage of collectivization that government fiscal policies so shrunk private sources of funds as to make voluntary support of religion impracticable, there might well then be merit in re-evaluating the historically rooted and contemporarily valued prohibition against state support of strictly sectarian activities.[87] But I do not believe that it has yet been persua-

---

87. *See* Giannella, *Religious Liberty, Nonestablishment and Doctrinal Development*

sively shown that that time has come.

XI.

Several scholars have urged that the Establishment Clause is largely designed to implement the Free Exercise Clause, so that when the Religion Clauses clash, the Establishment Clause must be subordinated to the Free Exercise Clause.[88] The leading decision of *Sherbert v. Verner*[89] may be read as supporting this view. In that case, Mrs. Sherbert, a mill worker and a Seventh Day Adventist, was discharged by her employer when she would not work on Saturday, the Sabbath day of her faith, after all the mills in her area adopted a six-day work week. South Carolina denied her unemployment compensation benefits for refusing to accept "suitable work," even though that would require her to work on Saturday. The Court held that this violated the Free Exercise Clause because "to condition the availability of benefits upon [her] willingness to violate a cardinal principle of her religious faith effectively penalizes the free exercise of her constitutional liberties."[90] Under the Court's Establishment Clause test, however, any government action that has a religious purpose is forbidden, and, therefore, a Sabbatarian exemption would appear to be unconstitutional. It seems indisputable that when the state excuses Mrs. Sherbert from taking otherwise suitable work because of her religious scruples, the purpose of the exemption is solely to facilitate her religious exercise.

To avoid the stark impact of its Establishment Clause approach, the Court may have either totally subordinated the Establishment Clause's "no-aid" mandate to the Free Exercise Clause, or simply balanced Mrs. Sherbert's right to Sabbatarianism under the Free Exercise Clause against the "no-aid" principle of the Establishment Clause and found the former weightier. Justice Brennan, author of the *Sherbert* opinion, had previously advocated this approach for resolving the establishment-free exercise conflict: "[T]he logical interrelationship between the Establishment and

---

(pt. 2): *The Nonestablishment Principle*, 81 HARV. L. REV. 513, 522-26, 537-55 (1968); Van Alstyne, *Constitutional Separation of Church and State: The Quest for a Coherent Position*, 57 AM. POL. SCI. REV. 865, 881-82 (1963).

88. *See, e.g.,* Moore, *The Supreme Court and the Relationship Between the "Establishment" and "Free Exercise" Clauses*, 42 TEX. L. REV. 142, 196 (1963).
89. 374 U.S. 398 (1963).
90. *Id.* at 406.

Free Exercise Clauses may produce situations where an injunction against an apparent establishment must be withheld in order to avoid infringement of rights of free exercise."[91]

If, in a balancing process, the Establishment Clause's prohibition of aid to religion is viewed only as an abstract principle rather than as a means for securing religious liberty, then it is not surprising that the Court found it wanting in *Sherbert*. On the other side of the balance was Mrs. Sherbert's grave, immediate, and concrete injury—the very type of injury that the Free Exercise Clause was meant to prevent. Indeed, if the Establishment Clause is so abstractly viewed, then it is difficult to imagine any situation where it would not be subordinated or outweighed when measured against a colorable free exercise claim.

Under my proposal, the Establishment Clause would not be so viewed. Rather it would serve the underlying values of both Religion Clauses by forbidding laws whose purpose is to aid religion—including exemptions for religion from general government regulations—if such laws tended to coerce, compromise, or influence religious beliefs.

Mrs. Sherbert's exemption would fail this test. First, since those who refused to work on Saturdays for nonreligious reasons, such as watching football games or spending the day with their children, would be denied unemployment benefits under South Carolina's scheme (and could constitutionally be denied them under the Court's ruling), the sole purpose of Mrs. Sherbert's exemption was to aid religion. Second, the exemption results in impairment of religious liberty because compulsorily raised tax funds must be used to subsidize Mrs. Sherbert's exercise of religion.

The situation produced by the Court's decision in *Sherbert* is distinguishable from that in which the state allows all unemployment compensation claimants to refuse work on one day of their choosing in order to pursue whatever outside interests they might have. Even though some claimants might use the day for religious exercise, government has not conditioned the grant of public funds on a religious use, nor in any other way restricted freedom of choice as to how the money will be spent. While taxpayers may rightfully complain if Mrs. Sherbert's exemption is granted on condition that she use it for religious purposes, they may not object to

---

91. School Dist. of Abington Twp. v. Schempp, 374 U.S. 203, 247 (1963) (Brennan, J., concurring).

Mrs. Sherbert's religious use of her leisure time. This is analytically the same as a welfare recipient's contributing part of his benefits to his church. Even though the state's money finds its way into the church's coffers, there is no violation of the Establishment Clause because the government has not conditioned the grant on the recipient's promise to use it for religious purposes. The government's secular goal of providing for the basic needs of indigents is served even though a particular recipient decides that one of his basic needs is religion.[92]

Does my proposal—which forbids a religious exemption for Mrs. Sherbert because it would coerce taxpayer's religious beliefs—simply subordinate the Free Exercise Clause to the Establishment Clause? I think not, because the religious liberty value at the core of both Religion Clauses demands that Mrs. Sherbert's right to freely exercise her religion not encompass the right to governmental assistance which infringes the religious freedom of others.

XII.

In a provocative article published fifteen years ago, Marc Galanter sought to justify exemptions for religious minorities from general government regulations on the ground that they do not constitute preferential aid to religion forbidden by the Establishment Clause but rather amount to no more than equalizing the position of these minorities with that of the majority.[93] He based his thesis on the persuasive premise that "[w]hatever seriously interferes with majority religious beliefs and practices is unlikely to become a legal requirement—for example, work on Sunday or Christmas."[94] Indeed, the statute involved in *Sherbert* is illustrative because, by prohibiting any disadvantage against employees who refused to work on Sunday because of their religion,[95] it "expressly save[d] the Sunday worshipper from having to make the kind of choice"[96] imposed on Mrs. Sherbert. Thus, special treatment for religious minorities, Galanter contended, is restorative or equalizing, granting them only "what majorities have by virtue of suffrage and rep-

---

92. See generally Choper, *supra* note 16, at 315-17.
93. Galanter, *Religious Freedom in the United States: A Turning Point?* 1966 WIS. L. REV. 217.
94. *Id.* at 291.
95. *See* 374 U.S. at 400.
96. *Id.* at 406.

resentative government."[97]

One difficulty that I have with this view is that it assumes the validity of certain advantages that religious majorities may create for themselves. But if what the majority obtains "by virtue of suffrage" itself contravenes the Establishment Clause, then providing the same benefit to religious minorities compounds the violation rather than eliminates it. Thus, the devotional Bible reading and Lord's Prayer programs struck down by the Court[98] could not have been cured, in my judgment, by reading from the Torah, the Koran, and works of secular philosophy on selected days of the month. In *Sherbert,* since the exemption for Sunday worshippers granted by South Carolina, as much as the exemption for Mrs. Sherbert mandated by the Supreme Court, served a religious purpose and involved religious coercion in the form of a tax subsidy for religious practice, it too would violate the Establishment Clause under my proposal.

But if the government policy that imposes burdens on minority religions has a secular purpose (as most such regulatory and tax programs do), and is thus itself immune to challenge under the Establishment Clause, I do not believe that Establishment Clause values should be ignored in situations where alleviating the burden or "restoring" the minority to a position of "equality" with the majority results in impairment of religious liberty. For example, even if members of a particular church demonstrated that, largely because of the financial burdens of government taxation, they had inadequate funds to buy vestments, it appears beyond dispute—at least in the absence of the wholly collectivized society hypothesized earlier[99]—that the Establishment Clause should forbid a state subsidy for this purpose. Moreover, even if a zoning ordinance, enacted to serve substantial public goals, excluded churches within many miles of a particular indigent person's home, it is plain that the historical and contemporary Establishment Clause command to avoid taxation in aid of religion should forbid the state's funding his weekly transportation to church.

Similarly, the Establishment Clause should be held to forbid the government's paying chaplains to minister to the religious needs of prisoners and military personnel. It may be that, under a

---

97. Galanter, *supra* note 93, at 291.
98. School Dist. of Abington Twp. v. Schempp, 374 U.S. 203 (1963).
99. *See* text accompanying note 87 *supra.*

Free Exercise Clause balancing test,[100] the state could not exclude chaplains who volunteer for these purposes. But the Establishment Clause makes it the financial responsibility of the church and not the state to attend to its members' religious needs.

I agree, however, that "restorative or equalizing" accommodations for religion that do not tend to interfere with religious freedom should be permissible, even when such accommodations impose substantial costs of other kinds on those who are not their beneficiaries. For example, if a state were to grant a Sabbatarian exemption from a Sunday closing law, a non-Sabbatarian merchant might well object on the ground that the religiously motivated exemption caused him financial injury because, being forced to close on Sundays, he lost business to Sabbatarian competitors.[101] But even though the non-Sabbatarian store owner probably suffers a far greater monetary loss than any individual taxpayer would suffer from most tax subsidies of religious activities, this *alone* would not produce a violation of the Establishment Clause under my proposal. Similarly, that other accommodations of religious exercise would impose substantial non-monetary costs on nonrecipients would not *itself* invalidate them. For example, granting a draft exemption to a religious objector probably means that a nonbeliever who would otherwise avoid being drafted will be required to serve. Exempting a religious child from the school requirement that she wear shorts in gym class deprives her nonbelieving classmates of the desired total uniformity of dress. Excising evolutionary theory from public school curricula in order to avoid offending devout believers in a religious theory of creation deprives nonbelieving children of meaningful knowledge.

However, these indirect social costs of religious accommodation—in contrast to the tax cost of a religious subsidy—do not themselves threaten the values undergirding the Establishment Clause. They do not tend to coerce, compromise, or influence the nonbeliever's religious beliefs. Unlike the tax cost in *Sherbert*, these indirect social costs are not required to satisfy the believer's needs. The Sabbatarian store owner who seeks to remain open on Sunday does not demand that the non-Sabbatarian be closed on Sunday so that the Sabbatarian may acquire the non-Sabbatarian's customers; they are an unsought benefit, and the Sabbata-

---

100. *See* Sec. XIV *infra*.
101. Arlans Dep't Store, Inc. v. Kentucky, 371 U.S. 218 (1962) (appeal dismissed for want of a substantial federal question), raised precisely this claim.

rian's free exercise claim could be fully satisfied without them. Nor does the religious pacifist need to have another serve in his place; the cost imposed on the nonbelieving draftee does not aid the exempted person's religious beliefs at all. Nor, on the factual premises discussed earlier,[102] is it necessary to the religious tenets of the fundamentalist that nonbelieving children fail to learn about Darwin. In contrast, Mrs. Sherbert claimed a constitutional right to tax funds to subsidize the observance of her Sabbath. The pocketbook injury to nonbelieving taxpayers was required to accomplish this religious end. The cost itself served a religious purpose, rather than resulting incidentally from the accommodation of religious exercise. If accommodations for religion impose religious costs on nonbelievers, then, under my proposal, they are forbidden by the Establishment Clause. But if such accommodations impose only nonreligious costs, then the Establishment Clause should be held to permit—or, indeed, the Free Exercise Clause may be interpreted to demand—that these costs of religious tolerance be paid.

XIII.

In a most sophisticated effort to resolve the tension between the Religion Clauses, Alan Schwartz, a decade ago, urged that accommodations for religious exercise should survive Establishment Clause challenge unless they result in the "imposition of religion,"[103] that is, they *actually influence* individuals to change their religious beliefs. His approach differs from mine in several important respects. First, it would apparently not invalidate a tax subsidy of religion unless it met this criterion. But, as we have seen, the Framers considered taxation in support of churches to be an especially reprehensible form of religious coercion,[104] a view confirmed by the contemporary value of protecting religious freedom. Under the "no imposition" approach, many such subsidies would seemingly be permissible, thus enabling government to finance most private religious activities—as opposed to public activities such as school prayers, which undoubtedly influence religious belief[105]—free of Establishment Clause constraints.

Second, under Schwartz's approach, government action that merely "helps implement a religious or irreligious choice indepen-

---

102. See text accompanying notes 82-83 *supra*.
103. Schwartz, *supra* note 64, at 692.
104. See notes 34-36 and accompanying text *supra*.
105. See Choper, *supra* note 14, at 368-77.

dently made,"[106] rather than actually influences religious beliefs, does not amount to imposition of religion, and thus passes the Establishment Clause hurdle. I believe that government programs with no secular purpose that intensify or meaningfully encourage even independently chosen beliefs should be held to violate the Establishment Clause. Otherwise, a modest public reward for regular attendance at the church of one's faith would be permissible.

Finally, Schwartz contends that although aid to religion may induce false claims of religious belief, "the Establishment Clause is not concerned with false claims of belief, only with induced belief."[107] But, as we shall see,[108] at least some initially false claims of belief, particularly those which require for their proof participation in religious exercise, will probably ripen into sincere belief.[109] Indeed, it also seems likely that strong temptations to adopt a particular religion will sometimes produce a sincere belief without any initial bad faith. Thus, government temptations that tend to influence religious choice, like other forms of religiously motivated action that tend to coerce or compromise religious freedom, jeopardize Establishment Clause values and should be proscribed.

XIV.

As indicated earlier, my proposal to reconcile the tension between the Religion Clauses focuses on when the Establishment Clause permits or prohibits government accommodations for religion. Although it does not speak to when the Free Exercise Clause mandates religious exemptions from secular government regulations, it does assist in the balancing process traditionally employed under the Free Exercise Clause by identifying the state interest that must be weighed against the religious burden imposed. If the Establishment Clause *permits* a religious exemption, the state

---

106. Schwartz, *supra* note 64, at 728.
107. *Id.*
108. *See* text accompanying notes 124-26 *infra*.
109. It is obviously impossible to gather precise information on the number of fraudulent claims for conscientious objector status, or on the number of such claims which ripened into true belief. It is interesting to note, however, that a number of handbooks published during the Vietnam War era recommended tactics for asserting questionable claims. One handbook, for example, suggested that "many who consider themselves to be 'selective objectors' find that they can qualify for CO status by taking what might be called an existential approach." CCCO, HANDBOOK FOR CONSCIENTIOUS OBJECTORS 4 (12th ed. 1972). It is also interesting to note that the percentage of registrants classified as conscientious objectors increased sharply in the late 1960s, a time of widespread political opposition to military service. *See* [1973] U.S. DIR. SELECTIVE SERV. SEMI-ANN. REP., JULY 1-DEC. 31, at 32.

interest to be balanced against the free exercise claim is that of *maintaining its program without religious exemptions*. If, however, the Establishment Clause *prohibits* a religious exemption, the state interest to be balanced is that of *preserving its entire program*, because only by abandoning it altogether could the free exercise claim be satisfied.

To illustrate, consider the hypothetical regulation requiring school children to wear gym shorts. We have already observed that a religious exemption would in no way coerce, compromise, or influence religious choice and is thus permissible under the Establishment Clause. In balancing the child's claim for exemption under the Free Exercise Clause, the state's interest would be that of complete uniformity of dress. The free exercise balancing process necessarily involves value judgments that may often be difficult. Whether a more refined analysis than naked interest balancing can be developed is beyond the scope of this discussion. Whatever the optimal approach may be, it would seem most unlikely that the aesthetic interest in complete uniformity could overcome the child's interest in not being compelled to violate her religious beliefs.

Similarly, in *Wisconsin v. Yoder*,[110] which held that the Free Exercise Clause demanded an exemption for Amish children from the state's requirement of school attendance until age sixteen, the Court correctly identified the relevant state interest as that of denying a religious exemption. Unless it could be shown that relieving the Amish of this government-created impediment to fulfillment of their religious tenets would tend to coerce, compromise, or influence religious choice—and it is extremely doubtful that it could—the exemption was permissible under the Establishment Clause. In contrast, in *Sherbert v. Verner* we have seen that my proposal would prohibit the state from granting a religious exemption from the "suitable work" requirement. Therefore, only by abandoning this requirement for *all* claimants as applied to Saturdays (or a day of the claimant's choice) could the state have satisfied Mrs. Sherbert's free exercise claim without running afoul of the Establishment Clause. Under the appropriate Free Exercise Clause balancing test, it seems likely under these circumstances that the state's interest in maintaining its requirement intact would have prevailed.

---

110. 406 U.S. 205 (1972).

The draft exemption cases present a further problem. The Court has never held that the Free Exercise Clause requires an exemption for those who object to military service on religious grounds. Indeed, as recently as 1971 in *Gillette v. United States*[111]—holding that the Free Exercise Clause does not require excuse of those whose religious beliefs prohibit participation only in particular wars—the Court strongly suggested that "relief for conscientious objectors is not mandated by the Constitution."[112] The central question for our purposes, however, is whether, contrary to prevailing doctrine,[113] Congress may grant a religious exemption without violating the Establishment Clause.

First, the Court's efforts in *Gillette* to the contrary notwithstanding, an exemption for persons whose objection to military service is based on "religious training and belief" cannot be found to have other than a religious purpose. In *Gillette*, the Court contended that this exemption had a "neutral, secular basis"[114] grounded in "considerations of a pragmatic nature, such as the hopelessness of converting a sincere conscientious objector into an effective fighting man . . . ."[115] But if Congress' aim were simply to exclude those who were especially poor risks for military combat, then its making "religious belief" an absolute ground of incapacity was plainly both under- and over-inclusive. Rather, the Selective Service Act's specific limitation to religious objectors demonstrated on its face—as the Court conceded—Congress' "attempt to accommodate free exercise values"[116] and its "respect for the value of conscientious action and for the principle of supremacy of conscience."[117]

Second, we have already observed that religious exemptions from conscription impose substantial costs on nonbelieving draftees who must take the religious objector's place, but that these "nonreligious" social costs are not themselves enough to condemn the exemption under the Establishment Clause.[118] Nonetheless, they do serve as a warning signal that the advantage for religion may be so great as to impermissibly induce nonbelievers to profess

---

111. 401 U.S. 437 (1971).
112. *Id.* at 461 n.23.
113. *Id.* at 452 n.17.
114. *Id.* at 452.
115. *Id.* at 452-53.
116. *Id.* at 453.
117. *Id.*
118. *See* text following note 101 *supra*.

religious belief and ultimately undergo genuine conversions.

The Selective Service Law of 1917, which exempted from combat duty only those religious objectors who belonged to "well-recognized" religious sects,[119] strikingly posed the danger of influencing people to adopt particular religions. The more broadly worded exemption in effect during the Vietnam War era—applying to any person "who, by reason of religious training and belief, is conscientiously opposed to participation in war in any form"[120]—was significantly less likely to induce people to join established churches. In addition, the Court's expansive reading of that provision[121]—making it available "if an individual . . . holds beliefs that are purely ethical or moral in source and content but . . . nevertheless impose upon him a duty of conscience to refrain from participating in any war at any time"[122]—minimized that danger still further. Still, professing a personal "religion" (as opposed to "essentially political, sociological, or philosophical considerations")[123] was enough to gain the enormous advantage of avoiding combat duty, and therefore would likely influence religious choice. Indeed, since the government was authorized to examine the sincerity of a claimant's religious beliefs,[124] it seems that at least some claimants would be induced to join established churches to corroborate their claims.[125] Even if not, potential draftees seeking exemption would have to formulate a statement of personal doctrine that would pass muster. This endeavor would involve deep and careful thought, and perhaps reading in philosophy and religion. Some undoubtedly would be persuaded by what they read. Moreover, the theory of "cognitive dissonance"[126]—which posits that to avoid madness we tend to become what we hold ourselves to be and what others believe us to be—also suggests that some initially fraudulent claims of belief in a personal religion would develop into true belief. Thus, a draft exemption for reli-

---

119. Selective Service Law of 1917, ch. 15, § 4, 40 Stat. 78 (1917).
120. 50 U.S.C. § 456(j) (1976).
121. *See* Welsh v. United States, 398 U.S. 333 (1970); United States v. Seeger, 380 U.S. 163 (1965).
122. Welsh v. United States, 398 U.S. 333 (1970).
123. United States v. Seeger, 380 U.S. 163, 173 (1965).
124. *See* Welsh v. United States, 398 U.S. 333 (1970); United States v. Seeger, 380 U.S. 163 (1965). *See also* United States v. Ballard, 322 U.S. 78 (1944).
125. *See* note 109 *supra*.
126. *See generally* L. FESTINGER, A THEORY OF COGNITIVE DISSONANCE (1957); Festinger & Carlsmith, *Cognitive Consequences of Forced Compliance*, 58 J. ABNORM. SOC. PSYCH. 203 (1959).

gious objectors threatens values of religious freedom by encouraging the adoption of religious beliefs by those who seek to qualify for the benefit.

Finally, in contrast to draft exemption, recall the case of the non-Sabbatarian merchant who coveted the Sabbatarian exemption from the Sunday closing law because he felt that it was more profitable to be open on Sundays than on Saturdays.[127] Perhaps it is possible that some such non-Sabbatarian would be led to misrepresent his religious beliefs to obtain the exemption. But I believe that the intrinsic motivational difference between conscientious opposition to war and the comparatively crass desire to obtain pecuniary gain makes it extremely unlikely that the non-Sabbatarian's actual beliefs would be influenced in the process. Therefore, the Establishment Clause should not bar the accommodation for religion.

Conclusion

My proposal for resolving the conflict between the two Religion Clauses seeks to implement their historically and comtemporarily acknowledged common goal: to safeguard religious liberty. It surely does not produce ready answers for every case involving instances of government action whose purpose is to aid religion—either because such aid is claimed under the Free Exercise Clause, because the state wishes to avoid antagonizing or burdening religious groups, or simply because the state otherwise wishes to assist religion as a private means. The proposal requires that a number of delicate, factual judgments be made—and some that I have advanced herein may well be subject to dispute. Nor have I attempted to set forth criteria for determining when an advantage to religion is so great as to impermissibly influence religious choice: that is left for case-by-case adjudication on developed factual records leavened by common sense. I have urged, however, that the Establishment Clause forbids such influence if accompanied by government action for a religious purpose.

Although the proposal will invalidate some accommodations for religion, I do not believe that it improperly diminishes the religious freedom guaranteed by the Constitution. For it is only when an accommodation would jeopardize religious liberty—when it would coerce, compromise, or influence religious choice—that it

---

127. *See* text accompanying note 101 *supra*.

would fail. To subordinate the Establishment Clause in such circumstances would be to permit—or, indeed, sometimes require—government to implement one person's religious liberty at the expense of another's.

GUIDELINES FOR THE FREE EXERCISE CLAUSE

J. Morris Clark *

> *Since Sherbert v. Verner, which held the free exercise clause to protect religious practice as well as religious belief, no clear legal principles have evolved to define when practice is protected and when it can be regulated by the state. The author describes the disadvantages of the ad hoc balancing of interests made necessary by the absence of standards. He proposes that when a conscientious refusal to perform a positive duty is at issue, a strong presumption be applied that the state can satisfy its interest by some less burdensome means than criminal prohibition: either by imposing an alternative burden on the objector or by performing the act for him, or both. Positive acts should also be specially privileged, the author says, when they are believed by the actor to be inexcusable moral duties and when they do not interfere with nonparticipants.*

IN 1878 the Supreme Court, in its first pronouncement on the free exercise clause of the first amendment, voiced the proposition that although laws "cannot interfere with mere religious belief and opinions, they may with practices."[1] The case itself, *Reynolds v. United States*,[2] involved polygamy, and no very sweeping assertion of governmental power would have been necessary to condemn a practice considered so particularly egregious in that day. Nonetheless, Chief Justice Waite bolstered his obiter with historical quotation from Thomas Jefferson's address to the Danbury Baptists, to the effect that man "has no natural right in opposition to his social duties."[3] Although both these quotations left open the possibility that some actions lay beyond the pale of regulation, the Court's failure to state the existence of any limitation on legislative power suggested that the scope of free exercise was circumscribed by the boundary between belief and act so long as a secular purpose for regulation existed.

Historically it is by no means certain that all or even most of the men who voted for the first amendment believed that government could exercise full control over the actions of religious men.[4] Several participants in the debate on the Bill of Rights urged that a conscientious refusal to serve in the militia should

---

* Member of the Massachusetts Bar. B.A., Yale, 1966; J.D., Harvard, 1969.
[1] Reynolds v. United States, 98 U.S. 145, 166 (1878).
[2] 98 U.S. 145 (1878).
[3] *Id.* at 164.
[4] *See* Freeman, *A Remonstrance for Conscience*, 106 U. PA. L. REV. 806, 808-13 (1958).

go unpunished,[5] and although a stipulation to this effect disappeared from the amendments,[6] the reasons for its demise are uncertain. It may be of course that no majority view existed concerning the boundaries of the free exercise clause at the time of its enactment,[7] and indeed Jefferson's assertion that natural rights do not conflict with social duties need amount to no more than a tautology.

Whether or not supported by history, however, the notion that freedom of religion encompasses only belief and not action has the merits of simplicity and relative ease of application. A plenary governmental power to regulate action was again implied in dictum by the Supreme Court during the 1930's when Mr. Justice Sutherland asserted that there existed no constitutional right of conscientious objection to armed service, stating that "unqualified allegiance to the Nation and submission and obedience to the laws of the land, as well those made for war as those made for peace, are not inconsistent with the will of God."[8] More explicitly, at least two academic commentators have cited the distinction between belief and action as basic to the courts' treatment of the establishment and the free exercise clauses.[9]

In the 1963 case of *Sherbert v. Verner*,[10] however, the Supreme Court rejected this simple dichotomy. Mrs. Sherbert, a Seventh-day Adventist, was denied unemployment compensation because she was unwilling for religious reasons to take jobs which would require her to work on Saturday. Writing for the majority, Mr. Justice Brennan stated that "[i]t is basic that no showing merely of a rational relationship to some colorable state interest would suffice [to justify the denial]; in this highly sensitive constitutional area, '[o]nly the gravest abuses, endangering paramount interests, give occasion for permissible limitation . . . .'"[11] Since the state had failed to show that the fund available for unemployment compensation could not be safeguarded if Sabbatarians were permitted to refuse Saturday work, the plaintiff prevailed.

---

[5] *See* 1 ANNALS OF CONG. 750–51 (1834) (remarks of Messrs. Sherman, Vining, and Stone); Freeman, *supra* note 4, at 812–13.

[6] The sixth amendment as originally passed by the House provided that "no person religiously scrupulous shall be compelled to bear arms in person." 1 ANNALS OF CONG. 766–67 (1834). This clause disappeared from the amendment in the Senate, whose debates were not reported.

[7] *See* Mansfield, *Conscientious Objection — 1964 Term*, in 1965 RELIGION AND THE PUBLIC ORDER 3, 59–60.

[8] United States v. Macintosh, 283 U.S. 605, 625 (1931).

[9] P. KURLAND, RELIGION AND THE LAW 22 (1962); Weiss, *Privilege, Posture and Protection: "Religion" in the Law*, 73 YALE L.J. 593, 608 (1964).

[10] 374 U.S. 398 (1963).

[11] *Id.* at 406, quoting Thomas v. Collins, 323 U.S. 516, 530 (1945).

In common sense terms the *Sherbert* decision seems correct enough. The consequences to the petitioner of the denial amounted to the complete loss of a living allowance, whereas the state's interest was minimal. Moreover, her action was compelled by an unquestionably sincere religious belief. Yet by its holding that some religious practices are protected even from laws not intended to affect the communicative aspects of belief, *Sherbert* introduced a new range of complexity into the free exercise clause. For the first time the Court had affirmed a duty to weigh the damage to an individual's freedom of conscience against the harm to the state's legislative scheme. Few commentators subsequent to *Sherbert* have doubted the need of the law to strike some balance between the two. Yet only one appears to have realized the difficulty, even the impropriety in terms of judicial process, of administering an ad hoc balancing test, of rendering decisions without some set of guidelines to import predictability and coherence into a series of constitutional cases.[12]

This article explores in detail the problems involved in ad hoc balancing and the many factors to be balanced. It then proposes the resolution of these factors into a set of administrable guidelines.

I. The Balancing Test and the Role of Courts

A. The Nature of Ad Hoc Judgments

Professor Giannella has stated the components of the free exercise balancing test he advocates as follows:[13]

> A thoroughgoing balancing test would measure three elements of the competing governmental interest: first, the importance of the secular value underlying the governmental regulation; second, the degree of proximity and necessity that the chosen regulatory means bears to the underlying value; and third, the impact that an exemption for religious reasons would have on the overall regulatory program. This assessment of the state's interest would then have to be balanced against the claim for religious liberty, which would require calculation of two factors: first, the sincerity and importance of the religious practice for which special protection is claimed; and second, the degree to which the governmental regulation interferes with that practice.

---

[12] Dodge, *The Free Exercise of Religion: A Sociological Approach*, 67 Mich. L. Rev. 679, 681–87 (1969).

[13] Giannella, *Religious Liberty, Nonestablishment, and Doctrinal Development: Part I. The Religious Liberty Guarantee*, 80 Harv. L. Rev. 1381, 1390 (1967). For a discussion of the difficulties inherent in ad hoc balancing, see Fried, *Two Concepts of Interests: Some Reflections on the Supreme Court's Balancing Test*, 76 Harv. L. Rev. 755, 758 (1963).

This statement of a balancing test will serve as a working illustration of the problems entailed by any process of ad hoc balancing in first amendment cases. One caveat should be noted at the beginning of this discussion. Nearly all hard constitutional decisions require a balancing of interests in some sense; even where the case turns on the meaning of bright-line principles the Court must engage in a process of evaluating and comparing the interests involved, a process justified ultimately only by the constitutional role given the Court by *Marbury v. Madison*.[14] Consequently the following criticisms of ad hoc balancing do not pretend to uncover problems with which courts by their nature cannot deal, but rather problems which it would be desirable to avoid by more refined rules of law if any can be established.

The first of these problems lies in the formlessness of any ad hoc balancing test, whether in the free exercise clause or elsewhere. As Professor Emerson has stated, "it frames the issues in such a broad and undefined way, is in effect so unstructured, that it can hardly be described as a rule of law at all."[15] The consequence of a lack of specific rules is not only to deprive individuals and prosecutors of an advance notion of their respective powers, but also to deprive the lower courts of guidance and the Supreme Court itself of the legitimacy normally conferred by reasoned decision.[16] Courts are compelled to invest great amounts of time in the compilation and evaluation of records reflecting individual and governmental needs in each case.[17] Finally, in an effort to avoid the inevitable appearance of arbitrary decision, the courts may too often defer to the legislature's judgment.[18]

In addition to these serious general problems, the particular interests involved in free exercise cases are subject to change from one area, time, or individual to the next, so that the uncertainties produced by an ad hoc test are particularly great. An elucidation of this problem requires a more specific look at the interests involved.

B. *The Governmental Interest*

The first element of the test quoted above is the "importance of the secular value underlying the governmental regulation." The purpose of almost any law can be traced back to one or another of

---

[14] 5 U.S. (1 Cranch) 137 (1803).
[15] T. EMERSON, TOWARD A GENERAL THEORY OF THE FIRST AMENDMENT 54 (1963).
[16] *Id.* at 54–56.
[17] *Id.* at 55.
[18] *Id.*

the fundamental concerns of government: public health and safety, public peace and order, defense, revenue. To measure an individual interest directly against one of these rarified values inevitably makes the individual interest appear the less significant. In order to avoid this pitfall the courts must look not at such highly generalized secular values but at the more particular values served by the chosen regulation.

There may be some few cases where no value of reasonable importance is served by a law. The requirement that all men of draft age carry registration cards and notices of classification has been attacked as one such instance.[19] Laws which bear no reasonable relation to the fulfillment of a secular goal generally violate the due process clause alone,[20] and can be disposed of without inquiry into problems of free exercise. However, the great majority of laws challenged on grounds of free exercise are not arbitrary. Surely this assertion applies to conscription, laws against polygamy, the requirement of jury service, and nearly all other laws challenged by religious objectors.

If a law is found to be reasonable, then the question of its importance is raised. The importance of a law should be measured not by all the benefits it confers on society, but by the incremental benefit of applying it to those with religious scruples. Its importance, in other words, should be the cost of resorting to a nonrestrictive or less restrictive alternative by exempting from the law's coverage those conscientiously opposed to the law.[21] Regulating conduct in some way other than the legislature has chosen usually involves some degree of cost, at least potentially, to the efficiency of any regulatory scheme. It is safer to bar all Communists from defense plants than only those who can be shown to have subversive motives; [22] easier to require all leaflets to carry the name of their sponsors than to seek out the sponsorship of fraudulent or libelous ones already distributed; [23] cheaper to run an unemployment compensation system requiring all workers to take Saturday work than allowing some to refuse it.[24] There have been only a few first amendment cases where the Court

---

[19] *See* 81 HARV. L. REV. 1347, 1349, 1351 (1968); p. 359 *infra*.

[20] *Cf.* Shelton v. Tucker, 364 U.S. 479 (1960); Bates v. City of Little Rock, 361 U.S. 516 (1960); NAACP v. Alabama *ex rel.* Patterson, 357 U.S. 449 (1958).

[21] *See* Braunfeld v. Brown, 366 U.S. 599, 607 (1961) ("[I]f the State regulates conduct by enacting a general law within its power, the purpose and effect of which is to advance the State's secular goals, the statute is valid despite its indirect burden on religious observance unless the State may accomplish its purpose by means which do not impose such a burden.").

[22] *Cf.* United States v. Robel, 389 U.S. 258 (1967).

[23] *Cf.* Talley v. California, 362 U.S. 60 (1960).

[24] *Cf.* Sherbert v. Verner, 374 U.S. 398 (1963).

265

could say with confidence that the protection of individual freedoms did not reduce the efficiency of the regulatory program at all.[25] The highly intuitive evaluation of this governmental cost by a court, based on information which may be sparse or at least difficult to accumulate, contributes a great deal of the uncertainty which Emerson finds in all ad hoc balancing tests.

An additional element of uncertainty is added in free exercise cases by the fact that the cost to the government frequently depends on the number of persons who can lay claim to the exemption. Unlike free speech claims, for example, claims of religious freedom do not require the invalidation of a law as to all who oppose it, but merely as to those with sincere religious or conscientious scruples. A religious privilege to smoke marijuana might be workable if only a handful of persons in the United States could establish the requisite religious interest, but absent assurance of this the right probably does not exist.[26] Similarly, the number of persons who invoke the privilege of conscientious objection to war has been considered by commentators to be a highly important fact in estimating whether a constitutional right to such objection should exist.[27] In *Sherbert v. Verner* itself, the Court defined the governmental interest as that in assuring that enough money would be left in the unemployment fund to support claimants against it, and in assuring that employers would not be seriously inhibited in scheduling necessary Saturday work; [28] the possible number of claimants of the privilege figured centrally in the majority's discussion.[29] In a footnote to his dissent, Mr. Justice

---

[25] Shelton v. Tucker, 364 U.S. 479 (1960), may, however, constitute one example.

[26] The Supreme Court decided two other constitutional questions presented by Leary v. United States, 383 F.2d 851 (5th Cir. 1967), *rev'd*, 395 U.S. 6 (1969), but declined to hear the question of the first amendment right to use marijuana for religious purposes, decided adversely to defendant below. 392 U.S. 903 (1968) (grant of certiorari).

[27] *See, e.g.*, Macgill, *Selective Conscientious Objection: Divine Will and Legislative Grace*, 54 VA. L. REV. 1355, 1381-82 (1968); Mansfield, *supra* note 7, at 45-46; Note, *The Conscientious Objector and the First Amendment: There But for the Grace of God . . . .*, 34 U. CHI. L. REV. 79, 103-04 (1966).

[28] 374 U.S. 398, 407 (1963).

[29] The Court remarked first that, of the 150 or more Seventh-day Adventists in petitioner's locality, only she and one other had failed to find suitable employment which did not require Saturday work. Second, the Court observed that the religious beliefs in question did not make their holders into nonproductive members of society, since they could realistically hope to find work. Third, the Court dismissed the argument that deceitful or fraudulent claims would be encouraged by a religious exemption, on the grounds that no argument concerning this danger had been made in the state courts and that the record did not sustain the contention. Justice Brennan added that even absent these facts it would be "highly doubtful whether such evidence [of fraudulent claims] would be sufficient to warrant a substantial infringement of religious liberties." *Id.*

Harlan treated the assertion that a constitutional privilege could depend on the number of persons who invoke it with an air of incredulity, stating, "[S]urely this disclaimer cannot be taken seriously, for the Court cannot mean that the case would have come out differently if none of the Seventh-day Adventists in Spartanburg had been gainfully employed, or if the appellant's religion had prevented her from working on Tuesdays instead of Saturdays." [30]

The difficulties pointed out by Justice Harlan are certainly serious ones. First, to condition a constitutional right on the number of persons who claim it could mean, for example, that the right which exists in Spartanburg, South Carolina, does not exist in a community with a large worker population of orthodox Jews or Seventh-day Adventists. In addition to the possibility of geographical discrimination, there exists the possibility that changes in the Sabbatarian population of a given locality will result in time in the nullification of a previously declared constitutional privilege.[31]

A second problem lies in the fact that courts are ill equipped to judge what exact number of conscientious objectors to a given law should tip the balance. Not only would any particular number chosen be arbitrary, but the permissible number of objectors might have to be made to vary according to the needs of the state at any particular moment. Such a defeasible immunity is suggested in the recent case of *United States v. Sisson*,[32] in

---

In his dissent, Justice Harlan responded to the majority's observation that the objectors remained productive by stating, "[n]or can the Court be suggesting that it will make a value judgment in each case as to whether a particular individual's religious convictions prevent him from being 'productive.' I can think of no more inappropriate function for this Court to perform." *Id.* at 420-21 n.2. In fairness to the majority, the reference to productivity should probably be read to mean that the state need not extend the basic purpose of its program, namely the compensation of members of the work force between jobs, to encompass persons whose religion prevents them from working at all. As discussed below, such limitations upon the grant of positive benefits should generally be permissible. *See* pp. 360-61 *infra*.

[30] 374 U.S. at 420-21 n.2.

[31] In *In re* Jenison, 375 U.S. 14 (per curiam), *vacating* 265 Minn. 96, 120 N.W.2d 515 (1963), the Supreme Court remanded for reconsideration in light of *Sherbert* the conviction of a woman who had refused jury duty for religious reasons. The Minnesota Supreme Court reversed itself, stating without elaboration the conclusion that harm to the state's interest in obtaining competent jurors had not been adequately demonstrated, and creating a constitutional right "until and unless further experience indicates that the indiscriminate invoking of the First Amendment poses a serious threat to the effective functioning of our jury system . . . ." 267 Minn. 136, 137, 125 N.W.2d 588, 589 (1963).

[32] 297 F. Supp. 902 (D. Mass. 1969), *jurisdictional decision postponed until hearing on merits*, 38 U.S.L.W. 3127 (U.S. Oct. 13, 1969) (No. 305). A case note on *Sisson* can be found on page 453 of this issue.

which Judge Wyzanski, for the district court, held that a conscientious objector had a constitutional right to an exemption from conscription for combat, but indicated that this right might not exist during a war involving defense of the homeland. However, any estimation of how large or close to home a war has to be to constitute a defense of the homeland would be extremely difficult for courts to make.

It has been suggested that should courts estimate that the national interest can tolerate an exemption to a given law and later have to reverse this decision, the legislature could respond by establishing a quota of objectors who may enjoy the exemption and then select that number by lot. This method has been urged for exemptions to the draft.[33] However, any such judicially established figure would suffer from arbitrariness.

Another possible solution to the problem of judging numbers is for courts to defer to legislative judgments modifying judicial pronouncements. Under this approach, legislatures could revoke any judicially created exemption to a statute. Legislatures have better capacities for fact finding than do courts, and are better equipped because of their electoral responsibility to draw arbitrary lines to settle questions of degree. Ultimate legislative authority would not render the initial judicial determination useless, for it would at least force the legislature to consider the issue specifically before denying an exemption to conscientious objectors. Legislative inertia might in many cases preserve the courts' initial judgments. On the other hand, judicial deference of this sort would give the legislature power to eliminate a personal right entirely, and freedom of religion is an area where majoritarian rule may be highly dangerous to unpopular or misunderstood minorities. The Court has stated at least once that congressional power to modify judicial interpretations of the Constitution cannot serve to narrow the scope of individual liberties declared by the Court previously.[34]

The above criticisms are mitigated to some extent by the fact that an estimation of the governmental interest does not entail calculating the number of probable objectors in every case. Some actions, such as polygamy, ritual human sacrifice, or the sacramental ingestion of LSD may in the eyes of the Court represent such dangers to the immediate participants that the practice cannot be tolerated regardless of numbers. Also, there are some cases where any exemption at all may defeat the governmental

---

[33] *See* Mansfield, *supra* note 7, at 73.
[34] Katzenbach v. Morgan, 384 U.S. 641, 651 n.10 (1966). *But see* Cox, *The Supreme Court, 1965 Term — Foreword: Constitutional Adjudication and the Promotion of Human Rights*, 80 HARV. L. REV. 91, 106 n.86 (1966).

purpose in a different way, as the conduct of business on Sunday by Sabbatarian merchants was held to defeat the state's interest in obtaining a day of entire public peace and quiet.[35]

In addition to the difficulty of estimating numbers of objectors and evaluating these numbers in terms of state needs, there remain two other variables which may affect the courts' estimation of the governmental interest. One is the difficulty of distinguishing truly religious objectors from those making false claims. Justice Brennan was able to minimize this problem in *Sherbert*, since Sabbatarianism is usually associated with other well defined religious beliefs and practices. In different contexts, however, the problem may prove more compelling. In *United States v. Leary*, the Fifth Circuit expressed concern that the religious use of marijuana by some individuals would give rise to fraudulent claims of privilege or greater ease of access to the drug by those not using it for religious purposes:[36]

> It would be difficult to imagine the harm which would result if the criminal statutes against marihuana were nullified as to those who claim the right to possess and traffic in this drug for religious purposes. For all practical purposes the anti-marihuana laws would be meaningless, and enforcement impossible. The danger is too great, especially to the youth of the nation, at a time when psychedelic experience, "turn on," is the "in" thing to so many, for this court to yield to the argument that the use of marihuana for so-called religious purposes should be permitted under the Free Exercise Clause.

In a number of areas where religious beliefs overlap with secular self-interest, and where the sincerity of religious belief may be harder to define than the sectarian belief in the sanctity of the Sabbath, the government may invoke both administrative difficulty and the broad possibility of error as legitimate factors militating against an exemption.

A final component in the computation of the government's interest in preventing exemptions concerns the practical power of the government to apply the law to objectors to whom it denies an exemption. In *Sherbert* enforcement amounted only to denial of financial benefits, and so lay entirely in the government's power. On the other hand, several thousand conscientious objectors to war have chosen to go to jail rather than enter the armed forces,[37] and many others would doubtless have followed

---

[35] Braunfeld v. Brown, 366 U.S. 599 (1961).
[36] 383 F.2d 851, 861 (5th Cir. 1967), *rev'd on other grounds*, 395 U.S. 6 (1969).
[37] White, *Processing Conscientious Objector Claims: A Constitutional Inquiry*, 56 CALIF. L. REV. 652, 674 (1968).

suit were it not for the traditional statutory exemption of many conscientious objectors to war.[38] The denial of an exemption might well result in greatly increased penal costs and personal bitterness, offset only by relatively small increases in armed services enrollment. In any event the degree of compliance a particular law will receive may be difficult to predict in advance if an exemption already exists.

C. The Religious or Conscientious Interest

1. The Policies Underlying the Free Exercise Clause. — The American concern for freedom of conscience arises in part from the extreme importance of religious principle in American history. Many Americans tend to believe that any scruple which is truly and genuinely religious probably cannot be very harmful to society at large. Perhaps as a generalization from this belief, as well as from a heritage of rugged individualism, most Americans also feel sympathy for the proposition that the theist's highest duty is to serve God and that the rationalist has reserved from the social contract the right to make and follow his own deductions concerning the fundamental meaning of life. However, these common prejudices of our culture do little to explain what individual acts the state can and cannot afford to tolerate.

To some extent the justifications for religious freedom duplicate those for freedom of speech. On several occasions the two interests have been conjoined in Supreme Court litigation,[39] and it appears that at least during the 'forties the Court attempted to identify the two, perhaps in an effort to show that the state did not place orthodox religious belief in a more favored position than any other persuasion.[40] However, any such identification of interests makes the free exercise clause redundant in light of the freedoms of speech and assembly. Nor can free speech justifications explain the right to refrain from Saturday work, as in *Sherbert*, or from jury duty, as in *In re Jenison*,[41] since the symbolic qualities of such acts are minimal and the believer's motivation is not primarily one of communication.

---

[38] Total pacifists, those who object to all war, are exempted from military service by 50 U.S.C. app. § 456(j) (1964). For the history of this exemption, see 1 SELECTIVE SERVICE SYSTEM, SPECIAL MONO. NO. 11, CONSCIENTIOUS OBJECTION 29–90 (1950).

[39] *See, e.g.,* West Virginia Bd. of Educ. v. Barnette, 319 U.S. 624 (1943); Murdock v. Pennsylvania, 319 U.S. 105 (1943); Cantwell v. Connecticut, 310 U.S. 296 (1940).

[40] *See* M. HOWE, THE GARDEN AND THE WILDERNESS 91–118 (1965).

[41] 375 U.S. 14 (per curiam), *vacating* 265 Minn. 96, 120 N.W.2d 515 (1963). *Jenison* is described in note 31 *supra*.

A second justification for free exercise therefore looks beyond its value as speech and suggests that religious or conscientious values frequently represent an idealism which serves a valuable function in society even though the idealist's conclusions may be rejected. Exemption of conscientious objectors to war, for example, may be tolerated as a valuable reminder to the nation that war is undesirable and that evil should be returned with good.[42] This theory does reflect one of the values protected by the free exercise clause, but it does not provide much guidance for judicial decisions. Unless a court is to assume the religious value of all religious practices, which surely is unlikely in the case of polygamy, for example, it must develop a sort of "rudimentary natural theology" to determine which deviant religious practices should be permitted to leaven national life and which should not. By implication the courts would also be forced to distinguish on moral grounds among the statutes which objectors challenged. Although Professor Giannella has defended this concept of a natural theology for courts,[43] it seems hard to formulate and harder still to defend. Why opposition to national defense should be judged valuable whereas drug-induced expansion of consciousness should not, for example, is far from clear. Indeed, opposition to Saturday work or jury service would seem so idiosyncratic in the light of a judicially developed natural theology that it could not qualify for an exemption. These difficulties could be avoided only by assigning all beliefs the same value.

A far more important interest protected by the free exercise clause relates to fairness to the individual. The violation of a man's religion or conscience often works an exceptional harm to him which, unless justified by the most stringent social needs, constitutes a moral wrong in and of itself, far more than would the impairment of his freedoms of speech, press or assembly. The argument is not merely that avoiding compulsion of a man's conscience produces the greatest good for the greatest number, but that such compulsion is itself unfair to the individual concerned. The moral condemnation implicit in the threat of criminal sanctions is likely to be very painful to one motivated by belief. Furthermore, the cost to a principled individual of failing to do his moral duty is generally severe, in terms of supernatural sanction or the loss of moral self-respect. In the face of these costs, the individual's refusal to obey the law may be inevitable, and therefore in some perhaps unusual sense of the word, involuntary.

---

[42] Mansfield, *supra* note 7, at 41.
[43] Giannella, *supra* note 13, at 1386, 1430-31.

An examination of the nature of conscientious compulsion, however, also demonstrates the difficulty of measuring the strength of conscience in particular cases.

The emotional sources and the strength of conscientious commitment to a principle vary from one individual to the next, and in the case of one individual, from one principle to the next.[44] Some principles held even by a conscientious individual are held lightly, either because the harm which attaches to violation of the principle is minimal, or because the individual is not thoroughly convinced of the correctness of the principle, or both. Many churches, like most political groups, have memberships whose dedication ranges from near-fanatical to insouciant. Moreover, men's consciences vary in strength. Some individuals as a matter of course transgress important principles which they profess to believe to be true; other men habitually stand firm even over matters of minute practical importance. To coerce a man's conscience on a principle which he holds lightly, or to coerce a man who holds all his principles at the mercy of expedience, does no great harm; the punishment of a man who has acted because he strongly believed in the necessity of his act places him in a very sore quandary.

However, the difficulty of distinguishing those who are conscientious from those who are not cannot obviate the necessity of doing so, assuming, as this article does, that fairness to the conscientious individual is a major purpose of the free exercise clause. A summary follows of the two primary bases of distinction which commentators and courts have suggested, although a complete review of the legal literature on the meaning of religion [45] transcends the purpose of this article.

---

[44] In a World War II study of conscientious objectors to war, the following observations were made:
> (a) No single factor could account for the conscientious objection of all the men .... There were wide variations within the categories of family, morals, personality, and religion. No single consequential emotion was found in all cases. [The objectors] present the usual differences which may be expected in young American manhood. (b) It was found that emotional factors do account for conscientious objection to war. Social pressures, ideologies, *et cetera* were influential in the pacifist decision only as they were weighted by emotions related to value-goals. (c) These emotions may be divided into positive and negative affects. The negative ones were found in these cases to be feelings of inferiority, guilt feelings and anxiety, feelings of insecurity, fear to condemn, over-dependence, and indignation. The positive emotions were loyalty to religious ideals, compassion, love, desire for justice, and willingness to stand alone. These emotional factors, attached to moral values, were highly influential.

Kelley & Johnson, *Emotional Traits in Pacifists*, 28 J. Soc. Psych. 275, 285 (1948).

[45] *See, e.g.*, Clancy & Weiss, *The Conscientious Objector Exemption: Problems in Conceptual Clarity and Constitutional Considerations*, 17 Me. L. Rev. 143, 160 (1965); Mansfield, *supra* note 7, at 33-34; Potter, *Conscientious Objection to Particular Wars*, 1968 Religion and the Public Order 44; Note, *supra* note 27.

2. *Approaches to the Definition of the Protected Religious or Conscientious Interest.* — Some commentators have attempted to define religious or conscientious belief in terms of subject matter rather than attempting a psychological analysis of a belief's place in the life of the believer. Professor Mansfield, for example, would define the kind of belief protected by the free exercise clause as [46]

> the affirmation of some truth, reality, or value. . . . [which] addresses itself to the basic questions to which man has always sought an answer, questions about the meaning of human existence, the origin of being, the meaning of suffering and death, and the existence of a spiritual reality.

Professor Mansfield asserts that the fundamental quality of belief can be separated from the psychological role which it plays in the life of the believer and argues that the former rather than the latter criterion should be used by the law.

A test based upon the type of belief claimed does have certain attractions. Whereas a judgment concerning the psychological role that a belief plays requires a difficult and intuitive factual determination in each case, as discussed below, a judgment concerning the subject matter of belief is capable of being generalized in legal rules. But probably no limited subject-matter definition can be framed to include all beliefs involving interests protected by the free exercise clause — that is, all beliefs involving strong conscientious compulsions. Professor Mansfield's definition succeeds only by being so general as to include nearly all belief whatsoever. Nearly all belief about right and wrong does deal with "basic questions to which man has always sought an answer" simply because any man who attempts to justify his action as right must relate it at some point in his thinking to some basic postulate concerning human life. Since for most people these basic postulates do concern the questions Professor Mansfield lists — the meaning of existence, of suffering and death, spiritual reality — Professor Mansfield's definition covers almost any certain belief that an action is "right." Furthermore, his definition does not provide a basis for defining the weight of a conscientious claim. It is a commonplace, of course, that traditional religious beliefs have justified behavior ranging from thoroughgoing pacifism to religious wars. Similarly, nontheistic conscientious belief may include a great range of attitudes. Beliefs on subjects normally considered political in nature are conscientious when held earnestly and deeply; for example, it is by no

---

[46] Mansfield, *supra* note 7, at 10.

means inconceivable that beliefs concerning race could be elevated to the level of moral persuasion.[47]

In sum, to attempt definition of a conscientious belief by reference only to its subject matter is to encounter those linguistic complexities which provide grist for moral philosophers. A brief excursion into some of the best of recent works in this highly erudite field [48] should convince the lawyer that for his own purposes such terms as "right," "moral," or "conscientious," are incapable of simple yet more precise definition.

One recent article has attempted to impose a narrower definition, arguing that only adherents of organized religions, sociologically identifiable as such, should be permitted to claim religious privileges.[49] But serious problems of arbitrariness would be raised by such a definition. If one accepts that the principal interest protected by the free exercise clause is the individual's interest in not being forced to violate the compelling requirements of conscience, then one must agree that the man who chooses to worship only at home may have very strong protected interests. The anomaly of a contrary result would be particularly striking where the religion was a humanistic one which emphasized individual ethics rather than group worship or even group membership. A man could easily hold identical beliefs with similar intensity without joining such a group. All this is not to say, of course, that church membership may not sometimes be evidence of sincerity.

A third approach to the definition of religious belief is that of psychological analysis. The two leading cases on the meaning of religion at present, *United States v. Seeger* [50] and the recent district court decision in *United States v. Sisson*,[51] suggest this interpretation.

In *Seeger* the Supreme Court avoided a direct interpretation of the Constitution by construing the statutory exemption of

---

[47] For example, in Clark v. Gabriel, 393 U.S. 256, 261 (1968), a black draft registrant claimed that because "the United States Government has willfully let the Negro be deprived of his rights . . . the debt of forced service claimed arbitrarily from all eligible men for the purpose of fighting for the United States rights is in the Negroes' case void." The Supreme Court considered only whether judicial review of such a case could be obtained under the principles of Oestereich v. Selective Service Bd., 393 U.S. 233 (1968), and did not pass on the merits of the claim. However, it is at least arguable that certiorari would not have been granted absent a colorable claim of statutory conscientious objection.

[48] *See* R. HARE, THE LANGUAGE OF MORALS (1952); P. NOWELL-SMITH, ETHICS (1954). *See generally* M. WARNOCK, ETHICS SINCE 1900 (2d ed. 1966).

[49] Dodge, *supra* note 12.

[50] 380 U.S. 163 (1965).

[51] 297 F. Supp. 902 (D. Mass. 1969), *jurisdictional decision postponed until hearing on the merits*, 38 U.S.L.W. 3127 (U.S. Oct. 13, 1969) (No. 305).

those opposed to all war "by reason of religious training and belief" [52] to include the humanistic beliefs of Seeger and his co-appellants. *Seeger* thus carries the implication that the broad definition was necessary to avoid a construction of the statute which would make it constitute an establishment of religion and, perhaps, a violation of free exercise.[53] As a practical matter, broad treatment of the the concept of religion has much to recommend it. Any attempt to define religion so as to include only theistic beliefs would mock common usage by excluding many Unitarians, Buddhists, and other persons normally thought of as religious. Furthermore, the gradations between the more "orthodox" religions and humanism are so infinitesimal and theologically complex that courts cannot safely attempt to draw distinctions among them. Finally, any attempt to distinguish religious from other beliefs without some convincing secular rationale justifying different treatment might constitute an establishment of religion.[54]

To admit that religion may include humanistic beliefs, however, does little to determine the difference between religious and secular persuasions. In making this distinction the *Seeger* court eschewed direct definition of religious belief and resorted instead to psychological analogy: the test of religiosity is "whether a given belief that is sincere and meaningful occupies a place in the life of its possessor parallel to that filled by the orthodox belief in God of one who clearly qualifies for the exemption." [55] The Court distinguished individuals holding such beliefs from "those persons who, disavowing religious belief, decide on the basis of essentially political, sociological or economic considerations that war is wrong and that they will have no part of it." [56]

A psychological analysis was also implied in *United States v. Sisson* [57] in which a district court held that the *Seeger* statutory construction failed to exempt a defendant who did not describe his conscientious belief as religious, and that therefore the relevant clause of the Selective Service Act was unconstitutional in its limitation to religious believers. Judge Wyzanski, for the court, described the beneficiaries of his opinion as those "motivated in their objection to the draft by profound moral beliefs which constitute the central convictions of their beings." [58] The court observed that "[w]hat another derives from the discipline of a

---

[52] 50 U.S.C. app. § 456(j) (1964).
[53] *The Supreme Court, 1964 Term*, 79 HARV. L. REV. 56, 115–16 (1965).
[54] *See* Clancy & Weiss, *supra* note 45, at 160.
[55] 380 U.S. at 166.
[56] *Id.* at 173.
[57] 297 F. Supp. 902 (D. Mass. 1969), *jurisdictional decision postponed until hearing on the merits*, 38 U.S.L.W. 3127 (U.S. Oct. 13, 1969) (No. 305).
[58] *Id.* at 911.

church, Sisson derives from the discipline of conscience. . . . He was as genuinely and profoundly governed by his conscience as would have been a martyr obedient to an orthodox religion." [59] Since the most important interest protected by the free exercise clause is the prevention of the severe psychic turmoil that can be brought about by compelled violations of conscience, a psychological definition of religious belief seems appropriate.

It seems likely, however, that no psychological analysis can provide the basis for a legal definition excluding any class of conscientious beliefs from protection.[60] Psychological theories as to the origins and functions of religious and conscientious belief differ widely from one school of analysis to another. Most schools would agree that no distinction between theistic and nontheistic belief can be justified by any consistently recurring difference between the mental roles these two types of belief play.[61] Psychoanalytically oriented psychologists, for example, explain both kinds of conscientious beliefs as related to the development of the superego. A child is said to identify with and copy certain attributes of his parents,[62] forming a "separate subsystem of the personality which reacts to the subject's behavior in the same way as the parent did." [63] This development is seen as the source of the urge in later life to respond to moral authority or to the authority of God.[64]

It is not clear, however, that psychoanalysts are prepared to

---

[59] *Id.* at 905.

[60] *See* Goldstein, *Psychoanalysis and Jurisprudence*, 77 YALE L.J. 1053, 1068–69 (1968); Stone, *Psychoanalysis and Jurisprudence Revisited*, in MORAL VALUES AND SUPEREGO DEVELOPMENT: A PSYCHOANALYTIC STUDY (S. Post ed., to be published).

[61] Conversation with Alan A. Stone, M.D., Assistant Professor in Psychiatry, Harvard Medical School; Lecturer in Psychiatry, Harvard Law School, at Harvard Law School, Oct. 22, 1969.

[62] Argyle, *Introjection: A Form of Social Learning*, 55 BR. J. PSYCHOL. 391 (1964).

[63] *Id.*; *see* S. FREUD, THE EGO AND THE ID 27 (Norton ed. 1961).

[64] S. FREUD, THE FUTURE OF AN ILLUSION 42 (1928). Psychoanalytic psychologists have emphasized the further changes in the superego during adolescence, when belief is likely to be more strongly influenced by group identification and by the individual's conscious thought. *See, e.g.,* Jacobson, *Adolescent Moods and the Remodeling of Psychic Structures in Adolescence*, 16 PSYCHOANALYTIC STUDY OF THE CHILD 164, 172, 174–75 (1961). Since these later developments are not so intimately associated with childhood sources of moral authority, they might be considered less compelling. However, this is clearly not always the case; compelling belief could be based on an adulthood conversion. Consequently religious belief could not fairly be limited to beliefs developed in childhood. It should also be emphasized that conscientious compulsion need not be related to the concepts of sin and guilt attendant upon western religions and philosophies. The Buddhist's dedication to a life of meditation, for example, should be treated as conscientious even though it may be compelled by a belief in the importance of achieving spiritual harmony rather than by guilt or fear of divine retribution.

state that all the strongly-held beliefs of persons with strong superegos should be considered religious. Nor, perhaps, are psychoanalysts prepared to describe to a jury whether a particular person's superego compels even his conventionally religious beliefs with sufficient strength that they should be granted first amendment protection.

The task of determining whether an individual acted according to principle or narrow self-interest is therefore a most difficult one for psychoanalysts where the two coincide. Any attempt to identify a dominant motive where two or more coexist is a complex psychological task, and even the individual may not be completely certain of his reasons. Psychoanalysts may also find such questions of motivation difficult, and the number of persons expert in psychology and available to administrative bodies is small.[65] Even if the question of motivation can be put aside by exempting from a law all those who sincerely hold a belief at all, the determination of sincerity in individual cases will frequently be arbitrary. It may often be necessary to assume, as does the Selective Service in judging claims of conscientious objection to war, that a history of subscription to a given belief means that actions related to it are motivated by principle.[66] Where no such evidence exists, one may assume that a person who consistently acts according to principle is conscientiously motivated even regarding a principle which he has only recently adopted.[67]

When the objector is a member of a traditional religion, it may in some cases be possible to determine the strength of his belief by the relationship it bears to the theology as a whole. Some sins are venial, others mortal.[68] But the difficulty of pronouncing judicially upon matters of theological complexity must be emphasized: as one recent Note has aptly observed, "where an act is ritualistic and the government contests its centrality to the particular religion the courts must act as the final arbiter in questions of religious doctrine — questions more appropriately decided by prelates than by judges."[69] The desire to avoid making theological distinctions has moved the Supreme Court to for-

---

[65] Conversation with Alan A. Stone, M.D., Assistant Professor of Psychiatry, Harvard Medical School; Lecturer in Psychiatry, Harvard Law School, at Harvard Law School, Mar. 18, 1969.

[66] *Cf.* Smith & Bell, *The Conscientious-Objector Program — A Search for Sincerity*, 19 U. PITT. L. REV. 695, 719-25 (1958).

[67] Conversation with Alan A. Stone, *supra* note 65.

[68] The possibility of making distinctions according to religious doctrine is discussed at pp. 362-63 *infra*.

[69] Note, *Free Exercise: Religion Goes to "Pot,"* 56 CALIF. L. REV. 100, 112 (1968).

bid judicial decisions on disputes of dogma in church property ownership disputes.[70]

These difficulties with the psychological test cannot be minimized. However, it is difficult to see how the central purpose of avoiding conscientious compulsion can be served other than by inquiring in individual cases, through a jury or other finder of fact, whether a man's conscience will be violated — whether his belief plays the same role in his life as does the sincere orthodox believer's faith in a theistic God.[71] That this judgment must be largely intuitive, and therefore more or less arbitrary, aided only in part by the science of psychology, is regrettable but true.

In conclusion then, it is submitted that the interest to be weighed on the individual's side of the balance in free exercise cases is always the same in kind, that is, the interest in avoiding punishment of an act which is compelled by conscience. However, the degree to which this interest exists — that is, the intensity of the compulsion — can be evaluated only as a factual matter in individual cases, not as a matter of law based on the kind of belief at issue. Consequently, the law can measure only the weight of the governmental interest, and not the individual interest, in Professor Giannella's balancing test. The rest of this article is concerned with the formulation of guidelines to determine which governmental costs should override this individual interest and which should not.

II. Guidelines for Free Exercise

Before attempting to assign principles to the free exercise clause, one might ask preliminarily whether the formulation of guidelines would not be as arbitrary a process as the ad hoc decisionmaking discussed earlier. Admittedly the history of the enactment of the Bill of Rights divulges no scheme for the first amendment, even in embryo, and the reference to the right of conscience which Congress considered for some time before dropping seems equally vacant. Yet as the expounder of the Constitution, the Court has a responsibility for developing that document and assigning it a purpose even when policy rather than history must control. The establishment of constitutional principle permits the Court to operate in the realm of philosophy and removes the suspicion of partiality which highly particularistic decisions may entail. Principles need not emerge full blown in any given decision,

---

[70] Presbyterian Church in United States v. Mary Elizabeth Blue Hull Memorial Presbyterian Church, 393 U.S. 440 (1969); Watson v. Jones, 80 U.S. (13 Wall.) 679 (1872).

[71] *See* Seeger v. United States, 380 U.S. 163, 166 (1965).

of course; yet to the extent that they do emerge they permit the individuals affected to calculate their rights in advance and act with confidence accordingly.

The guidelines which this article advocates can be stated at the outset: when an individual because of compelling conscientious belief refuses to perform any duty of positive action established by the state, there exists a constitutional presumption that the state can satisfy its needs either by performing the act on his behalf or by placing upon him an alternative burden of equal weight, or both. Unless it can overcome this presumption, the state may not attempt to coerce his will by civil contempt or punish his refusal to act by criminal sanctions. If the state can overcome the presumption — that is, if it can show that it has no other way to satisfy its needs — then a balancing of interests must be resorted to. The state may enforce all its laws prohibiting positive actions, except that a similar presumption of privilege exists concerning those actions whose performance an individual's conscience deems an inexcusable duty and which involve directly only himself and other fully consenting persons.

Before explaining the rationale and application of these guidelines, a word should be said concerning the nature of the presumptions they involve.[72] Presumptions serve to maintain a measure of judicial flexibility which would be lost by the establishment of hard and fast rules of law. However, it is essential that a presumption in the free exercise area not serve to reinstate the ad hoc system of judgments which has been criticized above. The following discussion will attempt to point out those few situations in which the presumption may be overcome, and the majority of cases in which it should not be.

A. *The Privilege to Refuse to Act*

In *Reynolds v. United States*,[73] the 1878 polygamy case, Chief Justice Waite contrasted an offense of inaction with "a positive act which is knowingly done, [where] it would be dangerous to hold that the offender might escape punishment because he religiously believed the law which he had broken ought never to have been made."[74] At first blush this distinction between malfeasance and nonfeasance seems arbitrary or formalistic. However, practical considerations give meaning to the distinction.

To begin with, there are very few positive acts which the state

---

[72] The Supreme Court may have established a similar presumption against the constitutionality of statutes limiting voting rights in Kramer v. Union Free School Dist., 393 U.S. 818 (1969).

[73] 98 U.S. 145 (1879).

[74] *Id.* at 167.

compels by the threat of criminal penalties without according individuals alternative options. These duties of positive action consist of military service, jury duty, the payment of taxes, and a few others. Those laws which Professors Hart and Sacks call modal duties [75] are not involved: the government may still prevent a man from the positive act of engaging in the restaurant business if he refuses the duty of serving customers regardless of race. However, the relatively small class of positive duties is a very important one analytically, for these laws alone face the individual with the sole alternatives of acting in violation of conscience or risking criminal punishment.

The difference between action and inaction is often considered an important moral distinction. Inaction frequently represents an individual's compromise between violating his conscience and actively interfering with the right of others to act in ways which he disapproves. The claim in effect is that of the individual to separate himself from the state without interfering with those who wish to support it. Thoreau recognized the distinction in *On the Duty of Civil Disobedience*: [76]

> It is not a man's duty, as a matter of course, to devote himself to the eradication of any, even the most enormous wrong; he may still properly have other concerns to engage him; but it is his duty, at least, to wash his hands of it, and, if he gives it no thought longer, not to give it practically his support. If I devote myself to other pursuits and contemplations, I must first see, at least, that I do not pursue them sitting upon another man's shoulders. I must get off him first, that he may pursue his contemplations too.

1. The Cost to the State of According the Privilege to Refuse to Act. — Given that a moral line can be drawn between action and inaction, the question remains whether the state can afford to provide the privilege. Some, such as Mr. Justice Fortas, have strongly asserted that it cannot.[77] But three distinct factors help reduce the cost of privileging inaction. First, the state can sometimes achieve its goals without infringing the individual's conscience by performing for him the act which he cannot perform voluntarily. Second, the state can place a substitute burden upon objectors which will serve to discourage claims of conscience which are not strongly felt. A third factor is the fact that for better or worse the finder of fact will almost inevitably consider

---

[75] H.M. Hart & A. Sacks, The Legal Process: Basic Problems in the Making and Application of Law 146 (tent. ed. 1958).

[76] H. Thoreau, *On the Duty of Civil Disobedience*, in Walden and Other Writings of Henry David Thoreau 635, 642 (Modern Library ed. 1937); *cf.* L. Tolstoy, The Kingdom of God Is Within You 236 (Estes ed. 1905).

[77] A. Fortas, Concerning Dissent and Civil Disobedience 33 (1968).

the degree of harm to the government in passing on the defendant's sincerity. We shall examine each of these principles in turn.

(a) *The Principle of False Conflict.* — In a well-known case in the District of Columbia Circuit, a blood transfusion was authorized to be given a Jehovah's Witness who revealed that an unconsented-to transfusion would not violate her conscience, even though she could not affirmatively authorize the transfusion herself.[78] This case illustrates a method the state can frequently use to achieve its ends without violating the individual's conscience. Conscience, it must be remembered, frequently makes demands only in regard to acts of will. Violation of duty, or sin, is usually regarded as impossible where the individual can do nothing to avert certain consequences. Thus, the state can often achieve its goals without conflicting with religious belief by performing the required acts for an objector. The conscientious refusal to pay taxes can be dealt with by attaching part of the taxpayer's bank account or other property;[79] voluntary payment is not strictly necessary. Similarly, inoculations against smallpox and other diseases can be administered involuntarily.[80]

Admittedly giving transfusions or inoculations without consent, or impounding a bank account instead of receiving a voluntary payment in the mail, does not necessarily safeguard the government's interest as well as criminal penalties would. If the withholding of taxes will not incur punishment, many more people may find it in their hearts to do so than would otherwise. Moreover, there may be additional costs involved in performing an action which the individual could have performed for himself: in the tax case, the cost of finding out where a bank account or other property is located, and of filling out forms to notify both the bank and the taxpayer of the action being taken. In the case of inoculation it might be difficult to identify those persons who had refused, and time would have to be spent going to their houses or places of employment to give the shot. Only in the case of the blood transfusion, where the patient is already in the hospital, is there very little additional difficulty. These objections are largely overcome, however, by the government's ability to impose alternative burdens, as discussed below.

The principle of false conflict does not apply, of course, if the proposed recipient of an inoculation or blood transfusion believes that he will be damned by receiving the injection regardless of

---

[78] Application of President & Directors of Georgetown College, Inc., 331 F.2d 1000 (D.C. Cir.), *cert. denied*, 377 U.S. 978 (1964). *See also* United States v. George, 239 F. Supp. 752 (D. Conn. 1965).

[79] *Cf.* Abraham J. Muste, 35 T.C. 663 (1961); N.Y. Times, Apr. 16, 1965, at 35, col. 2.

[80] *Cf.* Wright v. DeWitt School Dist., 238 Ark. 906, 385 S.W.2d 644 (1965).

whether he consents. Such a belief is by no means impossible, and indeed it has been said that Jehovah's Witness theology may command such an interpretation.[81] In such cases, the appropriate question would seem to be not whether the presumption against the use of criminal penalties should be overcome, but whether the presumption permitting the involuntary administration of the treatment should give way. Where only the health of the individual himself is concerned, as for example, in the case of a blood transfusion, involuntary administration should probably not be permitted. Where the health of a whole community may be seriously endangered, however, as in the case of a required vaccination during a smallpox epidemic, it is difficult to say that the individual should remain immune from treatment unless effective methods of quarantine are available.

There is a second category of cases in which the principle of false conflict does not provide a solution. These cases concern positive acts required by the law which involve activity which the government cannot perform for the individual. The duties of military or jury service provide prime examples. To the extent that national security depends on the country's ability to mobilize soldiers, national security will be diminished by the exercise of conscientious belief. There are a number of other positive acts which may also fit this description. If an individual does not fill out a tax return at all, it may be difficult for the Internal Revenue Service to collect the required information accurately. Similar considerations may apply to the filing of other required information with the government. For example, the requirement that all eighteen-year-old males register with the Selective Service System [82] may not be possible to accommodate without individual co-operation unless the individual lets the local board know who and where he is.

These, then, are situations of true rather than false conflict. They challenge the presumption against the use of criminal penalties by the government, for the government cannot obtain its ends through the objector without violating his conscience. The government may still be able to satisfy its needs, however, by replacing the duty with a civil burden.

(b) *The Principle of Alternative Burdens.* — The ability of the government to impose alternative burdens carries two major advantages. First, it enables the government to separate conscientious motives from motives of self-interest. When it is equally burdensome or more burdensome to claim a religious exemption than not to claim it, there is no motive for fraudulent

---

[81] Dodge, *supra* note 12, at 720–21.
[82] 50 U.S.C. app. § 453 (1964).

claims or claims by those with very minor conscientious scruples. (Some exemptions of course entail sacrifice by their very nature: no one who needs a blood transfusion is likely to refuse it out of self interest). Second, the state may by exacting a price for a religious exemption effectively eliminate any cost to itself.

In the case of conscientious objection to war, the government now imposes a duty of two years' alternative service.[83] For those who refuse noncombatant service as medics in the army, alternative service generally consists of civilian work in hospitals, usually in the United States, although other jobs in the national interest are available as well.[84] The government probably has power to make these requirements more stringent, at least in time of war, without their being struck down judicially as a penalty upon the exercise of religion.[85] In return for the benefits of civilian life, continuation of family relationships during the period of service, and the safety of avoiding warfare, alternative service could probably be increased from two to four or more years during wartime. Moreover, since many conscientious objectors apparently refuse to do medical service in battle areas only because noncombatant service now places them in the army itself,[86] many men could be sent to war areas without violation of conscience if assigned to a civilian-controlled body similar to the Red Cross or the ambulance corps of World War I.

Similarly, alternative burdens could be placed upon those who refuse to pay taxes voluntarily. By analogy to alternative service for conscientious objectors to war, such taxpayers could be assessed an amount equal to the increased cost of collection, including the cost of estimating income in cases where the objector refused to file a form at all. The same assessment might be made upon those who refuse to report for compulsory inoculations: the cost of trips to homes by health service agents could be assessed as part of a state or local tax on objectors.

There is some question as to the constitutional permissibility of alternative burdens. However, the courts have never as yet challenged the constitutionality of alternative service for objectors to war, and the requirement of a financial payment in lieu of alterna-

---

[83] *Id.* § 454(b) (1964); *id.* § 456(j) (Supp. III, 1968).

[84] *See* National Serv. Bd. of Religious Objectors, Civilian Work Agency List for Conscientious Objectors (Nov. 1967).

[85] The Japanese relocation cases, whatever the continuing validity of their direct holdings, do indicate that the war power justifies substantial regulation of civilian life. *See* Korematsu v. United States, 323 U.S. 214 (1944); Hirabayashi v. United States, 320 U.S. 81 (1943).

[86] *Cf.* CENTRAL COMM. FOR CONSCIENTIOUS OBJECTORS, HANDBOOK FOR CONSCIENTIOUS OBJECTORS 87-88 (10th ed. 1968).

tive service went unchallenged during the Civil War.[87] *Sherbert v. Verner* might be read for the proposition that the government must absorb the costs to society which result from the exercise of religious beliefs. However, it is not necessary to construe the case so broadly. There the "assessment" upon the individual bore no relationship to the cost created by her action; instead it amounted to the complete forfeiture of all unemployment benefits. Had the statute provided instead for the payment of slightly lower compensation to reflect the lower wages a five-day worker could expect to receive, it might have been valid. Moreover, *Sherbert* dealt not with a governmental prohibition but with conditions placed on public benefits, and, as set forth below, different considerations apply to this type of law.[88]

A somewhat more difficult case is *Murdock v. Pennsylvania*,[89] in which the Court held that a license fee for the door-to-door sale of reading material could not constitutionally be required of Jehovah's Witnesses selling religious tracts. The Court observed that "[t]he power to tax the exercise of a privilege is the power to control or suppress its enjoyment,"[90] and remarked broadly that a "state may not impose a charge for the enjoyment of a right granted by the Federal Constitution."[91] However, *Murdock* can be distinguished on two grounds. First, the license fee there was a precondition to the exercise of the right rather than a tax levied upon revenue or benefits obtained. The Court indicated by an analogy to the interstate commerce clause that a tax on revenue would be treated differently, observing that though a state "may not exact a license tax for the privilege of carrying on interstate commerce . . . it may tax the property used in, or the income derived from, that commerce, so long as these taxes are not discriminatory."[92] In contrast, the religious objector does obtain a profit of sorts in the situations just described, in that he avoids duties which other citizens must perform. This benefit is not likely to be of a sort normally subject to tax, of course, but nevertheless burdens imposed on them should probably survive *Murdock*. Burdens imposed as a factor of benefits cannot be swollen to a destructive size, as feared by the *Murdock* Court.

Murdock might be distinguished on the additional grounds that the sale of literature created no additional cost to the government and taxing it served no important governmental purpose. The Court observed that the license fee was not intended to pay for

---

[87] *See* 1 SELECTIVE SERVICE SYSTEM, *supra* note 38, at 36–37, 40–42.
[88] *See* pp. 360–61 *infra*.
[89] 319 U.S. 105 (1943).
[90] *Id.* at 112.
[91] *Id.* at 113.
[92] *Id.*

the policing of door-to-door solicitation."³ Refusals of positive duties, in contrast, may impose significant costs on the government, and taxing such refusals not only recoups these government losses but also serves to distinguish the person truly compelled by conscience from the individual who holds his belief lightly or not at all. Taxes no larger than necessary to recover losses to the government produced by refusals to act and to deter the insincere should be held to survive *Murdock*.

This rationale would permit the imposition of burdens even larger than the benefit obtained from refusals to act where government costs were great. The cost of finding him could be levied against a person who refused to be inoculated, for example, even though he obtained no secular benefit from his refusal. Some reasonable maximum would have to be attached to such a burden, of course, to prevent its serving as a penalty.

This system of limited civil burdens might be objected to on the ground that many fraudulent claimants who would not risk criminal sanctions would be willing to endure civil burdens. But this danger must be compared with the drawbacks of a system based on criminal deterrents. Many conscientious objectors to war, for example, would undoubtedly go to jail if no exemption in the law existed. Prison entails the forfeiture by the state of the objector's productive work and also entails a considerable financial investment in his custody. For these sums to be justified, the deterrent value of criminal penalties must be substantial. The question of the fairness of labeling a conscientious man a criminal also weighs heavily against applying such penalties.

It must also be remembered that the burden of proving conscientious motives for a refusal to act can itself constitute a very serious deterrent to inaction. A person conscientiously opposed to performing a given duty can be required actually to refuse to perform it before receiving a judicial declaration of his right to do so. A man who knows he will be jailed for refusing to file a tax form unless he can demonstrate that he acted not merely out of an urge to discomfort the government but in the belief that cooperation would be a moral wrong must be conscientious indeed to take the risk. It seems unlikely that fact-finding agencies will be misled by claims of conscience from individuals who act primarily from self-interest. If anything, the experience of conscientious objectors to war indicates that the fault will lie in the opposite direction.[94]

---

[93] *Id.* at 114.
[94] *See generally* Rabin, *Do You Believe in a Supreme Being — The Administration of the Conscientious Objector Exemption*, 1967 WIS. L. REV. 642.

The deterrent effect of risking conviction, in fact, will probably be so great that some sincere objectors will be frightened into cooperation. In some cases, this will reflect the fact that their conscientious compulsion is rather slight, but in other cases, deeply committed believers may be deterred because of extraneous factors, such as their need to stay out of jail to support their families. Although this injustice should perhaps be remedied by a constitutionally-imposed requirement of anticipatory adjudication on the merits of individual first amendment cases,[95] no such requirement has been imposed. The deterrent effect of the prospect of criminal prosecution must still be considered, therefore, in evaluating the effect of according the privilege.

(c) *The Role of the Jury.* — A further limitation upon the cost of the exemption is the role of the fact-finding body which decides questions of sincerity. The desirability of having juries rather than administrative agencies decide this question has already been discussed in the legal literature.[96] In deciding issues of sincerity, juries almost certainly are influenced by the importance of the state interest involved. The fact finder's perception of the claimant's sincerity naturally relates in greater or lesser degree to his view of the reasonableness of the claimant's beliefs. The ease with which a person could hold certain beliefs bears on the fact finder's decision as to whether a claimant does in fact hold them. Thus, in *Sisson*, Judge Wyzanski pointed out that the defendant's views on the Vietnam war were "reasonable" ones.[97] Finders of fact thus are influenced by their own perceptions of the morality of the act in question. This judgment in turn involves an evaluation of the harm which the type of objection at bar will do to the public interest. The result of this is that to a significant extent the same ad hoc judgments which prevent disastrous harm to the public interest but which inject an undesirable element of judicial arbitrariness into the law are made in the jury room.

It is not clear by any means that such judgments are permissible as a matter of law.[98] Furthermore, weighing of interests by juries impairs the predictability which the proposed guidelines seek to establish. But since this jury weighing is likely to take place whenever juries pass on the question of sincerity, it must be taken into account as another factor reducing the cost to the state of the immunity for conscientious refusals.

---

[95] This possibility is discussed in an article by Professor Henry Monaghan which will appear in the January issue of the *Harvard Law Review*.

[96] *See generally* White, *supra* note 37, at 667–76.

[97] United States v. Sisson, 297 F. Supp. 902 (D. Mass. 1969), *jurisdictional decision postponed until hearing on merits*, 38 U.S.L.W. 3127 (U.S. Oct. 13, 1969) (No. 305).

[98] *See* United States v. Ballard, 322 U.S. 78 (1944).

2. *Application to Particular Cases of the Presumption Against Criminal Penalties.* — The acceptability of these guidelines ultimately must rest on judges' intuition as to their practicability. The broad argument ultimately may stand or fall on intuitive judgments. However, the following examination of several particularly thorny types of conscientious claims can serve to demonstrate that the proposal is not clearly unworkable.

(a) *Medical Treatment.* — The refusal of medical treatment may endanger three different kinds of state interest: that in the safety of the individual who himself refuses treatment, that in the safety of children or others on whose behalf the individual refuses treatment, and that in the safety of the community at large to whom the individual might communicate disease. In most of these cases the presumption against criminal penalties should not be overcome.

The case of the individual who risks his own death by refusing medical treatment in a context where the state does not know of the illness and therefore cannot intervene is probably the easiest to dispose of. Criminal penalties would not normally be applied to such a person in any event, and they would do little to change the mind of one who already faces death or serious illness as a result of his belief. Such penalties would clearly be useless.

The criminal law is more likely to be brought to bear on the parents of a sick child who refuse to call medical help, but the same considerations should prevail. The loss or serious illness of a child would normally provide a much more serious impulsion to action than can the criminal law. Moreover, the parent's motive for refusing to call a doctor would normally be his belief that God would cure the child without the help of a doctor. In *Regina v. Wagstaffe*,[99] an English case cited in *Reynolds v. United States*,[100] the court held that such a belief negated the imputation of gross negligence.

The danger to the community of an individual's refusing inoculation need not be overwhelming, either. Again, the sincerity of the claimant cannot be questioned in most cases, since the threat of death or disease to the individual is great. Moreover, the community will often be able to identify those who have not been inoculated and administer the treatment involuntarily. Inoculation is usually required only in connection with some process in which the state is already involved, such as birth, education, and trips abroad. In these cases the state already makes an effort to locate and register the entire group concerned, and the extra

---

[99] 10 Cox Crim. Cas. 530, 533 (Cent. Crim. Ct. 1868); *cf.* State v. Sandford, 99 Me. 441, 59 A. 597 (1905) (dictum).
[100] 98 U.S. 145, 167 (1878).

effort necessary to ensure that every member of the group has been inoculated is slight. Much greater difficulties would arise if the state sought to inoculate the entire population of an area. Census lists and questionnaires might help locate many objectors, but some would probably be able to avoid detection, particularly when time was short. The harm caused by these objectors would depend on the nature of the disease and the inoculum. In most cases, uninoculated persons would be a threat only to other uninoculated persons, who would be very few where a thorough effort had been made to reach everyone.[101] In other cases, where even inoculated persons could catch the disease, the presumption against criminal penalties should be overcome, provided the state showed it had made a reasonable effort to locate objectors.

(b) *Conscientious Objection to Armed Service.* — The Supreme Court has never passed definitively on the issue of whether the Constitution requires an exemption for conscientious objection to war, although it is possible that it will do so in the near future in *United States v. Sisson*.[102] A number of dicta have indicated that no constitutional privilege exists, but their continued validity is in doubt. In *United States v. Macintosh*, the Court held that an alien could be denied naturalization for refusing on conscientious grounds to promise to bear arms for the United States. Mr. Justice Sutherland stated for the Court: [103]

> The conscientious objector is relieved from the obligation to bear arms in obedience to no constitutional provision, express or implied; but because, and only because, it has accorded with the policy of Congress thus to relieve him . . . .
>
> . . . .
>
> . . . We are a Christian people . . . according to one another the equal right of religious freedom, and acknowledging with reverence the duty of obedience to the will of God. But, also, we are a Nation with the duty to survive; a Nation whose Constitution contemplates war as well as peace; whose government must go forward upon the assumption, and safely can proceed upon no other, that unqualified allegiance to the Nation and

---

[101] However, even where injections normally prevent infection, the existence of a large population of uninoculated persons would pose some threat to inoculated ones, since the disease could then become endemic in the unvaccinated population. If the disease became endemic, inoculations would have to be obtained much more frequently, and since inoculation itself entails some risk to health, the community's interest in forced inoculation of objectors would be fairly great. Conversation with Alan A. Stone, *supra* note 61. In such a case, the presumption against forced inoculation should be overcome.

[102] 297 F. Supp. 902 (D. Mass. 1969), *jurisdictional decision postponed until hearing on merits*, 38 U.S.L.W. 3127 (U.S. Oct. 13, 1969) (No. 305).

[103] 283 U.S. 605, 623, 625 (1931) (dictum).

submission and obedience to the laws of the land, as well those made for war as those made for peace, are not inconsistent with the will of God.

Two other Supreme Court decisions subsequently used *Macintosh* as controlling precedent in holding that conscientious objectors who refused to participate in ROTC exercises could be excluded from a state university [104] and that conscientious objectors who could not guarantee to serve in the state militia could be excluded by a state from the practice of law.[105] Yet the *Macintosh* interpretation of the naturalization statute was later overruled,[106] and the accuracy of the *Macintosh* dictum on the constitutional right to conscientious objection has therefore been thrown into doubt as well. *United States v. Seeger* [107] can easily be read as based in part on the possibility that a nonstatutory right to conscientious objection exists.

There is some evidence that a constitutional exemption for conscientious objectors to war was contemplated by the drafters of the first amendment,[108] but the evidence is by no means conclusive, and the Court will have to formulate its decision on grounds of policy. Commentators who have approached the question from the perspective of ad hoc balancing have for the most part appeared friendly to the establishment of a constitutional right, at least with respect to objectors to all war.[109] The numbers of objectors have always been small,[110] and alternative service has been found to put them to useful national ends. Moreover, significant numbers of conscientious objectors who did not qualify for the statutory exemption have chosen to go to jail rather than serve,[111] so that denial of the exemption might achieve very little change in individual choices.

On the other hand, writers have stated the reservation that, should the number of conscientious objectors to all war increase

---

[104] Hamilton v. Regents of the Univ. of Cal., 293 U.S. 245 (1934).

[105] *In re* Summers, 325 U.S. 561 (1945).

[106] Girouard v. United States, 328 U.S. 61 (1946). *Girouard* did not purport to reach the constitutional issue. It is unclear whether the *Girouard* Court meant to permit naturalization even of persons who would not be exempt under the statutory exemption for pacifists, or not.

[107] 380 U.S. 163 (1965).

[108] *See* notes 4-6 *supra*.

[109] *See, e.g.,* Note, *supra* note 27.

[110] During World War II, 72,000 men out of 13,000,000 inducted claimed conscientious exemption, and 52,000 men were awarded it. The overall percentage of conscientious objectors in the drafted population since World War II has been 0.6%. 1 SELECTIVE SERVICE SYSTEM, *supra* note 38, at 53; Note, *supra* note 27, at 88.

[111] White, *supra* note 37, at 652.

significantly, or should the need for soldiers increase dramatically, as in time of war, the exemption could be revoked or at least limited to a quota, and individuals assigned to military service or alternative service by lot until the quota was filled.[112] The failings of this arrangement have been noted above.[113] It seems much more desirable to create a constitutional right which extends to all who merit it and which cannot be created and taken away periodically by governmental fiat.

The feasibility of permitting conscientious objection to particular wars as an exemption from military service has been thought more doubtful than that of permitting conscientious objection to all war. The number of objectors to particular wars would almost certainly be significantly higher than the number of total pacifists, or objectors to all war, who now qualify for exemption. The grounds of objection to a particular war are likely to be more political than conventionally religious.[114]

However, it is by no means clear that an exemption for selective objectors would so endanger the nation that it could not afford the exemption. First, it must be remembered that many young men have gone to jail or left the country rather than serve in the war in Viet Nam, which they conscientiously oppose. The deterrent power of civil burdens must therefore be measured against the partial ineffectiveness of the criminal law itself. Second, the government's putative ability to increase the difficulty of alternative service could, if acted upon, serve both to discourage claims of conscience by those not unalterably opposed to the war and to allay feelings of resentment in the rest of the community. Third, an objector could presumably be made to refuse induction before having his claim adjudicated. He would therefore run a serious risk of criminal penalties in the event he were found insincere. Fourth, it must be remembered that those persons actively opposed (and therefore presumably opposed in conscience) to the present war in Viet Nam probably constitute a rather small minority of the total student population, much less of the total population of men between eighteen and twenty-five. Many elements of that group consider military service a moral and patriotic obligation. Finally, the principle that the fact finder's reaction to the claimant's sincerity will depend on the fact finder's evaluation of the danger to the government seems especially applicable here. A jury would undoubtedly be more favorably disposed to a selective objector to the Viet Nam war than to an objector to World War II, though jury sympathy would probably not be over-

---

[112] Mansfield, *supra* note 7, at 46, 73.
[113] *See* p. 334 *supra*.
[114] *See* United States v. Kauten, 133 F.2d 703, 708 (2d Cir. 1943) (A. Hand, J.).

whelming in either case. To some extent, therefore, public opinion as to the strength of the state's interest seems likely to regulate the number of men who gain exemption from armed service. Mr. Justice Fortas has argued that many wars are unpopular until they are won, and that public opinion is at best a fickle indicator of the importance of a war to the nation's history.[115] So much is probably true. However, Justice Fortas does not go on to show that on average the officials who prosecute wars have been much more correct in the light of history than were the citizens who opposed them at the time. Surely it is at least arguable that a war is likely to be justified by compelling state interests only if the nation's citizens are sufficiently concerned to win it.

These arguments cannot of course demonstrate with any degree of certainty the cost to the state which a right of objection to particular wars would entail. However, they do seem to nullify any clear assumption that such an exemption from armed service would render the country incapable of defending itself or pursuing crucial national goals. The ultimate question is whether the right to conscientious objection can be trusted to the judgment of juries or whether it must be cut off by courts before that point. The benefit of operating by a clear rule should be kept in mind in making this judgment. Judge Wyzanski suggested in *Sisson* that the right to selective objection (or conscientious objection of any sort) could be ended if it became necessary to defend the homeland from attack.[116] However, any such determination raises much the same questions of fact and degree which had led Judge Wyzanski earlier in the same case to declare the legality of the Vietnam war a political question.[117] Such determinations, highly intuitive as they are, might better be left to juries in the limited context just described.[118]

(c) *Refusals of All Cooperation with the Government.* — A more difficult governmental problem in some ways even than the conscientious objector is the absolutist or resister who refuses alternative service as well as military service, and frequently also refuses to carry a draft card or register with the Selective Service System. Other individuals refuse to fill out income tax forms. There are at least three possible motives for such action, and the three may be interwoven in any given case. One motive is that of achieving publicity, as in cases where draft cards have been burned

---

[115] A. FORTAS, *supra* note 77, at 52–55.

[116] United States v. Sisson, 297 F. Supp. 902, 908 (D. Mass. 1969), *jurisdictional decision postponed until hearing on merits*, 38 U.S.L.W. 3127 (U.S. Oct. 13, 1969) (No. 305).

[117] 294 F. Supp. 515 (D. Mass. 1968).

[118] *Cf.* Sax, *Conscience and Anarchy: The Prosecution of War Resisters*, 57 YALE REV. 481, 493 (1968).

or turned in at public meetings. Most draft card cases in the courts, in fact, have been argued primarily on free speech grounds.[119] A second motive is that of disrupting governmental operations. This motive may be dominant in cases of refusals to file income tax forms or to pay certain taxes. A third motive is that of avoiding cooperation with a morally evil process.[120] This third motive is most likely to merit the protection of the free exercise clause, since it more probably than the others makes noncooperation a compelling duty.

It must be recognized that such refusals are difficult for the state to deal with, for it cannot always perform the acts on behalf of the individual, and alternative burdens may be difficult to impose. A refusal by a conscientious objector to perform alternative service would give him an inordinate benefit not shared by the rest of society, a situation which might give rise to feelings of resentment in the general population and stimulate fraudulent claims, or claims based on weakly-held beliefs.

On the other hand, the kind of philosophy which considers any cooperation at all with the government or certain of its operations to be wrong probably has relatively few strong adherents,[121] so few as to represent no threat either to the nation's revenues or to its national defense. The fact that noncooperators do represent a threat to the perception of legal fairness in the community at large means that juries would probably be extremely wary of granting exemptions and would probably do so only in cases of belief so clear cut that the individual would choose jail if denied the exemption. Consequently the state loses little if any of its deterrent power by granting the exemption. Furthermore, the government has little hope or aim of rehabilitation in the case of conscientious objectors in jail. Finally, it should be possible to impose a financial levy upon those who refuse alternative service as an additional deterrent.[122]

Certain objectors, however, should automatically be immune from charges of insincerity and from alternative burdens. Those permanently exempt from the draft by reason of physical incapacity, for example, should not be jailed. These individuals have nothing to gain by their refusal to register for the draft, and exempting them would give little encouragement to others to emulate them.

---

[119] *See, e.g.*, United States v. O'Brien, 391 U.S. 367 (1968); United States v. Edelman, 384 F.2d 115 (2d Cir. 1967), *cert. denied*, 392 U.S. 904 (1968); United States v. Miller, 367 F.2d 72 (2d Cir. 1966), *cert. denied*, 386 U.S. 911 (1967).

[120] *See* p. 346 *supra*.

[121] In 1965 it was estimated that there were less than 100 confirmed "absolutists" in the United States. Wall St. J., Sept. 22, 1965, at 16, cols. 4-5.

[122] *See* pp. 348-52 *supra*.

A separate observation should be made concerning the duty imposed by Selective Service System regulations that all men of draft age carry in their possession their registration certificate and notice of classification.[123] Various individuals object to this requirement on conscientious grounds, though most of the cases to reach the courts have turned on the issue of whether a particular method of disposing of the cards — usually burning — was protected by the free speech clause.[124] In 1968, in *United States v. O'Brien*,[125] the Supreme Court rejected the free speech claim. However, a refusal to carry draft cards for conscientious reasons should be made subject to criminal sanctions only if compelling reasons exist. Even though the government cannot perform the act of possessing cards for the individual or impose any meaningful equivalent burden, this appears to be one of the rare areas in which the statute performs no important function.[126]

(d) Refusals to Testify. — One case of a conscientious refusal to act which is likely to be unamenable to solution by alternate burdens or the principle of false conflict is that of the witness who refuses to testify.[127] In some cases, where it is clear that his testimony can be adequately replaced by the testimony of others or by written records, the objecting witness can be left free from criminal compulsion. But in other cases, the presumption that the state has adequate alternatives may be overcome. There, a balancing of state against individual interests will have to be resorted to, and a decision reached in the light of such factors as the importance of the witnesses' information and the gravity of the case. Refusals to testify in felony cases, for example, are less likely to be privileged than refusals to testify in misdemeanor cases and civil cases.

B. *The Power of the State to Burden Inaction by Withholding Positive Benefits*

Until now we have not dealt with the problem of the *Sherbert* case itself. There the law did not prohibit the Saturday Sabbath but withheld governmental benefits from those observing it. In addition to this claim of discrimination by Sabbatarians, it has been argued that the denial of state aid to parochial schools burdens the free exercise of Catholics and others who cannot in good

---

[123] 32 C.F.R. §§ 1617.1, 1623.5 (1969).
[124] *See* cases cited note 119 *supra*.
[125] 391 U.S. 367 (1968).
[126] *See* 81 HARV. L. REV. 1347, 1349, 1351 (1968).
[127] *See* People v. Woodruff, 26 App. Div. 2d 236, 272 N.Y.S.2d 786 (1966), *aff'd*, 21 N.Y.2d 848, 236 N.E.2d 159, 288 N.Y.S.2d 1004 (1968).

conscience attend public schools, by denying them educational benefits available to public school children.[128]

As a limiting principle upon *Sherbert*, it seems clear that the state should be free to assign reasonable purposes to its laws and distribute the laws' benefits accordingly even when this process excludes persons because of their religious objections. A pacifist who refuses to carry a gun could hardly claim denial of free exercise if he were barred from a police force, for example. Similarly, the unemployment fund involved in *Sherbert* need not have been made available to a Buddhist monk who believed it his duty to contemplate rather than work. It is because Mrs. Sherbert considered herself a worker and could realistically expect to find work that she came within the purposes of the statute at all. The rule in these cases should be that for judging other questions of the constitutionality of conditional benefits: namely, that the state must extend benefits or privileges to conscientious objectors as it does to all others unless such an extension would prevent the government from accomplishing the purpose of its program or unless the extension could not be related to the basic purposes of the program, liberally construed. Phrased differently, the government must demonstrate an interest "in ensuring that the benefit or facility extended is maintained for the purposes intended." [129] This permissive standard for burdens upon inaction is justified by the fact that the effects upon the individual of an arbitrary judicial decision are more bearable where they consist of the denial of a benefit rather than the imposition of criminal penalties, important though the former may be.

Such a test does permit a form of balancing in individual cases, yet the scope of such balancing is limited to the discovery of a rational relationship between the denial of a benefit and a legitimate governmental purpose. The range of such inquiry is relatively narrow. For example, in *Braunfeld v. Brown*,[130] where a Sunday closing law was upheld as applied to Orthodox Jewish merchants, the question was not whether the individual's interest in Saturday worship was greater than the state's interest in quiet Sundays, but rather whether business operations by scattered merchants on Sunday would affect the general public significantly at all. In answering such questions, however, the numbers of believers of a particular sort should not generally determine the outcome. Such estimates by courts can seldom be reliable in the absence of statistical evidence.

---

[128] *See* R. DRINAN, FEDERAL AID TO EDUCATION 24 (1962). For the counterarguments, see Freund, *Public Aid to Parochial Schools*, 82 HARV. L. REV. 1680 (1969).

[129] Note, *Unconstitutional Conditions*, 73 HARV. L. REV. 1595, 1600 (1960).

[130] 366 U.S. 599 (1961).

C. Privileges to Perform Positive Actions.

The right of individuals to act positively, in such a way as to harm others in the society, must by its nature be more restricted than the right to refrain from acting. Our civil order is based on the establishment of rights and interests, and the protection of these rights and interests from positive infringement. On the other hand, the essence of the theory of religious freedom as it has been outlined here lies in the freedom of men to run their own lives according to the dictates of conscience, and this freedom clearly implies some protection of affirmative acts. It may be possible to strike a balance between these two interests by the following proposition: where an individual's conscience demands of him as an inexcusable duty the performance of a positive act which can harm only himself and other fully consenting persons, that act cannot be prohibited by the state. The state may, however, prohibit other positive actions, even ones impelled by conscience.

This proposition is not as far-reaching as it may at first appear. For one thing, a great many conscientious duties of positive action are not in fact inexcusable. In almost all moral systems the duty to act is circumscribed by the fact that in some instances action may be impossible. The degree of impossibility, or impractibility, required to excuse performance of course varies with the individual and the duty concerned. For a Roman Catholic, for example, failure to attend Mass may be excused by a circumstance such as a broken car, even though in an emergency he might have walked the distance. In other words, most duties of positive action require a good faith effort on the part of the actor, but seldom heroics.

There are two main classes of exceptions to this generalization. The duty of proselytizing is generally one of the most difficult duties to excuse. The early Christian apostles underwent martyrdom because they refused to abandon the positive duty of testimony even in the face of persecution. The reason, of course, is that the salvation of souls is at stake, and a failure to act means that they will be lost. A somewhat related rationale applied to polygamy in the early Mormon Church, which believed that spirit children were born in heaven and had to be accommodated in the bodies of humans before they could return to heaven saved.[131] Reliable sources indicate that this belief still exists and that polygamy still flourishes among certain Mormon sects despite the

---

[131] *See* CHURCH OF JESUS CHRIST OF LATTER DAY SAINTS, DOCTRINE AND COVENANTS § 132 (1921).

sanctions of the law and the official disclaimer of the Mormon Church.[132]

A second class of action which cannot be excused by impossibility, or at least by criminal prohibition, consists of certain sacramental duties. Most sacramental rites are encompassed within the freedoms of speech and assembly, but some are not. In *People v. Woody* [133] the California Supreme Court held that the Native American Church, a religious assembly of American Indians, is entitled by the free exercise clause to the use of peyote in religious ceremonies. The court emphasized the essential nature of peyote in the religious life of the Indians: [134]

> Although peyote serves as a sacramental symbol similar to bread and wine in certain Christian churches, it is more than a sacrament. Peyote constitutes in itself an object of worship; prayers are directed to it much as prayers are devoted to the Holy Ghost. On the other hand, to use peyote for nonreligious purposes is sacrilegious.

In both the case of proselytizing and the case of ritual worship, action is essential not merely to placating or pleasing a deity but to the very life of the religion. Without testimony a religion would wither away and souls would be lost. Without worship, the believer would be cut off from God. This suggests that it may be possible to limit the exemption of positive conduct to acts deemed by the individual concerned to be absolutely necessary to communion with God or to the salvation of other souls.

The difficulty of deciding religious doctrine has already been mentioned.[135] However, most of the examples which critics have given of theological ambiguities do not arise in the free exercise context under discussion here.[136] The best way to demonstrate the feasibility of the test doubtless is to apply it to several test cases. It should be remembered that actions which harm nonconsenting persons need not be exempted no matter how necessary the act is deemed by one of the individuals concerned.

1. Sacramental Use of Wine During Prohibition. — During Prohibition Congress created an exemption in the Volstead Act for churches using wine for Communion, though such use was

---

[132] N.Y. Times, Dec. 27, 1965, at 18, cols. 7–8 ("It is entirely possible that more people live in polygamy today in Utah than did between 1852 and 1890, the period when the L.D.S. Church openly advocated it.").

[133] 61 Cal. 2d 716, 394 P.2d 813, 40 Cal. Rptr. 69 (1964).

[134] *Id.* at 721, 394 P.2d at 817, 40 Cal. Rptr. at 73.

[135] *See* p. 343 *supra*.

[136] *See, e.g.,* M. KONVITZ, RELIGIOUS LIBERTY AND CONSCIENCE: A CONSTITUTIONAL INQUIRY 78–79 (1968).

subject to licensing restrictions.[137] Would the Constitution compel such an exemption if Congress had not created it? It seems clear that such ritual use would not violate the purpose of the Act, which was intended to prevent broken homes, public drunkenness, and the consumption of large quantities of alcohol for hedonistic purposes. Communion wine is consumed in small quantities and on infrequent occasions. The fact that not all Christian churches might be able to show that the use of wine is "necessary" in the sense just described should not affect the outcome where ritual use would not violate the purposes of the Act.

2. *The Ritual Use of Other Drugs.* — The use of illegal drugs including marijuana and LSD, even for ritual purposes, does violate the purposes of the laws prohibiting them, which assume that use for any nonmedical purpose is harmful. Moreover, the use of such drugs is less tied to specific theological beliefs, and whatever religious attitudes are involved may be hard to distinguish from hedonism.[138] The cases thus far seem to indicate that most users do not claim that the drugs are truly essential to communion with God. Dr. Leary did not make that claim, nor have others convicted of the use of peyote and marijuana,[139] except for the Native American Church involved in the *Woody* case. Thus, effective drug laws could be maintained consistently with the privilege.

3. *Polygamy.* — Polygamy in the Mormon Church has at certain times been required as a means of bringing souls to God. For this reason it does not seem difficult to deem the practice necessary. On the other hand, the children born from polygamous relationships cannot very well be said to "consent" to the practice. The latitude of the state to regulate action on behalf of children is generally greater than to regulate the acts of adults alone,[140] and if proof of any real harm to children can be shown to result from polygamy, the state should have the power to condemn it.

4. *Faith Healing.* — In *United States v. Ballard*,[141] a case involving sale of allegedly fraudulent literature, the Court held that the government cannot inquire into the truth of representations of spiritual matters, but only into the sincerity with which they

---

[137] National Prohibition Act, tit. II, § 3, 41 Stat. 308 (1919).

[138] *See* Leary v. United States, 383 F.2d 851, 859–62 (5th Cir. 1967), *rev'd on other grounds*, 395 U.S. 6 (1969).

[139] *See id.*; People v. Mitchell, 244 Cal. App. 2d 176, 52 Cal. Rptr. 884 (Dist. Ct. App. 1966). *But see* State v. Bullard, 267 N.C. 599, 148 S.E.2d 565 (1966), *cert. denied*, 386 U.S. 917 (1967).

[140] *See, e.g.*, Prince v. Massachusetts, 321 U.S. 158 (1944). *See also* Ginsberg v. New York, 390 U.S. 629 (1968).

[141] 322 U.S. 78 (1944).

are made. A lower court has recently extended this holding to the sale of faith healing machines.[142] It seems possible to derive from these holdings the proposition that where an individual sincerely believes that a given practice will cure his own physical illness or that of others, even if he does not believe he has an inexcusable duty to practice faith healing he should be permitted to do so so long as the other participants consent, and so long as their consent has not been fraudulently obtained. State court cases prosecuting faith healers for practicing medicine without a license overlook the fact that such individuals do not hold themselves out as normal physicians but instead make spiritual claims whose truth the state is incapable of proving or disproving.

A harder problem is the handling of snakes by certain Pentecostal sects who believe that, when infused with the Holy Spirit, they will be immune from harm.[143] Although deaths have resulted and the practice is frequently prohibited by state law, it seems singularly irradicable.[144] It is by no means clear that snake handling is believed necessary to communion with God — rather, it seems more a test or sign of spiritual grace. In cases where it is regarded as an absolute necessity by believers it should be privileged.[145]

III. Conclusion

The principles or guidelines for the free exercise clause which have been set out above certainly do not remove the difficulty of judging the consciences of men. Whenever an exemption is created in the law for the purpose of protecting conscience, such judgments become necessary — and despite difficulties, it seems

---

[142] Founding Church of Scientology v. United States, 409 F.2d 1146 (D.C. Cir. 1969).

[143] *See* TIME, Nov. 1, 1968, at 86. The constitutionality of criminal penalties for handling poisonous snakes has been upheld in several state court cases. *See, e.g.*, Lawson v. Commonwealth, 291 Ky. 437, 164 S.W.2d 972 (Ct. App. 1942); State v. Massey, 229 N.C. 734, 51 S.E.2d 179, *appeal dismissed sub nom.* Bunn v. North Carolina, 336 U.S. 942 (1949). Neither of these opinions indicated that the believer considered snake handling an inexcusable duty.

[144] *See* TIME, Nov. 1, 1968, at 86.

[145] An interesting case in this connection is Mayock v. Martin, 157 Conn. 56, 245 A.2d 574 (1968), *cert. denied*, 393 U.S. 1111 (1969), in which the Connecticut Supreme Court justified the continued incarceration of an inmate of a mental institution on the grounds that he intended, if called upon by God, to cut off his foot as a free will offering. The opinion is confused, since it treats his claim as one arising under the first amendment, yet relegates him to continued detention as mentally ill. It seems unlikely that courts will confront a similar claim from a sane man.

much fairer except in extreme cases for the state to make such judgments than to label clearly conscientious men as criminals.

The guidelines here proposed provide a coherent theory for the first amendment: that a man compelled by his conscience can refrain from doing acts he regards as wrong without being called a criminal, and may pursue whatever religious activities he must so long as they affect only other persons similarly persuaded, but that he may not undertake by positive acts to infringe the security or freedom of others. The guidelines differ from a balancing test only in three significant ways: they apply a presumption that alternate means can be made to suffice, discount the state interest in protecting objectors from harm to themselves, and acknowledge the tendency of juries to take account of strong state interests. These changes have the practical effect of limiting the uncertainty of interest balancing to a few cases such as those involving plague or the availability of vital evidence for a judicial proceeding. In other cases, the balancing test is transformed into a clear and predictable privilege for the exercise of conscience.

ARTICLES
CHURCH-STATE SEPARATION: RESTORING THE "NO PREFERENCE" DOCTRINE OF THE FIRST AMENDMENT

Robert L. Cord*

I. Introduction

For almost four decades, since *Everson v. Board of Education* was decided in 1947,[1] the United States Supreme Court has sought with historical scholarship to justify its interpretation of the First Amendment injunction: "Congress shall make no law respecting an establishment of religion." While the Supreme Court has, on other occasions and subjects, employed a variety of arguments to justify its holdings,[2] in Church-State cases the Court has, for the most part, consistently relied on what it has said is the historical intent and mandate of the "founding fathers," especially Thomas Jefferson and James Madison.

In recent years, much has been written, debated, and decided about what, under the law, should be or is the proper relationship between religion and the state. Relevant today, these words also aptly describe concerns felt two centuries ago when, in 1785, James Madison and the Virginia State Assembly began the extensive deliberations that would ultimately yield the disestablishment of the Anglican Church and Jefferson's immortal "Bill for Establishing Religious Freedom."[3] Now, as then, our public agenda contains many issues that derive from our societal commitment to the concept of Church-State separation.

In 1785, the Virginia Assembly debated the comprehensive

---

* University Distinguished Professor and Professor of Political Science, Northeastern University. City College of New York, B.B.A., 1956; Syracuse University, Maxwell School of Citizenship and Public Affairs, M.A., 1958; Ph. D., 1967; Harvard Law School, Liberal Arts Fellow in Law and Political Science, 1971.
1. 330 U.S. 1 (1947).
2. *See, e.g.*, Payton v. New York, 445 U.S. 573, 591 n. 33 (1980) (current norms); Marbury v. Madison, 5 U.S. (1 Cranch) 137, 178-180 (1803) (constitutional text); Calder v. Bull, 3 U.S. (3 Dall.) 386, 388-389 (1798) (opinion of Chase, J.) (natural law).
3. 2 The Papers of Thomas Jefferson 1777 to June 18, 1779 (J.P. Boyd ed. 1950) [hereinafter cited as Papers], including the *Revisal of the Laws 1776-1786* [hereinafter cited as *Revisal*]. (Bill No. 82).

legislative proposals—some of which involved religion—generated almost a decade earlier by a "Committee of Revisors" of Virginia's laws,[4] dominated nominally and actually by its most prominent member, Thomas Jefferson.[5] Now, in 1985, a popular and re-elected President of the United States and a cadre of members in both houses of Congress call for, among other things, the re-introduction of prayer in our public schools and some form of aid to private sectarian schools or the parents (or both) whose children attend them. In 1785, the desired relationship between government and religion was forged in the heat of the political process. Now, two centuries later, that relationship is primarily molded in the judicial process; unlike the citizens of 1785, we have become increasingly accustomed to government by judiciary.

In its 1983 term, the United States Supreme Court laid to rest three Church-State questions. The Court held that a Minnesota law that provided a state income tax deduction for some public and private school expenses—including those that might be incurred by sending a child to a sectarian private school—did not violate the degree of separation between Church and State required by the Establishment Clause of the First Amendment.[6] Neither, the Court ruled, did prayers by a state-paid chaplain in the Nebraska legislature,[7] nor the presence of a municipally-owned nativity scene in a Christmas display in Pawtucket, Rhode Island.[8]

Subsequently, in its 1984 term, the Court decided several more important Church-State cases. Of greatest significance among those cases is *Wallace v. Jaffree*,[9] the Alabama "moment of silence" case. Challenged in *Jaffree*, for the first time, was the central doctrine of the *Everson* Court, to wit: that the Framers of the Establishment Clause intended thereby to erect a "high and impregnable wall of separation between Church and State,"

---

4. The "Committee of Revisors" was appointed by resolution of the General Assembly, printed under the date October 15, 1776 and included, in addition to Jefferson, George Mason (who declined to serve), Thomas Ludwell (who died before the Committee began its work), Edmund Pendleton, and George Wythe. Jefferson, Pendleton, and Wythe did the actual revision. PAPERS, *supra* note 3, at 312.

5. PAPERS, *supra* note 3, at 313.

6. Mueller v. Allen, 463 U.S. 388 (1983).

7. Marsh v. Chambers, 463 U.S. 783 (1983).

8. Lynch v. Donnelly, — U.S. —, 104 S. Ct. 1355, *reh'g denied*, — U.S. —, 104 S. Ct. 2376 (1984).

9. Wallace v. Jaffree, — U.S. —, 105 S. Ct. 2479 (1985).

one that would preclude any governmental activity that aided one religion, aided all religions, or preferred one religion over another. Irrespective of scholarly arguments that the quest for the original understanding of the Framers of the First Amendment is misconceived,[10] the facts are that the Court, with little objection from its own ranks, has claimed to have been successful in that search, and has used its historical findings to defend its Establishment Clause requirements. It is, therefore, most timely to re-examine the Supreme Court's Establishment Clause history inasmuch as that history—and consequently what the Court says the Clause forbids—is now very much in dispute.

---

10. For a general discussion about the limitations of the search for the intentions of the Framers in constitutional adjudication see Brest, *The Misconceived Quest for the Original Understanding*, 60 B.U.L. REV. 204 (1980).

To what extent, if at all, "history" should be used to determine constitutional requirements has spawned a seemingly endless and fascinating scholarly debate. *See, e.g.,* J. ELY, DEMOCRACY AND DISTRUST: A THEORY OF JUDICIAL REVIEW (1980); Berger, *The Scope of Judicial Review: An Ongoing Debate*, 6 HAST. CONST. L.Q. 527 (1979); Brest, *supra*; CROSSKEY, POLITICS AND THE CONSTITUTION OF THE UNITED STATES (1953) (2 vols.); Gangi, *Judicial Expansionism: An Evaluation of the Ongoing Debate*, 8 OHIO N.U.L. REV. 1 (1981); Monaghan, *The Constitution Goes to Harvard*, 13 HARV. C.R.-C.L. L. REV. 117 (1978).

This debate has, in part, been fueled by Supreme Court decisions holding that the Fourteenth Amendment incorporates the First, thus making the Establishment Clause's prohibitions applicable to the States. *See, e.g.*, R. BERGER, GOVERNMENT BY JUDICIARY: THE TRANSFORMATION OF THE FOURTEENTH AMENDMENT (1977); Avins, *Incorporation of the Bill of Rights: The Crosskey-Fairman Debates Revisited*, 6 HARV. J. ON LEGIS. 1 (1968); Black, *The Bill of Rights*, 35 N.Y.U.L. REV. 761 (1961); Brennan, *The Bill of Rights and the States*, 36 N.Y.U.L. REV. 761 (1961); Cord, *Neo-Incorporation: The Burger Court and the Due Process Clause of the Fourteenth Amendment*, 44 FORDHAM L. REV. 215 (1975); Crosskey, Charles Fairman, *'Legislative History,' and the Constitutional Limitations on State Authority*, 22 U. CHI. L. REV. 1 (1954); Fairman, *A Reply to Professor Crosskey*, 22 U. CHI. L. REV. 144 (1954); Fairman, *Does the Fourteenth Amendment Incorporate the Bill of Rights? The Original Understanding*, 2 STAN L. REV. 5 (1949); Frankfurter, *Memorandum on 'Incorporation' of the Bill of Rights into the Due Process Clause of the Fourteenth Amendment*, 78 HARV. L. REV. 746 (1965); Green, *The Bill of Rights, The Fourteenth Amendment and the Supreme Court*, 46 MICH. L. REV. 869 (1948); Henkin, *'Selective Incorporation' in the Fourteenth Amendment*, 73 YALE L.J. 74 (1963); Morrison, *Does the Fourteenth Amendment Incorporate the Bill of Rights? The Judicial Interpretation*, 2 STAN. L. REV. 140 (1949).

At the risk of continued criticism, *see, e.g.*, Gangi, Book Review, 7 HARV. J.L. & PUB. POL'Y. 581, 592-95 (1984) (reviewing R. CORD, SEPARATION OF CHURCH AND STATE: HISTORICAL FACT AND CURRENT FICTION (1982)), it seems to me that it does not serve the purposes of this article to join either of those contests here.

What is most relevant here is that the Supreme Court has used its American "history"—and little else—to justify its present Establishment Clause requirements. That fact alone makes an historical analysis germane, if not crucial, to any re-examination of present Supreme Court policy. It is not intended herein to consider whether that policy—once reviewed and, I hope, properly altered—should apply to the States; that argument remains, at least for me, for another day.

II. BACKGROUND

The facts of the *Everson* case are relatively uncomplicated. A 1941 New Jersey law authorized local school boards to "make rules and contracts for the transportation of . . . children to and from school, including the transportation of school children to and from schools other than a public school."[11] Pursuant to this state law, the Board of Education of Ewing passed a resolution providing for the reimbursement of transportation costs to parents who sent their children—by way of the public bus transportation system—to public schools and Roman Catholic parochial schools.[12] The reimbursements were to be paid out of local tax revenues.

Everson, a citizen and taxpayer in the Ewing school district, challenged both the New Jersey statute and the school board resolution under the New Jersey and United States Constitutions.[13] Although the state trial court found that the New Jersey statute conflicted with the state constitution,[14] the New Jersey Court of Errors and Appeals reversed, holding that neither the statute nor the resolution conflicted with either the state or the federal constitution.[15]

Everson appealed to the United States Supreme Court, asserting that both the state law and the school board's resolution violated the federal constitution in two ways. First, he argued that the enactments "authorized the State to take by taxation the private property of some and bestow it upon others, to be used for their own private purposes."[16] This, he alleged, was in violation of the Due Process Clause of the Fourteenth Amendment. Second, Everson contended that the statute and the resolution violated the Establishment Clause of the First Amendment, in that they "forced inhabitants to pay taxes to help support and maintain schools which are dedicated to,

---

11. 330 U.S. 1, 3. Among other things, the New Jersey statute provided that: Whenever in any district there are children living remote from any schoolhouse, the board of education of the district may make rules for the transportation of such children to and from school, including the transportation of school children to and from schools other than a public school, except such school as is operated for profit in whole or in part.
Id. at 3 n.1.
12. *Id.* at 3.
13. *Id.* at 4-5.
14. 132 N.J.L. 98, 39 A.2d 75 (N.J. Sup. Ct. 1944).
15. 133 N.J.L. 350, 44 A.2d 333 (N.J. Ct. of Errors and Appeals 1945).
16. 330 U.S. at 5.

and which regularly teach, the Catholic Faith."[17]

The Court quickly rejected Everson's first contention. It held that the States have broad police power to legislate for the public welfare, and that the Supreme Court should exercise extreme caution in striking down state legislation enacted under that power. According to the Court, the New Jersey legislature had not overreached the limitations imposed on that power by the Fourteenth Amendment.[18]

The Court turned next to Everson's second contention: that the New Jersey statute was a law respecting an establishment of religion. Before the Court could determine whether the statute violated the Establishment Clause, however, it first had to inquire about what governmental actions were prohibited by the Clause. For the answer, Justice Black and the majority looked to history:

> Whether this New Jersey law is one respecting an 'establishment of religion' requires an understanding of the meaning of that language, particularly with respect to the imposition of taxes. Once again, therefore, it is not inappropriate briefly to review the background and environment of the period in which that constitutional language was fashioned and adopted.[19]

III. THE "HIGH AND IMPREGNABLE WALL" THEORY

Justice Black's "review" for the Court included, as background, a discussion of religious intolerance in Europe and the transplanting of that evil in the American colonies. The inequities of religious establishments in America eventually engendered a movement for religious toleration, nowhere stronger than in Virginia, under the leadership of Thomas Jefferson and James Madison.[20] According to Justice Black, "[t]he people there, as elsewhere, reached the conviction that individual religious liberty could be achieved best under a government which was stripped of all power to tax, to support, or otherwise to assist any *or all religions*, or to interfere with the beliefs of any religious individual or group."[21] As a result, in 1785 and 1786, Madison fought and won his battle in the Virginia Assembly

---

17. *Id.*
18. 330 U.S. at 6-8.
19. *Id.* at 8.
20. *Id.* at 8-15.
21. *Id.* at 11 (emphasis added).

against the renewal of "Virginia's tax levy for the support of the established church."[22] In fighting that tax, Madison not only wrote his famous *Memorial and Remonstrance Against Religious Assessments* but, additionally, created the atmosphere in which the Assembly enacted Jefferson's famous Statute of Virginia for Religious Freedom.[23]

It should be carefully noted that Justice Black and the Court majority in *Everson* show no reluctance whatsoever in declaring what were the objectives and the intentions of the Framers of the First Amendment. "This Court," wrote Black, "has previously recognized that the provisions of the First Amendment, in the drafting and adoption of which Madison and Jefferson played such leading roles, *had the same objective and were intended to provide* the same protection against governmental intrusion on religious liberty as the Virginia statute."[24]

Although *Everson* was decided by a vote of five to four, there appears to have been unanimity on the Court about: (1) the minimal prohibitions that the Clause imposed on government; and (2) the method by which those restraints were ascertainable. In using history as their guide to identifying the objectives and intentions of the Framers of the Establishment Clause, the *Everson* dissenters were at one with the opinion of the Court.[25] Nor did they contest the following definition that Justice Black advanced in this first Establishment Clause case:

> The "establishment of religion" clause of the First Amendment means at least this: Neither a state nor the Federal Government can set up a church. Neither can pass laws which aid one religion, *aid all religions*, or prefer one religion over another. Neither can force nor influence a person to go to or to remain away from church against his will or force him to profess a belief or disbelief in any religion. No person can be punished for entertaining or professing religious belief or disbelief, for church attendance or non-attendance. *No tax in any amount, large or small, can be levied to support any religious activities or institutions, whatever they may be called, or whatever form they may adopt to teach or practice religion.* Neither a state nor the Federal Government can, openly or secretly, participate in

---

22. *Id.* at 11.
23. *Id.* at 12. The Statute is sometimes, as in the *Everson* opinions, referred to as the "Bill for Religious Liberty" or the "Bill for Establishing Religious Freedom."
24. *Id.* at 13 (emphasis added).
25. There were three written opinions in *Everson*. Justice Black wrote the opinion of the Court; Justice Jackson dissented, joined by Justice Frankfurter; and Justice Rutledge dissented, joined by Justices Frankfurter, Jackson, and Burton.

the affairs of any religious organizations or groups and vice versa. In the words of Jefferson, the clause against establishment of religion was intended to erect a "wall of separation between church and State . . . ."[26]

Many of these prohibitions, equated with the Establishment Clause by Justice Black, are verifiable by historical documentation. Regrettably, some significant ones are not. Likely more by design than by chance, Justice Black's opinion and both dissents omit any reference to words or deeds that would have run counter to the Court's final conclusion—that the First Amendment was intended by its Framers to erect a "high and impregnable wall" between Church and State.[27] A clear example of this history by omission is the Court's discussion of the events in the Virginia Assembly of 1785 and 1786.

Although the Court's opinion discusses at length Madison's *Memorial and Remonstrance* and Jefferson's Statute of Virginia for Religious Freedom, virtually nothing is said about other events that occurred in that Virginia legislative session. While it is true that on 31 October 1785, Madison, acting as Jefferson's surrogate,[28] introduced his "Bill for Religious Liberty"[29] in the Virginia Assembly, it is equally true that on the same day Madison also introduced Jefferson's bill for punishing—among other undesirable behavior—"sabbath breaking."[30] *Both* of these bills were enacted into Virginia law in 1786.[31] Additionally, there is no mention in *Everson* of another bill attributed to Jefferson which called for "Appointing Days of Public Fasting and Thanksgiving."[32] Madison also introduced this bill but it did not become law.[33] When all of these Madison-Jefferson actions are considered together, they hardly make a convincing

---

26. 330 U.S. at 15-16 (emphasis added).
27. *Id.* at 18.
28. PAPERS, *supra* note 3, at 307.
29. *Id.* at 545-547.
30. *Id.* at 555-556. Although Madison introduced Bill No. 84 of the *Revisal*, punishing sabbath breakers, the most accepted theory is that Jefferson was responsible for revising it and that it was one of some fifty-one bills that Jefferson drew up. PAPERS, *supra* note 3, at 318-20.
31. PAPERS, *supra* note 3, at 545-547 and 555-556.
32. *Id.* (Bill No. 85).
33. Unlike Bill Nos. 82 and 84, Bill No. 85 did not become Virginia law, but it was introduced by Madison. One manuscript copy indicates in the "Clerk's hand endorsed by T.J.: 'A Bill Concerning Public Fasts.' " *See* PAPERS, *supra* note 3, at 556. For a brief but more complete account of the involvement of Jefferson and Madison with the *Revisal* and the texts of Bill Nos. 82, 84, and 85, see R. CORD, SEPARATION OF CHURCH AND STATE: HISTORICAL FACT AND CURRENT FICTION 215-221, 249-250 (1982).

case for the *Everson* Court's "high and impregnable wall" theory. Instead these bills, taken together with Madison's *Memorial and Remonstrance*, lend support to an understanding of Church-State separation different from that of the *Everson* Court—one of state religious non-preference. Additional historical documents, generated in other states, as well as Virginia, during the constitutional ratification process, support the universality, as well as the substance, of this "no preference" interpretation.

IV. THE "NO PREFERENCE" DOCTRINE AND THE ESTABLISHMENT CLAUSE'S ORIGIN

The words that the First Congress eventually shaped into the First Amendment and its Establishment Clause were proposed by James Madison in the House of Representatives on 8 June 1789, four years after he wrote the *Memorial and Remonstrance*.[34] Madison—fully aware that several states had ratified the Constitution with the understanding that a series of constitutional amendments would be added to safeguard certain human rights from encroachment by the national government—called upon the House to act with swiftness tempered by reasonable care.[35]

Although several of the state ratifying conventions urged the protection of diverse individual rights, amendments guaranteeing freedom of religion were commonly suggested. On their face, these suggestions indicate that the States wanted to prevent the establishment of a national religion or the elevation of a particular religious sect to a preferred status and to prohibit interference by the national government with an individual's freedom of religious belief.[36] Specifically, the Maryland ratifying convention proposed an amendment stating: "That there be no national religion established by law; but that all persons be equally entitled to protection in their religious liberty."[37] The Virginia ratifying convention proposed a "Declaration or Bill of Rights" as amendments to the Constitution, of which Article Twenty stated, among other things, "that no particular religious sect or society ought to be favored or established, by

---

34. 1 ANNALS OF CONG. 434 (J. Gales ed. 1834) [hereinafter cited as ANNALS].
35. *Id.* at 427.
36. R. CORD, *supra* note 33, at 5-12.
37. J. ELLIOTT, 2 DEBATES ON THE FEDERAL CONSTITUTION 553 (1901) [hereinafter cited as DEBATES].

law, in preference to others."[38] The New York convention similarly declared: "That the people have an equal, natural, and unalienable right freely and peaceably to exercise their religion, according to the dictates of conscience; and that no religious sect or society ought to be favored or established, by law, in preference to others."[39] Resolutions passed by the North Carolina[40] and Rhode Island conventions[41] echoed Virginia's "Bill of Rights."

Madison's first draft of what ultimately became the Establishment Clause clearly shows this same "no preference" intent: "The Civil rights of none shall be abridged on account of religious belief or worship, nor shall any national religion be established . . . ."[42] Even after Madison's draft was changed by congressional committee deliberations, when asked in debate on the House floor what the re-worded clause meant, Madison said that he "apprehended the meaning of the words to be, that Congress should not establish a religion, and enforce the legal observation of it by law, nor compel men to worship God in any manner contrary to their conscience. . . . to prevent these effects he presumed the amendment was intended, and he thought it as well expressed as the nature of the language would admit."[43]

The resolutions passed by the Maryland, Virginia, New York, North Carolina and Rhode Island ratifying conventions, the original draft of Madison's religion amendment, the debate within the first House and Senate,[44] and Madison's final statement on the floor of the first House of Representatives support the "no preference" interpretation. In other words, insofar as religious establishment was concerned, the First Amendment

---

38. 3 DEBATES, *supra* note 37, at 659. Article Twenty read, in full, as follows:
That religion, or the duty which we owe to our Creator, and the manner of discharging it, can be directed only by reason and conviction, not by force or violence; and therefore all men have an equal, natural, and unalienable right to the free exercise of religion, according to the dictates of conscience, and that no particular religious sect or society ought to be favored or established, by law, in preference to others.
Id.
39. 1 DEBATES, *supra* note 37, at 328.
40. 4 DEBATES, *supra* note 37, at 244.
41. 1 DEBATES, *supra* note 37, at 334.
42. ANNALS *supra,* note 34, at 434.
43. *Id.* at 730.
44. For a detailed study and excellent analysis of the debates in the House and Senate regarding the Establishment Clause, see M. MALBIN, RELIGION AND POLITICS,THE INTENTIONS OF THE AUTHORS OF THE FIRST AMENDMENT (1978).

was intended by its framers to constitutionally forbid the establishment of a national church or religion, or the placing of any one religious sect, denomination, or tradition, into a preferred legal status—a status that was the essential characteristic of religious establishments.[45] Much of what the *Everson* Court said the Establishment Clause "means in the least" embraces

---

45. It has been suggested that the "no preference" interpretation of the Establishment Clause is faulty on at least two grounds. First, it has been argued that early American history indicates that many governmental actions, immediately before and after the addition of the First Amendment to the Constitution, bestowed a favored status upon Christians as opposed to non-Christian theists, thereby making untenable the proposition that the Founding Fathers intended the First Amendment to preclude federal religious partisanship. *See* Gangi, Book Review, *supra* note 10, at 599. The response to that application of the "no preference" doctrine must take into account the attitude that the Framers of the Establishment Clause had about religion. Professor Leo Pfeffer—perhaps the nation's most eminent absolute separationist scholar—has pointed out in his book CHURCH, STATE, FREEDOM 141-42 (1967) that, in the early days of the nation, the "number of professed non-Christians" was minute. Seeing their society as universally Christian—non-Christians not being thought numerous enough to constitute another distinct religious grouping—the adoption of the First Amendment was most likely not seen by its Framers and ratifiers as prohibiting the continued, and exclusive, use of Christian entities as means to reach valid secular ends unless, of course, the government's policy discriminated against some Christian groups in favor of others. Today, however, the application of the Establishment Clause's "no preference" doctrine requires different governmental practices.

In a religiously *homogeneous* society, governmental [policy] that in some way uses, touches, or benefits religion may be by definition nondiscriminatory. That seems to be the case in the United States when Christianity in its many varieties was used by the Federal Government in the eighteenth and much of the nineteenth centuries as a means of accomplishing secular goals. In twentieth century America that is no longer the case. The religious pluralism that now exists in the United States has as a consequence made the historic prohibitions of the Establishment Clause more delimiting of governmental actions. Today, because of the present *religious diversity* in the nation, public sponsored activities that were nondiscriminatory in the past can no longer be reconciled with the Establishment Clause's ban against placing any purely sectarian activity identified with one religious tradition into a preferred position.
R. CORD, *supra* note 33, at 165.

The second criticism of the "no preference" doctrine is that any interpretation of the concept that allows government to use religious institutions to accomplish valid secular ends prefers religion over nonreligion and thus violates the Establishment Clause. *See* Book Note, 97 HARV. L. REV. 1509, 1511 (1984). If one adopts that position— which basically assumes that nonreligion is a religion—all institutions used by government to reach valid legislative ends could be constitutionally assailed under the Establishment Clause. If a purely secular method were employed by government, it could be challenged as putting nonreligion into a constitutionally forbidden preferred position. The fallacy of that interpretation of the "no preference" doctrine is that it relies upon a *reductio ad absurdum*. Almost any legal principle taken to an extreme is likely to become somewhat absurd. For example, the First Amendment injunction that "Congress shall make no law . . . prohibiting the free exercise of [religion] . . . ." does not mean that unlawful acts may be committed as long as one truly believes them to be part of the free exercise of one's religion. Human sacrifice does not come under the Free Exercise Clause simply because one may believe it to be an essential religious sacrament. While I might agree that some non-theistic beliefs and values may occupy "a place in the life of its possessor parallel to that filled by the orthodox belief in God . . . ."—as the Supreme Court held in United States v. Seeger, 380 U.S. at 163, 166 (1965)— that

the "no preference" principle. With that part of the Court's definition—supported as it is by historical fact—I have no quarrel.[46]

V. THE *EVERSON* MAJORITY AS AMERICAN HISTORIANS

Government actions during the formative years of the Republic also lend support to the "no preference" interpretation of the Establishment Clause's prohibitions. They do not make credible the *Everson* Court's "high and impregnable wall" theory. For instance, none of the opinions in *Everson* explains the incongruity between what the Court says are the "least" commands of the Establishment Clause and the institution of the congressional chaplain system by the very Congress that wrote the First Amendment and recommended it to the States for ratification.[47] This is no small point, inasmuch as the *Everson* Court invoked nothing but history to substantiate its interpretation of the Clause.

A. *Financing Religious Activities: Chaplains*

The Court's opinion in *Everson* has the Establishment Clause precluding as unconstitutional, at a minimum, any government financial support for religious activities: "No tax in any amount, large or small, can be levied to support any religious activities or institutions, whatever they may be called, or whatever form they may adopt to teach or practice religion."[48] While I readily concede that such a position certainly follows from, and is reasonable in keeping with, the *Everson* Court's "high and impregnable wall" concept, it is historically clear that this was *not* part of the interpretation of Church-State separation embraced by Congressman James Madison and the other authors of the First Amendment. During the early days of the First Congress, a joint House-Senate Committee considered establishing a con-

---

does not, for me, necessarily transform itself into the concept that all non-theistic beliefs are essentially theistic ones.

46. Additionally, and for the same reason, I do not dispute that part of the *Everson* Court's definition that speaks to the lack of constitutional power vested with government "to compel [people] to worship God in any manner contrary to their conscience."

47. The wording of the Establishment Clause—"Congress shall make no law respecting an establishment of religion"—was accepted by the First House of Representatives on 24 September 1789, and by the First Senate the following day. M. MALBIN, *supra* note 44, at 14 nn.37-38

48. 330 U.S. at 16.

gressional chaplain system.⁴⁹ James Madison was one of the six members of the Committee.⁵⁰ "The result of their consultation was a recommendation to appoint two chaplains of different denominations—one by the Senate and one by the House—to interchange weekly."⁵¹ Accepting that report, the First House of Representatives on 1 May 1789, "proceeded by ballot to the appointment of a [House] chaplain . . . ."⁵² "Upon examining the ballots it appeared," the proceedings of the First Congress report, "that the Rev. William Linn was elected."⁵³ The Reverend Linn and his Senate counterpart, "the Right Reverend Doctor Samuel Provost,"⁵⁴ were paid $500 annually out of federal funds.⁵⁵

The First Congress did more than create a publicly financed chaplain system of its own. By statute enacted on 3 March 1791, it authorized the President, "by and with the advice and consent of the Senate" to appoint a chaplain for the "Military Establishment of the United States."⁵⁶ The compensation for this chaplain was to be "fifty dollars per month, including pay, rations and forage."⁵⁷ If the Establishment Clause means, as the Supreme Court in *Everson* claims, that no tax money in any amount large or small can be used to support "any religious activities or institutions, whatever they may be called, or whatever form they may adopt to teach or practice religion," then we are forced to the ludicrous conclusion that the First

---

49. CHAPLAINS IN CONGRESS AND IN THE ARMY AND NAVY, H.R. DOC. No. 124, 33d Cong., 1st Sess. (1854), *reprinted in* 2 REPORTS OF COMMITTEES OF THE HOUSE OF REPRESENTATIVES 4 (1854).
50. In addition to Madison, the House also chose Boudinot, Bland, Tucker, and Sherman to serve on this joint House-Senate committee. Oliver Ellsworth was the only member of the Senate to serve on the Committee. *Id.*
51. *Id.*
52. ANNALS, *supra* note 34, at 242.
53. *Id.* The technicality that the House did not agree to the text of what became the First Amendment until 24 September 1789, which was after Rev. Linn's selection, or that the First Amendment did not become part of the Constitution until 1791, does not alter the principle discussed here because the chaplain system remained in effect after ratification of the Amendment.
54. *Id.* at 968.
55. CHAPLAINS IN CONGRESS AND IN THE ARMY AND NAVY, *supra* note 49, at 4.
56. For the text of an act entitled "An Act for raising and adding another Regiment to the Military Establishment of the United States and for making farther [sic] provision for the protection of the frontiers," see 1st Cong., 3d Sess., ch. 28, § 5 (1791), *reprinted in* 1 THE PUBLIC STATUTES AT LARGE OF THE UNITED STATES OF AMERICA 222-23 (R. Peters ed.) [hereinafter cited as 1 U.S. STATUTES AT LARGE].
57. *Id.*, at § 6. The Second and Third Congresses also passed statutes authorizing Federal monies to be spent for military chaplains. *See* 2d Cong., 1st Sess., ch. 9, § 7 (1792), *reprinted in* 1 U.S. STATUTES AT LARGE, *supra* note 56, at 241; 3d Cong., 1st Sess., ch. 12, §§ 2 & 6 (1794), *reprinted in* 1 U.S. STATUTES AT LARGE, *supra* note 56, at 350-51.

Congress— including Representative Madison—either recommended to the States a proposed constitutional amendment, the substance of which they then immediately proceeded to violate, or did not understand what the proposed amendment, which they had authored, meant. Both of these propositions on their face are absurd. Yet they grow out of the *Everson* Court's overbroad interpretation of Church-State separation, which has held sway in most Establishment Clause decisions since 1947.

B. *Financing Religion for Public Policy Purposes: The Use of Treaties*

Federal financial support of religious activities was not limited to the appropriation of money to meet the salaries of Congressional and military chaplains. The *Everson* "high and impregnable wall" theory also cannot be squared with the history of financing of religious institutions to meet valid public policy objectives. Frequently, this took the form of Indian treaty obligations proposed and assumed by the new federal government of the United States.

In 1794, only three years after ratification of the First Amendment, President Washington concluded a treaty—proclaimed 21 January 1795—with the Oneida, Tuscarora, and Stockbridge Indians. The treaty obligated the United States to pay "one thousand dollars, to be applied in building a convenient church at Oneida." The church would replace one that the British had burned during the Revolutionary War.[58] Would church building through treaty pass constitutional muster under the *Everson* decision?

Washington was not alone in church building through treaty. On 31 October 1803, President Jefferson presented to the Senate for its advice and consent, a proposed treaty that his representative had negotiated "with the Kaskaskia Indians for the transfer of their country [to the United States] under certain reservations and conditions."[59] The treaty pledged the United

---

58. A Treaty Between the United States and the Oneida, Tuscarora, and Stockbridge Indians, dwelling in the Country of the Oneidas, art. IV, January 21, 1785, 7 THE PUBLIC STATUTES AT LARGE OF THE UNITED STATES OF AMERICA 47, 48 (R. Peters ed. 1861) [hereinafter cited as 7 U.S. STATUTES AT LARGE].

59. 1 A COMPILATION OF THE MESSAGES AND PAPERS OF THE PRESIDENTS: 1789-1897, at 363 (J. Richardson ed. 1901) [hereinafter referred to as A COMPILATION OF THE MESSAGES].

States to supply funds to help build a church and to support a Catholic priest in his priestly duties.[60] Almost a month later, Jefferson asked both houses of Congress to act "in their legislative capacity" to implement the treaty obligations.[61] When Congress granted Jefferson's request and appropriated the federal monies to pay the priest and help build his church, did it pass a law respecting an establishment of religion?

At least two other early presidents joined Washington and Jefferson in committing federal monies to church building by treaty. President Jackson, in an 1833 treaty with the Kickapoo Indians, committed thirty-seven hundred dollars of Federal funds "for the erection of a mill and a church . . . ."[62] President Van Buren's treaty with the Oneida Indians, in 1838, provided funds that were intended for the erection of both a church and a parsonage.[63]

In assuming these treaty obligations, not only was religion financed or otherwise aided by federal tax dollars, but those presidents and congresses closest to—and in some instances responsible for—the addition of the Establishment Clause to our Constitution did not interpret it as being a bar against the use of sectarian means to achieve what would otherwise be construed as constitutionally permissible secular ends.

C. *Financing Religion for Policy Purposes: Land Grants and Federal Monies*

Providing federal funds to support certain religious activity was not the only way that our early presidents and congresses aided sectarian institutions while using them to promote secular objectives. Large grants of land, as well as federal subsidies, were provided to religious societies that acted as federal gov-

---

60. A Treaty Between the United States of America and the Kaskaskia Tribe of Indians, December 23, 1813, 7 U.S. STATUTES AT LARGE, *supra* note 58, at 78. The Third Article of the Treaty in part provided: "And whereas, The greater part of the said tribe have been baptised [sic] and received into the Catholic church to which they are much attached, the United States will give annually for seven years one hundred dollars towards the support of a priest of that religion, who will engage to perform for the said tribe the duties of his office and also to instruct as many of their children as possible in the rudiments of literature. And the United States will further give the sum of three hundred dollars to assist the said tribe in the erection of a church." *Id.* at 79.
61. A COMPILATION OF THE MESSAGES, *supra* note 59, at 365.
62. A Treaty for the Cession of Lands, February 13, 1833, United States—Kickapoo Tribe of Indians, art. VI, 7 U.S. STATUTES AT LARGE, *supra* note 58, at 391-92.
63. A Treaty for the Cession of Lands, May 17, 1838, United States—Oneida Tribe of Indians, art. III, 7 U.S. STATUTES AT LARGE, *supra* note 58, at 566-67.

ernment surrogates in educating and "civilizing" the Indians. Madison and Jefferson were well aware of, and participated in, these practices.

Under the Articles of Confederation, the Continental Congress—in accord with a resolution of 27 July 1787, and "[o]n a report of a [committee] consisting of Mr. [Abraham] Clarke, Mr. [Hugh] Williamson and Mr. [James] Madison to whom was referred a memorial of John Etwein of Bethlehem, president of the brethrens society for propagating the Gospel among the Heathen"[64]—on 3 September 1788, ordered that three parcels of land, one adjoining each of the towns, Gnadenhutten, Shoenbrun, and Salem on the Muskingum, be conveyed to the Moravian Brethren at Bethlehem, Pennsylvania. The land was to be held in trust "for the sole use of the Christian Indians who were formerly settled there."[65] To insure that these lands, totaling twelve thousand acres, were used for the good of the Christian Indians, "a society was formed at Bethlehem by the members of the United Brethren, by the title of 'Society of the United Brethren for propagating the Gospel among the Heathen,' which met for the first time September 21, 1787, and was afterwards duly incorporated by the State of Pennsylvania, by an act dated February 27, 1788 . . . ."[66] Thereafter, this newly created evangelical arm of the United Brethren was incorporated "by the States of New Jersey, Ohio, and New York."[67]

In 1796, eight years after the ratification of the federal Constitution and five years after the addition of the First Amendment, the Fourth Congress passed "An Act regulating the grants of land appropriated for Military services and for the Society of the United Brethren, for propagating the Gospel among the Heathen."[68] As its name suggests, the Society was interested in more than simply managing the land set aside for Indians already converted to Christianity. While governing this

---

64. 34 JOURNALS OF THE CONTINENTAL CONGRESS: 1774-1789, at 485 (R. Hill ed. 1937).
65. *Id.* at 485-86; 33 JOURNALS OF THE CONTINENTAL CONGRESS: 1774-1789, at 429-30 (R. Hill ed. 1937).
66. PROGRESS OF THE SOCIETY OF THE UNITED BRETHREN IN PROPAGATING THE GOSPEL AMONG THE INDIANS, S. DOC. NO. 189, 17th Cong., 2d Sess. (1822), *reprinted in* 2 AMERICAN STATE PAPERS: INDIAN AFFAIRS 372, 374 (1834).
67. *Id.*
68. For the text of an act entitled "An Act regulating the Grants of Land appropriated for Military Services, and for the Society of the United Brethren, for propagating the Gospel among the Heathen," see 4th Cong., 1st Sess., chap. 46 (1796), *reprinted in* 1 U.S. STATUTES AT LARGE, *supra* note 56, at 490.

trust in the interests of the Christian Indians living on parts of this land, the Society also used some of the resources, derived from the cultivation of the lands and from the sale of land leases to white tenant farmers, to send out missionaries to convert souls "from among the neighboring heathen."[69]

Under the terms of the original federal statute, the opportunity to receive a land grant for the services specified in the Act was to expire on 1 January 1800. The Fifth Congress extended the deadline to 1 January 1802 by amending the law.[70] Subsequently, the cut-off date was, by further legislative enactments extended—twice by the Seventh Congress,[71] and once by the Eighth Congress—until finally set as 1 April 1805.[72] Even though these laws in effect paid, with enormous land grants held in a controlling trust, an evangelical Christian sect to spread and maintain Christianity among the Indians in the Ohio Territory, none were vetoed or challenged by the incumbent presidents as violating the degree of Church-State separation required by the First Amendment. Instead, the original bill was approved by President Washington, the next two were approved by President Adams, and the last three became federal law upon the approval and signature of President Jefferson.

Later presidents, through treaties with Indian tribes, also provided grants of federal lands to sectarian organizations, thereby supporting their religious activities. President Monroe, Madison's former Secretary of State, in a treaty with

---

69. PROGRESS OF THE SOCIETY OF THE UNITED BRETHREN IN PROPAGATING THE GOSPEL AMONG THE INDIANS, *supra* note 66, at 376-77.

70. For the text of an act entitled "An Act to amend the act intituled 'An Act regulating the grants of land appropriated for military services and for the Society of the United Brethren for propagating the Gospel among the Heathen,'" see 5th Cong., 3d Sess., ch. 29 (1799), *reprinted in* 1 U.S. STATUTES AT LARGE, *supra* note 56, at 724.

71. For the text of an act entitled "An Act in addition to an Act, intituled 'An Act, in addition to an act regulating the grants of land appropriated for military services, and for the Society of the United Brethren for propagating the Gospel among the Heathen,'" see 7th Cong., 1st Sess., ch. 30 (1802), *reprinted in* 2 THE PUBLIC STATUTES AT LARGE OF THE UNITED STATES OF AMERICA 155 (R. Peters ed. 1850) [hereinafter cited as 2 U.S. STATUTES AT LARGE]. For the text of an act entitled "An Act to revive and continue in force, and an act in addition to an Act intituled 'An Act in addition to an act regulating the grants of land appropriated for Military Services and for the Society of the United Brethren for propagating the Gospel among the Heathen,' and for other purposes," see 7th Cong., 2d Sess., ch. 30 (1803) *reprinted in* 2 U.S. STATUTES AT LARGE, *supra*, at 236.

72. For the text of an act entitled "An Act granting further time for locating military land warrants, and for other purposes," see 8th Cong., 1st Sess., ch. 26 (1804) *reprinted in* 2 U.S. STATUTES AT LARGE, *supra* note 71, at 271.

the Wyandots and other Indian tribes, proclaimed on 4 January 1819, granted United States land "to the rector of the Catholick Church of St. Anne of Detroit, for the use of said Church, and to the corporation of the said college, to be retained or sold, as the said rector and corporation may judge expedient, each, one half of three sections of land, to contain six hundred and forty acres . . . ."[73] Subsequently, President John Quincy Adams, in a treaty with the Osages and other Indian tribes, proclaimed on 30 December 1825, dedicated federal lands to a "Missionary establishment" engaged in "teaching, civilizing, and improving said Indians." Article 10 of the treaty provided:

> It is furthermore agreed on, by and between the parties to these presents, that there shall be reserved two sections of land, to include the Harmony Missionary establishment, and their mill, on the Marias des Cygne; and one section, to include the Missionary establishment, above the Lick on the West side of Grand river, to be disposed of as the President of the United States shall direct, for the benefit of said Missions, and to establish them at the principal villages of the Great and Little Osage Nations, within the limits of the country reserved to them by this Treaty, and to be kept up at said villages, so long as said Missions shall be usefully employed in teaching, civilizing, and improving, the said Indians.[74]

Additionally, despite Justice Black's *Everson* interpretation, that no tax money can—consistent with the Establishment Clause—be used "to support any religious activities or institutions, whatever they may be called, or whatever form they may adopt to teach or practice religion,"[75] the facts show that the United States directly subsidized many church schools, which were engaged in the federal government's program to teach, "civilize," and otherwise improve the Indians.[76] During the years from 1824 through 1831 alone, the *Annual Reports of the*

---

73. A Treaty for the Cession of Lands, January 4, 1819, United States—Wyandot and Other Tribes of Indians, art. XVI, 7 U.S. STATUTES AT LARGE, *supra* note 58, at 160, 166.

74. A Treaty for the Cession of Lands, December 30, 1825, United States—Great and Little Osage Tribe of Indians, art. X, 7 U.S. STATUTES AT LARGE, *supra* note 58, at 240, 242.

75. 330 U.S. at 16.

76. REPORT OF THE CONDITION OF THE SEVERAL INDIAN TRIBES, H.R. DOC. No. 182, 17th Cong., 2d Sess. (1822), *reprinted in* 2 AMERICAN STATE PAPERS: INDIAN AFFAIRS 275 (1834).

Commissioner of Indian Affairs substantiate that federal tax revenues supported religious schools run by the Society of the United Brethren, the American Board of Foreign Missions, the General Baptist Convention, the Hamilton Baptist Missionary Society, the Cumberland Missionary Board, the Synod of South Carolina and Georgia, the United Foreign Missionary Society, the Methodist Episcopal Church, the Western Missionary Society, the Catholic Bishop of New Orleans, the Society for Propagating the Gospel among the Indians, the Jesuits, the Protestant Episcopal Church of New York, the Methodist Society, and the Presbyterian Society for Propagating the Gospel.[77] This policy, of federal financing of church schools, continued throughout the nineteenth century until Congress ended it by statute in 1896.[78]

Did James Madison, when he recommended that Congress—under the Articles of Confederation—convey large tracts of government-owned land to the Moravian Brethren, compromise his *supposedly* strong held "conviction that individual religious liberty could be achieved best under a government which was stripped of all power to tax, to support, or otherwise to assist any or all religions?"[79] And did many presidents and congresses violate the *supposedly* "high and impregnable" wall between Church and State imposed by the Establishment Clause of the First Amendment, when they authorized the granting of Federal lands and monies to religious organizations that they might spread "the Gospel among the Heathen?" Or did Washington, Jefferson, Madison, their contemporaries, and many succeeding presidents and congresses have a far different view of the proper constitutional relationship between government and religion than did Justice Black and the entire *Everson* Court? Merely to pose these questions is to answer them. A thorough reading of early American history manifests that the Framers of the First Amendment did not intend to preclude every significant relationship between the federal government and religion. Their goal was to avoid what in part the *Everson*

---

77. 1 ANNUAL REPORTS OF THE COMMISSIONER OF INDIAN AFFAIRS, 1824-1832 (1976).
78. For the text of an act entitled "An Act Making appropriations for current and contingent expenses of the Indian Department and fulfilling treaty stipulations for fiscal year ending June thirtieth, eighteen hundred and ninety seven, and for other purposes," see 54th Cong., 1st Sess., ch. 398, "Support of Schools," *reprinted in* 29 THE PUBLIC STATUTES AT LARGE OF THE UNITED STATES OF AMERICA 321, 345 (1897) [hereinafter cited as 29 U.S. STATUTES AT LARGE].
79. 330 U.S. at 11.

Court rightly declared were the "cruel persecutions [that] were the inevitable result of government-established religions."[80] But, unlike the *Everson* Court, for the Framers—as the original Madison draft of the Establishment Clause manifests—an established religion connoted a religion, or religious tradition, that was favored and placed in a preferred status by the government.[81] It was this "evil" that the Framers sought to prevent.

Jefferson's 1803 treaty, and the federal land grant laws that he signed, created neither a national church, nor were they government acts designed to put any religious sect into a preferred national status. In the Kaskaskia Indian Treaty, the Catholic Church was funded because Catholic priests were working with those Indians, many of whom had become Catholics.[82] Therefore, it was sensible government policy to aid the Catholic Church in that instance. This was not favoritism toward the Catholic Church, because where it made sense to aid the United Brethren with federal land grants in the Ohio Territory, in that they were working with the Indians there, the Jefferson Administration followed the same policy. Additionally, the fact that schools of many different Christian denominations were funded during the federal government's policy to educate and "civilize" the Indians indicates an absence of preferential treatment.[83]

While the historical acts of collaboration between government and religion—documented and discussed above—are incompatible with the *Everson* Court's interpretation of the Establishment Clause, that is not the case when one assigns the "no-preference" meaning to the Clause. This very fact lends further support to the position that the "no-preference" interpretation of Church-State separation is the one that the Framers intended and the Founding Fathers embraced. Interpretations of the First Amendment that would prohibit *non-discriminatory* governmental aid to religion, especially in pursuit of a secular goal, are of a distinctly modern origin. In light of primary historical documents, it is faulty to attribute

---

80. *Id.* at 12.
81. "The Civil rights of none shall be abridged on account of religious belief or worship, nor shall any national religion be established, nor shall the full and equal rights of Conscience be in any manner, or on any pretext, infringed." ANNALS, *supra* note 34, at 434.
82. See the relevant part of the Treaty quoted *supra* in note 60.
83. 1 ANNUAL REPORTS OF THE COMMISSIONER OF INDIAN AFFAIRS, *supra* note 77.

these interpretations—as the *Everson* Court did—to Madison, Jefferson, and the other Founding Fathers.

VI. THE *EVERSON* MAJORITY AS LEGAL HISTORIANS

Regrettably, the *Everson* Court's judicial history is no more reliable than its recounting of the early history of the Establishment Clause. Prior to 1947, the Supreme Court had not, in any significant way, addressed itself to either the meaning or the scope of of the Establishment Clause's prohibitions on the power of Congress. That is why *Everson* is such an important First Amendment case. Nevertheless, Justice Black's *Everson* opinion mistakenly gives the impression that the Supreme Court had previously spoken to the substance of the Clause. "The meaning and scope of the First Amendment, preventing an establishment of religion or prohibiting the free exercise thereof, in the light of its history and the evils it was designed forever to supress," wrote Justice Black, "have been several times elaborated by the decisions of this Court . . . ."[84] To corroborate this statement, Justice Black essentially relies on six previous Supreme Court decisions:[85] *Terret v. Taylor*;[86] *Watson v. Jones*;[87] *Davis v. Beason*;[88] *Reynolds v. United States*;[89] *Reuben Quick Bear v. Leupp*;[90] and *Bradfield v. Roberts*.[91] Although these cases did address themselves in one way or another to the Free Exercise Clause, only two of them, *Bradfield v. Roberts* (1899) and *Reuben Quick Bear v. Leupp* (1908), may reasonably be identified as involving Church-State separation issues. Regardless of Justice Black's assertion to the contrary, not one of these cases cited supports the broad interpretation that the *Everson* court assigned to the Establishment Clause.

In *Bradfield v. Roberts*, Joseph Bradfield brought suit in the District of Columbia to prevent Providence Hospital—a corporation operated by the Sisters of Charity, a monastic order of the Roman Catholic Church—from receiving any public funds

---

84. 330 U.S. at 14-15.
85. *Id.* at 15, nn.21 & 22. The remainder of the cases cited in these footnotes concentrated on free-expression issues and contain little, if any, discussion of the proper scope of the Establishment Clause.
86. 13 U.S. (9 Cranch) 43 (1815).
87. 80 U.S. (13 Wall.) 679 (1872).
88. 133 U.S. 333 (1890).
89. 98 U.S. 145 (1879).
90. 210 U.S. 50 (1908).
91. 175 U.S. 291 (1899).

set aside by Congress for building construction on privately owned hospital grounds. Bradfield argued that such actions would provide money "to a religious society, thereby violating the constitutional provision which forbids Congress from passing any law respecting an establishment of religion."[92] Noting that the hospital's services were not confined to members of the Catholic faith, and that the act of incorporation did not even mention religion, the Supreme Court's apparently unanimous opinion held that the case was simply one of "a secular corporation being managed by people who hold to the doctrines of the Roman Catholic Church."[93] Hardly supporting Justice Black's "high and impregnable wall" theory, the Court in *Bradfield* further stated that a hospital run by a religious order was to be viewed as a secular corporation so long as it performed its purpose as stated in the articles of incorporation, despite the "alleged sectarian character of the hospital."[94] Not viewing the appropriations act as one respecting the establishment of a religion, as Bradfield had charged, the opinion of the Court, by Justice Peckham, avoided altogether defining the prohibitions imposed by the Establishment Clause.

In the *Reuben Quick Bear* case, a suit was brought against the Commissioner of Indian Affairs by members of the Sioux tribe to enjoin him from using Indian funds to pay, pursuant to a contract, the Bureau of Catholic Missions, a private sectarian corporation, for education provided some members of the tribe. In that case, however, "[t]he validity of the contract for $27,000 [was] attacked on the grounds that such contracts for sectarian education among the Indians [were] forbidden by certain provisos contained in the Indian appropriations acts of 1895, 1896, 1897, 1898, and 1899."[95] Chief Justice Fuller's opinion for the Court, consequently, did not define the limitations imposed on the federal government by the Establishment Clause, in that no contention was raised that the First Amendment was violated by the contract.

Terret v. Taylor, decided in 1815, involved disputed ownership of church property belonging to a particular Episcopal church in Virginia prior to the Revolution and to disestablishment.

---

92. *Id.* at 295.
93. *Id.* at 298-99.
94. *Id.* at 299.
95. 210 U.S. at 77.

Apart from reviewing some of the characteristics of the formerly established church in Virginia, the Court, through Justice Story, said little that can even remotely be interpreted as involving the First Amendment. In fact, both parties to the suit specifically recognized that "the Episcopal Church no longer retained its character as an exclusive religious establishment," so the issue of religious establishment was neither a factor nor addressed in the ownership dispute.[96]

Similarly, in *Watson v. Jones*, a schism within a church produced a legal battle over control of the church's property. As Justice Miller succinctly stated in the Court's opinion: "This is a case of a division or schism in a church. It is a question as to which of two bodies shall be recognized as the Third or Walnut Street Presbyterian Church . . . ."[97] Although the Court's opinion does discuss the two religious protections of the First Amendment, it can hardly be validly cited as one that sets forth the "meaning and scope" of the Establishment Clause.[98]

In *Davis v. Beason*, a brief definition of the Establishment Clause was mentioned in the Court's *obiter dicta*. While clearly stating that the only inquiry before the Supreme Court was one of jurisdiction of the trial court,[99] Justice Field nevertheless wrote that the First Amendment was in part "intended . . . to prohibit legislation for the support of any religious tenets, or modes of worship of any sect."[100] Given Justice Field's earlier remark about the sole issue before the Court, his statement about the First Amendment hardly makes a convincing rationale for defining this case as an Establishment Clause case.

Reynolds v. United States (1879) involved the past Mormon religious practice of polygamy. Even though Chief Justice Waite's

---

96. 13 U.S. (9 Cranch) at 49.
97. 80 U.S. (13 Wall.) at 717.
98. In this country the full and free right to entertain any religious belief, to practice any religious principle, and to teach any religious doctrine which does not violate the laws of morality and property, and which does not infringe personal rights, is conceded to all. *The law knows no heresy, and is committed to the support of no dogma, the establishment of no sect.* The right to organize voluntarily religious associations to assist in the expression and dissemination of any religious doctrine, and to create tribunals for the decision of controverted questions of faith within the association, and for the ecclesiastical government of all the individual members, congregations, and officers within the general associations, is unquestioned.

Id. at 728-29 (emphasis added).
99. 133 U.S. at 341.
100. *Id.* at 342.

opinion of the Court discussed the Establishment Clause,[101] there is nothing in the Court's opinion that adds any substance to the historical argument in defense of the broad interpretation of the Clause disputed here. Notwithstanding Waite's comments about the Establishment Clause, *Reynolds* is in essence a Free Exercise Clause case. The Court's opinion makes this extremely clear in holding that the freedom to act on one's religious belief is not absolute and can be appropriately tempered to the needs of society.[102] Wrote the Chief Justice for the Court:

> So here, as a law of the organization of society under the exclusive dominion of the United States, it is provided that plural marriages shall not be allowed. Can a man excuse his practices to the contrary, because of his religious belief? To permit this would be to make the professed doctrines of religious belief superior to the law of the land, and in effect to permit every citizen to become a law unto himself. Government could exist only in name under such circumstances.[103]

Upon examination of all the previous Supreme Court cases that Justice Black cites in *Everson*, it is evident that they provide no precedent of any significance for determining the "meaning and scope" of the First Amendment's Establishment Clause. While it may be conventional and even desirable legal practice to cite previous judicial decisions to bolster the Supreme Court's interpretation of the Constitution, cases cited that bear little if any relevance to the point being made do not serve well either to substantiate the Court's interpretation or to engender respect for its legal research and scholarship.

VII. Justice Jackson, Dissenting

Although the opinion of the Court in *Everson* held that the First Amendment mandated a "high and impregnable" wall of separation between Church and State, Justice Black and the majority did not see the refunding of public transportation fares to parents who sent their children to Catholic parochial schools as breaching that wall.[104] From that conclusion four justices dissented in two written opinions. For Justice Jackson, the Court's conclusion simply did not follow from the major-

---

101. 98 U.S. 145, 162-64.
102. *Id.* at 166.
103. *Id.* at 166-67.
104. 330 U.S. at 18.

ity's own arguments or its analysis of early American history. Almost mockingly, Justice Jackson made his point:

> [T]he undertones of the opinion, advocating complete and uncompromising separation of Church from State, seem utterly discordant with its conclusion yielding support to their commingling in educational matters. The case which irresistibly comes to mind as the most fitting is that of Julia who, according to Byron's reports, "whispering 'I will ne'er consent,' consented."[105]

What the majority had done in *Everson* was to embrace the "Child Benefit" theory that, when applied to the facts in the case, viewed the New Jersey statute, not as helping sectarian schools, but instead, as merely an exercise of the State's police power to protect children from traffic hazards on their way to school. As Justice Black put it: "The State contributes no money to the schools. It does not support them. Its legislation, as applied, does no more than provide a general program to help parents get their children, regardless of their religion, safely and expeditiously to and from accredited schools."[106]

Unconvinced, Justice Jackson countered, "I should be surprised if any Catholic would deny that the parochial school is a vital, if not the most vital, part of the Roman Catholic Church. . . . Catholic education is the rock on which the whole structure rests, and to render tax aid to its Church school is indistinguishable to me from rendering the same aid to the Church itself."[107]

Almost inevitably—as with virtually all Supreme Court justices from *Everson* to the present—Justice Jackson, like Justice Black before him, turned American historian: "There is no answer to the proposition . . . that the effect of the religious freedom Amendment to our Constitution was to take every propagation of religion out of the realm of things which could directly or indirectly be made public business expense."[108] One cannot help but wonder when reading this whether Washington, Adams, Jefferson, Madison, and the early congresses were aware of this proposition, to which "there was no answer." But, as historian, Justice Jackson truly shows his non-

---

105. 330 U.S. at 19.
106. 330 U.S. at 18. For a discussion of the "Child Benefit" theory, see R. CORD, *supra* note 33, at 105-08.
107. 330 U.S. at 24.
108. *Id.* at 26.

factual grasp of the history of the "religious freedom Amendment" with this symmetrical declaration: "This [religious] freedom was first in the Bill of Rights because it was first in the forefathers' minds . . . ."[109] If anything is historically clear about the First Amendment, it is that it is first in the Bill of Rights by *accident*, not by the "forefathers'" design.

When Madison proposed what eventually became the "religious freedom Amendment," in the first House of Representatives on 8 June 1789, he wanted it—and all other individual rights that he and some of the state ratifying conventions wanted constitutionally secured from invasion by the federal government—to be added to the ninth section of the first article of the Constitution.[110] Certainly, this establishes that Madison did not want the "religious freedom Amendment" first in a separate Bill of Rights. The fact that the "religious freedom Amendment" is in a Bill of Rights, not integrated into the rest of the body of the Constitution, is because Madison's placement suggestion was not accepted by the First Congress. But historian Jackson is wrong about the "minds" of the other forefathers as well.

The First Congress, in 1789, proposed twelve amendments to the States for ratification.[111] Only ten of the original twelve gained ratification and have subsequently become known as the "Bill of Rights."[112] The other forefathers, less Madison, could have put the religious freedom Amendment first among the twelve they proposed for ratification if, as Justice Jackson assures us, that was their desire. The framers of the Bill of Rights chose, however, to put the religious freedom amendment *third*.[113] It became the First Amendment to the Constitution quite by happenstance when the first two proposed amendments were not ratified by the requisite number of states. So much for Justice Jackson's historical reading of the "forefather's minds." The rest of Justice Jackson's relatively short dissent provides little more than what is discussed at greater length—but regrettably not with greater historical accuracy—in

---

109. *Id.*
110. ANNALS, *supra* note 34, at 434.
111. Resolution of the First Congress Submitting Twelve Amendments to the Constitution, *reprinted in* DOCUMENTS ON THE FORMATION OF THE UNION OF THE AMERICAN STATES 1063-65 (1927).
112. ENCYCLOPEDIA OF AMERICAN HISTORY 145-46 (R. Morris ed. 1976).
113. *See supra* note 111.

the dissent by Justice Rutledge, which Justice Jackson also joined.[114]

VIII. FABRICATING HISTORY: JUSTICE RUTLEDGE'S *EVERSON* DISSENT

"The *Everson* case seems in retrospect to be out of line with the First Amendment," wrote Justice Douglas in 1962.[115] Had Justice Douglas been committed to that view in 1947, he would have—in all probability—joined Justice Rutledge's *Everson* dissent, thus transforming it into the opinion of the Court. Virtually reckless in its disregard of indisputable historical facts concerning the Establishment Clause and the First Amendment, Justice Rutledge's *Everson* opinion was only one vote short of deciding that precedent-setting Church-State case.

As with Justice Black's majority opinion, Justice Rutledge's *Everson* dissent embraces the proposition that the Establishment Clause could and should be defined by history. In pursuit of the Clause's meaning and the Framers' intentions—both of which are of great import to him—Justice Rutledge also relies on the same historical documents and events invoked by Justice Black: Madison's "Memorial and Remonstrance,"[116] Jefferson's Virginia "Bill for Establishing Religious Freedom,"[117] and the events in the Virginia Assembly that culminated in disestablishment. Additionally, on the face of his opinion, Justice Rutledge finds little fault, if any, with the majority's definition of the minimal prohibitions which the Establishment Clause places on government.

The only substantive disagreement between the majority and dissenting opinions in *Everson* appears to be an uncompromising absolutist interpretation of Church-State separation embraced by the dissenters. As Justice Rutledge saw it, the First Amendment's purpose, in part, "was to create a complete and permanent separation of the spheres of religious activity and civil authority by comprehensively forbidding every form of public aid or support for religion."[118] The dissenters simply saw the "child benefit" theory as incompatible with the First

---

114. 330 U.S. 1, 28 (Rutledge, J., dissenting).
115. Engel v. Vitale, 370 U.S. 421, 443 (1962) (Douglas, J., concurring).
116. 330 U.S. at 31-38, 40-41.
117. *Id.* at 31, 35, 37-38, 40.
118. *Id.* at 31-32.

Amendment. Justice Rutledge, unlike the majority, argued that the Establishment Clause prohibited any tax money—even under the guise of "public welfare legislation"—to be used in such a way as to aid directly or indirectly any religious institution or activity.[119] Justice Rutledge warned that, by allowing the use of public funds for reimbursement of bus fare for parochial school children, *Everson* created a dangerous legal precedent that could logically culminate in a First Amendment devoid of all power to preclude any government aid to religious educational institutions.[120]

> [W]e are told that the New Jersey statute is valid . . . because the appropriation is for a public, not a private purpose, namely, the promotion of education, and . . . that all we have here is "public welfare legislation" . . . .
>
> If the fact alone be determinative that religious schools are engaged in education, thus promoting the general and individual welfare, together with the legislature's decision that the payment of public moneys for their aid makes their work a public function, then I can see no possible basis, except one of dubious legislative policy, for the state's refusal to make full appropriation for support of private, religious schools, just as is done for public instruction. There could not be, on that basis, valid constitutional objection.[121]

Unsatisfied with the majority's holding that the New Jersey statute did not violate the Establishment Clause, Justice Rutledge launched his own historical investigation. His scholarship and conclusions, however, prove to be even less commendable than those of the majority. In his quest for the original purpose and intent of the Establishment Clause, Justice Rutledge disregards any historical evidence which runs counter to his own absolutist interpretation. Erroneously, like the majority, he relies on historical documents which provide little insight into the Clause's origin. Further, Justice Rutledge's conclusions are seldom substantiated by reliable evidence. A brief analysis of his *Everson* dissent will illustrate its historical failings, its untenable arguments, and its contrary to fact conclusions.

After briefly reviewing the facts of *Everson*, Justice Rutledge begins his inquiry into the historical meaning of the Establish-

---

119. *Id.* at 49.
120. *Id.*
121. *Id.* at 49-50.

ment Clause by asserting that by it, "[n]ot simply an established church, but any law respecting an establishment of religion is forbidden."[122] Referring to Madison, he continues, "The Amendment was broadly but not loosely phrased. It is the compact and exact summation of its author's views formed during his long struggle for religious freedom."[123] With this statement, Justice Rutledge completely ignores two important considerations. First, James Madison was not the only author of the Establishment Clause. The final wording of the First Amendment was arrived at through a series of committee meetings, redrafts, and no doubt compromises. Although Madison was an important participant in this process, he can hardly be said to have been solely responsible for the result.

Second, if Madison did in fact seek to compactly and exactly sum up his views on religious freedom in what later became the First Amendment, would not those views more likely be reflected in his original wording of the Establishment Clause, rather than in the final draft arrived at through the legislative political process? As indicated earlier, Madison's original House proposal was a narrow one that, on its face, sought the prevention of "any national religion be[ing] established."[124] Justice Rutledge's statement is so far off base that it ignores completely that, had Madison's original religion amendment been accepted, the words "any law respecting an establishment of religion" would not even be in the Constitution.

Justice Rutledge does make an assessment of Madison with which I am in total accord. "Madison," he wrote, "could not have confused 'church' and 'religion', or 'an established church' and 'an establishment of religion.' "[125] This acknowledgement does not, however, aid Justice Rutledge's case for a broad interpretation of the Establishment Clause. As already discussed,[126] when on the House floor Roger Sherman in effect asked why the Establishment Clause was at all necessary, "inasmuch as Congress had no authority whatever delegated to them by the Constitution to make *religious establishments*?"[127] Unlike Justice Rutledge, Madison took the word "establish-

---

122. *Id.* at 31.
123. *Id.*
124. ANNALS, *supra* note 34, at 434.
125. 330 U.S. at 31.
126. *See supra* text accompanying note 43.
127. ANNALS, *supra* note 34, at 730.

ment" to mean an established national religion.[128]

Justice Rutledge's discussion of the First Amendment also ignores Madison's own statement about the purpose of the Establishment Clause. As previously indicated, through the Establishment Clause—as well as through the rest of the First Amendment and the Bill of Rights—Madison sought to satisfy some of the state ratifying conventions, which were concerned that the newly formed federal government might encroach on long recognized state authority and individual liberties. Madison's original draft of the religious freedom amendment was patterned after resolutions passed by these conventions, most of which reflected the "no preference" doctrine by insuring the individual's freedom of religious conscience and that no "particular religious sect or society [would] be favored or established, by law, in preference to others."[129] During his House exchange with Roger Sherman of Connecticut, Madison reiterated his purpose when he stated that the Clause

> had been required by some of the State Conventions, who seemed to entertain an opinion that [the Necessary and Proper Clause of the Federal Constitution] enabled [Congress] to make laws of such a nature as might infringe the rights of conscience, and establish a national religion; to prevent these effects [Madison] presumed the amendment was intended, and he thought it as well expressed as the nature of the language would admit.[130]

Completely untenable, when read in light of the then existent federal division of power, is Justice Rutledge's statement that

> The [First] Amendment's purpose was not to strike merely at the official establishment of a single sect, creed or religion, outlawing only a formal relation such as had prevailed in England and some of the colonies . . . . It was to create a complete and permanent separation of the spheres of religious activity and civil authority forbidding every form of public aid or support for religion.[131]

James Madison and the other framers of what became the First Amendment were well aware that the Amendment, if ratified, would place no such restrictions on the state governments.

---

128. *Id.*
129. DEBATES, *supra* note 38.
130. ANNALS, *supra* note 34, at 730.
131. 330 U.S. at 31-32.

They knew full well that no state religious establishment that existed prior to ratification of the Establishment Clause would be disestablished by operation of the Clause. Clearly, Madison, and the others, could not have expected those states that had retained established churches to ratify the First Amendment if they thought it would interfere with their own systems of religious support. As attested to by the continued existence of established churches in several states after the adoption of the First Amendment—the last one being disestablished in 1833—Justice Rutledge's sweeping statement, about the First Amendment's purpose, literally and historically makes no sense.[132]

Justice Rutledge also found meaning in the brevity of the First Congress's debate about the proposed religion amendment. In his discussion of the First Amendment's history, Justice Rutledge observed:

> By contrast with the Virginia history, the congressional debates on consideration of the Amendment reveal only sparse discussion, reflecting the fact that the essential issues had been settled. Indeed the matter had become so well understood to have been taken for granted in all but formal phrasing. Hence, the only enlightening reference shows concern, not to preserve any power to use public funds in aid of religion, but to prevent the Amendment from outlawing private gifts inadvertently by virtue of the breadth of the wording.[133]

Justice Rutledge either overlooked or disregarded the discussion on the floor of the House of Representatives, mentioned earlier, between Madison and Roger Sherman, in which Madison stated his own interpretation of the Establishment Clause. Although the discussion may have been sparse, it was far from unenlightening. Madison's own statement of what he apprehended the meaning of the Clause to be—"that Congress should not establish a national religion, and enforce the legal observation of it by law"[134]—is fatal to Justice Rutledge's con-

---

132. At the start of the American Revolution in 1775, nine of the thirteen colonies had established churches. By the time that the Constitutional Convention assembled in Philadelphia in 1787, only Georgia, South Carolina, Connecticut, Massachusetts, and New Hampshire had retained their religious establishments. After ratification of the Constitution and the First Amendment, disestablishment in the states continued, culminating with that of the Congregational Church in Connecticut in 1818, in New Hampshire in 1819, and in Massachusetts in 1833. For a brief but more complete discussion of disestablishment in the United States, see R. CORD, *supra* note 33, at 3-5.
133. 330 U.S. at 42.
134. ANNALS, *supra* note 34, at 730.

tention that the First Amendment sought to preclude any and all governmental support for religion. It is clear that at least James Madison, while a member of the First Congress and the original sponsor of a religion amendment, did not interpret the Amendment so broadly; any contrary interpretation is not warranted unless supported by equally impressive documentation.

Justice Rutledge may be accurate in stating that the sparseness of the discussion in Congress indicates that the essential issues had been settled. It nevertheless does not follow that the issues had been settled in favor of the expansive interpretation read into the Establishment Clause by Justice Rutledge and the entire *Everson* court. Members of the First Congress probably interpreted Madison's original wording of the Establishment Clause on its face—that no national religion should be established. The sparse discussion more likely indicates that most, if not all, of the members of the First Congress recognized and accepted the limits on the prohibitions incorporated into that original phrasing. Extensive discussion apparently was unnecessary because it was obvious what the Amendment purported to do; that is, it precluded preferential treatment by the federal government, of any one religion or sect, to the detriment of all others.

Justice Rutledge, like the majority, relies heavily on Madison's "Memorial and Remonstrance" in his development of the original meaning of the Establishment Clause. Such reliance is misplaced for several reasons. First, as indicated earlier, Madison was not the sole author of the Establishment Clause. Even if the "Remonstrance" was, as Rutledge would have us believe, "Madison's complete . . . interpretation of [the meaning of] religious liberty,"[135] it does not necessarily follow that this interpretation was completely and concisely incorporated into the Establishment Clause. In fact, given the nature of the legislative process by which the final wording of the Clause was formulated, it would have been difficult, if not impossible, for Madison to project his views into the Amendment to the exclusion of those of the other legislators.

Secondly, both Justice Rutledge and the majority ignore the clearly discriminatory nature of the Assessment Bill which Madison attacked in his "Remonstrance." That Bill provided

---

135. 330 U.S. at 37.

state funds *only* for teachers of the Christian religion. The inference that Madison was also averse to non-preferential support of religious activity *does not* necessarily follow from his "Memorial and Remonstrance." Here is Justice Rutledge's interpretation:

> With Jefferson, Madison believed that to tolerate any fragment of establishment would be by so much to perpetuate restraint upon that freedom. Hence he sought to tear out the institution not partially but root and branch, and to bar its return forever.
>
> In no phase was he more unrelentingly absolute than in opposing state support or aid by taxation. Not even "three pence" contribution was thus to be exacted from any citizen for such a purpose. Remonstrance, Par. 3. Tithes had been the lifeblood of establishment before and after other compulsions disappeared. Madison and his coworkers made no exceptions or abridgments to the complete separation they created. Their objection was not to small tithes. It was to any tithes whatsoever . . . .
>
> In view of this history no further proof is needed that the Amendment forbids any appropriation, large or small, from public funds to aid or support any and all religious exercises. *But if more were called for, the debates in the First Congress and this Court's consistent expressions, whenever it has touched on the matter directly, supply it.*[136]

Nowhere in Justice Rutledge's opinion or its footnotes is there cited any primary documentation corroborating his assertion that "[i]n view of this history, no further proof is needed that the Amendment forbids any appropriation, large or small, from public funds to aid or support any and all religious exercises. But if more were called for, the debates in the First Congress . . . supply it."[137] Instead, the records of the debates and actions of the First and subsequent Congresses contain primary documentation that is contrary to Justice Rutledge's position.

Already documented here are actions taken by the First and subsequent Congresses that indicate that the Amendment was not so broadly interpreted by its framers as by Justice Rutledge and the rest of the *Everson* Court. Take, for example: the First Congress's adoption of the congressional chaplain system, recommended by, among others, James Madison, and supported

---

136. *Id.* at 40-41 (emphasis added).
137. *Id.* at 41.

by public funds;[138] the First Congress's legislation providing for a chaplain for the Army, also paid for out of public monies;[139] and Acts of the Second and Third Congresses that extended the chaplaincy corps, and provided additional funding to support a chaplain for the Navy.[140] Surely, Justice Rutledge was not referring to the Congressional debates, over these and other measures already discussed here, to support his broad interpretation of the Establishment Clause. Notwithstanding Justice Rutledge's sweeping statements to the contrary, the First Congress spent much more than "three pence" of public funds to support the religious exercise of prayer in Congress alone.

Failing to cite any actions in the First Congress to support his absolute interpretation of the Establishment Clause, Justice Rutledge cites some previous Supreme Court decisions that allegedly confirm his First Amendment Church-State position.[141] While most of the cases cited have little, if anything, to do with the Establishment Clause,[142] Justice Rutledge relies for support mainly on *Reuben Quick Bear v. Leupp* (1898). The most germane statement he provides is in footnote 35 of his dissent:

> The decision most closely touching the question, where it was squarely raised, is *Quick Bear v. Leupp*, 210 U.S. 50. The Court distinguished sharply between appropriations from public funds for the support of religious education and appropriations from funds held in trust by the Government essentially as trustee for private individuals, Indian wards, as beneficial owners. The ruling was that the latter could be disbursed to private, religious schools at the designation of those patrons for paying the cost of their education. *But it was stated also that such a use of public moneys would violate both the First Amendment* and the specific statutory declaration involved, namely, that "it is hereby declared to be the settled policy of the Government to hereafter make no appropriation whatever for education in any sectarian school."[143] 210 U.S. 79

Contrary to what Justice Rutledge has written, neither at the

---

138. *See* CHAPLAINS IN CONGRESS AND IN THE ARMY AND NAVY, *supra* note 49; ANNALS, *supra* note 34, at 242.
139. *See* 1 U.S. STATUTES AT LARGE, *supra* note 56, at 222-23.
140. *See id.* at 241, 350-51.
141. 330 U.S. at 43 n.35.
142. *Id.* at 44 n.37. (There, Justice Rutledge discussed the constitutional prohibitions on religious qualifications for public office).
143. *Id.* at 43 n.35 (emphasis added and citation partially omitted).

page 79 of the *Quick Bear* case nor anywhere else in that case did the Supreme Court indicate that the use of public moneys for sectarian education would violate the First Amendment. In 1896, the federal Appropriations Act did declare, as settled policy of the federal government, that there would no longer be appropriations for Indian education in any sectarian schools, provided nonsectarian schools were available.[144] But what Justice Rutledge fails to mention is that this policy change was initiated by Congress, not by a court decision holding unconstitutional the previous congressional policy of aiding sectarian schools involved with Indian education.

Additionally, Justice Rutledge neglects to mention *Quick Bear* footnote 12, which indicates that in "1820, twenty-one schools conducted by different religious societies were given $11,838 by the United States Government and from that date until 1870 the principal educational work in relation to the Indians was under the auspices of these bodies" with financial aid by the national government.[145] Given this documentation, plus more in *Quick Bear* footnote 12,[146] Justice Rutledge can hardly bolster the accuracy of his claim that the First Amendment was historically seen as forbidding "any appropriation, large or small, from public funds to aid or support any and all religious exercises"[147] with appeals to *Quick Bear*. Instead, the major Supreme Court case that Justice Rutledge invokes to support his broad Establishment Clause interpretation contains—within its footnote—factual information that directly contradicts his conclusions.

Justice Rutledge's logic concerning the meaning to be given the word "religion" as used in the First Amendment is no more plausible than his conclusion as to the Amendment's purpose. Inasmuch as the word "religion appears only once in the Amendment," he argues,

> [i]t does not have two meanings, one narrow to forbid 'an establishment', and another, much broader, for securing 'the free exercise thereof.' 'Thereof' brings down 'religion' with its entire and exact content, no more and no less, from the first into the second guaranty, so that Congress and now the states are as broadly restricted concerning one as they are

---
144. 29 U.S. STATUTES AT LARGE, *supra* note 78, at 321, 345.
145. 210 U.S. at 58 n.12.
146. *Id.*
147. 330 U.S. at 41.

regarding the other.[148]

Yet, even as Justice Rutledge concludes, that "religion" should be construed as broadly in the Establishment Clause as in the Free Exercise Clause, he admits to limits on the freedoms protected by the Free Exercise Clause. For him, such limits arise when certain conduct constituting religious expression "trenches upon the like freedoms of others or clearly and presently endangers the community's good order and security."[149] Given his own argument about the equal vitality of both religious prohibitions in the First Amendment, how can Justice Rutledge logically maintain that the Establishment Clause provides for an absolute ban on governmental action while the Free Exercise Clause does not? Justice Rutledge's own logic compels that the governmental prohibitions imposed by the Establishment Clause, like the freedoms protected by the Free Exercise Clause, are not absolute.

Should a majority of the Supreme Court ever, retrospectively, find itself in agreement with Justice Douglas's concurrence in the *Engel* case,[150] and adopt Justice Rutledge's *Everson* dissent as "durable First Amendment philosophy," it could only do so by ignoring our constitutional forebearers and the First Amendment's history.

IX. CONCLUSION

During its 1982, 1983, and 1984 terms, the Supreme Court decided much that is significant for Establishment Clause law in general, and for the "no-preference" doctrine in particular. In *Mueller v. Allen*,[151] the Court in a five-to-four decision[152] upheld the constitutionality of a Minnesota state income tax deduction for expenses incurred by parents whose children attended elementary and secondary schools, including sectarian ones.[153]

---

148. *Id.* at 32.
149. *Id.*
150. 370 U.S. 421, 443.
151. 463 U.S. 388 (1983).
152. Justice Rehnquist, joined by Chief Justice Burger and Justices White, Powell, and O'Connor, wrote the opinion of the Court.
153. The Minnesota statute permitted a taxpayer to deduct from his or her computation of gross income the following:
> the expenses he has paid to others, not to exceed $500 for each dependent in grades K-6 and $700 for each dependent in grades 7-12, for tuition, textbooks and transportation of each dependent in attending an elementary or secondary school situated in Minnesota, North Dakota, South Dakota, Iowa, or Wisconsin, wherein a resident of this state may legally fulfill the state's

Calling the dissimilarity perceived by the majority between the Minnesota statute upheld in *Mueller* and the New York law struck down by the Court in *Committee for Public Education v. Nyquist*,[154] "a distinction without a difference,"[155] Justice Marshall, in dissent, would have voided the law in *Mueller* on the same grounds used by the Court in *Nyquist*.[156] Quoting from *Nyquist*, Justice Marshall wrote: "[T]he effect of the aid is unmistakenly to provide desired financial support for nonpublic sectarian institutions."[157]

More significant in *Mueller* for Establishment Clause law than the majority's sanction of the alleged sectarian aid was the reduced status that Justice Rehnquist's opinion for the Court assigned to the Church-State tripartite test of constitutionality, first used by the Court in *Lemon v. Kurtzman*.[158] Instead of identifying the "cumulative criteria" enunciated in *Lemon*[159] as the irreducible minimal requirements that a statute has to meet if challenged under the Establishment Clause, as had been the Court's practice for the previous decade, the Court took another tack. Justice Rehnquist essentially characterized the *Lemon* criteria as Justice Powell had—"no more than helpful signposts"—in his majority opinion ten years previously in *Hunt v. McNair*.[160] Accomplishing this status reduction, Justice Rehnquist, in *Mueller*, proceeded ultimately to employ the

---

compulsory attendance laws, which is not operated for profit, and which adheres to the provisions of the Civil Rights Act of 1964 and chapter 363.

The law specified that the "textbooks" referred to in the statute included books and other instructional materials and equipment used in elementary and secondary schools in teaching only those non-extracurricular subjects legally and commonly taught in public elementary and secondary schools in Minnesota. 463 U.S. at 390 n.1. The definition explicitly excluded materials "used in the teaching of religious tenets, doctrines or worship, the purpose of which is to inculcate such tenets, doctrines or worship . . . ." *Id.*

154. 413 U.S. 756 (1973).

155. 463 U.S. at 411.

156. Justice Marshall's dissent was joined by Justices Brennan, Blackmun, and Stevens. *Id.* at 404.

157. *Id.* at 406, quoting *Committee for Public Education v. Nyquist*, 413 U.S. at 783.

158. 403 U.S. 602 (1971).

159. The *Lemon* "three-part" test requires that to survive challenge under the Establishment Clause a statute: (1) must have a secular legislative purpose; (2) must have a principal or primary effect that neither advances nor inhibits religion; and (3) must not foster an excessive government entanglement with religion. *Id.* at 612-13.

160. Hunt v. McNair, 413 U.S. 734, 741 (1973). In *Hunt*, Justice Powell, joined by Chief Justice Burger and Justices Stewart, White, Blackmun, and Rehnquist, wrote the opinion of the Court. Justice Brennan, joined by Justices Douglas and Marshall, dissented. *Id.* at 749.

Lemon test, holding that the Minnesota statute did not violate the First Amendment.

If the Court's return to the *Hunt* interpretation of the *Lemon* test's status was somewhat revisionist in *Mueller*, one week later, Chief Justice Burger's opinion in *Marsh v. Chambers*[161] contained a departure from the Court's recent Establishment Clause decisions that was much more fundamental. In *Marsh*, a six-to-three majority of the Court[162] clearly embraced a test for determining the constitutionality of challenged or suspect governmental action under the Establishment Clause distinctively different from the test in *Lemon*.

Writing for the Court, Chief Justice Burger indicated that while "[s]tanding alone, historical patterns cannot justify contemporary violations of constitutional guarantees," in the case of opening a legislative session with prayers by a paid chaplain "there [was] far more . . . than simply historical patterns."[163] Regarding legislative chaplains, the Chief Justice continued,

> [H]istorical evidence sheds light not only on what the draftsmen intended the Establishment Clause to mean, but also on how they thought that Clause applied to the practice authorized by the First Congress—their actions reveal their intent. . . . It can hardly be thought that in the same week Members of the First Congress voted to appoint and to pay a Chaplain for each House and also voted to approve the draft of the First Amendment for submission to the States, they intended the Establishment Clause of the Amendment to forbid what they had just declared acceptable. . . . This unique history leads us to accept the interpretation of the First Amendment draftsmen who saw no real threat to the Establishment Clause arising from a practice of prayer similar to that now.[164]

Of great significance is the fact that the Chief Justice, who a dozen years earlier had carefully fashioned the Court's "three-part" test in *Lemon*, was now deciding an Establishment Clause case without invoking it. By so doing, the Court indicated that the *Lemon* test no longer held *exclusive* sway in such cases. Unmistakably, the Court in *Marsh* had embraced a history test, or at a minimum, a "unique history" test, the use of which estab-

---

161. 463 U.S. 783. *Mueller* was decided 29 June 1983 and *Marsh* on 5 July 1983.
162. Chief Justice Burger, joined by Justices White, Blackmun, Powell, Rehnquist, and O'Connor, wrote the opinion of the Court. 463 U.S. 783.
163. *Id.* at 790.
164. *Id.*

lished that, at least on one issue, a majority of the Court's present personnel[165] had overtly made a commitment to an *alternative* test to *Lemon* as determinative of at least one kind of contemporary Establishment Clause controversy. Seen as such, the Chief Justice's opinion was much disputed by Justice Brennan in a vigorous dissent.[166]

Justice Brennan's *Marsh* dissent is a masterful display of damage control.[167] First, by focusing on the Court's "unique history" statement,[168] he cleverly dismissed the majority's opinion as an aberration, because it did not use "[the Court's] settled doctrine"—the *Lemon* test—to determine the constitutionality of Nebraska's chaplaincy practice. The majority chose not to do so, he explained, because they then "would have [had] to strike it down as a clear violation of the Establishment Clause."[169] In this, Justice Brennan refused to acknowledge that a majority of the Court's members rejected the notion that the tripartite *Lemon* test, especially his broad interpretation of it, is an *inextricable* part of the Establishment Clause, and, in fact, were willing to use *other criteria* to judge practices alleged to violate that clause.

Second, Justice Brennan, whose own opinion significantly contains many appeals to the extremely selective Madison and Jefferson "history" characteristic of the *Everson* opinions,[170] in-

---

165. There have been no changes in the Supreme Court's composition since *Marsh* was decided in 1983.
166. Justice Brennan, joined by Justice Marshall, dissented. 463 U.S. 795. Justice Stevens dissented separately. *Id.* at 822.
167. Justice Brennan's dissent in *Marsh* is more than twice as long as the Court's opinion. *Id.* at 795-822.
168. *Id.* at 795.
169. *Id.* at 796. Justice Brennan's dissent, in several places, truly chided the Court's failure to use the *Lemon* test: "The Court makes no pretense of subjecting Nebraska's practice of Legislative prayer to any of the formal tests that have traditionally structured our inquiry under the Establishment Clause." *Id.* "I must begin by demonstrating what should be obvious: that, if the Court were to judge legislative prayer through the unsentimental eye of our settled doctrine, it would have to strike it down as a clear violation of the Establishment Clause." *Id.* "In sum, I have no doubt that, if any group of law students were asked to apply the principles of *Lemon* to the question of legislative prayer they would nearly unanimously find the practice to be unconstitutional." *Id.* at 800-01.
170. The selective history used, especially by Justices Black and Rutledge, is documented in Sections V and VIII of the text. Justice Brennan, in *Marsh*, 463 U.S. at 807-08, placed great emphasis on Madison's "Detached Memoranda," a document first published in 1946, which Madison wrote late in life. Fleet, *Madison's "Detached Memoranda*," 3 WM. & MARY Q. 534 (1946). It is somewhat amusing to note that Justice Brennan had previously dismissed—appropriately in my judgment— Madison's statements in the "Memoranda" when he wrote:

dicated his most important disagreement with the majority was with its "misguided" use of history.[171] Quoting from his concurrence in *Abington v. Schempp*,[172] where he had earlier criticized the use of an historical argument by others, even as he invoked one himself,[173] Justice Brennan wrote that "the Constitution is not a static document whose meaning on every detail is fixed for all time by the life experience of the Framers. To be truly faithful to the Framers, 'our use of the history of their time must limit itself to broad purposes, not specific practices.'"[174]

Whether the non-use of the *Lemon* test in *Marsh* was in fact an aberration by a momentary Court majority was raised again during the Court's 1983 term in *Lynch v. Donnelly*,[175] where the constitutionality of Pawtucket, Rhode Island's Christmas creche display was challenged. As in *Marsh*, decided the previous term, Chief Justice Burger wrote the Court's opinion[176] and Justice Brennan the major dissent. Even though there was an opinion of the Court, the four written opinions in *Lynch* revealed a much fragmented Supreme Court.[177]

While Justice Brennan, writing for four justices,[178] continued to indicate that the majority's failure in *Marsh* to utilize the *Lemon* criteria did indeed represent an "aberrant departure from [the Court's] *settled* method of analyzing Establishment Clause cases,"[179] the Chief Justice, writing for five justices,[180] held that the Court had "repeatedly emphasized [its] *unwillingness* to be confined to any *single test or criterion* in this sensitive

---

These arguments were advanced long . . . after the adoption of the Establishment Clause. They represent at most an extreme view of church-state relations, which Madison himself may have reached only late in life. He certainly expressed no such understanding of Establishment during the debates on the First Amendment . . . . And even if he privately held these views at that time, there is no evidence that they were shared by others among the Framers and Ratifiers of the Bill of Rights.

Walz v. Tax Comm'n, 397 U.S. 664, 684 n.5 (1970) (Brennan, J., concurring).
171. 463 U.S. at 816.
172. Abington v. Schempp, 374 U.S. 203, 230 (1963).
173. *Id.* at 237-38, 241, 294-95.
174. 463 U.S. at 816.
175. — U.S. —, 104 S. Ct. 1355 (1984).
176. *Id.*
177. The opinions in *Lynch* were written by Chief Justice Burger, *id.*; Justice O'Connor, *id.* at 1366; Justice Brennan, *id.* at 1370; and Justice Blackmun, *id.* at 1386.
178. Justice Brennan was joined in dissent by Justices Marshall, Blackmun, and Stevens. Justice Blackmun's dissent was joined by Justice Stevens.
179. 104 S. Ct. at 1371 n.2 (emphasis added).
180. Chief Justice Burger was joined by Justices White, Powell, Rehnquist, and O'Connor. Additionally, Justice O'Connor wrote a concurring opinion.

area."[181] Although the Court had "often found" the standards in *Lemon* useful in determining whether or not the Establishment Clause had been violated, the Chief Justice, documenting his point, wrote: "In two cases, the Court did not even apply the *Lemon* 'test.' We did not, for example, consider that analysis relevant in *Marsh* . . . . Nor did we find *Lemon* useful in *Larson v. Valente* . . . where there was substantive evidence of discrimination against a particular church."[182]

Divergence on the Court about the nature of the *Marsh* "history" test can also be seen in *Lynch*. Even as Justice Brennan emphasized that "the Court [in *Marsh*] concluded on the basis of . . . 'unique history' that the modern-day practice of opening legislative sessions with prayer was constitutional,"[183] the Court's opinion no longer employed the "unique history" terminology. Instead, the wording of Chief Justice Burger's opinion indicated that the "unique history" test—if indeed there had ever been one in *Marsh*— had metamorphosed into simply a "history" test. "The Court's interpretation of the Establishment Clause has comported with what history reveals was the contemporaneous understandings of its guarantees,"[184] wrote the Chief Justice. He then proceeded to discuss some specific and general American historical events, linked to the nation's "religious heritage," that the majority thought were relevant in acquiring an understanding of the First Amendment's Church-State prohibitions.[185] "This history," the majority hoped, "may help explain why this Court consistently has declined to take a rigid, absolutist view of the Establishment Clause. We have refused 'to construe the Religious Clauses with a literalness that would undermine the ultimate constitutional objective *as illuminated by history*,' " said the Court's opinion, quoting from *Walz v. Tax Commission*, but adding its own emphasis.[186]

Having said that, the *Lynch* majority then proceeded to employ the *Lemon* criteria holding that Pawtucket's creche had a secular purpose,[187] did not unconstitutionally advance religion,[188] and did not impermissibly entangle government with

---

181. 104 S. Ct. at 1362 (emphasis added).
182. *Id.* (citations omitted).
183. *Id.* at 1383.
184. *Id.* at 1354.
185. *Id.* at 1359-61 nn.1-5.
186. *Id.* at 1361. Walz v. Tax Comm'n, 397 U.S. 664, 671 (1970).
187. 104 S. Ct. at 1363.
188. *Id.* at 1364.

religion.[189] Given the outcome of the majority's application of *Lemon* to the facts in *Lynch*, there is no wonder that Justice Brennan's dissent reflected concern for the future of his version of the test: "[T]he Court's less than vigorous application of the *Lemon* test suggests that its commitment to those standards may only be superficial."[190] The most dramatic shift in Establishment Clause law, however, was to unfold during the 1984 term when the Supreme Court decided *Wallace v. Jaffree*,[191] the Alabama "moment of silent prayer or meditation" case.

Until the Supreme Court's 1984 term, no sitting justice had clearly and forcefully challenged *Everson*'s "high and impregnable wall" doctrine. That unity of Church-State ideology was shattered by Justice Rehnquist's dissent in *Wallace v. Jaffree*.[192] Adopting the "no preference" doctrine as his own, and presenting some of the historical evidence that supports it, Justice Rehnquist, in a single opinion, called into question some of the Court's most fundamental assumptions about the degree of separation between Church and State required by the Constitution.

For Justice Rehnquist, the historical evidence was clear that the Founding Fathers and the Framers of the First Amendment did not construe the Establishment Clause as prohibiting government from using non-preferential sectarian means to reach valid secular ends.[193] Nor did he accept the view that non-partisan aid to religious institutions are on their face constitutionally estopped.[194] Instead, Justice Rehnquist called unequivocally upon the present Court to consider carefully all the historical evidence,[195] and finally to probate it,[196] even if the outcome runs counter to the current majority's "impregna-

---

189. *Id.*
190. *Id.* at 1370-71.
191. — U.S. —, 105 S. Ct. 2479 (1985).
192. *Id.* at 2508. In *Wallace*, there were six written opinions. Justice Stevens, joined by Justices Brennan, Marshall, Blackmun, and Powell, wrote the opinion of the Court. *Id.* at 2481. In addition to joining the Court's opinion, Justice Powell wrote a concurring opinion. *Id.* at 2493. Justice O'Connor wrote an opinion concurring only in the Court's judgment. *Id.* at 2496. Additionally, there were three separate dissents: one by Chief Justice Burger, *id.* at 2505; Justice White, *id.* at 2508; and Justice Rehnquist, *id.* at 2508.
193. *Id.* at 2520.
194. *Id.* at 2512-13, 2520.
195. *Id.* at 2508-09, 2519-20.
196. *Id.* at 2519-20.

ble wall" metaphor.[197]

It is of course understandable why Justice Brennan—and those on the Court who usually agree with him in Establishment Clause cases—*now* caution against an overdependence on history to guide the judiciary, and others, in making or interpreting Establishment Clause law. Having successfully used their selective history to legitimize the infusion of the "high and impregnable wall" theory into the First Amendment, Justice Brennan and the other contemporary successors to Justices Black, Jackson, and Rutledge now want an end to further historical considerations because—as shown herein—their interpretation of the Establishment Clause cannot survive a full and careful historical scrutiny.[198] In brief, having obtained their goal of overbroadly defining the Establishment Clause's prohibitions through the selective use of early American history, Justice Brennan and the others now proclaim irrelevant the very same historical methodology that the Court majority has, since *Everson* to the present, used to justify its precedent-setting decisions in this very sensitive area of First Amendment law. Whatever else may be said about uses of history to determine and apply Establishment Clause principles to contemporary legal controversies, this technique of historical "special pleading"—that is, the simultaneous invocation of historical arguments when it suits one's cause and to deny their validity or importance when it does not—is, in my judgment, at best illogical, and at worst, an intellectually unacceptable double standard.

In calling for a re-examination of all Establishment Clause law beginning with *Everson*, Justice Rehnquist may be less of a lone dissenter than he appears.[199] Justice White, who indicated most recently in *Grand Rapids School District v. Ball*[200] that he had dissented in *Lemon v. Kurtzman*, has also taken the position that he, too, would be willing to see if the Establishment Clause's history supports the sweeping prohibitions assigned to it by the *Everson* Court.[201] Both justices have long been unhappy with

---

197. *Id.* at 2508, 2516-17.
198. For a comprehensive analysis, see R. Cord, *supra* note 33, especially chs. 7 & 8 at 102-211, and the documents in the Addenda at 241-302.
199. Although there were three dissenters in *Wallace*, neither of the other two joined Justice Rehnquist's opinion.
200. Grand Rapids School Dist. v. Ball, — U.S. —, 105 S. Ct. 3216, 3249 (1985) (White, J., dissenting).
201. 105 S. Ct. at 2508.

the *Lemon* test. They indicated, almost a decade ago in *Roemer v. Bd. of Public Works of Maryland*, that the test ought to be modified or abandoned and that other criteria should be fashioned to determine the substance of Establishment Clause law.[202] It appears that only the desire to write some of that law brought Justices White and Rehnquist back into judicial collaboration with other members of the Court, who were themselves bound to the *Lemon* criteria.[203] However, unlike *Roemer* in 1976, the recent re-emergence of the "no preference" doctrine offers the Court another basis with which to view not only Establishment Clause cases, but also some Free Exercise and other cases that seem to arise out of the present Court's application of the *Lemon* criteria.[204]

While there assuredly will continue to be some uncertainty about what the Establishment Clause forbids—a problem with most, if not all, First Amendment guarantees— an uncompromising application of the "no preference" doctrine in future cases promises not only to return to the principles of separation between Church and State embraced by the First Amendment's framers, but also to go a long way toward extricating the Supreme Court from the present time- consumptive case-by-case analysis evident in this area of constitutional law.[205] While by no means a panacea, a return to the "no preference" doctrine will assuredly provide lower appellate courts, and those of original jurisdiction, a clearer understanding of what offends the Establishment Clause than the Supreme Court's present use, or in some cases the non-use, of one of the current varieties of *Lemon*.

One thing is certain. Justice Rehnquist did not stake out his Establishment Clause course lightly, nor is his *Jaffree* opinion a casual commitment. His invocation of his *Jaffree* dissent in two subsequent Church-State cases decided by the Supreme Court

---

202. Roemer v. Board of Pub. Works of Maryland, 426 U.S. 736, 768-69 (1976) (White, J., concurring). Justice Rehnquist joined in Justice White's opinion.
203. In Committee for Public Education and Religious Liberty v. Regan, 444 U.S. 646 (1980), Justices White and Rehnquist re-embraced the *Lemon* test in a five-to-four split decision. Justice White, joined by Chief Justice Burger, and Justices Stewart, Powell and Rehnquist, wrote the opinion of the Court. Justice Blackmun dissented in an opinion joined by Justices Brennan and Marshall. Justice Stevens dissented separately.
204. NLRB v. Catholic Bishop of Chicago, 440 U.S. 490 (1979); Brandon v. Board of Educ. of Guilderland, 635 F.2d 971 (2d Cir. 1980); Lubbock Civil Liberties Union v. Lubbock Ind. School Dist., 669 F.2d 1038 (5th Cir. 1982); Witters v. Washington State Comm'n for The Blind, 102 Wash. 2d 624, 689 P.2d 53 (1984).
205. R. CORD, *supra* note 33, ch. 7 at 166-211.

late in its 1984 term[206] indicates that he has decided to do on the Court all he can to restore the Establishment Clause's "no preference" doctrine.

---

206. Grand Rapids School Dist. v. Ball, — U.S. —, —, 105 S. Ct. 3216, 3231 (1985); Aquilar v. Felton, — U.S. —, —, 105 S. Ct. 3232, 3243 (1985).

THE SUPREME COURT AS NATIONAL SCHOOL BOARD*

Edward S. Corwin†

As a student at the University of Michigan a half century ago I had frequent occasion to attend convocations, lectures, and concerts in University Hall. Each time my eyes were confronted with the words, emblazoned on the wall over the great organ, "Religion, morality, and knowledge, being necessary to good government and the happiness of mankind, schools and the means of education shall forever be encouraged." These words are from the famous Northwest Ordinance which was enacted in 1787 by the last Congress of the Confederation,[1] and which from the provision it makes for the establishment of public schools is the matrix of the public school system of a great part of the United States. Two years later many of the same men, representatives of the same people, sitting as the first Congress under the Constitution, proposed the following amendment to the Constitution: "Congress shall make no law respecting an establishment of religion, or prohibiting the free exercise thereof. . . ." Do these words represent a fundamental change in attitude on the part of the American people on the question of what relation should subsist between public education and the teaching of religion? Prima facie it seems doubtful,[2] but that it is so, nevertheless, is the implication of the decision on March 8, 1948, of the United States Supreme Court in *Illinois* ex rel. *Vashti McCollum v. Board of Education of Champaign County*.[3]

The facts and holding in the case may be set forth as follows:

A local board of education in Illinois agreed to the giving of religious instruction in the schools under a "released time" arrangement whereby pupils, whose parents signed "request cards," were permitted to attend religious-instruction classes conducted during regular school hours in the school building by outside teachers furnished by a religious council representing the various faiths, subject to the approval and supervision of the superintendent of schools. Attendance records were kept and reported to the school authorites in the same way as for other classes; and pupils not attending the religious instruction classes were required to continue their regular secular studies.

The Court held, in an opinion by BLACK, J., that this arrangement was in violation of the constitutional principle of separation of Church and State, as expressed in the First Amendment and made applicable to the states by the Fourteenth Amendment, and accordingly that the state courts below had acted erroneously in refusing relief to the com-

---
* This is a revision of an article published in 43 Thought 665 (1948).
† McCormick Professor of Jurisprudence (emeritus), Princeton University.
[1] July 13, 1787, 1 Stat. 51, n., Art. III.
[2] The doubt becomes doubly doubtful when we recall that Congress re-enacted the Northwest Ordinance in 1791!
[3] 333 U. S. 203 (1948).

plainant, parent and taxpayer, against the continued use of school buildings for such religious instruction.

This conclusion was supported further in a separate concurring opinion by FRANKFURTER, J., in which the historical backgrounds of the principle of separation of Church and State, and of "released time" arrangements, are considered at length. Justices JACKSON, RUTLEDGE, and BURTON joined in this opinion; and Justices RUTLEDGE and BURTON also concurred in the opinion written by Justice BLACK.

JACKSON, J., in an additional opinion, although concurring in the result, expressed doubt as to the standing of the complainant to raise the question at issue, and also felt that the relief granted, prohibiting all religious instruction in the schools, was too broad and indefinite.

REED, J., dissented on the ground that the co-operative "released time" arrangement did not involve either an "establishment of religion" or "aid" to religion by the state, sufficient to justify the Supreme Court in interfering with local legislation and customs.[4]

The holding and the opinions accompanying it raise all sorts of questions. "Released time" programs prior to the decision operated in some 2,200 communities spread over forty-six states.[5] Are all of these programs rendered unconstitutional by the ruling in the *McCollum* case, or only those which are conducted in public school buildings? Justice Frankfurter, after characterizing the Champaign plan as "a conscientious attempt to accommodate the allowable functions of Government and the special concerns of the Church within the framework of our Constitution,"[6] says that some released-time programs may be constitutional, others unconstitutional, and which are the one or the other must await "close judicial scrutiny"[7] as cases arise. From the point of view of persons vested with the responsibility of administering the public school system of the country, this is not exactly a consoling utterance. And positively disturbing to all public educational authorities, both those at the school level and those at the college and university level, is Justice Jackson's[8] suggestion that the holding may contain a threat to courses on religion and religious history, or even to courses in art, philosophy, and literature, which can hardly be taught without reference to religion, the seed-bed of them all.[9]

In fact, the decision seems to have fully satisfied very few people. Even Mrs. McCollum is disappointed in the final outcome, to date, of her efforts. What she asked for was a judicial mandate that

would ban all teaching of the Scriptures. She especially mentions as an example of invasion of her rights "having pupils learn and recite such statements, 'The Lord is my Shepherd, I shall not want.'" And she objects to teaching that the King James version of the Bible "is called the Christian's Guide Book, the Holy Writ and the Word of God," and many other similar matters.[10]

[4] 92 L. Ed. 451 (1948).
[5] McCollum v. Board of Education, 333 U. S. 203, 224-225 n. 16 (1948).
[6] *Id.* at 213.   [7] *Id.* at 225.   [8] *Id.* at 236.
[9] A great many state constitutional provisions seem likely to undergo Supreme Court scrutiny under the *McCollum* decision. See FREDERIC J. STIMSON, THE LAW OF THE FEDERAL AND STATE CONSTITUTIONS OF THE UNITED STATES III, §§ 2-48 (1908).
[10] McCollum v. Board of Education, *supra* note 5, at 234-235.

She also avows a distaste for the word "sin." Yet all that the Court did was to remand the cause to the State Supreme Court "for proceedings not inconsistent with this opinion,"[11] a directive with which the latter court complied by banning the Champaign system. Comments the lady, according to the Champaign *News-Gazette:*

> I am right back where I started from three years ago. I have wasted all this time and money without an order prohibiting the schools from aiding and abetting in carrying on these classes. The schools should be definitely ordered against corralling students for religious classes. I told Mr. Dodd [her attorney] that I was dissatisfied and wanted to appeal. I believe we will take any further action that is open to us.[12]

My interest in this case is, however, not in the question of its practical soundness, but in that of its constitutional soundness; in the question, in brief, whether the Constitution *does* require that all public-supported education be kept strictly secular. Some comparatively recent decisions suggest the contrary. In the *New Jersey Bus* case,[13] which was decided thirteen months prior to the Champaign case, it was held that the state is not inhibited from aiding religious instruction incidentally to the exercise by it of the police power for the protection of the health and safety of school children on the way to school; while in 1930, in *Cochran v. Louisiana*,[14] it was held that children attending parochial schools could be made beneficiaries of that state's free textbook law without offense to the Constitution. The interest of the statute, said the Court, "is education, broadly; its method comprehensive. Individual interests are aided only as the common interest is safeguarded."[15] Federal appropriations in support of free lunches for school children embrace parochial schools, presumably on the same justification. The parochial school is regarded as a distributing agency of social benefit, including education. Are these holdings invalidated by the *McCollum* decision?

I

We encounter the characteristic almost at the outset of Justice Black's "Opinion of the Court" in his brusque dismissal of the question whether Mrs. McCollum's own interest in the constitutional issue raised by her was sufficient to entitle the Supreme Court, under the rules governing judicial review, to decide it.[16] The basic principle involved was stated by Justice Sutherland for the Court a quarter of a century ago, in these words:

We have no power *per se* to review and annul acts of Congress on the ground that they are unconstitutional. That question may be considered only when the justification for some direct injury suffered or threatened, presenting a justiciable issue, is made to rest upon such

[11] *Id.* at 212.
[12] Speech delivered before National Council of Catholic Women, Convention in New Orleans, September 11, 1948, by George E. Reed of Washington, member of the Council's legal department.
[13] Everson v. Board of Education, 330 U. S. 1 (1947).
[14] 281 U. S. 370 (1930).
[15] *Id.* at 375.
[16] McCollum v. Board of Education, *supra* note 5, at 206-207.

an act. Then the power exercised is that of ascertaining and declaring the law applicable to the controversy. It amounts to little more than the negative power to disregard an unconstitutional enactment, which otherwise would stand in the way of the enforcement of a legal right. *The party who invokes the power must be able to show not only that the statute is invalid but that he has sustained or is immediately in danger of sustaining some direct injury as the result of its enforcement, and not merely that he suffers in some indefinite way in common with people generally.*[17]

The *McCollum* case originated, to be sure, in the courts of Illinois and was decided by them prior to its appeal to the Supreme Court, on writ of certiorari; but that fact does not alter the situation so far as the question above posed is concerned. In the words of Justice Frankfurter, dealing in 1939 in the case of *Coleman v. Miller*[18] with a situation which was on all fours with the one before us:

To whom and for what causes the courts of Kansas [*sc.* Illinois] are open are matters for Kansas to determine. But Kansas can not define the contours of the authority of the federal courts, and more particularly of this Court. It is our ultimate responsibility to determine who may invoke our judgment and under what circumstances. . . .

It is not our function, and it is beyond our power, to write legal essays or to give legal opinions, however solemnly requested and however great the national emergency. . . our exclusive business is litigation. The requisites of litigation are not satisfied when questions of constitutionality though conveyed through the outward forms of a conventional court proceeding do not bear special relation to a particular litigant. The scope and consequences of our doctrine of judicial review over executive and legislative action should make us observe fastidiously the bounds of the litigious process within which we are confined. *No matter how seriously infringement of the Constitution may be called into question, this is not the tribunal for its challenge except by those who have some specialized interest of their own to vindicate, apart from a political concern which belongs to all.*[19]

While these words are from a dissenting opinion, they voice on this particular issue the views of the Court as a whole, as is shown by its explicit ruling that Coleman had a sufficient interest to entitle him to prosecute the case before it. In the *McCollum* case, nevertheless, Justice Black brushes aside the question of the materiality of Mrs. McCollum's interest in these curt words: "A second ground for the motion to dismiss is that the appellant lacks standing to maintain the action, a ground which is also without merit. *Coleman v. Miller*, 307 U. S. 433, 443, 445, 464."[20] The passages thus cited in no wise challenge Justice Sutherland's position;

[17] Frothingham v. Mellon, 262 U. S. 447, 488 (1923). (Italics supplied.) It should be noted that formerly the vast majority of constitutional cases arose out of the effort of some official agency or of some private individual to enforce legislation which the defendant in the case attacked as unconstitutional. There can be no doubt as to the *special* interest of such a defendant in having the constitutional question passed upon. The practice which has developed within the last half century of raising the question of constitutionality in suits for injunctions alters the picture somewhat. But it is as to taxpayers' suits that the doctrine of direct or special injury is most evidently relevant. See 16 C. J. S. *Constitutional Law*, §§76, 80-82 (1939).
[18] 307 U. S. 433 (1939).
[19] *Id.* at 462-464. (Italics supplied).
[20] McCollum v. Board of Education, *supra* note 5, at 206.

to the contrary, they assume its correctness. It is clear that the learned Justice had as much, and as little, right to cite *Coleman v. Miller* in support of his ruling as he would have had to invoke the Book of Revelations.

Of the remaining members of the Court sitting in the *McCollum* case, Justice Jackson alone expresses any qualms as to the right of the Court to exercise its jurisdiction. Comparing the case with the *New Jersey School Bus* case mentioned earlier, he says:

> ... in the *Everson Case* there was a direct, substantial and measurable burden on the complainant as a taxpayer to raise funds that were used to subsidize transportation to parochial schools. Hence, we had jurisdiction to examine the constitutionality of the levy and to protect against it if a majority had agreed that the subsidy for transportation was unconstitutional.
>
> In this case, however, any cost of this plan to the taxpayers is incalculable and negligible. It can be argued, perhaps, that religious classes add some wear and tear on public buildings and that they should be charged with some expense for heat and light, even though the sessions devoted to religious instruction do not add to the length of the school day. But the cost is neither substantial nor measurable, and no one seriously can say that the complainant's tax bill has been proved to be increased because of this plan. I think it is doubtful whether the taxpayer in this case has shown any substantial property injury.[21]

"Incalculable and negligible" sums up with substantial accuracy the purport of the extensive finding of facts by the Circuit Court of Champaign County, in which Mrs. McCollum instituted her action. Besides, what of the opposed public interest —why should not that have been considered by the Court? In fact, it always has been considered in cases in which taxpayers have sought to challenge the constitutional validity of expenditures from the national fisc, with the result that no such challenge has succeeded thus far.[22] Why the same rule should not be observed in the case of local expenditures is hard to see; and especially disappointing is the indifference shown on this occasion by those two or three members of the Court who have so frequently in recent years protested their love for the federal system and deplored its impairment.

I should like to point out, moreover, that a strange difference appears to exist today between public school buildings and public parks in respect to their availability for religious uses. In the *Lockport* case,[23] which was decided three months after the *McCollum* case, it was held by a vote of five justices to four that an ordinance of the city of Lockport, New York, which forbids the use of sound amplification devices except with the permission of the chief of police was unconstitutional as applied in the case of a Jehovah's Witness who used sound equipment to amplify lectures in a public park on Sunday, on religious subjects. The proposition for which the case seems to stand is that when a municipality establishes a public park it thereby renders the park a potential forum for any blatherskite politician or

---

[21] *Id.* at 233-234. See also Transcript of Record, p. 69. The state Supreme Court agreed. *Id.* at 274-275.
[22] See note 17 *supra*.   [23] Saia v. New York, 334 U. S. 558 (1948).

whirling deverish who wishes to peddle his doctrinal wares over a public address system, and that a park for quiet uses, to serve the amenities of civilized living, is unconstitutional.[23a]

At any rate, the discrepancy between the two holdings is apparent. In one it is held that a school board may not constitutionally permit religious groups to use on an equal footing any part of a school building for the purpose of religious instruction to *those who wish to receive it*. By the other the public authorities are under a *constitutional obligation* to turn over public parks for religious propaganda to be hurled at all and sundry whether they wish to receive it or not. The Court seems to cherish a strange tenderness for *outré* religious manifestations which contrasts sharply with its attitude toward organized religion.

But it appears that Mrs. McCollum had a second string to her bow, and that her appeal for the Court's protection was based also on her right and duty as *parent*. This ground for the Court's intervention is, if possible, even flimsier than the one just considered. What it simmers down to is the contention that plaintiff's son James Terry was subjected, in consequence of his non-participation in the program, to "embarrassment" and "humiliation." These allegations too, like those regarding the expense of the program, the court of first instance found to be unsubstantiated by "the great preponderance of evidence," a circumstance to which Justice Black makes no allusion.[24] But even had the weight of testimony been otherwise, still the problem raised would seem to have been one of school discipline, to be settled in the principal's office, rather than one of constitutional interpretation for the Supreme Court at Washington. Besides, so far as anything to the contrary appears, had James Terry and his parent made proper application, the school authorities would have willingly assigned accommodations where the two of them might have foregathered during the released time period to confer with regard to their common faith—or lack of it.[25]

[23a] In *Kovacs v. Cooper*, 336 U. S. 77, decided January 31, 1949, the Court sustained a Trenton Ordinance which banned from that city's streets all loud speakers and other devices which emit "loud and raucous noises." The decision is asserted by three of the four dissenters to it to amount to a flat overruling of the decision in the *Saia* case, and I am inclined to agree with them. So much the better, say I. Justice Frankfurter's concurring opinion in the *Kovacs* case deserves special attention for its criticism of Justice Reed's reference, in his opinion for the Court, to "The preferred position of freedom of speech." *Id*. at 88. Justice Frankfurter follows a review of other similar dicta in recent opinions with the observation that the claim that any legislation which restrains "liberty" in the sense of the First and Fourteenth Amendments considered together, is "presumptively unconstitutional," "has never commended itself to a majority of this Court." *Id*. at 94-95. I wish to add that, even were it otherwise, still the Court would not be warranted in taking jurisdiction of a case which involved such a restraint, on the mere application of a person who had not shown sufficient direct injury because of the restraint in question.

[24] McCollum v. Board of Education, *supra* note 5, at 232. Transcript of Record, p. 68. It appears that Mrs. McCollum herself considers James Terry to be something of a "problem child," unable to get along with other children.

[25] This question occurs to me: Suppose that Jehovah's Witnesses' children should complain that they were "embarrassed," etc., in consequence of their not participating along with other school children in saluting the flag, would that render the salute requirement invalid for all school children? At least, their grievance would seem to be fully as substantial as James Terry's.

To conclude this phase of the *McCollum* case—which may in the long run prove to be its most important phase—I wish to make two observations. The first is that Justice Black's brusque disposal of the question of Mrs. McCollum's *locus standi* in court to maintain her action reduces—or elevates—the doctrine of "special interest" to a jurisdictional fiction. All that anyone has to do to get the Court to pass on the constitutionality of a state statute or administrative order, under the First Amendment at any rate, is to allege that its enforcement will involve expense and that he is a taxpayer; neither of which allegations appears to be traversable, otherwise the Court must have paid some heed to the Illinois court's findings of fact. Whether the Court is wise in thus enlarging its jurisdiction in an area in which its performance has been in the past so obviously at the mercy of the individual prepossessions of its members, and is consequently so spotted with self-contradictions and inconsistencies, prompts a doubt—one which its holding in the case at bar is not calculated to dispel.

My second observation is advanced more diffidently. It is that under the principles governing award of mandamus, if the Champaign School Board had peremptorily refused the use of public school rooms for the released-time program, the backers of the plan would have had a far stronger case against the board than Mrs. McCollum had. Their combined interest in compelling a fuller use of public property to the creation and maintenance of which they contributed as taxpayers would have been impressive. Moreover, it would have been an *affirmative* interest. Mrs. McCollum, it seems to me, ought to have asked for an *injunction*, not *mandamus*.

II

People of the State of Illinois ex rel. *Vashti McCollum, Appellant v. Board of Education of School District No. 71, Champaign County* was welcomed by the Court with open arms, as affording it a grand opportunity to break a lance—or several of them—in behalf of the "constitutional principle"—as it is asserted to be—of Separation of Church and State. Actually, the Constitution does not mention this principle. In fact, it does not contain the word "church," nor yet the word "state" in the generic sense except in the Second Amendment, in which a "well regulated militia" is asserted to be "necesary to the security of a free state"; even the word "separation" fails to put in an appearance. These singular omissions—singular, if what the Framers wanted was "Separation of Church and State" in the Court's understanding of it—are now supplied by the Court by the interpretation which it affixes to the "establishment of religion" clause of the First Amendment. The Court's theory, which was stated in the first instance by Justice Black in his opinion for the Court in the *New Jersey Bus* case, is that, under this clause, supplemented by the word "liberty" of the Fourteenth Amendment, "Neither a state nor the Federal Government can [1] set up a church"; [2] "pass laws which aid one religion,

[3] aid all religions, or [4] prefer one religion over another."[26] For this reading of the clause the Court relies primarily on historical data. *Do historical data, on the whole, sustain it?* The answer is, not in such a way or such a sense as to vindicate the *McCollum* decision.

So far as the *National Government* is concerned, the first of the above four propositions is true; originally, indeed, it came near being the whole truth; as to the *states* it is not, as we shall see, *necessarily* true even today. Of the remaining assertions, the second may be ignored as ambiguous; the third is untrue historically; the fourth is true. In a word, what the "establishment of religion" clause of the First Amendment does, and *all that it does, is to forbid Congress to give any religious faith, sect, or denomination a preferred status;* and the Fourteenth Amendment, in making the clause applicable to the states, does not add to it, but *logically curtails it.*

Where, then, did Justice Black get his confident reading of the "establishment of religion" clause? He got it from Justice Rutledge's dissenting opinion in the *New Jersey Bus* case, which in turn is based largely on James Madison's *Memorial and Remonstrance Against Religious Assessments* of 1785.[27] At that time—four years *before* the First Amendment was framed—a proposal was pending in the Virginia Assembly to levy a tax for the benefit of "teachers of the Christian religion." The father of the measure was Patrick Henry, but it was also supported outside the Assembly by Washington, Marshall, and other great names. Madison, on the other hand, with the recent successful fight for the disestablishment of the Episcopal Church in mind, fought the measure tooth and nail, fearing that if it was enacted that body would have its foot in the stirrup for a fresh leap into the saddle. The keynote of the *Remonstrance,* which summed up his opposition, is sounded in the following passage:

Who does not see that the same authority which can establish Christianity, in exclusion of all other Religions, may establish with the same ease any particular sect of Christians, in exclusion of all other Sects? That the same authority which can force a citizen to contribute three pence only of his property for the support of any one establishment, may force him to conform to any other establishment in all cases whatsover?[28]

As those very words show, however, Madison's conception of an "establishment of religion" in 1785 was precisely that which I have set forth above—*a religion enjoying a preferred status.* The same conception, moreover, underlies the state constitutions of the day, when they deal with the subject.[29] It also underlies all but one

---

[26] Everson v. Board of Education, *supra* note 13, at 15.

[27] *Id.* at 63 ff, quoting II THE WRITINGS OF JAMES MADISON 183-191 (Hunt ed. 1901).

[28] Justice Rutledge's dissenting opinion in Everson v. Board of Education, *supra* note 13, at 65-66, quoting II THE WRITINGS OF JAMES MADISON 183, 186 (Hunt ed. 1901).

[29] See I FRANCIS NEWTON THORPE, THE FEDERAL AND STATE CONSTITUTIONS, COLONIAL CHARTERS, AND OTHER ORGANIC LAWS OF THE STATES, TERRITORIES, AND COLONIES NOW OR HEREAFTER FORMING THE UNITED STATES OF AMERICA 567 (Dela); III *id.* 1890 (Mass.); IV *id.* 2454 (N. H.); V *id.* 2597 (N. J.), 2636 (N. Y.), 2793 (N. C.); VI *id.* 3255 (S. C.).

of the proposals from the states which led to the framing of the First Amendment in the first Congress. Thus Virginia proposed that "no particular religious sect or society ought to be favored or established, by law, in preference to others"—a formula which North Carolina reiterated word for word, and which New York reiterated save for the word "particular." Only New Hampshire, concerned for her own "establishment," wanted a broader prohibition, one that would keep Congress out of the field of religion entirely.[30]

But, it may well be asked, what bearing do the views which Madison advanced in 1785 in a local political fight regarding the subject of religious liberty in Virginia have on the question of the meaning of the First Amendment? Justice Rutledge's theory is (1) that Madison was the author of the First Amendment, and (2) that he must have intended by the ban which is there imposed on Congress's legislating "respecting an establishment of religion" to rule out the kind of legislation which he had opposed in Virginia four years earlier. Neither of these positions is correct.

As originally introduced into the House of Representatives by Madison, the proposal from which the religion clauses of the First Amendment finally issued read as follows:

The civil rights of none shall be abridged on account of religious belief or worship, nor shall any national religion be established, nor shall the full and equal rights of conscience be in any manner, or on any pretext, infringed.[31]

These words Madison later elucidated thus:

... he apprehended the meaning of the words to be, that Congress should not establish a religion, and enforce the legal observation of it by law, nor compel men to worship God in any manner contrary to their conscience ... if the word "national" was inserted before religion, it would satisfy the minds of honorable gentlemen. He believed that the people feared one sect might obtain a pre-eminence, or two combine together, and establish a religion to which they would compel others to conform. He thought if the word "national" was introduced, it would point the amendment directly to the object it was intended to prevent.[32]

In short, "to establish" a religion was to give it a preferred status, a pre-eminence, carrying with it even the right to compel others to conform. But in fact, before Madison's proposal was passed by the House and went to the Senate it had been changed to read: "Congress shall make no law establishing religion, or to prevent the free exercise thereof, or to infringe the rights of conscience"; and in the Senate this proposal was replaced by the following formula: "Congress shall make no law establishing articles of faith or a mode of worship or prohibiting the free exercise of religion."[33] That is, Congress should not prescribe a national faith, a possibility

---

[30] III THE DEBATES IN THE SEVERAL STATE CONVENTIONS ON THE ADOPTION OF THE FEDERAL CONSTITUTION 659 (Jonathan Elliott ed. 1836); I *id.* 326; IV *id.* 244, 251. See also II *id.* 553.
[31] I ANNALS OF CONG. 434 (1789-1791).
[32] *Id.* at 730-731.
[33] Records of the United States Senate, September 9, 1789, United States National Archives, cited

which those states with establishments of their own—Massachusetts, New Hampshire, Connecticut, Maryland, and South Carolina—probably regarded with fully as much concern as those which had gotten rid of their establishments. And the final form of the First Amendment, which came from a committee of conference between the two houses, appears to reflect this concern. The point turns on the significance to be attached to the word "respecting," a two-edged word, which bans any law *disfavoring* as well as any law *favoring* an establishment of religion. As will be seen in a moment, Story's reading of the First Amendment makes "respecting" the pivotal word of the "no establishment" clause.

To come back for a moment to Madison. Thanks to his exertions, Henry's bill was defeated, and unquestionably his *Remonstrance* should be given considerable credit for this result. But political management also played a role, and no unimportant one. The great problem was to overcome the tremendous influence which Henry's oratory exerted in the Virginia Assembly. Writing Madison at this time from Paris, Jefferson said: "What we have to do, I think, is devotedly to pray for his death." Madison, however, had a better scheme. Relying on Henry's vanity, he concocted a movement to make him Governor, and Henry took the bait, hook, line, and sinker, thus automatically removing himself from the Assembly and destroying his brain-child.[34]

Yet it is probably due to his part in this fight that in his later years Madison carried the principle of separation of church and state to pedantic lengths, just as he did the principle of the separation of powers. In his essay on *Monopolies,* which was written after he left the presidency (probably long after), he put himself on record as opposed to the exemption of houses of worship from taxation, against the incorporation of ecclesiastical bodies with the faculty of acquiring property, against the houses of Congress having the right to choose chaplains to be paid out of national taxes, which, said he, "is a palpable violation of equal rights, as well as of Constitutional principles,"[35] and also against chaplains in the Army and the Navy. He states, indeed, that as President he was averse to issuing proclamations calling for days of thanksgiving or prayer, but was in some instances prevailed upon to

---

in Appellees' Brief (Messrs. Franklin, Peterson, Rall, and Fisk) in the *McCollum* case, *supra* note 5. Here attention is drawn to the fact that the Virginia legislature postponed ratification of the third proposed amendment (Amendment I of the first ten amendments) until December 15, 1791 (III ANNALS OF CONG. 54), by which time they had already received the approval of the required three-fourths of the state legislatures. The leaders in opposition to the First Amendment voiced their objections in the following terms: ". . . although it goes to restrain Congress from passing laws establishing any national religion, they might, notwithstanding, levy taxes to any amount for the support of religion or its preachers; and any particular denomination of Christians might be so favored and supported by the general government, as to give it a decided advantage over the others, and in the process of time render it powerful and dangerous as if it was established as the national religion of the country." Evidently, as Appellees' Brief remarks, Virginians, who, after all, were the ones most familiar with the Virginia concept of religious freedom, did not interpret the First Amendment as living up to the spirit or the letter of the Virginia Bill for Establishing Religious Freedom. Brief, pp. 53-54.

[34] IRVING BRANT, JAMES MADISON, THE NATIONALIST 345-346 (1948).
[35] Fleet, *Madison's "Detached* [sic] *Memoranda,"* 3 WILLIAM AND MARY Q. 534, 558 (3d Ser.) (1946).

affix his name to proclamations of this character at the request of the houses of Congress.[36] In all these respects, of course, Madison has been steadily overruled by the verdict of practice under the Constitution, as the data assembled by Justice Reed in his dissenting opinion show.[37]

To conclude this—the Madisonian—phase of our subject: the importance attached by Justice Rutledge in the *School Bus* case to Madison's *Memorial and Remonstrance* of 1785 as interpretive of the First Amendment is obviously excessive. First, the *Remonstrance* antedated the framing of the amendment by four years; second, Madison himself never offered it as an interpretation of the amendment; third, he was not the author of the amendment in the form in which it was proposed to the state legislatures for ratification; fourth, even had he been, the *Remonstrance* itself is excellent evidence that "an establishment of religion" meant in 1785 a religion, sect, or denomination enjoying a privileged legal position; finally, Madison himself asserted repeatedly as to the Constitution as a whole that "the legitimate meaning of the Instrument must be derived from the text itself."[38] Rejecting in a recent case the proposition that the Fourteenth Amendment, but more particularly the "due process" clause thereof, was intended to impose upon the States all of "the various explicit provisions of the first eight Amendments," Justice Frankfurter said: "Remarks of a particular proponent of the Amendment no matter how influential are not to be deemed part of the Amendment. What was submitted for ratification was his proposal, not his speech."[39] And Madison was not even the proponent of the First Amendment in its final form!

But Justice Rutledge, and the Court also, urge the authority of Jefferson as an interpreter of the First Amendment, although, being in Paris at the time, Jefferson had no hand in framing it. The reason for the Court's deference to the third president is that in 1802 he wrote a letter to a group of Baptists in Danbury, Connecticut, in which he declared that it was the purpose of the First Amendment to build "a wall of separation between church and state."[40] What, then, was Jefferson's idea of such a wall? So far as it bears on the question of religion in the schools, it certainly does not support the position of the Court in the *McCollum* case. Dealing with the subject with respect to his own recently established University of Virginia, Jefferson wrote in 1822:

> It was not, however, to be understood that instruction in religious opinion and duties was meant to be precluded by the public authorities, as indifferent to the interests of society. On the contrary, the relations which exist between man and his Maker, and the duties resulting from those relations, are the most interesting and important to every human being, and most incumbent on his study and investigation. The want of instruction in the various creeds of religious faith existing among our citizens presents,

[36] *Id.* at 551-562.
[37] McCollum v. Board of Education, *supra* note 5, at 253-255.
[38] III THE WORKS OF JAMES MADISON 228, 552 (Phila. 1867).
[39] Adamson v. California, 332 U. S. 46, 64 (1947).
[40] SAUL K. PADOVER, THE COMPLETE JEFFERSON 518-519 (1943).

therefore, a chasm in a general institution of the useful sciences ... A remedy, however, has been suggested of promising aspect, which, while it excludes the public authorities from the domain of religious freedom, will give to the sectarian schools of divinity the full benefit the public provisions made for instruction in the other branches of science ... It has, therefore, been in contemplation, and suggested by some pious individuals, who perceive the advantages of associating other studies with those of religion, to establish their religious schools on the confines of the University, so as to give to their students ready and convenient access and attendance on the scientific lectures of the University; and to maintain, by that means, those destined for the religious professions on as high a standing of science, and of personal weight and respectability, as may be obtained by others from the benefits of the University.... Such an arrangement would complete the circle of the useful sciences embraced by this institution, and would fill the chasm now existing, on principles which would leave inviolate the constitutional freedom of religion, the most inalienable and sacred of all human rights, over which the people and authorities of this state, individually and publicly, have ever manifested the most watchful jealousy; and could this jealousy be now alarmed, in the opinion of the legislature, by what is here suggested, the idea will be relinquished on any surmise of disapproval which they might think proper to express.[41]

And again:

... by bringing the sects together, and mixing them with the mass of other students, we shall soften their asperities, liberalize and neutralize their prejudices, and make the general religion a religion of peace, reason, and morality.[42]

The eager crusaders on the Court make too much of Jefferson's Danbury letter, which was not improbably motivated by an impish desire to heave a brick at the Congregationalist-Federalist hierarchy of Connecticut, whose leading members had denounced him two years before as an "infidel" and "atheist." A more deliberate, more carefully considered evaluation by Jefferson of the religious clauses of the First Amendment is that which occurs in his Second Inaugural: "In matters of religion, I have considered that its free exercise is placed by the constitution independent of the powers of the general government."[43] In short, the principal importance of the amendment lay in the separation which it effected between the respective jurisdictions of state and nation regarding religion, rather than in its bearing on the question of the separation of church and state. For the rest, it is not irrelevant to the major subject opened up by the Court's decision to note that Jefferson regarded religion as "a supplement to law in the government of men," as "the alpha and omega of the moral law"—an attitude closely akin to that voiced in the Northwest Ordinance.[44]

Finally, I wish to adduce the evidence afforded by some important systematic

---

[41] *Id.* at 957-958.

[42] 12 THE WORKS OF THOMAS JEFFERSON 272 (Ford ed. 1905). These passages are both quoted by Justice Reed in a footnote, 333 U. S. 203, 245, 246 n. 11.

[43] 1 MESSAGES AND PAPERS OF THE PRESIDENTS 379 (Richardson ed. 1896).

[44] 7 THE WRITINGS OF THOMAS JEFFERSON 339 (H. A. Washington ed. 1854); 1 *id.* at 545. For the latter reference, I am indebted to J. M. O'NEILL, RELIGION AND EDUCATION UNDER THE CONSTITUTION. This work, now in press, is a devastating assault upon the *McCollum* decision from several angles.

works on the subject of constitutional interpretation, as to the meaning of the term "an establishment of religion." The first of these, although the Court seems to have overlooked it entirely in its researches on the present occasion, carried vast authority a century ago, especially north of the Potomac. I refer to Story's *Commentaries on the Constitution*. Interestingly enough, with one important exception, Story's hard-bitten New England views are quite in line in this instance with those of the Virginians. The exception is that according to Story, while the "no establishment" clause inhibited Congress from giving preference to any sect or denomination of the Christian faith, it was not intended thus to withdraw the Christian religion as a whole from the protection of Congress. Thus he wrote:

> Probably at the time of the adoption of the Constitution, and of the amendment to it, now under consideration, the general, if not the universal sentiment in America was, that christianity ought to receive encouragement from the state, so far as was not incompatible with the private rights of conscience, and the freedom of religious worship. An attempt to level all religions, and to make it a matter of state policy to hold all in utter indifference, would have created universal disapprobation if not universal indignation.[45]

Nor was it the purpose of the Amendment to discredit state establishments of religion, but simply "to exclude from the National Government all power to act on the subject."

> The situation ... of the different states equally proclaimed the policy, as well as the necessity of such an exclusion. In some of the states, episcopalians constituted the predominant sect; in others, presbyterians; in others, congregationalists; in others, quakers; and in others again, there was a close numerical rivalry among contending sects. It was impossible, that there should not arise perpetual strife and perpetual jealousy on the subject of ecclesiastical ascendency, if the national government were left free to create a religious establishment. The only security was in extirpating the power. But this alone would have been an imperfect security, if it had not been followed up by a declaration of the right of the free exercise of religion, and a prohibition (as we have seen) of all religious tests. Thus, the whole power over the subject of religion is left exclusively to the state governments, to be acted upon according to their own sense of justice, and the state constitutions; and the Catholic and the Protestant, the Calvinist and the Arminian, the Jew and the Infidel, may sit down at the common table of the national councils, without any inquisition into their faith, or mode of worship.[46]

A generation later Cooley's famous work on *Constitutional Limitations* appeared, the province of which is the constitutional restraints imposed by the state constitutions of that date on the state legislatures. In striking contrast to the passage just quoted from Story, Cooley's work records the disappearance of religious establishments from the state constitutions. His conception of "an establishment of religion" is, however, still the same as that of Story, Madison, and Jefferson, *viz.*, "a sect ...

---

[45] JOSEPH STORY, COMMENTARIES ON THE CONSTITUTION §1874 (1833).
[46] *Id.* §1879.

favored by the State and given an advantage by law over other sects."[47] And in his later *Principles of Constitutional Law,* Cooley is more explicit: "By establishment of religion is meant the setting up or recognition of a state church, or at least the conferring upon one church of special favors and advantages which are denied to others [citing 1 TUCK. BL. COMM., App. 296; 2 *id.,* App. Note G.]. It was never intended by the Constitution that the Government should be prohibited from recognizing religion—where it might be done without drawing any invidious distinctions between different religious beliefs, organizations, or sects."[47a]

III

All in all, it is fairly evident that Justice Rutledge sold his brethren a bill of goods when he persuaded them that the "establishment of religion" clause of the First Amendment was intended to rule out all governmental "aid to *all* religions." However, the First Amendment, taken by itself, is binding only on Congress; and the legislation involved in the *McCollum* case was state legislation. The *immediate* basis of the decision in this case was, in fact, the "due process" clause of the Fourteenth Amendment; or more strictly speaking, the word "liberty" there. In other words, the theory of the case is that the Fourteenth Amendment renders the ban of the First Amendment on an establishment of religion applicable also to the states. Whence came this theory; and to what, logically, does it lead?

I shall deal with these questions in a moment. But first I wish to comment briefly on Justice Frankfurter's supplemental opinion in the *McCollum* case, in which he is joined by three other justices. For while the opinion throws no additional light on the meaning of the "establishment of religion" clause, it does have bearing on the broader subject of religion in the schools.

The opinion is a well-documented sketch of the secularization of public school education in the United States, a reform effected—so far as it has been effected—purely by the political process, unaided up to this point by the Supreme Court. An outstanding figure in the fight on *sectarianism* in the schools was Horace Mann, who lived and wrought in Massachusetts in the second quarter of the last century. Of him Justice Frankfurter writes:

In Massachusetts, largely through the efforts of Horace Mann, all sectarian teachings were barred from the common school to save it from being rent by denominational conflict. The upshot of these controversies, often long and fierce, is fairly summarized by saying that long before the Fourteenth Amendment subjected the States to new limitations, the prohibition of furtherance by the State of religious instruction became the guiding principle, in law and feeling, of the American people.[48]

This account of things requires some amplifying. Any implication that he was

---

[47] COOLEY, CONSTITUTIONAL LIMITATIONS* 469 (2d ed. 1871).
[47a] COOLEY, PRINCIPLES OF CONSTITUTIONAL LAW 224-225 (3d ed. 1898). It is perhaps worth noting that it is in Tucker's *Blackstone* (1803) that Madison's and Jefferson's Virginia and Kentucky Resolutions were first elevated to the rank of an authoritative gloss on the Constitution.
[48] McCollum v. Board of Education, *supra* note 5, at 215.

totally opposed to religious instruction in the schools Mann himself would have denied vehemently. Summing the matter up, Culver writes in his authoritative work on the subject:

> It is true that Mr. Mann stood strongly for a "type of school with instruction adapted to democratic and national ends." But it is not quite just to him to contrast this type of school with the school adapted to religious ends, without defining terms. Horace Mann was opposed to sectarian doctrinal instruction in the schools, but he repeatedly urged the teaching of the elements of religion common to all of the Christian sects. He took a firm stand against the idea of a purely secular education, and on one occasion said he was in favor of religious instruction "to the extremest verge to which it can be carried without invading those rights of conscience which are established by the laws of God, and guaranteed to us by the Constitution of the State." At another time he said that he regarded hostility to religion in the schools as the greatest crime he could commit. Lest his name should go down in history as that of one who had attempted to drive religious instruction from the schools, he devoted several pages in his final Report—the twelfth—to a statement in which he denied the charges of his enemies.[49]

At another point, Justice Frankfurter quotes President Grant's "famous remarks" in 1875 to a convention of the Army of Tennessee, and his message to Congress of the same year, asking for a constitutional amendment which, among other things, would forbid the use of public funds for sectarian education, and attacking the exemption of church property from taxation.[50] Acting on these suggestions James G. Blaine introduced a resolution providing that "no State shall make any law respecting an establishment of religion" and prohibiting any appropriation of public school money by any state to sectarian schools. The proposal was adopted by the House overwhelmingly, but was lost in the Senate.[51] Down to 1929 it had been reintroduced some twenty times, without result. The proposal assumes, of course, that it was necessary in order to fill a gap in the Constitution. Conversely, the Court's reading of the "due process" clause of the Fourteenth Amendment in the *McCollum* case assumes that any such amendment would be superfluous.

That the Fourteenth Amendment would make the Bill of Rights applicable to the states was frequently asserted in the congressional debates on the former, but this circumstance lends little if any support to the holding in the *McCollum* case. For one thing, the Court can hardly rely on it and at the same time reject the conception of the "establishment of religion" clause which prevailed in 1868. If history is to be followed on the one point, it cannot fairly be abandoned on the other. Again,

---

[49] RAYMOND B. CULVER, HORACE MANN AND RELIGION IN THE MASSACHUSETTS PUBLIC SCHOOLS 235 (1929). With this statement of Mann's position it is interesting to compare the following extract from a colloquy of Justice Frankfurter with counsel for the School Board, in the course of the argument at Washington: "MR. JUSTICE FRANKFURTER. I put my question again: We have a school system of the United States on the one hand, and the relation it has to the democratic way of life. On the other hand we have the religious beliefs of our people. The question is whether any kind of scheme which introduced religious teaching into the public school system is the kind of thing we should have in our democratic institutions." J. M. O'NEIL, *op. cit. supra* note 44, at 234.

[50] McCollum v. Board of Education, *supra* note 5, at 218.

[51] M. A. MUSMANNO, PROPOSED AMENDMENTS TO THE CONSTITUTION 182 (1929).

the expectations of its framers regarding the operation of the amendment rested mainly on two ideas, both of which were early discredited by the Court itself. The first of these was that the "privileges and immunities of citizens of the United States" protected by the amendment covered the whole realm of civil rights; the second was that Congress's legislative power under Section V of the amendment would be equally extensive. Thus the application of the Bill of Rights to the states would be effected by congressional action; the notion that the Court would have any hand in the business was not widely entertained.[51a]

The Court itself, however, had different ideas. In the famous *Slaughter House Cases*[52] of 1873 it adopted a conception of "privileges and immunities of citizens of the United States" which extruded all "fundamental" rights from the term. In the *Civil Rights Cases*[53] ten years later it pared down Congress's powers under the fifth section of the amendment to the bare disallowance of state legislation violative of the first section—a function better left to the processes of judicial review. The subsequent judicial history of the Fourteenth Amendment has in the main been the history of the Court's interpretation of the due process clause; but of this history the only phase of interest in the present connection is that which involves the word "liberty" in that clause. In 1898, thirty years after the adoption of the amendment, the Court, responding to the pressure of preponderant legal opinion in the country, at last adopted a definition of "liberty" embracing "freedom of contract," and especially freedom of contract in the sphere of employer-employee relations.[54] More expansive conceptions of the term, on the other hand, it steadily repelled throughout the next quarter of a century.[55] Even as late as 1922 we find it using the following words:

> Neither the Fourteenth Amendment nor any other provision of the Constitution of the United States imposes upon the States any restrictions about "freedom of speech" or the "liberty of silence."[56]

Following the first World War, however, the Court began shifting its position; and in the notable case of *Pierce v. Society of Sisters*,[57] decided in 1925, it held that the word "liberty" in the Fourteenth Amendment protects the rights of parents to guide the education of their children, and hence the right to send them to

---

[51a] In his dissenting opinion in Adamson v. California, 332 U. S. 46, 68ff. (1947), Justice Black argues that the Fourteenth Amendment adopts the Bill of Rights in toto and quotes from the congressional debates on the former to prove the point, relying especially on speeches by Representative Bingham of Ohio and Senator Howard of Michigan. He overlooks the fact that both these high authorities expected that the application of the Bill of Rights to the states would be effected by congressional legislation. See the Appendix compiled by Justice Black to his opinion, 332 U. S. 92-123, especially at pp. 93, 94, 95, 97, 98, 101, 106, 107, 110, 112, 114, 115, 117, and 118.

[52] Slaughter House Cases, 16 Wall. 36 (U. S. 1873).

[53] Civil Rights Cases, 109 U. S. 3 (1883).

[54] Holden v. Hardy, 169 U. S. 366 (1898).

[55] On this and the following paragraph, see my LIBERTY AGAINST GOVERNMENT 134-168 (1948).

[56] Prudential Insurance Co. v. Cheek, 259 U. S. 530, 543 (1922).

[57] 268 U. S. 510 (1925).

parochial schools rather than the public schools, if they so choose. And on this basis, the Oregon compulsory school law, which made it impossible, practically, for children to attend parochial schools, was pronounced unconstitutional. As I shall point out in a moment, the holding in the *McCollum* case is logically incompatible with the decision just mentioned. Finally, in this same year, 1925, the Court, in the well-known *Gitlow* case,[58] tentatively adopted the thesis that the word "liberty" in the Fourteenth Amendment includes freedom of speech and press as recognized in the First Amendment; and this tentative thesis has since become a firm part of the Court's jurisprudence. In many recent cases, most of which involve Jehovah's Witnesses, the same doctrine has, moreover, been applied to religious liberty.[59]

That the Court was warranted by a considerable line of recent decisions in taking the position in the *McCollum* case that if the "released time" program there involved amounted to an invasion of anybody's freedom of religion it was unconstitutional, is clear. Indeed, whether the program did this or not was, properly speaking, the only question before the Court; and the talk about "an establishment of religion" was entirely beside the point *unless the "released time" program of the Champaign schools involved an establishment of religion of such a nature as to deprive the plaintiff in the case of feedom of religion.* That is to say, the Fourteenth Amendment does not authorize the Court to substitute the word "state" for "Congress" in the ban imposed by the First Amendment on laws "respecting an establishment of religion." *So far as the Fourteenth Amendment is concerned, states are entirely free to establish religions, provided they do not deprive anybody of religious liberty.* It is only *liberty* that the Fourteenth Amendment protects. And in this connection it should not be overlooked that contemporary England manages to maintain as complete freedom of religion as exists in this country alongside an establishment of religion, although originally that establishment involved a ban upon all other faiths.[60]

Vital, therefore, to the Court's argument in the *McCollum* case is the proposition that such children in the Champaign schools as came under the program were *coerced* to do so by virtue of the fact that they were gathered there—"recruited" is the Court's word—in consequence of the state compulsory school law. The answer is that no children were admitted to the program unless their parents formally requested that they be, and the choice of the parent must be imputed to the child. There is still, of course, the coercion exercised by the parent, but it seems unlikely that the Court is out to emancipate children from their parents!

[58] Gitlow v. New York, 268 U. S. 652 (1925).
[59] Cantwell v. Connecticut, 310 U. S. 296 (1940); West Virginia State Board of Education v. Barnette, 319 U. S. 624 (1943), and cases there cited.
[60] In the *Cantwell* case, cited above, it is stated incidentally (p. 303) that the Fourteenth Amendment makes the "establishment of religion" clause of the First Amendment operate with the same force on the states as it does on Congress; but this statement is based on the idea that an establishment signifies "compulsion by law of the acceptance of . . . [a] creed or the practice of . . . [a] form of worship." *Ibid.* Story, on the other hand, holds that an ecclesiastical establishment may be perfectly compatible with full freedom of religion for all sects. JOSEPH STORY, COMMENTARIES ON THE CONSTITUTION §1872 (1833).

This is not to say, however, that there was no question of coercion involved in this case and involved in a very significant way, although one which appears to have escaped entirely the careful diligence of the Court. I recur to my reference a paragraph or two back to the decision in 1925 in *Pierce v. Society of Sisters*,[61] in which an Oregon compulsory school law was set aside as impairing the right of parents, who wished their children to attend parochial schools, to guide the education of their children. Two observations seem called for. In the first place, it is an inevitable implication of the case that compulsory school laws which *permit* attendance at parochial schools are constitutional, notwithstanding the compulsion which is thereby lent such schools in "recruiting" pupils. This compulsion is, in fact, immensely more evident than that which was put upon pupils to avail themselves of the Champaign "released time" program. In the second place, the parental right which was vindicated in the *Pierce* case, whatever else it is, must also be reckoned to be an *element of the right which the Constitution guarantees to all to "the free exercise" of their religion*. The question accordingly arises whether this right is confined to parents who can afford to send their children to parochial or other private schools; whether, in other words, parents who must for financial or other reasons send their children to the public schools have no right to guide their education to the extent of demanding that the education there available shall include some religious instruction, provided nobody's freedom of religion is thereby impaired? *All in all, it seems clear that the Court, by its decision in the* McCollum *case, has itself promulgated a law prohibiting "the free exercise" of religion, contrary to the express prohibition of the First Amendment!*

To summarize the argument against the decision in the *McCollum* case: In the first place, the justification for the Court's intervention was trivial and directly violative of restrictions hitherto existing on judicial review. In the second place, the decision is based, as Justice Reed rightly contends,[62] on "a figure of speech," the concept of "a wall of separation between Church and State." Thirdly, leaving this figure of speech to one side, the decision is seen to stem from an unhistorical conception of what is meant by "an establishment of religion" in the First Amendment. The historical record shows beyond peradventure that the core idea of "an establishment of religion" comprises the idea of *preference;* and that any act of public authority favorable to religion in general cannot, without manifest falsification of history, be brought under the ban of that phrase. Undoubtedly the Court has the right to make history, as it has often done in the past; but it has no right to *remake* it. In the fourth place, the prohibition on the establishment of religion by Congress is not convertible into a similar prohibition on the states, under the authorization of the Fourteenth Amendment, unless the term "establishment of religion" be given an application which carries with it invasion of somebody's freedom of religion, that is, of "liberty." Finally, the decision is accompanied by opinions and by a mandate

[61] See note 57 *supra*.
[62] McCollum v. Board of Education, *supra* note 5, at 247.

which together have created great uncertainty in the minds of governing bodies of all public educational institutions. And, of course, as is always the case, the Court's intervention is purely negative. It is incapable of solving the complex problem with which forty-six states and 2,200 communities have been struggling by means of the "released time" expedient. With the utmost insouciance the Court overturns or casts under the shadow of unconstitutionality the "conscientious attempt" of hundreds of people to deal with what they have considered to be a pressing problem in a way that they have considered to be fair and just to all.

Finally, this question may be asked: Is the decision favorable to democracy? Primarily democracy is a system of ethical values, and that this system of values so far as the American people are concerned is grounded in religion will not be denied by anybody who knows the historical record. And that the agencies by which this system of values has been transmitted in the past from generation to generation—the family, the neighborhood, the church—have today become much impaired will not be seriously questioned by anybody who knows anything about contemporary conditions. But what this all adds up to is that *the work of transmission has been put more and more upon the shoulders of the public schools.* Can they, then, do the job without the assistance of religious instruction? At least, there seems to be a widely held opinion to the contrary.

I wonder just how the shade of Justice Holmes would comment on this decision. I can imagine the late Justice repeating some words which he used in a dissenting opinion in 1921:

There is nothing that I more deprecate than the use of the Fourteenth Amendment beyond the absolute compulsion of its words to prevent the making of social experiments that an important part of the community desires, in the insulated chambers afforded by the several States, even though the experiments may seem futile or even noxious to me and to those whose judgment I most respect.[63]

Indeed, he might even feel called upon to repeat his gibe about judges being "naïf, simple-minded men"[64] one mark of naiveté being a preference for slogans over solutions.

And what would the Court answer? Perhaps it might adopt the words of Justice Jackson in a recent case:

We [the Court] act in these matters not by the authority of our competence but by force of our commissions. We cannot, because of modest estimates of our competence in such specialties as public education, withhold the judgment that history authenticates as the function of this Court when liberty is infringed.[65]

[63] Truax v. Corrigan, 257 U. S. 312, 244 (1921). The "watchfulness of state interests against exuberant judicial restrictions," which Holmes gave expression to in the passage just quoted, is praised by Justice Frankfurter with warm enthusiasm in his MR. JUSTICE HOLMES AND THE SUPREME COURT 86-88 (1938). See also his recent opinion in Adamson v. California 332 U. S. 46, 59, 62.
[64] HOLMES, COLLECTED LEGAL PAPERS 295 (1921).
[65] West Virginia State Board of Education v. Barnette, *supra* note 59, at 640.

This is a plea in confession and avoidance which can by no means be granted. It is not to be presumed that the Constitution puts burdens on the Court in the discharge of which with appropriate modesty it must still risk disaster for the country. The decision in the *McCollum* case, however, is not a "modest" decision. Instead it is to be grouped with those high-flying *tours de force* in which the Court has occasionally indulged, to solve "forever" some teasing problem—slavery, for example, in the *Dred Scott* case[66]—or to correct, as in the *Pollock* case,[67] "a century of error."

In my opinion the Court would act wisely to make it clear at the first opportunity that it does not aspire to become, as Justice Jackson puts it, "a super board of education for every school district in the nation."[68]

[66] Dred Scott v. Sanford, 19 How. 393 (U. S. 1856).
[67] Pollock v. Farmers Loan and Trust Co., 157 U. S. 429 (1895).
[68] McCollum v. Board of Education, *supra* note 5, at 237.

RELIGIOUS FREEDOMS IN THE UNITED STATES: A TURNING POINT?[†]

Marc Galanter[*]

Introduction

Obscured from view by the clamor over religious observances in the public schools and more recently by proposals for aid to religiously affiliated schools, an inconspicuous but potentially momentous shift in judicial notions of religious freedom has taken place. I shall attempt here to examine some recent developments and to contrast the emerging but still inchoate view of religious liberty with earlier and competing views. I shall try to indicate some of the directions in which these present tendencies may proceed and some of the problems that may ensue. In doing this, I shall try to suggest a conceptual framework which may be useful for considering problems of religious liberty in the United States and for making cross-national comparisons.

I begin with the notion that freedom of religion is not an undifferentiated or unidimensional condition or concept, but is a constellation of overlapping and sometimes conflicting claims for specific freedoms, each trying to borrow the immense prestige of the general notion of religious liberty. I shall attempt to analyze the notion of religious liberty into its components, to portray recent developments in a few areas, and to assess their implications for the whole pattern of religious liberty. As components I intend to use the kinds of claims made upon governmental bodies to recognize, certify, or implement some interest in respect to religion.[1] I shall group some of these claims into types in accordance with the stance or posture toward religious interests that government is requested to take.

In describing the way in which American courts have responded to such claims, I shall be concerned in detail with only three areas: first, freedom from those admittedly "secular" regulations which prohibit activity to which the claimant accords positive

---

[†] An earlier version of this article was presented at the annual meeting of the American Political Science Association, Washington, D.C., Sept. 8-11, 1965.
[*] Assistant Professor in the Social Sciences, University of Chicago. B.A., 1950, M.A., 1954, J.D., 1956, University of Chicago.
  I am indebted to Miss Eleanor Perlmutter for her assistance, and to Mr. Steven Boyan and Prof. Mark Haller for valuable comments on portions of this article. Needless to say, the views expressed here are my own and should not be attributed to any of them.
[1] I have attempted to use freedom in a descriptive rather than a normative sense. Unless the context indicates otherwise, the term is used throughout simply to indicate something that somebody wants to do. Obviously unrestricted freedom (in this sense) of religion—or of anything else—is not desirable, or even conceivable, since such desires conflict.

religious significance;[2] second, freedom from those admittedly "secular" regulations which require activity accorded negative religious significance;[3] and third, freedom to define what is religious.[4] But before proceeding to discuss the recent developments in respect to these sorts of claims, I would like to put them in context by sketching very briefly what I conceive to be the whole constellation of claims for religious freedom.[5] The list I present is a tentative one, and is intended to be illustrative rather than exhaustive. Another list, compiled for another purpose, might contain a few items more or a few less. For present purposes the

---

[2] See *M infra*.
[3] See *N infra*.
[4] See *O infra*.
[5] The following categories, I believe, are comprised in the general notion of religious freedom in the United States. For ease of reference, I have set them out at this point, in the order in which each is discussed in the text, together with brief illustrations where appropriate.

A. *Freedom from religious compulsion.* For example, one may not be forced to entertain or express specific religious views, or to perform specific religious practices, or to contribute tax money for religious purposes.

B. *Freedom from persecution or discrimination because of religious beliefs or practice.* For example, one may not be subjected to religious tests for public office or for the enjoyment of public benefits.

C. *Freedom from state-sponsored religion.* One may not be subjected to religious instruction, ceremony, or symbolism under the aegis of governmental authority. For example, Bible reading in schools.

D. *Freedom from state use of religious standards.* For example, the state may not evaluate actions by religious standards, such as heresy, sacrilege, or desecration of the Sabbath.

E. *Freedom to enlist state co-operation in carrying out religious purposes.* For example, courts may lend their aid in enforcing religious trusts.

F. *Freedom to obtain (from government) opportunities to implement religious values.* For example, the state may provide religious facilities for prisoners and soldiers.

G. *Freedom from private interference with one's religious beliefs and practices.* For example, freedom from disturbance of religious worship.

H. *Freedom of religious association and the freedom of association to maintain autonomous internal government.*

I. *Freedom of religious choice.* This is the freedom to change or retain one's religious views, practices, or affiliations.

J. *Freedom to transmit and implant religious views in the next generation.* For example, parental freedom to supervise the religious training of children.

K. *Freedom to express, publish, distribute, and teach religious views.*

L. *Freedom from compelled disclosure of religious views.* For example, freedom not to divulge the contents of religious communications or the existence of religious views.

M. *Freedom from governmental restrictions upon activities accorded positive religious significance.* That is, freedom from (a) direct prohibitions (e.g., on snake handling or polygamy), and (b) indirect burdens (e.g., Sunday laws).

N. *Freedom from governmental compulsion to perform an act accorded negative religious significance.* For example, army service, flag saluting, or vaccination.

O. *Freedom to define the religious or sacred.*

366

exact number is not as important as the notion that religious freedom is multiplex and that its component elements are not necessarily harmonious; in some cases they reinforce one another, in others they conflict. The boundaries between these items are not always sharp; the categories overlap. But I think that each has a core that is not covered by the others and that adds something distinctive to the notion of religious liberty.

At this point, a few preliminary remarks about the categories I have chosen may be in order. First, I have included several instances that are more felicitously phrased as "freedom from" rather than "freedom to." I do not believe there is any ultimate validity to this distinction. For every freedom "to" is a freedom from governmental or other restraints on the protected act. And every freedom "from" here implies a freedom to engage in activities without the imposition of certain kinds of restraints or influences.

Second, some of these freedoms are closely associated with the free exercise clause of the first amendment. But freedom of religion has a wider scope. Other of these claims may find their principal constitutional basis in the establishment clause;[6] the first amendment freedoms of speech, press, and assembly; the due process clauses; the equal protection clause; or the no religious tests provision of article VI. In general the list moves roughly from those freedoms distinctly covered by the establishment clause, through an area of overlap, to those distinctly covered by the free exercise clause. Or, to put it another way, it moves from those situations in which government attempts to promote or protect some religion (or religions) with which it is identified or associated, through those situations in which government attempts to promote or protect the religion of some private persons, to situations in which government is not engaged in protecting or promoting anyone's religion, but is pursuing some other secular interest.

Third, not every claim mentioned under each of these headings is of full constitutional stature. Some are vindicated on statutory or common-law grounds; others are not vindicated at all. Under each heading we may identify some core of constitutionally vindicated claims, surrounded by a penumbra of statute and common law vindicating similar claims, and finally instances in which similar claims have been denied. We are not dealing with a two-valued logic in which state recognition of a claim is either constitutionally obligatory or constitutionally prohibited. On the contrary, at least four responses are possible: (1) the claim may be found

---

[6] On the freedoms implicit in the establishment clause, see Abington School Dist. v. Schempp, 374 U.S. 203, 222 (1963); Engel v. Vitale, 370 U.S. 421, 430 (1962); Torcaso v. Watkins, 367 U.S. 488 (1961). I shall not be concerned with the meaning of "establishment" except as it relates to claims for various religious liberties.

to be one which the Constitution requires to be vindicated in a particular situation; (2) the claim may be one which the Constitution permits to be vindicated where statute or common law so provides; (3) the claim may be a permissible one in this sense, yet fail because no such provision is extant; and (4) a claim may be one which the state is constitutionally forbidden to recognize. Thus we have zones of constitutional requirement and prohibition surrounding an area of permissibility.[7] But it should be noted that the shape of the constitutional zones has a profound impact on the way in which courts will construe statutes and give effect to common-law rules; and conversely, adjudications which are not technically constitutional may give us some indication of the content of the constitutional zones.

I. Some Religious Freedoms in the United States

A. Freedom From Religious Compulsion

One is free from the use of official force to compel one to entertain or express certain religious beliefs or to observe certain religious practices. One cannot be punished for expressing disagreement with specified religious beliefs or for failing to observe these practices.[8] Government has no power to compel ceremonial affirmations which violate the religious beliefs of the claimant.[9] But there may be some marginal cases in which government does support religious compulsion by private parties, as, for example, by upholding parental freedom to supervise the religious training of children.

One is also free from compulsory payments of taxes in order to support religious beliefs or practices.[10] But again we reach a borderline where this freedom may be limited by government spending public funds or giving tax exemptions in the course of implementing other claims to religious freedom.[11]

B. Freedom From Religious Discrimination

Closely connected with freedom from religious compulsion is freedom from governmental penalties (and exclusion from benefits) for failure to subscribe to particular religious tenets or to

---

[7] Many matters that are within the "permissible" area in the sense that there has been no definitive constitutional adjudication may eventually be in one of the constitutional zones. Also, state constitutional provisions regarding religion often are more detailed than the first amendment and may give definitive answers within the state. On the relation of federal and state constitutional requirements, see KATZ, RELIGION AND AMERICAN CONSTITUTIONS (1964).

[8] See Everson v. Board of Educ., 330 U.S. 1, 15 (1947). The most notable contrary practice is compulsory attendance at religious services at the service academies.

[9] West Virginia State Bd. of Educ. v. Barnette, 319 U.S. 624 (1943).

[10] Everson v. Board of Educ., 330 U.S. 1, 16 (1947).

[11] See *F, H, K,* and *M infra.*

perform certain religious practices.[12] The Constitution explicitly forbids religious tests for federal offices. In the past those unwilling to subscribe to generalized religious requirements have sometimes been disqualified by states from various public functions. But it is now clear that any religious test for any governmental benefit, state or federal, is unconstitutional. It does not matter that the benefit is a "privilege" rather than a right. No government may use tests which distinguish among believers or between believers and nonbelievers.[13] Yet in carrying out private purposes government may impose religious conditions, as I shall show in subsequent sections of this article.[14]

C. *Freedom From State-sponsored Religion*

Like the two freedoms discussed above, this is an "establishment" freedom. It is now clear that there is an enforceable right not to be subjected to religious instruction, ceremony, or symbolism in situations where these are highly sanctioned by governmental authority. Thus religious instruction under public school auspices is unconstitutional,[15] as are Bible reading and recitation of prayers sponsored by public schools.[16] Several things should be noted here. First, the governmentally sponsored religion need not be compulsory; it offends even where participation is voluntary (in the sense that one can request an exemption). Second, such

---

[12] Everson v. Board of Educ., 330 U.S. 1, 15-16 (1947).
[13] Torcaso v. Watkins, 367 U.S. 488 (1961). See also Schowgurow v. State, 213 A.2d 475 (Md. 1965), in which the Maryland Court of Appeals reversed a Buddhist's conviction for murder, finding "the inevitable result of the Supreme Court's decision in *Torcaso* to be that the exclusion of persons from jury service because of their lack of belief in a Supreme Being is in violation of the Federal Constitution." *Id.* at 480.
[14] See *E, H, I,* and *J infra.*
[15] Illinois *ex rel.* McCollum v. Board of Educ., 333 U.S. 203 (1948). *Cf.* Zorach v. Clauson, 343 U.S. 306 (1952). In terms of this article, these cases can be seen as instances in which state responsiveness to claims of freedom to obtain from government opportunities to implement religious values is challenged for infringing claims of freedom from state-sponsored religion. There are important distinctions of fact between the two cases. In *McCollum*, public school personnel and facilities were used to recruit the children for the religious classes; the public school superintendent screened possible participants for suitability; and the religious instructor came onto public school premises and occupied the teacher's position of authority at the head of the classroom. In *Zorach*, recruitment was done by the churches; there were no limitations on participation; the instruction was off the premises; and the religious instructor presumably had to establish his authority independently, rather than assuming that of the teacher. Yet the obtrusive similarity of the use of the compulsory school laws to detain the nonparticipating pupils seemed to escape the attention of the writer of the majority opinion in *Zorach*, who thought the case involved "nothing more" than an instance in which the school "can close its doors or suspend its operations as to those who want to repair to their religious sanctuary for worship or instruction." 343 U.S. at 314.
[16] Abington School Dist. v. Schempp, 374 U.S. 203 (1963); Engel v. Vitale, 370 U.S. 421 (1962).

claims (like *A* and *B supra*) can be vindicated by nonbelievers or by those who are offended for other than religious reasons. Third, (unlike *M* and *N infra*), rather than merely carving out an exception to an otherwise valid governmental regulation, a successful claim of the type under discussion here involves a right to have the offending instruction, ceremony, or symbolism deleted in its entirety. One has not only a right to abstain personally, but a further right to secure the elimination of the entire practice. One is entitled to protection not only from being forced to participate but also from any detriment attendant upon securing a special exemption.

One further feature of this claim should be noted. It seems to have a special applicability—or at least availability—to children.[17] This is due in part to the rules of standing combined with the fact that children are subjected to continuous official supervision in schools more than are most adults.[18] But it is also due to the fact that children are considered more susceptible to religious imposition and to the symbolism of governmental authority.[19]

D. *Freedom From State Use of Religious Purposes, Standards, and Instrumentalities*

The state may not pursue religious objectives. The Supreme

---

[17] It is noteworthy that three of the four cases in which the Supreme Court has struck down arrangements as violations of the establishment clause have involved claims made on behalf of children. Abington School Dist. v. Schempp, 374 U.S. 203 (1963); Engel v. Vitale, 370 U.S. 421 (1962); Illinois *ex rel.* McCollum v. Board of Educ., 333 U.S. 203 (1948). On the other hand, the establishment claims of adults were rejected in Everson v. Board of Educ., 330 U.S. 1 (1947) (taxpayers), and the *Sunday Closing Law Cases*: Gallagher v. Crown Kosher Super Market, 366 U.S. 617 (1961); Braunfeld v. Brown, 366 U.S. 599 (1961); Two Guys from Harrison-Allentown, Inc. v. McGinley, 366 U.S. 582 (1961); McGowan v. Maryland, 366 U.S. 420 (1961) (merchants). An adult establishment claim has prevailed only in Torcaso v. Watkins, 367 U.S. 488 (1961), and that case seems to be based on free exercise considerations as well. The courts have vindicated various free exercise claims at the behest of adults. But except for the *Barnette* case, which was decided on a broader ground, no assertion of free exercise on behalf of a child has been vindicated by the Supreme Court. See Prince v. Massachusetts, 321 U.S. 158 (1944). Generally, claims involving children are said to assert the parents' right to control the religious upbringing of their child. But it should be noted that the children as well as the parents were parties in the *Schempp* case.

[18] Only those "directly affected" by such practices may complain. This includes school children and their parents, but not taxpayers. *Cf.* Doremus v. Board of Educ., 342 U.S. 429 (1952).

[19] See Mr. Justice Brennan's suggestion that a claim for freedom from religious ceremony might apply with less force in the case of such "mature adults" as legislators who are, unlike children, in full control of their movements. Abington School Dist. v. Schempp, 374 U.S. 203, 299 (1963). He also noted that children are particularly susceptible to peer group pressure, thus making the cost of seeking exemption higher than for adults. *Id.* at 290. *Cf.* State *ex rel.* Weiss v. District Bd., 76 Wis. 177, 200, 44 N.W. 967, 975 (1890).

Court clearly indicated in the *Sunday Closing Law Cases* that it upheld these laws only because it found that neither their main purpose nor their principal effect was religious.[20] In *Abington School Dist. v. Schempp*, on the other hand, it found that the purpose of the ceremonies was clearly religious and therefore unconstitutional.[21]

Whatever the objective, the state cannot use religious standards to define public offenses. The Supreme Court, while striking down a provision that allowed censorship of the sacrilegious on free speech grounds, indicated that outrage of sacramental values cannot be a crime.[22] On the other hand, there are instances in which the state may employ religious standards in carrying out private purposes—for example, enforcing testamentary bequests and adjudicating disputes over church property.[23] Again, the state also enforces many policies which express the "witness" of various religious groups. Many of the fundamentals of our criminal and civil law correspond to religious injunctions; many recent "reforms" from prohibition to civil rights are thought to be inspired by religious conscience. The state may carry out such policies as long as they are not concerned with what is ordinarily deemed to be religious practice.[24]

The state cannot ordinarily employ religious instrumentalities to achieve secular public purposes. It may not employ ceremonial Bible reading to instill discipline or provide moral training in the schools where other means are available;[25] it may not involve religious functionaries in the process of effecting marital reconciliations.[26] On the other hand, there may be cases in which religious instrumentalities can be used to carry out specific functions which are not in themselves regarded as religious, such as public health.[27] Finally, there are some instances in which the state must permit public functions to be performed by private religious institutions in order to implement other religious freedoms.[28] Thus the state may require compulsory education of all school-age children, but is bound to permit the operation of private religious schools that meet reasonable requirements.[29]

---

[20] Gallagher v. Crown Kosher Super Market, 366 U.S. 617 (1961); Braunfeld v. Brown, 366 U.S. 599 (1961); Two Guys from Harrison-Allentown, Inc. v. McGinley, 366 U.S. 582 (1961); McGowan v. Maryland, 366 U.S. 420 (1961). All of these cases were decided on May 29, 1961.
[21] Abington School Dist. v. Schempp, 374 U.S. 203, 223 (1963).
[22] Joseph Burstyn, Inc. v. Wilson, 343 U.S. 495 (1952).
[23] See *E* and *H infra*.
[24] See *E infra*.
[25] Chamberlin v. Dade County Bd. of Pub. Instruction, 377 U.S. 402, *reversing* 160 So. 2d 97 (Fla. 1964).
[26] People *ex rel.* Bernat v. Bicek, 405 Ill. 510, 91 N.E.2d 588 (1950).
[27] Bradfield v. Roberts, 175 U.S. 291 (1899); Schade v. Allegheny County Institution Dist., 386 Pa. 507, 126 A.2d 911 (1956).
[28] See *J infra*.
[29] Pierce v. Society of Sisters, 268 U.S. 510 (1925).

Presumably, like the three foregoing claims, claims in this category can be vindicated not only by a claimant who asserts "religious" objections but by anyone.[29a] It is clear that for purposes of vindicating these claims for freedom from governmental religion, the offending religion is religion as conventionally understood rather than as understood by the claimant.[30]

E. Freedom To Enlist State Co-operation in Carrying Out Religious Purposes

The state may be used to transmit and enforce religious values among private parties. Thus the state will enforce religious trusts,[31] and most courts are willing to enforce religious requirements or restrictions in wills.[32] But only a few courts will enforce antenuptial agreements regarding the religious training of children.[33]

While the state will not compel individuals to conform to the standards of the religious groups to which they belong, it does uphold the internal order of religious associations. It recognizes their form of government, respects their decrees about internal disputes, and decides property disputes in accordance with their rules. Ordinarily it refrains from interference with their disciplinary measures, but in some cases it actively enforces them.[34]

While the state may lend support to private religious undertakings, it cannot be used to enforce in the wider society those religious values which are obviously sacramental or theological.[35] Yet the state will not prevent a religious association from enforcing religious requirements on nonmembers who purport to observe these standards.[36]

Values which are religiously sanctioned may be promoted by the state if they are separable from the sacramental and ceremonial

---

[29a] State v. Madison, 213 A.2d 880 (Md. 1965) (belief in God requirement for grand jury service invalidated at instance of defendant not himself a member of the excluded class).

[30] See part II *infra*.

[31] See ZOLLMAN, AMERICAN CIVIL CHURCH LAW ch. 7 (1917). *Cf.* Quick Bear v. Leupp, 210 U.S. 50 (1908) (funds held by the federal government in trust for Indians could be disbursed to religious schools at the designation of the Indians).

[32] See, *e.g.*, Gordon v. Gordon, 332 Mass. 197, 124 N.E.2d 228, *cert. denied*, 349 U.S. 947 (1955).

[33] See note 68 *infra*. Factors limiting the enforcement of such agreements include the primacy of the child's welfare, the freedom of the other parent, and of the child.

[34] See, *e.g.*, Bonacum v. Harrington, 65 Neb. 831, 91 N.W. 886 (1902).

[35] See C and D *supra*.

[36] On judicial response to the efforts of associations for insuring the observance of the Jewish dietary laws by merchants who purport to deal in Kosher goods, see Hygrade Provision Co. v. Sherman, 266 U.S. 497 (1925); S. S. & B. Live Poultry Corp. v. Kashruth Ass'n of Greater N.Y., Inc., 158 Misc. 358, 285 N.Y.S. 879 (Sup. Ct. 1936).

aspects of religion and do not involve obviously religious tests in their application. A great many ordinary criminal laws and laws regarding sexual activity, family arrangements, drinking, gambling, and so forth, are at least for many the expression of religious conscience. Although there is some disagreement about the propriety of religious groups seeking official enforcement of their views in such matters, there is no doubt that the mere correspondence of legal regulation with religious imperative does not make the law invalid.[37]

F. *Freedom To Obtain (From Government) Opportunities To Implement Religious Values*

This is a freedom that is severely limited by the first four categories set out above. But there is a constitutional right for religious persons and groups to use public streets and parks for religious activities.[38] On the other hand, religious groups can apparently be excluded from the afterhours use of public school buildings that are available for other kinds of voluntary groups.[39]

The main thrust of this type of claim is in situations where governmental action has deprived persons of normal opportunities for pursuing religious activity without state co-operation. Thus government must provide opportunities for prisoners[40] and soldiers,[41] because it has put them in special environments in which the normal opportunities for religious activity are absent. In this respect, religion seems to occupy a special position, for it does not appear that government has similar obligations in regard to political expression. Apparently government may remove one from political society, but not from religious society.

A claim of this type was put forward in the school prayer cases, where it was asserted that compulsory detention of school children during part of the day deprived them of opportunities for religious activity and that this authorized the government to provide facilities for them.[42] This was rejected by the Supreme Court. On the other hand, some adjustment in school timetables for this purpose is permissible.[43] It is not clear just what degree

---

[37] See McGowan v. Maryland, 366 U.S. 420, 442 (1961).

[38] See, *e.g.*, Fowler v. Rhode Island, 345 U.S. 67 (1953); Kunz v. New York, 340 U.S. 290 (1951); Niemotko v. Maryland, 340 U.S. 268 (1951); Jamison v. Texas, 318 U.S. 413 (1942).

[39] State *ex rel.* Greisiger v. Grand Rapids Bd. of Educ., 153 Ohio St. 474, 92 N.E.2d 385, *cert. denied*, 340 U.S. 820 (1950); McKnight v. Board of Pub. Educ., 365 Pa. 422, 76 A.2d 207 (1950), *appeal dismissed*, 341 U.S. 913 (1951).

[40] See cases cited note 193 *infra*.

[41] See Abington School Dist. v. Schempp, 374 U.S. 203, 226 n.10 (1963); *id.* at 296 (Brennan, J., concurring).

[42] This view of the matter was advanced by Mr. Justice Stewart, dissenting, *id.* at 312, and was rejected by the Court, *id.* at 225-26: "[Free exercise] has never meant that a majority could use the machinery of the State to practice its beliefs." See *id.* at 298 (Brennan, J., concurring).

[43] *Cf.* Zorach v. Clauson, 343 U.S. 306 (1952).

of governmental control over the environment must take place before provision of religious opportunities becomes a governmental responsibility. But even short of such a point, religious groups have a right to participate in governmental programs, such as urban redevelopment, in which government is responsible for restructuring a wide section of the environment.[44] Where government controls the use of land and buildings by zoning and building requirements, there are situations when it may not exclude the use of buildings for religious purposes—at least not without providing equivalent opportunities without too great inconvenience.[45]

G. Freedom From Private Interference With Religion

The state provides ordinary protection and services for religious undertakings. It also acts positively to protect the right to carry on religious activities without private interference. Most states make it a criminal offense to disturb a religious meeting by noise or intrusion—even where this limits the religious expression of the interloper.[46] But the state is limited in acting positively to provide an atmosphere free of religious hostility and free of that which is religiously offensive. The state may protect persons against overt private discrimination on religious grounds in such areas as employment or housing.[47] It may possibly act to protect the reputation of a religious group—at least from those verbal assaults likely to lead to a breach of the peace.[48] But the state cannot suppress religious communications which might offend the hearer's religious sensibilities. Even when they arouse severe animosity, the state cannot protect against exaggeration, vilification, and abuse "in the realm of religious faith."[49] Presumably the state cannot make blasphemy or sacrilege criminal offenses.[50]

The state will not act affirmatively to prevent the discharge of an employee who refuses to join a union on the grounds that his religion forbids him to belong to an organization of which unbelievers are members.[51] But where the streets of a town are privately owned, property rights do not avail to limit religious activities on those streets; they may be utilized as if they were pub-

---

[44] 64th St. Residences, Inc. v. City of New York, 4 N.Y.2d 268, 150 N.E. 2d 396, 174 N.Y.S.2d 1, cert. denied, 357 U.S. 907 (1958).
[45] See note 199 infra.
[46] See, e.g., Jones v. State, 219 Ga. 848, 136 S.E.2d 358 (1964).
[47] See, e.g., WIS. STAT. §§ 111.31, 66.40(2m) (1963).
[48] Beauharnais v. Illinois, 343 U.S. 250 (1952); but cf. Kunz v. New York, 340 U.S. 290 (1951).
[49] Cantwell v. Connecticut, 310 U.S. 296 (1940).
[50] See Joseph Burstyn, Inc. v. Wilson, 343 U.S. 495 (1952); contra, State v. Mockus, 120 Me. 84, 113 Atl. 39 (1921).
[51] Wicks v. Southern Pac. Co., 231 F.2d 130 (9th Cir.), cert. denied, 351 U.S. 946 (1956); Otten v. Baltimore & O.R.R., 205 F.2d 58 (2d Cir. 1953).

lic.[52] On the other hand, a private hospital may exclude religious functionaries from performing ritual circumcisions there.[53]

H. Freedom of Religious Association

Freedom of religion includes a freedom to form and join associations devoted to religious purposes. Such associations may form corporations, acquire property, and set up continuing bodies.[54] A very wide degree of internal autonomy within such religious associations is protected by the Constitution. Religious bodies have their own rules and procedures for dealing with internal disputes, deviance from ritual and social rules, and change in their procedures. The form of internal government, the parties who are to exercise it, and the application of its rules to disputants may not be interfered with by government.[55] Where government is called upon to vindicate the civil and property rights of disputants, it must respect the recognized authorities within the association. Religious associations may expel or discipline their adherents in accordance with their domestic rules.[56] Government may not interfere with such disciplinary measures and may sometimes enforce them.

At common law, such bodies enjoy immunity from tort liability; these associations, or at least some of their activities, enjoy immunity from certain forms of taxation—in some states by constitutional provision and in all places by statute.[57]

I. Freedom To Choose and Change Religion

Ordinarily each individual is free to choose (or discover) his religious beliefs, practices, and affiliations. The state cannot influence his choice by rewards or penalties.[58] The right of choice

---

[52] Marsh v. Alabama, 326 U.S. 501 (1946).

[53] Zlotowitz v. Jewish Hospital, 193 Misc. 124, 84 N.Y.S.2d 61 (Sup. Ct. 1948).

[54] Two states forbid incorporation of religious associations. VA. CONST. art. I, § 59; W. VA. CONST. art. VI, § 47. Cf. President Madison's veto of a charter of incorporation for a religious body, 3 STOKES, CHURCH AND STATE IN THE UNITED STATES 414 (1950).

[55] Kreshik v. Saint Nicholas Cathedral, 363 U.S. 190 (1960); Kedroff v. Saint Nicholas Cathedral, 344 U.S. 94 (1952). Cf. Watson v. Jones, 80 U.S. (13 Wall.) 679 (1872). Cf. earlier prescriptions of the form of church government, e.g., Robertson v. Bullions, 11 N.Y. 243 (1854).

[56] Thus a university controlled by a religious order may expel a student for willful violation of ecclesiastical law, consisting of participating in a civil marriage. Carr v. Saint John's Univ., 17 App. Div. 2d 632, 231 N.Y.S. 2d 410, aff'd, 12 N.Y.2d 802, 187 N.E.2d 18, 235 N.Y.S.2d 834 (1962).

[57] On tax exemptions, see Kauper, *The Constitutionality of Tax Exemptions for Religious Activities*, in THE WALL BETWEEN CHURCH AND STATE 95 (Oaks ed. 1963); Van Alstyne, *Tax Exemptions of Church Property*, 20 OHIO ST. L.J. 461 (1959).

[58] Presumably it may not influence his choice by exposing him to religious symbolism, indoctrination, and the like. But it is unclear how

of younger children is clearly limited by the parental control over their religious training and activity.⁵⁹ For adults, there are some limits which ensue from government carrying out private purposes and upholding the decisions of religious associations. Thus, for example, one cannot receive communion or attend a religious meeting where this violates the rules of the religious group.⁶⁰

Religious associations, as well as individuals, enjoy a right to choose and change their doctrines, practices, and affiliations. Independent religious bodies may change any of these things; but in some states a majority cannot divert property specifically endowed for certain doctrines to the support of different ones,⁶¹ or change denominational affiliation.⁶² Those religious groups which are part of larger bodies with representative or hierarchical government are limited in ability to change by the fact that courts will enforce the will of the higher church authorities against a local majority.⁶³ In church disputes the law supports the "regular" faction against insurgents. But courts will not interfere with innovations which are introduced by established authorities according to established procedures.⁶⁴

J. Freedom To Transmit and Implant Religion in Children

A parent ordinarily has a right to supervise the religious training of his children.⁶⁵ However, this may occasionally be limited because of the child's welfare,⁶⁶ and it is limited by the child's own free choice of religion as he gets older.⁶⁷ Where parents are

---

much the state may be inhibited from influencing such religious choices by exposing individuals, particularly children, to influences which are not religious in a doctrinal or pedagogical sense. For example, it has been suggested that public schools are not forbidden to expose a child to "objective" study of the Bible, of comparative religion, and the history of religion. Abington School Dist. v. Schempp, 374 U.S. 203, 225 (1963).

⁵⁹ See *J infra*.
⁶⁰ See *G* and *H supra*.
⁶¹ See, *e.g.*, Mitchell v. Church of Christ, 221 Ala. 315, 128 So. 781 (1930); Davis v. Scher, 356 Mich. 291, 97 N.W.2d 137 (1959).
⁶² See, *e.g.*, Reid v. Johnston, 241 N.C. 201, 85 S.E.2d 114 (1954); Kemp v. Lentz, 46 Ohio L. Abs. 28, 68 N.E.2d 339 (Ct. App. 1943).
⁶³ See, *e.g.*, Watson v. Jones, 80 U.S. (13 Wall.) 679 (1872); Board of Trustees v. Richards, 58 Ohio Op. 219, 130 N.E.2d 736 (C.P. 1954).
⁶⁴ See McGinnis v. Watson, 41 Pa. St. 9 (1861).
⁶⁵ The parent enjoys the same right to give the child *no* religious training. Welker v. Welker, 24 Wis. 2d 570, 129 N.W.2d 134 (1964). While the parental right includes teaching his child that war is wrong, it does not include urging him not to register for the draft. Warren v. United States, 177 F.2d 596 (10th Cir. 1949), *cert. denied*, 338 U.S. 947 (1950).
⁶⁶ Custody may be lost or denied because the parent's opposition to blood transfusion poses a hazard to the child's health or well-being. Battaglia v. Battaglia, 9 Misc. 2d 1067, 172 N.Y.S.2d 361 (Sup. Ct. 1958); Salvaggio v. Barnett, 248 S.W.2d 244 (Tex. Civ. App.), *cert. denied*, 344 U.S. 879 (1952).
⁶⁷ Hehman v. Hehman, 13 Misc. 2d 318, 178 N.Y.S.2d 328 (Sup. Ct. 1958) (thirteen-year-old has "right" to choose his religion); Martin v. Martin,

separated, the parent with custody enjoys the right. Most courts will not enforce antenuptial or separation agreements about the religious upbringing of the child.[68] On the other hand, some states undertake to vindicate the right of the natural parent to transmit his religion to a child he gives for adoption.[69]

A parent does not have a right to withhold his child from all secular schooling or from secular schooling that he thinks is religiously detrimental.[70] But he does have a right to send him to a religious school which meets the requirements of the state's education laws. Religious societies have a right to operate such schools.[71] Parents may not inculcate religion by practices which violate school attendance laws—even to observe their Sabbath or religious holidays[72]—or child labor laws.[73]

---

308 N.Y. 136, 123 N.E.2d 812, 127 N.Y.S.2d 851 (1954) (thirteen-year-old's religious preference subsumed under welfare). *But cf.* Prieto v. Saint Alphonsus Convent of Mercy, 52 La. Ann. 631, 27 So. 153 (1900) (parent may remove seventeen-year-old girl from convent which she entered without consent for purpose of becoming a nun).

[68] See, *e.g.*, Stanton v. Stanton, 213 Ga. 545, 100 S.E.2d 289 (1957). This seems to be the prevailing view. However, some courts have enforced such agreements. See, *e.g.*, Ramon v. Ramon, 34 N.Y.S.2d 100 (Dom. Rel. Ct. 1942).

[69] Insofar as these "religious matching" statutes operate irrespective of the choice of the natural parent, they appear to vindicate an interest of the religious group in its potential members. See, *e.g.*, Petition of Goldman, 331 Mass. 647, 121 N.E.2d 843 (1954), *cert. denied*, 348 U.S. 942 (1955). See Paulsen, *Constitutional Problems of Utilizing a Religious Factor in Adoptions and Placement of Children*, in THE WALL BETWEEN CHURCH AND STATE 117 (Oaks ed. 1963); Pfeffer, *Religion in the Upbringing of Children*, 35 B.U.L. REV. 333 (1955).

[70] *In re* Currence, 42 Misc. 2d 418, 248 N.Y.S.2d 251 (Family Ct. 1963) (unapproved school of Ancient Divine Order of Melchisadech); Application of Auster, 198 Misc. 1055, 100 N.Y.S.2d 60 (Sup. Ct. 1950), *aff'd*, 278 App. Div. 656, 104 N.Y.S.2d 65, *aff'd*, 302 N.Y. 855, 100 N.E.2d 47, *appeal dismissed*, 342 U.S. 884 (1951); People ex rel. Shapiro v. Dorin, 99 N.Y.S.2d 830 (Dom. Rel. Ct.), *aff'd sub nom.* People v. Donner, 302 N.Y. 857, 100 N.E.2d 48, *appeal dismissed*, 342 U.S. 884 (1951) (parents believed that all systematic secular education was prohibited by Jewish law and sent child to a school which did not meet state requirements); State v. Hershberger, 77 Ohio L. Abs. 487, 150 N.E.2d 671 (Juv. Ct. 1958), *rev'd*, 83 Ohio L. Abs. 63, 168 N.E.2d 12 (Ct. App. 1959) (Mennonite refusal to attend public schools); State v. Hershberger, 103 Ohio App. 188, 144 N.E.2d 693 (1955) (Mennonite attendance at school with unqualified teachers); Commonwealth v. Beiler, 168 Pa. Super. 462, 79 A.2d 134 (1951) (Amish refusal to attend high school and expose children to university-educated teachers).

[71] See Pierce v. Society of Sisters, 268 U.S. 510 (1925); State v. Hershberger, 103 Ohio App. 188, 144 N.E.2d 693 (1955).

[72] *In re* Currence, 42 Misc. 2d 418, 248 N.Y.S.2d 251 (Family Ct. 1963) (withdrawal of child for Melchisadech Sabbath, noon Wednesday to noon Thursday, not permitted); Commonwealth v. Bey, 166 Pa. Super. 136, 70 A.2d 693 (1950) (Mohammedan parents cannot keep children out of school on Fridays); Ferriter v. Tyler, 48 Vt. 444 (1876) (Catholic children absent for Corpus Christi day).

[73] Prince v. Massachusetts, 321 U.S. 158 (1944).

K. Freedom of Religious Expression

The Constitution protects all kinds of religious utterances, spoken, written, or by symbols, direct or mediated, individual or group. It protects not only prayers, worship services, and sermons, but also "addresses," solicitation of funds, proselytization, and sales of religious literature.[74] Not only are direct prohibitions forbidden but also prior censorship, subsequent penalties, onerous licensing requirements, and special taxation. Religious expression is certainly subject to less restriction than is "commercial" solicitation[75] and perhaps even less than political and other first amendment speech.[76] It is subject to limitations to secure public order and other important interests.[77]

This freedom of expression may sometimes give way to other religious freedom claims. For example, the right of a teacher to express religious convictions by the wearing of distinctive religious garb or insignia does not prevail against a claim for freedom from religious symbolism under state sponsorship.[78] But freedom of religious expression does prevail over a claim for state protection from insult to religious sensibilities.[79]

L. Freedom From Compelled Disclosure of Religious Views

Along with freedom of religious expression should be mentioned certain privacy claims—claims for a right not to divulge the contents of religious communications or the existence of religious views. Most states recognize the privileged nature of the minister-

---

[74] Fowler v. Rhode Island, 345 U.S. 67 (1953); Niemotko v. Maryland, 340 U.S. 268 (1951); Follett v. McCormick, 321 U.S. 573 (1944); Martin v. City of Struthers, 319 U.S. 141 (1943); Murdock v. Pennsylvania, 319 U.S. 105 (1943); Jamison v. Texas, 318 U.S. 413 (1943); Cantwell v. Connecticut, 310 U.S. 296 (1940).

[75] *Compare* Jamison v. Texas, *supra* note 74, *and* Martin v. City of Struthers, *supra* note 74, *with* Valentine v. Christiansen, 316 U.S. 52 (1942), *and* Breard v. Alexandria, 341 U.S. 622 (1951).

[76] See Follett v. McCormick, 321 U.S. 573 (1944); Murdock v. Pennsylvania, 319 U.S. 105 (1943); Saladin, *Relative Ranking of the Preferred Freedoms: Religion and Speech*, in 1964 RELIGION AND THE PUBLIC ORDER 149 (Gianella ed. 1965).

[77] Cox v. New Hampshire, 312 U.S. 569 (1941) (relatively minor restriction on religious liberty justified by necessity of avoiding disorder ensuing from unlicensed parades); Gara v. United States, 178 F.2d 38 (6th Cir. 1949), *aff'd by equally divided court*, 340 U.S. 857 (1951) (religiously motivated advice against registration for draft punishable as incitement); People v. Parker, 397 Ill. 305, 74 N.E.2d 523 (1947) (religious freedom no defense against contempt conviction for improper letters to grand jury foreman); Hopkins v. State, 193 Md. 489, 69 A.2d 456 (1949), *appeal dismissed*, 339 U.S. 940 (1950) (minister convicted for violating state prohibition of signs advertising his services in performing marriages).

[78] See, *e.g.*, Zellers v. Huff, 55 N.M. 501, 236 P.2d 949 (1951); Comment, *Religious Garb in the Public Schools—A Study in Conflicting Liberties*, 22 U. CHI. L. REV. 888 (1955). See C *supra*.

[79] Cantwell v. Connecticut, 310 U.S. 296 (1940). See G *supra*.

communicant relationship.[80] A federal court recently ruled that the free exercise clause barred a suit for slander consisting of statements to church authorities.[81] And it has been suggested that one cannot be put to the necessity of publicly expressing disbelief.[82] Whether government can require a person to state his religion for census purposes has never been adjudicated.[83]

M. Freedom From Governmental Prohibition of Activity Accorded Positive Religious Significance

Here, and in the section which follows, it may be assumed that from the government's point of view the regulation is entirely nonreligious in purpose. Under this heading I shall discuss (1) direct prohibitions—those in which the government forbids the commission of an act that has religious significance for the claimant (*e.g.*, polygamy, solicitation in violation of child labor laws, snake handling, the use of peyote, fortunetelling, faith healing, and religious meetings in prisons), and (2) indirect burdens—those in which the government does not directly prohibit the religiously valued activity, but prohibits or requires something else that makes it expensive or burdensome (*e.g.*, cessation of work on a day other than one's Sabbath, and zoning and building regulations). Freedom of religion has been raised as a defense against governmental attempts to enforce all of these regulations, and until recently it has proved almost totally unavailing.

The classic instance of direct prohibition is Mormon polygamy. In *Reynolds v. United States*,[84] the Supreme Court upheld the federal bigamy conviction of a Mormon who took a second wife in accordance with accepted doctrine of his church—having received permission from church authorities and having been married according to the practices of that church. The Court found that the first amendment deprived Congress "of all legislative power over mere opinion, but . . . left [it] free to reach actions which were in violation of social duties or subversive of good order."[85] The Court had no doubt that Congress was fit to determine what

---

[80] See Hogan, *A Modern Problem on the Privilege of the Confessional*, 6 LOYOLA L. REV. 1 (1951); Note, *Privileged Communications to Clergymen*, 1 CATHOLIC LAW. 199 (1955).

[81] Cimijotti v. Paulsen, 230 F. Supp. 39, 41 (N.D. Iowa 1964) ("A person must be free to say anything and everything to his Church, at least so long as it is said in a recognized and required proceeding of the religion and to a recognized official of the religion.").

[82] Abington School Dist. v. Schempp, 374 U.S. 203, 289 (1963) (Brennan, J., concurring).

[83] It should be noted that the proposed (but later cancelled) religious census was opposed on a variety of grounds, including both establishment and free exercise arguments (Christian Science forbids religious enumerations). For an analysis of the dispute, see FOSTER, A QUESTION ON RELIGION (Inter-University Case Program No. 66, 1961).

[84] 98 U.S. 145 (1878).

[85] *Id.* at 164.

were "social duties" in regard to marriage and family. While marriage is "from its very nature a sacred obligation, [yet it is] ... in most civilized nations, a civil contract, and usually regulated by law."[86] Thus "it is within the legitimate scope of the power of every civil government to determine whether polygamy or monogamy shall be the law of social life under its dominion."[87] The first amendment does not change this since it covers only opinions, not actions.[88]

Does the amendment create an exception for religious objectors? Are "those who make polygamy a part of their religion ... excepted from the operation of the statute"?[89] To allow this would be "dangerous" for it would "make the professed doctrines of religious belief superior to the law of the land, and in effect ... permit every citizen to become a law unto himself."[90] Thus while laws "cannot interfere with mere religious belief and opinions, they may with practices."[91]

Since it solved the problem by defining the appropriate spheres of religious and civil authority, it was not necessary for the Court to evaluate polygamy. Yet the Court indicates that "polygamy has always been odious among the northern and western nations of Europe . . . ."[92] It has always been punishable. Its consequences are immense. Upon the form of marriage, "this most important feature of social life," depends the form of the state. "In fact, according as monogamous or polygamous marriages are allowed, do we find the principles on which the government of the people, to a greater or less extent, rests."[93] In an early and unheralded use of social science findings, the Court cites the learned opinion of the day that "polygamy leads to the patriarchal principle . . . which . . . when applied to large communities, fetters the people in stationary despotism, while that principle cannot long exist in connection with monogamy."[94]

In two later cases, the Supreme Court upheld, respectively, a test oath which excluded polygamists from voting, and the with-

---

[86] Id. at 165.
[87] Id. at 166.
[88] The Court does not explain how this belief-action distinction is compatible with the text of the first amendment's religion clauses. For presumably that religion whose free exercise may not be prohibited is the same religion respecting whose establishment Congress may make no law. For the latter purpose, religion includes practices as well as beliefs. Congress may not require "overt acts" any more than it may require the holding of religious opinions. The answer seems to lie in the Court's view that, after all, religion has to do with opinions and closely related activities.
[89] Ibid.
[90] Id. at 167.
[91] Id. at 166.
[92] Id. at 164.
[93] Id. at 165-66.
[94] Id. at 166.

drawal of the charter of the Mormon Church.[95] In these cases the Supreme Court resists the notion that polygamy is a genuinely religious tenet.[96] While the main Mormon Church officially gave up polygamy in 1890, prosecutions of fundamentalists who continued to adhere to polygamy have reached the same result.[97] The last time the Supreme Court drew close to the merits of polygamy as an issue of religious freedom was in 1946, when it upheld the conviction of a fundamentalist Mormon under the Mann Act, which prohibits the interstate transportation of females for "'any . . . immoral purpose.' "[98] The courts have uniformly refused to consider the possibility that the free exercise of religion might require recognition of differences in systems of marriage—even though these same courts refer to marriage as "a sacred obligation" and "holy estate" which was until relatively recently regulated by ecclesiastical law, and even though every state permits marriages to be performed by authorized religious personnel.[99]

---

[95] Late Corp. of the Church of Jesus Christ of Latter-Day Saints v. United States, 136 U.S. 1 (1890); Davis v. Beason, 133 U.S. 333 (1890).
[96] See N infra.
[97] State v. Barlow, 107 Utah 292, 153 P.2d 647 (1944), *appeal dismissed sub nom.* Barlow v. Utah, 324 U.S. 829 (1945). For a non-Mormon example, see Long v. State, 192 Ind. 524, 137 N.E. 49 (1922). Children of a polygamous marriage were found "neglected" and the parents deprived of custody because a polygamous home is an immoral place, unfit for children. *In re* Black, 3 Utah 2d 315, 283 P.2d 887, *cert. denied*, 350 U.S. 923 (1955).
[98] Cleveland v. United States, 329 U.S. 14, 16 (1946). Mr. Justice Douglas, for the majority, cited favorably the earlier observations that polygamy was odious to Northern and Western Europeans, a return to barbarism, and contrary to the spirit of Christianity. "The establishment or maintenance of polygamous households is a notorious example of promiscuity. The permanent advertisement of their existence is an example of the sharp repercussions which they have in the community." *Id.* at 19. Although they might have different ramifications, these polygamous practices, long branded as immoral in the law, are of the "same genus as the other immoral practices covered by the Act." *Ibid.* "Whether an act is immoral within the meaning of the statute is not to be determined by the accused's concepts of morality. Congress has provided the standard." *Id.* at 20. Mr. Justice Murphy, in a remarkable dissent which observes that different religions might imply different moralities, would not include polygamous marriage among the "immoral practices" of the statute. He observed that "polygyny is a form of marriage built upon a set of social and moral principles. It must be recognized and treated as such." *Id.* at 26.

Other recent Mormon prosecutions fared less well in the Supreme Court. In Musser v. Utah, 333 U.S. 95 (1948), the Court reversed, on grounds of vagueness, a conviction of Mormons for conspiracy to commit acts injurious to public morals (by counseling and advising plural marriage). In Chatwin v. United States, 326 U.S. 455 (1946), the conviction of a polygamist under a federal kidnapping statute was set aside on the ground that the facts would not support a finding of kidnapping.
[99] Most states permit variations in the form of solemnizing a marriage to accord with the religion of the parties. See TORPEY, JUDICIAL DOCTRINES OF RELIGIOUS RIGHTS IN AMERICA ch. 7 (1948). A state statute limiting the

Similarly, freedom of religion has been held not to protect those who deemed palm reading to be a religious practice against laws forbidding commercial fortunetelling.[100] It has not availed against statutes prohibiting the handling of snakes in religious services.[101] Nor can faith healers use religious liberty as a defense in prosecutions for the unlicensed practice of medicine.[102] Nor has it protected religious performances against statutes regulating noise[103] and obscenity,[104] or religious pretensions against prosecutions for fraud.[105] In the period before 1940, there is only one case in which a claim of religious liberty was a successful defense against such a direct prohibition.[106] However, there are a number of explicit statutory exemptions for religious activities,[107] and in a number of cases courts have construed statutes to exclude religious practices from their scope.[108] And there were innumerable

---

power to solemnize marriages to those clergymen affiliated with any religious group listed in the federal census of religious bodies has been held an unconstitutional violation of religious freedom. *In re* Saunders, 37 N.Y.S.2d 341 (Sup. Ct. 1942). It should be noted that the United States does recognize polygamous marriages among American Indians. See Bartholomew, *Recognition of Polygamous Marriages in America*, 13 INTERNATIONAL AND COMPARATIVE L.Q. 1022 (1964).

[100] See, *e.g.*, McMasters v. State, 21 Okla. Crim. 318, 207 Pac. 566 (1922).

[101] Hill v. State, 38 Ala. App. 404, 88 So. 2d 880, *cert. denied*, 264 Ala. 697, 88 So. 2d 887 (1956); Lawson v. Commonwealth, 291 Ky. 437, 164 S.W.2d 972 (1942); State v. Massey, 229 N.C. 734, 51 S.E.2d 179, *appeal dismissed sub nom.* Bunn v. North Carolina, 336 U.S. 942 (1949); Harden v. State, 188 Tenn. 17, 216 S.W.2d 708 (1948). Nor is religious motivation a good defense in a prosecution for death due to snake handling. Kirk v. Commonwealth, 186 Va. 839, 44 S.E.2d 409 (1947).

[102] See, *e.g.*, People v. Handzik, 410 Ill. 295, 102 N.E.2d 340, *cert. denied*, 343 U.S. 927 (1952). However, some medical licensing statutes in terms do not apply to religious practices. See, *e.g.*, People v. Cole, 219 N.Y. 98, 113 N.E. 790, 148 N.Y.S. 708 (1916), where the court ruled that a Christian Science practitioner could not be convicted of violating a statute which exempted "the practice of religious tenets of any church." But church practice is not a good defense where the healer uses the ordinary instrumentalities of medicine. People v. Vogelgesang, 221 N.Y. 290, 116 N.E. 977, 158 N.Y.S. 1126 (1917).

[103] See, *e.g.*, State v. White, 64 N.H. 48, 5 Atl. 828 (1886).

[104] Knowles v. United States, 170 Fed. 409 (8th Cir. 1909); Delk v. Commonwealth, 166 Ky. 39, 178 S.W. 1129 (1915) (vulgarity in the pulpit a breach of the peace).

[105] Crane v. United States, 259 Fed. 480 (9th Cir. 1919); New v. United States, 245 Fed. 710 (9th Cir. 1917), *cert. denied*, 246 U.S. 665 (1918).

[106] State v. De Laney, 1 N.J. Misc. 619, 122 Atl. 890 (Sup. Ct. 1923) (religious defense upheld against statute barring commercial fortunetelling).

[107] For example, the exemption for sacramental wine in the Prohibition Act, the exemptions for Christian Science healers in many medical practice acts, and exemptions for "religious sacramental" use of peyote in several state narcotics acts.

[108] Notably in Church of the Holy Trinity v. United States, 143 U.S. 457 (1892), where the Court found that Congress, in making it illegal to bring aliens into the country to work, could not have intended to include a church which hired a foreign minister.

"exemptions" created by the inaction of enforcement officials.[109]

Until the last few decades claims in this category were generally disposed of under what David Manwaring calls the " 'secular regulation' rule: There is no constitutional right to exemption on religious grounds from the compulsion of a general regulation dealing with non-religious matters."[110] Manwaring finds this rule applied almost invariably by both state and federal courts before 1940 and often since. It should be emphasized that the general regulation deals with matters which are nonreligious in the general community estimation, though they may be quite essentially religious in the view of the minority whose practice is thereby prohibited. When using such an approach, the courts were unconcerned about the nature of the religious motivations for the prohibited acts; it was enough to establish that the regulation was indeed a legitimate secular one which the state had power to make for the population generally. It then followed that in the absence of a statutory exemption it was equally applicable to those whose religious practices it prohibited.

The application of this rule was not deemed a significant impingement upon religious liberty, for religious liberty was visualized primarily as freedom from religious persecution.[111] Most of the cases were decided under state constitutional provisions rather than under the first amendment,[112] and the state provisions emphasize freedom of religious profession and worship and freedom from specifically religious oppressions rather than freedom from secular regulations.[113] For example, when a nineteenth-century Massachusetts court refers to the "unrestricted liberty in their religion" which is enjoyed by all, it is clear that what it refers to is immunity from punishment or persecution for religious opinions. But religious freedom does not require any concession to the varying practices of different religions; indeed, such concessions would amount to a forbidden connection between church and state.[114] Thus in the Mormon cases, the Supreme Court identifies the free exercise guaranteed by the first amendment with freedom from taxes and punishments and from compelled conformity to religious standards.[115] This view is expressed most eloquently

---

[109] An example may be found in *In re* Black, 3 Utah 2d 315, 283 P.2d 887, *cert. denied*, 350 U.S. 923 (1955), where an isolated polygamous village existed for over twenty-five years.

[110] MANWARING, RENDER UNTO CAESAR—THE FLAG-SALUTE CONTROVERSY 51 (1962). (All italicized in original.)

[111] *I.e.*, A and B *supra*, sometimes also C and D *supra*.

[112] The first case to hold that the first amendment's religion clauses are fully incorporated by the fourteenth amendment and applicable against the states is Cantwell v. Connecticut, 310 U.S. 296 (1940). *Cf.* Hamilton v. Regents of the Univ. of Cal., 293 U.S. 245 (1934).

[113] MANWARING, *op. cit. supra* note 110, at 40.

[114] Commonwealth v. Cooke, 7 AMERICAN L. REGISTER 417 (Police Court of Boston, Mass. 1859).

[115] Davis v. Beason, 133 U.S. 333, 342 (1890); Reynolds v. United States, 98 U.S. 145, 162 (1878).

by Mr. Justice Frankfurter in the first flag-salute case, where he limits religious freedom to a ban on measures directed against particular sects, not as applying against general regulations which work special hardship on some because of their religious beliefs.[116]

The past few years have seen a radical shift in the treatment of claims of this type.[117] The roots of this new dispensation are to be found in the religious solicitation cases of the 1940's.[118] The holdings in most of these cases are at least as much on grounds of freedom of speech and press as freedom of religion. Yet taken together these cases established that religious freedom, along with speech and press, is involved in such activities as sidewalk preaching, house-to-house solicitation, and sale of religious books; that the religious character of this activity is to be assessed at least in part by the views of the claimants and not wholly by "objective" standards;[119] that religious freedom is a substantive freedom which did more than protect from invidious discrimination; that it covers not only belief, but also action; and that restrictions on such action must meet some kind of test of validity under the circumstances—a test akin to, if not identical with, that applied to restrictions on speech and press. In addition, there is some indication that at least those religious activities which are what might be called the sacramental core of religion are perhaps in a specially favored position.[120]

In *Cantwell v. Connecticut*,[121] the Court abandoned the belief-action distinction which had been an important component of the secular regulation rule. It found that the first amendment's guarantee of free exercise "embraces two concepts,—freedom to believe and freedom to act. The first is absolute but, in the nature of things, the second cannot be. Conduct remains subject to regulation for the protection of society."[122] At that moment the Court

---

[116] Minersville School Dist. v. Gobitis, 310 U.S. 586 (1940). Compare his dissent in West Virginia State Bd. of Educ. v. Barnette, 319 U.S. 624, 653-54 (1943), where he reiterates that religious freedom "terminated disabilities, it did not create new privileges." He continued,

> The essence of the religious freedom guaranteed by our Constitution is therefore this: no religion shall either receive the state's support or incur its hostility. . . . [I]t is not enough to strike down a nondiscriminatory law that it may hurt or offend some dissident view. . . . It is only in a theocratic state that ecclesiastical doctrines measure legal right or wrong.

[117] As recently as 1956 an eminent student of the field could conclude that "the religious liberty which is protected by the Constitution is essentially freedom of religious thought and expression; it does not include conduct which violates the criminal law, offends public morals, or interferes with the legitimate exercise of the police power for the protection of public safety and health." CUSHMAN, CIVIL LIBERTIES IN THE UNITED STATES: A GUIDE TO CURRENT THOUGHT AND EXPERIENCE (1956).

[118] See K supra.
[119] See O infra.
[120] See note 76 supra.
[121] 310 U.S. 296 (1940).
[122] Id. at 303-04.

embarked upon a search for some principle for saying just how far action was protected. "In every case the power to regulate must be so exercised as not, in attaining a permissible end, unduly to infringe the protected freedom."[123] The Court then reversed Cantwell's conviction for breach of the peace on the ground that his communication "raised no . . . clear and present menace to public peace and order . . . ."[124] No clear test emerged out of such cases, although there were further expressions of a "clear and present danger" formula.[125] But having given up the belief-action distinction and with it the secular regulation rule, and foreswearing an absolute immunity, the Court had to find some way to weigh or balance the interests involved.

In *Prince v. Massachusetts*,[126] the defendant was convicted of violating Massachusetts' child labor laws by permitting her nine-year-old niece to sell religious magazines on a street corner in the evening. The girl and her aunt were both, according to Jehovah's Witness doctrine, ordained ministers. The girl "believed it was her religious duty to perform this work and failure would bring condemnation 'to everlasting destruction at Armageddon.' "[127] The Court finds it must balance "the rights of children to exercise their religion, and of parents to give them religious training and to encourage them in the practice of religious belief . . ." against "the interests of society to protect the welfare of children . . . ."[128] While the state cannot wholly prohibit this form of adult activity, this "does not mean it cannot do so for children."[129] For "the state's authority over children's activities is broader than over like actions of adults."[130] Given the "harmful possibilities" inherent in this kind of activity, the state may prohibit this conduct—that is, the state may for good reason prohibit some of the ways of accomplishing the religious training and indoctrination of children. *Prince* was the last important free exercise case decided by the Supreme Court until 1961.[131]

So far this discussion has dealt with direct prohibitions of the performance of religiously sanctioned acts. However, the decisive change came not in cases of this type, but in cases dealing with burdens on the performance of religious duties which were less

---

[123] *Id.* at 304.
[124] *Id.* at 311.
[125] *Cf.* the concurring opinion of Justices Black and Douglas in West Virginia State Bd. of Educ. v. Barnette, 319 U.S. 624 (1943). A clear and present danger test was employed by the district court in the *Barnette* case, 47 F. Supp. 251, 253-54 (S.D.W. Va. 1942).
[126] 321 U.S. 158 (1944).
[127] *Id.* at 163.
[128] *Id.* at 165.
[129] *Id.* at 168.
[130] *Ibid.*
[131] For a compilation of the intervening religious freedom cases in which the Court dismissed appeals or denied certiorari, see MANWARING, *op. cit. supra* note 110, at 245.

direct than outright prohibition or onerous taxes and licensing requirements. It came in the area of "indirect burdens." It is significant that the first major breakthrough came in the area of Sunday laws. Generally, religious objections to indirect burdens had fared no better than objections to direct prohibitions.[132] But the treatment of Sunday laws was somewhat distinctive. Generally, Sunday regulations were upheld on the ground that there were valid secular purposes underlying them and that they were not religious in nature.[133] However, statutory exceptions for Sabbatarians were common, and the obvious religious flavoring of Sunday laws led several courts to concede that a genuine religious scruple might prevail.[134]

Sunday laws came before the Supreme Court in four cases in 1961. In two of them the objectors did not make any freedom of religion claim, but only asserted that the law was religious in intent and thus a forbidden establishment (see D supra). The Court rejected this argument, finding that the primary, if not the exclusive, purpose and effect of the laws were secular.[135] In the other two cases,[136] the objectors were Orthodox Jewish merchants who argued that the application to them of Sunday closing laws interfered with their free exercise of religion by subjecting the practice of their religion to severe economic burdens, since they had to close on Sunday as well as on Saturday, as required by their religion. The Court accepts that freedom to act in accord with one's religious convictions is not absolute. But then it distinguishes *Reynolds* and *Prince* on the ground that there "the religious practices themselves conflicted with the public interest."[137] However, the Sunday law "does not make unlawful any religious practices of appellants; the Sunday law simply regulates a secular activity . . . ."[138] It makes the practice of their religious beliefs

---

[132] See, *e.g.*, Heisler v. Board of Review, 156 Ohio St. 395, 102 N.E.2d 601, *appeal dismissed*, 343 U.S. 939 (1952); Kut v. Albers Super Markets, 146 Ohio St. 522, 66 N.E.2d 643 (1946); *cf.* cases cited notes 196-99 *infra*.

[133] See, *e.g.*, *Ex parte* Andrews, 18 Cal. 679 (1861). *But cf.* District of Columbia v. Robinson, 30 App. D.C. 283 (Ct. App. 1908), where a law was construed as actually enforcing Sunday observance and was struck down.

[134] Specht v. Commonwealth, 8 Pa. 312 (1848); City Council v. Benjamin, 2 Strob. 508 (S.C. Ct. App. 1848). Compare the Bible-reading cases, where the religious flavor was even more unalloyed and where many of the statutes contained exemptions for conscientious objectors. See BOLES, THE BIBLE, RELIGION AND THE PUBLIC SCHOOLS (1961); MANWARING, *op. cit. supra* note 110, at 43-44.

[135] Two Guys From Harrison-Allentown, Inc. v. McGinley, 366 U.S. 582 (1961); McGowan v. Maryland, 366 U.S. 420 (1961).

[136] Gallagher v. Crown Kosher Super Market, 366 U.S. 617 (1961); Braunfeld v. Brown, 366 U.S. 599 (1961). The religious freedom claims in *Gallagher* are similar to those in *Braunfeld*, and the Court's brief discussion in the former incorporates the detailed consideration in the latter. Gallagher v. Crown Kosher Super Market, *supra* at 631.

[137] Braunfeld v. Brown, 366 U.S. 599, 605 (1961).

[138] *Ibid.*

more expensive. Thus it presents them with an option between financial sacrifice and omission of religious observance which the Court finds "wholly different" from that presented in cases where legislation makes the religious activity itself unlawful.[139]

The Court finds that such indirect financial burdens on religious observance are not unique and would be difficult for legislators to avoid in view of American religious diversity. Economic disadvantage to adherents of some religions is not "an absolute test for determining whether the legislation violates the freedom of religion protected by the First Amendment."[140] But this does not mean that any indirect burden can be justified. Burdens, even if indirect, may be invalid infringements of freedom of religion.

If the purpose or effect of a law is to impede the observance of one or all religions or is to discriminate invidiously between religions, that law is constitutionally invalid even though the burden may be characterized as being only indirect. But if the State regulates conduct by enacting a general law within its power, the purpose and effect of which is to advance the State's secular goals, the statute is valid despite its indirect burden on religious observances *unless the State may accomplish its purpose by means which do not impose such a burden.*[141]

With the italicized words the Court does not merely modify the secular regulation test, but substantially abandons it.[142] The "no alternative means" requirement means that in every such case it is not sufficient merely to determine the secular character of the regulation, but that it is also necessary to ascertain the feasibility of alternative means of regulation.[143]

The Court then undertakes to evaluate the availability of such alternative means. It dismisses the notion that a one-day-in-seven statute would serve the state's ends. Then it takes up the question of an exemption for those who observe another Sabbath and finds that "to permit the exemption might well undermine the State's goal of providing a day that, as best possible, eliminates the atmosphere of commercial noise and activity."[144] Again, enforcement problems would be multiplied; an exception might provide

---

[139] *Id.* at 606.
[140] *Id.* at 606-07.
[141] *Id.* at 607. (Emphasis added.)
[142] By requiring attention to "effects" as well as purposes of the law, this standard implies that the Court will evaluate the impact of the regulation upon the religious practice—something that it did not have to do under a straight secular regulation rule where it was sufficient for the Court to determine that the purpose or object of the law was properly secular.
[143] As the Court points out, *id.* at 607 n.4, such a requirement was foreshadowed in some of the license tax cases where the Court suggested that the government could satisfy its revenue needs without imposing onerous restrictions on religious colporteurs.
[144] *Id.* at 608.

Sabbatarians with economic advantages over their Sunday-observing competitors; the exception might thus offer inducements to bad faith claims and necessitate inquiries into religious sincerity; exempted establishments would be induced to use religious standards in hiring. In view of all of these speculative difficulties, the Court could not conclude that there were in fact such alternative means available and upheld the Pennsylvania statute.

Mr. Justice Brennan's dissent, in which Mr. Justice Stewart joined, attempts to approach the case "from the point of view of the individuals whose liberty is—concededly—curtailed by these enactments."[145] He finds that the first amendment prohibits putting "an individual to a choice between his business and his religion."[146] The economic burden on religion, "this clog upon the exercise of religion, this state-imposed burden on Orthodox Judaism, has exactly the same economic effect as a tax levied upon the sale of religious literature."[147] Such a burden can be justified only by "a compelling state interest" in the object of the regulation to outweigh the freedom of religion "in the constitutional scale."[148] Unlike *Reynolds*, it is not an interest in stamping out "a practice deeply abhorred by society . . . ."[149] And unlike *Prince*, which involved "the State's traditional protection of children," the Jewish merchants "are reasoning and fully autonomous adults."[150] It is not an interest in having everyone rest one day a week, but only "the mere convenience of having everyone rest on the same day."[151] For there is "the alternative route of granting an exemption for those who in good faith observe a day of rest other than Sunday."[152] Dismissing the Court's objections to this alternative as "more fanciful than real"[153] and considering the fact that such exemptions have proved workable in a number of states, he finds that there was in fact a suitable alternative means and that the state was constitutionally obligated to use it.[154]

Just over two years after it had decided the *Sunday Closing Law Cases*, the Supreme Court spent what was perhaps its most eventful day on religion cases. In *Abington School Dist. v. Schempp*,[155] the Court held that school programs prescribing Bible

---

[145] *Id.* at 610.
[146] *Id.* at 611.
[147] *Id.* at 613.
[148] *Id.* at 613-14.
[149] *Id.* at 614.
[150] *Ibid.*
[151] *Ibid.*
[152] *Ibid.*
[153] *Id.* at 615.
[154] *Id.* at 614-16.
[155] 374 U.S. 203 (1963). The Court disposed of the case on establishment grounds and found it unnecessary to consider whether these programs were a violation of the free exercise clause. However, the opinions,

reading and recitation of the Lord's Prayer violated the establishment clause. In a less celebrated judgment on the same day, *Sherbert v. Verner*,[156] we find the dawn of a new day for religious freedom claims. A Seventh Day Adventist textile worker was discharged by her employer for unwillingness to work on Saturday and was unable to obtain other employment since she would not take Saturday work.[157] Her claim for unemployment compensation was denied on the ground that she was not "available for work" as required by statute, since she failed to accept suitable work. Mr. Justice Brennan, writing for the Court, finds that this denial of benefits was a burden on the free exercise of her religion. The pressure on her to omit her religious observance "puts the same kind of burden upon the free exercise of religion as would a fine imposed against appellant for her Saturday worship."[158] The state cannot condition public benefits, whatever their purpose, so that they operate "to inhibit or deter the exercise of First Amendment freedoms."[159]

Thus the secular purpose of the law does not settle the question. Quoting from the majority opinion in *Braunfeld v. Brown*, Mr. Justice Brennan finds that " '[i]f the purpose or effect of a law is to impede the observance of one or all religions or is to discriminate invidiously between religions, that law is constitutionally invalid even though the burden may be characterized as being only indirect.' "[160] There is discrimination here, for South Carolina protects

---

particularly that of Mr. Justice Brennan, considered in great detail the relation of the free exercise and establishment provisions of the first amendment. In Mr. Justice Clark's opinion for the majority, the "purpose and effect" language of the Chief Justice in *Braunfeld* was elaborated into a test for forbidden establishments. "The test [is] . . . what are the purpose and the primary effect of the enactment? . . . [T]o withstand the strictures of the Establishment Clause there must be a secular legislative purpose and a primary effect that neither advances nor inhibits religion." *Id.* at 222.

[156] 374 U.S. 398 (1963).
[157] The same question had come before several state courts. Two Ohio cases deny compensation on the ground that the unwillingness to work was for merely personal reasons. Heisler v. Board of Review, 156 Ohio St. 395, 102 N.E.2d 601, *appeal dismissed*, 343 U.S. 939 (1952); Kut v. Albers Super Markets, 146 Ohio St. 522, 66 N.E.2d 643 (1946). But the Ohio court read a subsequent amendment making "risk to the claimant's health, safety and *morals*" relevant to suitability of work to mean that violation of her religious scruples was a risk to her morals within the meaning of the statute. Tary v. Board of Review, 161 Ohio St. 251, 254, 119 N.E.2d 56, 58 (1954). Similarly, two other state courts reached the same result by statutory construction. Swenson v. Employment Security Comm'n, 340 Mich. 430, 65 N.W.2d 709 (1954) (Sabbatarian is "available for work" within meaning of statute); *In re* Miller, 243 N.C. 509, 91 S.E.2d 241 (1956) ("work that requires one to violate his moral standards is not ordinarily suitable work within the meaning of the statute").
[158] Sherbert v. Verner, 374 U.S. 398, 404 (1963).
[159] *Id.* at 405.
[160] *Id.* at 404.

Sunday observers from such burdens.[161] But for Mr. Justice Brennan this religious discrimination merely compounds the unconstitutionality of the scheme.[162] The Court deliberately avoids deciding on the narrower discrimination ground and proceeds to consider the circumstances under which a measure which indirectly impedes free exercise may be valid.

A burden on free exercise may be "justified by a 'compelling state interest in the regulation of a subject within the State's constitutional power to regulate . . . .' "[163] Such a showing must be more than a "showing merely of a rational relationship to some colorable state interest . . . ."[164] " 'Only the gravest abuses, endangering paramount interests, give occasion for permissible limitation.' "[165] The state can cite none here except the possibilities of spurious claims. Thus the state interest asserted is "wholly dissimilar to the interests which were found to justify the less direct burden upon religious practices in *Braunfeld v. Brown* . . . ."[166] The *Braunfeld* statute was "saved by . . . a strong state interest in providing one uniform day of rest for all workers."[167]

Not only must the state show that such a "compelling" interest is present, but having done so "it would plainly be incumbent upon the [state] . . . to demonstrate that no alternative forms of regulation would combat such abuses without infringing First Amendment rights."[168] In *Braunfeld* the administration of exemptions appeared to present problems of such magnitude that such an exemption "would have rendered the entire statutory scheme unworkable."[169] But in the present case there is presumably no such justification for not having an exemption. The exemption is, by implication, an acceptable and available "alternative," and the state is constitutionally compelled to utilize it.

The majority opinion indicates that the state is clearly obligated to excuse a refusal to work for religious reasons, even if it makes no similar indulgence for refusals stemming from nonreligious reasons.[170] Concurring, Mr. Justice Stewart approves, for he finds

---

[161] South Carolina provides that when textile plants operate on Sunday " 'no employee shall be required to work on Sunday . . . who is conscientiously opposed to Sunday work . . . .' " Nor may he be subject to any loss of seniority or other penalty because of this refusal. *Id.* at 406.
[162] *Ibid.*
[163] *Id.* at 403, quoting from NAACP v. Button, 371 U.S. 415, 438 (1963).
[164] 374 U.S. at 406.
[165] *Id.*, quoting from Thomas v. Collins, 323 U.S. 516, 530 (1945).
[166] 374 U.S. at 408.
[167] *Ibid.*
[168] *Id.* at 407.
[169] *Id.* at 409.
[170] In Judson Mills v. South Carolina Unemployment Compensation Comm'n, 204 S.C. 37, 28 S.E.2d 535 (1943), the South Carolina Supreme Court denied compensation to a woman who was "unavailable for work" because, unable to get a babysitter, she refused to work on Saturday.

that "the guarantee of religious liberty embodied in the Free Exercise Clause affirmatively requires government to create an atmosphere of hospitality and accommodation to individual belief or disbelief. . . . [O]ur Constitution commands the positive protection by government of religious freedom . . . for each of us."[171] He asserts that the holding is in conflict with the Court's "insensitive and sterile construction of the Establishment Clause,"[172] and that it is inconsistent with *Braunfeld*, since the burden here is "considerably less onerous," the statute is not a criminal one, and the economic loss is temporary rather than permanent.[173]

It is precisely the preferential treatment of religious over other reasons for unavailability for work that disturbs Mr. Justice Harlan, joined in dissent by Mr. Justice White. Asserting the traditional secular regulation rule, he finds "the fact that these personal considerations [which made her unwilling to work on Saturdays] sprang from her religious convictions . . . wholly without relevance to the state court's application of the law. . . . She was denied benefits just as any other claimant would be denied benefits who was not 'available for work' for personal reasons."[174] While he would allow "that at least under the circumstances of this case it would be a permissible accommodation of religion for the State, if it *chose* to do so, to create an exception to its eligibility requirements [for religious objectors] . . . ,"[175] he cannot subscribe to the conclusion "that the State is constitutionally *compelled* to carve out an exception to its general rule of eligibility in the present case."[176] While an exception might be compelled in extreme cases, it is inappropriate here "in light of the indirect, remote, and insubstantial effect of the decision below on the exercise of appellant's religion . . . ."[177] Indeed he discerns establishment limitations which point to the same answer because the decision of

---

[171] 374 U.S. at 415-16.
[172] *Id.* at 414.
[173] *Id.* at 417. Mr. Justice Harlan (joined by Mr. Justice White), dissenting, agrees that *Braunfeld* is overruled. *Id.* at 421. In a separate opinion, Mr. Justice Douglas concurs on the ground that the first amendment forbids "interference with the individual's scruples or conscience . . . . [G]overnment cannot exact from me a surrender of one iota of my religious scruples . . . ." *Id.* at 412. Unfortunately the opinion fails to mention how religious "scruples" are to be distinguished from any act sanctioned by religion. We are given a few examples of scruples from near and far: prayer, holidays, carrying weapons (Sikh *kirpans*), distributing pamphlets, abstention from swearing, and avoiding meat. It is not clear whether we are to conclude that every act expressing such a scruple is protected by the first amendment. On sensitivity to religious scruples, see the majority opinion in Cleveland v. United States, 329 U.S. 14 (1946), discussed in note 98 *supra*.
[174] Sherbert v. Verner, 374 U.S. 398, 420 (1963).
[175] *Id.* at 422.
[176] *Id.* at 423.
[177] *Ibid.*

the majority requires "direct financial assistance to religion . . . ."[178]

We now come full circle from indirect burdens back to direct prohibition of a religious practice. In the first and so far the most notable application of *Sherbert* by a state court, the Supreme Court of California utilized the *Sherbert* test to overturn the conviction of Navaho members of the Native American Church for unauthorized possession of narcotics. In *People v. Woody*,[179] defendants were apprehended while performing a religious ceremony which involved the use of peyote. The court finds that "the statutory prohibition most seriously infringes upon the observance of the religion."[180] The religious interest is a weighty one, for peyote "is the *sine qua non* of defendants' faith. . . . [It is] the sole means by which defendants are able to experience their religion . . . ."[181]

The burden then rests upon the state to indicate a compelling reason for prohibition. The court finds that the record does not support "the state's chronicle of harmful consequences of the use of peyote"[182] which included an assertion that the Indians used peyote in place of medical care, the threat of indoctrination of small children, and possible encouragement of a propensity to use other drugs. The court emphatically rejects the argument that the state may ban peyote because it "'obstructs enlightenment and shackles the Indian to primitive conditions'. . . ."[183] The state has no general mandate to promote such uninvited enlightenment. The court finds *Reynolds* distinguishable, for there is no compelling interest in prohibiting peyote: "the degree of danger to state interests in *Reynolds* far exceeded that in the instant case. The court in *Reynolds* considered polygamy as a serious threat to democratic institutions and injurious to the morals and well-being of its practitioners."[184]

Thus the state has no compelling interest in prohibiting this use of peyote sufficient to outweigh the Indians' interest in using it. But the state argues that it has no alternative means. It objects to making a religious exception because fraudulent assertions of religious immunity might make impossible the effective enforcement of its narcotics laws. This, too, is rejected because "the state produced no evidence that spurious claims of religious immunity would in fact preclude effective administration of the

---

[178] *Ibid.* It is difficult to see how a "compelled" exception could be a forbidden establishment where one which was imposed by legislative policy would not be.
[179] 61 Cal. 2d 716, 40 Cal. Rep. 69, 394 P.2d 813 (1964).
[180] *Id.* at 720, 40 Cal. Rep. at 72, 394 P.2d at 816.
[181] *Id.* at 725, 40 Cal. Rep. at 76, 394 P.2d at 820.
[182] *Id.* at 722, 40 Cal. Rep. at 74, 394 P.2d at 818.
[183] *Id.* at 723, 40 Cal. Rep. at 74, 394 P.2d at 818.
[184] *Id.* at 725, 40 Cal. Rep. at 76, 394 P.2d at 820.

law or that other 'forms of regulation' would not accomplish the state's objectives."[185] Thus such cases as *Braunfeld* and *Prince* are distinguishable as instances in which the administrative problem of exceptions is of such magnitude as to render the whole statute unworkable.[186] Having "weighed the competing values," the court concludes that "the weight of freedom of religion" in using peyote is "heavy," while the weight of the state's "'compelling interest'" is "relatively light."[187]

On the same day the California court heard a habeas corpus petition from one not an Indian, a "self-styled 'peyote preacher' and 'way-shower,' [who] acted as spiritual leader of a group of [six] individuals . . . ."[188] The group lived together and Grady "selected their food, taught them deepbreathing exercises, how to pray, 'and in general how to love the Christian life.'"[189] He provided and prepared peyote for the group and claimed that it was used for religious purposes. According to Grady, peyote "'is a very spiritual plant because it gives you direct contact with God, or in other words, proceeds on all four planes of consciousness simultaneously, and when used for prayer the best thing that can happen to you.'"[190] Reading *Woody* as forbidding the state from prohibiting the use of peyote "in connection with bona fide practice of a religious belief," the court granted habeas corpus.[191] But finding that unlike Woody, Grady had not proved that his asserted belief was "an honest and bona fide one," the court sent the case back for a factual determination of "whether defendant actually engaged in good faith in the practice of a religion."[192]

Before I leave claims of this type, another line of cases should be mentioned which involves restrictions on the religious practices of prison inmates. In a number of recent cases, Black Muslim prisoners have brought suits against prison officials to remove restrictions on religious practices ranging from receipt of newspapers, visitation by religious advisors, and obtaining copies of a chosen version of the Koran, to holding unsupervised meetings and having the time of prison meals determined by Muslim procedure in order to facilitate their Ramadan fasting. In most of these cases, there was a charge of religious discrimination since, while comparable facilities or privileges were available to inmates of other persuasions, prison authorities imposed special restrictions on Muslims. All the courts concede that religious freedom covers acts as well as beliefs, and that any greater restrictions on one

---

[185] *Id.* at 723, 40 Cal. Rep. at 75, 394 P.2d at 819.
[186] *Id.* at 725, 40 Cal. Rep. at 76, 394 P.2d at 820.
[187] *Id.* at 727, 40 Cal. Rep. at 77, 394 P.2d at 821.
[188] *In re* Grady, 61 Cal. 2d 887, 888, 39 Cal. Rep. 912, 913, 394 P.2d 728, 729 (1964).
[189] *Ibid.*
[190] *Ibid.*
[191] *Ibid.*
[192] *Ibid.*

religious group must be justified by special circumstances. On the whole, the courts have applied a clear and present danger standard (or something akin to it) to determine when such discriminations are permissible.[193] In none of these cases has any court upheld a claim for any treatment different from that accorded other prisoners.[194] There is some difference over the kind of evidence necessary to support a finding of the requisite danger and over the weight to be given to administrative convenience.[195] This standard has developed independently of *Sherbert*. As in *Sherbert*, however, the courts are involved in balancing or weighing interests—discipline and the welfare of some prisoners against other prisoners' free exercise claims.

Finally, mention should be made of other kinds of indirect burdens. The religious character of its work does not exempt a religious association from liability under a workmen's compensation law,[196] or from conformity to the Fair Labor Standards Act.[197] It is difficult to specify the standards which prevail in the area of building and zoning regulations. Courts usually limit their consideration to the particular regulation in issue; and general principles play a restricted role in these cases. However, there are a few cases in which religious freedom claims have succeeded in

---

[193] Banks v. Havener, 234 F. Supp. 27 (E.D. Va. 1964) (prison officials must allow Muslims to practice their religion on a nondiscriminatory basis so long as there is no clear and present danger to the orderly functioning of the institution); Brown v. McGinnis, 10 N.Y.2d 531, 180 N.E.2d 791, 225 N.Y.S.2d 497 (1962) (requisite "dangers" cannot be shown by journalistic speculation). See *In re* Ferguson, 55 Cal. 2d 663, 673, 12 Cal. Rep. 753, 757, 361 P.2d 417, 421 (1961) (ban reasonable where activities "present a serious threat to the maintenance of order" and serious risk of harm to prison officials).

[194] Claims for special dietary consideration were put forth in several cases, but the issue has never been decided. *E.g.*, Banks v. Havener, *supra* note 193. Apparently some prison authorities have provided special pork-free meals for Muslim prisoners. In Childs v. Pegelow, 321 F.2d 487 (4th Cir. 1963), the court held that prison officials who agreed to provide Muslim prisoners with a pork-free meal before sunrise and after sunset during the fast month of Ramadan need not calculate the time of sunset according to Muslim procedures. "There is no charge here of discrimination against plaintiffs by way of interference with the practice of their religious beliefs . . . . The plaintiffs are, in fact, seeking special privileges because of their religious beliefs, privileges not extended to the other inmates." *Id.* at 490.

[195] *Compare* the rejection of "mere speculation" in Brown v. McGinnis, 10 N.Y.2d 531, 180 N.E.2d 791, 225 N.Y.S.2d 497 (1962), *with* Cooper v. Pate, 324 F.2d 165 (7th Cir. 1963), *rev'd per curiam*, 378 U.S. 546 (1964). For a case which gives greater weight to administrative convenience than those in note 193 *supra*, see Williford v. People, 217 F. Supp. 245 (N.D. Cal. 1963), where the court upheld a blanket restriction because piecemeal treatment might lead to lessening of efficiency.

[196] See, *e.g.*, Meyers v. Southwest Region Conference Ass'n of Seventh Day Adventists, 230 La. 310, 88 So. 2d 381 (1956).

[197] Mitchell v. Pilgrim Holiness Church Corp., 210 F.2d 879 (7th Cir.), *cert. denied*, 347 U.S. 1013 (1954).

securing exemption from such regulations. In more cases, the religious group has prevailed on some other ground. But a religious freedom claim is in itself usually insufficient to obtain exemption from building codes, fire and safety regulations, and offstreet parking requirements.[198] On the other hand, the application of zoning requirements which entirely exclude churches and their subsidiary institutions from residential neighborhoods has often been found to be a violation of religious freedom.[199]

N. Freedom From Governmental Requirements of Actions Accorded Negative Religious Significance

This freedom is closely related to the one discussed immediately above. Courts dealing with problems of either of these types freely employ precedents involving the other. Here, too, a successful claim does not necessarily confer a right to eliminate the offensive requirement for everyone; generally it only carves out an exception. We are again dealing with activities in which the governmental regulation is admittedly nonreligious in purpose. But here the individual defines that requirement as having a negative religious significance for him. There are many more instances of this type than of the positive religious type. They may conveniently be grouped into four general areas of regulation: (1) required civic duties, *e.g.*, compulsory military service, jury duty, and compulsory ROTC at state universities; (2) compulsory education and its incidents, *e.g.*, objections to secular education generally or education past a certain age, attending classes on religious holidays, the use of motion pictures in classes, and the teaching of social dancing; (3) health measures, *e.g.*, vaccination, physical examination, X-ray examination, blood tests before marriage, blood transfusions, and fluoridation; and (4) economic and general measures, *e.g.*, crop limitations, compulsory union membership, social security payments, and photograph requirements for driver's licenses.

In the claims of positive religious significance,[200] we could distinguish between direct prohibitions of the religiously valued act

---

[198] See, *e.g.*, Portage Township v. Full Salvation Union, 318 Mich. 693, 29 N.W.2d 297 (1947), *appeal dismissed*, 333 U.S. 851 (1948); Allendale Congregation of Jehovah's Witnesses v. Grosman, 30 N.J. 273, 152 A.2d 569 (1959). *But cf.* Board of Zoning Appeals v. Jehovah's Witnesses, 233 Ind. 83, 117 N.E.2d 115 (1954) ("balancing of interests" between police power and religious freedom; unwillingness to vary offstreet parking requirements is unreasonable restriction on freedom of worship). See generally Curry, Public Regulation of the Religious Use of Land (1964).

[199] See, *e.g.*, Ellsworth v. Gercke, 62 Ariz. 198, 156 P.2d 242 (1945); State *ex rel.* Wenatchee Congregation v. City of Wenatchee, 50 Wash. 2d 378, 312 P.2d 195 (1957). *But cf.* Corporation of the Presiding Bishop of the Church of Jesus Christ of Latter-Day Saints v. City of Porterville, 90 Cal. App. 2d 656, 203 P.2d 823 (4th Dist. 1949).

[200] See M *supra*.

and those regulations which merely made it more expensive. It is more difficult to put claims of the present type on such a directness-indirectness scale. But we may distinguish among the following types of claims, which generally move from flat requirements of the distasteful act to merely making it onerous or expensive to avoid it. I shall briefly survey the pre-1963 law under several headings and then review some recent developments.

The first situation is that in which the offensive act is an unconditional requirement, and here freedom of religion has seldom been sustained as a sufficient defense for failing to perform the requirement. In respect to draft registration,[201] for example, the exemption of conscientious objectors from combatant service and of clergymen from all military service is said to be a privilege extended by Congress and not a constitutional right to exemption.[202] On the other hand, objection to jury duty has been upheld on constitutional grounds.[203] But a person may be compelled to be vaccinated in spite of religious objections.[204] A statutory duty to provide medical care for children has uniformly been enforced against religious objections,[205] and government may intervene to require religiously offensive medical care for a child.[206] Nor can an objection that secular studies or prolonged education is religiously offensive avoid the statutory duty to provide education in such subjects,[207] up to the school-leaving age.[280]

Similar results obtain where the offensive act is a mandatory condition for the use of a governmental facility and the government requires the use of this facility or some costly private equivalent. It is uniformly held that government may require

---

[201] See, e.g., United States v. Henderson, 180 F.2d 711 (7th Cir.), cert. denied, 339 U.S. 963 (1950).

[202] See In re Summers, 325 U.S. 561 (1945); United States v. Macintosh, 283 U.S. 605 (1931). Thus, who is a clergyman for purposes of enjoying the exemption depends on the intention of Congress, not on the meaning attached to the term by the members of a religious group. See, e.g., Rase v. United States, 129 F.2d 204 (6th Cir. 1942).

[203] United States v. Hillyard, 52 F. Supp. 612 (E.D. Wash. 1943) (on clear and present danger test). Cf. Commonwealth v. Lesher, 17 S. & R. 155 (Pa. 1828).

[204] Jacobson v. Massachusetts, 197 U.S. 11 (1905). This clearly applies to adults as well as to children. Religious objections are dismissed with all others in a much-quoted dictum.

[205] See, e.g., People v. Pierson, 176 N.Y. 201, 68 N.E. 243 (1903); Owens v. State, 6 Okla. Crim. 110, 116 Pac. 345 (1911).

[206] People ex rel. Wallace v. Labrenz, 411 Ill. 618, 104 N.E.2d 769, cert. denied, 344 U.S. 824 (1952); State v. Perricone, 37 N.J. 463, 181 A.2d 751 (1962). Recent developments in regard to compulsory blood transfusions for adults are treated subsequently in this article.

[207] People ex rel. Shapiro v. Dorin, 199 Misc. 2d 643, 99 N.Y.S.2d 830 (Dom. Rel. Ct.), aff'd, 302 N.Y. 857, 100 N.E.2d 48, cert. denied, 342 U.S. 884 (1951).

[208] Commonwealth v. Beiler, 168 Pa. Super. 462, 79 A.2d 134 (1951).

children in public schools to submit to vaccinations,[209] physical examinations,[210] and to attend on their religious holidays;[211] but a religious objection was permitted to override a requirement that children participate in a class in coeducational social dancing.[212] The only instance in which the Supreme Court has dealt with a requirement of this type was in the flag-salute cases. In the first case, Mr. Justice Frankfurter upheld the secular regulation rule in this area.[213] In the second, *West Virginia State Bd. of Educ. v. Barnette*, Mr. Justice Jackson, for the majority, found that the state had no power to compel ceremonial affirmations regarding beliefs—at least where the refusal did not affect the rights of others.[214] Exceptions for religious—but not only religious—objections are required in such cases. But, the *Barnette* decision does not cover situations in which government clearly has the power to act in pursuit of some interest such as health or educational requirements.

So too, where the offensive act is a mandatory condition for obtaining governmental certification to pursue normal and innocent activities and such certification is a governmental monopoly. A blood test requirement for a marriage license has been upheld against religious objections;[215] and in its only confrontation with this kind of case, the Supreme Court upheld the disqualification for the bar of an applicant who would not take an oath that he would perform military service in time of war.[216] In like fashion, religious objections are apt to be unavailing where the offensive act is a governmentally imposed condition for engaging in normal and innocent activities or enforcing rights incident to such activities. A religious objection to crop allotments is not a good defense in a prosecution for illegal marketing of wheat.[217] A husband's religiously motivated avoidance of proper medical treatment

---

[209] See, *e.g.*, Mosier v. Board of Health, 308 Ky. 829, 215 S.W.2d 967 (1948). All vaccination cases usually refer to Jacobson v. Massachusetts, 197 U.S. 11 (1905), which was not itself a case of religious objection, but in which the Court indicated that religious objections would stand in no better stead.

[210] Streich v. Board of Educ., 34 S.D. 169, 147 N.W. 779 (1944).

[211] See note 72 *supra*.

[212] Hardwick v. Board of School Trustees, 54 Cal. App. 696, 205 Pac. 49 (3d Dist. 1921). Here, the social dancing class was not specifically required by the state education law. The court, while respecting the parents' religious scruples, indicated that it would treat objections based on "morals or conscience" in the same way.

[213] Minersville School Dist. v. Gobitis, 310 U.S. 586 (1940).

[214] 319 U.S. 624 (1943).

[215] Peterson v. Widule, 157 Wis. 641, 147 N.W. 966 (1914).

[216] *In re* Summers, 325 U.S. 561 (1945). Until 1946, unwillingness to take a similar oath required by the Naturalization Act disqualified an alien for citizenship. United States v. Macintosh, 283 U.S. 605 (1931). This was reversed by statutory construction in Girouard v. United States, 328 U.S. 61 (1946).

[217] United States v. Kissinger, 250 F.2d 940 (3d Cir. 1958).

disqualifies a widow from collecting a workman's compensation claim against the employer.[218] Where the offensive act is a condition for engaging in normal and innocent activities and is imposed by private parties, the same results are reached. Thus the courts will not enjoin dismissal of a worker who objects to becoming a member of a union as required by contract between union and employer.[219]

Finally, where the offensive act is a condition for the use of public services and facilities whose use is not mandatory but whose replacement is expensive, courts have reached the same conclusion. Thus a requirement of a physical examination for enrollment in a state-supported university has been upheld against religious objections.[220] A requirement of participation in an ROTC program as a condition of matriculation at a state university has been upheld by the Supreme Court.[221] The fact that the students could not afford to attend a private university was said to be "without significance."[222] Fluoridation provides another instance of this type. It has uniformly been held that a city need not refrain from fluoridating its water supply because the consumption of fluoridated water is religiously offensive to some.[223]

Thus the free exercise clause of the first amendment and the analogous provisions of state constitutions have afforded little protection to religious noncompliance of the type under consideration here. Except for the exemptions allowed in the jury-service and social-dancing cases, courts uniformly denied any constitutional right to exemption from such regulations. The single exception is *Barnette*, which includes religious along with nonreligious objectors, but which is limited to narrow facts. However, there are in this area a number of statutory exemptions designed to accommodate religious scruples,[224] and courts have on

---

[218] Martin v. Industrial Acc. Comm'n, 147 Cal. App. 2d 137, 304 P.2d 828 (2d Dist. 1956).
[219] See note 51 *supra*.
[220] State *ex rel.* Holcomb v. Armstrong, 39 Wash. 2d 860, 239 P.2d 545 (1952) (utilizing clear and present danger test).
[221] Hamilton v. Regents of the Univ. of Cal., 293 U.S. 245 (1934); Hanauer v. Elkins, 217 Md. 213, 141 A.2d 903 (1958) (ROTC requirement upheld where objectors had already served two years in civilian "alternative service").
[222] 293 U.S. at 262.
[223] Baer v. City of Bend, 206 Ore. 221, 292 P.2d 134 (1956) (religious freedom preferred: measure here bears only remotely on religious practice). Religious objections are ignored in Kraus v. City of Cleveland, 121 N.E.2d 311 (Ohio Ct. App. 1954), *aff'd*, 163 Ohio St. 559, 127 N.E.2d 609 (1955), *appeal dismissed*, 351 U.S. 935 (1956); Dowell v. City of Tulsa, 273 P.2d 859 (Okla. 1954), *cert. denied*, 348 U.S. 912 (1955). See also deAryan v. Butler, 119 Cal. App. 2d 674, 260 P.2d 98 (4th Dist. 1953); Chapman v. City of Shreveport, 225 La. 859, 74 So. 2d 142 (1954).
[224] Most notable are the exemptions for religious objectors in the Selective Service Act and the Naturalization Act. Congress has recently added a religious exemption to the Social Security Act. Statutory exemptions for

occasion construed statutes to create or extend these exemptions.[225] Officials administering such regulations, too, have created by tacit agreement or mere nonenforcement a great many exemptions which are not to be found in the law books.[226]

Recent developments may portend some changes in this area. The *Sherbert* rule was soon applied to the situation in which government requires an act to which a subject gives negative religious significance. In *In re Jenison*,[227] the Supreme Court of Minnesota had upheld a thirty-day sentence for contempt for a woman's refusal on religious grounds to serve on a civil jury. The court found no constitutional right to refuse; the burden on her religion was less than that on a religious objector to military conscription who admittedly enjoyed no constitutional right to exemption. Indeed, all Minnesota citizens enjoyed a state constitutional right to jury trials, and her refusal to serve thus affected the interests of others. In a brief memorandum decision, the Supreme Court vacated the judgment and remanded for further consideration in the light of *Sherbert*.[228] Upon remand, the Supreme Court of Minnesota concluded that "there has been an inadequate showing that the state's interest in obtaining competent jurors requires us to override relator's right to the free exercise of her religion."[229] The court held that until further experience might indicate that such an exemption posed "a serious threat to the effective functioning of our jury system, any person whose religious convictions prohibit compulsory jury duty shall . . . be exempt."[230]

Jenison did not involve a prohibition of a religiously significant activity (as in *Woody*); nor did it involve an indirect burden on such an activity (as in *Sherbert*). It involved a direct command from the state to perform a religiously offensive act. In this respect it is closer to *Barnette* than to any other case decided by the Supreme Court. Since the Court's brief memorandum decision did not refer to *Barnette*, it remains unclear whether it covers situations other than compelled statements and ceremonial affirmations.[231] Again, the *Jenison* decision goes beyond *Barnette*,

---

religious objectors to oaths are common. See TORPEY, JUDICIAL DOCTRINES OF RELIGIOUS RIGHTS IN AMERICA (1948). For an example of a statutory exemption from medical test requirements, see Kolbeck v. Kramer, 84 N.J. Super. 569, 202 A.2d 889 (L. 1964).

[225] *Cf.* Girouard v. United States, 328 U.S. 61 (1946).

[226] For example, the plaintiff in Kolbeck v. Kramer, 84 N.J. Super. 569, 202 A.2d 889 (L. 1964), had gone through twelve years of public school without meeting the inoculation requirement. Each time enforcement was attempted, he withdrew from school until the requirement was waived.

[227] 265 Minn. 96, 120 N.W.2d 515 (1963).

[228] 375 U.S. 14 (1963).

[229] *In re* Jenison, 267 Minn. 136, 137, 125 N.W.2d 588, 589 (1963).

[230] *Ibid.*

[231] It might be argued that the verdict which a juror must return is just the sort of compelled statement which is covered by *Barnette*. However,

for it turns on specifically religious objections; the Minnesota court believes that it is now faced with the problem of determining which claims are in fact religious. And, while Mr. Justice Jackson in *Barnette* pointed out that refusal to salute the flag did not affect the rights of others, there is in *Jenison* at least an indirect connection between the duty to serve on a jury and the rights of others to jury trial.

To what extent does the application of *Sherbert* to claims of this negative type portend any change in the existing law? The first vaccination case in which *Sherbert* was cited came to the usual result.[232] The Supreme Court of Arkansas found *Sherbert* was remote in its facts from the area of public health. There was some concession to *Sherbert* language in its formulation of the general rule: "their freedom to act according to their religious beliefs is subject to a reasonable regulation for the benefit of society as a whole. We reaffirm that the health regulation in question is a reasonable exercise of police power on a subject of paramount and compelling state interest and, therefore, is valid."[233] But there was no trace of any burden placed on the state to show that no alternative was feasible. Indeed, the court read earlier vaccination cases as not requiring it to hear the claimant's arguments about the lack of necessity for this requirement.[234] In spite of the apparent balancing, it is clear that there are two factors present here which make the court regard the case as entirely distinguishable from *Sherbert*. First, it deals with children over whom the state may, says the court, exercise a broader authority. Second, the claimants' acts here may affect others: "rights of religious freedom cease when they transgress upon the rights of others."[235]

Sherbert received a somewhat more hospitable reception in *Sheldon v. Fannin*,[236] where the court held that children could not be compelled to stand while the national anthem was being played. The court employed a mixture of the *Barnette* and *Sherbert* approaches, rephrasing *Barnette* in terms akin to the *Sherbert* balancing test. Religious freedom is subject to reasonable restrictions, but "where . . . a particular application of a general law

---

the analogy fails to convince, for there is clearly more to a juror's duties than making a statement about one's beliefs. Nor is the statement entirely of a ceremonial or ritual nature.

[232] Wright v. DeWitt School Dist. No. 1, 385 S.W.2d 644 (Ark. 1965).
[233] *Id.* at 648.
[234] *Id.* at 647. Plaintiffs argued that the fact that unvaccinated children had been attending school for many years and that there had been no smallpox in the county for at least fifty years indicated the absence of any clear and present danger to public health.
[235] *Id.* at 648. The court cites the first *Jenison* case as illustrating the proposition that freedom must give way to the "rights of society as a whole."
[236] 221 F. Supp. 766 (D. Ariz. 1963).

not protective of some fundamental State concern materially abridges free expression or practice of religious belief, then the law must give way to the exercise of religion."[237] The court finds the facts close to *Barnette*; indeed the interest in national unity present in *Barnette* was a weighty one, while here the sole justification for the dismissal stems from the disciplinary problems which would ensue upon permitting the children to remain seated.

In other recent developments, several courts for the first time addressed the question of compelling adults to submit to religiously offensive blood transfusions. In the first case, the Supreme Court of New Jersey ordered a woman, thirty-two weeks pregnant, to undergo a transfusion which hospital authorities asserted was necessary to save her unborn but quick child.[238] The court found that the unborn child was entitled to its protection. Since the "welfare of the child and the mother are so intertwined and inseparable," the transfusions might be administered "if necessary to save her life or the life of her child . . . ."[239] The court found it unnecessary to decide whether such intervention might be undertaken to save the life of an adult whose religious beliefs forbade blood transfusions.

In the second case a single judge of the Court of Appeals of the District of Columbia signed an emergency "order" allowing a hospital to administer a transfusion to a twenty-five-year-old married woman, mother of a seven-month-old child, who had lost a considerable amount of blood from a ruptured ulcer. The judge later wrote an opinion on the matter,[240] suggesting a number of justifications for the issuance of the order, including the state's paternal authority over someone who was "as little able competently to decide for herself as any child would be."[241] Furthermore, "the patient had a responsibility to the community to care for her infant. Thus the people had an interest in preserving the life of this mother."[242] Again, since her religion did not command her to die but only to withhold consent from a transfusion, a court-ordered transfusion allowed her to live without violating her religious tenets. Finally, there was the suggestion that a patient who has voluntarily entered a hospital and placed the responsibility for her treatment upon its staff may not retain a right to veto its judgment in emergencies. A full bench of the court denied a petition for a rehearing, leaving open the question

---

[237] *Id.* at 774.
[238] Raleigh Fitkin-Paul Morgan Memorial Hosp. v. Anderson, 42 N.J. 421, 201 A.2d 537, *cert. denied*, 377 U.S. 985 (1964).
[239] *Id.* at 423, 201 A.2d at 538.
[240] Application of the President & Directors of Georgetown College, Inc., 331 F.2d 1000, *rehearing en banc denied*, 331 F.2d 1010 (D.C. Cir.), *cert. denied*, 377 U.S. 978 (1964).
[241] 331 F.2d at 1008.
[242] *Ibid.*

whether the proceeding had ever been properly before the court and whether the order had any legal validity.[243]

In neither of these cases did the courts consider any religious freedom cases other than the child transfusion cases, which they extended to cover these adults. But in *In re Brooks' Estate*,[244] the Supreme Court of Illinois for the first time decided a case in favor of the religious objector to a transfusion. An older woman without minor children was dying. During the several years in which she had been under the doctor's care, she steadfastly refused to accept transfusions. When she was so weakened that she was incompetent, the hospital obtained an order appointing a conservator authorized to consent to the transfusion in order to prolong her life. The court, hearing the case after her death, ordered the appointment expunged.

Religious freedom was "absolute" and "subject only to the qualification that the exercise . . . may properly be limited by governmental action where such exercise endangers, clearly and presently, the public health, welfare, or morals."[245] The court found that all of the cases in which religious objections were overriden prevented "practices . . . immediately deleterious to some phase of public welfare, health or morality."[246] Unlike earlier transfusion cases which dealt with the welfare of children, the principal here was a competent adult with no minor children. The court found in her refusal no clear and present danger and found the order an interference with her basic constitutional rights.

It is difficult to discern to what extent a compelling interest test along the lines of *Sherbert*, *Jenison*, and *Woody*—or a clear and present danger test of the sort that seems to flourish in spite of the lack of recent encouragement from the Supreme Court—will change any of the law regarding claims of this type.[247] The question, of course, is what factual dimensions will emerge as important in the application of such a test. Some of these dimensions I shall discuss in a later part of this article; but for the moment it may be concluded that the test applies in cases in-

---

[243] Of the nine judges sitting, three dissented on the ground that there was no rehearing to be denied, since the judge who issued the order had had no competence to issue it. Of the majority, one judge concurred on the ground that the issue was moot, another on the ground that no case or controversy was presented.

[244] 32 Ill. 2d 361, 205 N.E.2d 435 (1965).

[245] *Id.* at 369, 205 N.E.2d at 441.

[246] *Id.* at 370, 205 N.E.2d at 442.

[247] So far, it cannot be said that there has been any great change. The jury exemption had been permitted earlier; Sheldon v. Fannin, 221 F. Supp. 766 (D. Ariz. 1963), is clearly covered by *Barnette*; the adult transfusion case is clearly distinguishable from earlier cases on its facts, and the result there relied on a clear and present danger test rather than using "compelling interest" language. For some other instances in which the clear and present danger test was employed, see notes 193, 203 & 220 *supra*.

volving (1) direct prohibitions of religiously valued acts, (2) indirect burdens on religiously valued acts, and (3) requirements which violate religious precepts. It may apply to other areas of the first amendment beyond religious claims.[248] To some undetermined extent, it does not matter whether the objections to such prohibitions, burdens, or requirements are religious or not: *Barnette* protects all opinion, religious or otherwise, from compelled ceremonial affirmations.[249] But beyond this, the constitutionality of such prohibitions, burdens, or requirements—and the applicability of statutory exemptions for religious objectors—may depend on whether the objection is a religious one. This, in turn, brings us to the last type of religious freedom claim: the right to define what is religious.

O. Freedom To Define the Religious

This rough schematic sketch of the religious freedoms indicates that activity deemed religious sometimes occupies a distinctive place in the eyes of the law. But who is to determine what is or is not religious? How is it to be determined? What is the role of the claimant's own characterization? This claim, obviously, is not asserted in isolation, but always in the context of some other religious claim. It is the key to invoking all of the freedoms that have been mentioned above.

What is the "religion" whose "free exercise" may not be prohibited? The Mormon cases again provide a convenient starting point. In *Reynolds v. United States*, the Supreme Court finds "the true distinction between what properly belongs to the church and what to the State" in a statement of Madison's in which he distinguishes between "the field of opinion" on the one hand and "overt acts" on the other.[250] By the first amendment, then, "Congress was deprived of all legislative power over mere opinion, but was left free to reach actions which were in violation of social

---

[248] Several courts have been very receptive to *Sherbert* in cases not involving religion. The Supreme Court of California, upsetting the dismissal of a county officer for political activity under a state analogue of the Hatch Act, found his first amendment rights could be curtailed only if the state could show a "compelling interest" in limiting these, that a "rational relationship to some colorable state interest" was insufficient, and that the state must show that no alternative forms of regulation were available to it. Fort v. Civil Serv. Comm'n, 61 Cal. 2d 331, 38 Cal. Rep. 625, 392 P.2d 385 (1964). Again the compelling interest and no alternative means formula was used to invalidate regulations on receipts of propaganda mail. Heilberg v. Fixa, 236 F. Supp. 405 (N.D. Cal. 1964), *aff'd sub nom.* Lamont v. Postmaster Gen., 381 U.S. 301 (1965). Neither Mr. Justice Douglas's opinion for the Court nor Mr. Justice Brennan's concurring opinion referred to *Sherbert*.

[249] Another case allowing exemptions on a ground of conscientious scruples broader than the merely religious is Hardwick v. Board of School Trustees, 54 Cal. App. 696, 205 Pac. 49 (3d Dist. 1921).

[250] 98 U.S. 145, 163 (1878).

duties or subversive of good order."[251] The Court does not deny that polygamy is indeed a religious practice for the defendant, for it says the question before it is "whether those who make polygamy a part of their religion are excepted from the operation of the statute."[252] They are not, of course, for while the laws "cannot interfere with mere religious belief and opinions, they may with practices."[253]

Having identified the protected part of religion with opinion, the *Reynolds* Court had no need to define which actions were religious, for actions were to be measured by nonreligious qualities. However in *Davis v. Beason*,[254] eleven years later, the Supreme Court did undertake to define religion. Voters in the Territory of Idaho were required to swear that:

> I am not a bigamist or polygamist; that I am not a member of any order, organization or association which teaches, advises, counsels or encourages its members, devotees or any other person to commit the crime of bigamy or polygamy, or any other crime defined by law, as a duty arising or resulting from membership in such order, organization or association, or which practises bigamy, polygamy or plural or celestial marriage as a doctrinal rite of such organization; that I do not and will not, publicly or privately, or in any manner whatever teach, advise, counsel or encourage any person to commit the crime of bigamy or polygamy . . . .[255]

In upholding the validity of the test oath, the Court had to do more than limit religious freedom to opinion, for here the actions proscribed included expression of opinion. The Court was not willing to countenance the suggestion that Mormon opinion respecting polygamy was actually a religious belief. Where the *Reynolds* Court seemed to accept as religious what the Mormons put forward as such, the *Davis* Court is interested in an objective test of religion independently of the views of the Mormons. "The term 'religion' has reference to one's views of his relations to his Creator, and to the obligations they impose of reverence for his being and character, and of obedience to his will."[256] Combining this with the belief-action distinction, the Court views the scope of religious liberty as permitting each "to entertain such notions respecting his relations to his Maker and the duties they impose as may be approved by his judgment and conscience, and to exhibit his sentiments in such form of worship as he may think proper, not injurious to the equal rights of others . . . ."[257]

But the Court is not willing to admit that the Mormon belief in

---

[251] *Id.* at 164.
[252] *Id.* at 166.
[253] *Ibid.*
[254] 133 U.S. 333 (1890).
[255] *Id.* at 334.
[256] *Id.* at 342.
[257] *Ibid.*

polygamy is included. "To call . . . advocacy [of polygamy] a tenet of religion is to offend the common sense of mankind."[258] Polygamy is recognized as a crime "by the general consent of the Christian world in modern times"[259] and "crime is not the less odious because sanctioned by what any particular sect may designate as religion."[260]

In the same year the Court upheld an act of Congress to annul the charter of the Mormon Church and forfeit most of its real estate.[261] Here the Court finds that the Mormon Church was not really a religious or charitable corporation, for one of its principal tenets, polygamy, is merely supposed or imagined to be religious. The "pretence [that it is] . . . a religious belief" is undone by "the enlightened sentiment of mankind."[262] This enlightened sentiment is clearly that of the western Christian world. Polygamy is "a blot on our civilization," and "contrary to the spirit of Christianity and of the civilization which Christianity has produced in the Western world."[263] The Thugs of India "imagined that their belief in the right of assassination was a religious belief; but their thinking so did not make it so."[264] Similarly, the state may prohibit "open offenses against the enlightened sentiment of mankind, notwithstanding the pretence of religious conviction . . . ."[265]

These Mormon cases, taken together, suggest an image of religion which has been widely accepted by American courts until recently. In the first place, there is a more or less territorial division between religion and other things;[266] the realm or sphere of religion covers beliefs respecting divinity, moral teachings derived therefrom, and forms of worship. Second, the legitimate occupants of this realm are those views and practices which involve theistic notions—and only those which are not so outrageous or preposterous as to be obviously beyond the pale. Finally, the demarcation of disputed boundaries may properly be undertaken by courts.

Such a view of religion has been present in most judicial encounters with religious issues until fairly recently—for example, in determining what qualified as a religious trust,[267] or construing

---

[258] *Id.* at 341-42.
[259] *Id.* at 343.
[260] *Id.* at 345.
[261] Late Corp. of the Church of Jesus Christ of Latter-Day Saints v. United States, 136 U.S. 1 (1890).
[262] *Id.* at 49-50.
[263] *Id.* at 49.
[264] *Ibid.*
[265] *Id.* at 50.
[266] It was the *Reynolds* case, of course, which revived and popularized Jefferson's "wall of separation" metaphor. 98 U.S. at 164.
[267] See, *e.g.*, Stephan's Estate, 129 Pa. Super. 396, 195 Atl. 653 (1937). But for a broader view, see Estate of Hinckley, 58 Cal. 457, 512 (1881).

a tax exemption for religious activities,[268] or determining what qualified as religion for purposes of free exercise claims.[269] But within the last twenty years, each component of this view has eroded. The exclusion of outrageous matters was the first to go, followed more recently by the distinction between theistic and nontheistic beliefs. In this process the extent to which courts can impose any "objective" standards has been seriously curtailed.

In *United States v. Ballard*,[270] the leaders of the "I Am" movement were convicted of mail fraud. They were charged with soliciting funds by falsely representing that they had been selected as divine messengers by Saint Germain, given supernatural power to cure all diseases, and the like. The trial judge instructed the jury that it was not to consider the truth of these religious beliefs, but only whether or not the defendants believed them. The court of appeals reversed on the ground that a conviction required that their representations be proved false as well as insincere. Defendants appealed on the ground that the first amendment prevented even the good faith of their religious beliefs from being tested. The majority of the Supreme Court agreed with the trial court that the first amendment precludes the submission to the jury of "the truth or verity of respondents' religious doctrines or beliefs . . . ."[271] The preposterous character of these doctrines did not place them outside the boundary of religion, for religious freedom

> embraces the right to maintain theories of life and of death and of the hereafter which are rank heresy to followers of the orthodox faiths. . . . The First Amendment does not select any one group or any one type of religion for preferred treatment. It puts them all in that position.[272]

---

[268] See, e.g., People ex rel. McCullough v. Deutsche Evangelisch Lutherische Jehovah Gemeinde Ungenderter Augsburgischer Confession, 249 Ill. 132, 94 N.E. 162 (1911).

[269] See Mr. Chief Justice Hughes, dissenting in United States v. Macintosh, 283 U.S. 605, 633-34 (1931):
> The essence of religion is belief in a relation to God involving duties superior to those arising from any human relation. . . . One cannot speak of religious liberty, with proper appreciation of its essential and historic significance, without assuming the existence of a belief in supreme allegiance to the will of God. . . . The battle for religious liberty has been fought and won with respect to religious beliefs and practices, which are not in conflict with good order, upon the very ground of the supremacy of conscience within its proper field. What that field is, under our system of government, presents in part a question of constitutional law and also, in part, one of legislative policy . . . .

[270] 322 U.S. 78 (1944).

[271] *Id.* at 86. Mr. Justice Jackson, dissenting, suggested that the first amendment protects representations respecting matters of religious faith and experience from being tested for their sincerity. *Id.* at 92-95. For an instructive discussion, see Weiss, *Privilege, Posture and Protection: "Religion" in the Law*, 73 YALE L.J. 593 (1964).

[272] 322 U.S. at 86-87.

But the *Ballard* case deals with religious beliefs. So long as a belief-action distinction prevailed (with the secular regulation rule applied to action), it was not necessary to decide what actions were religious or religiously motivated, since these were treated on a par with actions proceeding from other motives. But when free exercise was broadened to include a freedom to act, the question arose as to which actions were religious ones. In *Cantwell v. Connecticut*, a licensing regulation was struck down because it empowered a state official "to determine whether the cause is a religious one . . . ."[273] This was a question of prior censorship. Could a court or jury after the fact decide by some objective standard that an activity was or was not religious? The retreat from the view that it could is illustrated in the solicitation and licensing cases.

In *Jones v. Opelika*,[274] the defendants' claim that the solicitations were religious was not controlling in characterizing those activities. Mr. Justice Reed, writing for the majority, would not concede that the distribution and selling of literature was "a religious rite." He saw an important distinction between restrictions "upon the religious rite itself" on the one hand and, on the other, upon "sales . . . partaking more of commercial than religious . . . transactions . . . ."[275] While "the mind and spirit of man remain forever free . . . his actions rest subject to necessary accomodation to the competing needs of his fellows."[276] His own religious characterization of his actions does not overcome his fellows' characterization of them as a commercial transaction subject to ordinary regulation. For the dissenters, however, the defendants' view of their activities as religious was an important element in characterizing this activity as protected by the first amendment.

In *Murdock v. Pennsylvania*,[277] the "objective" view lost ground. The majority found that "this form of religious activity occupies the same high estate under the First Amendment as do worship in the churches and preaching from the pulpits."[278] Mr. Justice Reed in dissent maintains that it cannot be said that "these sales of religious books are religious exercises."[279] One who sells religious books at a price is not "performing a religious rite [and] . . . worshipping his Creator in his way."[280] The majority indicates that this form of distribution is a venerable type of religious activity. But it is still asserted that this is an objective determination, involving more than the estimate of the religious claimants. "[W]e do not intimate or suggest in respecting their

---

[273] 310 U.S. 296, 305 (1940).
[274] 316 U.S. 584 (1942).
[275] *Id.* at 596, 598.
[276] *Id.* at 594.
[277] 319 U.S. 105 (1943).
[278] *Id.* at 109.
[279] *Id.* at 131.
[280] *Id.* at 132.

sincerity that any conduct can be made a religious rite and by the zeal of the practitioners swept into the First Amendment."[281]

Some years later, in *Fowler v. Rhode Island*,[282] the Court announced that it was disqualified from making such an "objective" determination of whether something is religious or not. "[A]part from narrow exceptions not relevant here . . . it is no business of courts to say that what is a religious practice or activity for one group is not religion under the protection of the First Amendment."[283] Here, the Court overturned a conviction for the violation of an ordinance which was applied to permit sermons in a public park but to forbid an "address" by Jehovah's Witnesses. It is not clear how far beyond such conventionally religious activities as sermons, meetings, and proselytization one may proceed before encountering the narrow exceptions referred to, which include at least polygamy. In any event, it seems that in connection with all activities such as "services," courts will accept the claimant's characterization of his activity as religious. Whether it is then protected by the first amendment is yet another matter.

The theistic component of the older judicial view of religion has undergone similar erosion. In *Torcaso v. Watkins*,[284] the Supreme Court held that a state could not make declaration of belief in God a condition for appointment as a notary public. Such a condition on any public benefit puts state power "on the side of one particular sort of believers . . . ."[285] This is a forbidden establishment. For government may not "aid those religions based on a belief in the existence of God as against those religions founded on different beliefs."[286] If the state cannot grant benefits to those who profess a belief in God over those who do not, can it deem the former "religious" and the latter "nonreligious"?

This issue has confronted courts primarily in the construction of those statutes giving special exemptions to religious activities. In several recent cases, provisions granting tax exemptions to places of religious worship have been interpreted to include nontheistic groups.[287] The courts felt they were constitutionally inhibited from differentiating among theistic and nontheistic beliefs. To avoid constitutional questions, they interpreted religion broadly in terms of the social function of the group rather than the content of its beliefs.[288]

---

[281] *Id.* at 109.
[282] 345 U.S. 67 (1953).
[283] *Id.* at 69-70.
[284] 367 U.S. 488 (1961).
[285] *Id.* at 490.
[286] *Id.* at 495.
[287] Washington Ethical Soc'y v. District of Columbia, 249 F.2d 127 (D.C. Cir. 1957); Fellowship of Humanity v. County of Alameda, 153 Cal. App. 2d 673, 315 P.2d 395 (1st Dist. 1957).
[288] In the *Fellowship of Humanity* case, *id.* at 692, 315 P.2d at 406, the question
    is the objective one of whether or not the belief occupies the same

The definition of religion issue finally came before the Supreme Court during the last term. The 1940 Selective Training and Service Act exempted any conscientious objector "who, by reason of religious training and belief, is conscientiously opposed to participation in war in any form."[289] Federal courts divided over the meaning of "religious training and belief"; some held that religion necessarily involved a concept of deity,[290] while others rejected a theistic component and measured religious belief in terms of inner compulsion, extending the exemption to cover

> place in the lives of its holders that the orthodox beliefs occupy in the lives of believing majorities, and whether a given group that claims the exemption conducts itself the way groups conceded to be religious conduct themselves. The content of the belief, under such test, is not a matter of governmental concern.

The court finds that the activities of the Fellowship of Humanity—Sunday meetings, group singing, collections, speeches, and announcements—"are similar to those of the theistic groups . . . ." *Id.* at 698, 315 P.2d at 410. Thus the Fellowship was a "religion" within the meaning of the state constitutional provision giving tax exemptions to places of religious worship. To avoid questioning the constitutionality of this provision, the court adopts a broad definition of religion:

> Religion simply includes: (1) a belief, not necessarily referring to supernatural powers; (2) a cult, involving a gregarious association openly expressing the belief; (3) a system of moral practice directly resulting from an adherence to the belief; and (4) an organization within the cult designed to observe the tenets of belief. The content of the belief is of no moment.

Id. at 693, 315 P.2d at 406. It has been observed that the court in *Fellowship of Humanity* does not actually apply all of these criteria. Comment, *Defining Religion: Of God, the Constitution and the D.A.R.*, 32 U. CHI. L. REV. 533, 548 (1965).

In the *Washington Ethical Soc'y* case, *supra* note 287, the court found the group a religious society within the meaning of the statute. Although the group did not believe in a Supreme Being, it had "Leaders" who preach, conduct services for naming, marrying, and burying members and rendering them spiritual guidance; they have weekly services with Bible readings, sermons, and meditation. 249 F.2d at 128.

[289] 54 Stat. 889 (1940). The Draft Act of 1917 excused only those objectors who were members of "any well-recognized religious sect or organization at present organized and existing and whose existing creed or principles forbid its members to participate in war in any form . . . ." 40 Stat. 78 (1917).

Under the present statute, one may be exempted even if he is not a member of a pacifist sect or organization. United States v. Alvies, 112 F. Supp. 618 (N.D. Cal. 1953); United States v. Everngam, 102 F. Supp. 128 (S.D.W. Va. 1951). But where the claimant ascribes his beliefs to a church, the court may ascertain whether the church holds the tenets ascribed to it. Roberson v. United States, 208 F.2d 166 (10th Cir. 1953); Head v. United States, 199 F.2d 337 (10th Cir. 1952), *cert. denied*, 345 U.S. 910 (1953). The "war in any form" provision in the present statute has been interpreted not to bar exemptions for Jehovah's Witnesses who are willing to fight in the Battle of Armageddon. Sicurella v. United States, 348 U.S. 385 (1955).

[290] Notably Berman v. United States, 156 F.2d 377 (9th Cir.), *cert. denied*, 329 U.S. 795 (1946).

philosophical pacifists.²⁹¹ In 1948, Congress attempted to clarify its meaning by adding the following provision:

> Religious training and belief in this connection means an individual's belief in a relation to a Supreme Being involving duties superior to those arising from any human relation, but does not include essentially political, sociological, or philosophical views or a merely personal moral code.²⁹²

Congress thus appeared to incorporate the theistic interpretation into the statute and to repudiate the broader view. Again, the courts differed in their treatment of the new provision. Three cases, representing different treatments of this provision, came before the Supreme Court in *United States v. Seeger*.²⁹³ In one, the court of appeals found the statute constitutional and denied exemption to a nontheistic objector.²⁹⁴ In a second, the statute was broadly construed and exemption allowed for a pacifist who believed in "Godness" and a "Supreme Reality."²⁹⁵ In a third, the Supreme Being requirement as applied to one who believed in "goodness and virtue for their own sakes" was held to be an unconstitutional discrimination against objectors whose views were "internally derived."²⁹⁶

In *Seeger*, the Supreme Court held that all three objectors came within the statutory language. The congressional requirement of "belief in relation to a Supreme Being" was interpreted to mean a

> belief that is sincere and meaningful [and that] occupies a place in the life of its possessor parallel to that filled by the orthodox belief in God of one who clearly qualifies for the exemption. Where such beliefs have parallel positions in the lives of their respective holders we cannot say that one is "in a relation to a Supreme Being" and the other is not.²⁹⁷

In view of the diversity of conceptions of religion in the United States—and with an eye to "the ever-broadening understanding of the modern religious community"²⁹⁸—the Court concludes that Congress, "in keeping with its long-established policy of not picking and choosing among religious beliefs,"²⁹⁹ used the expression "Supreme Being" to indicate that the broadest sense of religion was meant. It "was merely clarifying the meaning of religious

---

²⁹¹ United States *ex rel.* Reel v. Badt, 141 F.2d 845 (2d Cir. 1944); United States *ex rel.* Phillips v. Downer, 135 F.2d 521 (2d Cir. 1943). These cases exempted philosophical pacifists, relying on dicta in United States v. Kauten, 133 F.2d 703 (2d Cir. 1943), where a "political" objector was denied exemption.
²⁹² 62 Stat. 613 (1948).
²⁹³ 380 U.S. 163 (1965).
²⁹⁴ Peter v. United States, 324 F.2d 173 (9th Cir. 1963).
²⁹⁵ United States v. Jakobson, 325 F.2d 409 (2d Cir. 1963).
²⁹⁶ United States v. Seeger, 326 F.2d 846 (2d Cir. 1964).
²⁹⁷ 380 U.S. at 166.
²⁹⁸ *Id.* at 180.
²⁹⁹ *Id.* at 175.

training and belief so as to embrace all religions . . . ."³⁰⁰

The ambit of "all religions," the Court implies, cannot be drawn in terms of traditional theism. In order to cover them all, "Supreme Being" is taken to refer not to "the orthodox God" but to "the broader concept of a power or being, or a faith, 'to which all else is subordinate or upon which all else is ultimately dependent.' "³⁰¹

If religion embraces all beliefs which fulfill this psychic function, by what test is the trier of fact to decide if what is claimed to be religious is in fact so? The Court says that "it is essentially an objective one, namely, does the claimed belief occupy the same place in the life of the objector as an orthodox belief in God holds in the life of one clearly qualified for exemption?"³⁰² Assuming that by "orthodox belief in God" the Court means conventional or widespread kinds of belief that the trier of fact is more likely to have encountered, how is he to assess and compare the psychic role played by orthodox and novel beliefs?

The Court does not indicate what it has in mind when it speaks of the position or place that a belief in God holds or occupies in the life of an orthodox believer. Apparently it envisions such a belief as "meaningful" and "paramount," and other beliefs as "subordinate" to it or "dependent" upon it.³⁰³ It seems questionable whether triers of fact have the resources to discern the relationships, logical or causal, among a person's beliefs. The Court seems to have discarded the congressional preference for theistic views over nontheistic ones and to have substituted a reading which prefers grandiose and pretentious scruples over more modest, empirical, and tentative exertions of conscience.

What weight is to be given to the self-estimate of the registrant in making this occult determination? "In such an intensely personal area . . . the claim of the registrant that his belief is an essential part of a religious faith must be given great weight. . . . The validity of what he believes cannot be questioned."³⁰⁴ Inquiries regarding

> the existence of the registrant's "Supreme Being" or the truth of his concepts . . . are . . . foreclosed to Government. . . .

---

³⁰⁰ *Id.* at 165.
³⁰¹ *Id.* at 174.
³⁰² *Id.* at 184.
³⁰³ At the risk of putting too much store by the Court's formulation, it may be pointed out that there is an ambiguity in such terms as "paramount," "subordinate," and "dependent." In determining whether one of a person's beliefs is dependent on another, it makes a great difference if we take dependence in the sense of causal connection or logical derivation. There is no reason to assume a correspondence between causal and logical accounts of the presence of a given belief. The Court seems to visualize the relation between opinions as deductive and hierarchic—on the model of a rather conceptualistic view of legal reasoning.
³⁰⁴ 380 U.S. at 184.

> Local boards and courts . . . are not free to reject beliefs because they consider them "incomprehensible." Their task is to decide whether the beliefs professed by a registrant are sincerely held and whether they are, *in his own scheme of things, religious.*[305]

But once the "threshold question of sincerity"[306] has been answered, it is difficult to see what there is of an "objective" nature about the Court's test.

In the process of avoiding the constitutional question, the Court has broadened its notion of religion to include all beliefs which are sincere, meaningful, and paramount in the lives of their holders. Thus the theistic element of the earlier view of religion is supplanted, and with it the application of any "objective" criterion of the boundaries of religion is rendered extremely difficult. There now remains no valid test of the content of a claimed religious belief—neither its truth, good sense, comprehensibility, theism, or its acceptance by an organized group. Courts may, at the most, apply general tests of psychic function—or, when dealing with institutions, of institutional form and functions.[307] Courts may test the sincerity of the claimant, but his characterization of his beliefs or activities as religious would seem to play a major, if not an exclusive, role in deciding whether they are. Recent decisions by several courts concur in this new latitudinarianism. Courts have set aside administrative determinations to the effect that the Black Muslim sect is not a religion because of the admixture of social and political doctrines[308] or because it is dedicated to hate and is "different from orthodox Islam."[309] Nor can a state decide that an individual's objection to vaccination based on a personal belief that God will keep him healthy is not a truly religious objection entitled to enjoy an exemption extended to other religious objectors who are members of organized groups.[310]

---

[305] *Id.* at 184-85. (Emphasis added.)
[306] *Id.* at 185.
[307] This judicial movement must be seen against the background of changes in prevailing conceptions of religion in the wider community. Among many religious thinkers and teachers—and slowly filtering out to a wider constituency—there has been a general movement away from the picture of religion that inspired the earlier legal view. See Stahmer, *Defining Religion: Federal Aid and Academic Freedom,* in 1963 RELIGION AND THE PUBLIC ORDER 116 (Gianella ed. 1964). A decline in the stress on the efficacy of doctrinal correctness to secure religious merit, the rising level of education, increased interreligious dialogue, and ecumenicism, to mention only a few factors, have made religious spokesmen less inclined to take a narrow prescriptive view of religion. On the score of increasing sophistication, it is instructive to compare the reactions of American religious spokesmen to the *Schempp* decision with those elicited by *McCollum,* fifteen years earlier.
[308] Fulwood v. Clemmer, 206 F. Supp. 370 (D.D.C. 1962).
[309] Bryant v. Wilkins, 45 Misc. 2d 923, 258 N.Y.S.2d 455 (Sup. Ct. 1965).
[310] Kolbeck v. Kramer, 84 N.J. Super. 569, 202 A.2d 889 (L. 1964).

II. Digression: The Definition of Religion and the Establishment Clause

The breakdown of any "content" test in defining religion for purposes of assessing free exercise claims raises the question whether "religion" means the same thing for establishment purposes. The equivalence of religion for purposes of the two clauses is suggested, of course, by the text of the first amendment and has been adverted to by some courts and writers.[311] But if we begin with the broad definition which is emerging in the free exercise area and work back to establishment, this equivalence leads to somewhat paradoxical results. Is the government forbidden to adopt and enforce policies which express paramount convictions or ultimate concerns?[312] Is it forbidden to support teachings which embody or proceed from such convictions or concerns?[313] Are such teachings and policies "religious" merely because they occupy a parallel position in the thoughts of their advocates or proponents? Even where they are not claimed to be "religious"? If religion embraces a whole class of beliefs when they are claimed to be such by their adherents, does it include all the beliefs of that class when no such claim is made for them? Or when the religious characterization is attached by someone other than the adherent himself? Is the teaching of secular subjects in religious schools a secular matter because the school authorities deem it such? Or is it a religious matter because opponents of aid to schools deem it religious? If government is constitutionally disabled from saying that something is nonreligious when its practitioners say that it is religious, is it similarly disabled from saying that something is religious when its practitioners say that it is not?

The broad, permissive, and subjective notion of religion is not applied in establishment cases. In *Schempp*, the test of a forbidden establishment is whether a governmental action has as its purpose or primary effect "the advancement or inhibition of religion."[314] But how is such a measurement to take place if religion includes all beliefs which occupy in the minds of their adherents a position parallel to that of the conception of God in the minds of

---

[311] *Cf.* the dissent of Mr. Justice Rutledge in Everson v. Board of Educ., 330 U.S. 1, 32 (1947), to the effect that everything protected by the free exercise clause cannot be established.

[312] In *Seeger*, the opinion of the Court notes approvingly theologian Paul Tillich's phrase "ultimate concern" as the definition of religion. 380 U.S. at 187. In the remainder of this article, this phrase is employed as a shorthand expression for the *Seeger* pronouncements on the definition of religion. *Cf.* Berman v. United States, 156 F.2d 377 (9th Cir.), *cert. denied*, 329 U.S. 795 (1946), where the court rejected the inclusion of moral views within the religion covered by the first amendment, on the ground that Congress was empowered to make laws regarding morals.

[313] See Stahmer, *supra* note 307, at 127.

[314] Abington School Dist. v. Schempp, 374 U.S. 203, 222 (1963).

orthodox believers? Surely legislation whose purpose or effect is to advance human dignity, equality, national destiny, freedom, enlightenment, and morality might come within such a test. But it is clear that there is no intention or possibility of using such a standard for testing establishment claims.

In undertaking to decide whether something is an establishment, the Supreme Court utilizes a much narrower concept of religion. In the *Sunday Closing Law Cases*, the Court found that in spite of the "unmistakably religious origin" of such laws, they have "for the most part . . . been divorced from the religious orientation of their predecessors."[315] They aim at a common day of repose and recreation, and the Court does not find that their "purpose or effect is religious."[316] In *Engel v. Vitale*, however, composition of a prayer by the state was an unwarranted performance of a "purely religious function."[317] But the Court there notes that there is "no true resemblance" between such an "unquestioned religious exercise" and such practices as "reciting historical documents . . . which contain references to the Deity or . . . singing officially espoused anthems which include the composer's professions of faith in a Supreme Being . . . ."[318] In *Schempp*, Bible reading and recitation of the Lord's Prayer were "religious exercises."[319]

> But even if its purpose is not strictly religious, it is sought to be accomplished through readings, without comment, from the Bible. Surely the place of the Bible as an instrument of religion cannot be gainsaid, and the State's recognition of the pervading religious character of the ceremony is evident . . . .[320]

On the other hand, the Court indicates that objective study of the Bible and of religion would not have this character.[321]

The effect and purpose of government action are not to be assessed by the religious sensibilities of the person who is complaining of the alleged establishment. It must be essentially religious in some widely shared public understanding. In other contexts it is admitted that what is or is not religious is not a given on which all agree. The boundaries of religion differ with the preconceptions, religious or otherwise, of the observer. But if some things are not to be established, then there must be some public meaning by which these things can be identified.[322] If "religion" for free

---

[315] Gallagher v. Crown Kosher Super Market, 366 U.S. 617, 624, 626 (1961).
[316] *Id.* at 630.
[317] 370 U.S. 421, 435 (1962).
[318] *Id.* at 435 n.21.
[319] 374 U.S. at 224.
[320] *Ibid.*
[321] *Id.* at 225.
[322] Such a meaning may be identified with common understanding—or with the nature of things. See, *e.g.*, Mr. Justice Black for the majority in Illinois *ex rel.* McCollum v. Board of Educ., 333 U.S. 203, 212 (1948): "[T]he First Amendment rests upon the premise that both religion and

exercise purposes extends to that which is distinctive about a particular religion, "religion" for establishment purposes is confined to some common areas of concern. No one doubts that governmental imposition of compulsory education, health, and war measures are not religious in purpose and effect (though most religious groups approve of them). On the other hand, such things as worship, prayer, sacraments, and communion are religious for establishment purposes, because they are commonly regarded as religious. This double standard is clearly articulated in *Sheldon v. Fannin*,[323] where the question before the court was whether Jehovah's Witness children might be required to stand during the singing of the Star-Spangled Banner. (The school authorities had excused them from the singing itself.) The requirement was challenged on both establishment and free exercise grounds. The court denied that the requirement amounted to an establishment of religion, for the establishment clause "looks to the majority's concept of the term religion"; but there was a restriction on their free exercise of religion, for the free exercise clause looks to the minority's.[324] The claimants' view of religion controls the characterization of their objection as a religious one. But it does not control the characterization of the government's action. Thus some popular or conventional notion of religion, as distilled and rationalized by the courts, is the religion that cannot be established. But the use of such a view of religion in free exercise cases is itself constitutionally impermissible.

Further, it is clear that the perspective from which the effect of a measure on religion is to be assessed differs in establishment and in free exercise cases. In establishment cases, the "advancement" or "inhibition" of religion is measured by the views of the marketplace. It is assumed without question that financial aid and compulsory religious exercises "advance" or "aid" religion. Of course, many religious sensibilities would reject such an assessment. Again, it is assumed that persecution and martyrdom "inhibit" religion, though from the perspective of a particular faith these tribulations might be evaluated differently.[325] On the

---

government can best work to achieve their lofty aims if each is left free from the other within its respective sphere." *Cf.* Mr. Justice Jackson's view that the distinction between secular and sectarian is a matter of prepossessions. *Id.* at 37-38.

[323] 221 F. Supp. 766 (D. Ariz. 1963). The double standard is also discussed in Van Alstyne, *Constitutional Separation of Church and State: The Quest for a Coherent Position*, 57 AM. POL. SCI. REV. 865, 873 (1963).

[324] 221 F. Supp. at 775.

[325] Mr. Justice Douglas, concurring in *Schempp*, 374 U.S. at 229, is even more specific. He finds that the establishment clause "forbids the State to employ its facilities or funds in a way that gives any church, or all churches, greater strength in our society than it would have by relying on its members alone." Assuming that "churches" and "religion" are commensurate terms, it is clear that the "strength" of churches is to be measured in the scales of worldly power.

other hand, the perspective of the religious adherent is used in assessing denial of free exercise. It is in his view, not in common estimation, that Saturday work, jury duty, or the absence of peyote are religious deprivations.

III. THE NEW DISPENSATION: PROBLEMS AND PROSPECTS

The new judicial solicitude toward religious objection and the broad permissive definition of religion have emerged when American law is undergoing salient changes which provide a new context for the problem of religious exceptions. Forbearance toward religious scruples can be seen as a response to the problem of reconciling personal liberty with increasing governmental activity. Government at all levels is increasingly a source of regulations touching many aspects of life previously subject only to nongovernmental controls. Just as the public operation of schools has been the classic source of establishment problems, so the staple source of free exercise problems is the multifarious regulations of the welfare state: compulsory education, financing of higher education, control over business hours, child labor, licensing of occupations and activities, union activity, use of land and buildings, health measures, and old age security. In regulating each of these things, government tends to make majority notions into normative standards; enjoyment of benefits and sometimes avoidance of penalties are conditional upon acceptance of prevailing notions about health, education, hours of work, age of retirement, and the like. The majority standards thus "established" by government are not in common estimation religious. Yet for some minorities they collide painfully with religious commands and prohibitions.

At the same time there has been a change in the notion of governmental responsibility with respect to personal freedom. Older views stressed governmental abstention as a condition (if not the substance) of freedom. But increasingly, affirmative governmental intervention is invoked to provide resources and opportunities for desired freedoms. Government responds to such appeals by structuring and controlling some part of the social environment to provide the opportunities desired by the "majority" or some sizable group. As government exercises control over more aspects of the environment, it becomes more difficult for a minority to opt out of the system or to form an enclave beyond its reach. In this setting, the question of exceptions for religious objectors normally arises after the government has intervened in response to larger groups in the society to implement their values by structuring the social environment in a way that makes it difficult for a minority to adhere to its religious convictions. Must government then provide for the minority a legal enclave as a substitute for the territorial or social enclave that was formerly available?

416

Concurrently with these changes in the sphere and responsibilities of government, there has been a significant change in the relation of the "higher law" promulgated by higher appellate courts and the "local law" put into effect by police, school boards, zoning boards, and local judges. It is well known that there is no one-to-one correspondence between what higher courts say and what lower courts, school boards, and the police do. The latter may extend, refine, ignore, distort, or subvert the law established by the higher courts.[326] The higher law does deflect the actions of these lower officials toward the standards promulgated by the higher courts. But the law in operation at any given place and time is some combination of these elevated national standards and more parochial understandings and concerns. There is some evidence to suggest that the deflecting power of the higher courts is even less in matters dealing with religion than in other fields.[327]

We have now entered a period in which the discrepancy between higher law and local practice is being radically diminished.[328] Previously there were widespread arrangements, both avowed and *sub rosa*, by which local authorities permitted what the higher courts said was impermissible and forbade what these courts said was protected. A multilevel legal system, staffed by locally recruited personnel, permitted variation in substance behind the veneer of doctrinal uniformity. Beyond this, local deviation from national norms was legitimated by limitations on the scope of central authority and standards. And the powerlessness and isolation of many dissenters provided fewer calls for extra-local intervention.

The relationship between higher and local legal authorities is undergoing a profound change. Authoritative national standards are being elaborated in more fields and local legal practice is required to align itself with these standards. In part this is due to the increased assertiveness of central authorities; higher courts are more assertive, less tolerant of local deviance. It is also a function of the increasing ease of communication, increased education, and the diffusion of political skills and resources which enables dissident groups to assert claims under the higher law and thereby bring officials to account by resort to the political process or to the courts. Thus as government intervention increases, so

---

[326] See, *e.g.*, Murphy, *Lower Court Checks on Supreme Court Power*, 53 AM. POL. SCI. REV. 1017 (1959); Note, *Evasion of Supreme Court Mandates in Cases Remanded to State Courts Since 1941*, 67 HARV. L. REV. 1251 (1954).
[327] DIERENFELD, RELIGION IN AMERICAN PUBLIC SCHOOLS (1962); Patric, *The Impact of a Court Decision: Aftermath of the McCollum Case*, 6 J. PUB. L. 455 (1957); Sorauf, *Zorach v. Clauson: The Impact of a Supreme Court Decision*, 53 AM. POL. SCI. REV. 777 (1959).
[328] The most notable current examples are in the fields of racial equality and criminal procedure. But a similar movement is discernible generally in the civil liberties field. See ROCHE, THE QUEST FOR THE DREAM (1963).

does the capacity of dissidents to assert and vindicate claims for religious freedom. All these factors operate to bring the higher law to bear on the local scene. The role of the higher courts in matters of civil liberty is being transformed from that of remote legitimators of local political powers to intermediaries who, in response to a diversity of claimants, control or at least deflect these powers.

The discrepancy between higher law and local practice did not always work to the disadvantage of religious objectors. Most of the exceptions which did exist were not granted by legislatures or found constitutionally obligatory by higher courts—they were the product of prosecutory inaction. Groups which did not have the dual misfortune to be both powerless and offensive to local opinion had a good chance to have their eccentricities respected. But as welfare measures move from local political control to impersonal bureaucratic administration, the possibility of such enclaves declines. Such agencies as the Social Security Administration are not likely to carve out an exception in the absence of legislative or judicial command.

In the remainder of this paper, I shall attempt to assess some of the consequences of the dual movement from, first, the secular regulation rule to a balancing test that allows exceptions for religious objectors, and, second, from a narrower to a more permissive definition of religion. In the first place, a number of previously settled questions are at least open to question. Although the courts in *Sherbert* and *Woody* scrupulously distinguished many of the previous cases—*Reynolds, Jacobson, Prince, Braunfeld*—it is difficult to believe that a sustained adherence to the compelling interest-no alternative means test would not bring about different results in at least some important cases. The denial of a constitutional basis for religious exemptions from the draft, the constitutionality of compulsory ROTC in state universities, the constitutionality of conditioning an occupational license upon willingness to bear arms, the constitutionality of prohibitions on snake handling—and perhaps of polygamy—all require re-examination. The denials of religious exceptions in various health, economic, and educational provisions deserve at least a fresh evaluation.

Second, when this forbearance toward religious objection is combined with the new permissiveness in defining religion, other kinds of possibilities come into view. Dissidents of all kinds— nudists, LSD users, racists, utopians, and groups as yet unimagined—can be expected to present claims for religious freedom.[329]

It is abundantly clear that not every claim for exemption from religiously offensive laws will be vindicated. As innumerable

---

[329] On religious claims in behalf of "consciousness-expanding drugs," see any issue of the Psychodelic Review.

courts have pointed out, a flat exemption for religious objection would give to every individual with sufficient zeal the prerogative of deciding which laws were to be binding on him. Such a doctrine would, as Cardozo said, "carry us to lengths that have never yet been dreamed of."[330] But for the first time the courts have committed themselves to giving religious objections some weight in determinations of constitutionality. They must now fashion some methods of deciding which claims are to be allowed and which are not. I shall attempt to ascertain some of the dimensions along which such tests might lie.

Sincerity

It seems well established that the good faith of religious claims may be tested by the courts and by other agencies as well.[331] This will dispose of some claims,[332] but to believe that it will not leave many more is seriously to underestimate the human capacities for commitment and invention.[333]

The One and the Many

At one time claims for religious exemption might be limited by requiring that the religious scruple be one shared with some recognizable group. The right to an exemption might be conditioned upon membership in a group with appropriate tenets.[334] In view of the new judicial sensitivity to distinctions among religions, it

---

[330] Hamilton v. Regents of the Univ. of Cal., 293 U.S. 245, 268 (1934). "The conscientious objector, if his liberties were to be thus extended, might refuse to contribute taxes in furtherance . . . of any other end condemned by his conscience as irreligious or immoral. The right of private judgment has never yet been so exalted above the powers and the compulsion of the agencies of government." *Ibid.* See PEACEMAKER MOVEMENT, HANDBOOK ON NON-PAYMENT OF WAR TAXES (1963), for a description of uneven governmental responses to such activities.

[331] United States v. Seeger, 380 U.S. 163 (1965). It is clear that the Court envisions that such determinations will be made by draft boards as well as by courts.

[332] For a recent example of disposition on this ground, see Dobkin v. District of Columbia, 194 A.2d 657 (D.C. App. 1963) (Jew who customarily worked on Sabbath cannot complain of trial then).

[333] There may be some as yet unspecified limits upon the testing of sincerity. The difficulties of separating the issue of good faith from that of truth and the dangers inherent in literal application of misrepresentation rules to religious appeals were eloquently urged by Mr. Justice Jackson, dissenting in United States v. Ballard, 322 U.S. 78, 92-95 (1944). This view commands some scholarly following. See, *e.g.*, Jones, *Church-State Relations: Our Constitutional Heritage*, in RELIGION AND CONTEMPORARY SOCIETY 184 (Stahmer ed. 1963); Weiss, *Privilege, Posture and Protection: "Religion" in the Law*, 73 YALE L.J. 593 (1964).

[334] See the exemption in the 1917 Draft Act, note 289 *supra*. *Cf. In re* Nissen, 138 F. Supp. 483 (D. Mass. 1955) (member of church which did not teach pacifism does not qualify as conscientious objector by reason of religious training and belief under provisions of Naturalization Act). *Contra, In re* Hansen, 148 F. Supp. 187 (D. Minn. 1957).

is at least doubtful that such a standard can now be employed to disqualify unaffiliated objectors.³³⁵ But suppose the exemption is conditional on the existence of a group norm which makes the public requirement superfluous? A recent amendment to the Social Security Act exempts members of those sects who the Secretary of Health, Education, and Welfare finds are conscientiously opposed to insurance and habitually provide for their dependent members.³³⁶ If the courts may determine what is a religious institution on the basis of institutional function, may the government distinguish among religions on the ground that some fulfill different functions for their members?

Time

One way to settle conflicts between governmental and religious authority is to ask who got there first. This evidently was in the mind of the *Reynolds* Court, which was reassured by the fact that the ban on polygamy long antedated the religious revelation which sanctioned it.³³⁷ (On the other hand, the Court was not impressed by the fact that legal regulation of the marriage relationship had moved from ecclesiastical to political authorities only relatively recently in legal history.) In some instances—for example, peyote and snake handling—the religious practices antedate the prohibition. In *Woody*, the court noted that peyote religion has a long history.³³⁸ But the duration of the claimant's affiliation was not a decisive factor; the same court extended its holding to cover a latecomer in *In re Grady*.³³⁹

While novelty might be relevant to good faith, it would not appear open to the state to distinguish between old and new religions³⁴⁰ or to disqualify new areas of religious concern in a particular religion.³⁴¹ Such a temporal distinction would put the

---

³³⁵ Kolbeck v. Kramer, 84 N.J. Super. 569, 202 A.2d 889 (L. 1964) (state forbidden to exclude individual objector while exempting members of recognized sects). *Cf.* Hardwick v. Board of School Trustees, 54 Cal. App. 696, 205 Pac. 49 (3d Dist. 1921) (views different from those of everyone else in state entitled to same weight as those of organized group).

³³⁶ N.Y. Times, July 31, 1965, p. 8, col. 4.

³³⁷ Compare the situation in India and Israel, where long-practiced polygamy was only latterly discovered to be obnoxious to the state. In both countries, *Reynolds* was favorably received by courts upholding the ban.

³³⁸ 61 Cal. 2d at 720, 40 Cal. Rep. at 72, 394 P.2d at 817. *Cf.* the emphasis on the age-old character of the religious activities in Murdock v. Pennsylvania, 319 U.S. 105 (1943).

³³⁹ 61 Cal. 2d 887, 39 Cal. Rep. 912, 394 P.2d 728 (1964).

³⁴⁰ See United States v. Ballard, 322 U.S. 78 (1944); *cf. In re* Grady, 61 Cal. 2d 887, 39 Cal. Rep. 912, 394 P.2d 728 (1964); Bryant v. Wilkins, 45 Misc. 2d 923, 258 N.Y.S.2d 455 (Sup. Ct. 1965). But compare the recent amendment to the Social Security Act which exempts only members of sects founded before December 31, 1950.

³⁴¹ The 1917 Draft Act exemption was only for existing sects which included opposition to war in their then existing doctrines. If a flat cutoff on

courts in the business of prescribing what matters were religious for whom. To apply it symmetrically would not only be inconvenient in an era of rapid government movement into such traditional areas of religious concern as care of the poor and aged, but would prevent government from regulating religious practices that changing social conditions make intolerable.[342]

High and Low

Another method of deciding which claims to allow is to manipulate the definition of religion so that it includes that which is acceptable and excludes that which is not.

Thus Harrop Freeman, who is ardently in favor of exceptions for religious objectors, would not extend this preferential treatment to everything which purports to be religion. For him, "religion" in the first amendment "included the great systems of religion recognized by civilization. It did not include the forerunners of religion, often referred to as primitive or barbaric."[343] According to Professor Freeman, we should "start protecting action taken in conformity with civilized religion. Specifically, [we should protect] . . . the right of love and conscience against the State, as the highest precept of all high religion."[344]

How are courts to distinguish high civilized religions from low or barbaric religions? Professor Freeman assures us that "the distinction is well recognized by all authorities in the field."[345] It may be doubted that such unanimity can be discerned without considerable selectivity in choosing authorities. A distinction of high and low religion can only be made from a particular perspective of what is high and low in human affairs. Whether this perspective is called religious or not, it will correspond closely to the viewpoint of some religions and not others. Thus it can lead to easy acceptance of "the right of love and conscience [rather than justice, truth, release, self-knowledge, or salvation] . . . as the highest precept of all high religion."

Even if one could say that certain religions were high and others low, this standard seems to assume that religions are monolithic entities. But in fact the "great systems of religion recognized by civilization" are themselves families of sects and cults whose beliefs

---

new groups is unconstitutional, the question would then arise whether a time period might be specified as a warrant of good faith and seriousness. For example, would a fifteen-years-in-existence requirement be less objectionable than a cutoff date?

[342] As, for example, in the communities where introduction of night shifts makes daytime house-to-house solicitation onerous. *But see* Martin v. City of Struthers, 319 U.S. 141 (1943).

[343] Freeman, *A Remonstrance for Conscience*, 106 U. PA. L. REV. 806, 824 (1958).

[344] *Id.* at 826.

[345] *Id.* at 824.

and practices may range from the most elevated and refined to the most narrow and bloody. Such contrasts are found not only between sects, but may be combined in a single group in the most surprising combinations.[346]

Finally, there is the notion of protecting action which is "in conformity with civilized religion." Does it matter if the act of conscience is not in conformity with that religion as interpreted by its authoritative interpreters? Whose interpretation of conformity is controlling? Does not the right of conscience extend to disagreement with religious authorities about the implications of religious tenets? But, if so, how can courts decide what is in conformity with civilized religion without setting themselves up as arbiters of disputed questions of religious doctrine—a task they have long and justifiably avoided?[347]

Center and Periphery

If the problem cannot be solved by managing the definition of religion or by some unchanging demarcation of spheres, the alternative that appears less avoidable is an attempt at some measurement of the degree to which the religious practice for which an exception is claimed is "central" or "essential" or "integral" to the claimant's religion. Does it make a difference if the religious practice which is forbidden is a crucial sacramental act or a sit-in at an air force base? Or whether the offensive act which is required of the claimant is combatant service in the armed forces or the use of fluoridated water?

We find premonitions of such a distinction in earlier cases. Indeed the belief-action distinction was an implicit affirmation that it was belief, prayer, and worship which comprised the central and essential core of religion. As a rough approximation, we might say that the earlier judicial image of religion envisioned a sacramental core surrounded by concentric circles of action, each

---

[346] Professor Freeman chides the *Reynolds* Court for classifying polygamy as a relic of barbarism along with ritual murder, human sacrifice, and the immolation of widows. Yet the last of these was approved until very recently by quite respectable elements within what is admittedly one of the civilized religions.

[347] For a few instances in which officials have undertaken to repel free exercise claims by instructing adherents in their religion, see Williford v. People of Cal., 217 F. Supp. 245 (N.D. Cal. 1963); *In re* Ferguson, 55 Cal. 2d 663, 12 Cal. Rep. 753, 361 P.2d 417 (1961) (request for Koran not proper because "it does not appear that they seek the standard Mohammedan scriptures"); Bryant v. Wilkins, 45 Misc. 2d 923, 258 N.Y.S.2d 455 (Sup. Ct. 1965) (prison authorities said that Black Muslims were not truly Muslim, but a "sham"); Commonwealth v. Beiler, 168 Pa. Super. 462, 79 A.2d 134 (1951) (court refused to entertain state's contention that Dortricht Creed did not bar Amish from school attendance after the eighth grade).

more external and less purely religious than the last.³⁴⁸ The further from the core of belief and worship that a particular activity lay, the less weight it would be accorded in assessing free exercise claims.³⁴⁹

A distinction between center and periphery is implicit in the solicitation cases of the 1940's. In *Jones v. Opelika*, Mr. Justice Reed for the majority saw an important distinction between restrictions upon the "religious rites" on the one hand, and "sales partaking more of commercial than religious or educational transactions" on the other.³⁵⁰ This estimate of the Witnesses' activity was rejected in *Murdock v. Pennsylvania*, where the Court found this form of distribution to be a species of evangelism combining preaching and distribution of religious literature: "this form of religious activity occupies the same high estate under the First Amendment as do worship in the churches and preaching from the pulpits."³⁵¹ While rejecting the use of conventional estimation to determine the protected core of religion, this and subsequent cases do seem consistent with the notion that only this core is protected.³⁵²

The same sort of standard reappears in the recent cases. In *Sherbert*, Mr. Justice Brennan had no difficulty in concluding that abstention from Saturday work was "a cardinal principle of her religious faith . . . ."³⁵³ We are not told what makes it cardinal but we may assume that it has something to do with the fact that she worships on Saturday.³⁵⁴

---

³⁴⁸ This picture of religion is probably derived from—and is in any event compatible with—the major kinds of Christianity found in the United States. It may be somewhat less congenial to other religions in which the center of religious gravity is the moral ordering of public life. See Hodgson, *A Comparison of Islam and Christianity as Frameworks for Religious Life*, 32 DIOGENES 49-74 (1960).
³⁴⁹ *Cf.* Cardozo, J., concurring in Hamilton v. Regents of the Univ. of Cal., 293 U.S. 245, 267 (1934) (ROTC participation is not "so tied to the practice of religion as to be exempt . . . from regulation by the state.").
³⁵⁰ 316 U.S. 584, 598 (1942).
³⁵¹ 319 U.S. 105, 109 (1943). Mr. Justice Reed, dissenting, was even more emphatic in urging his rite-periphery distinction. It cannot be said "that these sales of religious books are religious exercises." One who sells religious books "at a price" is not "performing a religious rite, [or] . . . worshipping his Creator in his own way." He points out that this distribution must be classed with other things such as maintaining orphanages, teaching the young, and healing the sick, which are "in a sense, religious practices but hardly such examples of religious rites as are encompassed by the prohibition [sic] against the free exercise of religion." *Id.* at 131-32. Mr. Justice Reed would apply the same distinction in the establishment area as well. Illinois *ex rel.* McCollum v. Board of Educ., 333 U.S. 203, 248 (1948) (dissenting opinion).
³⁵² *Cf.* Fowler v. Rhode Island, 345 U.S. 67 (1953). See text accompanying note 285 *supra*.
³⁵³ 374 U.S. 398, 406 (1963).
³⁵⁴ *Cf.* id. at 404.

In *People v. Woody*, the court found that the use of peyote was "the central event" of the religious meeting; peyote was more than a sacramental symbol, it "constitutes in itself an object of worship" which members of the church regard as an object of prayers, a teacher, and a protector.[355] Thus prohibition of its use removes "the theological heart of Peyotism."[356] The ceremony at which peyote is sacramentally used "composes the cornerstone of the peyote religion."[357] It is clear that the court regards the centrality of peyote as an important factor. It finds *Reynolds* distinguishable because "polygamy, although a basic tenet in the theology of Mormonism, is not essential to the practice of the religion; peyote, on the other hand, is the *sine qua non* of defendants' faith. It is the sole means by which defendants are able to experience their religion . . . ."[358]

Thus each of the cases in which a prohibition or an indirect burden has been held unconstitutional involves some determination that the activities prohibited or burdened were indeed central or essential to the religion involved. All of them involve the core of worship, sermons, or sacrament—very much along the lines of the conventional notion of religion employed in dealing with establishment claims.[359] But such a distinction is not evident in the cases involving religiously offensive requirements. The Supreme Court in *Seeger* seems to imply that an exemption is justified only when the objection to war is an essential element in the religious faith of the claimant.[360] But in *Jenison*, for example, there was no attempt to ascertain how essential or central avoidance of jury duty was to the woman's religion.[361] Is a center-periphery distinction of any help here or in dealing with claims involving some form of religious activity remote from the conventional "core"—such as invading an air force base or congregating during an air raid drill, raising all the wheat one can, or

---

[355] 61 Cal. 2d at 721, 40 Cal. Rep. at 73, 394 P.2d at 819.
[356] *Id.* at 722, 40 Cal. Rep. at 74, 394 P.2d at 818.
[357] *Id.* at 720, 40 Cal. Rep. at 72, 394 P.2d at 817.
[358] *Id.* at 725, 40 Cal. Rep. at 76, 394 P.2d at 820.
[359] See pp. 265-68 *supra*. Mr. Justice Brennan suggests that the solution to the central paradox of the first amendment may lie in distinguishing "essentially religious" activities from others. Abington School Dist. v. Schempp, 374 U.S. 203, 231, 294-95 (1963). On the vicissitudes of the Indian experience with distinguishing the "essential" part of religion, see Parameswara Rao, *Matters of Religion*, 5 J. OF THE INDIAN L. INSTITUTE 509 (1963); Subramaniam, *Freedom of Religion*, 3 J. OF THE INDIAN L. INSTITUTE 323 (1961).
[360] 380 U.S. at 184-85.
[361] *In re* Jenison, 267 Minn. 136, 125 N.W.2d 588, *reversing* 265 Minn. 96, 120 N.W.2d 515 (1963). In its original opinion, the Minnesota Supreme Court found the burden on conscience less in the case of a jury objector than in the case of a war objector who might be ordered to kill contrary to his convictions. Since the latter did not enjoy a constitutional right to exemption, a fortiori, neither did the former. *Id.* at 100, 120 N.W.2d at 517.

avoiding vaccination?[362]

Can the courts properly undertake to determine which activities are central or essential to religions and which are not? To determine what is central or essential to *all* religion would reintroduce the discarded and unworkable notion that some activities are by nature secular and some religious. Depending on one's point of view, virtually any activity can be religious: travel may be pilgrimage; eating or not eating may be the observance of feasts, fasts, or dietary laws; clothing may be required habit or forbidden indecency; medical practices may be required (circumcision) or forbidden (blood transfusions or contraception); war may be prescribed (*jihad*) or forbidden. But if the courts cannot determine what activities are religious per se, may they determine whether the particular activity (or avoidance) before them is central or essential to the particular religion in question?

Just as the religious character of an activity is dependent on a particular religious perspective, so is its centrality or essentiality. Most religious groups have their own authoritative traditions and their own methods of identifying authoritative interpreters, and these in turn have their own techniques of deciding on the relative importance of various elements in that tradition and the admissibility of innovations in it. A court might make its own determination independently of these received interpreters. On the other hand a court might decide to rely on these religious authorities, if it could identify them. Courts sometimes resort to these methods in settling church property disputes. But when courts undertake to determine who are the reigning church authorities or whether there has been a departure from "fundamental" doctrines, they are seeking the general understanding of a defined group. But such determinations in free exercise cases would leave them open to charges of discriminating against the claims of someone who had a deviant or idiosyncratic interpretation of the religion to which he claimed he adhered.[363] Does it matter if the practice or omission is essential to him, even if it is not to his coreligionists? Should not the same reasons that impel courts to accept the claimant's characterization of his activ-

---

[362] *Cf.* Baer v. City of Bend, 206 Ore. 221, 292 P.2d 134 (1956), where the court observed that fluoridation "bears only remotely, if at all, upon the religious practices of any individual . . . ." *Id.* at 236, 292 P.2d at 139. But *cf.* State v. Amana Soc'y, 132 Iowa 304, 109 N.W. 894 (1906), quoted favorably in *Seeger*, where the Iowa Supreme Court said that what the devotee regards as "an essential tenet of his faith" cannot be denounced as nonreligious. *Id.* at 315, 109 N.W. at 898.

[363] This has in fact happened in some cases. See Roberson v. United States, 208 F.2d 166 (10th Cir. 1953) (where registrant ascribed his objections to combatant service to a church, the court may ascertain the tenets of the church to see if it holds these views). Compare the use of theological panels by draft boards to advise them whether registrants are bona fide ministers or students for the ministry. Eagels v. United States *ex rel.* Samuels, 329 U.S. 304 (1946).

ity as religious prohibit them from imposing their own view of how central or essential the activity is to his religion?

Some test along these lines is suggested as soon as religious exceptions are proposed, for after all, the purpose of such exceptions is to vouchsafe to each what is most important to him. To decide how much of a burden a governmental measure imposes, one must know how "essential" is the practice forbidden (or the deviation commanded). There seems little doubt that considerations of this type will continue to play a role in evaluating the claims of religious objectors. It remains to be seen whether there is a test of centrality that will not get courts deeply involved in questions of religious doctrine. The cases do suggest a few lines along which courts might proceed: *Woody*, for example, would ask whether the prohibition of the practice in question will prevent the carrying out of other religious practices. Cases of physical dependency may be clear—and in this peyote may be almost unique—but how are the courts to assess the ritual or sacramental dependency between one religious act and another? Some of the zoning cases ask in effect if there are any alternatives available. Again, the availability of an alternative building site can be readily assessed; but what about the availability of alternative sacramental performances? In short, centrality seems to be a one-way street. A court inclined to credit the claimant's estimate of the essential character of his practice may weigh this in the balance; a court disinclined to credit it can hardly undertake to decide the centrality issue on its own. However, it may look into the question of good faith. Or, passing by centrality in silence, it may find that some other requirement for an exception is missing.

The Price Tag

Closely connected with the problem of the centrality of the religious practice is the question of how heavy the burden upon free exercise is. Outright prohibitions of religious practice are rare; indirect burdens which make it difficult or expensive are more common. Until recently there was no need to calculate the cost of a private alternative to using some public facility which was only available on religiously offensive conditions.[364] In the license tax cases it was indicated that the effect of a financial exaction on religious expression amounted to an infringement of free exercise.[365] But these are "direct" burdens—at least in the sense that the activity taxed was itself a religious performance. There is no indication in these cases that the amount of the tax was of any consequence.

---

[364] *Cf.* Hamilton v. Regents of the Univ. of Cal., 293 U.S. 245 (1934), where the fact that the objector could not afford a private college was held to be "without significance" for the constitutional question.

[365] Follett v. McCormick, 321 U.S. 573 (1944); Murdock v. Pennsylvania, 319 U.S. 105 (1943).

In *Sherbert v. Verner*,[366] the Supreme Court for the first time struck down a measure as an onerous though indirect burden. *Sherbert* deals with a restriction on income—and a temporary one, at that—and gives no indication just how severe a financial burden is required. The severity of such restrictions is difficult to estimate. Is it more of a burden to deprive someone of twenty-two weeks of unemployment compensation than to make a business less profitable—or unprofitable and unsustainable?[367] Apparently so, though the Court does not explain how this calculation is made.[368] Are poor textile workers more easily burdened beyond constitutional endurance than prosperous butchers? Is capacity to pay to be taken into account in assessing the weight of the burden?

So far we have dealt with restrictions on income. Presumably the financial burden is the same when it consists of a requirement of outlay to find an equivalent to some public facility available only upon some religiously offensive condition (*e.g.*, compulsory ROTC at a state university). This might be remedied by an exception. But suppose the very use of the public facility is deemed offensive and the state requires the use of a private alternative. For example, is there an obligation to relieve people of the financial burden if they find their children's attendance at a secular public school religiously offensive?[369]

Police and fire protection and elementary schooling became free public services within the past century and a half. We may expect higher education, medical care, and numerous other services now on the private market to become so in the not too distant future. As more services are provided by government and more aspects of the environment are subjected to governmental regulation, must government arrange to avoid expense or inconvenience to the free exercise of religion? Where government exercises total control, it may be required to provide opportunities for religious expression. But short of such overall control, how much state intervention into a field is necessary to create an obligation to administer it to avoid expense and inconvenience to those who wish to utilize governmental services or meet governmental requirements without violating their religious scruples?

---

[366] 374 U.S. 398 (1963).

[367] See Braunfeld v. Brown, 366 U.S. 599 (1961).

[368] Both the dissenting opinion and Mr. Justice Stewart's concurring opinion in *Sherbert* disagreed with the Court's estimation of the relative burdens in *Sherbert* and *Braunfeld*. 374 U.S. at 417, 421.

[369] See the remarks of Mr. Justice Brennan in Abington School Dist. v. Schempp, 374 U.S. 203, 242 (1963), in which he implies that the state is forbidden to inhibit freedom of choice by diminishing the attractiveness of either alternative. If it is no business of the state to influence the choice between private and parochial schools, is it then forbidden to permit one to be more expensive than the other? See Mr. Justice Rutledge's more sanguine estimate of the price of religious liberty in Everson v. Board of Educ., 330 U.S. 1, 53, 59 (1947) (dissenting opinion).

Beyond this lies the question of whether the burdens need be financial. May the forbidden burden be psychological or social? Do people enjoy a right to be protected from humiliation and embarrassment as well as from financial loss?[370] Does the seriousness and stigma of criminal proceedings make such regulations more burdensome than mere financial detriment?[371]

Compelling Interests and Alternative Means

After the religious claim and the burdens upon it are evaluated, the state's interests and alternatives must be weighed so that a balancing can take place. The first question that arises is the nature of the "compelling interest" that the state must have. Does this mean merely a compelling interest in the object of the general regulation, or does it mean a compelling interest in *not* having some less religiously onerous alternative? I think the cases indicate that it means both. For if it meant only a compelling interest in the object to be secured by the general regulation, surely the state could always meet the test; the interest of the state in such matters as defense, health, financial security, administration of justice, and control of narcotics is generally thought to be compelling.[372] The test as actually applied in *Braunfeld*, *Sherbert*, *Jenison*, and *Woody* is whether the state has a compelling interest in *not* having an alternative arrangement. It must have a compelling interest in the marginal difference—not in the whole regulation. But this is a difficult test for the state

---

[370] *Compare* Mr. Justice Brennan's concurring opinion in Abington School Dist. v. Schempp, 374 U.S. 203, 289 (1963), *with* the concurring opinion of Mr. Justice Jackson *and* the dissenting opinion of Mr. Justice Reed in Illinois *ex rel.* McCollum v. Board of Educ., 333 U.S. 203, 233, 241 (1948) (no religious freedom problem in humiliation and embarrassment).

[371] As suggested by Mr. Justice Harlan, dissenting in Sherbert v. Verner, 374 U.S. 398, 421 (1963).

[372] There is language in *Sherbert* to the effect that the compelling interest must be a "paramount" rather than a merely colorable state interest. *Id.* at 406. But since the Court proceeds to distinguish the case before it from *Braunfeld* on the ground that the interests in the latter were sufficiently important, we may assume that the state interest need be no more paramount than the interest in an atmosphere of repose and recreation, or the like. Such a view turns up again in Sheldon v. Fannin, 221 F. Supp. 766, 774 (D. Ariz. 1963), where the court says that "where . . . a particular application of a general law not protective of some fundamental State concern materially abridges free expression or practice of religious belief, then the law must give way . . . ." The district court has no difficulty in concluding that the interest in classroom discipline is not sufficiently compelling to warrant denial of an exemption. But such a finding does not in any way depend upon limiting compelling interests to "paramount" or "fundamental" ones. Such a distinction would not only put the courts in the business of deciding niceties of political philosophy, but it would lead to anomalous results. The state would be unable to restrict A's religious liberty to prevent serious harm to B, but it would be able to restrict it to avoid incidental annoyance in forwarding its own "paramount" interests or "fundamental" concerns.

to meet. How can it show a compelling interest in not excusing a few religious objectors from a Sunday law, a health requirement, or a tax measure?

It should be noted that there are two kinds of alternative means. One is to revamp the general regulation so as to remove the religiously offensive feature—for example, by replacing a Sunday law with a one-day's-rest-in-seven law, by replacing a monogamous marriage law with one which permits other forms of marriage, and so on. But in no case has a court held any such possible alternative form of general regulation one which the state was constitutionally obliged to take.[373] The second kind of alternative is a religious exemption or exception, which leaves the general regulation intact but permits noncompliance with it for religious reasons. It is this kind of alternative that the courts have held to be constitutionally obligatory in *Sherbert, Jenison,* and *Woody*—but not in *Braunfeld.*

In what cases, then, does the state have a compelling interest in the avoidance of this "exception" alternative? The kinds of interests the state may have can roughly be divided into avoidance of (1) expense and administrative inconvenience, and (2) interference with implementation of public policy.[374] It would be a rare case in which, theoretically, no alternative means are possible. Hence, it is almost always a question of cost—in money and resources. The cost may be nothing or negligible—as it was in *Sherbert*, or as it might be in excusing someone from compulsory ROTC. On the other hand, the cost might be prohibitively great—for example, the cost of a second water system to supply unfluoridated water.

Most cases will fall somewhere in the middle. In *Braunfeld*, the additional administrative burden of a religious exception was thought to be a valid (if not itself conclusive) reason for avoiding it. But in *Sherbert* and *Woody*, the mere possibility of fraudulent claims was not sufficient. Courts must then decide how much time, money, effort, and efficiency the state must sacrifice in order to provide an alternative. The courts have not indicated just how far out of its way the state may reasonably be expected to go. Must it go further out of its way for a sizable minority than for a single eccentric? Are burdens cumulative? It would be strange if what was unconstitutional in a place with a sizable number of Orthodox Jews or Seventh Day Adventists was constitutional where there was a lone Sabbatarian.

---

[373] *But cf.* West Virginia State Bd. of Educ. v. Barnette, 319 U.S. 624 (1943), where it was held in effect that the state would have to find some alternative method of promoting national unity that did not involve compulsory affirmations of belief.

[374] These categories, of course, are not sharply distinguishable, for every expense and inconvenience diminishes the resources available for effectuating policy.

Second, suppose the granting of an exception interferes with some state policy. Presumably it always will to some extent. *Braunfeld* indicates that the state might conclude that exceptions would be fatally disruptive to its policies of providing a Sunday atmosphere of repose and recreation and discouraging religious preference in private employment. But suppose the threatened disruption is even more remote and speculative—for example, the threat to the administration of justice in *Jenison* or the threat to the defenses of Illinois in *Summers*.[375] Or suppose the state policy which is disrupted is one which aims primarily at securing the welfare of the objecting party himself—as in blood transfusion cases? Or those who voluntarily consort with him—as in snake-handling cases?

Here we may invoke a distinction with a long history in libertarian thought and read "compelling interest" to mean prevention of tangible harm to specifiable others without their consent.[376] Such a standard permits us to classify the cases along somewhat different lines. First there are those in which the state's asserted interest is primarily in the welfare of the party who has the religious objections—for example, blood transfusions. Second, there are cases where the asserted state interest is in the welfare

---

[375] *In re* Summers, 325 U.S. 561 (1945); *In re* Jenison, 265 Minn. 96, 120 N.W.2d 515, *rev'd*, 267 Minn. 136, 125 N.W.2d 588 (1963).

[376] See MILL, *On Liberty*, in ESSENTIAL WORKS OF JOHN STUART MILL 249 (Lerner ed. 1965). The various components of this standard were suggested from time to time by Mr. Justice Jackson. *Cf.* West Virginia State Bd. of Educ. v. Barnette, 319 U.S. 624, 630 (1943); Douglas v. City of Jeannette, 319 U.S. 157 (1943) (dissenting opinion). It is most elaborately suggested in his opinion in Prince v. Massachusetts, 321 U.S. 158 (1944). Concurring in the result, he dissented from the grounds of affirmance. Expressing his dissatisfaction with the age distinction by which the Court upheld the prohibition of a child's performance of an activity that the Court had recently held to be of great religious significance to Jehovah's Witnesses, he suggested a different
> method of establishing limitations which of necessity bound religious freedom.
>
> My own view may be shortly put: I think the limits begin to operate whenever activities begin to affect or collide with liberties of others or of the public. Religious activities which concern only members of the faith are and ought to be free—as nearly absolutely free as anything can be. But beyond these, many religious denominations or sects engage in collateral and secular activities intended to obtain means from unbelievers to sustain the worshippers and their leaders. . . . All such money-raising activities on a public scale are, I think, Caesar's affairs and may be regulated by the state . . . .

Id. at 177-78. It is difficult to see just how the narrower principle is derived from the broader effect-on-nonmembers test. Did a nine-year-old's street corner selling "affect or collide with the liberties of others"? How does merely addressing an appeal to the public affect them? It is difficult to resist the conclusion that Mr. Justice Jackson was speaking with at least one eye to the earlier house-to-house solicitation cases with their aggressive intrusions on privacy. But he does not attempt to distinguish the relatively passive distribution involved in *Prince*.

of those who are voluntarily consorting with the objector and exposing themselves to whatever dangers he presents—usually other members of the religious group, as is the case with snake handling, polygamy, fortunetelling, and faith healing. Third, there are those where the religious act or omission has some possible effect on unconsenting others, but in a gross and diffuse way—refusal of jury duty and army service, crop limitations, compulsory union membership, or Sunday law violations. Finally, there are those acts or omissions which affect specifiable individuals in tangible and measurable ways: the householders whose privacy is disturbed by insistent religious solicitors,[377] the employer liable for the death of a workman who refused standard medical treatment,[378] or the child entitled to support from a father whose religious duties forbade gainful employment.[379]

If we take "compelling interest" to mean a threat to the tangible interests of unconsenting others, we can then see whether the religious exception is an acceptable "alternative." There are some clear cases at each end of the scale. The exceptions in *Woody* and *Sherbert* would not seem to involve any tangible detrimental effects on others. The adverse effects are speculative and remote; and if they did occur, they would be widely diffused rather than impinging heavily on specifiable individuals. But between such cases at one end of the scale and the child support case at the other, there is a vast middle range of instances in which the probability and extent of the impact on others is not clear. In *Jenison* there was clearly a potential impact on a specifiable class of persons—litigants seeking jury trials. Is it really likely that exemption of religious objectors from jury duty will deprive someone of his right to a jury trial? The Minnesota Supreme Court found an "inadequate showing" that exemptions were "a serious threat to the effective functioning of our jury system . . . ."[380] Here courts can readily estimate the effects. But is it likely that others will be damaged by allowing some children to go unvaccinated in a county that has been free of smallpox for fifty years? Or that others will suffer if polygamy is permitted? Is it incumbent upon the state to demonstrate that such effects are overwhelmingly probable? A distinct possibility? Does a more remote possibility suffice where the magnitude of the danger is greater?

The determination of the degree of danger involves some very

---

[377] See Martin v. City of Struthers, 319 U.S. 141 (1943).
[378] Martin v. Industrial Acc. Comm'n, 147 Cal. App. 2d 137, 304 P.2d 828 (2d Dist. 1956).
[379] Pencovic v. Pencovic, 45 Cal. 2d 97, 287 P.2d 501 (1955) (father was head and founder of a religious society which would not increase its "gifts" to him for purposes of increasing support payments to minor child).
[380] 267 Minn. at 137, 125 N.W.2d at 589. The court did not consider another class of parties affected: those who might be called to jury duty as the result of the granting of exceptions.

vexing questions. Often the probability of adverse effects is a question of numbers. An exemption may be harmless precisely because few people avail themselves of it. For example, a few polygamous marriages might have little effect on other than consenting parties, but a larger number might deplete the supply of potential wives for nonpolygamists. But can numbers affect constitutionality, so that tiny sects are entitled to exemptions where larger ones are not? If an exemption is constitutionally obligatory because it is bearable, can the successful operation of a statutory exemption in itself elevate the exemption from statutory to constitutional status?

If we read "compelling interest" to mean an interest in preventing harm to unconsenting others, we encounter the problems of assessing the quality of that consent. Are concepts of fraud and misrepresentation relevant for the purpose of vitiating apparent consent?[381] And are children capable of genuine consent to parental religious foibles? When do they become capable of the quality of consent that will exclude the state from protecting them from their own religious proclivities or those of their parents?

Parents and Children

If we consider the somewhat differing position of children and adults in relation to the religious freedoms, we touch upon what is perhaps the ultimate dilemma of the first amendment. Religious freedoms are ones which children, soldiers, and others who do not enjoy full rights of citizenship enjoy—unlike, for example, political freedom or freedom of movement. In some instances we have seen that children enjoy "more" religious freedom than do adults. For example, in vindicating their claims to be free of religious ceremony and symbolism they have a stronger claim than Congressmen and "mature adults." Yet in other instances, like compulsory medical treatment or street corner solicitations, children may have less religious freedom than adults.

What explains the different positions of children in regard to establishment claims on the one hand and free exercise claims on the other? Presumably children need greater freedom from establishments because they are less mobile, less formed in their attitudes, more malleable, more susceptible to authority. Adults, on the other hand, are in control of their movements, more firm in their convictions, and less susceptible to the pretenses of authority. When it comes to free exercise claims, children are presumably less able to entertain views of their own, less equipped to assess the consequences, and again they are more susceptible to external authority—though this time it is that of the parents rather than the state. In short, the Constitution can be thought of as giving

---

[381] *Cf.* United States v. Ballard, 322 U.S. 78 (1944).

the child greater insulation from nonfamilial religious influences, but less freedom of performance. Or, to put it another way, children have primarily a freedom for the formation of conscience but less freedom to exercise it.

The religious freedom of children is usually visualized as a freedom to be inculcated and shaped, as if each child were a dormant member of the parental faith, waiting to be drawn out of his chrysalis by appropriate indoctrination. It is rarely conceived of as a freedom for the child to explore, to experiment, to encounter, and to examine alternative views and practices. While adults are free to exercise their consciences, children are free to form theirs along the parental model. Thus, in *Illinois ex rel. McCollum v. Board of Educ.*, students were only admitted to religious classes "'upon the express written request of parents, and then only to classes designated by the parents.'"[382] While the members of the Court differed over whether a parent might thus affirmatively employ state instrumentalities to mold the religious conscience of his child, no one denied that the parent had such a prerogative. Similarly, such bland common denominator exertions as the Regents' Prayer or Bible reading are seen by their proponents not as an official rival to the parental faith, but as something akin to the popular food additive which, having no flavor of its own, brings out the flavors which lie hidden in various foodstuffs. Religion in schools is supposed to be similarly free of sectarian flavor and in a similar miraculous way a sprinkle should elicit the respective religious flavors inhering in the children.

If parents cannot employ the machinery of the state to mold the conscience of the child, may they object to the state's implanting that which they consider detrimental to that conscience? The parent does not have a right to shield his child from all learning in secular subjects. Does he have a right to shield his child from a comparative religion course or from "objective" study of the Bible? More than from an economics course that he finds distasteful or immoral? If the state can inculcate in the child habits and attitudes in regard to citizenship, hygiene, and language which do not conform to those of the parent, may it also do so in matters of religion? Not in matters that are popularly regarded as religious, for here the state has no competence. While in other matters, the state may promulgate received opinion, it may not do so with what is in common estimation religion.

But suppose the matters are not commonly regarded as religious, but are religiously offensive in the parental eye: for example, that war may be justifiable, that creation took place some billions of years ago, that worldly endeavor is laudable. Is the state incom-

---

[382] 333 U.S. 203, 207 n.2 (1948). Compare Mr. Justice Frankfurter, concurring on the ground that the secular public school avoids divisive conflict by "leaving to the individual's church and home, indoctrination in the faith of his choice." *Id.* at 217.

petent to impart to the child anything that might influence his ultimate concerns and paramount beliefs? Public institutions, like others, do convey basic perspectives to the child; they influence views about ultimate things. How may we reconcile the right of the state to provide the best nonreligious education with the parent's right to insulate his child from religiously offensive views? Surely a parent has no right to have everything that offends him removed from the public schools.[383] His claim at most can be a claim for withdrawal. Since it is a free exercise claim,[384] it is immaterial that the matters are nonreligious in public estimation. In such claims, it is the claimant's characterization of religion that is controlling. By the compelling interest test such withdrawal should be permitted unless unconsenting others are adversely affected. Is the child an "other" whom the state may protect from parental shortsightedness? Is he capable of genuine consent?[385]

If the parent can insulate the unformed conscience of the child from what is in common estimation religion, may the state insulate the same unformed child from what is in the parental estimate religion? It may do so when it intervenes to protect his temporal welfare and substitutes its judgment for that of the parent who refuses medical attention to the child, keeps him out of school, or takes him along to distribute religious literature on street corners at night. But may the state undertake to protect the child from "oppressions" that interfere with his capacity for eventually making his own decisions about ultimate things? If the state can require literacy and other skills to make the child a good and useful citizen, may it require him to know some science, history, and comparative religion to make available to him the intellectual resources of the whole society in order to make choices about ultimate meanings?[386]

---

[383] Of course, the parent may to some extent protect the child from offensive views on such matters by sending his child to a private school or educating him at home. In religious matters, however, he can have the offending material kept out of the school entirely. Teaching on these other things may express accepted views, but there are no accepted views on religion.

[384] See J supra.

[385] Compare the Minersville school superintendent's denunciation of the adverse ruling of the court of appeals as "based . . . on the assumption that little children have the right and ability to formulate religious beliefs and conscientious objections." MANWARING, RENDER UNTO CAESAR— THE FLAG-SALUTE CONTROVERSY 116 (1962).

[386] If the state may properly expose children to a variety of points of view, even those which are offensive to their religions, may the state exclude from its presentation those viewpoints which are in common estimation religious. Cf. Jones, Church-State Relations: Our Constitutional Heritage, in RELIGION AND CONTEMPORARY SOCIETY 156 (Stahmer ed. 1963). Or, to turn this around, may the state exclude certain secular knowledge because it may interfere with religious preconceptions? In Scopes v. State, 154 Tenn. 105, 289 S.W. 363 (1927), the court found that a law prohibiting the

This brings us to a veritable thicket of questions to which religious groups give widely varying answers. What is the nature of the religious capacity of the child? Is he capable of exercising religious conscience? Is religious conscience a faculty of mature individuals which depends on knowledge and experience? Or is it a special faculty which operates independently of external experience and worldly knowledge? Does such a conscience contribute to citizenship? Any answers are going to be more congenial to some religions than to others.[387]

These questions have a secular and public side. Is our pluralistic society to be an "open society" in which people enjoy freedom of choice in basic lifestyle upon condition of undergoing preparation for choice by contact, exposure, and exchange in the social and intellectual arena of the wider society? Or is it to be a diverse society in which groups that prefer withdrawal and self-segregation are tolerated? Are "closed" subgroups to be permitted to perpetuate their self-contained isolation by the inculcation and isolation of their young? Or must they compete for the ideological loyalty of their young in the wider social arena?

Robert Dixon discerns in the first amendment a commitment to "an open and common society" which values shared experience and free association rather than self-segregation.[388] But it is not essential or perhaps even desirable for an open and pluralistic society that each of its components has the same open and pluralistic character. The larger society may have something to gain from the toleration and encouragement of relatively self-contained communities. Again we reach a question of costs and amounts. At what point are the enrichments of diversity outweighed by the virtues of enlightenment?[389] At what points do the tensions en-

---

teaching of the theory of evolution did not violate the state constitutional provision forbidding "preference . . . to any religious establishment or mode of worship," since "the denial or affirmation of such a theory does not enter into any recognized mode of worship." *Id.* at 118, 289 S.W. at 366-67.

[387] Mr. Justice Jackson, dissenting in Everson v. Board of Educ., 330 U.S. 1, 23-24 (1947), observes that the public school
> is organized on the premise that secular education can be isolated from all religious teaching so that the school can inculcate all needed temporal knowledge and also maintain a strict and lofty neutrality as to religion. The assumption is that after the individual has been instructed in worldly wisdom he will be better fitted to choose his religion.

He points out that this view is "more consistent" with Protestant than Catholic views.

[388] Dixon, *Religions, Schools and the Open Society: A Socio-Constitutional Issue*, 13 J. Pub. L. 267 (1965).

[389] "In a mass society, which presses at every point toward conformity, the protection of a self-expression, however unique, of the individual and the group becomes ever more important. The varying currents of the subcultures that flow into the mainstream of our national life give it depth and beauty." People v. Woody, 61 Cal. 2d 716, 727, 40 Cal. Rep. 69, 77, 394 P.2d 813, 821 (1964).

gendered by diversity endanger the unity of the society? It seems doubtful to me that the first amendment supplies any clear guide one way or the other; it protects exposure and exchange, but it also gives some protection to those who wish to insulate themselves.

Establishment Limitations

In some eyes religious exceptions and exemptions not only encounter difficulties in application, but also contravene the establishment clause. Such a view has been taken by a few courts,[390] but current decisions do not support this objection.[391] Nevertheless, these objections are worth considering, since they raise the general problem of the nature of constitutional limitations on governmental recognition of free exercise claims, and thus the relationship between the first amendment's religion clauses.

At the outset it is difficult to see that exceptions have any of the coercive power of establishment in its various historic meanings. It takes considerable conceptual perseverance to think of Seventh Day Adventists, Orthodox Jews, Quakers, or Jehovah's Witnesses as members of an established state religion. Again there is not the element of institutional collaboration that is thought to characterize establishments. As Mr. Justice Brennan said in *Sherbert*, the exception "does not represent that involvement of religious with secular institutions which it is the object of the Establishment Clause to forestall."[392]

The establishment argument may take a broader ground. First, it may be said that a religious exemption is an establishment because it constitutes aid to religion.[393] It should be clear that aid (in the sense of facilitating the avowed objectives of some person or group) is not in itself a decisive test of an establishment. Indeed, we are often told on good authority that there is no greater aid to religion than its strict separation from the state.[394]

---

[390] City of Shreveport v. Levy, 26 La. Ann. 671 (1874) (Sabbatarian exception violates state constitutional provision forbidding preferment of any sect). *Cf.* Commonwealth v. Cooke, 7 AMERICAN L. REGISTER 417 (Police Court of Boston, Mass. 1859).
[391] Sherbert v. Verner, 374 U.S. 398 (1963); Commonwealth v. Arlan's Dep't Store, 357 S.W.2d 708 (Ky.), *appeal dismissed*, 371 U.S. 218 (1962); George v. United States, 196 F.2d 445 (9th Cir.), *cert. denied*, 344 U.S. 843 (1952). Compare the abrupt disposition of the establishment argument in the *Selective Service Draft Law Cases*, 245 U.S. 366, 389-90 (1918).
[392] Sherbert v. Verner, 374 U.S. 398, 409 (1963).
[393] See the opinion of Mr. Justice Douglas, dissenting from the dismissal of appeal in Arlan's Dep't Store v. Kentucky, 371 U.S. 218 (1962).
[394] Mr. Justice Black, writing for the majority in Illinois *ex rel.* McCollum v. Board of Educ., 333 U.S. 203, 212 (1948), states that "the First Amendment rests upon the premise that both religion and government can best work to achieve their lofty aims if each is left free from the other within its respective sphere." *Cf.* Engel v. Vitale, 370 U.S. 421, 431-32 (1962) (majority opinion of Black, J.). More succinctly, Mr. Justice Douglas, con-

Besides this there is probably nothing that aids religion more, in the mundane reckoning by which an outsider may calculate such advantage, than those measures for the welfare of the general public which provide for the security of persons and property, police and fire protection, safe drinking water, and good roads. Such aid is clearly permissible since it is not directed specifically to religious institutions and in most cases benefits individuals selected by nonreligious criteria, who in turn give their energies and resources to religious purposes. The chain of unconstitutionality is broken by the intervention of individual choice.

But suppose people are chosen for a particular beneficial treatment on the ground that their objection to a general regulation is a religious one. Is an arrangement to relieve religious objectors of what would otherwise be an oppressive and disadvantageous regulation an establishment because it facilitates their religious observance or their financial well-being? We come here to the second facet of the argument: that such aid is an establishment because the religion of those excepted is "preferred" over other religions or over nonbelievers. The Supreme Court of Kentucky, upholding a Sabbatarian exemption to a Sunday closing law, found that the law did not prefer the religion of the groups protected thereby; rather it avoided penalizing them for observing another Sabbath.[395] In *Sherbert*, Mr. Justice Brennan rejected the notion that there was any preferment involved: the exemption is "nothing more than the governmental obligation of neutrality in the face of religious differences . . . ."[396]

The relationship between "neutrality" and "religious differences" is the heart of the problem. There is general agreement that the first amendment enjoins upon the state some kind of neutrality in regard to religion. But neutrality is in itself an equivocal standard. American law is in the larger sense not neutral among religions. In defining the boundaries within which neutrality must operate, the first amendment is a charter for religion as well as for government.[397] It is congenial to those religions which favor private and voluntary observance rather than those which favor official support of observance. It favors those religions which prefer social and spiritual sanctions over those which would employ official force to support their social and ritual prescriptions.

---

curring in *Engel*, tells us that "the First Amendment teaches that a government neutral in the field of religion better serves all religious interests." *Id.* at 443.

[395] Commonwealth v. Arlan's Dep't Store, 357 S.W.2d 708 (Ky.), *appeal dismissed*, 371 U.S. 218 (1962).

[396] 374 U.S. at 409.

[397] Religion is not merely a datum for constitutional law, unaffected by it. It is, in part, the product of that law. The American legal setting has made, and presumably will continue to make, a profound contribution toward shaping religion in the United States. Compare the remarks of Mr. Chief Justice Hughes, note 269 *supra*.

It favors groups which are not exclusive in their claims and are willing to tolerate the presence of alternative and hostile views. It is not so congenial to religions which purport to supply obligatory principles for the governing of society or believe that it is necessary to extirpate error.

Neutrality, then, does not mean a regime equally congenial to all; this would be a self-contradictory ideal so long as religions differed in their views of a good regime. It means a regime in which all are treated alike. But people may be so different in important respects that the application to them of the same rule impinges on them differently. May "religious differences" ever be a difference which the state takes into account in deciding that people are not alike? Is the neutrality required of the state neutrality in the sense of similarity of treatment regardless of differential impact? If so, then religion cannot be a relevant basis of classification. But if neutrality means comparability of effect or impact, then we may have to sort people out by their vulnerability to certain things.

Which of these neutralities is required? *Sherbert* suggests that when others are not thereby disadvantaged, the state must move from strict neutrality (identical treatment with indifference to varied effects) to a broader neutrality (differentiated treatment to achieve comparability of effects). The state must, in *Sherbert*, extend unemployment benefits "to Sabbatarians in common with Sunday worshippers."[398] Here it was clear that the state was already solicitous of the scruples of Sunday worshippers, though not of Saturday ones.[399] In such a case, it is easy to appreciate that the exception is restorative or equalizing. It puts the minority in the same position that the majority enjoys. The exception prefers the religious minority only if it is looked at in isolation. Once it is looked at as a counterbalance to a wider regulation which has already accommodated the religious scruples of the majority, it is seen not as preferential, but as restorative.

In this respect, *Sherbert* is the direct descendant of the *Sunday Closing Law Cases*. There the members of the Court, with one exception,[400] found no establishment in permitting the state to accomplish an admittedly secular purpose in a way that incidentally accommodated the majority religious groups.[401] But if the

---

[398] 374 U.S. at 409.
[399] See note 161 *supra*.
[400] Mr. Justice Douglas read the establishment clause as forbidding any law which puts the force of government behind any religious practice in spite of an admixture or overlay of secular purposes. McGowan v. Maryland, 366 U.S. 420, 564, 571 (1961).
[401] The majority of the Court indicates that since the preponderant purpose of the law is secular, a slight admixture of helpfulness to religion is not enough to invalidate it. Gallagher v. Crown Kosher Super Market, 366 U.S. 617, 627 (1961). Mr. Justice Frankfurter (with whom Mr. Justice Harlan joins) seems to go further and sees no establishment limita-

state can thus accommodate the majority, may it not then restore the balance by an equivalent concession to the minority where this accommodation of the majority disadvantages the minority? While such a "restorative" position applies in the case of Sabbatarian exemptions from Sunday laws, where the state has already accommodated the religious majority, does it also apply to draft exemptions, compulsory ROTC, and health regulations, where there is no special concession to the majority?

But can it be said that the kind of disparity found in *Sherbert* between the treatment of majority and minority is a unique or unusual thing? Whatever seriously interferes with majority religious beliefs and practices is unlikely to become a legal requirement—for example, work on Sunday or Christmas. And whatever the majority considers necessary for its religious practice is quite unlikely to be prohibited by law. And whatever the majority finds religiously objectionable is unlikely to become a legal requirement—for example, medical practices which substantial groups find abhorrent, like contraception, sterilization, euthanasia, or abortion. Exceptions then, give to minorities what majorities have by virtue of suffrage and representative government. The question is not whether the state may prefer these minorities, but whether it may counterbalance the natural advantages of majorities.

We come to a third facet of the establishment argument. To administer a religious exemption, the state must distinguish between religious objectors and others. Is the employment of a religious classification in itself a violation of the establishment clause? The first amendment religion clauses have been read as forming a single standard which forbids any use of religion as a ground of classification.[402] This would preclude the state from using religion as a ground for issuing special dispensations. Religiously motivated activities (or omissions) would stand on exactly the same ground as similar activities impelled by nonreligious motives.

But should the first amendment be read to prohibit all religious classifications? Neutrality in the sense of avoidance of religious classifications is clearly one of the central themes in the American legal disposition toward religion. But it does not describe the whole of that disposition. Rather than a single comprehensive principle, American law has provided an armory of alternative responses to claims for religious freedom. These include not only neutrality (in the sense of avoidance of religious classifications), but also notions of separation and accommodation. All of these

---

tion unless the purpose of the enactment is primarily (or perhaps purely or exclusively) religious. McGowan v. Maryland, 366 U.S. 420, 465-67 (1961).

[402] See KURLAND, RELIGION AND THE LAW: OF CHURCH AND STATE AND THE SUPREME COURT 16-18 (1962).

responses have some grounding in constitutional history and current practice. At present, religion in America is not entirely on a par with other activities, as the no-classification principle would imply; in some respects religion occupies a unique and exceptional position because of the concurrent impulses toward separation and accommodation. Thus government is prohibited from aiding or promulgating specifically religious values in the same ways that it may aid and promulgate political, educational, esthetic, and recreational values.[403] At the same time government cannot regulate religious activities to the same extent that it may regulate other activities.[404]

The pattern in which these alternative responses to religious claims have been combined has been changing throughout our history. There are at present broad areas in which the appropriate response is fairly clear. In other areas there is overlap and ambiguity. The principle of no religious classifications does not offer us a standard for selecting the response appropriate in each case. Instead it proposes to eliminate the ambiguities by eliminating separation and accommodation as distinct elements in this pattern. It discards these elements of the multiplex tradition on the ground that a single neutrality principle can better serve the agreed objectives of the first amendment's religion clauses.[405] But while there is indeed a wide area of agreement on the ends to be served by these clauses, there are also disagreements that are more than differences about the methods for achieving given ends. The legal posture toward religion is ambiguous not only because of disagreement about means, but because both official and lay understandings have invested these clauses with a simultaneous commitment to a number of things which are not wholly compatible: to avoidance of religious strife and freedom of religious expres-

---

[403] Compare the dissenting opinion of Mr. Justice Jackson in Everson v. Board of Educ., 330 U.S. 1, 26 (1947), in which he discerned "a difference which the Constitution sets up between religion and almost every other subject matter of legislation, a difference which goes to the very root of religious freedom . . . ." That is, the first amendment takes "every form of propagation of religion out of the realm of things which could directly or indirectly be made public business and thereby be supported in whole or in part at taxpayers' expense." *Ibid.*

[404] Some outstanding examples of this special position are the following. (1) While religious claims may be tested for sincerity, they are uniquely immune from being tested for truth, credibility, and comprehensibility. See p. 264 *supra*. (2) Religious bodies enjoy an immunity from state interference in their internal government which is greater than that enjoyed by other associations. Kedroff v. Saint Nicholas Cathedral, 344 U.S. 94 (1952). (3) Claims for religious freedom will be vindicated on behalf of persons who ordinarily cannot press other first amendment claims—children and prisoners, for example, and perhaps soldiers. See pp. 284-88 *supra*. (4) Religious claims are in some instances to be characterized as such by the subjects themselves, and this characterization cannot be challenged by a court.

[405] See KURLAND, *op. cit. supra* note 402, at 111-12.

sion; to immunity for religious activities and to majority rule; to the promotion of an open society and the protection of the closed sect; to equal treatment in law and to the promotion of equality in fact; to provision of a congenial environment for religion and abstention from aid to religion. The problems of selecting and combining these varied impulses in particular situations seem unavoidable. The problems would exist even if the no-classification principle were expanded to cover the field. I, for one, am not convinced that they would be appreciably closer to resolution.

We come to the fourth and final facet of the establishment argument. It is said that the state cannot distinguish between religious noncompliance and noncompliance based on some other ground, thereby putting religious dissenters in a better position. In *Sherbert*, the state was apparently under no compulsion to extend similar indulgence to one whose objection to Saturday work stemmed from personal, political, or recreational motives. What makes religion a suitable ground for differentiation?

If religion includes whatever is central and paramount and pervasive in the individual's life, then we may distinguish between patterns of action that are based on central and pervasive beliefs and actions subject to expediential alteration. May the state differentiate between people who are acting on beliefs that occupy this central position in their lives and those whose objection is based on circumstantial and transient grounds?

In matters of politics, esthetics, charity, entertainment, and economics, there is freedom of opinion and expression; but actions are subject to regulation, and government may to some extent ordain normative standards of action in these things. But government has no power to decide or promulgate what is normative in matters of religion. For example, government may legislate standards of child care (while respecting differing opinions on the subject), but it may not make certain religious practices normative. In matters of religious action as well as opinion, there is to be no majority rule. And if government has less power to promulgate norms of action in what is religion in common estimation, it may perhaps use a different standard in forbearing from action that touches what is religious in some private estimation. Disabled from establishing the ultimate concerns of the majority, government may be permitted to exercise greater forbearance where it promulgates standards which inadvertently impinge on the ultimate concerns of the minority. It may be allowed to distinguish between action which touches ultimate concerns on the one hand, and the more transient and expediential ones on the other.

What lies just behind the establishment objection and is so troubling to many critics of exceptions is not any establishment in the historic sense, but the particularism that is involved in measuring by religious criteria the applicability of rules to different people. Such particularism seems to abandon our general impersonal territorial law, oriented to the offense (or transaction) and to substitute special law dependent on the personal qualities of the actor. The Court in *Reynolds* observed that such a course would introduce a new element into our law. This "new" element is of course a very old one. In the long historical view, it is the incidence of laws along strict territorial lines that is the new element. Many matters that we consider to be naturally subject to regulation along territorial lines were once regulated along communal lines. Modern law has shifted regulative power from communal groups to territorial majorities—that is, to geographically concentrated minorities. Exceptions for religious objectors do not represent a return to personal law in the old style—for individuals enter the exempted class by choice rather than by ascription. But exceptions are a departure from territoriality designed to give to minorities who cannot get representation through the political process those same protections from oppression that the majority obtains through the political process.

The understanding that there is to be no official position in matters of religion secures this to the majority, for the religious matters in which there can be no official position are those matters defined as religious by the majority. But minorities may have different definitions of what is religious; there is an overlap between what the minority thinks of as religious matters, in which there should be no majority rule, and what the majority thinks of as nonreligious matters, subject to majority rule. The question then is whether the state should forbear to enforce its views in this area of overlap in those instances where it can get along without the compliance of the minority.

Where the state does forbear and creates an exception, may it do so for only some religionists and not for all?[406] *Torcaso* and *Seeger* seem to imply that any exception for religious dissenters must extend to all who qualify as religious under the broad permissive sense of ultimate concern or paramount conviction, for government may not choose among religions.[407] May government distinguish between systems of ultimate belief which label themselves as religious and those which do not?[408] May it justify the

---

[406] See State ex rel. Heck's Inc. v. Gates, 141 S.E.2d 369, 385 (W. Va. 1965), where the court upheld a Sunday closing law which contained a Saturday exemption against a free exercise challenge of Muslim and Druse merchants who observe Friday as their Sabbath.

[407] United States v. Seeger, 380 U.S. 163 (1965); Torcaso v. Watkins, 367 U.S. 488 (1961).

[408] Can government deny similar forbearance to such groups as communists, who seem to have all the characteristics of religion under the new test except the use of the religious tag? See Comment, *Defining Religion: Of God, the Constitution and the D.A.R.*, 32 U. CHI. L. REV. 533, 553 n.101 (1965). Presumably such a differentiation should be required to meet the same compelling interest test.

use of a narrower category for some particular purpose by showing a compelling interest in refusing to extend the exception to the full ambit of those who qualify under the broad definition of religion?[409]

What is the value of governmental forbearance in the marginal area: is it a good thing that people be free to endanger themselves by avoiding medical treatment or fondling snakes or to be imposed upon with messages from Saint Germain? Most religious exceptions involve things over which reasonable men (in the current fashion) do not differ. The question, though, is not whether we think these exceptions lead to good results but whether we may employ our "reasonable" perspective in making this assessment. Should we not permit private judgment to prevail in assessing the results to the objector himself and confine ourselves to evaluating the results to the community of government's withholding its hand? Where such forbearance fails to protect others, there need be no exception. Perhaps the strongest justification for exceptions is to habituate society to respect people's judgments about their own welfare and to induce an appreciation of the limits of our ability to set people right. But while exceptions may thus induce a general tolerance of dissent that is more valuable than the minor untidiness of administration, there are on the other hand genuine dangers in extensive use of religion as a standard in public life. The possibilities for exacerbating tensions among groups are obvious and need not be detailed here.

Conclusion

If religious exceptions do not automatically violate establishment limitations, it still remains unclear at what point they are not merely permitted but are required by the free exercise clause. As we have seen, a number of factors are involved: the good faith of the claimant and the extent of the burden on his free exercise, which in turn involves an assessment of the centrality of the practice to his religion as well as the cost to him of the prohibition or requirement. On the government's side there is the determination of the importance of the regulation, the nature and probability of adverse effects on others, and the cost and feasibility of alternatives.

The difficulty of combining these into a standard to serve as a genuine guide to courts faced with claims for religious exemptions suggests that courts should enter this area with extreme caution. Cases at the end of the scale, where considerations of centrality, burden, and lack of adverse effects overlap and reinforce each other diverge quickly into situations involving imponderable calculations of religious centrality or the quality of consent (particularly by children), and the probability of indirect but adverse ef-

---

[409] See text accompanying note 336 *supra*. For some examples of judicial response to such differentiation, see notes 193, 195 & 406 *supra*.

fects. Certainly courts should be hesitant to create constitutionally obligatory exemptions in situations where the bearableness of the exemption turns on numbers. It would be unseemly if an exemption lost its constitutional status when the religious group or groups that utilized it became too numerous.

It should be recalled that a court ordinarily has other options: it may sometimes read a religious exemption into the statute before it without unfair distortion; or it may simply indicate to the legislature that an exemption is permissible there. This has the advantage of leaving the final say to a legislature better equipped to assess shifting probabilities of harm. Even a limited judicial response of this kind may steer legislatures toward sensitivity to the problems of religious minorities in the welfare state.

The use of the religious exemption device raises fundamental questions about the shape of our society—questions which are not within the exclusive competence of courts to answer. In an era when both religion and government are undergoing rapid change, the lack of a single comprehensive principle for responding to all claims for religious freedoms may not be entirely a disadvantage. The existence of competing and overlapping principles in this area can give courts and legislatures flexibility in making past understandings relevant to emerging experience. Case law, after all, is among other things a way of getting along with a plurality of principles which need not be integrated in the abstract, but only in specific concrete contexts. Such a piecemeal case law process of resolution, aiming at a workmanlike development of middle-level principles, may do more to clarify particular areas of the law than attempts to find a single comprehensive principle to dispose of all religious freedom problems. Just as the Constitution, no matter how thick the gloss, does not provide a remedy for every injustice, so it does not contain satisfactory answers to all intellectual problems.

HARVARD LAW REVIEW

RELIGIOUS LIBERTY, NONESTABLISHMENT, AND DOCTRINAL DEVELOPMENT
PART I. THE RELIGIOUS LIBERTY GUARANTEE

Donald A. Giannella *

> *The content given the religious freedom guarantees of the first amendment has changed significantly as the role of government has become more pervasive. While the principle of "strict neutrality" formerly could reconcile the free exercise and the establishment clauses, the increasing scope of governmental regulation has led to conflict between these clauses as individuals have sought on religious grounds to escape the regulatory grasp of government. The problem is particularly difficult when the effectiveness of the regulatory scheme may be impaired if numerous exceptions are granted. Professor Giannella examines the elements of the balancing test applied by the courts in assessing religious liberty claims, and concludes by analyzing the problem of defining "religion" for first amendment purposes.*

I. INTRODUCTION

THE enduring hope that our democracy rests on a demonstrable rule of law rather than an apparent rule of men has inspired legal scholars to search for neutral principles of constitutional law. Such an enterprise involves the formulation of general principles — rules where possible — to guide judicial decision making so that it can rest "on analysis and reasons quite transcending the immediate result that is achieved."[1] Most appropriately, serious efforts have been made to discern such principles in the sensitive area encompassed by the two religion clauses of the first amendment.[2] Not too surprisingly such efforts have failed the acid test of predicting the outcome of constitutional litigation.

---

* Professor of Law, Villanova Law School; A.B., Harvard, 1951, LL.B., 1955.

[1] Wechsler, *Toward Neutral Principles of Constitutional Law*, 73 HARV. L. REV. 1, 15 (1959).

[2] P. KURLAND, RELIGION AND THE LAW (1962) [hereinafter cited as KURLAND]; Weiss, *Privilege, Posture and Protection: "Religion" in the Law*, 73 YALE L.J. 593 (1964).

The most cogent and celebrated attempt has been that of Professor Kurland, who neatly synthesized both clauses into a unitary principle of strict neutrality.³ According to this principle "religion may not be used as a basis for classification for purposes of governmental action, whether that action be the conferring of rights or privileges or the imposition of duties or obligations." ⁴ But, the Supreme Court has rejected this principle in both *Sherbert v. Verner*,⁵ which compelled South Carolina to extend unemployment compensation benefits to claimants who refused to accept available employment when to do so would interfere with the observance of their Sabbath, and *In re Jenison*,⁶ which vacated, for reconsideration in light of *Sherbert v. Verner*, a Minnesota court's judgment holding a woman in contempt of court for refusal to serve as a juror because of religious scruples. A few commentators have criticized the Court for its decisions in these cases,⁷ but they seem to be in the minority. Even Professor Kurland does not seem unduly disturbed by the results of these cases.⁸ He is resigned to the fact that the Court is determined to avoid endowing constitutional doctrine with the clean and simple lines which satisfy the sensibilities of the legal craftsman. He does, however, yearn wistfully for coherence in results. Of course, all who subscribe to a rule of law which requires the rational exposition of judgment and the achievement of the minimal consistency necessary to satisfy elementary notions of justice will concur in this wish.

The free exercise and establishment clauses express an underlying relational concept of separation between religion and secular government. This concept must be continually reformulated if it is to adapt to changing ideas concerning the types of human experience encompassed by the term "religion" and the kinds of action within the proper domain of the state. Any attempt to articulate a relational concept of separation in one or more fixed formulae may well be unsatisfactory since environmental circumstances change so rapidly. As to the free exercise clause, for instance, it is axiomatic that its scope must vary with

---

³ KURLAND.
⁴ *Id.* at 18.
⁵ 374 U.S. 398 (1963).
⁶ 375 U.S. 14 (1963). The Supreme Court of Minnesota reversed the conviction. 276 Minn. 136, 125 N.W.2d 588 (1963) (per curiam).
⁷ *See, e.g.,* Weiss, *supra* note 2, at 620-22.
⁸ Kurland, *Foreward — Church and State in the United States: A New Era of Good Feelings,* 1966 WIS. L. REV. 215.

the breadth of governmental regulation if the individual is to enjoy some minimum of freedom of action in religious matters. In a political society characterized by significant governmental disability and wide personal autonomy, religious interests need not make special claims to achieve a wide zone of immunity. But in a society where governmental regulation is pervasive and individual freedom generally limited, religious interests must make special claims vis-à-vis the state if they are to enjoy an equally wide ambit of action. Similarly, the establishment clause embodies a concept of separation of church and state which takes on precise meaning only in light of prevailing assumptions as to the appropriate sphere of action for each institution. As the role of the state, with the passage of time, transcends traditional boundaries and assumes new dimensions, the idiomatic meaning of "separation" must be revised to conform with the new realities if original purposes and expectations are to be realized.

Any critical frame of reference for evaluating the Court's performance in the area of religious liberty must rest in significant part on history. However, any thoroughgoing effort to interpret the religion clauses of the first amendment by resorting to the original understanding of the authors and ratifiers of the Constitution is apt to be regarded as a misguided, if not dangerous enterprise.[9] Certainly, attempts to resolve twentieth century church-state problems by asking ourselves how the entire pantheon of the founding fathers would have resolved them will prove futile.[10] Perhaps more conducive to a coherent resolution would be a resort to the thinking of one man, such as Madison, who played a more or less decisive role in the formulation of the religion clauses. But even though such resort would provide *an* answer, it is unlikely that this answer would be both a constitutionally appropriate and politically satisfactory resolution of present-day problems. For when we turn to Madison's theories concerning religious freedom and nonestablishment, we must inevitably find them encrusted with certain implicit assumptions which were products of prevailing social, political, and economic conditions. Doctrinal formulations designed to achieve certain ends may achieve indifferent or perverse results when the assumptions on which they rest change. As the social, political, and

---

[9] *See* School Dist. of Abington Township v. Schempp, 374 U.S. 203, 232-41 (1963) (Brennan, J., concurring).

[10] Summers, *The Sources and Limits of Religious Freedom*, 41 ILL. L. REV. 53, 55-58 (1946).

economic milieu evolves, so must the content given the first amendment.

Resort to the past, therefore, should not attempt to capture the intentions of the founding fathers in rigidly precise verbal formulae; instead, the proper objective of an historical search should be the determination of the "historic purpose of the First Amendment." [11] In other words, the Court, in giving content to the first amendment, should attempt to incorporate the human purposes and values underlying it. We find considerable agreement as to the core values and purposes embodied in the free exercise clause, even though the main thrust of the establishment clause has been the subject of considerable disagreement among legal scholars.[12] The difficult problems of interpreting the free exercise clause arise when its values are interpolated into a context of problems and needs not anticipated by the authors of the Constitution; these difficulties might well compel the Court to follow a highly particularistic approach, and to a considerable extent this has proven unavoidable.

The more recent free exercise cases frankly adopt a balancing of competing interests test. But this approach involves certain hazards, since a balancing test tends to substitute subjective judgment for objective standards. The choice, however, need not be between an inflexible, formalistic approach and an unprincipled, wholly intuitive process of decision making. Ad hoc judgment can be subjected to more or less objective criteria.[13] The human values and political objectives influencing our constitutional ideals can be defined with some degree of clarity; the means whereby these values and ends are to be attained can undergo critical analysis and rationalization; guidelines can be established to direct the accommodation of competing ends and values; and in those hopefully few cases where a head-on conflict is unavoidable, a hierarchy of values and ends can be elaborated. If subjected to this analysis, prevailing judicial decisions interpreting the free exercise clause can fit into a more or less rational pattern. Unfortunately, and perhaps inevitably, this coherence may simply

---

[11] Jones, *Church-State Relations: Our Constitutional Heritage*, in RELIGION AND CONTEMPORARY SOCIETY 156, 173 (H. Stahmer ed. 1963).

[12] The establishment clause is treated at length in Part II of this article to appear in a future issue.

[13] Professor Freund suggests that "A course of decisions may be principled without being doctrinaire." P. FREUND & R. ULICH, RELIGION AND THE PUBLIC SCHOOLS 12 (1965).

be the result of rationalization after the fact of decision and may do little to illuminate the course of future judgment.

This paper attempts to provide a rather simple scheme of the elementary factors weighed by the Court in evaluating religious liberty claims. As a corollary to this inquiry I will try to indicate the impact of expanding government on the development of doctrine concerning the free exercise clause. The Court's performance in this area is examined critically to determine if it accords with the enduring consensus that religious liberty is one of the most fundamental and important values in American life. Some of the Court's decisions appear to fall short of this mark.

This shortcoming, I believe, is the result of judicial acquiescence in the sometimes unpalatable fact that democratic government acts to reinforce the generally accepted values of a given society and not merely the fundamental ones which relate to its political structure. There is language in the second flag-salute case [14] that might be taken to indicate the contrary, and the non-establishment principle is sometimes regarded as forbidding government preferences in a wide area of behavior traditionally encompassed by the term private morality; [15] but in fact, the Court has not adopted a balancing test that turns on careful assessment of conflicting needs and vindication of the ones shown to be more compelling, though some recent cases imply that this is the proper approach. Instead, it has followed a course that ultimately intimates a judicial approval of established orthodox values. The Mormon polygamy cases [16] and the cases upholding compulsory vaccination requirements stand as recurring testaments to the Court's preference for prevailing morality over the religious liberty of radical dissenters.

Contemporary changes in the traditional understanding of what is religious must also be taken into account to equip eighteenth

---

[14] West Virginia State Bd. of Educ. v. Barnette, 319 U.S. 624, 642 (1943) (dictum). Mr. Justice Jackson, speaking for the Court, said: "If there is any fixed star in our constitutional constellation, it is that no official, high or petty, can prescribe what shall be orthodox in politics, nationalism, religion, or other matters of opinion or force citizens to confess by word or act their faith therein." Mr. Justice Jackson here was clearly referring to freedom of opinion only, and to symbolic acts expressing internal commitment. It is most unlikely that he meant to indicate the government's inability to require conformity of behavior to accepted moral norms, such as monogamy.

[15] Henkin, *Morals and the Constitution: The Sin of Obscenity*, 63 COLUM. L. REV. 391, 407–11 (1963).

[16] *E.g.*, Cleveland v. United States, 329 U.S. 14 (1946); Davis v. Beason, 133 U.S. 333 (1890); Reynolds v. United States, 98 U.S. 145 (1878).

century ideas of religious liberty for their work in the twentieth century. Some attention will be given to the difficulties created by changing concepts of religion. The frequently expressed hope that the Court will not undertake to decide what is religious seems to be a vain one, and I am led to the reluctant conclusion that the Court must adopt some elementary natural theology when presented with a claim that does not rest on an articulated body of doctrine fitting into traditionally accepted categories of what is religious.

II. Historical Evolution of the Religious Liberty Concept

The original constitutional consensus concerning religious liberty was an outgrowth of Protestant dissent and humanistic rationalism, the viewpoints that dominated the thinking of the authors of the Constitution.[17] These two perspectives conjoined to place the individual conscience beyond the coercive power of the secular state. For the Protestant dissenter there was a Higher Power claiming his ultimate allegiance. For the rational humanist the individual was anterior to the state; in the social contract with the state he had properly reserved the right to his opinions and beliefs on matters of ultimate concern. This respect for the inviolability of conscience lies at the heart of the free exercise clause of the first amendment.[18]

The free exercise clause must also be measured in terms of the limited historic evils against which it was directed. Government oppression had generally been of two kinds: direct restraints on belief and worship, and imposition of civil disabilities because of religious affiliation.[19] In the post-revolutionary era, these twin evils could be eliminated and inviolability of conscience secured against the federal government by simply placing matters of religion beyond the competence of the central government. The political philosophy of such leading exponents of religious liberty as Jefferson and Madison led them to favor local government of limited powers, devoted essentially to the maintenance of basic social order by a series of purely negative restraints. The possibility that such limited government would encroach upon free-

---

[17] D. Fellman, Religion in American Public Law 8 (1965); M. Howe, The Garden and the Wilderness 1–10 (1965); A. P. Stokes & L. Pfeffer, Church and State in the United States 3–4 (1964).

[18] See Freeman, *A Remonstrance for Conscience*, 106 U. Pa. L. Rev. 806 (1958).

[19] C. Antieau, A. Downey & E. Roberts, Freedom from Federal Establishment 10–29 (1964).

dom of religious action was minimal once the subject of religion was divorced from the political sphere. This was particularly true of the federal government, which possessed only those limited powers expressly delegated to it by the Constitution.

The first important religious liberty case to be decided by the Supreme Court, *Reynolds v. United States*,[20] rested on the principle that religion "was not within the cognizance of civil government." The rule adopted by that case was that the free exercise clause in effect protected only religious belief. Religiously motivated action was to be subjected to the police power of the state to the same extent as would similar action springing from other motives. This distinction between belief and action was adequate to achieve the purposes of the free exercise clause in a rural, agrarian society, for under it not only freedom of belief would be insured, but also a significant degree of religious expression. Furthermore, the notion of freedom of religious belief carries with it the correlative idea of freedom of expression in ceremonial forms. Although the Court did not advert to this point, it seems unlikely that it would have permitted interference with symbolic religious rituals unless they infringed significantly upon the public health, welfare, or morals. If not, the free speech guarantee of the first amendment would assure protection for such forms of expression. That guarantee would also protect the freedom to proselytize, which could have been limited by the legitimate exercise of the police power pursuant to a strict reading of the *Reynolds* test because of attendant potential for public annoyance and discomfort.

Professor Kurland finds the *Reynolds* decision to be essentially sound because it rests in the final analysis on the strict principle of neutrality, despite the Court's inartistic reliance on the dubious action-belief distinction.[21] An excerpt from Jefferson's letter to the Danbury Baptists, relied on by the *Reynolds* Court, indicates that the principle of strict neutrality probably most nearly expresses the original understanding of the free exercise clause; it also reveals the limitations of that principle. Jefferson had written: [22]

> Believing with you that religion is a matter which lies solely between man and his God; that he owes account to none other for his faith or his worship; that the legislative powers of the govern-

---

[20] 98 U.S. 145, 163 (1878).
[21] KURLAND at 22.
[22] Quoted in 98 U.S. at 164 (emphasis added).

ment reach actions only, and not opinions, — I contemplate with sovereign reverence that act of the whole American people which declared that their legislature should "make no law respecting an establishment of religion or prohibiting the free exercise thereof," thus building a wall of separation between church and State. Adhering to this expression of the supreme will of the nation in behalf of the rights of conscience, I shall see with sincere satisfaction the progress of those sentiments which tend to *restore man to all his natural rights, convinced he has no natural right in opposition to his social duties.*

The italicized language betrays the presupposition that there are correlative limitations on man's "social duties" to match his "natural rights," because the conviction that a man has no natural right in opposition to his social duties assumes we are considering basic, widely recognized duties such as refraining from ritualistic murder or the ceremonial use of dangerous animals. The language is not at all convincing if we consider the "social duty" of refraining from the use of sacramental wine during national prohibition; only slightly more convincing if we consider the "social duty" of refraining from labor on the common day of rest; and hardly relevant if we consider the "social duty" which requires a claimant for unemployment benefits to stand ready to work on Saturday.

The style and scope of twentieth century government has led to its involvement with ends and values of varying importance. In addition, as the examples concerning prohibition and unemployment compensation demonstrate, the regulatory means selected to attain these ends and values do so with varying degrees of proximity and necessity. An absolute ban on the consumption and manufacture of alcoholic beverages serves on its outer limits only the end of efficient and effective enforcement; limited use of alcohol for sacramental purposes would not be inconsistent with any of the other ends sought by prohibition. For those who take inviolability of conscience as seriously as did the founding fathers, the minimal governmental interest in absolute prohibition could hardly justify the serious interference with worship entailed by a ban on sacramental wine. Failure to grant an exception for such ceremonial uses because of adherence to the strict principle of neutrality would subvert the historic purpose of the free exercise clause.

It must be recognized, however, that to grant an exemption from general governmental regulations solely for religious reasons violates the historic purpose of the establishment clause. As Professor Howe has pointed out, that clause rested on an eighteenth century political theory of federalism which disabled the national government from taking positive action to make religious liberty effective.[23] Although he recognizes that the framers of the Constitution may have believed religious liberty to be the most important substantive civil right, he concludes that the first amendment only codified a guarantee insuring religion immunity from interference by the *federal* government, with the states free to adopt their own practices and policies in this area; and it was not conceived as giving rise to a right in the individual to have that government help him pursue his religious aims.

It seems most unlikely that the authors of the first amendment appreciated the inner tension between the two religion clauses. Now that this conflict has emerged with the increased scope of governmental activity and has become complicated because of the first amendment's applicability to the states under the fourteenth amendment,[24] it is necessary to accommodate the two clauses. This accommodation requires a value judgment as to which one is to become dominant when there is a conflict — the one premised on a vital civil right, or the one premised on an outmoded eighteenth century political theory. The resolution was preordained — to pose the conflict is to resolve it. Despite its invocation of the principle of neutrality, the Supreme Court in *Sherbert v. Verner*[25] held that the state must make special provision to relieve religious liberty from restrictions imposed by generally legitimate governmental regulations. The neutrality which the Court had in mind must have been similar to that proposed by Professor Katz,[26] resting primarily on the free exercise clause and permitting the state to relieve religious liberty from state-imposed burdens.

This reading of the first amendment demands a balancing test — where the interest of the state incidentally giving rise to interference with religious liberty is minor and the religious interest burdened is substantial, the historic purpose of the free exercise clause would suggest that the state be compelled to grant an

---

[23] Howe, *The Constitutional Question*, in FUND FOR THE REPUBLIC, RELIGION AND THE FREE SOCIETY 49, 51-52 (1958).
[24] Illinois *ex rel.* McCollum v. Board of Educ., 333 U.S. 203 (1948) (establishment clause); Cantwell v. Connecticut, 310 U.S. 296 (1940) (free exercise clause).
[25] 374 U.S. 398 (1963).
[26] *See* W. KATZ, RELIGION AND AMERICAN CONSTITUTIONS (1964); Katz, *Freedom of Religion and State Neutrality*, 20 U. CHI. L. REV. 426 (1953).

exemption. Recent decisions of the Supreme Court indicate a trend toward adoption of such a balancing test, especially evident in *Sherbert*: "It is basic that no showing merely of a rational relationship to some colorable state interest would suffice [to justify a substantial infringement of religious liberty]; in this highly sensitive constitutional area, '[o]nly the gravest abuses, endangering paramount interests, give occasion for permissible limitation' . . . ." [27]

A thoroughgoing balancing test would measure three elements of the competing governmental interest: first, the importance of the secular value underlying the governmental regulation; second, the degree of proximity and necessity that the chosen regulatory means bears to the underlying value; and third, the impact that an exemption for religious reasons would have on the over-all regulatory program. This assessment of the state's interest would then have to be balanced against the claim for religious liberty, which would require calculation of two factors: first, the sincerity and importance of the religious practice for which special protection is claimed; and second, the degree to which the governmental regulation interferes with that practice.

III. Weighing the Interests: The Public Interest

Judicial inclination to be more explicit in assessing the governmental interest than in evaluating the competing religious claim suggests that the critical element in a religious liberty case is assessment of the governmental interest. In making this assessment great attention has been given to the importance of the underlying secular value involved and the proximity and necessity of the regulatory means to achieve it. In some of the more recent decisions there is language indicating that the courts are also calculating the costs of a limited exemption for religious reasons, but this approach has been given effect in only certain limited circumstances. A survey of the cases decided since 1940 will give some idea of the comparative weight given by the courts to different elements of the public health, welfare, and morals when they come into conflict with claims for religious liberty.

A. *Public Health and Safety*

Of the traditional categories of the police power, the courts rank health and safety very highly when they conflict with claims

---

[27] 374 U.S. at 406 (citation omitted).

of religious liberty. In *Sherbert* the Supreme Court observed that cases upholding legislative restrictions on religious liberty involved religious practices which "invariably posed some substantial threat to public safety, peace or order." [28] In support of this proposition the Court cited *Jacobson v. Massachusetts*,[29] in which it had upheld a state compulsory vaccination requirement. Although *Jacobson* was decided prior to extension of the free exercise clause to the states under the fourteenth amendment, it has since been cited by state courts as authority for the constitutionality of various health and safety measures. For example, state courts have overridden claims of religious liberty in allowing the criminal prosecution of faith healers who practice medicine without a license,[30] the prohibition of snake handling as part of religious ceremonies,[31] and the compulsory vaccination of school children.[32] As the North Carolina Supreme Court has put it, when public safety is pitted against religious liberty "[t]he authorities are at one in holding that the safety of the public comes first." [33]

In most of these cases the evil, such as smallpox, was assuredly grave, and the regulatory means chosen, such as compulsory vaccination, was directly and most effectively aimed at the hazard involved. But little consideration was given to whether a religious exemption could properly be tolerated because of its minimal impact on the scheme of regulation. This question was raised in the guise of clear and present danger rhetoric in a recent Arkansas case, *Wright v. DeWitt School District*,[34] where parents sought an order exempting their children, on religious grounds, from a compulsory vaccination prerequisite for school attendance. The complaint alleged that there was no immediate, grave or present danger of a smallpox epidemic, and in support of this assertion averred that no case of the pox had occurred in the county for more than fifty years and that complainant's children had regularly attended school without being vaccinated. Plaintiff urged

---

[28] *Id.* at 403.

[29] 197 U.S. 11 (1905).

[30] *E.g.*, People v. Handzik, 410 Ill. 295, 102 N.E.2d 340 (1951), *cert. denied*, 343 U.S. 927 (1952); State v. Verbon, 167 Wash. 140, 8 P.2d 1083 (1932).

[31] *E.g.*, Kirk v. Commonwealth, 186 Va. 839, 44 S.E.2d 409 (1947); Lawson v. Commonwealth, 291 Ky. 437, 164 S.W.2d 972 (1942).

[32] *E.g.*, Cude v. State, 237 Ark. 927, 377 S.W.2d 816 (1964); Mosier v. Barren County Bd. of Health, 308 Ky. 829, 215 S.W.2d 967 (1948); Vonnegut v. Baun, 206 Ind. 172, 188 N.E. 677 (1934).

[33] State v. Massey, 229 N.C. 734, 735, 51 S.E.2d 179, 180, *appeal dismissed sub nom.* Bunn v. North Carolina, 336 U.S. 942 (1949).

[34] 238 Ark. 906, 385 S.W.2d 644 (1965).

reversal of a dismissal on the ground that the defendant's demurrer had admitted the facts alleged. The Arkansas Supreme Court upheld the dismissal, but avoided the embarrassment of repudiating the clear and present danger test by taking "judicial notice of the very nature of this loathsome disease and that it presents a clear and ever present danger which is best controlled by health measures such as the one in question." [35] The opinion did not, on the other hand, conclude that exemption for religious purposes *alone* would present a clear and present danger of epidemic; it did not even consider this question.

It is hard to reconcile this approach, which accurately reflects prevailing judicial attitudes, with the historic purpose of the free exercise clause. Although *Wright* is rationalized as requiring claims for religious liberty to yield when they infringe the rights of others,[36] a limited exemption from vaccination probably creates a risk — and a minimal one at that — only for those who avail themselves of it. Presumably others will be protected by the generally widespread system of vaccination.

There are two possible justifications for failure to investigate the substantiality of the risk arising from a limited exemption. One rests on the fact that the compulsory vaccination cases, like many others concerning matters of health, usually involve children. The state, as *parens patriae*, is justified in exercising a certain degree of control over the child to insure his minimal well-being.[37] The second is attributable to the presence of another value hovering in the background when serious diseases are involved — the public sense of security. This element reinforces the frequently expressed concern for the rights of others, but this only states the conclusion. It could be argued that just as religious rights cannot unduly infringe upon other rights, neither can the latter encroach upon the former.

What adjustment should the courts make when the right to religious liberty comes into conflict with the right to move freely without the imagined fear of contracting a loathsome disease? A utilitarian calculus would vindicate a choice made in favor of maximum security because the overwhelming majority would feel the need for it. Striking such a balance apparently achieves the legitimate end of favoring the felt needs of the majority; it also works, however, to vindicate a hierarchy of values in which the

---

[35] *Id.* at 909, 385 S.W.2d at 646.
[36] *Id.* at 912–13, 385 S.W.2d at 648.
[37] *See* p. 1395 *infra.*

religious liberty of the unconventional ranks rather low. In the matter of vaccination the public demands maximum security so fervently because it so weakly appreciates the claim of those who wish to escape vaccination. Consider the contemporary hazard to small children from drownings in backyard pools. The danger of drowning is statistically much greater than the current risk of smallpox,[38] though even in our present state of national affluence it is doubtful that the number of pool owners constitutes a substantial percentage of our population. Yet the suggestion that such pools be prohibited or subjected to costly safety requirements, such as mechanical pool covers, would undoubtedly meet great resistance and fail. Thus, despite the creation of a hazard which is apparently greater than would be entailed by religious exemption from vaccination, the backyard swimming pool is tolerated, indeed is approved, because of the high esteem given to physical fitness in our conception of the good life.

The North Carolina Supreme Court is undoubtedly correct in placing public safety first. But is it consistent with the ideal expressed in the first amendment to have religious liberty show greater deference to public safety than is required of the leisured pursuits of the affluent? There are legislative bodies which have recognized that religious liberty deserves at least a corresponding degree of tolerance and have granted a religious exemption from compulsory vaccination requirements.[39] It is doubtful, however, that the courts will compel such deference, the sweeping dictum of *Sherbert*[40] notwithstanding. Although the courts are frequently regarded as the keepers of the majority's conscience, the kind of religious tolerance which exempts individuals from public health requirements should perhaps be expressed by the legislature, which is directly responsible to the electorate. The courts may, with some justification, be reluctant to force the community to expose itself to even the smallest risks, especially where the evil involved is such that should disaster strike the courts would incur intense bitterness.

---

[38] In the one to four year age group accidental drownings are the third most frequent cause of death, and a large percentage arise from drownings in private pools. Klebba, *Accidental Deaths in the United States* in ACCIDENTS 25 (U.S. Dept. of Health, Educ. and Welfare reprint 1965). No deaths from smallpox have been reported in the United States since 1960. N.Y. Times, Nov. 20, 1966, § 4, at 8, col. 3 (city ed.).

[39] For an example of such an exemption, as well as the problems it creates, see State v. Miday, 263 N.C. 747, 140 S.E.2d 325 (1965).

[40] P. 1390 *supra*.

People v. Woody,[41] the California decision upholding the use of peyote in religious ceremonies despite a general criminal prohibition, does indicate something of a shift in judicial attitude, but not one radical enough to reverse the holdings in the compulsory vaccination cases. Drug addiction and severe mental disturbance undoubtedly pose grave hazards to public health, safety, and order; but even the prosecution conceded in argument both that there is no permanent deleterious effect on the physical health of peyote users and that the drug is non-addictive. Rather, the public health grounds urged on appeal by the prosecution were the tendency of Indians to resort to peyote as a substitute for medical care and its propensity to induce the use of habit-forming drugs. Both arguments were rejected because of the insufficiency of evidence on the record. Thus, unlike the compulsory vaccination cases, the court found that the regulatory means selected — the absolute prohibition of peyote — was not closely related to the alleged public health objectives. Nevertheless, a difference in mood, indicating increased judicial respect for the religious liberty claim, could be discerned. Whereas judicial notice had sufficed to support the claimed effectiveness of compulsory vaccination in the *DeWitt* case, the California Supreme Court searched the record closely for evidence to substantiate the state's claims, and found it wanting. Relying heavily on the Supreme Court's opinion in the *Sherbert* case, the California court demanded that proof be adduced to support the compelling interest of the state and found "untested assertions" inadequate to justify limitation of religious liberty.

Another aspect of the court's reasoning is encouraging for those who would grant liberal religious exemptions when the exemptions would have minimal impact on the total scheme of regulation. The state had put forward as an additional reason to deny exemption the difficulties of enforcement that would be engendered by its grant. Reference was made to the danger of spurious claims and the difficulty of determining whether the asserted religious beliefs were sincerely held. In rejecting this reason the court necessarily calculated the impact of a religious exemption, but it did so only for the limited purpose of determining whether the exemption might create problems of enforcement against those not exempted. The court did not purport to measure the extent to which the general effectiveness of a highly desirable statute would be lessened by the removal of the exempted class from its

---

[41] 61 Cal. 2d 716, 394 P.2d 813, 40 Cal. Rptr. 69 (1964).

coverage, yet this would seem to be the critical determination.

A final distinction should be noted in contrasting *Woody* with the compulsory vaccination cases. The *Woody* court emphasized that the consumption of peyote was central to the worship of the Native American Church. Absolute prohibition of its use would make the practice of that religion impossible. This continuing and devastating degree of interference with religious liberty stands in sharp contrast to the more limited impact on a person's total religious orientation caused by a single instance of compulsory vaccination.

If *Sherbert* does mark a shift in the Supreme Court's attitude, as *Woody* would lead us to believe, some existing precedents may be seriously limited, if not overruled. Among the cases giving broad vent to the public health concept, the Supreme Court's decision in *Prince v. Massachusetts* [42] seems most vulnerable. In that case the Supreme Court upheld a statutory ban on the public sale of periodicals and other publications when applied to minor Jehovah's Witnesses distributing religious pamphlets on the public streets. The Court's opinion recognized that the state, as *parens patriae*, was properly concerned not only with the well-being of the child, but also with "the healthy, well-rounded growth of young people into full maturity as citizens, with all that implies" [43] in a democracy. But against this heightened interest of the state in his welfare stands the child's claim to religious liberty, diminished by reason of his minority. The Court said: "Parents may be free to become martyrs themselves. But it does not follow they are free, in identical circumstances, to make martyrs of their children before they have reached the age of full and legal discretion when they can make that choice for themselves." [44]

This passage suggests an ideological rift between the Court's views concerning religious liberty and the views of those invoking the protection of the free exercise clause. To the latter, religious liberty as an ideal meant essentially the absence of governmental restraint on the activities of young and old alike as they sought to do God's will. To the Court, religious liberty as an ideal required the free and voluntary choice of a person come of age. Consequently, the Court's concern for the child's freedom to engage in religious activities, which were hazardous to his physical

---

[42] 321 U.S. 158 (1944).
[43] *Id.* at 168.
[44] *Id.* at 170.

and mental growth, was limited by its very conception of religious liberty.

However, even after giving weight to the increased concern of the state in well-developed citizens on the one hand and discounting the claim to religious liberty because of the child's minority on the other, *Prince* seems to clash with the mood expressed in *Sherbert*. In *Prince* the Court went so far as to hold that the state could prohibit the child from public distribution of religious literature even when accompanied by an adult, but it is difficult to conceive how in these circumstances there was substantial danger that the child would be subject to the evils against which the prohibition was directed. As Mr. Justice Murphy observed in his dissenting opinion: "The state . . . has completely failed to sustain its burden of proving the existence of any grave or immediate danger to any interest which it may lawfully protect." [45] If by requiring the state to show more than a rational connection between a public health regulation and the end to which it is directed the *Woody* opinion has accurately interpreted *Sherbert*, the authority of the *Prince* case has been seriously undermined.

B. *Public Peace and Order*

The necessity of maintaining the public peace is one aspect of public safety which the courts have very effectively harmonized with religious liberty. Here the Supreme Court has turned to the "clear and present danger" test enunciated in the free speech cases;[46] this seems most appropriate in this area where most of the risks of public disturbance arise from provocative religious expression. Actual breaches of the peace, even religiously motivated, of course cannot be tolerated in organized society. The issue is the degree of freedom to be extended to activities which threaten to bring about breaches of the peace. Absent the existence of a widespread religious conspiracy to subvert the existing social order, the evils threatened, though serious, can usually be managed effectively by application of the police power after the commencement of an actual disturbance. Regulatory provisions designed to restrain free religious expression must therefore be limited to occasions when there is an immediate threat of public disturbance. In effect, the "clear and present danger" test reduces the process of balancing competing interests to a general formula for cases where the religious interest in free speech is

---

[45] *Id.* at 174.
[46] Cantwell v. Connecticut, 310 U.S. 296 (1940).

opposed to the public interest in curbing more or less limited breaches of the peace.

C. *Public Welfare Regulations*

Public welfare regulations not concerned with health, safety or maintenance of public peace encompass a multitude of activities and seek a multitude of ends. Because of this variety generalizations are hazarded at the risk that the particular facts of a given case may warrant a unique result. However, it is safe to say that governmental interests in this area generally have not been considered as compelling as in the area of public health and safety. But, this generalization must be further refined by examining the cases within the analytical framework of two categories: the first contains police regulations relating to public comfort and convenience; and the second contains economic regulations affecting substantial social and individual interests.

1. Public Comfort and Convenience. — Religious liberty is almost always ranked above public comfort and convenience. As one commentator has put it: [47]

> It is not enough to justify state restraint that the religious expression or conduct be considered absurd by majority public opinion or even that it be offensive or annoying to the majority, or to other groups, in the community. If there is no demonstrable threat to public health, safety, or morals, the exercise of religious conviction is outside the sphere of lawful public regulation.

Accordingly, outright prohibition [48] of, or requirement of a license [49] for the distribution of religious literature on the public streets, and even on the privately owned common thoroughfares of a company town,[50] have been struck down; an ordinance prohibiting the ringing of door bells or sounding of knockers by persons distributing advertising circulars was also invalidated in *Martin v. Struthers* [51] when applied to the door-to-door distribution of handbills announcing a religious meeting. All of these cases involved Jehovah's Witnesses, a fact enhancing the claim for exemption because of the importance to that denomination of hand distribution of religious tracts.[52] Although these cases were

---

[47] Jones, *supra* note 11, at 181.
[48] Schneider v. State, 308 U.S. 147 (1939).
[49] Lovell v. City of Griffin, 303 U.S. 444 (1938).
[50] Marsh v. Alabama, 326 U.S. 501 (1946).
[51] 319 U.S. 141 (1943).
[52] *See* pp. 1419–20 *infra*.

decided on freedom of speech grounds, the involvement of the free exercise of religion gave the claims added weight. Thus, the Supreme Court, in *Breard v. City of Alexandria*,[53] sustained from a free speech attack an ordinance prohibiting home solicitation by peddlers when applied to solicitors for subscriptions to literary periodicals, distinguishing *Struthers* on the ground that it involved a noncommercial invitation to religious services.

However, the state may place public comfort and convenience above claims for religious exemption when the activities involved are unnecessary to the pursuit of important religious objectives. Thus, although a municipal ordinance licensing the use of sound trucks to disseminate religious doctrine in public places was struck down,[54] the Court suggested that the noise involved could be controlled by regulating decibels as well as the hours and place of public discussion.[55]

Where the regulatory scheme has implications extending beyond comfort and convenience and touching upon public health and safety, the attitude of the courts stiffens. The *Prince* case [56] exemplifies such a disposition, as does *Cox v. New Hampshire*,[57] where the Supreme Court upheld a licensing requirement for parades on public streets. In the latter case, the Court was convinced that public safety required control of parades to keep open heavily traveled roads. But the decision was tempered by the observation that there was ample opportunity for the public expression of religious views on city streets without the necessity of staging a parade. The latter observation indicates that the Court here viewed the claim to parade freely as one chiefly involving religious speech rather than a religious service. This characterization aided it in striking a balance in favor of the governmental interest in avoiding traffic congestion because the ban on parades did not unduly hamper the Jehovah's Witnesses in reaching the public with their message.

2. *Economic Regulations.* — The courts will not require the state to grant an exemption from economic regulations to religious interests if a preferential benefit would be conferred. Exemption under these circumstances would not simply relieve the religious practitioner from a burden on the free exercise of religion, but would also turn the regulatory scheme into a device for ad-

---

[53] 341 U.S. 622 (1951).
[54] Saia v. New York, 334 U.S. 558 (1948).
[55] *Id.* at 562.
[56] 321 U.S. 158 (1944). *See* pp. 1395–96 *supra*.
[57] 312 U.S. 569 (1941).

vancing a particular religion. Such a preference would violate the nonestablishment principle, regardless of the interpretation given the establishment clause,[58] and engender the interreligious disputes and rivalries which that clause was meant to avoid. Thus, the general rule appears to be that religious exemptions from economic regulations are denied where uniformity of treatment goes to the essence of the regulatory scheme.

A typical economic regulation requiring uniform treatment to achieve its goals of market control and social justice is the governmental limitation of agricultural production. Accordingly, no farmer is permitted to market or use wheat beyond his allotted quota on the basis of religious scruples.[59] An economic regulation of the variety not requiring uniformity of treatment was involved in *Sherbert*.[60] The requirement that Mrs. Sherbert stand ready to accept suitable work was designed to protect South Carolina's unemployment insurance fund from claims inspired by indolence. Recognition of Mrs. Sherbert's claim accorded with the central aims of the unemployment compensation scheme to alleviate individual hardship caused by enforced unemployment and really did not conflict with the purpose of the requirement to accept suitable work. On the other hand, to condition the payment of benefits on her willingness to accept work on the Sabbath did involve a substantial, albeit an indirect burden on the practice of her religion. Thus, applying a balancing test and in the absence of proof demonstrating the magnitude of the risk that the insurance fund would be depleted by spurious claims, the Court's allowance of an exemption was both easily made and appropriate. But Mr. Justice Brennan, writing for the majority, went further and said that "even if the possibility of spurious claims did threaten to dilute the fund and disrupt the scheduling of work, it would plainly be incumbent upon the appellees to demonstrate that no alternative forms of regulation would combat such abuses without infringing First Amendment rights."[61]

The sweep of this language would appear to augur well for re-

---

[58] The broadest reading given the establishment clause would outlaw all aids to religion. Everson v. Board of Educ. 330 U.S. 1, 15 (1947); *see also id.* at 33 (Rutledge, J., dissenting). The narrowest reading would outlaw state action which tended to confer preferential benefits on particular sects or members of particular sects. C. ANTIEAU, A. DOWNEY & E. ROBERTS, *supra* note 19, at 205.

[59] United States v. Kissinger, 250 F.2d 940 (3d Cir.), *cert. denied*, 356 U.S. 958 (1958).

[60] Sherbert v. Verner, 374 U.S. 398 (1963).

[61] *Id.* at 407.

ligious liberty claims; even thoroughly secular programs would have to be structured, so far as possible, to avoid interfering with substantial claims of religious freedom. Read in the context of the Court's decision, however, this language is not quite so revolutionary. In Mr. Justice Brennan's view, the central purpose of the statute was provision of public benefits for those suffering because of enforced unemployment. For the state to withhold such benefits because of the claimant's decision to observe the tenets of her religion raised the question of whether the state would be withholding public benefits on the basis of an unconstitutional condition, the sacrifice of free exercise rights. It may be that the state must be especially careful in placing ancillary conditions on public benefits; only those conditions which achieve their ends with the least possible interference with religous liberty are permissible.

Mr. Justice Harlan, joined in dissent by Mr. Justice White, viewed the statute differently. He emphasized that the main purpose of the legislation was to provide relief when *"work was unavailable"*;[62] if for personal reasons, including religious ones, a claimant chose to reject available work, the benefits of the program were forfeited. Whereas Mr. Justice Brennan emphasized the public benefit aspects of the legislation, Mr. Justice Harlan seemed to emphasize its character as an economic measure to counteract the impact on the economy of widespread unemployment. But the majority's position accords more closely with the realities, for unemployment compensation programs, including South Carolina's, invariably excuse a claimant from taking available work when there are compelling personal reasons for rejection, such as hazard to health.[63] If these excuses are consistent with the overall objectives of unemployment compensation programs, the first amendment calls for at least similar departures from uniformity in recognition of religious scruples which dictate the refusal of Saturday work by a conscientious Sabbatarian.

The limited scope of the *Sherbert* case is suggested by the failure of the Court to overrule *Braunfeld v. Brown*,[64] which had held that the first amendment does not require exemption from Sunday closing laws for an Orthodox Jewish merchant who observes Saturday as the Sabbath and thereby suffers loss of business on two days rather than one. Indeed, three members of the Court,

---

[62] *Id.* at 419 (italics original).
[63] *E.g.*, S.C. CODE ANN. § 68-114(3)(b) (1962).
[64] 366 U.S. 599 (1961).

among them the two dissenters, thought that *Sherbert* required an overruling of *Braunfeld*. Justices Harlan and White emphasized the potentially greater interference with religious freedom caused by Sunday closing laws than that caused by the loss of unemployment benefits, for in *Braunfeld* one of the defendants had alleged that enforced closure on Sunday would eventually force him out of business. The financial loss of invested capital and the foreclosure of a congenial and satisfactory means of livelihood seem more onerous costs of religious observance of the Sabbath than the loss of temporary economic benefits suffered by Mrs. Sherbert.

There are cogent reasons, however, to distinguish the *Braunfeld* case from *Sherbert*, notwithstanding the compelling religious interest in the former case. At first glance one might be disposed to classify Sunday closing laws as simply involving the secular values of public convenience and comfort. This was Mr. Justice Brennan's dissenting view in *Braunfeld*, so it was easy for him to require the state to rank personal religious liberty over collective comfort and convenience. He did, however, recognize that the idea of a common day of rest implies uniformity of impact. Consequently, an exemption from such a regulation would do more than entail difficulties of administration. It would directly interfere with the underlying purpose of the statute. Thus, exemption from the Sunday closing laws would involve greater deference by the state to religious interests than was involved in the *Sherbert* case, where dispensation from the Saturday work requirement actually advanced the fundamental welfare purpose of the legislation to alleviate individual hardship. However, even taking this into account, it is difficult to quarrel with Mr. Justice Brennan's conclusion that the free exercise clause should require religious exemptions if the only cost would be a Sunday which was a little noisier and a little busier.[65]

In writing the majority opinion for the Court in *Sherbert*, Mr. Justice Brennan distinguished the *Braunfeld* case on two grounds. First, he adverted to the administrative problems of enforcing a ban which operated in part on two days rather than one, a difficulty compounded by the necessary inquiry into the sincerity of those claiming a religious exemption. But, even granted that the danger of spurious claims might be greater where loss of Sunday profits rather than loss of unemployment benefits is concerned, this difficulty does not clearly outweigh the claim for religious liberty. The fact that many jurisdictions have managed to tolerate

---

[65] *Id.* at 614.

Sabbatarian exemptions indicates that they are feasible from an enforcement point of view; the public interest in public comfort and convenience can apparently be served to a significant extent even with the religious exemption.

Although Sunday closing legislation can be categorized as merely promoting the interest in public convenience and comfort, it impinges on very substantial business interests. Since a necessary and primary effect of the regulation is therefore economic, the demand for uniformity of treatment is much greater than when only public convenience is involved. Hence, the second of Mr. Justice Brennan's distinctions is very weighty. He adverted to the possibility that the exempted class might obtain so great an economic advantage as to render the statutory scheme unworkable. If the religious exemption were to confer a preferential economic benefit, it would pose a conflict with the nonestablishment principle. Although an exemption from Sunday closing laws for Sabbatarians is only designed to redress the imbalance that arises when conscientious Sabbatarians must refrain from labor and commerce on two days instead of one, the exemption may overshoot this mark. The absence of competition on Sunday may generate profits in excess of those that could be made on a general business day. An unqualified exemption for Sabbatarians might occasion such a degree of competitive strife as to generate strong pressures to remove the Sunday closing mandate altogether. Thus, if exemptions are to be allowed they should be carefully tailored to remove the more oppressive effects of Sunday closing laws while limiting the possibility of economic preferences.

An acceptable minimum exemption might not remove all the disadvantages created by the closing laws. The size of the Sabbatarian business establishment could be a limiting factor, for the larger the business organization, the greater is the likelihood that a competitive advantage will accrue from exemption and the greater would be the concern of competitors. It would seem that consequences of the Sunday closing laws bear most heavily on the small merchant, who is the one most apt to be forced out of business by adverse conditions.[66] Accordingly, a limited exemption in favor of the small family-run business might be allowed.[67] But the difficulties involved demand empirical investigation, thus

---

[66] *See, e.g.,* People v. Finklestein, 38 Misc. 2d 791, 239 N.Y.S.2d 835 (Crim. Ct., New York City), *aff'd per curiam,* 41 Misc. 2d 35, 244 N.Y.S.2d 727 (Sup. Ct. 1963), *aff'd,* 14 N.Y.2d 608, 198 N.E.2d 265, 248 N.Y.S.2d 889, *cert. denied,* 377 U.S. 1006 (1964).

[67] Such an exemption is found in the New York Sunday Closing statutory scheme. N.Y. PEN. LAW § 2154 (McKinney Supp. 1966).

putting the legislature in a better position than the judiciary to structure an exemption scheme. On the other hand, should Justices Harlan and White in a subsequent Sunday closing law case feel bound by *Sherbert* to grant a religious exemption, and should the *Braunfeld* dissenters — Justices Brennan, Douglas, and Stewart — maintain their original position, *Braunfeld* will be overturned. Such a coalition, however, would seem unlikely.

D. *Public Morality*

In refusing to grant Mormons an exemption from federal laws prohibiting bigamy, the Court in *Reynolds* observed that the free exercise clause could never excuse criminal conduct. This per se approach, which always ranks public morality over religious liberty, reflects the sound judgment that when criminal prohibitions are consistent with general due process limitations protecting the liberty of all citizens, no special exception should be made for religious liberty. But if this per se approach is to be adopted, the problem of classifying criminal conduct becomes extremely important. The distinction between *malum prohibitum* and *malum in se*, perhaps discredited in other areas, is a useful concept for our purposes. Those offenses designed to serve only the ends of public health, safety, or welfare by the imposition of fines and imprisonment, the *mala prohibita*, are appropriately subjected to the balancing approach when there is conflict with religious liberty. Prohibitions based on the moral censure of society, the *mala in se*, constitute the "true crimes" which must be penalized uniformly throughout the entire community.

Objection might be taken to the per se approach itself on the ground that it violates the spirit if not the letter of both religion clauses by always elevating the morality of the majority over the religious liberty of the individual. But where the morality of the majority, as enacted into law, clearly reflects important secular values, no problem arises. The state is only engaging in its basic functions when it protects life by the law of homicide and property by the law of theft. But when it seeks to protect the aspirational aspects of morality, *i.e.*, those precepts and values designed to improve the quality of the individual's life and to elevate the tone of interpersonal relationships, problems arise. This kind of morality is analogous to religion; indeed, its origins will frequently be located in religious values and its continued acceptance may depend in large part on the continuing vitality of those values.

Professor Henkin has suggested that the enforcement of this

morality may violate the establishment clause.[68] To avoid this violation he would require government regulation to serve only "apparent, rational and utilitarian social purpose[s]."[69] He maintains that "a state may not legislate merely to preserve some traditional or prevailing view of morality."[70] An extension of this reasoning would carry the notion of strict governmental neutrality toward religion to its logical, but impossible, extreme. This extension requires a state extricated from its history and culture, then somehow programmed anew to create a society in which property and social relationships are arranged with justice but without deep inquiry into basic religiously-based human values. But if at its inception the society is characterized by social inequality, why should the state, on utilitarian grounds, require the elite to diminish the aristocratic quality of their life in order to encourage the proliferation of what may be a highly inferior mass culture? Assuming that some neutral principle of equality would be desirable, should we strive for an equality of opportunity — thereby creating an aristocracy of the intelligent, vigorous and enterprising — or an equality of treatment based on a highly altruistic concern? In its welfare programs, should the state play the role of social engineer and be guided by a scientific behaviorism, or should it recognize the dignity of the individual and work to encourage and increase his capacity for self-determination and self-development. In short, this reductio ad absurdum clearly suggests that some basic values must be chosen as a framework to guide the regulation of the state's activity and the individual's conduct. Of necessity this framework will reflect the values of a society's culture, and these values will have been largely influenced by religion. The Bill of Rights itself gives constitutional force to a certain conception of man, a conception that is the outgrowth of the Judaeo-Christian tradition. Accordingly, our substantive criminal law, as well as our criminal procedure, is inextricably entwined with religiously-based moral values. Professor Henkin himself seems to recognize this when he says that "laws against incest or polygamy, for example, now reflect mores and institutions — in particular, the family — that are the fabric of our society."[71] In short, the secular and the spiritual are so tightly interwoven that they cannot be successfully separated. For

---

[68] Henkin, *supra* note 15, at 407-11.
[69] *Id.* at 402.
[70] *Id.*
[71] *Id.* at 409.

example, the institution of marriage ultimately rests on a view of the nature of mankind (or womankind) that defies "ultilitarian" analysis. It springs from religious origins, is oriented to our basic ethos, and in turn influences our society. Marriage law, then, is an instance where the state can legitimately support a cultural institution born of religious values.

Concluding that the state can support at least some of our morals without violating the establishment clause, two questions yet remain unanswered. First, what morals can be appropriately enforced by the criminal law of the state? Second, should special exceptions be made for free exercise purposes? The first question is beyond the scope of this paper and remains extremely controversial, with the debate to date inconclusive. At one extreme is the libertarian approach taken by Professor H.L.A. Hart, who would dissuade the state from enforcing criminal sanctions against conduct which does not harm others in an immediate, tangible and specific fashion.[72] At the other extreme, Lord Devlin postulates [73] that a society derives its quality and identity from its prevailing moral code — the commonly shared ideas that direct and sustain collective judgment, common endeavor and the prevailing social institutions. For him the dissolution of the moral core of a society means the dissolution of that particular society. Consequently, he would have the state commit the full force of its coercive powers to maintain society's basic morality.

Regardless of the view adopted, I believe that the enforcement of public morals cannot admit of exception for religious claims. If one prefers Hart's view — the law of crimes being restricted to antisocial behavior clearly injurious to important and tangible interests of other members of society — application of the balancing test to such criminal laws would always result in a denial of exemption. In other words, a per se rule is appropriate. If instead Devlin's views are adopted, one might be tempted to conclude that distinctions could and should be made between different moral offenses; only the more serious ones fundamental to society's prevailing institutions would be enforced without exception, while religious exemptions would be allowed from the lesser ones. For instance, exemptions might be allowed for gambling, fornication, or the consumption of narcotics by those who engage in such practices to fulfill religious obligations, but none would be permitted from laws prohibiting incest or polyg-

---

[72] H.L.A. Hart, Law, Liberty and Morality (1963).
[73] P. Devlin, The Enforcement of Morals (1965).

amy. But a full adoption of Devlin's approach eliminates the need for drawing such distinctions since a particular moral norm is to be enforced by the criminal law only after an evaluation of its importance. Under this refined approach, gambling, for example, might simply not be subjected to criminal sanction.

It would seem that Hart and Devlin agree that criminal sanctions should be used to control antisocial conduct that society simply cannot tolerate; but there is a significant rift between them in determining what is intolerable. Hart's test hinges on measuring the harmful effect of the conduct on others, whereas Devlin's test turns on whether a right-minded member of society would find the practice in question so abominable that its mere existence would be an offense. It can be argued that Lord Devlin relies too much on the depths of irrational emotion for the important determination of the proper scope of moral offenses. A dispassionate assessment of the matter might indicate that a plurality of moralities should be tolerated. Tolerance of deviant behavior, although difficult psychologically, might have only very limited sociological consequences that would not seriously undermine the moral character or climate of a society. But Devlin will not concede this much. Although he recognizes that a society without a common religion can exist, he does not believe that a society without a common morality is viable. Accordingly, he concludes that "[t]he suppression of vice is as much the law's business as the suppression of subversive activities . . . ."[74] Once this proposition is accepted, special pleading for vice under the cloak of religion compounds the subversion because it implies that the common morality is out of joint with a standard claiming to represent the highest and finest in man. In short, to warrant criminal sanctions the morality must be so important that it cannot allow of a religious exemption.

Up to now American jurisprudence has reflected sentiments similar to those of Lord Devlin, and will probably do so for some time to come. This judicial predisposition may explain a recent North Carolina decision, *State v. Bullard*,[75] which upheld a statute prohibiting the use and possession of peyote and marijuana when applied to a college student who had both substances in his possession, allegedly for religious purposes. In an unsatisfactory opinion the North Carolina Supreme Court appeared to rely on the now generally discredited belief-action distinction of *Rey-*

---
[74] *Id.* at 13-14.
[75] 267 N.C. 599, 148 S.E.2d 565 (1966).

nolds,[76] but what really may have moved the court is revealed in this excerpt: [77]

> The defendant may believe what he will as to peyote and marijuana and he may conceive that one is necessary and the other is advisable in connection with his religion. But it is not a violation of his constitutional rights to forbid him, in the guise of his religion, to possess a drug which will produce hallucinatory symptoms similar to those produced in cases of schizophrenia, dementia praecox, or paranoia, and his position cannot be sustained here — *in law nor in morals.*

The use of narcotics is generally regarded as a vice, or at least has been until recently, largely because it is believed to be destructive of industriousness, clear-headedness, and self-reliance — virtues traditionally thought to provide a keen edge to our national character, energy for our system of free enterprise, and vitality to our national purpose. Therefore, if one is to follow Lord Devlin's test, the case seems clear for suppression.

But under this view *Woody*,[78] which permitted the use of peyote by members of the Native American Church, would seem hopelessly wrong. A simple explanation, and perhaps a dispositive one, can be found in the philosophical distance between California and North Carolina. Whereas North Carolina seemed to intimate that the use of peyote was intrinsically immoral, California treated it strictly as conduct subject to criminal sanction in order to protect the public health. At no point did the California Attorney General raise the question of morality, though he did raise the question of acculturization by suggesting that peyotism was the manifestation of a tribal culture which stood as an obstacle to Indian adaptation to modern society. The California Supreme Court rejected this analysis out of hand, for it smacked too much of a paternalistic behaviorism. An indirect attempt by the state to eliminate a lawful, albeit backward tribal ethos is not to be equated with its direct coercive protection of the dominant moral climate of a society. The California court's libertarian views, which led it to see this crime as a public welfare offense, were revealed when it said:[79] "In a mass society, which presses at every point toward conformity, the protection of a self-ex-

---

[76] 98 U.S. 145 (1878); *see* p. 1387 *supra.*
[77] 267 N.C. at 604, 148 S.E.2d at 569 (emphasis added).
[78] People v. Woody, 61 Cal. 2d 716, 394 P.2d 813, 40 Cal. Rptr. 69 (1964).
[79] 61 Cal. 2d at 727, 394 P.2d at 821, 40 Cal. Rptr. at 77.

pression, however unique, of the individual and the group becomes ever more important."

This explanation of the *Bullard* and *Woody* cases is somewhat disturbing because it suggests that the religious liberty of the individual will sometimes turn on how a state characterizes its statutory offenses. However, the resulting lack of uniformity may simply be inevitable in our federal system. For example, all states may not seek to ban the use of peyote and marijuana, or some may prohibit their use but exempt religious practices from the ban. Of course, this variety of treatment could be minimized somewhat if the Supreme Court were to place limits on the types of offenses which can be considered *mala in se* for purposes of the free exercise clause. In making this determination, the Court might look to the number of states that do not criminally prohibit the particular activity.

There is yet another ground, however, for distinguishing and reconciling these decisions. It could be argued that a narrow exemption should be granted for carefully delimited sacramental practices which do not conflict with the underlying moral purpose of the legislative prohibition. For instance, the use of sacramental wine was hardly one of the corrupting evils that national prohibition sought to eradicate, though it was proper to place conditions and limitations on the use of such wine to insure that it was not diverted for improper purposes.[80] Thus, the result in *Woody* can be justified if one regards only the regular use of peyote as a corrupting practice, although the sacramental wine analogy is vulnerable because the wine's use for ritualistic purposes is not intoxicating whereas the religious use of peyote is hallucinatory. Nonetheless, the practices of the Native American Church are in fact limited. Only a prescribed amount of peyote is used once a week as part of a fairly well-defined ritual, with the purpose of achieving a communal experience of union with God. Indeed, use of peyote for other purposes is considered blasphemous. On this basis the California court could have concluded that such limited sacramental use was quite distinct from a religiously inspired use which advocates reliance on peyote as a way of life.

On the other hand, the defendant in *Bullard* was a member of the Neo-Native American Church, which did not appear to have

---

[80] *Cf.* Shapiro v. Lyle, 30 F.2d 971 (W.D. Wash. 1929) (upholding licensing and other restrictions on use of sacramental wine pursuant to the National Prohibition Act).

a traditional body of teachings on the use of peyote. His reliance on the drugs did not appear to be strictly limited. Marijuana as well as peyote was found in his possession; and while he alleged that use of peyote was necessary for his practice of religion he only claimed of his use of marijuana that it was "most advisable." [81] Defendant's expansive views may have led the court to doubt the sincerity of his religious protestations. But even if he were sincere, the North Carolina court probably would have concluded that he had made the use of peyote a dominant way of life rather than a way to experience God in a highly restricted ritual.

E. *Civic Duties*

The civic responsibilities of the citizen range over a broad field of activities and, like public welfare regulations, are difficult subjects for generalization since these duties represent governmental interests of varying importance. Three civic duties frequently in conflict with religious scruples — payment of taxes, jury duty, and military service — will be examined to determine the appropriateness of a balancing approach in this area.

1. Taxes. — The enforced payment of taxes, despite religious objections to either the levy itself or to the purpose for which public funds are to be spent, presents the easiest problem. To avoid conferring a preferential economic benefit on the basis of religion a per se approach always upholding the priority of the governmental interest is appropriate. The danger of preferential economic treatment in violation of the establishment clause might be avoided if exception were conditioned on a compensating donation to a charitable or beneficial enterprise operated under secular auspices, but this would be difficult to administer.

Nonestablishment apart, we have here an economic regulation which requires uniformity of treatment to satisfy the principle of distributive justice. Moreover, when the religious objection goes not to the power of the government to levy a particular kind of tax but to the use of the funds raised, the interest of the government takes on an added dimension. Whatever the dissenter's avowed purposes and actual motives, his refusal to pay all or part of his taxes operates, in effect, not as a personal withdrawal from a particular government program, but as an attempt to subvert it. Organized government cannot tolerate this kind of dissent, and

---

[81] 267 N.C. at 602, 148 S.E.2d at 568.

refusals to pay taxes on this ground have been given short shrift in the courts.[82]

This analysis would suggest that the action of Congress which will exempt the Amish from payment of the social security tax [83] is ill advised and possibly a violation of the nonestablishment principle. However, two factors may sap the strength of these objections. First, the legislative exemption requires the Amish to make adequate provision for the support of the elderly in their communities. This substantially reduces the danger of conferring a preferential economic benefit in violation of the establishment clause or the principle of distributive justice. Secondly, the social security system is a government-operated insurance program — a special kind of governmental undertaking. Because of its special function the concept of withdrawal without disruption is at least plausible. On the other hand, this argument loses much force in light of the fact that socialized insurance is premised on the compulsory participation of all.

2. *Jury Duty.* — Jury service presents a problem ideally suited for balancing analysis: Although the governmental interest in securing jurors is a most important one, the cost of a religious exemption is negligible. The burden of jury service falls on a relatively small segment of the population. Numerous exemptions exist for various personal reasons, and religious liberty could probably be added to the list without noticeable effect. Also, in terms of the governmental interest itself, there is good reason to pay greater deference to religious objections to jury duty than to other personal excuses. A juror who professes that it is contrary to his religious scruples to pass judgment on others could hardly be expected to fulfill his civic duty satisfactorily.

The recent about-face executed by the Minnesota Supreme Court in *In re Jenison* on the issue of jury duty supports this conclusion. The Minnesota court had first ruled [84] that the obligation of the citizen to participate in the governmental process of maintaining civil order outweighed his claims for religious exemption. But on appeal the United States Supreme Court reversed and remanded the case to the Minnesota high court for reconsideration in light of its recent decision in *Sherbert*.[85] On remand the Minnesota Supreme Court then reversed its prior rul-

---

[82] Abraham J. Muste, 35 T.C. 913 (1961); *cf.* Massachusetts v. Mellon, 262 U.S. 447 (1923).

[83] INT. REV. CODE of 1954, § 1402(h), *added by* Social Security Amendments of 1965, Pub. L. No. 89-97, § 319(a), 79 Stat. 391-92.

[84] *In re* Jenison, 265 Minn. 96, 120 N.W.2d 515 (1963).

[85] 375 U.S. 14 (1963).

ing and held that religious scruples were to be respected and exemption from jury service granted until further experience indicated that "indiscriminate invoking of the First Amendment" was interfering with the effective functioning of the jury system.[86]

This reversal reflected a refinement of balancing analysis, for instead of simply weighing the social value of compulsory jury duty against the claim of religious liberty, as it had done at first, the Minnesota court calculated the impact of a religious exemption on the state's interest and found it prima facie to be so negligible as not to warrant interference with religious freedom. *Sherbert* is thus viewed, as it was in *People v. Woody*,[87] as placing on the state the burden of coming forward with proof demonstrating the degree to which a religious exemption will interfere with the purposes of a regulatory program. But *Jenison* might even be construed as going beyond both *Sherbert* and *Woody* in recognizing a religious liberty claim. The claim put forward by Mrs. Jenison, unlike that advanced by Mrs. Sherbert, went directly against the basic purpose of the governmental regulation involved — having one judged by his peers. The court was measuring the direct social cost of tolerating effective dissent from the state's programs; it was not just assessing the difficulties of administration that would be created by a religious exemption, as was done in the *Sherbert* and *Woody* cases. On the other hand, *Jenison* may not have extended *Sherbert* or *Woody*. To portray Mrs. Jenison's claim as flying directly into the face of the jury duty requirement may be inaccurate. A person whose religious beliefs proscribe the passing of judgment on others may be incapable of providing a satisfactory trial by peers. Furthermore, uniformity is not highly prized or necessary in this area, as evidenced not only by numerous explicit personal exemptions but also by the number of eligible persons never called to serve.

3. Military Service. — Conscientious objection from military service raises a conflict of interest most difficult to resolve. National security represents perhaps the most compelling collective interest of any society; moreover, unconditional exemption would confer a very substantial economic benefit on those who could continue to pursue their private interests while their fellow citizens were conscripted into military service. Finally, denial of special treatment might well accord with the views of the founding fathers, for conscientious objectors to participation in the Rev-

---

[86] *In re* Jenison, 267 Minn. 136, 137, 125 N.W.2d 588, 589 (1963).
[87] *See* pp. 1394–95 *supra*.

olutionary War incurred the hostility of many committed to the struggle against England.[88] Indeed, a proposed amendment to the Constitution which would have exempted conscientious objectors from military service was never enacted by the House Committee of the Whole sitting to consider the religion clauses of the first amendment.[89]

Although the Supreme Court has never had occasion to pass squarely on this question, through the years it has spoken as if exemption for conscientious objectors rests on legislative grace rather than constitutional right.[90] If this were the view at a time when the nation was but an isolated minor power, it seems that the total mobilization required by modern warfare and the leading role of the United States in foreign affairs would make even stronger the case for giving constitutional priority to the nation's demands should Congress repeal the present exemption.

However, there are compelling reasons that support exemption. The moral revulsion of the convinced conscientious objector at the thought of taking human life is great. Military conscription of such men necessarily entails grave interference with conscience. Their refusal to serve elicits great sympathy and respect, not because of the religious origins of their objection, but because of their display of high ethical concern. Although the stance of the conscientious objector necessarily implies criticism of the exist-

---

[88] *See* 1 CONSCIENTIOUS OBJECTION 34-36 (Selective Service System Special Monograph No. 11, 1950).

[89] The proposed Bill of Rights debated by the Committee of the Whole of the House of Representatives contained a provision exempting religious conscientious objectors from military service. A motion to have this clause struck out was defeated during debate. 1 ANNALS OF CONG. 749-51 (1789). Nonetheless the Bill of Rights as adopted contained no such clause.

[90] One of the first cases decided that Congress had required the promise to bear arms in defense of the nation as a condition for naturalization. United States v. Macintosh, 283 U.S. 605 (1931). The Court there was faced with the argument that since citizens could not be forced to bear arms in a war contrary to their conscientious objections, Congress did not intend to place an inconsistent burden on those seeking naturalization. The Court answered this argument with the observation that exemption from military service on religious grounds was based on a congressional policy of exempting conscientious objectors rather than constitutional right. Because Congress has continued to allow this exemption, the Court has never had occasion to reexamine this dictum. The holding of the *Macintosh* case itself has been overruled. Girouard v. United States, 328 U.S. 61 (1946). Nevertheless, two intervening decisions tend to support the *Macintosh* dictum. *In re* Summers, 325 U.S. 561 (1945) (upholding a refusal of Illinois courts to admit to the bar an otherwise qualified candidate because he was a conscientious objector); Hamilton v. Regents, 293 U.S. 245 (1934) (upholding expulsion from a state university for a religiously based refusal to enroll in a required course in military training).

ing order, he is not subversive of social aims and values. Rather, he seeks to elevate the practices of our society, compromised by the need to survive in an imperfect world, to the universally held ideals of peace and brotherhood. To exempt those who uncompromisingly adhere to these ideals stands not only as a mark of the nation's civilized character but acts also as a restraining influence in an age whose material progress has spawned the most horrible weapons of destruction. In addition to this intangible yet highly important reason for exemption is a more ponderable consideration which detracts from the desirablity of drafting conscientious objectors — the truly committed ones will not permit themselves to be led off to war; they will simply be led off to jail.

Difficulties arising because of the exemption's bestowal of economic benefits can be overcome. Those who object only to combatant service can be assigned a special noncombatant status in medical or similar units. Those who object to any direct support of combat can be excused from military service on condition that they undertake some equivalently onerous service to the public. Ever since the heavy demands made on the nation by World War I, some kind of substitute personal service has always accompanied the exemption of conscientious objectors.

Throughout its history the nation has shown continued respect and deference to religious scruples, providing some kind of exemption from the military service.[91] This undeviating practice, manifesting as it does both an enduring understanding of the ideal scope of the free exercise principle and the lesson from experience that such exemption is feasible, could well provide the basis for constitutional doctrine. However, a number of fluid circumstances would probably affect the Court's judgment, making it difficult to fix the outlines of such a constitutional doctrine. For instance, it might compel exemption in time of peace, but be reluctant to do so in time of major war; or, it might conclude that the maximum protection guaranteed by the free exercise clause is a narrow exemption excusing conscientious objectors from com-

---

[91] The First Continental Congress resolved in 1775 that it would recognize the rights of those who would not bear arms because of religious scruples. 2 JOURNALS OF THE CONTINENTAL CONGRESS 189 (1905). In the Civil War the federal draft eventually was made to include a conscientious objector provision providing for noncombatant duty. Act of Feb. 24, 1864, ch. 13, § 17, 13 Stat. 9. During World War I Congress passed the Draft Act of 1917 which exempted conscientious objectors who were affiliated with historic peace churches. Act of May 18, 1917, ch. 15, 40 Stat. 78. Exemption was broadened to include all those who have conscientious objection because of religious training and belief by the Selective Training and Service Act of 1940, 54 Stat. 889.

batant service only. On the other hand, it is unlikely that the Court will ever be driven to an articulation of the contours of such an exemption. Instead, the Court might deliver a forceful constitutional message to the legislature without making any declaration of unconstitutionality; or, it might achieve transformation of the draft laws through the process of statutory interpretation.[92]

The recent decision in *United States v. Seeger*[93] is an illustration of this technique. The 1940 Selective Service Act extended exemption from military service to any person "who, by reason of religious training and belief, is conscientiously opposed to participation in war in any form."[94] Disagreement developed among the circuit courts as to whether this language required a belief in God as a condition for exemption.[95] In 1948 Congress acted, presumably to resolve this conflict, by legislating a statutory definition of "religious training and belief" which required "belief in a relation to a Supreme Being."[96] Seeger, who denied any belief in God, nonetheless claimed exemption on the grounds that his religious convictions prevented him from taking part in preparation for war. The Second Circuit reversed a denial of exemption to Seeger, holding that the due process clause of the fifth amendment requires equal treatment of all persons who have conscientious objections based on religious beliefs, even nontheistic ones.[97] The Supreme Court affirmed the Second Circuit's judgment, but not on constitutional grounds. It interpreted the 1948 statute defining religious training and belief in terms of "belief in a relation to a Supreme Being" as not having added to or changed the previously existing requirements for exemption. It then found that Seeger's pacifist convictions were based on religious training and belief because they were formed in part by a Roman Catholic upbringing and by wide acquaintance with and respect for Quaker views. The Court concluded that for purposes of the Selective Service Act the term religion includes a sincere and meaningful belief which occupies in the life of its possessor a place parallel to that filled by the God of those admittedly qualifying for the exemption.[98]

---

[92] *Cf.* Greene v. McElroy, 360 U.S. 474 (1959); Vitarelli v. Seaton, 359 U.S. 535 (1959).

[93] 380 U.S. 163 (1965).

[94] 54 Stat. 889.

[95] *Compare* United States v. Kauten, 133 F.2d 703 (2d Cir. 1943) (A. Hand, J.), *with* Berman v. United States, 156 F.2d 377 (9th Cir.), *cert. denied*, 329 U.S. 795 (1946).

[96] Universal Military Training and Service Act, 50 U.S.C. § 456(j) (1964).

[97] 326 F.2d 846 (2d Cir. 1964).

[98] 380 U.S. at 166.

There are some thorny problems ahead, however, which cannot be solved by statutory manipulation. For example, Congress has made it abundantly clear that exemption is available only to those who object to "war in any form." Yet there is much to be said on free exercise grounds in favor of extending the exemption to those who object to particular wars. Objection to service in so-called unjust wars finds support in various religious traditions,[99] and to deny exemption to these dissenters while granting it to those who object to all wars smacks of preferential treatment for particular religious beliefs.

Despite the seeming injustice of this narrow exemption and its inconsistency with the nonestablishment principle, the likelihood that the Court will broaden it to include dissenters to particular wars is at best remote. There are differences in the philosophical and sociological implications of a limited as contrasted with a broad exemption and these may be substantial enough to offer a rational basis justifying difference in treatment. The consistent pacifist dissents from the history of nations; his position does not single out his own country for adverse judgment. The state can give such views limited recognition without contradicting its own war effort; exemption of only thoroughgoing pacifists stands as a mark of the nation's continuing adherence to the ideal of peace. But how can the state justify exempting those who refuse military service on the ground that their nation is an unjust aggressor? Such an objection, no matter how religious or how philosophical its origins, immediately expresses a political judgment at odds with the nation's war effort. Resting as it does on a consequential analysis of the nation's involvement and objectives in the war, it cannot be distinguished readily, if at all, from a nonreligious, nonconscientious dissent from the wisdom or desirabilty of the government's policy. In *United States v. Kauten,* Judge Augustus Hand offered such reasoning as the explanation of congressional failure to exempt dissenters from a particular war: [100]

> There is a distinction between a course of reasoning resulting in a conviction that a particular war is inexpedient or disastrous and a conscientious objection to participation in any war under any circumstances. The latter, and not the former, may be the basis of exemption under the Act. The former is *usually* a political

---

[99] For a discussion of the just war doctrine from a Protestant perspective, see P. RAMSAY, WAR AND THE CHRISTIAN CONSCIENCE (1961); R. BAINTON, CHRISTIAN ATTITUDES TOWARD WAR AND PEACE (1960). For a survey of a Catholic doctrine in support of a refusal to serve in an unjust war, see F. STRATMANN, WAR & CHRISTIANITY TODAY 98-109 (J. Doebele transl. 1956).

[100] 133 F.2d 703, 708 (2d Cir. 1943) (emphasis added).

objection, while the latter, we think, may justly be regarded as a response of the individual to an inward mentor, call it conscience or God, that is for many persons at the present time the equivalent of what has always been thought a religious impulse.

Conscientious objection to the use of certain weapons or strategies of war presents a more difficult problem. Since this objection rests on a general standard which expresses on its face an ethical or religious concern, and does not turn on the political objectives and involvement of the nation in a particular war, it would appear to merit the same treatment as conscientious objection to war in any form. On the other hand, the determination of whether a particular war has reached the point of escalation that renders it immoral poses issues closely related to those raised by military and political critics of national policy.

In determining the treatment to be given objectors to particular wars, the Court would probably try to avoid an analysis involving these ideological overtones. Rather, should it decide that there are no constitutional grounds for exempting conscientious objectors to particular wars, it will probably rationalize their different treatment on practical grounds. Two come quickly to mind. First, much can be made of the deleterious effect on national morale in war time if persons who quarrel with the political objectives of the government are excused from the military service. This rationale is actually a tacit acquiescence in the idea that a nation which is involved in a struggle momentous enough to require its citizenry to sacrifice their very lives cannot permit any of them to withdraw their support from the particular cause because they question its wisdom or justice. Second, it can be argued that the danger of spurious claims will be increased if the exemption is extended to objectors to particular wars, since past conduct of the claimants would not provide much of a basis by which to test the sincerity of their objections. But this argument should be dispositive only if actual experience proved it to be a substantial obstacle to the workings of military conscription.

IV. Weighing the Interests:
The Religious Interest

One of the drawbacks of the balancing approach is that it complicates the role of the courts in dealing with religious liberty. Conversely, one of the virtues of the strict neutrality approach is that neither the sincerity nor the importance of the individual's religious beliefs need be considered by the court; the constitutionality of government action turns entirely on its own character rather than on a comparative evaluation of the competing religious and public interests.

A. Sincerity of Religious Belief

While the Supreme Court has recently expressed some reservations concerning the propriety of examining the sincerity of religious beliefs,[101] state courts have frequently done so.[102] Of course, a minimal inquiry is necessary to avoid making a mockery of both religion and government; religious liberty is hardly served by exempting a merchant from appearing in court on Saturday because he claims to be a Sabbatarian when he regularly conducts his business on that day.[103] Protection of religious conscience lies at the heart of the free exercise clause; where the individual's conduct is repeatedly at variance with his avowed religious duties, restriction on his religious liberty is entirely academic — no serious injury is done to his conscience.[104]

Only once, in *United States v. Ballard*,[105] has the Supreme Court directly touched on governmental inquiry into religious sincerity. In that case, a criminal prosecution for fraud, defendants had used the mails to solicit contributions, representing themselves to be divine messengers with supernatural powers. The Court — with no expressed dissent on this point — held that to examine the truth or falsity of these representations would violate the first amendment. Chief Justice Stone, joined by Justices Roberts and Frankfurter, while regarding this point as irrelevant, saw no constitutional obstacle to examining defendant's state of mind, "a fact as capable of fraudulent misrepresentation as . . . one's physical condition or the state of his bodily health." [106]

Mr. Justice Jackson disagreed, taking the position that the first amendment prohibits determination not only of the truth or falsity of the defendant's religious beliefs but also of his subjective commitment to them. He wrote: [107]

---

[101] *E.g.*, Sherbert v. Verner, 374 U.S. 398, 407 (1963) (dictum).

[102] *E.g., In re* Grady, 61 Cal. 2d 887, 394 P.2d 728, 39 Cal. Rptr. 912 (1964); *In re* Jenison, 267 Minn. 136, 125 N.W.2d 588 (1963).

[103] Dobkin v. District of Columbia, 194 A.2d 657 (D.C. Ct. App. 1963).

[104] *See* Mansfield, *Conscientious Objection — 1964 Term*, 1965 RELIGION & PUB. ORDER 3, 23.

[105] 322 U.S. 78 (1944).

[106] *Id.* at 90.

[107] *Id.* at 92–95 (dissenting opinion).

In the first place, as a matter of either practice or philosophy I do not see how we can separate an issue as to what is believed from considerations as to what is believable. . . . If we try religious sincerity severed from religious verity, we isolate the dispute from the very considerations which in common experience provide its most reliable answer.

In the second place, any inquiry into intellectual honesty in religion raises profound psychological problems. . . . [Religious] experiences, like some tones and colors, have existence for one, but none at all for another. They cannot be verified to the minds of those whose field of consciousness does not include religious insight. When one comes to trial which turns on any aspect of religious belief or representation, unbelievers among his judges are likely not to understand and are almost certain not to believe him.

And then I do not know what degree of skepticism or disbelief in a religious representation amounts to actionable fraud. . . . It is hard in matters so mystical to say how literally one is bound to believe the doctrine he teaches and even more difficult to say how far it is reliance upon a teacher's literal belief which induces followers to give him money.

. . . .

The chief wrong which false prophets do to their following is not financial. The collections aggregate a tempting total, but individual payments are not ruinous. . . . The wrong of these things, as I see it, is not in the money the victims part with half so much as in the mental and spiritual poison they get. But that is precisely the thing the Constitution put beyond the reach of the prosecutor, for the price of freedom of religion or of speech or of the press is that we must put up with, and even pay for, a good deal of rubbish.

Mr. Justice Jackson's arguments are especially persuasive in cases where government would otherwise act to protect gullible citizens from spurious religious movements; a monitoring of the sincerity of religious leaders should be placed beyond the powers of the government. However, precluding inquiry into sincerity seems inappropriate when individuals make claim for special treatment vis-à-vis the state. In the latter instance the entire community, including those who have doubts about either the validity or the sincerity of the claimant's beliefs, deserve protection from the dilution of governmental programs which would result if preferred status were given to insincerely held claims.

B. Importance of Religious Practices

Not wishing to appear to pass on religious questions, the courts frequently do not indicate the criteria they use in assessing the importance of the religious practices involved. The Supreme Court has apparently disclaimed the existence of general standards for such a measurement,[108] but this cannot possibly mean that the claimant's assessment of the religious importance of his claim must always be taken at face value. For instance, if special treatment is sought for a certain practice only because of its cultic significance, its importance should be measured in light of the teachings of the particular sect.[109] In the past, most claims presented under the free exercise clause have rested on elaborately articulated bodies of religious doctrine. The courts have thus had objective standards, albeit ones established in effect by various faiths, for measurement of the importance of religious observances.

As might be expected, one can discern in the pattern of decisions certain judicial predispositions which reflect the predominant western religious tradition of our culture. In accordance with the theistic tradition of the West, upon which almost all religious liberty claims have rested until recently, the cases give greatest weight to practices concerning worship of the deity.[110] Sacramental practices that are presumed to be occasions of God's grace are ranked very highly; there is a judicial tendency to accord the highest place to those practices believed to effect a transignification of some part of the material order and invest it with divine attributes. This tendency was manifest, for example, in *People v. Woody*,[111] the California decision finding the religious interest in peyotism of members of the American Native Church to be most essential.[112] For members of that religion peyote is a central object of worship, holding a place analogous to that of the Holy Spirit in the Christian tradition.

Some decisions of the Supreme Court reflect the attitude that religious exercises take on added weight if they are regarded as prescribed forms of worship by their practitioners. In *Murdock*

---

[108] *See* Fowler v. Rhode Island, 345 U.S. 67 (1953) (dictum).

[109] *But see* State v. Miday, 263 N.C. 747, 140 S.E.2d 325 (1965) (dictum).

[110] *See* Galanter, *Religious Freedoms in the United States: A Turning Point?*, 1966 WIS. L. REV. 217, 274-76.

[111] 61 Cal. 2d 716, 394 P.2d 813, 40 Cal. Rptr. 69 (1964).

[112] *See* p. 1395 *supra*.

v. Pennsylvania [113] the Court struck down a municipal license tax on peddling when it was applied to the distribution of religious literature by Jehovah's Witnesses. The tax did not impose a heavy burden on the distribution of religious literature; it was a nondiscriminatory levy on activities having the earmarks of a commercial enterprise when viewed from a secular perspective. In addition, the tax might have been considered a just exaction for the police protection extended to the religious peddler on the city's streets.[114] Despite the apparent balance in favor of the governmental interest, the Court held the license tax invalid as a clear violation of the first amendment because it was in effect a levy on the practice of religion itself. In reaching this conclusion for the Court, Mr. Justice Douglas equated the distribution of religious literature by Jehovah's Witnesses with worship: [115]

> The hand distribution of religious tracts is an age-old form of missionary evangelism. . . . It is more than preaching; it is more than distribution of religious literature. It is a combination of both. Its purpose is as evangelical as the revival meeting. This form of religious activity occupies the same high estate under the First Amendment as do worship in the churches and preaching from the pulpits. It has the same claim to protection as the more orthodox and conventional exercises of religion.

In the later *Sherbert* case Mr. Justice Brennan, writing for the Court, concluded that observance of the Sabbath was a "cardinal principle" of the faith of a Seventh-day Adventist.[116] There was no discussion of this point and none was necessary, for Mr. Justice Brennan could rely on an audience conversant with the Judaeo-Christian tradition and appreciative of the importance of resting on the Sabbath.

Ethical commands enforced by religious sanctions are not regarded as highly as religious services offered directly to the deity. This can, in part, be explained by the fact that governmental regulations which conflict with ethical-religious standards sometimes do not seriously interfere with them in terms either of intensity or duration.[117] But this disposition is to be explained in other part by the fact that the courts, conditioned by a religious tradition that is God-centered, regard worship of the deity

---

[113] 319 U.S. 105 (1943).
[114] *See id.* at 140 (Frankfurter, J., dissenting).
[115] *Id.* at 108–09.
[116] 374 U.S. at 406.
[117] *See* p. 1423 *infra*.

as the heart of the religious experience. Ethical claims, unlike purely devotional observances, may be viewed as relating primarily to social rather than spiritual experience and therefore not regarded as basic to the practice of religion. Whatever a theologian might make of such a distinction, the California Supreme Court seemed to find it of some substance in distinguishing *Reynolds* from its decision in *Woody*: [118] "Polygamy, although a basic tenet in the theology of Mormonism, is not essential to the practice of the religion; peyote, on the other hand, is the *sine qua non* of defendants' faith." The willingness and ability to draw this distinction makes easier the state's refusal to yield to ethical-religious claims sharply opposed to those parts of the prevailing moral code which have been incorporated into the criminal law.[119]

As for religious scruples that command a higher or more encompassing ethic than does the prevailing moral code, thereby bringing the individual into conflict with societal regulations, one senses that the courts will show greater deference to these scruples, especially if they are related to the mainstream of the Judaeo-Christian-Humanist tradition. Religious claims resting on concern and respect for fellow humans may well be accorded greater judicial respect than those resting on some seemingly arbitrary divine command. At least this might explain in part the greater protection accorded to conscientious scruples against the killing or even judging of human beings than that granted to religious objections against vaccination or blood transfusion. If greater weight is given, albeit subconsciously, to a religious ethic when it has strong humanitarian overtones, this may be both proper and inevitable, for in adopting the free exercise clause the founding fathers had in mind moral and spiritual values, as well as libertarian ones. They were more interested in permitting the free development of the finest qualities in man than in achieving freedom for freedom's sake.[120]

C. *Extent of Governmental Interference*

When we turn to judicial assessment of the extent to which a challenged governmental regulation interferes with religious practices or commands, we find explicit, common-sense criteria

---

[118] People v. Woody, 61 Cal.2d 716, 725, 394 P.2d 813, 820, 40 Cal. Rptr. 69, 76 (1964).

[119] *See* pp. 1403–09 *supra*.

[120] *See* Freeman, *supra* note 18.

at work. An absolute prohibition of an important religious activity is not as likely to stand as is a less restrictive regulation. Thus, the fact that the absolute ban in *Woody* made impossible the ceremonial use of peyote — the central act of worship in the Native American Church — weighed heavily in favor of the free exercise claim. In contrast, building and zoning restrictions which make the erection and maintenance of places of worship more costly and difficult, although not impossible, do not usually yield to the religious claim. Thus, it was held in *Corporation of the Presiding Bishop v. City of Porterville*[121] that churches can be excluded from highly restricted residential areas without violating the free exercise clause. Mr. Justice Douglas, later explaining the summary dismissal of an appeal from this case, noted that the effect of the ordinance upon free exercise was "relatively small and the public interest to be protected [was] substantial . . . ."[122] However, complete exclusion from a residential, suburban municipality might be successfully challenged on free exercise grounds.[123] Indeed, by applying a balancing test, some courts[124] have found that ordinances excluding churches must yield to the free exercise clause, while others[125] have reached the the same result by finding that the ordinances make arbitrary and unreasonable discriminations contrary to substantive due process.

These cases, involving expense and inconvenience to religious institutions, are to be contrasted with those involving economic sacrifices and difficulties on the part of the individual. In *Sherbert*[126] the Supreme Court recognized that even indirect burdens on religious liberty can be improper when the effect is to condition the individual's religious practices on a substantial financial sacrifice.

Government regulations that compel action contrary to conscience probably are regarded as more serious interferences with religious liberty than those which merely subject more or less passive religious dissenters to government action. This may account in part for the Supreme Court's decision[127] to excuse Je-

---

[121] 90 Cal. App. 2d 656, 203 P.2d 823, *appeal dismissed*, 338 U.S. 805 (1949).

[122] American Communications Ass'n v. Douds, 339 U.S. 382, 397 (1950).

[123] *See* J. CURRY, PUBLIC REGULATION OF THE RELIGIOUS USE OF LAND 49 (1964).

[124] *E.g.*, Board of Zoning Appeals v. Decatur Ind. Co. of Jehovah's Witnesses, 233 Ind. 83, 117 N.E.2d 115 (1954).

[125] Ellsworth v. Gercke, 62 Ariz. 198, 156 P.2d 242 (1945). *See generally* 1 A. & C. RATHKOPF, THE LAW OF ZONING AND PLANNING, ch. 19, § 1 (3d ed. 1960).

[126] 374 U.S. 398 (1963).

[127] West Virginia Bd. of Educ. v. Barnette, 319 U.S. 624 (1943).

hovah's Witness school children from the compulsory flag salute while upholding in another case [128] a prohibition against the street distribution of religious literature by youngsters. It also helps explain the more liberal judicial attitude toward exemption from jury duty and the military draft than toward excuse from compulsory vaccination and similar health requirements imposed on a passive subject. This distinction has at least been suggested in a few blood transfusion cases, though with the perhaps questionable result of compelling Jehovah's Witnesses to accept such medical treatment.[129] In these cases the courts have concluded that the objecting patients would regard a judicial decree as transferring responsibility for the blood transfusions from their consciences to the court, but one questions whether the inviolability of conscience is truly respected when a court is so quick to utilize the doctrine of "superior orders."

But there is another aspect of compulsory health requirements that tends to minimize their impact on the free exercise of religion — they usually are of very limited duration; their effects are soon dissipated and do not seriously hamper the individual's continued practice of his religion as a rule. One can only speculate whether these courts would have decided differently had the religious doctrines involved maintained that the ingestion of human blood marked one as a lost soul forever.

V. The Expanded Concept of Religion

A discussion of religious liberty is not complete unless something is said about the definition of religion for constitutional purposes. A good part of my discussion concerning assessment of the religious interest assumed that the claimant will rely on traditional theistic beliefs and an articulated body of doctrine, which the courts can learn through expert testimony. When this assumption is not operative, it is more difficult to assess the weight to be given a religious claim, but this is hardly sufficient reason to deny such a claim out of hand, for to deny religious freedom to the unorthodox believer would be a perversion of the "historic purpose" invested in the free exercise clause by both the humanists and the Protestant dissenters.

As a practical matter, however, the individual who founds his

---

[128] Prince v. Massachusetts, 321 U.S. 158 (1944).

[129] Application of the President & Directors of Georgetown College, 331 F.2d 1000 (D.C. Cir.), *cert. denied*, 377 U.S. 978 (1964); United States v. George, 239 F. Supp. 752 (D. Conn. 1965).

own sect, has an insignificant number of followers, and professes a very rudimentary body of doctrine, may find it difficult to persuade either the trier of fact of his sincerity or the court of the importance to himself of his religious beliefs. This, simply, is to be attributed to the lack of an adequate frame of reference against which to test the claimant's assertions. Thus, there is a tendency to show greater deference to those religions which have achieved a significant communion among men.

The case of the nontheistic but committed humanist who seeks to assert a religious liberty claim presents the most troublesome theoretical and practical difficulties. The language and history of the free exercise clause militate against the recognition of such a claim. Consequently, some scholars suggest that humanist claims to freedom of conscience must be protected, if at all, by constitutional provisions other than the free exercise clause.[130] It has been suggested that where freedom of belief and expression are involved, the free speech provisions of the first amendment provide the necessary protection;[131] where freedom of action is at issue, the due process and equal protection clauses have been advanced as substitutes for first amendment protection.[132]

However, there are other commentators [133] who believe that the free exercise clause realizes its "historic purpose" when the concept of inviolability of conscience is expanded to accommodate changing notions of religion. They regard the fundamental purpose of the free exercise clause to be the guarantee of freedom for the individual's spiritual development. But the realm of the spirit is wide — in its broadest sense it extends beyond religion to encompass all the forms of art and philosophy. Only a particular, fundamental aspect of the realm of the spirit is embodied in the concept of religion. That branch of modern religious thought which is strongly influenced by Paul Tillich's thinking refers to this realm as that area dealing with matters of ultimate concern. In this view religion encompasses those beliefs and world-views which illuminate the "very ground of our being"

---

[130] M. Howe, *supra* note 17, at 156; Gorman, *Problems of Church and State in the United States: A Catholic View*, in D. Oaks, The Wall Between Church and State 41, 47 (1963).

[131] Gorman, *supra* note 130.

[132] M. Howe, *supra* note 17, at 156, 165. The Second Circuit adopted this theory in exempting from the military service a registrant who had conscientious objections but did not believe in God. United States v. Seeger, 326 F.2d 846 (2d Cir. 1964), *aff'd* 380 U.S. 163 (1965).

[133] Stahmer, *Defining Religion: Federal Aid and Academic Freedom*, 1963 Religion & Pub. Order 116, 122–28.

and which invest life with ultimate meaning and direction.[134]

Although these concepts are very abstract for judges and lawyers, the Supreme Court appears ready to adopt them. In *United States v. Seeger*,[135] the Court admitted that its decision had been influenced by modern theological thought in general and that of Tillich in particular. This development was not too surprising in light of the Court's earlier decision in *Torcaso v. Watkins*,[136] where Mr. Justice Black said that nontheistic religions, such as Buddhism, were included within the protection afforded by the free exercise clause and listed both ethical culture and secular humanism as religions.[137] It is true that the *Seeger* definition is only an interpretation of the term religious belief as used in the Selective Service Act. Nonetheless, it seems to suggest the Court's ultimate definition of religion for constitutional purposes.[138]

Though it might seem expedient for the Supreme Court to restrict application of the free exercise clause to traditional types of religious belief, leaving protection of other claims of conscience to the equal protection and due process clauses, it actually makes little difference under which amendment nontheistic claims are protected. Problems of judicially defining, or at least of judicially intuiting the essence of religion are present in any event, since the equal protection clause requires a standard for comparison. In other words, the equal protection clause only requires that a nonreligious claim of conscience receive the same treatment as a religious one if they are alike in relevant respects. The "relevant respects" would appear to be the quality and intensity of the psychological and ideological forces behind a religious belief or obligation, and hence the treatment to be accorded a nontheistic claim would hinge on the answer to this question: Does the claimed belief occupy the same place in the life of the objector as an orthodox belief in God holds in the life of one clearly entitled to protection under the free exercise clause? Yet this is the very test adopted by the Supreme Court in *Seeger*.

Contrary to Mr. Justice Clark's characterization of this test as "simple of application," [139] it is little more than a point of departure and gives minimum guidance to courts in determining

---

[134] *Id.* at 128–31.
[135] 380 U.S. 163, 187 (1965). *See* p. 1414 *supra*.
[136] 367 U.S. 488 (1961).
[137] *Id.* at 495 n.11 (dictum).
[138] Mansfield, *supra* note 104, at 8–9.
[139] 380 U.S. at 184.

what beliefs are fundamental enough to be taken seriously as matters of ultimate concern. Though such a general and vague standard engenders uncertainty, it has two virtues. First, it acknowledges that the Court should proceed gingerly in this area, for any attempt at a final and definitive statement concerning religion may violate the spirit of both religion clauses as times change. Second, a broadly written definition permits a flexible approach under which the question of whether a particular personal ideology is to be protected can be answered in terms of the precise claim being advanced. One readily acquiesces in the broadest definition of religion when the issue before the court involves qualification for public office; [140] however, when the issue is fluoridation of water, one expects a far more restrictive definition. In the former case protection of the sphere of the spirit and intellect from improper state invasion is involved; in the latter, care should be taken lest exemption from social duties is granted because of strong political or philosophical objections.

In *Seeger* the Court noted two trends in modern religious thought. One was the shift from transcendental and supernatural perspectives to a greater emphasis on the immanence of meaning in the natural order. The second was the tendency in some religious quarters to move from a theocentric to an anthropocentric focus. Both of these developments tend to erode the distinction between the sacred and the secular, between religion and culture; they also highlight the ethical content of religion. One consequence might be that modern nontheistic religions will have fewer claims that are protected by the free exercise clause — it will be extremely difficult to find an analogue to the sacramental worship of God in their practices. Nonetheless, there will be attempts to characterize certain practices having no transcendental referent, but which are meant to advance the individual's emotional and spiritual development, as religious activities worthy of protection under the free exercise clause. In this category would fall the use of drugs and hallucinogenic agents, deviant sexual practices, and other behavior undertaken for its unusual psychological effects.[141] To the extent that such practices are forbidden by the criminal law, because contrary to public morality,

---

[140] *See* Torcaso v. Watkins, 367 U.S. 488 (1961).

[141] The recent establishment of the League for Spiritual Development by Dr. Timothy Leary portends sustained efforts by those who advocate the use of drugs for more expansive self-realization to draw about them the protective mantle of the free exercise clause.

no problem arises so long as the courts continue to deny all exemptions from criminal statutes of this kind. But a problem does arise when the practices run afoul of public welfare regulations, particularly if the regulation is directed at eliminating what is considered to be a menace to psychological health, as where the use of peyote or LSD is banned.

These practices should be denied the status of religious claims for two closely related reasons. First, denial of exemption for these practices does not create problems for the individual's conscience similar to those created by traditionally religious claims to freedom of worship. Personal alienation from one's Maker, frustration of one's ultimate mission in life, and violation of the religious person's integrity are all at stake when the right to worship is threatened. Although the seeker of new psychological worlds may feel equally frustrated when deprived of his gropings for a higher reality, there is not the same sense of acute loss — the loss of the Be-all and End-all of life.[142]

Secondly, such pursuits do more than seek limited exemption from regulations that have been designed to serve psychological or "mental health" purposes, if you will. They quarrel with those very ends. They tend to be as subversive of the existing secular order as conduct made criminal because it is offensive to public morality. Indeed, the state's interest in maintaining normality in personal behavior is akin to its interest in maintaining public morality. If we are to take issue with a society that places limitations on the individual's psychological experience, we should do so across the board on general libertarian grounds and not seek a special exemption for "religious" reasons.

Thus far courts have recognized exemptions from regulations relating to psychological purposes only when the behavior was limited to well defined ceremonial occasions.[143] By limiting ex-

---

[142] This point can cut the other way. Since the traditional believer has faith in a beneficent Almighty who towers above the state, he can find consolation and support that will carry him over a period of trial and tribulation; not so for the one who is still searching for the secret of fulfillment. He may be totally deprived of what little he finds in life that makes it worthwhile. However, to adopt a sympathetic view toward the nontheistic claim would be to equate the free exercise of religion with the pursuit of happiness. The happily married man may find his total fulfillment in his family; but this hardly provides a religious basis for exemption from the draft. The blissful enjoyment of rich psychological vistas, whether new or old, cannot describe the heart of the religious experience for free exercise purposes, because such a definition would merge secular and religious values and eliminate the historical and theoretical basis for special treatment of the latter. *See* Mansfield, *supra* note 104, at 34.

[143] *See* p. 1408–09 *supra*.

emption to these occasions, the favored behavior either had no impact whatsoever in subtracting from the purposes of the regulation (the sacramental wine exemption from national prohibition) or it was directly related to the worship of God and strictly limited in intensity, time, and place by a theological system of discipline (peyotism in the Native American Church). Thus, the indiscriminate use of hallucinogenic agents, in accordance with some private religious mystique, would have extremely difficult sledding in the courts. Even if the courts prove reluctant to remove from the shield of the first amendment all consciousness expanding practices which are unrelated to an established and clearly defined theology, they will probably scrutinize such claims with a very cold eye. In such cases the courts are likely to be especially stringent in requiring proof of the defendant's "sincerity." For instance, the California Supreme Court in *In re Grady* [144] required the petitioner, who sought to be released from prison after a conviction for illegal possession of peyote, to prove that his claim for religious exemption was based on honest and bona fide beliefs. Though the California court was probably not placing a special burden of proof on the petitioner,[145] it would not be too surprising if a self-styled peyote preacher were to find it impossible to convince the trier of fact of his "religious sincerity"; there would be a persistent suspicion that he had nothing more in mind than an adventuresome journey into the realm of the psyche.

A different problem presents itself when an individual who does not believe in a supernatural or personal God asserts conscientious objection to certain conduct because of its injurious effects on his fellow man. The courts will probably be more prone to recognize that this ethical belief may be held with such a degree of intensity that its violation occasions the same interior revulsion and anguish as does violation of the law of God to the pious. However, the problem of definition here becomes complicated, for more than the intensity of the reaction must be taken into account; its quality must also be akin to religious guilt and an-

---

[144] 61 Cal. 2d 887, 394 P.2d 728, 39 Cal. Rptr. 912 (1964).

[145] The *Grady* case involved a habeas corpus proceeding and it appears that at the defendant's trial the first amendment defense had not been put in issue. Consequently, the California Supreme Court remanded the case for trial on this point and petitioner Grady was required to produce sufficient evidence to support his allegation of religious motivation. Such a burden would be imposed on anyone who raised this defense. The California Supreme Court said nothing that would indicate it was placing a special burden on Grady because he did not refer to an established theology or cult, although as a practical matter he might face special difficulties in convincing the trier of fact that religion was his guiding light.

guish. Otherwise, the man of intense personal, political, philosophical, or even aesthetic loyalties, could claim a religious exemption whenever some cause moved his emotions to an extreme.

Most likely to be recognized will be ethical objections that involve serious concern for the dignity and basic welfare of one's fellow men. Indeed, it is hard to conceive of another human concern that so justly deserves treatment similar to that accorded man's anxiety to do the will of God. But there must be something fundamental about the objections; [146] the offensive conduct must require the objector to deny the "very ground of his being." Although such a test may appear impossible of application in the abstract, intuitive application nevertheless appears to be possible. The Seventh Circuit recently found [147] that a draftee who did not believe in a "Supreme Being . . . outside of man," did not know of any "after life," and had no knowledge as to man's mission in life except "to help other men," was entitled to the religious exemption from military service. Although it found it difficult to state exactly what the claimant's "religious" beliefs were, the court nonetheless concluded that they were of the kind considered sufficient in *Seeger*.

Actually, the difficulties of determining an individual's right to special treatment are not much greater in the case of the nonbeliever than in the case of many theists. Of course, if the theist's church takes a clear position on the activity involved the inquiry has a determinate frame of reference: is the claimant truly devoted to the fundamental dogmas of his church? But if the claimant's religious faith does not categorically proscribe the particular conduct, the trier of fact must determine whether the claimant's objection is grounded in his religious beliefs. The issue of sincerity, or degree of commitment, becomes inextricably bound up with the question of the religious basis for the objection.

A most powerful influence on the trier of fact in resolving the question of sincerity will undoubtedly be the extent to which the claimant appears to be willing to undergo personal sacrifice for his beliefs. Both the sincerity and the religiousness of his objection will be more readily accepted if he evidences the same degree of selflessness to his beliefs as is expected of the committed religionist when allegiance to the fundamental tenets of his faith is being tested. In *Kauten* Judge Augustus Hand referred to readiness to make a thoroughly selfless commitment as the hall-

---

[146] Mansfield, *supra* note 104, at 29.
[147] United States v. Stolberg, 346 F.2d 363 (7th Cir. 1965).

mark of a religious belief in one not believing in God.[148] But that case involved a conscientious objector to the draft, a situation in which it is much easier to test the degree of commitment because of the trying consequences of claiming exemption. It will be far more difficult to test the religious sincerity of other claims, such as claims demanding an exemption from jury service.[149] The courts can only hope that as a practical matter they will be spared from making such decisions with any degree of frequency.

Cases in which the courts have readily extended statutory tax exemptions for religious activities to organizations based on nontheistic beliefs [150] do not express a broad attitude in conflict with the above observations. These cases involved organizations devoted to high ethical ideals that have gained wide recognition in our society; the courts have justly concluded that since they promote the common good just as religious associations do, these organizations properly fall within the tax exemption statutes. One of these cases, *Fellowship of Humanity v. County of Alameda*,[151] has suggested a broad and frequently quoted definition of religion:

> Religion simply includes: (1) a belief, not necessarily referring to supernatural powers; (2) a cult, involving a gregarious association openly expressing the belief; (3) a system of moral practice directly resulting from an adherence to the belief; and (4) an organization within the cult designed to observe the tenets of belief.

The emphasis on a cultic bond and a body of established doctrine does not lend much encouragement to the undisciplined mystic who seeks unlimited license to escape, in any way he sees fit, into his own private world.

This much seems certain: regardless of whether the Court elects to proceed under the free exercise clause or the due process and equal protection clauses, it must formulate some kind of rudimentary natural theology in order to evaluate nontheistic religious claims. One may quarrel with the two main proposi-

---

[148] United States v. Kauten, 133 F.2d 703 (2d Cir. 1943) (dictum).

[149] *But see In re* Jenison, 267 Minn. 136, 125 N.W.2d 588 (1963) (fact that relator had gone to jail rather than purge herself of contempt by undertaking jury service demonstrated to the court her sincerity and depth of commitment).

[150] Washington Ethical Soc'y v. District of Columbia, 249 F.2d 127 (D.C. Cir. 1957); Fellowship of Humanity v. County of Alameda, 153 Cal. App. 2d 673, 315 P.2d 395 (1957).

[151] 153 Cal. App. 2d at 693, 315 P.2d at 406.

tions I suggest — first, that nontheistic practices seeking to advance individual psychological and spiritual development are to be denied equal status with sacramental acts of worship; and second, that only those nontheistic conscientious objections that are based on an intensely felt, selfless, and thoroughgoing personal commitment to the brotherhood of man should receive treatment equal to theistically based scruples. But if the Court does not adopt broad guidelines similar to these, it will have to evolve some other neotheological criteria to separate the dross from the gold.

DATE DUE

KF 4749 .A2 B55 1990 v.1

35874

Religious freedom.

HIEBERT LIBRARY
Fresno Pacific College - M.B. Seminary
Fresno, CA 93702

DEMCO